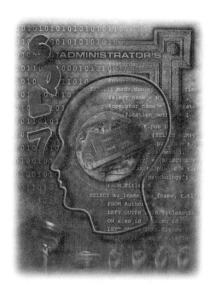

Microsoft® SQL
Server™ 7.0
Administrator's
Guide

Ron Talmage

A Division of Prima Publishing

A Division of Prima Publishing

Prima Publishing and colophon are registered trademarks of Prima Communications, Inc.

Prima Publishing, Rocklin, California 95677

Publisher: Matthew H. Carleson

Managing Editor: Dan J. Foster

Senior Acquisitions Editor: Deborah F. Abshier

Acquisitions Editor: Jenny L. Watson

Project Editor: Kevin Harreld

Technical Reviewers: Richard Campbell, Jeff Winchell

Copy Editor: Robert Campbell

Interior Layout: Marco Sipriaso and Scott Wyss of CWA, Inc.

Cover Design: Prima Design Team

Indexer: Sharon Hilgenberg

ISBN: 0-7615-1389-2

Library of Congress Catalog Card Number: 98-65195

Printed in the United States of America

99 00 01 02 03 HH 10 9 8 7 6 5 4 3 2

To my mother, Jean C. Talmage, my first and best teacher.

Acknowledgments

I want to thank Kevin Knoepp and Curt Beardsley of GTE Enterprise Solutions (formerly True North Technology) for giving me my start in SQL Server several years ago, and allowing me to continue DBA work while undertaking this book. Thanks to Edna Brennan and Rob Arnold for encouraging me to start and continue on this book while teaching for ST Labs. Thanks also to Karen Watterson of Pinnacle Publishing for her encouragement and technical feedback.

Thanks to my colleagues Jeff Winchell and Rod Paddock for their friendship and encouragement, and both Jeff and Richard Campbell for incisive and helpful technical editing. Thanks to Kevin Harreld, Robert Campbell, and Debbie Abshier of Prima Publishing, for their support and effort to get the book put together.

Thanks also to fellow members of the Pacific Northwest SQL Server Users Group, especially Richard Waymire and Kalen Delaney, for many helpful technical exchanges at the meetings. We all owe a debt of gratitude to the Microsoft SQL Server group for a great product and for the February 1998 Sphinx Developer's Conference. Finally, I want to thank Shawn Aebi of Microsoft, and my fellow SQL Server MVPs, for a great learning experience and good company at the MVP Summit last November.

About the Author

Ron Talmage is senior database developer with GTE Enterprise Solutions in Kirkland, WA. He is also a part-time SQL Server instructor for ST Labs, in Bellevue, WA. Ron is a SQL Server MVP and MCP, with MCSD certification. He writes regularly for SQL Server Professional, and contributes to other SQL Server publications. He is also president of the Pacific Northwest SQL Server Users Group. You can reach him at **RonTalmage@compuserve.com.**

Contents at a Glance

Contents

Chapter 5   Configuring   119

Chapter 6   Connectivity   149

Chapter 22   Database Load Testing   615

Introduction

Microsoft SQL Server 7.0 is more than just the latest version of SQL Server, it's a complete revision. Microsoft terms it a "defining release," meaning that SQL Server 7.0 is built on a new architectural platform that will support many subsequent releases in the years to come.

SQL Server 7.0 greatly simplifies database administration and development. In fact, it redefines the role of the SQL Server database administrator. You no longer need a full-time administrator for smaller databases, which used to require one, and with SQL Server 7.0 you can manage more servers with larger databases than ever before. The result: You can move on to managing larger and more complex database applications. The aim of this guide is to give you a solid practical knowledge of SQL Server 7.0 for administering and developing database applications. Every chapter contains analysis, practical tips, and hints that go beyond the SQL Sever 7.0 documentation.

Organization

Part I of this guide gives you an overview of SQL Server 7.0, starting with some background concepts, and then moving on to its architecture. Chapter 1 discusses the background context of relational database theory, the SQL database language, and the database software industry. Chapter 2 illustrates how SQL Server 7.0's architecture follows the general structure of relational database management systems.

Part II takes you through the tasks required for setting up SQL Server 7.0. Installing, upgrading, configuring, and connecting to SQL Server is very easy if you choose just the defaults and restrict yourself to the simplest hardware. These chapters give you additional information to confidently depart from the default choices.

Part III covers SQL Server 7.0 administration. Though all aspects of SQL Server administration (backup, security, data transfer, and scheduling) are made easier and more powerful with 7.0, it's still important to know what happens behind the scenes so you can prepare for the unexpected.

Part IV covers the management of data using built-in SQL Server 7.0 utilities and Transact-SQL (SQL Server's dialect of the SQL query language.) To successfully manage SQL Server 7.0, you must know how to define data storage, manipulate data, and write Transact-SQL scripts, stored procedures, and triggers. All of these topics and more, including transactions and the English Query utility, are covered in this part.

To be useful, a database system must perform well. Part V focuses on information you can use to measure and improve SQL Server 7.0 peformance. There are numerous utilities to assist in the task, and you'll learn about all of them: the index tuning wizard, current activity, SQL Profiler, and the SQL counters added to the Windows NT Performance Monitor. You end with a treatment of database load testing, in which you learn a number of ways to load and stress SQL Server and measure the outcome.

Part VI of this guide deals with the integration of SQL Server 7.0 with other servers and services. You'll learn about distributing queries across many SQL Servers as well as other OLE DB data providers. You'll also learn about replicating data from a SQL Server to other servers. Finally, you'll learn about the new OLAP service, a separate server and database system designed specifically for querying statistical aggregations of summarized database data, often in a data warehouse setting.

References for each chapter are collected at the end of the book, followed by a bibliography of sources used in the writing of this book. Also, an appendix tells you what you can find on the CD-ROM included with this book.

Conventions Used in this Book

As you read through this book, you will discover specific design features that point out helpful information. Please pay special attention to the following elements as you are reading:

NOTE

Notes identify information that is related to the discussion at hand, but may need special attention. Many notes refer you to places where you can find additional information.

TIP

Generally, tips call out information that you can use to make a task easier. Applying these tips can speed up your use of SQL Server 7.0 and make you more productive.

WARNING

Warnings mark critical information. Some steps or information can be dangerous if used improperly; the icon draws your attention to information you should be aware of before proceeding.

♦ Code, items that appear onscreen, and Internet/Web addresses. A special `monospace` typeface is used in this book to make code, command syntax, Internet addresses, and so on easier to distinguish. Output results of program commands are formatted as *`italic monospace`*.

♦ Long code lines. The code-continuation character is used when one line of code is too long to fit on one line of the book. Here's an example:

```
strMsg = strMsg + Chr(10) + Chr(13)+"The error was caused by: "
➥ & Err.Source & "."
```

When typing these lines, you would type them as one long line without the code-continuation character.

Though SQL Server 7.0 is a broad and complex product, it's easy to learn and use on the surface. You can tackle complex tasks using tools that are intuitive and flexible. I hope you find SQL Server 7.0, as I do, intellectually satisfying to learn, and a pleasure to manage.

PART I

SQL Server 7.0 Overview

Chapter 1

Background

In This Chapter

◆ Database management systems (DBMSs)

◆ Server-side computing

◆ Influences of the relational model and ANSI SQL on SQL Server 7

◆ The relational model, database design, and normalization

◆ OLTP and DSS data

To get some control over SQL Server 7's power and complexity, it's a good idea to approach it with some background information about the database industry. In this chapter, I'll outline the basic concepts needed to understand the purpose and context of SQL Server 7, its features, and tools. If you're new to relational database systems and would like a general understanding of the influences on the database industry, then this chapter is for you.

Your first step will be to learn to place SQL Server 7 squarely in the context of a database management system (DBMS). Database management systems are a class of software products meant to manage and control databases.

Second, you'll understand that SQL Server 7 has evolved in the context of server-side computing in the 1990s, starting with the traditional client/server model, and evolving with industry trends. Recently SQL Server has adapted to other server-side roles, including Internet, multitier, and distributed server applications. SQL Server 7's use of OLE DB takes the SQL Server product line into new areas with distributed queries, the ability to execute queries across heterogeneous data sources.

Third, you'll see that SQL Server is a relational SQL DBMS. In other words, it's a DBMS that is based on the relational model of database management, and influenced by the ANSI SQL-92 language standard. Your third background component will be a general understanding of the relational model, database design levels, normalization, and influences on SQL Server's evolution.

Finally, you'll see that nowadays database data generally consists of two kinds: OLTP and DSS. OLTP stands for *online transaction processing*, the use of data to store the dynamic data based on transactions taking place over time. This is also often called operational data. DSS stands for *decision support systems*, the kind of data used for making decisions (relatively static data, including a lot of historical data with aggregations). Often this is called analytical data. With your last framework component, you'll learn that SQL Server has always been a good OLTP DBMS, but with SQL Server 7, Microsoft has added numerous new features and enhanced the query engine to support very large databases in a DSS context.

Database Management Systems (DBMS)

A database management system, abbreviated as DBMS, is a specific type of software product that is meant to manage databases. Each database managed by a DBMS is just a collection of data stored according to some specifications.

To get a better perspective on why DBMS software such as SQL Server is popular, let's start by considering the basic components of a database application.

Presentation, Business Rules, and Data Access Services

At the 30,000 foot level, you can view data-oriented software applications as consisting of three services to the user:

♦ Presentation: presenting and receiving data from the user

♦ Business rules: validating data according to business rules

♦ Data access: storing and retrieving data from disk

These services are shown graphically in Figure 1-1.

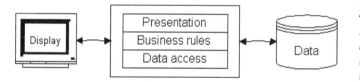

FIGURE 1-1

Data-oriented applications consist of three services to the user: presentation, business rules, and data access.

Often applications make no distinction among these different roles and will weave together codes for presentation, validation, and data access throughout the application. These are often called monolithic applications, because everything is bound up with the application. The application programmer is responsible for presenting and receiving data from the user, validating the data, and storing the data. Monolithic applications started on mainframes but have also been written on minicomputers, Unix systems, and desktop PCs.

However, real progress has been made by separating these different roles, logically at first, and then physically into separate application components.

Database Management Systems

An important breakthrough occurred in the late 1960s. Application developers separated data access services and business rules from the presentation services. Separating the data access services into another application made it possible to develop database management systems as general-purpose software products.

Initially operating on mainframe computers, and later in the 1970s on minicomputers, these database systems act as independent software applications that store and retrieve data. At first they only had data access services, but later they gained the capability of validating business rules, as illustrated in Figure 1-2.

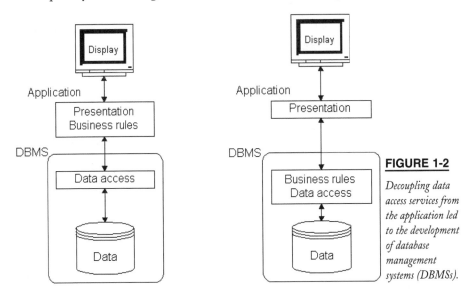

FIGURE 1-2

Decoupling data access services from the application led to the development of database management systems (DBMSs).

This breakthrough created the overall class of software known as database management systems. By having a separate software product to handle data, you save the cost of having to rewrite or even reinvent data storage routines with each new application. Instead, applications only need to communicate with the DBMS, and let it handle the data.

There is a difference between a database and a DBMS. A database is an organized collection of data, whereas a database management system stores and maintains databases. A database includes the data tables, indexes, constraint rules, dependencies, triggers, and stored procedures that make the database behave in a particular way. But it's always contained in a DBMS. The DBMS is the vendor's software that provides data storage and retrieval, a query engine, administrative tools, and other utilities to manage databases.

A DBMS is a very complex software product and as such can have bugs and flaws of its own. The database developer and administrator must be aware of them and often work around them.

In the late 1960s and early 1970s, the IBM researcher and mathematician E.F. Codd proposed the relational model for database management systems. Applying formal set theory to the storage and manipulation of data, Codd proposed that database systems should show data to users as sets of data, which could be visualized as tables. This way, the user's view of the data gained independence from the physical implementation by the DBMS. All links between the tables should be shown not by any physical pointers, but by actual data values. You'll examine the relational model more closely later in this chapter.

Database management systems that follow the relational model are called relational database management systems, or RDBMSs. As the first RDBMSs were being prototyped, researchers realized that they needed a query language to interact with the data. The SQL language was proposed in the early 1970s and implemented later in the decade on various relational database prototypes. When IBM adopted it in the early 1980s as the query language for DB2, it became an industry standard. Since then it has become widely used, and ANSI committees have been formed to write various standards. The current SQL standard is ANSI SQL-92, which was released in 1992. (A further SQL standard, called SQL-3, is close to release. However, observers are skeptical that it will have as much influence as SQL-92.)

For more informaton on the DBMS architecture of SQL Server, see Chapter 2, "Architecture."

Server-Side Computing

At first, all DBMS applications resided on centralized host systems such as mainframes and minicomputers. But with the explosive growth in the 1980s of computing power on the desktop, a second breakthrough in database application technology occurred. More powerful desktop PCs and workstations made it possible to decentralize the database application's computing needs and locate the application's presentation services apart from the database system.

Host-Based Systems

When a database application resides on a central host and is accessed by remote terminals, the application is called "host-based," as you see illustrated in Figure 1-3.

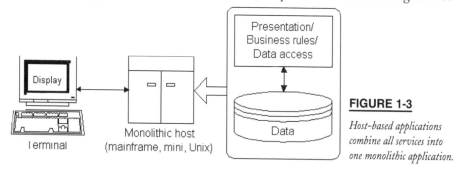

FIGURE 1-3

Host-based applications combine all services into one monolithic application.

There are many variations on host-based systems, and the diagram in Figure 1-3 is just a simple model. It is a distilled picture, meant to drive home the essential characteristics of an entire generation of database applications with centralized presentation, business rules, and data access services. There were important exceptions to this simplified model. In some ways anticipating thin-client computing, mainframe computers often implemented terminal servers that offloaded the presentation services from the central mainframe.

The great advantage of host-based systems is their centralized management of everything. The great disadvantage is that everything is centralized, including the presentation services that could be much more easily managed on the desktop. When terminals are replaced by PCs running terminal emulation software, a huge amount of PC computing power goes to waste.

File-Server Database Applications

During the late 1980s and early 1990s, the growing power of PC computers and networks led to multiuser applications using desktop databases such as Access, FoxPro, Paradox, and dBASE. These database applications adopt a file-server architecture for sharing data. They place the data access engine on the desktop computer and centralize their data in files on the LAN server, as shown in Figure 1-4.

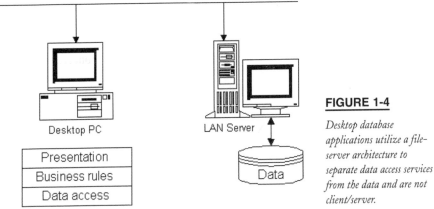

FIGURE 1-4

Desktop database applications utilize a file-server architecture to separate data access services from the data and are not client/server.

Because these products place the database engine on the desktop and share their data on a file-server, they are not considered server database systems. Rather they are usually called desktop or file-server database systems. Because the shared data is somewhat exposed on the LAN server, desktop database systems do not provide the security and transactional characteristics of a server DBMS such as SQL Server. On the other hand, they can be simpler to develop with and are certainly easier to manage, for smaller amounts of data, than a server database.

The Client/Server Breakthrough

Another important breakthrough occurred when developers first created applications that could place the database system on one central server computer and use the desktop computer's power for presentation and business rules. This client/server model aimed to balance the computing load between the server and the users' desktop computers. As server DBMSs added functionality, and server hardware became more powerful, even the business rules could migrate into the database, as shown in Figure 1-5.

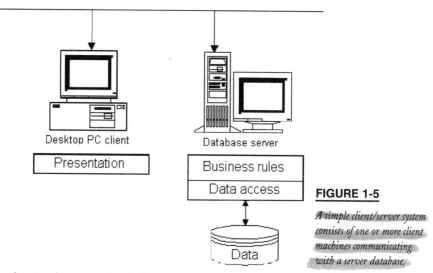

FIGURE 1-5

A simple client/server system consists of one or more client machines communicating with a server database.

In the simplest case, the desktop part of a client/server application is called the "client side" of the application, and the database, located on some server machine, is called the "server side." A further separation of an application's business rules into a separate component has led to distributed database systems and multitier client/server systems.

NOTE

It's not really necessary to put the client part of an application on a different computer from the server. It is quite possible to run the client software on the server, or place a server database on the client machine.

In the development of client/server applications, it was always possible to place the business rules with the client or the server, or to split the business rules between the two. As relational databases added programmable features such as stored procedures and triggers in the late 1980s, it became possible to embed a greater number of business rules in the database. However, it's probably true that some business rules (data validations) always end up in the client, so the picture of standard two-tier client/server applications was more like that shown in Figure 1-6.

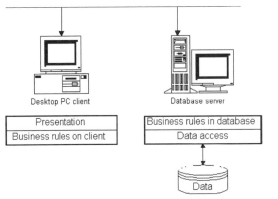

FIGURE 1-6

Typical two-tier client/server systems often placed business rules in both the client application and the database server.

However, there are limits to the amount and complexity of business rules that can be embedded in a server database. The natural next step for large and complex applications was to separate business rules from both the server database and the client application and give them their own server. This led to the three-tier concept.

Three-Tier Client/Server

The next step in the evolution of database applications was to further decouple the business rules from the presentation services. This has since come to be called "three tier" or middle-tier client/server, where the "middle" tier is now the business rules application logic, as shown in Figure 1-7.

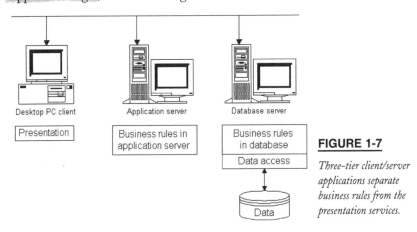

FIGURE 1-7

Three-tier client/server applications separate business rules from the presentation services.

Even in three-tier applications, it's common to put at least some of the business rules in the database. That way, the data remains protected from invalid entries made by other applications, bugs in the current applications, or random interactive users.

However, some vertical market client/server applications such as SAP achieve the ability to work with a number of different server DBMSs by putting no business rules logic in the database at all.

Internet Database Applications

Among the first middle-tier applications in the Microsoft world were OLE automation servers. But middle-tier computing has really taken off recently with the use of Web servers in the middle tier, as shown in Figure 1-8.

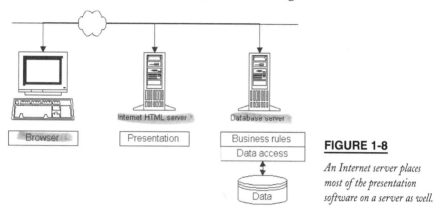

FIGURE 1-8

An Internet server places most of the presentation software on a server as well.

The Internet server provides an interesting twist, because by putting the presentation software on the server, it makes the client even thinner. All it needs is a browser. Because of this, some think that an Internet server configuration is no longer client/server at all.

Multitier Client/Server

In addition to having a multiple number of clients, a system might also have a multiple number of servers. In that case, a transaction monitor such as Microsoft Transaction Server (MTS) can distribute the data among several database servers, as illustrated in Figure 1-9.

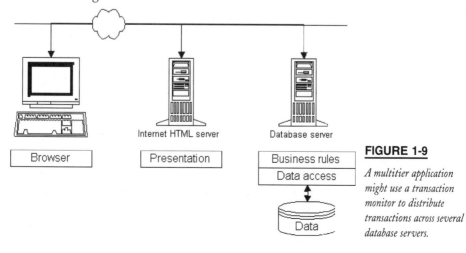

FIGURE 1-9

A multitier application might use a transaction monitor to distribute transactions across several database servers.

In addition, an Internet server might be added to the mix as well. In fact, Microsoft bundles Transaction Server with its Internet server software, IIS.

Another configuration might have several servers replicating data to each other, with no intervening monitor. You'll look at SQL Server replication in Chapter 24, "Replication."

Mobile Computing

Because the general purpose of SQL Server 7 is to run on the back end, that is, on a server machine, SQL Server 7 will also run on Windows 95 and 98. That way, it can run on laptop or other portable computers that must disconnect and reconnect occasionally. This adds a new wrinkle to client/server, as illustrated in Figure 1-10.

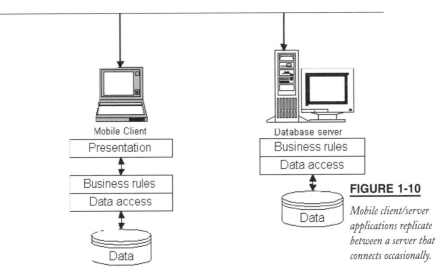

FIGURE 1-10

Mobile client/server applications replicate between a server that connects occasionally.

What makes this possible is SQL Server 7's merge replication, which you'll examine in Chapter 24. It's interesting to note that because the mobile computer has a temporary copy of the main database, it also may have business rules embedded in its database—to prevent the user from entering invalid data while disconnected.

Client/server technology continues to evolve in many directions, mixing and matching its components to serve a variety of needs. The key enabler of this technology is the relational database.

NOTE

To learn more about SQL Server's connectivity options, see Chapter 6, "Connectivity." For more information about OLE DB and distributed queries, see Chapter 23, "Distributed Data."

Influence of the Relational Model and ANSI SQL on SQL Server 7

The evolution of SQL Server 7 as a relational database depends on two outside industry influences, the relational model and the ANSI SQL standard, as you can see in Figure 1-11.

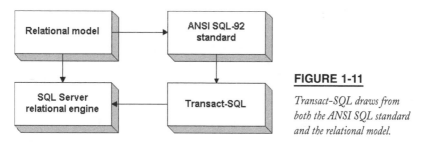

FIGURE 1-11

Transact-SQL draws from both the ANSI SQL standard and the relational model.

Even though the relational database model and the ANSI SQL-92 standard are not software products at all, they still have a direct influence on the development of SQL Server.

The Relational Model

In 1969, the IBM mathematician E.F. Codd first formulated the theory or model of relational database systems. He based his ideas on the application of set theory to data structures. During the 1970s, researchers worked out most of the fundamental operations that could be applied to data organized in sets. A few prototype relational database systems were built, and many more were proposed, but the first commercial relational database systems, including IBM's mainframe DB2, were introduced in the early 1980s. Since that time, the relational DBMS model has become the dominant type of DBMS for storing database data.

The relational model serves as a theoretical guide for how relational databases should present data to users, and what the results of user operations on the data should look like. (It's not a model of how the data should actually be stored.) If a DBMS follows the relational model's rules, then the results of performing relational operations on the data can be predicted or proven with mathematical certainty.

TIP

It's important to know which commands in Transact-SQL conform to the SQL standard. If there's a choice between formulating a Transact-SQL command using the ANSI SQL syntax on the one hand, and in a nonconforming way on the other, usually it's better to choose the ANSI SQL way.

Microsoft implements well-known relational algorithms in SQL Server's relational query engine. Industrial and academic researchers have built and refined these algorithms for over 25 years, and DBMS vendors often adapt them into their products. In this way, the relational model has a direct influence on SQL Server's relational query engine, and an indirect influence on Transact-SQL through the ANSI SQL standard.

The ANSI SQL Standard

When it comes time to start defining database tables and loading them with data, your main relationship with SQL Server will be through its query interface language, called Transact-SQL. The commands in Transact-SQL allow you to define tables, populate them with data, and retrieve data back from them. Most Transact-SQL commands are based on a standardized set of commands called ANSI SQL.

The ANSI SQL committee consists of representatives from across the database software industry. The committee's current standard is called ANSI SQL-92, or SQL-92 for short. SQL-92 is not a database product, just a set of standards defining the SQL language.

The ANSI SQL committee has defined the SQL standard with the relational model in mind. However, it's important to note that ANSI SQL does not always implement the relational model. The ANSI SQL standard falls short of being fully relational in several places. As a result, there's industry pressure on the ANSI SQL committee to improve the language and change it where it deviates from the relational model.

Because the initial ANSI SQL standards (SQL-87 and SQL-89) were very primitive, Sybase, and later Microsoft, developed extensions to the SQL language, called Transact-SQL. Some elements of Transact-SQL are present because the SQL standard does not supply commands that a commercial DBMS must have, but sometimes those extensions reflect older conventions and oddities that should be avoided.

> **TIP**
>
> A good understanding of the relational model is very helpful when designing databases. Neither Transact-SQL nor the ANSI SQL standard treat database design; they simply work with tables you've already decided upon. The relational model, however, is defined at a level where design decisions can be analyzed and examined.

There is a constant drive among DBMS vendors to implement the parts of the ANSI SQL standard that would enhance their products and make them more attractive and useful to customers, and Microsoft is no exception. SQL Server 7 is entry-level ANSI SQL-92 compliant, which places it among the most ANSI SQL–compatible of the relational database systems. SQL Server 7 has implemented many new features that are ANSI standard, as you'll learn in Chapter 12, "Data Definition," and Chapter 13, "Data Manipulation." You'll also learn that many advanced features of ANSI SQL are still not implemented in SQL Server.

NOTE

By understanding both the relational model and the SQL standard, you can get a better understanding of SQL Server 7—where it's been and where it's likely to go in the future. For more information about the relational model, see the next section of this chapter. For more about SQL Server's relational engine, see Chapter 12, "Data Definition." For more about Transact-SQL, see all of Part IV, "Managing Data."

The Relational Model and Database Design

SQL Server is a relational DBMS, which means it presents data to you in a relational format. In this section you'll find out about what it means for a DBMS to be relational. In addition, you'll learn about the levels of database design, how to read database design diagrams, and how the process of data normalization in the relational model works.

In 1969, the IBM mathematician E.F. Codd first formulated the theory of relational database systems. He based his ideas on the application of set theory to data structures. During the 1970s, researchers worked out most of the fundamental operations that could be applied to data organized in sets. A few prototype relational database systems were built, and many more were proposed, but the first commercial relational database systems, including IBM's mainframe DB2, were introduced in the early 1980s. Since that time, the relational DBMS has become the dominant method for storing database data. It's important to learn about the relational model because it plays a role in how SQL Server 7 is designed and implemented.

So why is it called the relational model?

Relations

The relational model of data gets its name from treating sets of data as a mathematical relation. It's actually quite simple. First, let's look at an example of a mathematical relation, and then see how it applies to data.

Consider the "greater-than" relation between integers. To simplify your example, let's restrict your consideration to the integers 1, 2, 3, and 4. These four integers will be your domain.

When you consider just those four numbers, you know that:

4 > 3,

4 > 2,

4 > 1,

3 > 2,

3 > 1, and

2 > 1

This can be expressed as the collection or set of ordered pairs of numbers,

{<4, 3>, <4, 2>, <4, 1>, <3, 2>, <3, 1>, <2, 1>}

From a mathematical standpoint, this set of ordered pairs characterizes the greater-than relation for the four integers 1, 2, 3, and 4.

Each ordered pair is called a tuple, and the set of all the tuples of the relation defines the relation. The greater-than relation is a binary relation, but relations can have a higher order: There are ternary (three elements in each tuple) relations, and so on.

To create the tuples of your simplified greater-than relation, you picked a set of two numbers from your domain {1,2,3,4}. You chose one number from the integer domain for the first of the ordered pair, and you picked another appropriate number from the same domain for the second member of the pair. You only chose those numbers for which the greater-than relation is true.

Now your simple greater-than relation is a set, so you can apply the set operations of union, difference, and so on to it. In other words, you could make a union of one subset with another, find an intersection, or perform other similar operations. This becomes important when dealing with data.

Now here's the important point. In addition to seeing your greater-than relation as a set of tuples, you can also see it as a table of data. Let's call the table "1to4GreaterThan" and give it two columns:

1to4GreaterThan	
Col1	Col2
4	3
4	2
4	1
3	2
3	1
2	1

The rows of the table are just the tuples of the relation, and therefore you can view the table as a representation of the simplified greater-than relation!

Now apply these principles to some database data. Instead of using the set of integers from 1 to 4, use a subset of the actual data from the Authors table in the SQL Server 7 sample pubs database. The Authors table includes a set of available author ids, namely the domain of author ids (au_id):

```
{'172-32-1176', '213-46-8915', '238-95-7766'}
```

There are 23 actual values in the Authors table (and roughly 999,999,997 more possible values), but for brevity let's just look at the first three.

There's also a domain of author last names:

```
{'White', 'Green', 'Carson'}
```

and first names:

```
{'Johnson', 'Marjorie', 'Cheryl'}
```

If you restrict your attention to these three domains, and just three values in each domain, you can form a small version of the Authors relation. Just choose the elements from each domain and make the ordered triples:

```
<'172-32-1176', 'White', 'Johnson'>,
<'213-46-8915', 'Green', 'Marjorie'>, and
<'238-95-7766', 'Carson', 'Cheryl'>
```

The basis for your choosing which values to put together is the truth of statements like this:

> There is an author with id "172-32-1176" that has a last name of "White" and a first name of "Johnson."

If you take your triples and make a set, you get:

```
{<'172-32-1176', 'White', 'Johnson'>, <'213-46-8915', 'Green', 'Marjorie'>, <'238-
95-7766', 'Carson', 'Cheryl'>}
```

You can represent the set as a table called Authors, which is the way you see it using SQL commands:

au_id	au_lname	au_fname
172-32-1176	White	Johnson
213-46-8915	Green	Marjorie
238-95-7766	Carson	Cheryl

As you can see, a table is a natural representation of a relation. In this case the relation is something like, "there is an author with id au_id that has a last name of au_lname and a first name of au_fname." All you have to do is decide the column header names, which normally come from the domains you defined earlier. (In the relational model, they're called attributes, not column headers.)

So the relational model of data gets its name by treating tabular data as instances of mathematical relations. E.F. Codd actually called them *time-varying relations*, to allow a relation to have its tuples (rows) change over time. Technically speaking, if you add or change a row, you make a new relation, so there's a need to define the unvarying form of the relation, which for Codd is the time-varying relation. C.J. Date, another relational database pioneer, calls them *relation variables*, or *relvars*, also to indicate that a relation's tuples can vary.

Sets versus Lists (Sequences)

It's also possible to look upon a table less as a logical set of rows, but more as a physical list of records, so that one record's the beginning of the list, another the second, and so on, forming a sequence. This is how file-processing systems such as COBOL and desktop databases treat their data. They often refer to files, records, and fields to define the data storage. When opening a table's file, these products will use a record pointer to position themselves at some row in the table. They also have commands to move forward and backward, skipping to the end or jumping to the beginning.

In the relational model, in ANSI SQL and Transact-SQL, you generally ignore the order of the rows in a table and look upon the table as a set of rows, not a list (exceptions are the ORDER BY and cursors). Generally the standard SQL commands do not explicitly rely on the order of the data.

WARNING

When you look at a table as a sequential list, you break the set-theoretic connection to relations, because sets do not have any order. Therefore it's important to keep in mind that in the relational model, the table's data will be stored in some physical order, but the relation itself, at a logical level, does not have any physical order.

The terminology for referring to data across list-processing systems, the SQL language, and the relational model, can be summarized as follows:

List-Processing Systems	SQL Language	Relational Model
file	table	relation
field	column	attribute
record	row	tuple

When dealing with ANSI SQL and Transact-SQL, you will use the SQL terminology of table, column, and row.

NOTE

Transact-SQL does provide a way to process a table as a list, through a cursor. You'll learn more about cursors in Chapter 15, "Basics of Transact-SQL Programming."

Relational Tables

Among the many components of the relational model, perhaps the most important one concerns the way you refer to the data. In a fully relational DBMS, said Codd, all data must appear to the user as organized into relational tables. Originally, Codd defined a relational table as something like the following:

> A relational table is a table of data with unique rows and single-valued columns.

Therefore, a relational table allows neither duplicate rows nor repeated data in its columns. (Recently, theorists such as Chris Date have proposed allowing multi-valued columns in relational tables.) What's fundamental is that in the relational model, you can only refer to part of the data by referring to the data values themselves. If the rows are not unique, then there is no way in the data itself to tell the data apart.

There are good reasons that the relational model forbids duplicate rows in a table. Consider the following data from the actual Pubs sales table:

stor_id	ord_num	qty	title_id
6380	6871	5	BU1032

Suppose you add a duplicate row:

stor_id	ord_num	qty	title_id
6380	6871	5	BU1032
6380	6871	5	BU1032

What does the second row, the duplicate, really mean? Surely it is either a separate sale or not.

◆ If it's a separate sale, shouldn't it have a distinct order number?

◆ If it is part of the original order, shouldn't you have just one sale with a quantity of 10?

◆ If it is truly a duplicate, then is it a mistake? How can you tell?

The upshot, according to the relational model, is that there is never any genuine meaning to duplicate rows in a data table, and therefore they should be eliminated.

Ironically, while ANSI SQL and Transact-SQL make it possible to enforce this rule on your tables, they also make it possible to violate it! In fact, there are many situations where SQL commands return results that contain duplicates. This is just one instance among several of a gap between the relational model and the SQL language. On the whole, though, the SQL language does implement the aims of the relational model.

NOTE

In SQL Server 7, you can store duplicate rows in tables. It's up to you to place uniqueness constraints on a table.

Relational Database System Features

Originally, Codd proposed a set of 12 rules (actually 13, because there was a rule 0) for any database system to call itself "relational." Then in 1990, he expanded the list to over 300 rules! Without getting into that kind of detail, you can see a number of other common features of relational database systems.

1. Candidate, Primary, and Alternate keys: When a data table has no duplicate rows, you can use the data values themselves to identify each row. A candidate key is a column or combination of columns that will remain unique in a table. Because there may be more than one column or combination of columns making each row unique, there can be more than one candidate key in a table.

   The primary key is a candidate key that the designer decides should always be unique and perhaps also be the link to other tables with related data. SQL Server has support for primary and foreign keys, and you can create other candidate keys. A candidate key that is not a primary key is called either an alternate or secondary key.

2. Data Manipulation: A relational DBMS must, according to Codd, provide the ability to retrieve, insert, update, and delete rows. Although many alternative query languages were originally proposed, the winner and still champion in the database world is SQL (short for "structured query

language"). SQL Server uses the SQL SELECT, INSERT, UPDATE, and DELETE commands to manipulate data.

3. Transactions: Another important characteristic of relational databases is that they can execute their commands as a complete logical unit of work. In SQL Server, one or more operations on the data can be placed within a transaction, so that the entire group of operations takes place completely or not at all. If the transaction fails, the database can recover into a stable state.

4. Concurrent Access: A relational database must also provide support for concurrent access, namely handling multiple users simultaneously. To do this SQL Server employs locking methods. SQL Server will lock rows, and sometimes entire pages or tables, so that operations on the data by many users will not interfere with each other. That way, SQL Server can always provide a consistent view of the data to each user.

5. Catalog: A relational DBMS must support a set of relational tables about the data, called a catalog, which stores data about the database. SQL Server stores catalog data in the data tables of the master database, as well as system tables of every database.

6. Views: A relational database must also support views, which are derived tables based on the relational tables. In SQL Server, you can create persistent views based on tables in a database. (Because views are not permanent tables, they do not have primary keys.)

Database Design

Let's review two major components of database design. Entity-Relationship diagramming gives a bird's eye view of the major design constraints on your database tables, and normalization is the process of removing redundant data by identifying each table's primary key and all its dependent attributes.

Database Design Diagrams

The primary purpose of a relational database application is to ensure that all operations against the data happen according to the business rules laid out for the database. Many or most of these rules are encoded by the table design and enforced by constraints that implement the design. If the database design has flaws, or the implementation does not match the design, then the resulting database application will fail to enforce those business rules. Sometimes it can work the other way: You may not know what the business rules are and have to infer them from the design.

Database diagrams are used to represent the data model for a database, and the activity of producing an accurate database diagram is often called data modeling. Data modeling occurs at three important levels: conceptual, logical, and physical.

Conceptual Data Modeling

Conceptual data modeling takes place independently of the choice of the type of database. In other words, at the conceptual level, you make no commitment to whether the database will be relational, object-oriented, or even flat-file. The diagram in Figure 1-12 shows a sample of two kinds of conceptual modeling components, based on a fact taken from the Pubs sample database.

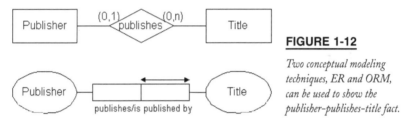

FIGURE 1-12

Two conceptual modeling techniques, ER and ORM, can be used to show the publisher-publishes-title fact.

At the conceptual level, it is conventional to keep the entity names singular, and to attempt to identify the basic facts about entities and their relationships among each other. Both diagrams in the figure represent the fact that publishers publish titles.

Attributes

The diagram in Figure 1-12 only shows two entities and their relationships; no attributes are shown. This is common in conceptual level design, but you can easily add the attributes to either the ER diagram by attaching them to either the entity or the relationship, as shown in Figure 1-13.

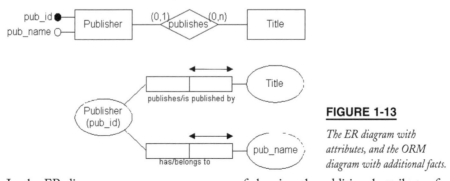

FIGURE 1-13

The ER diagram with attributes, and the ORM diagram with additional facts.

In the ER diagram, you now see one way of showing the additional attributes for Publisher, namely the publisher id (pub_id), and the publisher name (pub_name). Because the ORM diagram does not distinguish entities and attributes (they are all just objects), you simply add the fact that a publisher has a name.

Relationships

In all levels of database modeling, the numeric aspect of the relationship determines the relationships. There are really two kinds of choices: cardinality and optionality. Basically, you map one entity to the other, deciding whether each side of the relationship is one or many, and whether it is optional or mandatory. So for example, in the relationship of publishers to titles, the cardinality is that it is a one-to-many relationship. Then for optionality, you decide whether the publisher is mandatory or optional for the title, and whether the title is mandatory for the publisher. It turns out that there are two basic publisher-to-title optionality possibilities:

- ◆ Publisher mandatory for title: Each title has exactly one publisher.
- ◆ Publisher optional for title: Each title has zero or one publisher.

There are also two basic title-to-publisher possibilities:

- ◆ Title mandatory for publisher: Each publisher has at least one or more titles.
- ◆ Title optional for publisher: Each publisher has zero or more titles.

NOTE

A variation on cardinality is the specification of an actual number, so that the relationship is a one to a specific number: one entity is associated with exactly some number of related entities. For example, a baseball team might be associated with exactly 17 players.

Let's look at a specific example. In the ER portions of Figures 1-12 and 1-13, the publisher entity is related to the title entity by the relationship "publishes." The numbers on either side of the relationship diamond symbol indicate the cardinality of the relationship, in the format (min, max). The (0,1) on the left side shows the minimum and maximum numbers of publishers per title: The minimum number of publishers per title is zero (hence a publisher need not publish a title), whereas the maximum number of publishers for any given title is 1. The (0, n) on the right shows the number of titles per publisher: the minimum number of titles per publisher is zero, meaning that a title needn't have a publisher. The n indicates that the maximum number of titles per publisher is an indefinitely large number.

In the ORM (Object-Role Modeling) diagram in the same figures, the publisher object plays a publishing role with the title object. This diagramming technique has a slightly different way of showing cardinality. Instead of a relationship, you have a predicate between the two objects. The predicate has a one-way direction indicated by which side of the predicate box you look at. The left side of the box represents the "x publishes y" predicate, which goes from publisher to title; the right side of the box represents the "y is published by x" predicate, which goes from title to publisher. The arrow over the right-hand predicate indicates uniqueness: Each title is unique when paired with publishers. With these symbols, you get the same cardinality information that the ER diagram showed with numbers: that each publisher publishes zero or more titles, and each title is published by zero or one publisher.

Both ER and ORM are considered conceptual modeling techniques because they do not specify exactly what form the entities and their attributes should take. They could become tables in a relational DBMS, or objects in an object-oriented DBMS.

NOTE

Conceptual modeling is very useful when gathering and documenting database requirements. For more information about conceptual modeling and database requirements, see the references for this chapter in the Appendix.

Logical Data Modeling

Logical data modeling assumes that the type of database has been chosen, but that no commitment has been made to any particular vendor's product. So at the logical level, you would commit to a relational database, with tables for publishers and titles, for example, but not yet to SQL Server. Often ER diagrams can be translated to the logical level or built from an existing database into a logical model. For example, Figure 1-14 shows an ER diagram produced by reverse-engineering the Pubs database.

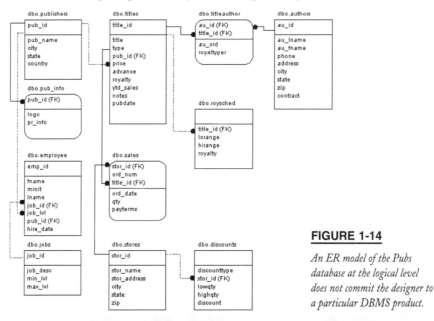

FIGURE 1-14

An ER model of the Pubs database at the logical level does not commit the designer to a particular DBMS product.

The type of ER model you see in Figure 1-14 is called IDEF1X. It is quite common and a U.S. government standard. Other ER styles (most notably the crow's foot) are somewhat less common.

Each of the boxes in Figure 1-14 show an entity, and each entity will ultimately correspond to a table in the database. Each entity consists of a number of attributes that are listed in the entity box (unlike the conceptual level modeling, which listed them outside the entity.) Take a look at the publishers table, for example, shown in Figure 1-15.

FIGURE 1-15

The publishers table has one primary key and a number of other attributes.

The pub_id attribute is the primary key, or primary identifier, of the publisher entity. The remaining attributes are listed below the primary key. Relationships between entities can be translated into relationships between tables, as you can see in Figure 1-16.

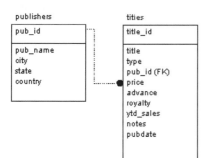

FIGURE 1-16

The publishers table has a relationship with the titles table.

The large dot at the end of the line connecting the publishers table and the titles table is the IDEF1X way of indicating that any one publisher publishes zero or more titles, showing that publisher is in a one-to-zero-or-more relationship with titles. In addition, the fact that the line itself is dashed indicates that this is not an identifying relationship: the pub_id attribute is not part of the titles primary key.

Physical Data Modeling

Physical data modeling is the activity of diagramming a database that belongs to a specific DBMS. You can use the same ER diagramming techniques to do this, because many ER tools will reverse-engineer a SQL Server database.

However, SQL Server 7 provides its own tool for physical data modeling, called the Database Designer (formerly the Visual Data Tools). Its style is similar to that of an

ER diagram, with some limitations. You can see a SQL Server Database Diagram of the pubs database in Figure 1-17.

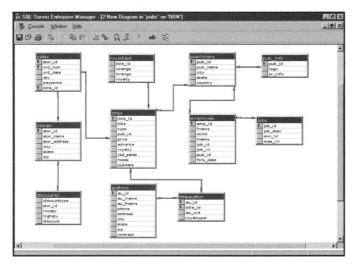

FIGURE 1-17

A SQL Server 7 physical database diagram of the pubs database.

The reason that SQL Server 7 database diagrams represent database modeling at the physical level is that they are not DBMS independent. In other words, these diagrams are bound to SQL Server. This is not a criticism. Because SQL Server's diagramming can work at the physical level, it can help you modify a database design in place. (I'll cover the SQL Server Database Design tool in the next section.)

Many-to-Many Relationships

A last type of entity relationship is not shown in the pubs ER diagram, called the *many-to-many* relationship, where each entity can associate with many of the other entities. Normally, many-to-many relationships are shown only at the conceptual level. For example, the diagram in Figure 1-18 shows the many-to-many relationship between title and author: Each title can have many authors, and each author can be the author of many titles.

FIGURE 1-18

A many-to-many relationship, at the conceptual level, shows each entity in a relationship to many of the other entities.

Many-to-many relationships are normally only stated at a conceptual level, because in order to implement them in a relational DBMS, and therefore to get to the logical level, they have to be resolved into two one-to-many relationships. So you can translate a conceptual many-to-many relationship by creating an association entity and assigning the original entities a one-to-many relationship to it. Figure 1-19 shows the same authors-title relationship translated into an IDEF1X representation at the logical level.

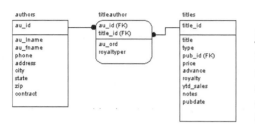

FIGURE 1-19

You can translate a single many-to-many relationship at the conceptual level into two one-to-many relationships at the logical level.

If you did not make this translation, the tables would not be in first normal form, a requirement of the relational model. This is a good point for to look into the normalization process.

Physical Database Design with the Visual Data Tools

For physical database design with SQL Server 7, there's no better tool to use than the Database Diagramming tool, also called the Visual Data Tools utility, built into SQL Server 7's Enterprise Manager. To use it, all you need to do is drill down to a particular database in Enterprise Manager's tree view, right-click, and choose New Database Diagram, as shown in Figure 1-20.

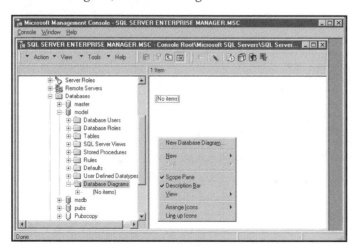

FIGURE 1-20

You can start a new database diagram in Enterprise Manager by right-clicking and choosing from the pop-up menu.

After the window has opened up for a new diagram, you can reverse-engineer a database by dragging and dropping tables from the database into the new diagramming area. In addition, a wizard lets you identify which tables you'd like to bring over.

After you have a set of tables, you can add, edit, and delete relationships between the tables by dragging and dropping from a primary key to a foreign key. In addition, if the tables already have a foreign key relationship, the diagramming tool will automatically draw the appropriate one-to-many relationship, as you can see in Figure 1-21.

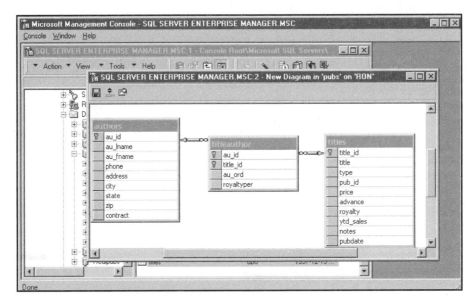

FIGURE 1-21

You can create relationships by dragging from primary key to foreign key.

The one side of the relationship is represented by the key symbol, and the many side is represented by the infinity symbol.

NOTE

The Database Diagramming Tool is a physical modeling tool because it maintains a one-to-one relationship between entities in the diagram and the tables in the database, and because it is specific to SQL Server databases.

Normalization

An important check on Entity Relationship modeling is normalization, the process of removing redundant data in order to prevent anomalies during insert, update, and delete operations. In a nutshell, it has the effect of splitting tables with redundant data into a greater number of tables that no longer contain redundant data. Recall that a relational table has no duplicate rows. As E.F. Codd first defined it, the normalization process applies to relational tables with single-valued columns and no duplicate rows.

Normalization and Database Design

It is quite possible to have redundant data in your database design. The ER modeling process does not force normalization at all. (On the other hand, ORM diagrams are automatically normalized.)

> **NOTE**
>
> It is possible to design un-normalized databases using ER diagramming tools. However, ORM diagramming tools can automatically generate fully normalized database designs from valid ORM conceptual schema diagrams. So if you use ER diagramming methods, you may still need to take your design through the normalization process.

Normalization and OLTP versus DSS Data

In the next section of this chapter, you'll look more closely at the difference between online transaction processing (OLTP) systems and decision support systems (DSSs). An OLTP system has a relatively high demand for modifications to the data (letting "modifications" cover inserting, updating, and deleting) and a relatively low demand for extracting data. By way of contrast, a DSS system has a relatively low demand for modifications to the data, but a high demand for extracting data.

> **NOTE**
>
> Normalization applies most usefully to OLTP systems. It is common in DSS systems to normalize initially and then introduce denormalizations in order to enhance query performance.

Repeating Groups within the Columns

You might find repeating groups of data in a table, keeping it from being a relational table, in at least a couple of ways.

Take a look at the following table that uses some data from the Pubs database. The table represents a many-to-many relationship between authors and titles. It is not even a candidate for normalization, because it is not a relational table at all, as you can see in Table 1-1.

Table 1-1 **Repeating Groups of Data within Columns Requires Something like a Comma to Separate the Data**

au_id	au_lname	title_id	title	au_ord
409-56-7008	Bennet	BU1032	The Busy Executive's Database Guide	1
213-46-8915	Green	BU1032, BU2075	The Busy Executive's Database Guide, You Can Combat Computer Stress	2,1

Notice the repeating data inside the columns of the second row: The values are not "atomic," because they are separated from each other by commas. The table is trying to say that Green is an author with two titles, BU1032 and BU2075. The only way you can tell is by the comma between the titles.

> **NOTE**
>
> Recently C. J. Date argues that repeating groups of data within a single column does not violate first normal form, and thus he abandons the "atomicity" requirement.

This kind of internal grouping occurs occasionally in databases, usually when people have not planned ahead and need to store multiple lists inside a single column. You'll often see it in comments. But it's fraught with problems. Searching and updating become notoriously difficult, for example, because you have to scan the data to find the place in the column's string to either extract or change the data.

Repeating Groups of Columns

To make it into a relational table, you must give the ord_num, qty, title_id, and title columns single values. Sometimes you'll see tables that give separate columns to each data item but really just pull out the repeating groups into their own columns, as you can see in Table 1-2.

Table 1-2 **Repeating Columns Is an Alternative Way of Repeating Data in a Nonnormal Fashion**

au_id	au_lname	title_id1	title_id2	title1	title2	au_ord1	au_ord2
409-56-7008	Bennet	BU1032		The Busy Executive's Database Guide		1	
213-46-8915	Green	BU1032	BU2075	The Busy Executive's Database Guide	You Can Combat Computer Stress!	2	1

In the preceding table, the columns for title_id1 and title_id2 repeat, indicating that title1 and au_ord1 belong to title_id1, and so on. You now have a relational table, but it is not in first normal form, because it still has repeating groups in the column names, even if each individual column is atomic. Among the many problems in the preceding table, note that if you want to add a new title for the second author, you have to add a whole new set of columns!

> **NOTE**
>
> The major problem with repeating groups of data in columns is that inserting additional data requires a new set of columns. In a DSS system, however, repeating groups of data can sometimes improve performance.

First Normal Form

"A table is in first normal form (1NF) if and only if its columns are single-valued (sometimes called atomic) and there are no repeating groups of data inside the columns or in the column names."

This means a 1NF table cannot have repeating groups of data within its columns, nor can it have repeating columns. You can remove the repeating groups from the preceding example, and as long as the table has at least one candidate key, it will be in first normal form. The preceding table is not in first normal form, because it has repeating groups of line number columns. It is simpler and more flexible to just give each title its own row in the table, as you can see in Table 1-3.

Table 1-3   A Table in First Normal Form May Still Contain Redundant Data

au_id	au_lname	title_id	title	au_ord	pub_id	pub_name
409-56-7008	Bennet	BU1032	The Busy Executive's Database Guide	1	1389	Algodata Infosystems
213-46-8915	Green	BU1032	The Busy Executive's Database Guide	2	0736	New Moon Books
213-46-8915	Green	BU2075	You Can Combat Computer Stress!	1	1389	Algodata Infosystems

You've added two new columns, pub_id and pub_name, for publisher id and publisher name, respectively, so that you can see the entire three-step process of normalization with the same set of data. Now you have the authors-titles table in first normal form.

What is the primary key for the new table? Since all the columns have duplicate values vertically, you'll have to choose a combination of columns. Note that the combination of author id and title id is unique, so let's choose au_id and title_id as the primary key.

NOTE

You can reproduce the authors-titles table with the following query:

```
SELECT ta.au_id,
            (SELECT a.au_lname FROM authors a
            WHERE a.au_id = ta.au_id) AS au_lname,
            (SELECT t.title_id FROM titles t
            WHERE ta.title_id = t.title_id) AS title_id,
            (SELECT t.title FROM titles t
            WHERE ta.title_id = t.title_id) AS title,
            ta.au_ord,
            (SELECT pub_id FROM titles t
            WHERE ta.title_id = t.title_id) AS pub_id,
            (SELECT pub_name FROM publishers p, titles t
            WHERE ta.title_id = t.title_id and p.pub_id = t.pub_id) AS
        pub_name
        FROM titleauthor ta
        WHERE au_id = '213-46-8915' or au_id = '409-56-7008'
```

Because this table is in first normal form, all the data must depend on the primary key, as shown in Figure 1-22.

FIGURE 1-22

A dependency diagram of the titles-authors table shows how the remaining columns depend on the primary key.

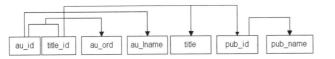

The dependencies that are shown by the arrow lines in Figure 1-22 are called "functional dependencies," or FDs. The goal of normalization is to make all the dependencies depend only on the primary key, because by doing that, you can eliminate the redundancies in the data. As long as those extra dependencies are combined where they shouldn't be, you will have redundant data.

The redundant data causes what are called "update anomalies." For example, in your current authors-titles table, if you insert a new author and title, you have to repeat an enormous amount of data: title, au_lname, and pub_name. If you change the name of a title, you have to change it throughout the entire table. Finally, if you delete an author-title row, you might end up deleting both the author and the title, as well as the publisher, from the entire system.

NOTE

Relational database theorists such as Chris Date have weakened the first normal form requirement to allow nonatomic complex objects as values of a column's table. This change accommodates the Object/Relational type of database, which can contain and query across complex objects such as pictures and drawings in a relational table.

Second Normal Form

"A table is in second normal form (2NF) if it's in first normal form and all the column values depend on the whole primary key, not just part of the primary key."

If a table has a single column as the primary key, your normalization process just skips this step.

Because the authors-titles table does have a compound primary key, you need to see what columns depend on only part of the primary key. Note in Figure 1-22 that au_lname depends only on au_id, and title depends only on title_id. You can change the table into second normal form by separating out an authors and titles table so that you don't have to repeat the author last name and title, as you can see in Table 1-4.

Table 1-4   **Separating Out the Columns That Depend on Only Part of the Primary Key Brings the Authors-Titles Table into Second Normal Form, but Not Yet Third Normal Form**

Titles:

title_id	title	pub_id	pub_name
BU1032	The Busy Executive's Database Guide	1389	Algodata Infosystems
BU2075	You Can Combat Computer Stress!	0736	New Moon Books

Authors:

title_id	au_name
213-46-8915	Green
409-56-7008	Bennet

Titleauthor:

au_id	title_id	au_ord
409-56-7008	BU1032	1
213-46-8915	BU1032	2
213-46-8915	BU2075	1

With the extraneous data removed to other tables, the authors-titles table is now very close to the titleauthor table in Pubs, so it gets a new name. The authors table is quite simple; there's no more work to do there. But look at the titles table: it contains what's called a "transitive dependency," which keeps it from being in third normal form. You can see this clearly if you look at the dependency diagrams for all three tables in Figure 1-23.

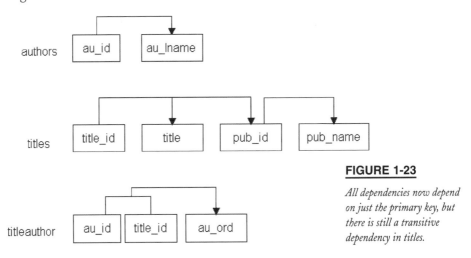

FIGURE 1-23

All dependencies now depend on just the primary key, but there is still a transitive dependency in titles.

The titles table contains what's called a transitive dependency because pub_name depends on pub_id, which in turn depends on title_id.

Third Normal Form

"A table is in third normal form (3NF) if it's in 2NF and all the column values depend only on the primary key, and there are no transitive dependencies."

Looking at the titles table, notice that it's pretty obvious that you ought to just take out the publisher name and make another table for it, just as you did for authors. When you do that, you end up with a new publishers table and a revised titles table. The whole set of four remaining tables is shown in Table 1-5.

Table 1-5   The Original Data in Third Normal Form Takes Up Four Tables

Titles:

title_id	title	pub_id
BU1032	The Busy Executive's Database Guide	1389
BU2075	You Can Combat Computer Stress!	0736

Publishers:

pub_id	pub_name
1389	Algodata Infosystems
0736	New Moon Books

Authors:

au_id	au_lname
213-46-8915	Green
409-56-7008	Bennet

Titleauthor:

au_id	title_lname	au_ord
409-56-7008	BU1032	1
213-46-8915	BU1032	2
213-46-8915	BU2075	1

There are more levels of normalization, having to do with some rather involved problems with compound keys. Normalization is based on a well-developed theory of functional dependency that is beyond the scope of this book. Because most third normal form tables will also be in fifth normal form, there is often no need to normalize further.

Denormalization

Denormalization is the process of selectively introducing redundancies into normalized tables. Developers will do this in DSS systems to improve query performance or make reporting easier.

However, the best practice is to normalize first and selectively denormalize later, only after you're sure you've removed redundancies. Because SQL Server performs best with normalized tables, certain kinds of denormalization could affect query performance detrimentally.

> **NOTE**
>
> A good general rule is that OLTP database tables should be normalized as fully as possible. On the other hand, DSS database tables, such those in a data warehouse, are often read-only and can be selectively denormalized for query and reporting reasons.

OLTP and DSS Data

A broad distinction is made in the type of databases stored in current DBMS software, based on the use of the data. If the database has data that is updated frequently, it's often called OLTP, short for online transaction processing. All the relational databases, including Microsoft SQL Server, were originally designed and built with OLTP activity in mind. Most of the important database applications in the first decades of database software have been in the OLTP arena, and many of them continue to be.

In recent years, demand has grown for databases that serve the inverse use of data, namely data that is queried frequently but updated only infrequently. The general umbrella term for this type of approach has been DSS, short for decision-support system. DSS systems have been around for a long time but have come into their own in the 1990s because of the special demands for company or corporate-wide data access, along with much faster hardware and software, and easy-to-use query and reporting tools.

In particular, the buzzword "data warehouse" has come to indicate a centralized corporate DSS database. Special-purpose DBMS products such as Red Brick and NCR's Teradata are specifically built for data warehousing applications.

> **NOTE**
>
> Sometimes OLTP data is also called operational data, suggesting the dynamic nature of the database application. By way of contrast, DSS data is often relatively static and is sometimes called analytical data.

It is common for small systems to combine elements of both OLTP and DSS in a database. For larger amounts of data, however, it's much more common to store these two types of data in separate databases, on separate servers. In fact, OLTP data and DSS data for large databases currently have a somewhat inverse relationship, as you can see in Figure 1-24.

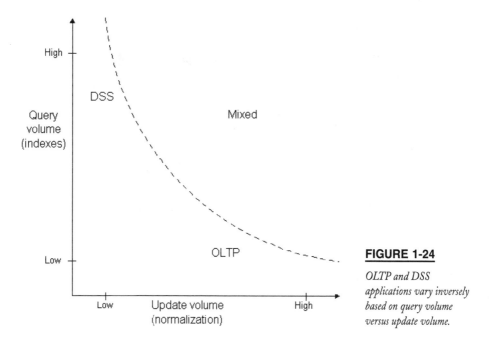

FIGURE 1-24

OLTP and DSS applications vary inversely based on query volume versus update volume.

As the need and market for data warehousing applications has risen, relational DBMS vendors have tried to keep pace by improving their query and indexing facilities.

Microsoft has made it a major goal for SQL Server 7 to support data warehousing applications. The relational engine's query processor has been completely revised, with additional optimization techniques for data warehousing. The query engine includes support for hash and merge joins, and it can adapt its optimizer for joins in star and snowflake schemas. You'll learn about a new SQL Server 7 tool called the SQL Server Profiler (which can be used to monitor the performance of queries) in Chapter 21, "Monitoring Performance." You'll learn about the Index Tuning Wizard and the Query Analyzer's new graphical showplan in Chapter 19, "Tuning Queries."

A specialized part of DSS applications concerns complex analysis of data, often called OLAP, short for online analytical processing. This does not necessarily imply the presence of a data warehouse, but it does imply a transformation of OLTP data into a separate format with summaries and aggregates that can be analyzed by the user. To learn about SQL Server 7's OLAP Server, which provides tools for data analysis, see Chapter 25, "OLAP Services."

Summary

SQL Server 7 is a relational database management system, one of a class of software products that store and manage databases. It started with client/server computing and has evolved with industry trends, to server multi-tier and Internet applications. Because SQL Server 7 uses OLE DB, it can execute queries across heterogeneous data sources. Because SQL Server is a relational SQL DBMS, it is based on the relational database model, the ANSI SQL-92 standard. SQL Server began as primarily an OLTP-oriented DBMS, but SQL Server 7 incorporates special new join technologies for DSS applications as well.

With this background framework in place, let's now take a brief look at SQL Server 7.0's architecture.

Chapter 2

Architecture

In This Chapter

◆ The structure of a server DBMS

◆ SQL Server architecture

◆ SQL Server origins

◆ The SQL Server learning curve

One of the best aids you can have in administering SQL Server is knowledge of its architecture. A good model of SQL Server's structure can help you organize your own knowledge of the product and make sense of the requirements for using SQL Server.

Structure of a Server DBMS

SQL Server is a back-end or server database system, not a file-server database system. In other words, it's a software system that provides data services to the entire network, in a client/server context. In this section, you'll examine the general structure of a server DBMS, and in the next section, you'll drill down into SQL Server's architecture.

DBMS Engine and Utilities

A server database system generally consists of two sets of components: the DBMS engine, and the utilities to administer and query the DBMS. It's important to note that the DBMS utilities are client applications, as shown in Figure 2-1.

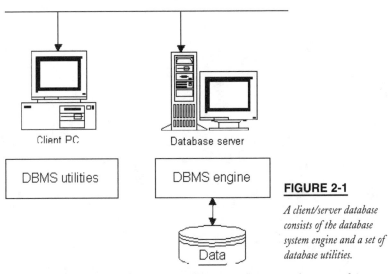

Client PC

Database server

DBMS utilities

DBMS engine

Data

FIGURE 2-1

A client/server database consists of the database system engine and a set of database utilities.

As client applications, the database system utilities use the same drivers to access the database that custom applications do. They do not have any privileged position.

Normally, you'd run the database system utilities on a separate machine from the server, perhaps to manage a server or set of servers in production. But it's also common to install the utilities on the server as well. There are many reasons for having the database system utilities and the DBMS on the same computer, including emergency work on the server machine, as well as developing or learning the system on your desktop.

A Typical Server DBMS

Now let's examine the DBMS engine. The primary purpose of any server DBMS is to store data in a format that can be shared. To support shared data, a DBMS must also have components to allow and control multiple users' querying and updating the data. Therefore, the DBMS must have a query interface component, often called the query processor.

In addition, the DBMS must update and retrieve data stored physically on disk. That data is stored in a special format recognized by the DBMS as database data. So data storage and retrieval must be a major component of a DBMS, which I'll call the data access engine. Figure 2-2 shows these components at a high level.

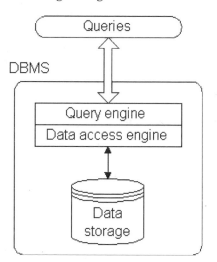

FIGURE 2-2

A typical server DBMS consists of query processor and data access engine components.

The Query Interface

The query processor must handle several kinds of queries. Users must be able to send commands that define storage structures, populate them with data, and retrieve the data. In addition, client/server database systems often provide the capability of compiling DBMS commands into stored procedures that users can invoke. Finally, every DBMS has a set of utility commands that administrators can use for maintenance on the databases. These queries are summarized in Figure 2-3.

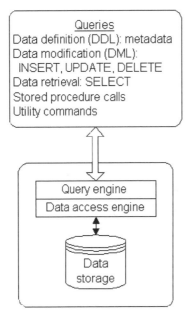

FIGURE 2-3

Every DBMS must be able to handle several kinds of queries.

The query processor must handle commands to define and modify objects such as tables and indexes. These commands make up the data definition language, or DDL. Current database systems use the CREATE and DROP commands from the SQL language to accomplish these tasks. The results of these commands are stored as metadata, that is, data about the database data.

The query processor must also handle commands to update the data. These commands compose the data manipulation language, or DML. In most of today's database systems, these are the SQL commands INSERT, UPDATE, and DELETE. For data retrieval, database systems generally provide the SQL SELECT command.

Database systems also may handle calls to compiled query execution plans. Because stored procedures can be executed on demand, the query processor must be able to recognize calls to invoke them.

Finally, utility commands are needed for database maintenance purposes. These include backup and restore commands, as well as consistency checks. Users must be able to execute these commands on demand, so the query processor must recognize them.

Security and Transactions

Let's drill down a step further into the DBMS engine. The DBMS must provide two kinds of control in order to handle shared access. The DBMS must control user access to the data, which means it must manage data security. The DMBS must protect the data from unauthorized access, and it must limit the extent of access among authorized users. The DBMS component to do this is commonly called the Security Manager.

Another type of control that the DBMS must provide is the ability to keep data consistent during simultaneous updates. This is generally accomplished by treating user updates as transactions. Transactions are logical units of work that succeed or fail as an entire group. The component that handles them is usually called the Transaction Manager.

A simple model of this architecture is shown in Figure 2-4.

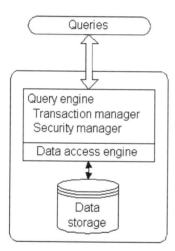

FIGURE 2-4

A server database must provide security and transaction handling.

Both security and transactions are all-pervasive, so they're shown in the diagram as standing between the query processor and the data access engine. All client requests for data retrieval and update must pass through both of them.

An extensive security system allows a DBMS to protect the data from unauthorized access at a variety of levels. Many database systems, SQL Server 7 included, can restrict access at the database, table, row, and column levels.

The transaction processing capability ensures that a single command, or a group of commands that are wrapped in an explicit transaction, will be executed atomically: They will be entirely executed or entirely aborted, and no partial updates will occur. Transaction management has the added advantage of providing for recovery. When the database server machine is restarted after losing power or having some other nondestructive crash, the DBMS will process all unfinished but committed transactions before going online. If the crash is destructive, backups of the transaction log can be applied to make the databases current again.

Database Storage Elements

You can go down one step further in the model, into the database storage. Relational databases store data in tables. An additional requirement of relational databases is that they store metadata, that is, data about the database and data tables, in a database as tables. These metadata tables are commonly called "system tables." Accordingly, a relational DBMS must store data tables, system tables, and the code of stored procedures and triggers on disk, as shown in Figure 2-5. (SQL Server 7 stores only the source code of stored procedures and triggers; prior releases of SQL Server also stored the compiled code.)

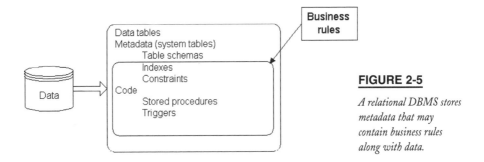

FIGURE 2-5

A relational DBMS stores metadata that may contain business rules along with data.

The system tables for a relational DBMS contain data about the user's data tables. These tables contain table schemas that define the data tables, provide information about indexes on those tables, and include constraints that limit the ranges of values that can be stored in the data tables.

Database systems store the business rules about the data in those constraints, and also in triggers and potentially in stored procedures. All these components, in particular constraints and triggers, act to enforce rules about the data that are defined for the application.

I've built up the general concepts of a relational database this way in order to detail SQL Server 7 as a relational database. It's now time to examine SQL Server's architecture in particular.

SQL Server 7 Architecture

Now let's apply the overall model of a server DBMS to SQL Server 7. What you find is that SQL Server follows the basic RDBMS model but its architecture is more complex and feature-rich.

The SQL Server DBMS Engine and Utilities

A full installation of Microsoft SQL Server 7 consists of two basic groups of modules: the client management tools, and the SQL Server engine itself. Normally you install both the management tools and the DBMS on the same machine, in case you need to administer SQL Server on the server machine. You can also install the management tools (sometimes also called "client utilities") on a separate machine. That allows you to administer many SQL Servers from one machine. The latter configuration is shown in Figure 2-6.

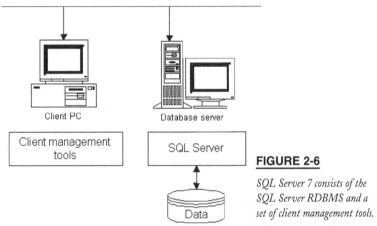

FIGURE 2-6

SQL Server 7 consists of the SQL Server RDBMS and a set of client management tools.

The client management tools are numerous. You'll examine them in detail when you look at SQL Server Setup in Chapter 3. For now, let's drill further down into the SQL Server DBMS architecture.

The SQL Server RDBMS Subsystems

The SQL Server relational DBMS consists of two independent subsystems: the relational engine, which corresponds to the query processor; and the storage engine, which corresponds to the data access component of relational database systems. The high-level structure of the SQL Server DBMS is shown in Figure 2-7.

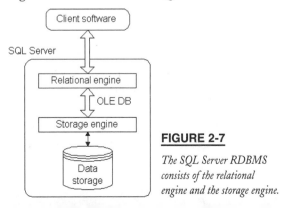

FIGURE 2-7

The SQL Server RDBMS consists of the relational engine and the storage engine.

The relational engine processes queries, whereas the storage engine stores and retrieves data. In prior versions of SQL Server, query processing and data storage were implemented by one SQL Server engine. However, with SQL Server 7, these two functions are separated out into two independent subsystems. The relational engine communicates with the storage engine via low-level OLE DB.

Both engines are OLE DB providers. The relational engine is an OLE DB service provider, which means that it can receive requests from active data objects (ADOs) and communicate with them. However, the relational engine has numerous other communication components as well. The storage engine is an OLE DB data provider, meaning that it controls SQL Server data and can communicate with OLE DB service providers, which are normally query engines like the relational engine.

The Relational Engine

The purpose of the relational engine is to process queries for SQL Server data. To do this, it must perform a number of functions, as shown in Figure 2-8.

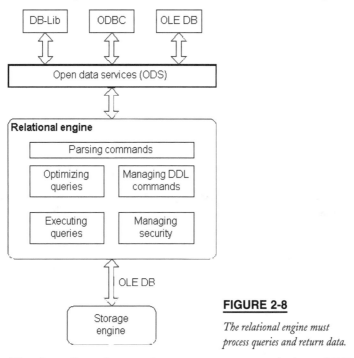

FIGURE 2-8

The relational engine must process queries and return data.

The Open Data Services layer receives commands from OLE DB, ODBC, and legacy DB-Library clients. Connectivity components unpack the network messages into their content, which for SQL Server is a format called Tabular Data Stream, or TDS. You'll examine how that format is transmitted in Chapter 6, "Connectivity."

After the relational engine receives incoming client requests, it parses the commands, checking their syntax and translating them into an internal format. When you receive a syntax error from a query, it is the command parser that detects the error and sets the error number and message. If the command either modifies or extracts data, the relational engine will optimize it, building a query tree, choosing indexes and the table sequence for the query.

The relational engine also checks security: for every retrieval and update, the user must be authorized to access the data. Permissions to data can be set for an entire database, or to desired tables, views, and stored procedures within the database. At these levels, users can have SELECT, INSERT, UPDATE, DELETE, and EXECUTE privileges. In addition, roles can be defined, and users assigned to a role. You'll learn more about security in Chapter 9, "Security." The relational engine must also handle DDL (data definition) commands. It will resolve and then execute a DDL statement such as a CREATE or ALTER TABLE.

The Storage Engine

The purpose of the storage engine is to store and retrieve data. Consequently, it must manage the data and index pages, the transaction log, the memory cache, and locking, so that many simultaneous requests to retrieve and update tables can be managed. These functions are illustrated in Figure 2-9.

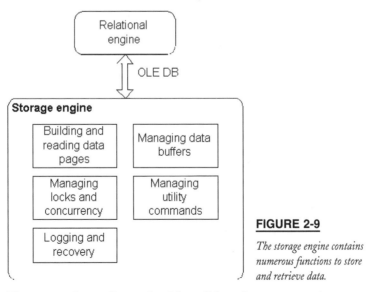

FIGURE 2-9

The storage engine contains numerous functions to store and retrieve data.

To manage the reading and writing of data, the storage engine must manage accesses and changes to data pages in memory, load data and index pages into memory, and manage the data cache.

The storage engine must also manage transactions: it ensures that any change to data is logged, and it also provides the service for recovery. Every SQL DML command is treated individually as a transaction, and client software can define transactions containing several commands. The commands within a transaction must either completely succeed (in the case of a commit), or completely fail (in the case of a rollback). All changes are written ahead to the transaction log, which can be used for restoring the database to its original state in the case of a system failure. You'll learn more about the transaction log, as well as backup and recovery, in Chapter 8, "Backup and Restore."

Another function of the storage engine is to manage locks. SQL Server stores all data in 8 kilobyte pages, and in order to protect data affected by a transaction, pages, rows, or tables must be locked and restricted for the current transaction's use for the duration of the transaction. During intensive updating operations, there is much contention for data by competing transactions. SQL Server's storage engine dynamically adjusts locks to the row and page, always seeking the most efficient way to maintain concurrency and efficiency. You'll learn more about SQL Server's locking and other performance issues in Chapter 20, "Concurrency Tools."

Distributed Queries

By separating the relational engine from the storage engine, and using the public standard OLE DB as the communication method between them, SQL Server can distribute queries across diverse data sources. That is, you can use the relational engine to query data from more than just its local storage engine. You can use it to query any OLE DB data provider, such as other remote SQL Servers, Oracle databases, ODBC data sources, and Microsoft Jet engine databases.

The capacity for distributed queries makes it easier to manage data across multiple database servers and generate reports across a wide variety of data sources. You can expect to see the number of data sources increase as other vendors write OLE DB data provider interfaces to their products.

Database Storage

When you look at what's stored in SQL Server databases, you find the same elements that generally hold for relational DBMSs, with a few new features, as shown in Figure 2-10.

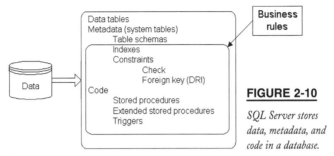

FIGURE 2-10

SQL Server stores data, metadata, and code in a database.

System tables in each database contain table schemas and index definitions, as well as definitions of all other objects such as constraints, triggers, and stored procedures.

SQL Server offers several kinds of constraints: declared and bound defaults, check constraints, rules, and foreign key constraints. Default constraints specify default values for columns, values that will be inserted automatically into the table if no other value was specified. Check constraints limit the values of columns to certain ranges or formats. Rules are a limited and somewhat obsolete form of check constraint, and are falling out of favor. Foreign key constraints validate the existence of column values against key values in another table. All these constraints are database-specific and stored in the database they affect.

SQL Server 7 stores the source code for triggers and stored procedures in its databases. Triggers are code attached to tables and are executed or "fired" when a data modification event such as INSERT, UPDATE, or DELETE occurs against the table. Stored procedures contain code that can be executed at will. Extended stored procedures provide an interface to the execution of external DLLs written in C++.

SQL Server Origins

Microsoft initially licensed SQL Server from Sybase, who first developed SQL Server as a client/server database on the Unix platform. Microsoft first deployed that version of SQL Server on the OS/2 platform in 1988, as you can see in Figure 2-11.

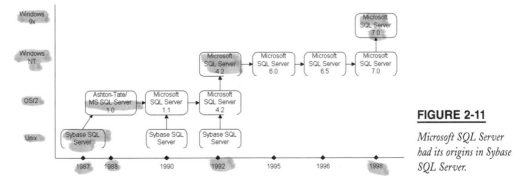

FIGURE 2-11

Microsoft SQL Server had its origins in Sybase SQL Server.

When talking about the many iterations of SQL Server, it's helpful to distinguish releases from versions. A release is a major product event, and you can expect to see dramatic changes from release to release. The initial version of a release will change incrementally as you apply the improvements provided by that release's service packs. Each service pack results in a new version of a given release.

The earliest release of MS SQL Server you will probably ever see in production is 4.21a, which runs on both OS/2 and Windows NT 3.1/3.51. This is also the last release of SQL Server that Microsoft kept synchronized with Sybase, and also the last release that runs on OS/2.

The next release was version 6.0, which Microsoft supports only on Windows NT 3.51. Microsoft revamped the administrative utilities and introduced new database engine facilities that diverged somewhat from the Sybase version of SQL Server. The next release, SQL Server 6.5, runs on both Windows NT 3.51 and Windows NT 4.0. The current release, SQL Server 7.0, only runs on Windows NT 4.0 (with the NT Service Pack 2 or later). For more detailed histories of SQL Server, see the notes for this chapter in the Appendix, "References."

Developing with SQL Server

Developing applications with SQL Server presents some special challenges, because an essential part of the application is on the back end, and not always visible to front-end developers. The best practice is to have separate SQL Servers for development, testing, and production, as shown in Figure 2-12.

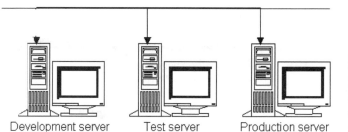

Development server   Test server   Production server

FIGURE 2-12

The best practice in SQL Server development is to separate the phases, often on separate servers.

During initial development, and especially after you've deployed a database application, as an administrator you can't allow developers to create new code on the production server. Instead, it's become common to give them limited access to a development server, where data can be corrupted and restored easily with no risk to the production system. Then, when changes are ready to pass testing or QA, they can be applied to a test system.

The test server often runs parallel to the production system, with a copy of live data, and with scripts to simulate production activity. Impacts of changes on performance can be simulated or predicted, based on the behavior of the test server.

Only when changes pass QA can they be applied to the production server. In each case, and at each step, it's important that the database administrator be involved. The DBA must ensure that the test system is truly in sync with the production system, that proposed changes meet coding and other standards, and that the production system can be rolled back to the prior working state if necessary.

Three Types of Database Careers

Career opportunities with SQL Server have evolved that correspond to the three phases mentioned previously, as shown in Figure 2-13.

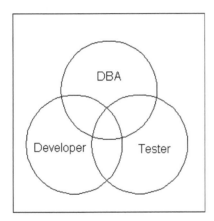

FIGURE 2-13

Three career paths have emerged in large SQL Server and other database installations.

The database administrator (DBA) maintains the database: its security, backups, configuration, and performance. A DBA will typically monitor a database on a daily basis and set up alerts that will e-mail or page the DBA when trouble arises.

The database developer typically designs the database, lays out its specification, and writes the trigger and stored procedure code that ensures the data integrity of the system.

The knowledge required for a DBA overlaps the knowledge required for a database developer. The database developer and administrator share much of their knowledge but have specialty areas that do not overlap.

The database tester is a relatively new role in the database world. As SQL Server applications become more complex and the data more valuable, it has become vital that people who are trained to look for likely trouble spots in the database test the database.

Summary

The architecture of the SQL Server 7 DBMS consists of a relational engine and a storage engine. The relational engine parses and executes queries, while the storage engine manages transactions and reading and writing data. Because the relational and storage engines use OLE DB to communicate, you can distribute SQL Server 7 queries across diverse data sources. The best practice is to separate the SQL Server development process into development, test, and production systems.

With these concepts in place, you can now examine the specifics of SQL Server. You'll start with setting up SQL Server, then move on to administration, managing data, and performance issues.

PART II

Setting Up SQL Server 7.0

Chapter 3

Installing

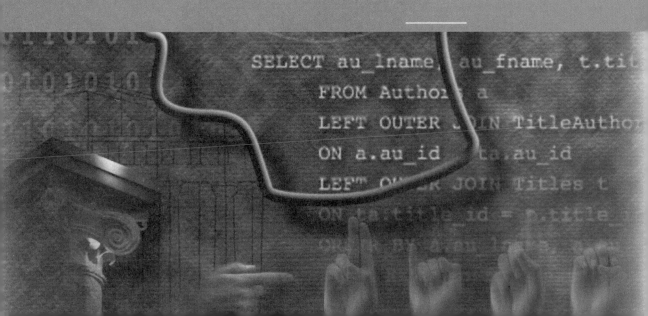

In This Chapter

- ◆ SQL Server products, releases, and versions
- ◆ Planning a new installation
- ◆ Installing SQL Server 7.0 for the first time
- ◆ Changing installation options after installation
- ◆ Uninstalling SQL Server
- ◆ Unattended installation
- ◆ Installed tools
- ◆ Tutorial: Inspecting an installation
- ◆ Troubleshooting installations
- ◆ Installation inspection checklist

Setting up SQL Server 7 is easy, but there's still a lot to understand that goes on behind the scenes. In this chapter, you'll take a look at installation issues, then move on to upgrading, configuring, and connectivity in the following chapters.

The SQL Server installation process is easy to run, but gives you no guarantee that the installation will be successful or meet your needs. If you don't make sure that your hardware and software are compatible, and that you've made the right installation decisions, chances are good that the install will sooner or later give you problems.

The purpose of this chapter is to help you avoid those problems in the first place, or if necessary solve them. You'll see how to plan a new installation, what decisions are involved in the installation process, how to use Setup after installation to change some options, how to uninstall, and how to troubleshoot a bad installation.

SQL Server Products, Releases, and Versions

Probably the first issue you must address before installation is, Which SQL Server product are you going to install? You have several choices here.

With its initial release, SQL Server 7.0 has several product variations:

- ◆ The Standard Edition of SQL Server 7 runs on Windows NT Server only (either standard or Enterprise.) It is the full SQL Server product, and takes advantage of Windows NT-specific security features.
- ◆ The SQL Server 7 Enterprise Edition runs only on Window NT Server Enterprise Edition, can address the larger RAM space that

Windows NTEE allows, and it can participate in Microsoft Cluster Server (MSCS.)

◆ The Small Business Edition comes with the Back Office Small Business Server. It is also a version of the SQL Server standard edition that is limited to 50 connections and 10GB data per database. You can upgrade this version to the Standard Edition.

◆ The SQL Server 7 Desktop Edition, designed for Windows NT Workstation and Windows 95 and 98, is optimized for desktop performance and is not designed for large databases or large numbers of users.

◆ Finally, the Microsoft Data Engine, also known as MSDE, is a redistributable component of Office 2000 and Visual Studio, made up of the relational and storage engines of SQL Server. It is limited to about 10 users maximum, and 2GB of data per database.

All the above products, except for the MSDE, deliver both the SQL Server DBMS relational and storage engines, as well as various tools. Let's take a closer look.

SQL Server: DBMS and Management Tools

SQL Server 7 comes with two collections of software: the SQL Server 7 RDBMS and its management tools, as shown in Figure 3-1.

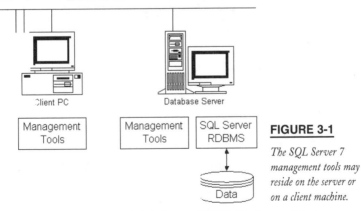

FIGURE 3-1

The SQL Server 7 management tools may reside on the server or on a client machine.

The Server includes the SQL Server RDBMS, along with the supporting services of SQL Agent and the Distributed Transaction Server. The management tools are a set of utilities that behave as clients to SQL Server and are essential for managing the DBMS.

The management tools can reside on the server as well as on client machines. They are your initial method of gaining access to SQL Server. Normally when you install the SQL Server database system, you will also install its management tools and operate them on the server. But you can install the tools by themselves on a client machine and then manage SQL Server over the network. You might choose to do so if you wanted to manage one or more SQL servers from your desktop but don't need to install the entire database system.

Finally, as you'll see later in this chapter, you can also install the SQL Server RDBMS without the tools, if you choose a minimum installation.

SQL Server Management Tools

The SQL Server management tools consist of a number of executables that are actually client software. These include:

- ◆ SQL Server Enterprise Manager (a Microsoft Management Console snap-in)
- ◆ SQL Server Query Analyzer
- ◆ SQL Server Client Configuration tool
- ◆ SQL Server Service Manager

Because they are client software, they may use client DLLs to run, including, for example, the SQL Server ODBC driver. It's important to remember that when you're running these tools on the database server, they are still running as client software for SQL Server.

SQL Server Releases and Versions

SQL Server 7 comes in a number of releases and versions. A SQL Server release is a major product issue with an identifying number, such as 6.0, 6.5, or 7.0. All three of these releases have major differences. You can see the release number on the installation CD, or on the Enterprise Manager.

SQL Server releases are the major divisions of the products over time. The earliest release of MS SQL Server you will probably ever see in production is 4.21a, which ran on both OS/2 and Windows NT 3.1 and 3.51. This is also the last release of SQL Server that Microsoft kept synchronized with Sybase, and also the last release that runs on OS/2.

The next releases were version 6.0, which Microsoft supports only on Windows NT 3.51, and 6.5, which is supported on both Windows NT 3.51 and 4.0. The current release is SQL Server 7, which is supported on Windows NT 4.0, as well as Windows 95 and 98.

Service Packs (Versions)

A SQL Server version is the build number of the release. That number increases as you add patches to the product by applying service packs.

Each version of SQL Server has follow-up patches called service packs. Service packs normally fix a number of bugs and occasionally introduce new features. It is generally a good idea to apply the latest service pack, though not always. If you have a production system that is running just fine, there's no strong motivation to apply a service pack that may have a slight possibility of breaking your application. (It's been known to happen!) Also, it's a bit wiser to apply a new service pack to a development or test system first, or wait for the feedback of other DBAs concerning a service pack's reliability, before applying it yourself to a production system.

TIP

When you install SQL Server service packs, you may have to stop other services, such as SQL Server, SQL Agent, Full Text Search (MSSearch), OLAP Services, and MS DTC services.

Planning a New Installation

It's a common practice in the PC world to install a software product first and read the manuals later. It's only when the installation fails, or it refuses to continue, or the product does not operate that we are forced to read the manuals.

In the case of installing SQL Server 7, it's even truer that a little planning can prevent a lot of pain and grief. As you'll learn in this section, there are numerous hardware and software requirements for installing SQL Server. I'll end this section with a checklist to assist you in planning an installation.

Hardware Requirements

SQL Server has some minimum hardware requirements. First of all, it is restricted to CPUs that run Windows NT and Windows 95/98. For Windows NT, that means an Intel 486/33 or better, or the DEC Alpha AXP processor. For Windows 95 or 98, the Intel chip will be required.

NOTE

SQL Server 7 drops support for MIPS computers.

Second, SQL Server requires that the machine have enough RAM. 32MB is considered by Microsoft to be the baseline, but any production or test system should have at least 64MB of RAM. If you're just learning SQL Server, and/or you know that you'll only be dealing with small amounts of data, then 32MB may be sufficient.

Third, SQL Server requires about 150MB of free disk space for the installation process, if you're doing a Typical or Custom install that adds the management tools. For the Minimum installation, this number is somewhere around 100MB. This does not include data for databases, so for a production or test system, you need to make sure you have the free space needed for your data. This calculation may not be easy, because you may not know how much space your data will take up in SQL Server, or how dynamic it will be. In addition, you need to budget disk space for SQL Server's temporary database (tempdb), and for your databases' transaction logs. The best solution is often to work with a system where it will be easy to add new disk storage if necessary.

Many hard disk subsystems come with caching controllers, but this can present problems for SQL Server and recovery. SQL Server tells the operating system to write all transactions to the appropriate transaction log disk file immediately. SQL Server relies on those writes going immediately to disk. If they don't, and the system crashes, SQL Server may not be able to recover a database. Consequently, if you're using a write-back caching controller, you should disable the write-back mechanism. Some caching controllers have on-board battery backups for the cache and can support a database server. You can find out about this from the maker of the card. If they're not sure what you're asking about, either disable the caching or get a new card.

SQL Server 7 is supported only on Windows NT 4.0 with the NT Service Pack 3 or better. For Windows 95, there are no such restrictions, but it is always safer to use the most current versions of the operating systems. These hardware requirements are summarized in the following table:

	Windows NT	Windows 9x
Processor	Pentium 166 or compatible Digital Alpha AXP	Pentium 166 or compatible
RAM	32MB (64MB Enterprise)	32MB
Required Disk Space	180MB (Full) 170MB (Typical) 65MB (Minimum)	180MB (Full) 170MB (Full) 65MB (Minimum)
OS Version	NT 4.0 with SP4 or later	Windows 95 and 98
Internet Explorer	IE 4.01 with SP1 or later	IE 4.01 with SP1 or later
Networking	Networking installed	Networking installed

NT Hardware Compatibility

If you're installing SQL Server on Windows NT, it's not enough to just have the right CPU, RAM, and disk. You also need to ensure that the hardware is compatible with NT. If your machine came with Windows NT preinstalled by its manufacturer, it's probably a safe bet that it's compatible! But if you're not sure, you can run the NTHQ software from Microsoft. You can obtain this program from the Microsoft Web site using the following URL:

http://www.microsoft.com/ntserver/info/hwcompatibility.htm

You run NTHQ by putting the program on a floppy disk and booting your NT machine. (NTHQ contains its own loader, so it does not use the OS installed on disk.) When it runs, it may report some machine components as unknown. When that happens, it may be the case that the hardware is compatible, just newer than the software recognizes. Usually computer and component makers are aware of whether their products are NT 4.0 compatible and will state so on their Web sites. However, it is wise to be cautious of any hardware components that NTHQ reports as unrecognized.

Hard Drive Stressing

SQL Server can make rather intense demands on a server's hard drive. Because your data is stored on the hard drive, in some ways it is the most important component of the system. How can you be sure that your hard drive subsystem will hold up? Microsoft also provides a method of stress-testing a hard drive, using the program called the SQL Server Hard Disk Stress Utility, SQLIO.EXE and SQLHDTST.EXE. SQLIO.EXE continually reads and writes data in 8K pages, and is meant to stress a hard drive's I/O capabilities for SQL Server 7.0. SQLHDTST.EXE, on the other hand, reads and writes data in 2K pages, the unit used by earlier releases of SQL Server. You can get SQLIO.EXE on the 1999 Back Office Resource Kit or later, and SQLHDTST on earlier versions of the Back Office Resource Kit. As you can see in Figure 3-2, SQLHDTST has a number of parameters that you can set. (SQLIO.EXE was not available at press time.)

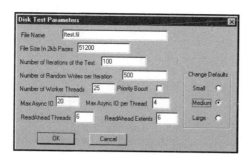

FIGURE 3-2

The SQLHDTST SQL Server Hard Disk Stress Utility will stress your I/O subsystem in 2K page reads and writes.

You specify a file name and file size that you want the stress test to write. Then you choose a number of iterations, which essentially determines how long the test will run. You can tweak the other parameters to match what you think SQL Server will use, though it's easier to just use the defaults. You can also let SQL Server size the test by choosing the Small, Medium, or Large option. Microsoft recommends boosting the number of iterations and letting a machine run for a weekend in order to simulate 7 x 24 activity. You can increase the stress on the CPU by running a second or third instance, choosing different file names for each.

> **TIP**
>
> The current SQL Server Hard Disk Stress Utility is oriented toward SQL Server 6.5's I/O. Watch the Microsoft Web site to see when Microsoft replaces it with a SQL Server 7 version.

The SQL Server Hard Disk Stress Utility is an excellent way to trigger a certain class of hard disk failures on a machine. If a problem will show up under intense disk activity, the utility will likely find it. It's much better to find this out early than to have it occur in production.

Estimating Hardware Requirements

How powerful a machine do you need? It's normally not enough just to satisfy the minimum. If you have some sense of the number of users you will have and amount of data that you need, Compaq, Hewlett-Packard, and other server makers offer white papers on the subject.

The Compaq Web site also has the Compaq ProLiant Sizer for Microsoft SQL Server. It's a free utility to aid in sizing a production server based on database size, transactions per second, and availability requirements. The version is oriented toward SQL Server 6.5, but a SQL Server 7 version should be out soon. You can download the Compaq Sizer utility from the Compaq Web site:

http://www.compaq.com/solutions/enterprise/database-mssqlsizer.html

RAID and SMP Systems

One of the best investments you can make for a production SQL Server is an efficient hard drive subsystem. Because SQL Server will use Windows NT's multithreading capability, it can do simultaneous reads and writes on separate SCSI hard drives. If the hard drive system is SCSI, you can stripe the drives so that a logical drive actually is spread across several hard drives.

SMP (symmetric multiprocessing) systems contain multiple CPUs. SQL Server will support multiple processors, and you'll see performance increases on CPU-intensive tasks and queries with additional processors. A good approach is to buy a machine capable of using additional processors and then add them as you experience 70 percent or higher use of the current CPUs.

Software Requirements

In addition to hardware requirements, there are numerous software requirements for the correct operation of SQL Server.

Computer Name

SQL Server will attempt to get its own name from the computer name. If the computer name is not a legal SQL Server name, SQL Server will finish installing, but it will not be able to enter a name for itself in its system tables. With no server name, replication cannot work and other activities will also fail. Legal SQL Server names start with a letter or underscore, followed by alphanumeric characters including the backslash (\), dollar sign ($), pound sign (#), and underscore (_).

TIP

In SQL Server 6.5, the dash (–), backslash (the domain separator, \), and space are not legal SQL Server characters. The computer name, logins for users, and other identifiers cannot use those characters. For integrated security, where SQL Server uses NT logins, SQL Server 6.5 would map the dash to a pound sign, the backslash to an underscore, and the space to a dollar sign ($). In SQL Server 7, dashes and backslashes are now legal, though the space is still not a legal SQL Server 7 character in the computer name, login id, and other identifiers.

Networking

You also need to make sure you have networking capability installed into either Windows 95/98 or Windows NT. Under Windows NT, if you do not have a network card installed on the machine, you can choose the MS loopback adapter as the networking card. It will appear in the list of possible network cards when you install NT networking. The MS loopback adapter is a software emulation of a networking card that will allow NT to install networking services. Because networking cards are so inexpensive, it's probably better to just put a card in the machine, and then install NT networking. That way you have a card if you need to hook up to a network. If you are going to install SQL Server 7 on an NT machine and you can see that it does not have networking services installed, you'll have to get the NT installation CD and install networking. Otherwise, the SQL Server 7 install will not succeed.

If your NT machine does not have a network card but you've installed RAS, then networking services have been installed and SQL Server 7 will also install. However,

SQL Server will attempt to use the dial-up connection as the network login, and some have reported this to be slow. It's better to at least have the loopback adapter as a network card, or simply buy a card and install networking services.

SQL Server 7 will install equally well on NT Server and NT Workstation. However, NT Workstation does have a limitation of 10 other client machines connecting to it simultaneously. This will limit the number of connections that SQL Server can accept from other workstations when installed on NT Workstation.

SMS Requirements

You can use SMS version 1.2 or later to install SQL Server 7 across multiple machines.

Important Planning Decisions

You must make three crucial decisions during a SQL Server installation:

♦ You must decide on the character set that SQL Server 7 will use to store all your character data.

♦ You must choose the sort order that SQL Server will use to sort data and build indexes.

♦ You must choose the Unicode collation for Unicode data types.

WARNING

What makes these decisions important is that you cannot change a SQL Server's character set or sort order without rebuilding system tables and losing your current databases. You can only restore from backups with the same compatible character set and sort order.

These are irreversible decisions, in the sense that if you want to change a SQL Server's character set or sort order, you must unload your data, uninstall and then reinstall SQL Server, and then reload and potentially rebuild your data.

Other decisions include the networking libraries and protocols to install, which are not irreversible. You can modify your choices online. However, SQL Server will not work properly without the correct network library choices.

A final decision concerns the NT user accounts that you assign for SQL Server and SQL Agent to use as NT logins. This decision can also be postponed, and I'll cover it in depth as I discuss installation. You'll examine all these decisions in more detail in the next section, "Installing SQL Server for the First Time."

Installation Planning Checklist

The following checklist summarizes the items you should look for before installing SQL Server:

❑ Make sure that the machine on which you are installing SQL Server is running Windows NT 4.0 or Windows 9x. (Note that NT Workstation has an upper limit of 10 other computers connecting to it.)

❑ If you are installing onto Windows NT Server in a networked environment, make sure your production SQL Server machine is not an NT primary or backup domain controller. Your database performance may suffer when your database server must also handle login validations.

❑ Make sure that the machine has at least 32MB of RAM. If this is an NT production server, it should have at least 64 MB of RAM.

❑ If the machine has SQL Server 6.5 or 6.0 on it currently, make sure that you are prepared to do an upgrade. Only one instance of SQL Server 7 can run on a single machine. If so, back up your 6.x databases before the upgrade process.

❑ Make sure networking services (and a network card or the MS loopback adapter) have been installed on NT.

❑ Make sure you have enough free disk space for the installation process (about 180MB for the full SQL Server, 98MB for the minimum installation.) You should also have budget free disk space for all your database data, transaction logs, and SQL Server's own temporary database, tempdb.

❑ Make sure the computer's name does not contain spaces. The computer name must begin with a letter or underscore.

❑ Decide on a character set, sort order, and Unicode collation before installing.

❑ Find out which net libraries you will need.

Installing SQL Server 7.0 for the First Time

You have three ways to install SQL Server 7: Typical, Minimum, and Custom. If you're just learning SQL Server, for example, and installing it on your desktop or at home, just choose the Typical installation, accept all the defaults that Setup offers you, and your installation will be fast and simple.

However, if you are installing into a production, development, or test environment, the typical way may not be correct for you. You will need to involve yourself in the Setup decisions and override the defaults if necessary.

Setup Preliminaries

You start the SQL Server Setup program by inserting the CD in your CD-ROM drive or running the autorun.exe program from the CD.

> **T IP**
>
> When you first start the Setup program, it will take a few seconds to initialize. After you see the Welcome screen and click on Next, you'll see the first set of decisions you need to make. These decisions are:

- ◆ Whether the installation is to be local or remote
- ◆ Whether you want to install the server components or just the management tools
- ◆ What type of installation you want: Typical, Compact, or Custom
- ◆ If you are including the server component, whether you are licensing per seat or per user

The overall flow of Setup up to this point is summarized in Figure 3-3.

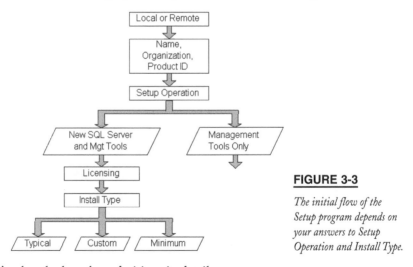

FIGURE 3-3

The initial flow of the Setup program depends on your answers to Setup Operation and Install Type.

Let's take a look at these decisions in detail.

Local or Remote

Your first decision concerns whether to make a local or remote installation. You can install SQL Server or its Management Tools on the local machine (the machine you're currently using) or on a remote machine, provided you have administrative permissions to it. Figure 3-4 shows these choices.

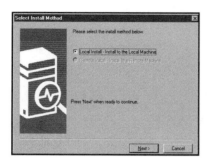

FIGURE 3-4

You can install SQL Server locally or remotely.

If you are installing remotely, you must supply the remote computer name and the path to the computer.

After this dialog box, you'll be asked for your Name, Company, and Product ID. You can get your product ID from the CD jewel case. Because this screen is so straightforward, we do not include a copy of it here.

Convert Existing SQL Server Data

SQL Server 7 will convert an existing SQL 6.0 or 6.5 system in place. Setup displays the Convert dialog box, shown in Figure 3-5.

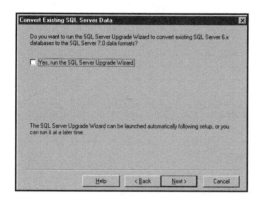

FIGURE 3-5

Setup will ask if you want to convert a SQL Server 6.0 or 6.5 database.

This option does run the Upgrade Wizard after the installation has completed. If you want to convert an existing SQL Server 6.0 or 6.5 server to SQL Server 7, you should first back up the SQL 6.x databases. For more information about upgrading, see Chapter 4, "Upgrading."

Note that this option only applies to Windows NT, because SQL Server 6.0 and 6.5 only ran on Windows NT.

You will also be asked whether you want to run the Upgrade Wizard after the installation. It's not necessary to run it now, because you can run it later from the SQL Server menu.

Setup Type

You are next asked about the type of setup—Typical, Custom, or Minimum installation—as you can see in Figure 3-6.

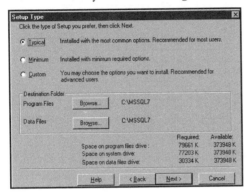

FIGURE 3-6

In Setup Type you choose whether to install SQL Server in a Typical, Minimum, or Custom mode.

You also choose drivers for server and data locations.

The Typical installation is a quick way to get SQL Server 7 up and running, using the defaults that it assigns for the several decisions covered in the Custom installation. The Minimum installation leaves out the Management Tools.

To understand what happens next, it's a good idea to see the overall flow of the Setup program, as shown in Figure 3-7.

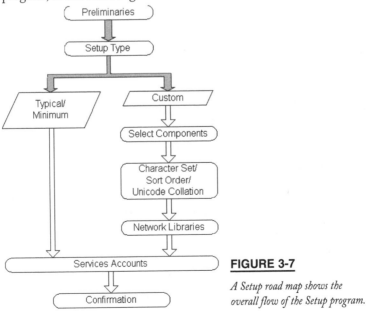

FIGURE 3-7

A Setup road map shows the overall flow of the Setup program.

A quick look at the diagram in Figure 3-7 shows you that the Custom operation includes quite a number of choices not present in the Typical and Minimum installation.

Typical Installation

The Typical installation is by far the simplest. Under Windows 95 and 98, it bypasses all choices entirely. However, if you choose to change any options at the Confirmation screen, you will be right back in the Custom path.

For Windows NT, you still have three decisions to make in the services accounts dialog box: the SQL Server login, SQL Server Agent login, and auto-start for SQL Server and SQL Agent. After you're finished with these, you'll also reach the Confirmation screen. Again, however, once you make any changes you'll be right back in the Custom path.

The Typical setup option removes most of the decisions you need to make, but only because the SQL Server Setup program is making them for you in the form of default options. Those defaults are usually acceptable in a learning situation, as on your desktop or at home, but they may not be acceptable in a production, development, or test environment.

The Typical option is something of a mixed blessing. You can use it to avoid making certain decisions about character set, sort order, file locations, and such. However, this only works if you're willing to accept the defaults provided by the Setup program. Obviously, you are better off knowing about these defaults, in case you need to change them.

WARNING

The Typical installation may give some defaults that are unexpected. Unless you are prepared to accept all of the defaults, use the Custom option.

The Typical setup can save you a great deal of time if you can accept all of the defaults. Eventually you'll want to know more about these decisions, so they are documented in this section following the Custom path section just ahead.

Minimum Installation

The Minimum installation does not install the management tools or the Books Online, and it is a very easy process. Like the Typical installation, it makes a number of default decisions for you. You can find out more about these defaults by looking at the sections right after "Custom Installation."

Custom Installation

The Custom installation path takes you sequentially through all of the various decisions that must be made for any SQL Server installation, and it shows you the default choices offered by the Setup program. All of those decisions are discussed one by one in the following sections.

Select Components

The next option you'll see is the choice called Select Components. These choices concern the parts of SQL Server that you may install. At this point, you can decide to include only client utilities and exclude the server, and also not to install the Books Online, as you can see in Figure 3-8.

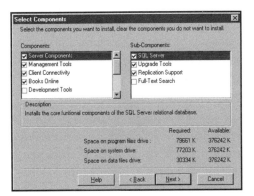

FIGURE 3-8

The Select Components dialog box lets you choose what to install.

NOTE

It's always a good idea to install Books Online with your server. If you do, when you are working on that server, perhaps under extreme pressure, they'll be close at hand.

Also, note that the disk space requirements are summarized at the bottom of the dialog box, and the summary reflects the choices you make in the dialog box. Note also that a certain amount of space is required on the system drive, that is, the drive with the operating system, no matter where you choose to install programs and data.

Character Set/Sort Order/Unicode Collation

The next dialog box concerns the choices you must make regarding character data.

Character Set

The character set is the set of valid characters that SQL Server uses to store character data. Normally a character set consists of all the possible characters that can be stored in a byte, namely 255 possible characters.

SQL Server has some character sets that use two bytes to store each character, namely the double-byte character sets (DBCS). However, if you must store this kind of data, the Unicode character data types will probably work better for you.

Across all of the single-byte character sets, the lower 128 values are constant. Only the upper 128 of the total 256 values vary. This choice applies only to character data, so it applies to the character, character varying, and text data types in SQL Server. Other types of data, such as numbers and dates, are unaffected.

The character set dialog box in the installation process looks like that in Figure 3-9.

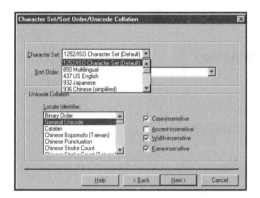

FIGURE 3-9

You must also choose a character set for non-Unicode character data in SQL Server.

The choice is important because your server will not be able to transfer data or participate in replication with other servers unless they all have the same character set. The default for SQL Server 6.5 is 1252-ISO (Latin 1 or ANSI), which is the character set used by Windows.

Other character sets include code page 850 (multilingual), which includes characters for American and European languages, and code page 437 (U.S. English), which contains some graphics characters not usually stored in databases. Code page 437 is also known as the OEM code page, because it's used by Windows to emulate MS-DOS upper-order characters.

Microsoft recommends using code page 850 if you need a multilingual installation compatible with most European languages.

TIP

It is important to make sure your computer uses the same character set as any other SQL servers with which it must communicate, and the same character set as the one used by SQL Server 6.x, if you are upgrading.

The remaining Asian character sets use double-byte character sets for character storage.

Sort Order

SQL Server offers quite a large number of possible choices for sort order. The sort order determines how the server will sort the character data. It affects the results of queries, the order in which the data will be stored and returned to the user, how indexes will be built and stored, and—in the case of tables with clustered indexes on character columns—how the data will be arranged. However, it does not affect the content of any data, unlike the character set choice. The Sort Order dialog box in the installation process looks like Figure 3-10.

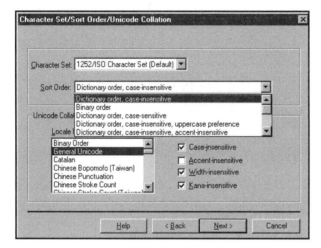

FIGURE 3-10

Choosing the sort order during setup

The default sort order is dictionary order, case-insensitive, which means that the letter 'A' will sort along with 'a'. In the case of binary order, the underlying binary values of the character determine the sort order. If you choose case-sensitive, you'll see the uppercase values first. The following table shows how to look at the first few choices:

Sort Order	Sorted Example
Dictionary order, case-insensitive	AaAAabBbbBCccC...ZzZ
Binary order	AAABBCC...ZZ...aabbbcc...z
Dictionary order, case-sensitive	AAAaaBBbbCCcc...ZZz

Most SQL Server installations use the default sort order, namely dictionary order, case-insensitive. The reason is that the alternatives all have problems.

For example, benchmarks have shown that the binary sort order has a small performance advantage over all the others during the sort process. However, the results are sorted in such an odd order that most client software would have to re-sort the data for presentation purposes anyway, and you would lose the performance gain.

Also, choosing a case-sensitive option produces the unpleasant side effect of forcing all of your queries to be case-sensitive as well. All table and column names must be spelled exactly, to the upper- and lower-case, in your queries.

Again, you should find out what your organization uses as a standard, or just use the default.

> **TIP**
>
> If you need to transfer data between servers that have different character sets or sort orders, you can use the Distributed Transformation Services, discussed in Chapter 10, "Importing and Exporting Data." As in the case of the character set choice, however, if you decide to change your sort order later, you must reinstall SQL Server and rebuild your databases.

Unicode Collation

SQL Server provides the ability to store Unicode character data, and accordingly you need to specify the collation (sort order) for Unicode data as well, as shown in Figure 3-11.

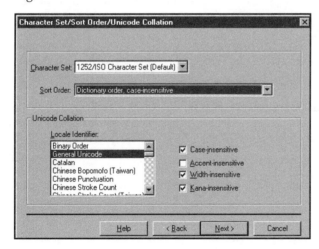

FIGURE 3-11

Choosing the Unicode collation

It's best to choose the default and keep the Unicode collation as close as possible to the character set sort order. If you don't accept the default that SQL Server offers, the Upgrade Wizard may have trouble converting constraints from a SQL 6.x database. If you choose a different sort order for the Unicode data than for your character data, you may have trouble converting data between Unicode and character data, when the data involves upper-order characters.

Additional Unicode choices are listed to the right, including case insensitivity, which is the default and matches the single-byte character set choice.

Network Libraries

The next dialog box chooses the server's network libraries, as you can see in Figure 3-12.

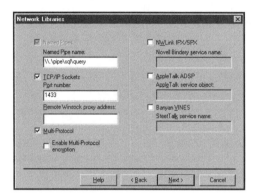

FIGURE 3-12

The Networking Libraries dialog box asks you to choose the server-side network libraries for SQL Server.

NOTE

It's important to see that these networking libraries are used by SQL Server on the server and are not used by client software. The tool for choosing client software is the Client Configuration Tool.

As the default, SQL Server 7 under Windows NT will install Named Pipes, TCP/IP, and Multi-Protocol. These options are additive, and you can change them later.

Named Pipes is the mechanism for named pipe connections, and the default pipe is listed in the dialog box. If you want to change that pipe, do so after installation. However, you should always leave Named Pipes installed.

TCP/IP is necessary if you have clients connecting to SQL Server via TCP/IP. The default port id for SQL Server 7 is 1433, and this should be left as is. It is the standard socket assigned to SQL Server by the Internet Assigned Number Authority (IANA).

Multi-Protocol is a network library that allows Windows NT remote procedure calls (RPCs). It supports encryption of data over the wire, so it can be a good WAN solution.

TIP

To have integrated security in SQL Server 7, you must be using either Named Pipes or Multi-Protocol. Also, both of these net libraries provide the ability to browse a network for other SQL servers.

Services Accounts

Notice how the Windows 95/98 Typical install option jumps immediately to a confirmation screen, whereas the Windows NT Typical path does not. That's because SQL Server 7 and its scheduler, the SQL Agent, are both NT services, whereas on Windows 95 and 98, SQL Server runs as a regular user program, not a service. Because of the nature of services on NT, you have to assign NT logins to SQL Server and SQL Agent, and often it's important to assign them network privileges as well.

You can assign two kinds of NT login accounts to SQL Server: a local system account, or a domain (user) account. The system account has Administrator privileges on the local machine but no privileges at all to other machines on the network. The domain account is a login like any others given to users, except that it will be used by SQL Server and/or SQL Agent.

The dialog box for choosing SQL Server's login is shown in Figure 3-13.

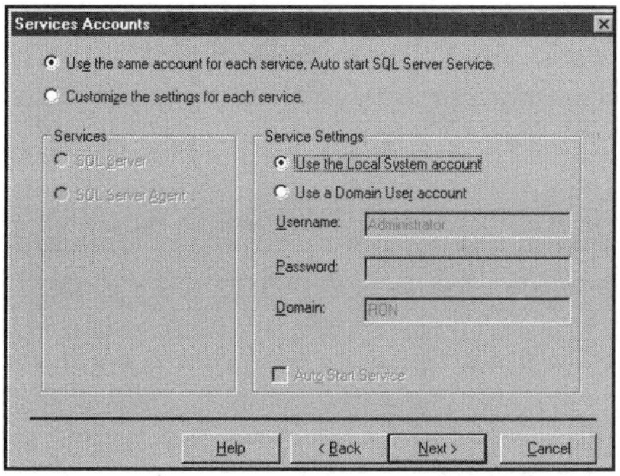

FIGURE 3-13

You are asked to provide a login for SQL Server.

You can choose a system account to start with and add a user account later. You can more easily manage a network with many SQL servers if you establish a common account that every SQL Server machine uses.

WARNING

Make sure that the account you establish for SQL Server has administrator privileges on the current machine, and sufficient network privileges if you need to access network resources. For example, if you want to back up a database to a different machine while online, the SQL Server login account will need access to the other machine.

SQL Agent Login

SQL Agent is the scheduler and task manager for SQL Server 7. It is the utility that performs tasks on an automated basis for the current server and others as well. To have it manage other servers, you must give it an NT account that has network privileges.

> **TIP**
>
> In order to work with replication, the current machine's SQL Agent must have an NT user account with administrator privileges on the current machine, and network privileges.

The rationale for SQL Server Agent logins is the same as for SQL Server.

Auto-Start for SQL Server and SQL Agent

Also, you have the opportunity to have SQL Server and SQL Agent automatically start as services when the NT operating system first starts up.

> **WARNING**
>
> Auto-starting SQL Server is important for security: If SQL Server is not running, your data files are exposed to anyone who has access rights to the folders containing them. Someone with write access could accidentally (or maliciously) delete them, for example. But when the SQL Server service is running, it will use all data and log files exclusively. When exclusively used, they cannot be read, copied, or deleted by any other user on the network.

If you have chosen Auto-Start for SQL Server and/or SQL Agent, they will start up immediately when NT boots, before any users log into the system. If you do not auto-start them now, you can change this option later using Setup or the Windows NT Control Panel Services dialog box.

Confirm Setup

After the Auto-Start screen, you'll be asked what name you'd like for the SQL Server 7 menu folder, and then you'll come to the Confirm Setup dialog box. You can change any of the options by just walking the Wizard backward.

If you're installing the Standard or Enterprise versions, you'll next go to the Licensing option.

Licensing

The SQL Server DBMS requires licensing, so Setup will now ask you about it, as you can see in Figure 3-14. There are two kinds of licenses for SQL Server: per server and per seat, as you can see in the figure. Per server refers to the act of licensing SQL Server for a given number of users at any time, irrespective of who those users are. Per seat refers to licensing each user individually, assigning one client license to each.

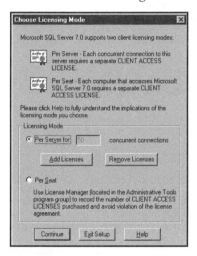

FIGURE 3-14

You are asked to choose per server or per seat licensing for SQL Server.

Per server licensing is more economical if you have occasional users and not many SQL servers. A per server license merely specifies a maximum number of licensed users for the server.

Per seat licensing is more economical if you have many SQL servers and users that need to connect to each of them. Then you can just purchase one client license for each user's "seat," no matter how many SQL servers they connect to. After you confirm the licensing agreement, the installation process begins.

Changing Installation Options after Installation

You can change a number of installation options after an install, through a number of utilities.

Changing Character Data Options

You can change the character set and sort order after installation by running the rebuldm.exe program, short for rebuild master. When you run it, from the Start/Run dialog box or the NT command prompt, you'll see the dialog box shown in Figure 3-15.

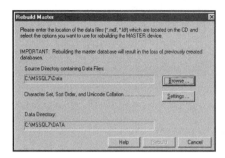

FIGURE 3-15

The Rebuild Master program will rebuild the master database, as well as reinstall the other system and sample databases.

First you need to find the location of the master database files. After you do that, you can change the character set, sort order, and Unicode collation. Just press the Settings button, and you'll see the same Character Set/Sort Order/Unicode Collation dialog box that you saw during installation.

WARNING

Rebuilding the master database with changes in character data settings will render any of your user databases unreadable.

Changing the Server Network Libraries

You can change SQL Server's network libraries by running the Server Network Utility from the Start, Programs, SQL Server 7.0 menu sequence. It will let you change the same options you chose for the server during installation, as you can see in Figure 3-16.

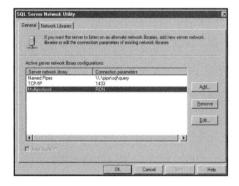

FIGURE 3-16

You can change the server-side network libraries using the Server Network Utility.

Any change here affects connectivity to the server, so it must be done with care. However, no changes are made to any data as a result of changing these values. To make the values take effect, stop and restart SQL Server.

Uninstalling SQL Server

To remove SQL Server, either choose the Uninstall SQL Server 7.0 option from the SQL Server 7.0 menu, or run the Add/Remove Programs dialog box from the Control Panel. You'll also find out about an automated way to uninstall SQL Server in the next section.

When Setup removes SQL Server, it will remove all Registry entries for SQL Server and related files, as shown in Figure 3-17.

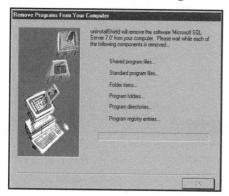

FIGURE 3-17

The Uninstall program will remove Registry entries and program files.

Setup will leave your data and backup files in the old MSSQL directories.

WARNING

Make sure you have backed up your data before removing data files.

Unattended Installation

You can automate the install and uninstall process using several command files that come with the SQL Server CD.

The sql70ins.bat command file uses the sql70ins.iss initialization file to perform a Typical installation, whereas the sql70cst.bat command file uses the sql70cst.iss initialization file to perform a Custom installation. The sql70cst.bat file consists of these lines of code:

```
@ echo off
rem          Performs SQL Server 7.0 Standard Edition Unattended
rem      for NT Server
cls
if '%PROCESSOR_ARCHITECTURE%'=='' goto Win9x
echo *
```

```
echo      Unattended install for SQL Server 7.0 is starting.
echo *
echo *
echo      Waiting for SQL Server 7.0 Setup to finish...
rem last changed 2-05-97 12:00
rem =================================
rem What Platform?
rem =================================
@echo on
start /wait %PROCESSOR_ARCHITECTURE%\setup\setupsql.exe -s -fi "sql70cst.iss"
@echo off
goto END
:Win9x
echo "Use the Desktop Edition version of this file: deskecst.bat"
:END


:DONE
```

Notice that the batch file tests for the type of processor (Intel or Alpha) using the %PROCESSOR ARCHITECTURE% system variable, to run the appropriate version of the setup.exe program. The –s and –f1 switches on the command indicate a silent install and the initialization file location.

The sql70cst.iss initialization file consists of a number of InstallShield options that you can customize. The appearance is similar to an INI file, as you can see in the following fragment:

```
[InstallShield Silent]
Version=v5.00.000
File=Response File
[DlgOrder]
Dlg0=SetupMethod-0
Count=12
etc.
```

For an unattended client installation, the sql70cli.bat command file uses the sql70cli.iss initialization file and performs an unattended client-tools-only installation.

A set of desktop unattended install files also appears in the root drive of the CD, each beginning with "deske": deskecli.bat for the client, deskecst.bat for custom, and deskeins.bat for standard.

> **NOTE**
>
> In SQL Server 6.5, you could perform an unattended install, but not an unattended uninstall or removal. Now, in SQL Server 7, you can do both.

You can also use the sql70rem.bat command file to remove SQL Server.

Rebuilding the Registry

Occasionally it is possible to end up with a Registry corruption. You might, for example, abort the removal of SQL Server, leaving it only half-uninstalled. Often that action corrupts the SQL Server Registry entries, making it impossible to either finish the removal or reinstall over the partially uninstalled system.

You can cause Setup to rebuild the Registry, without rebuilding any system databases, with the Rebuild Registry tool, regrebld.exe, which you run from the command line. It's located in the ..\MSSQL\BINN directory. You can run it without any parameters, and it will simply rebuild the SQL Server 7.0 Registry.

Or, you can use it to back up and restore the Registry, with –Backup and –Restore options.

The SQL Server Registry Keys

When SQL Server finishes its installation, it puts version and configuration information about SQL Server in the following Registry key:

HKEY_LOCAL_MACHINE\SOFTWARE\Microsoft\MSSQLServer

In addition, the following three keys contain information about SQL Server and the SQL Executive scheduler as services:

HKEY_LOCAL_MACHINE\SYSTEM\CurrentControlSet\Services\MSSQLServer

HKEY_LOCAL_MACHINE \SYSTEM\CurrentControlSet\EventLog\

Application\MSSQLServer

HKEY_LOCAL_MACHINE\SYSTEM\CurrentControlSet\Services\SQLServerAgent

Installed Tools

All the GUI-related components of SQL Server are shown in the program group that appears in Figure 3-18, though there are a number of console tools as well. Upon installation, your SQL Server 7.0 program group will look like Figure 3-18.

FIGURE 3-18

The program group for SQL Server 7

GUI Tools

The major GUI tools installed with SQL Server are shown in Table 3-1.

Table 3-1 The Program Group Items Installed by SQL Server Setup

Client Network Utility	Configures the client network library and DB-Library
Enterprise Manager	The main GUI utility for managing SQL databases
MSDTC Administrative Console	A utility to manage the Distributed Transaction Coordinator (DTC)
Performance Monitor	A SQL Server configuration for the NT performance monitor
Profiler	A method of inspecting queries and events occurring on a server
Query Analyzer	A visual query utility
Server Network Utility	A utility to change the server's network library
Service Manager	A utility to start and stop various SQL Server services
Uninstall SQL Server	Runs InstallShield to uninstall SQL Server

Console Tools

In addition to the GUI tools, additional tools run from the NT console (or command window, cmd.exe).

One is BCP, the bulk copy program. This is a fast data loader but is somewhat more difficult to use than the Data Transformation Services utility (DTS). For more information, see Chapter 10, "Importing and Exporting."

Another is OSQL, which is a query utility similar to the Query Analyzer, except that it runs from the NT command window. When you want to automate your queries, specifying an input script and capturing the output to a file, OSQL and its older sibling, ISQL, are the utilities to use. For further discussion, see Chapter 13, "Data Manipulation."

ISQL, also a query utility, uses DB-Library and not ODBC, and it cannot work with the new Unicode and GUID data types. It is provided for backward compatibility.

The last to mention is SQLSERV.EXE, the SQL Server database engine. You can start and stop SQL Server from the NT console without using any of the GUI tools. As you will see later, some emergency operations may require you to start SQL Server from the command line.

GUI versus Non-GUI Commands

Significant changes and improvements have been made to the MS SQL Server GUI over the years. If you go from one version to the other, you'll notice significant differences in the GUI tools. However, utility commands and system stored procedures often remain essentially the same, though new stored procedures or new parameters get added as time goes by.

Consequently, because the GUI tends to change and utilities and stored procedures are relatively constant, it's often more convenient to use the stored procedures across multiple versions than the GUI tools. On the other hand, the GUI tools are easier to learn and work with initially. Most people tend to learn the GUI tools first, whereas experienced SQL Server administrators and developers tend to use the system stored procedures whenever possible.

In this book, you'll see a balance struck between the GUI and non-GUI ways of doing things: It is important to learn both.

Tutorial: Inspecting an Installation

The following tutorial takes you through some steps that will assist you in verifying an installation. To inspect a SQL Server installation, you must:

♦ Make sure the SQL Server engine is running.

♦ Register the server with Enterprise Manager.

♦ Connect to the server with Enterprise Manager and verify key server objects.

♦ Connect to the server with the Query Analyzer and verify the server name and version.

1. Starting the SQL Server Service

You first need to find out whether SQL Server can run. When SQL Server is first installed, it will not be running as a service. To start it, start the Service Manager utility. Make sure you choose the SQL Server service. The service control icons appear in a dialog box, as shown in Figure 3-19.

FIGURE 3-19

The Service Manager can stop and start SQL Server.

If you're on a network, you can use the Server pull-down list to find a server. Normally, though, on the current machine, just make sure that the machine name is in the Server pull-down list.

To start SQL Server, double-click on the Start/Continue icon. After a couple of seconds, you should see the server icon turn green, with the message "MSSQLServer - Running" appearing in the status bar.

- ◆ It's a good idea to stop and restart SQL Server by clicking on the appropriate icons. Make sure that it remains running for at least five seconds or so.
- ◆ If it stops, record the error message and check the NT event log. It could indicate a failed installation.
- ◆ If the icon is grayed out (disabled), and the service will not start, check the Windows NT Event Log. The installation may have failed.
- ◆ When you've verified that SQL Server is running, you can close the Service Manager dialog box. (SQL Server will keep running.)
- ◆ If you cannot get SQL Server to run, then you may need to uninstall and reinstall it.

Note that the server name appears in the dialog box. This is the machine name. The Service Manager dialog box shows SQL Server's NT service name, MSSQLServer.

You can also start and stop SQL Server in the Services dialog box (from the NT Control Panel), as shown in Figure 3-20.

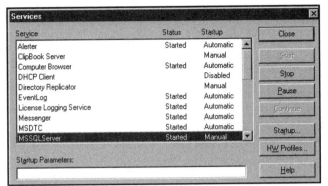

FIGURE 3-20

The Services dialog box from Control Panel, showing SQL Server's entry

In addition, you can use the commands:

```
net start mssqlserver
net stop mssqlserver
```

from the NT console or command window. This comes in handy when you need to start or stop SQL Server from within a batch or command file.

You can also run SQL Server, not as a service but as a regular program, by invoking it from the NT console command line:

```
sqlserv -f
```

This is sometimes necessary for maintenance purposes.

2. Registering the SQL Server with Enterprise Manager

If you are on the server machine, or if you are on a machine that has the SQL Server Management Tools and you have sufficient permissions, you can inspect the server with the Enterprise Manager. This section assumes you have some ability to connect to a SQL Server installation with SQL Server's own tools.

Enterprise Manager is the easiest tool you can use to check SQL Server's installation and configuration. It is a GUI utility that provides a tree view of the servers available on the network along with all their components. It can connect to all SQL servers and their databases on a domain, provided you have permissions to log into the servers.

Start up the Enterprise Manager by double-clicking on its icon. To see any SQL Server from EM, you must first register the server. The SQL Server install process will automatically register your local server. For any other servers, you must register the server.

When you register a SQL Server in Enterprise Manager, you'll use either the Register Wizard or the Register dialog box. The Register SQL Server Wizard walks you though a set of steps that actually just fill in the same data as the Register SQL Server dialog box, so it is of only limited value.

The actual Register SQL Server dialog box is shown in Figure 3-21.

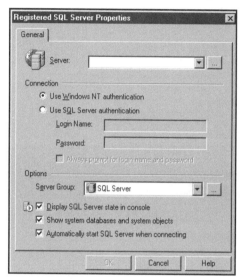

FIGURE 3-21

The Register SQL Server Properties dialog box

Here, you must fill in the server name, which is the same as the machine name. (You can also use the shortcut '(local)' or a period (.), but the actual server name is better.)

For a fresh installation, if you do not use NT authentication, you must use the standard login id of sa, with no password. The sa login stands for system administrator, a login that has unlimited rights to the database. If you do not have an sa password, you will have to use a login that has been set up for you at that server.

Assuming your NT login has permissions to the server machine, you can use NT authentication to register the server, or use SQL Server authentication and use the sa login and no password.

Notice the options at the bottom. These options allow you to toggle the display of the server state in the EM, whether to show system databases and objects in the EM tree view, and whether to start SQL Server (if the service is not running) when you try to connect.

This dialog box is actually just the Properties dialog box for the SQL Server you are registering. You can always recover these options, even if you rely on the Register SQL Server Wizard, through this Properties dialog box. Click on the OK button next. If you put in a bad server name, you'll get a message from ODBC like the one in Figure 3-22.

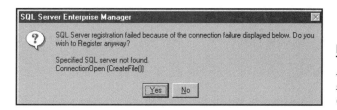

FIGURE 3-22

Registering an unknown server name produces an ODBC error message.

If you know that you've got the server name and login correct, you can go ahead, register anyway, and then start the server from inside the Enterprise Manager. It makes no sense to register a server that doesn't exist, though EM will let you.

If you have the correct server name but your login or password is incorrect, you'll get the message shown in Figure 3-23.

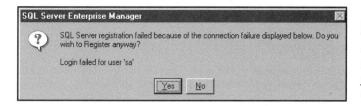

FIGURE 3-23

If you do not type the correct login or password, you'll receive an ODBC error message.

Under these circumstances, because you can't connect to the server, there's no sense in registering it. (However, if you enter a bad login or password with the correct server name, and if you have administrator privileges on that machine, you can start and stop the server, even though you cannot connect to it.) After you've registered the server without error, you can connect to it.

If you cannot register the server, and you know you have the server name, login, and password correct, examine the error message. You may need to uninstall and reinstall SQL Server.

3. Connecting to SQL Server and Examining Objects

After you've registered the server, and if the server is running, you can establish a connection to it by clicking on the + sign next to the server name. In the resulting dialog box, you'll see the objects belonging to that server as you drill down into the tree, as you can see in Figure 3-24.

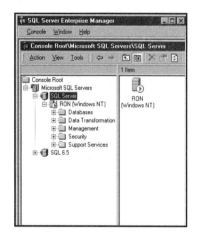

FIGURE 3-24

The Enterprise Manager tree view showing services and databases

You should check a number of things in a fresh installation right after you connect with Enterprise Manager:

◆ Check SQL Agent and make sure it can run, by drilling down into the Management node and starting it. If its icon is not green, right-click on it and select Start from the menu. If SQL Agent does not start and remain running, on a fresh installation, then you can look for telltale errors in the error log.

◆ Check the databases. You should see master, model, msdb, pubs, Northwind, and tempdb. If any of these are missing on a fresh installation, then the installation is suspicious.

If you are not looking at a fresh installation, there are a couple of exceptions to the preceding list that may not indicate a failed installation so much as someone else's activity:

◆ Often DBAs will remove the sample databases, pubs and Northwind.

◆ If a prior user gives SQL Agent an NT login that has since become invalid, it will not be able to start. However, this does not reflect on the quality of the install.

In both these cases, the installation is probably OK.

4. Querying SQL Server Using the Query Analyzer

Another other major tool for inspecting a SQL Server installation is the Query Analyzer. You can bring it up by itself or from the Enterprise Manager. Within Enterprise Manager, you can find it in the Tools menu. If you've connected to a SQL Server and drilled down into its objects, the Tools menu launches the Query Analyzer using your Enterprise Manager SQL Server login. Otherwise, if you launch it by itself, or without drilling down into a SQL Server in Enterprise Manager, you'll have to provide a login.

To use the query window to help validate an installation, you can enter two commands into it, as you can see in Figure 3-25.

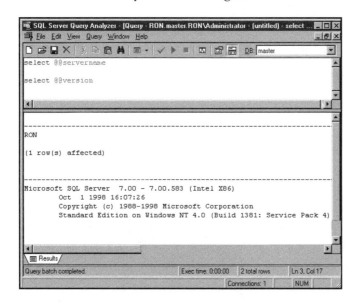

FIGURE 3-25

You can enter either of two commands within the Query Analyzer to help inspect your installation.

The query tool allows you to enter and execute either standard SQL statements or the extensions to SQL known as Transact-SQL. You simply type the commands into the top pane. You can click on the green triangle to execute the commands, and the results will show up in the lower results pane of the window.

You can choose a particular database in the Database list box. You can also use Control+E (^E) or Alt+X to execute the commands. The Query Analyzer will attempt to execute all that you've typed in, or just the amount of text that you select.

When you enter:

```
select @@version 'Version'
```

```
select @@servername 'Servername'
```

the Query Analyzer returns the results of these two Transact-SQL system variables: the current version of your SQL Server, and the server's name. The results of both commands are showing in the results pane of Figure 3-25.

For the version, notice that the full version here is 7.00.xxx. As service packs become available for SQL Server 7, other build numbers will show up.

For example, the build numbers for SQL Server 6.0 and 6.5 releases are:

6.00.121 Gold

6.00.124 SP1

6.00.139 SP2

6.00.151 SP3

6.50.201 Gold

6.50.213 SP1

6.50.240 SP2

6.50.252 SP3 (withdrawn)

6.50.258 SP3

6.50.281 SP4

6.50.415 SP5

By inspecting the build number, you can infer which service packs have been installed. Special patches or "hot fixes" may have other build numbers.

TIP

You can execute a query with Ctrl+E or Alt+X rather than clicking on the green arrow. Also, if you select one or more lines in the query window, just the selected text will be executed.

◆ Although generally it is a good idea to use the most recent service pack, you should learn what the consensus is among DBAs about each service pack before installing it.

◆ If the servername value is null, as you can tell when (null) appears as the value in the results pane, then something went wrong during installation. Unless SQL Server has a valid server name, it cannot participate in replication. Sometimes that can be fixed by issuing the following command, substituting the correct server name for <machine name>:

```
sp_adduser <machine name>, local
```

◆ If you connect to a server and the query window database pull-down list remains empty, you should uninstall and reinstall. If it lists only some of the databases or does not list one you recently created, quit the query window, right-click over the Databases node in the Enterprise Manager tree view and choose Refresh, and then restart the query window.

◆ You should verify that SQL Agent service will start, using Enterprise Manager or the Service Manager dialog box.

◆ You can determine the character set and sort order from within SQL Server by issuing the command:

```
exec sp_helpsort
```

from the query tool. Your result will look something like that in Figure 3-26.

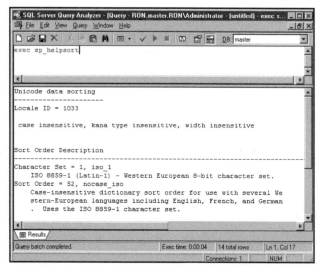

FIGURE 3-26

You can determine the current character set and sort order by executing the system stored procedure sp_helpsort.

The descriptions of the character set and sort order may not exactly match the names you saw in the installation screens. You have to interpolate a bit to see their matches. For example, in the preceding character set, you actually have to read fairly deeply before it says "case insensitive."

5. Inspecting the Server Log

An essential part of inspecting a SQL Server installation is to read the server log right after SQL Server starts and you've connected to it in Enterprise Manager. It is also another way to find the version, character set, and sort order. You can find the server log by drilling down within Enterprise Manager to a server's Log entry and choosing the current one, as shown in Figure 3-27.

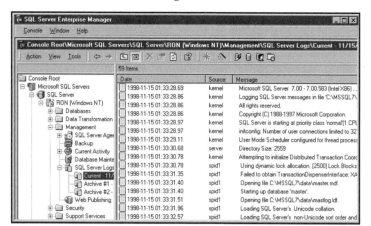

FIGURE 3-27

A SQL Server's server log also shows the version, character set, and sort order.

The version will show at the beginning of the log, and the character set and sort order, some number of lines later. The number of lines depends on the number of databases SQL Server brings up and additional messages that might occur.

It's a good idea to get into the habit of reading SQL Server 7's error log. It can contain information and error messages that can speed up your troubleshooting.

> **TIP**
>
> On a new installation, you should read the error log and make sure that no severe errors have been reported. Statements about recovering databases are normal.

Troubleshooting Installations

The Setup program is very reliable, but occasionally some things can go wrong. The following list contains a number of possible problems you may encounter, and some ways they can be solved.

1. The Setup program appears to succeed, but SQL Server will not start

Make sure you have NT networking installed. If necessary, use the Microsoft loopback adapter as your networking card.

2. The uninstall process failed

Rebuild the Registry using the regrebld utility, and retry the removal process.

3. Rebuilding the Registry will not work

When even rebuilding the Registry from Setup does not seem to clear out botched Registry settings, you can at least remove all the Registry entries, and all files, and then retry the installation from the CD. Delete the following keys from the Registry:

```
HKEY_LOCAL_MACHINE\SOFTWARE\Microsoft\MSSQLServer

HKEY_LOCAL_MACHINE\SYSTEM\CurrentControlSet\Services\MSSQLServer

HKEY_LOCAL_MACHINE \SYSTEM\CurrentControlSet\EventLog\

Application\MSSQLServer

HKEY_LOCAL_MACHINE\SYSTEM\CurrentControlSet\Services\SQLServerAgent
```

After you've deleted these Registry keys, delete the folders that contained your original installation of SQL Server. Then retry Setup.

4. The MSDB or Pubs databases did not install

Occasionally something may go wrong with the installation scripts that Setup runs to install the MSDB and Pubs databases. If the MSDB database does not install, something went wrong with the installation process. It's a vital database, required by SQL Server Agent and replication. Even if just the Pubs database, which is just a sample database, does not install, that event may mask more serious problems.

In either case, the safest thing to do is uninstall and reinstall SQL Server. If you are confident that the installation is otherwise good, you may just install the databases individually, by applying the scripts found in \MSSQL\INSTALL:

```
\Mssql7\Install\Instmsdb.sql
\Mssql7\Install\Instpubs.sql
```

in the Query Analyzer.

5. The Server name is null

If your computer name is not a legal name for SQL Server, Setup may finish the installation process, but eventually SQL Server will fail: Replication will not install, or other things may go wrong. You can correct the problem by changing the computer name within NT to a legal SQL Server format, removing the spaces, for example. Then you can restart SQL Server and see whether it picks up the computer's name. If it does, then check the server name again with:

```
SELECT @@servername
```

If it's OK, you're fine. If not, use the `sp_addserver` stored procedure mentioned in the last section to add the legal name to the local server:

```
exec sp_addserver 'MyServer', local
```

If you've added too many names or want to take some server names back out, you can use:

```
exec sp_dropserver 'BadServerName'
```

Installation Inspection Checklist

The following checklist summarizes the previous points concerning how to inspect an installation.

- ❏ Make sure that the SQL Server service will start and stay running. If it does not, check for error messages in the NT Event Viewer's Application log.
- ❏ Make sure you can register and connect to the SQL Server from Enterprise Manager using either a trusted connection or the sa login.
- ❏ Drill down and make sure that you can start SQL Agent and that it stays running.
- ❏ Make sure that the master, model, msdb, tempdb, and pubs databases are present.
- ❏ Make sure you can start the Query Analyzer and inspect the version, server name, and character set and sort order.
- ❏ Make sure you are running with the most current tested service pack.
- ❏ Read the SQL Server error log and make sure that the messages are all normal.

Summary

Installing SQL Server 7.0 is an easy process but can involve complex decisions regarding character set, network libraries, and login accounts. If you plan your installation and think through these decisions, the installation process should be smooth. After you've installed SQL Server 7, you may want to upgrade some older SQL Server databases, and that's the topic of the next chapter.

Chapter 4

Upgrading

In This Chapter

- ◆ Why upgrading is necessary
- ◆ Planning an upgrade
- ◆ Developing an upgrade plan
- ◆ Using the Upgrade Wizard
- ◆ Compatibility levels

If you've got one or more SQL Server 6.x or 4.2 databases in production, you will eventually want to upgrade them to SQL Server 7.0. Microsoft provides a utility to assist you in this task called the Upgrade Wizard.

If ever there was a time to "measure twice, cut once," it's before an upgrade. The more careful your plan, and the better your analysis, the greater degree of confidence you can have that the upgrade will succeed. Consequently, you'll start by examining the fundamental decisions, analysis, and planning that will go into a successful upgrade, and then you'll examine the tools you can use to complete the process.

NOTE

This chapter occasionally refers to SQL Server objects that will be covered later in the book. If you are new to SQL Server 7.0 or are installing SQL Server for the first time, you may want to skip this chapter and return to it when you want to know more about upgrading.

Let's clarify what an upgrade is. For this discussion, an upgrade takes an existing Microsoft SQL Server 6.x production system and converts it to a SQL Server 7.0 system. If the production system is using a different DBMS, such as Oracle or Access, let's call it a migration rather than an upgrade. In this chapter you're going to deal with upgrading an existing SQL Server DBMS only. (For information about SQL Server 4.21, see "Upgrading from SQL Server 4.21", later in this chapter.)

WARNING

Upgrading is an activity fraught with risk. It is much more critical than installing SQL Server for the first time, because you may be dealing with a server's data that is in production.

The purpose of upgrading, then, is to take all the database objects and their data from the current SQL Server 6.x database and copy them to a SQL Server 7.0 server.

Why Upgrading Is Necessary

Why is upgrading necessary? Why isn't the process as easy as applying a simple patch? Or why isn't it as simple as upgrading from SQL Server 6.0 to 6.5, where the database data files remained intact?

Changes to Storage Structures and Engine

The reason you must go through a complex upgrade process, and can't simply apply a patch, is that SQL Server 7.0 makes fundamental changes to the SQL Server storage structures and storage engine. SQL Server 7.0 increases all page storage from 2K to 8K pages, for example. In addition, 7.0 uses a bitmapping page addressing technique embodied in global allocation maps. So both the page size and addressing format change, and this affects the entire database.

Therefore a lot of work must be done to the data; an upgrade cannot be a simple copy. The upgrade process must copy all your data into a new set of data files with a new format.

NOTE

Upgrading is a one-way process, from SQL Server 6.x to SQL Server 7.0. There is no option to convert a SQL Server 7.0 database into SQL Server 6.x.

Microsoft has done its best to make the upgrade process as simple and straightforward as possible, through the use of the Upgrade Wizard. If your database systems are relatively simple, without complex trigger and stored procedure code, there is every likelihood that the upgrade process will be very smooth. If your database systems are complex, though, you need to be aware that something might go wrong. The Upgrade Wizard may even find problems in your databases of which you were unaware.

No matter what your situation, though, it's best to be well prepared for your upgrade, and that is the focus of the next section.

Preparing for an Upgrade

You can divide the preparation for an upgrade into three phases:

- Fundamental decisions about an upgrade strategy
- Planning the upgrade
- Analysis of your current system

Planning an Upgrade

It would be either bold or foolish, or likely both, to proceed with an upgrade of a production system without going through the phases just outlined. These fundamental decisions concern strategy: What tools will you use, and how, to effect your upgrade?

Decision 1: Upgrade to the Same Machine or to a Different Machine

On a server-by-server basis, you must determine whether it's possible or necessary to upgrade on the same machine or to a different machine. If you have plenty of free disk space, or a fast tape drive, you may want to upgrade your system in place and later, after you inspect it, put it into production. This is the option illustrated by Figure 4-1.

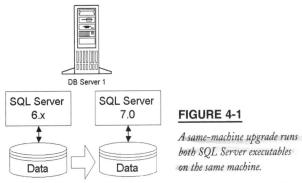

FIGURE 4-1

A same-machine upgrade runs both SQL Server executables on the same machine.

When you run a same-machine upgrade, you actually install SQL Server 7.0 on the same machine as your SQL Server 6.x, though you do not run them simultaneously. If you use the Upgrade Wizard provided by Microsoft, it will alternate starting and stopping each of the servers.

On the other hand, some of your servers may be making maximum use of their disk space, and there's simply no choice but to upgrade to a new machine. You can see this scenario illustrated in Figure 4-2.

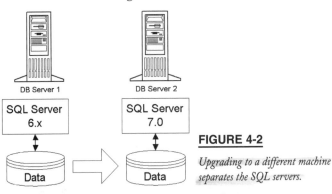

FIGURE 4-2

Upgrading to a different machine separates the SQL servers.

If you use the Upgrade Wizard to upgrade to a different machine, you'll drive the upgrade process from the SQL Server 7.0 machine.

Let's examine the advantages and disadvantages to each choice.

Same-Machine Upgrade

A same-machine upgrade gets your system back into production quickly, with SQL Server 7.0 as the production DBMS, if the machine has plenty of disk space available. Microsoft recommends free space of at least 1.5 times the amount of disk space your data currently takes. If the upgrade does not work, and you have plenty of free disk space, you can stop the 7.0 SQL server and restart the 6.x server in order to get your server back into production.

However, if the upgrade process runs out of space and has to delete some of the 6.5 devices, you'll have to restore from a backup in order to bring the machine back into production.

> **WARNING**
>
> An important limitation here is that a same machine upgrade requires that the machine be running Windows NT 4.0 SP4 or later. If your server is running NT 3.51, you must upgrade the operating system first. Microsoft will support SQL Server 6.x on Windows NT 4.0 SP4 for the purposes of upgrading.

Different Machine Upgrade

If you upgrade to a new machine, the number of tasks you have to perform is greater, because you'll have to carefully rename your servers so that the new machine can go into production. Although this does complicate the process, it does leave your former production machine untouched, as a backup.

Replication

If your servers participate in replication, you must first upgrade the distribution server or the server with the distribution database.

> **WARNING**
>
> The MSDB database, which stores replication information, changes dramatically between SQL Server 6.x and 7.0. Replication tasks will be upgraded into the 7.0 server with default schedules, not their 6.x schedules.

You cannot use the new features of SQL Server 7.0 replication until you've upgraded all of your replication servers to 7.0.

An Upgrade Decision Matrix

The following table summarizes the basic options for same machine and different machine upgrades.

	Same Machine	Different Machine
Requires NT 4.0 on the source server	Yes	No
Requires NT 4.0 on the target server	Yes	Yes
Supports replication	Yes	Yes

Using a Test Server in an Upgrade

No matter what type of upgrade you choose, upgrading a test system first and inspecting the result for errors is by far the safest way to learn and plan the upgrade process.

A good test system will reproduce the RAM and hard disk volume configuration of the production system. It need not duplicate the CPU speeds, or the exact hard drive types. For example, your production system might be a dual Pentium II with 512MB RAM. The disks may consist of drives C, D, and E, where they are RAID 0, RAID 1, and RAID 5 respectively. In this case, your test system should be a Pentium II system with 512MB RAM, but it need not be a dual-processor system. Similarly, the test system need not have RAID drives, but it should duplicate the volumes C, D, and E.

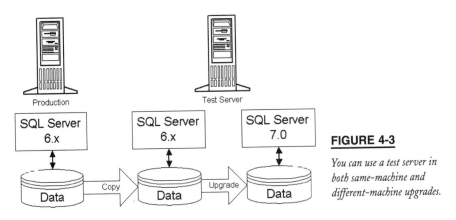

FIGURE 4-3

You can use a test server in both same-machine and different-machine upgrades.

After the test system hardware has been established, the software should exactly match the production system. The test machine should have the same NT service packs and network configuration of the production machine. In addition, the test server's SQL Server executables, data and log locations, backup locations, and other files should match as closely as possible.

In a same machine upgrade, you would install SQL Server 6.x on your test machine, build your devices to match production, and copy data over from the production machine. Then you can either upgrade the test system alone, as a same-machine upgrade, or upgrade the test server to a different machine.

In many cases, however, it may be impossible to duplicate the production scenario on test systems. Test systems tend to be smaller, less powerful servers than the production machines, and they may not be able to store as much data as the production machine. Also, the production environment may involve too many servers and/or may be involved in replication scenarios, making it cost-prohibitive to duplicate in a test environment.

Even in complex environments, however, it can pay to duplicate some of the more complex and critical databases on a test machine and then go through a dry run of the upgrade process.

Decision 2: Use the Upgrade Wizard or Upgrade Manually

Another decision is, will you use the Upgrade Wizard? Or instead, will you use your own handmade process, using scripts to re-create the database objects, and BCP to transfer the data?

The obvious advantage to using the Upgrade Wizard is that it can make the upgrade process rather easy and fast: It can do in one step something that would take you many steps by hand. In an environment with many servers to upgrade, you may have no choice. The time it would take to manually upgrade the servers could be prohibitive. You may require the ease of use provided by the Wizard.

The Upgrade Wizard is comparatively fast. It can upgrade a 1-gigabyte database in less than an hour, and an 80-gigabyte database in less than 15 hours.

On the other hand, if you have just one or a few servers to upgrade, you may want to keep the upgrade process under your control. Even then there's a potential use for the Upgrade Wizard: If you decide to do the upgrade in a more manual fashion yourself, you can still use it to jump-start your scripts.

TIP

The best approach for deciding whether to use the Upgrade Wizard is to examine it, use it on a test system, inspect the results, and see if they are satisfactory. Also, get a sense of the SQL Server community's view of the upgrade process, either through user groups or Internet news groups.

Decision 3: Consolidate or Separate Data

You may look upon the process of upgrading as an opportunity to change some database structures and either consolidate or separate data. After having a legacy system in production for some time, you may be acutely aware of what you'd like to change.

However, the 7.0 Upgrade Wizard will simply reproduce the current design and will not assist you in any redesign effort.

If you do want to redesign the database somewhat, your best bet may be to use the Upgrade Wizard to upgrade your current database system into a staging area in SQL Server 7.0 and then use the Data Transformation Services (DTS) to transfer data into the redesigned area. For more information about DTS, see Chapter 10, "Importing and Exporting Data."

Analyzing Your Current Systems

When analyzing your upgrade tasks, there are a number of factors that you should take into account.

Complexity

First of all, how complex are your systems? Complex databases are far more likely to develop trouble spots than simple ones. Replication can further complicate the situation.

If you have applied standards for your directory and database file names, you may have to make some allowances. If you're doing a same-machine upgrade, you won't be able to have the SQL Server 6.x and SQL Server 7.0 executables in the same directory. In addition, the Upgrade Wizard will enforce the .mdf extension for the first data file of a database, and .ndf for the remaining data files. It will also enforce the .ldf extension for the log file.

Quoted Identifiers

Inspect your stored procedures and determine whether they use double quotes as string delimiters. The ANSI SQL-92 standard specifies that strings must be delimited only by single quote marks, and it reserves the use of double quote marks for identifiers such as table and column names. In SQL Server 6.5 and 7.0, SET QUOTED IDENTIFIERS ON will enforce the ANSI standard. If you've already developed with that in mind, you can leave the setting ON in the Upgrade Wizard. On the other hand, if your system has stored procedures or triggers that use double quotes for string delimiters, you will need to have QUOTED IDENTIFIERS OFF during the upgrade. You can set this in the Upgrade Wizard.

ANSI Nulls

Inspect your table schemas and determine whether table columns allow nulls by default. If they do not, you will need to have ANSI_NULLS OFF during the upgrade. Also, if your stored procedure or trigger code uses the = NULL or NULL constructs instead of the ANSI standard IS NULL or IS NOT NULL, then you will want to have ANSI_NULLS OFF. For more information about how SQL Server 7.0 behavior with nulls differs from SQL Server 6.5, see Chapter 12, "Data Definition."

References to System Tables

Inspect your 6.x stored procedures to see if they make changes to the system tables. Because the system tables change in 7.0, there is some chance those stored procedures will no longer work.

WARNING

The Upgrade Wizard will not convert stored procedures that make references to system tables.

Upgrading from SQL Server 4.21

If you are upgrading a SQL Server 4.21 database, and you are going to use the Upgrade Wizard, you have additional tasks to perform. You must first upgrade the database to 6.x and then run the Upgrade Wizard. Directions for upgrading a 4.21

NOTE

You cannot directly upgrade from a SQL Server 4.21 system to 7.0. You must first upgrade the 4.21 system to 6.x, and then upgrade the latter system to 7.0.

server to 6.x are in the Books Online and are straightforward.

You need to run the 6.x CHKUPG.EXE utility against the 4.21 database. It will check the 4.21 database for incompatible keywords, and for the presence of text in the database's syscomments system table for all stored procedures and triggers.

You apply the upgrade by installing SQL Server 6.x on the 4.21 server and then rerunning the 6.x Setup program and choosing Upgrade. After you've upgraded the 4.21 server, do not forget to apply the latest service pack to the 6.x server. Because this upgrade is one-way only, and after the upgrade process the 4.21 server is no longer usable in production, you would be wise to run the upgrade on a second machine.

Upgrading from SQL Server 6.0

Although the Upgrade Wizard supports SQL Server 6.0, a problem arises if you

> **NOTE**
>
> For the purposes of upgrading, Microsoft will support SQL Server 6.0 on Windows NT 4 SP4.

want to upgrade the 6.0 server in place, that is, on the same machine. Normally Microsoft requires NT 4.0 SP4 for SQL Server 7.0, and SQL Server 6.0 is only supported on NT 3.51.

If you are not comfortable with running SQL Server 6.0 under NT 4.0, you should avoid a same-machine upgrade from 6.x to 7.0 and perform a different-machine upgrade instead.

Of course, if you are upgrading to a different machine, the Upgrade Wizard can run against NT 3.51 on the source machine. You simply make sure that you are running the Wizard from a SQL Server 7.0 system running on NT 4.0 SP4.

Upgrading from SQL Server 6.5

If you are running SQL Server 6.5 on NT 3.51, you have the same problem just mentioned for SQL Server 6.0: You cannot perform a same-machine upgrade unless the operating system has first been upgraded to NT 4.0 with NT SP4 or later.

Consequently, if you are running 6.5 on NT 3.51 and intend to perform a same-machine upgrade, you have to factor in the steps and time to upgrade the NT operating system as well. This includes all the necessary drivers, the network options, and the NT service packs. Obviously, the potential for error greatly increases with the increased number of tasks.

An Upgrade Analysis Checklist

The following checklist summarizes the prior discussion. All of the following issues should bear on your analysis of your current system.

❏ Plan to upgrade a test system first. Secure a test system that is as close a copy of production as is feasible. If you use the Upgrade Wizard, check for errors in the upgrade folder.

❏ Have a disaster plan in place, so that if the upgrade process fails, you can restore the production environment.

❏ If you are doing an in-place upgrade, the server must use NT 4.0 with NT SP3 or later. If you are upgrading to a second computer with SQL 7.0, it must be running NT 4.0 with NT SP3 or later.

❏ Make sure that the SQL 6.x server and 7.0 server services each are using domain logins, not the local system account.

❏ Make sure the default database for the sa login on the 6.x machine has been set to the master database.

❏ Determine what logins on your 6.x server contain special 6.x characters: underscore (_) for backslash /, pound sign (#) for dash (–). The Upgrade Wizard will copy them and a new set of logins with the dash and domain sign in place. This may impact your new production environment.

❏ Inspect your stored procedures and determine whether they use double quotes as string delimiters. If so, you will want to have QUOTED IDENTIFIERS OFF during the upgrade.

❏ Inspect your 6.x stored procedures to see if they make changes to the sys tem tables. The Upgrade Wizard will not convert stored procedures that make references to system tables. Also, it will not convert stored procedures that are compiled with encryption.

❏ Inspect your table schemas and determine whether table columns allow nulls by default. If they do not, you will need to have ANSI_NULLS OFF during the upgrade.

❏ Identify all dependent databases and plan to upgrade them simultaneously.

❏ If doing an in-place upgrade, make sure that you have double the disk space available.

Developing an Upgrade Plan

You have a number of items to consider when developing your upgrade plan. Most of them relate to disaster protection. Because you're upgrading a production system, you must prepare for the worst and plan to restore your older system if the upgrade does not succeed.

Note that you must remove your servers from production during the upgrade. It's just good policy: You cannot allow clients to change data during the upgrade process, under pain of losing data. In any case, the Upgrade Wizard will not operate unless it can get exclusive use of both the 6.x and 7.0 servers and their databases.

If something goes wrong during the upgrade, or if you discover errors that you cannot accept, or if your client applications cannot operate correctly with the resulting upgraded server, then you will have to back out of the process and put the old server back into production.

The 6.x Server

You need to plan to take care of a number of items on the 6.x server before actually upgrading. These items correspond to the kind of backups you would make in planning for recovery from a disaster, plus a few things that are specific to the Upgrade Wizard.

For the Wizard to operate properly, you must make sure that the server's name is the same as the computer name. You can check this with both

```
SELECT @@servername
```

and

```
SELECT name FROM sysservers
```

Make sure that you have the recommended amount of RAM allocated to your 6.x server. The following table shows the Microsoft recommendation from the 6.x Books Online:

Machine Memory (MB)	SQL Server Memory (MB)
32	16
48	28
64	40
128	100
256	216
512	464

You should also ensure that your 6.x tempdb database is at least 25MB in size. Preferably it is on its own device, but that is not required.

Your 6.x server should be running at least SQL SP3 or later for either 6.0 or 6.5. Also, before upgrading you should shut down replication and make sure that all transactions logs have been dumped. Doing a CHECKPOINT will cause SQL Server 6.x to write all data in RAM out to disk (though the Upgrade Wizard will stop and restart the 6.x server anyway, causing the checkpoint.)

On your 7.0 server, make sure that you don't fix any RAM allocation; let it determine its own RAM dynamically.

Finally, before upgrading, shut down all utilities and services related to SQL Server 6.x or 7.0, including the SQL Server service as well as the SQL Executive on 6.5 and the SQL Agent on 7.0. That will help guarantee that the Upgrade Wizard's utilities can gain exclusive access to each server.

An Upgrade Planning Checklist

You can use this checklist as a starting point for your own conversion. You will need to add items to match your own particular environment.

- ❏   Take all the 6.x servers you intend to upgrade out of production.
- ❏   Back up the server's Registry.
- ❏   Back up all 6.x databases, including master and msdb.
- ❏   Make sure each 6.x server's @@servername matches its sysservers system table entry and the machine name.
- ❏   Make sure that the 6.x server's tempdb database device is at least 10MB in size.
- ❏   For upgrading, a SQL Server 6.0 must have SP3 (build 151) applied. A SQL Server 6.5 server must have SP4 (build 283) or later applied.
- ❏   Configure memory on the 6.x machine to the Microsoft-recommended amount, based on the amount of physical RAM in the machine.
- ❏   Let the SQL Server 7.0 server dynamically configure its own memory; do not fix any memory setting manually.
- ❏   Shut down all SQL 6.x replication and make sure the 6.x transaction logs are empty.
- ❏   Disable all SQL 6.x startup stored procedures, that is, remove their startup status using the sp_unmakestartup system stored procedure.
- ❏   In a replication scenario, if the distribution database is on its own machine, then upgrade it first, before the publishers and subscribers. If the distribution server is on the same machine as the publisher, then you can upgrade either the publisher or the subscriber first.
- ❏   After the upgrade finishes, verify that the SQL Server 7.0 databases and data are in place, and inspect the \MSSQL7Upgrade folder for errors.

Using the Upgrade Wizard

After you've made the important decisions and have planned your upgrade carefully, running the Upgrade Wizard is quite easy. You will confront a number of decisions along the way, as well as some known problems, so it's worthwhile to take a look at the more important dialog boxes.

The Upgrade Process

When you start up the Upgrade Wizard, you'll first pass through a welcome dialog box, and then you'll see the Data and Object Transfer dialog box, as shown in Figure 4-4.

FIGURE 4-4

The Data and Object Transfer dialog box presents you with an initial set of options.

Export and Import

Your first option is to include objects or data, or both. When initially testing the upgrade, you might want to stage the upgrade, and just choose objects, to make sure that the upgrade utilities are truly scripting and capturing them. But during an actual upgrade, you would normally choose both objects and data.

> **NOTE**
>
> Do not use the Upgrade Wizard to attempt to replicate data from a 6.x system to a 7.0 system. It will always re-create the entire target database. Similarly, you cannot synchronize 7.0 data after an upgrade: The upgrade process will start over from the beginning when you rerun it.

Data Transfer Method

The Upgrade Wizard can transfer data either through a named pipe, which really implies via temporary disk files, or through a tape system. The recommended amount of free disk space to use the named pipe method is twice the amount of space used by your databases.

Using a tape system is a viable option if you are low on disk space and can afford to let the tape hold the intermediate objects and exported data. Normally you would only do this on a single-machine upgrade. However, be aware that on a same-machine upgrade, using the tape system will delete the 6.x data on your server. If the process fails for any reason, you will need to implement recovery procedures already in place.

Verification

Normally you will want to validate the object creation on the new server as well as exhaustively verify data integrity. The validation process involves running DBCC on all the 6.x databases before the transfer.

The exhaustive verification does much more checking. When you choose this option, the Upgrade Wizard uses a utility called DBCHECK.EXE to compare schemas and data between both new and old systems based on CRC (cyclical redundancy checks) and rowcounts. Because these operations will add time to the upgrade process, you might skip them during a dry run.

Identifying Server Names and Logins

The next dialog box you see asks you for your server names, sa login passwords, and any special startup parameters, as shown in Figure 4-5.

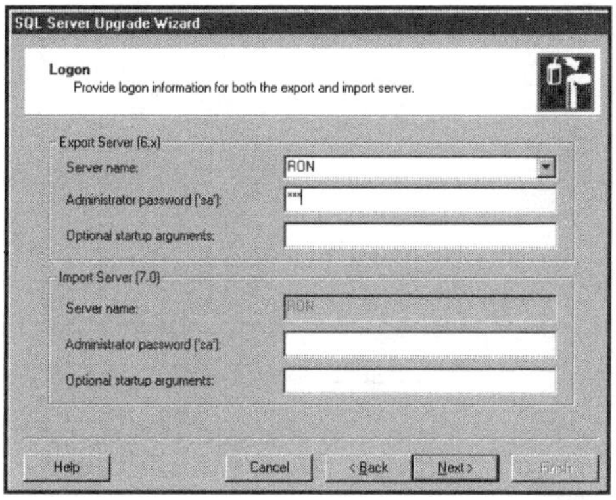

FIGURE 4-5

When you identify the servers, you are in effect choosing either a same-machine or different-machine upgrade.

Normally you would just supply the sa passwords. But if you have special trace flags that you use for starting up your servers, be sure to enter them here. In effect, here is where you are choosing whether to upgrade to the same machine or a different machine, based on the server name choices in this dialog box.

A few things are worth noting here. First of all, notice that you identify only a 6.x server in the first section of the dialog box. As you learned earlier in this chapter, this utility will not upgrade SQL Server 4.21 servers. In addition, you cannot upgrade to a Windows 98 or Windows 95 system. You must upgrade to SQL Server on Windows NT 4.0 SP4 or later.

The upgrade process may make significant changes to your 6.x system, if you are doing a same-machine upgrade. It modifies the 6.x distribution database if the 6.x server is a distribution server. Also, it will delete 6.x data devices if you use the tape backup method of upgrading.

Scripting Code Page Selection

In the next dialog box, you choose the scripting code page, as shown in Figure 4-6.

FIGURE 4-6

You should normally accept the default for the scripting code page.

This additional option exists because occasionally the 6.x server will have a different code page than the SQL Server 7.0 server to which you are upgrading. If they are different, choose the SQL Server 7.0 code page here. Because this is rare, you can normally just accept the default.

Selecting Databases

After you click on the Next button, the Upgrade Wizard finds the available databases to upgrade on your 6.x server. The result is the dialog box in Figure 4-7.

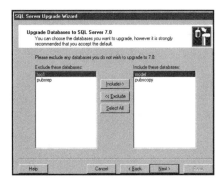

FIGURE 4-7

The Layout Utility finds the databases available for upgrading and lets you select a subset.

A few things are worth noting here. The master and pubs databases are not listed. The Model database, which serves to carry default settings for all new databases, is an option, though. (The pubs sample database cannot be upgraded.)

As you will see in a couple of pages, the master database will be upgraded if you choose to upgrade the server configuration in a later dialog box. Similarly, the msdb database, which contains scheduling information, will be upgraded if you choose to include SQL Executive settings in the same later dialog box.

WARNING

You must include all databases that have dependencies on each other for the upgrade to succeed. If you omit any dependent databases from the included list, the resulting upgrade may not work; certain scripts may fail due to missing objects on the 7.0 system.

Database Creation

After you've chosen the databases to upgrade, you can then choose how to create the corresponding databases on the SQL Server 7.0 target, as shown in Figure 4-8.

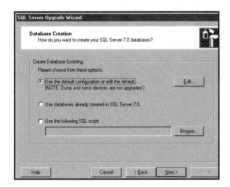

FIGURE 4-8

You must next decide how and where to create the upgraded 7.0 databases.

As you can see, you can use the default configuration or edit the default, use databases already created in SQL 7.0, or use a script to create the databases.

In the default configuration, the Upgrade Wizard will create databases on your SQL 7.0 server with the same names as exist on the 6.x server. The new files will be given names that match the current database names. There will be one file for data, and one for the log, each in its own file group.

You can inspect and edit the default by pressing the Edit button. The resulting dialog box shows you the proposed files, as shown in Figure 4-9:

FIGURE 4-9

You can see the initial layout of data and log files that the Upgrade Wizard will create.

In order to see the actual file names and full paths for locations, click on the Advanced button. The result is the dialog box shown in Figure 4-10.

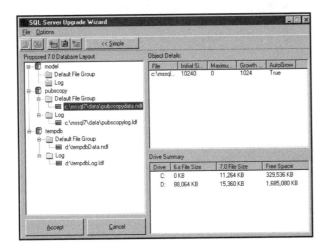

FIGURE 4-10

You can see the file locations and paths by clicking on the Advanced button.

In addition to file location information, notice that you can also see the file group default growth characteristics in the upper-right pane of the dialog box.

You can edit the locations, and also edit the default settings for the files, by selecting a particular file, right-clicking, and choosing the Properties option. The result is the dialog box shown in Figure 4-11.

FIGURE 4-11

You can also edit the properties of each file.

The dialog box in Figure 4-11 gives you most of the options you normally have when creating a database file in SQL Server 7. For more information about these options, see Chapter 7, "Managing Databases."

System Configuration

After you've navigated all of the previous dialog boxes and accepted their values, you move next to the System Configuration dialog box, as you can see in Figure 4-12. Here is where you choose to upgrade the master as well as msdb databases, among other things.

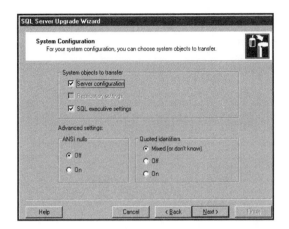

FIGURE 4-12

The System Configuration dialog box lets you choose how many configuration items you would like to upgrade.

The System Objects options let you choose first of all whether to upgrade the Server Configuration. Checking this option will transfer logins and other configurations from the 6.x master database to the 7.0 database. Conversely, if you leave this blank, your logins will not be transferred.

The second check box lets you choose replication settings. This option will be disabled if your server does not have replication installed. The last option to check concerns SQL Executive settings. If you want to transfer your scheduled jobs over to the 7.0 SQL Agent, you need to check this box.

Under Advanced settings, you see two choices. The first concerns ANSI nulls. If you've developed your 6.x database using SET ANSI_DEFAULTS ON, or SET ANSI_NULLS ON, then you can choose the On option. If not, you should leave the option at the default Off value.

The second advanced setting deals with quoted identifiers. As discussed earlier in this chapter, if any of your stored procedure or trigger code uses double quotes for delimiting strings, you should leave this option at the Mixed or Off values. Only if you've consciously developed your objects with quoted identifiers in mind should you use the On value.

For more information about ANSI nulls and quoted identifiers, see Chapter 12, "Data Definition."

Confirmation

The next screen lets you inspect your choices, as shown in Figure 4-13.

FIGURE 4-13

You can inspect your choices for confirmation purposes before beginning the actual upgrade.

If any of the choices need reworking, you can navigate back with the Previous button to change them.

Executing the Upgrade

After you click on the Finish button, the Upgrade Wizard utilities kick into gear and start the upgrade process. The tasks will be executed in the order you see them in the task list. A sample progress dialog box is shown in Figure 4-14.

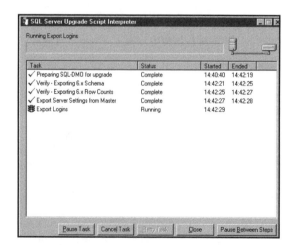

FIGURE 4-14

You can see the upgrade tasks listed as they are completed during the upgrade process.

If you do nothing else at this point, the Upgrade Wizard will proceed with all the tasks it determines are necessary to complete the upgrade. You can, however, interrupt and restart the process.

Notice all the options that are available to you during this execution. You can pause and resume any one of the tasks or cause all tasks to pause between steps. If you choose to pause between steps, you'll need to answer dialog boxes for each step that needs to execute.

You can also cancel a task—and therefore the entire upgrade. In this case, when you restart the Wizard, it will detect the point at which it left off and resume the process. This gives you the ability to halt a lengthy upgrade if necessary and resume it later. When you next start up the Wizard, you'll be presented with a dialog box that asks if you'd like to restart your upgrade, as shown in Figure 4-15.

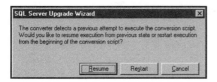

FIGURE 4-15

You can restart an interrupted upgrade and continue where you left off.

As you can see, you can either resume the process or restart.

Upgrade Complete

When the upgrade is complete, you'll be presented with a dialog box stating so, and the task dialog box will also indicate that the upgrade completed.

NOTE

Just because an upgrade completed does not mean that there were no errors. You must examine the upgrade directory for error files and inspect them to be assured that no errors occurred.

Also, at this point the Wizard will present you with information about the upgrade in a file format that you can use Notepad to examine, as shown in Figure 4-16.

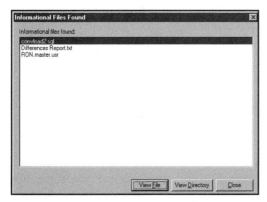

FIGURE 4-16

You can selectively view error files generated by the upgrade process.

These informational files contain results that are not errors but could still indicate problems. You need to satisfy yourself that they present no problem by inspecting them. You can just double-click on any of them and they will open in Notepad.

Interpreting the Upgrade Wizard Results

If you used the Upgrade Wizard, you must ensure that your upgrade proceeded correctly by examining the SQL Server 7.0 upgrade directory. There you will find files indicating the results of the upgrade process, as shown in Figure 4-17.

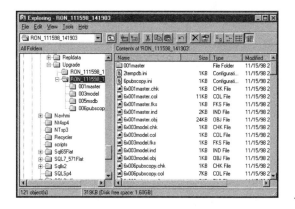

FIGURE 4-17

The results of the Upgrade Wizard are in a parent directory for the upgrade as a whole, with subdirectories for each database.

In Figure 4-17, you can see how the parent directory name is formed: The server name has the date and time appended to it to form the name. In effect, this provides a time stamp for each upgrade. Within the upgrade, each upgraded database is given a directory with the database ID followed by the name of the database.

You can find global results of the upgrade in the parent upgrade directory. Any scripts that failed will have an err in the file name. The .out files contain the output of the scripts at each stage.

Known Problems

No matter how much a program like the Upgrade Wizard tries to automate the upgrade process, some details are bound to arise in a complex system that it overlooks or cannot handle. Here are some examples:

1. In order to bring over stored procedure and trigger code, the Wizard's utilities must find the source text intact in your 6.x syscomments database tables. If you have deleted any text from syscomments (to hide your source code, for example), you will have to manually apply that code to your new server.

2. If you use the T-SQL system stored procedure sp_rename to rename a stored procedure or trigger, sp_rename does not update the source code of a stored procedure or trigger in syscomments to reflect the new name. Consequently, the source code that will be brought over to the new server

will still contain the old name. When the script is rerun on the new server, the stored procedure will take on the old name.

3. If a stored procedure simply references a system table, it may not work on the new server because system tables have changed in SQL Server 7.0.

4. Stored procedures that are created dynamically within other stored procedures will not be transferred. You will have to rerun the original stored procedure in order to create the inner stored procedure.

Compatibility Levels

When you upgrade a SQL Server 6.x database to SQL Server 7.0, the resulting 7.0 database will be assigned a compatibility level of 60 or 65, depending upon the original server. This is done to give stored procedure and trigger code behavior that matches earlier versions of Transact-SQL, in the case where SQL Server 7.0 has modified the behavior of certain commands. To determine the current compatibility level of a database, just execute

```
EXEC sp_dbcmptlevel, <database name>
```

For example, in the previous upgrade,

```
EXEC sp_dbcmptlevel, 'pubscopy'
```

shows that the new database has the compatibility level set to 65.

> **WARNING**
>
> When a database is in an older compatibility level, the new Transact-SQL constructs of SQL Server 7.0 are not available. SELECT TOP n, for example, only works if the database has a compatibility level of 70. For a detailed list, see the Books Online, `"sp_dbcmptlevel."`

You can change a database's compatibility level by adding the number on the end of the same command. For example,

```
EXEC sp_dbcmptlevel, 'pubscopy', 70
```

will change the compatibility level of the pubscopy database to 7.0.

Summary

The SQL Server 7.0 Upgrade Wizard makes the upgrade process relatively simple, as long as you make sure you plan your upgrade and understand the requirements. Then the Wizard becomes an indispensable tool. After you've upgraded some databases, or even if you haven't, you must consider how to configure SQL Server 7 for your application, which I'll cover in the next chapter.

Chapter 5

Configuring

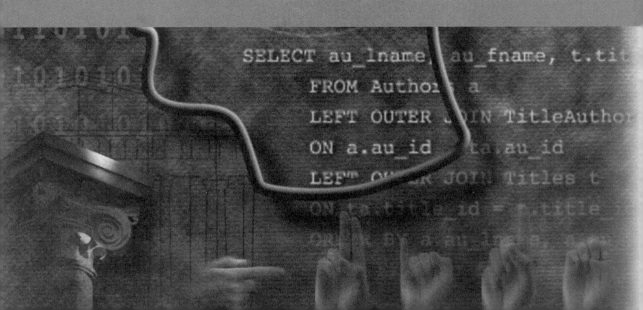

In This Chapter

- ◆ Configuring with the Setup program
- ◆ The Enterprise Manager Server Properties dialog box
- ◆ More `sp_configure` Options
- ◆ The Windows NT Services dialog box
- ◆ Other startup parameters

SQL Server 7.0 breaks new ground among relational database systems by automatically configuring its memory and other run-time settings. Traditionally, database systems have required that expert DBAs manually tune a system to configure a new installation correctly. With SQL Server 7.0, most of that tuning is done dynamically. In the words of one of SQL Server's architects, "We've left most of the knobs in there, even though you don't need to use them." The knobs are the tuning parameters, or the configuration settings.

Sometimes, though, you will need to use the knobs, set some configurations, and tune some parameters. This will happen especially when you have a larger system that is not performing the way you want. Then you'll need to probe beneath the surface and find out what all the "knobs" do!

NOTE

You will find that many SQL Server 6.x configuration options have been either retired or made dynamic in SQL Server 7. You may get the feeling that some knobs are missing, and some knobs no longer need you to turn them. The result is a much more smoothly operating database system.

You actually have several ways to configure SQL Server. You can set most of your server's configuration options using the server's Properties dialog box in Enterprise Manager. As you'll see, this dialog box actually writes to the database and the Registry behind the scenes. I'll cover all its options, plus the remaining advanced configuration settings that do not appear in the dialog box.

NOTE

Not all of the configuration options are available for Windows 98 and Windows 95. Because they lack the security authorization and multithreading capabilities of Windows NT, they lack many of the configuration options available to SQL Server under Windows NT.

After I've covered the server Properties dialog box, you'll see a few other places that you can set some configuration options, including the SQL Server setup program, the Control Panel Services dialog box, and the Connection Properties dialog box in Enterprise Manager. I'll cover these at the end of the chapter.

Configuring with the Setup Program

Before you look at the extensive list of server configuration items in SQL Server, it's a good idea to recall that there are two important server-level configurations that you must use the Setup program to change. They are covered in Chapter 3, "Installing," and I'll just summarize them here.

1. Character set, sort order, and Unicode collation: If you run the rebuild master program (rebuildm.exe) after installation, you can change the server's character set, sort order, and Unicode collation. Changing these options is drastic, because once you do, your entire system will be rebuilt, and any current user database files will be detached and no longer readable by that server.

2. Change network support: You can change the mix of network libraries that the server will load when starting up, by using the Server Network Utility. It is important that the SQL server have all the network libraries in place that the client machines require. For more information about network libraries, see Chapter 6, "Connectivity."

The preceding choices do partially configure the server, but they require external programs. A great many more configuration items are to be found in Enterprise Manager and in the sp_configure system stored procedure.

The Enterprise Manager Server Properties Dialog Box

The easiest tool for configuring an individual SQL Server is the server's Properties dialog box that you'll find when you register a SQL Server in Enterprise Manager. It's a standard GUI dialog box, and it's easy to use, but its ease of use can hide what's really going on. Before I get into particular configurations, let's examine the dialog box and the commands it emits behind the scenes.

Starting the Server Properties Dialog Box

After you've registered a server, you can bring up the server's Properties dialog box. To bring up the Properties dialog box, you can right-click over the server name and choose the Properties option from the pop-up menu, as shown in Figure 5-1.

FIGURE 5-1

You can right-click over a server name and choose Properties from the pop-up menu to get the server Properties dialog box.

Alternatively, you can select the server name in the Enterprise Manager tree view, click on the Action menu, and select Properties. In either case, you bring up a tabbed dialog box that allows you to inspect and change server-wide configuration properties. You can see a picture of the initial dialog box in Figure 5-2.

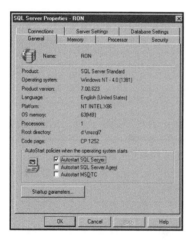

FIGURE 5-2

The server Properties dialog box is the GUI interface to many, but not all, of SQL Server's configuration options.

This dialog box behaves in a standard Windows tabbed dialog box fashion. But the easy GUI can hide what's really going on.

Behind the Scenes

For each setting in the dialog box you change, behind the scenes Enterprise Manager sends one of two kinds of commands to SQL Server's query engine. One kind includes calls to the system stored procedure, sp_configure, which changes values in the master database sysconfigures system table. The other kind includes calls to the extended system stored procedure, xp_regwrite, which writes to the Registry. The relationship of the Properties dialog box to these underlying actions is shown in Figure 5-3.

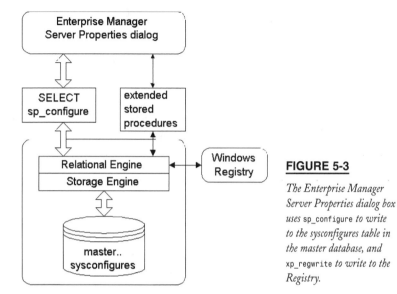

FIGURE 5-3

The Enterprise Manager Server Properties dialog box uses sp_configure *to write to the sysconfigures table in the master database, and* xp_regwrite *to write to the Registry.*

To read one set of configuration values from the database, EM sends a SQL SELECT command to the relational engine, which retrieves data from the sysconfigures table, a system table in the master database. To read a different set of configuration values from the Registry, EM sends the xp_regread extended stored procedure to the relational engine, which then calls an external .DLL to read Registry values. (EM also sends the extended stored procedure xp_msver to read some information about the server version. It sometimes uses xp_regenumvalues as well to read collections of Registry values.)

Enterprise Manager has the relational engine execute the system stored procedure sp_configure to write to the sysconfigures table, and it executes the system extended stored procedure xp_regwrite to write to the Registry.

In the next several pages, you'll learn not just the GUI way of configuring SQL Server, but also the sp_configure and xp_regwrite commands. After that, you'll examine the remaining sp_configure options that the dialog box does not show.

TIP

The advantage of being aware of the configuration commands in addition to the Server Properties dialog box is that you may find yourself needing to configure SQL Server without having Enterprise Manager available. When that happens, and it eventually will, you can use these commands to configure the server. Also, you will know what the Properties dialog box is doing behind the scenes and therefore have a much deeper knowledge of SQL Server.

Using the `sp_configure` System Stored Procedure

Before you start looking at particular configurations, it's important that you know how to use the `sp_configure` stored procedure, because you'll soon be seeing references to it. Basically, you execute it using the Query Analyzer. The Query Analyzer is a client application like Enterprise Manager. With it you can enter commands and then send them to the SQL Server relational engine, which will use its query processor to parse, compile, and execute it. You'll learn much more about the Query Processor in Chapter 12, "Data Definition."

Executing `sp_configure` in the Query Analyzer

You can either bring up the Query Analyzer by itself from the Windows Start Menu or launch it from Enterprise Manager from the Tools menu. After you bring it up, it will give you a window into which you can type commands. For example, Figure 5-4 shows you the Query Analyzer with one of the `sp_configure` options, "user connections." (This change will take effect when SQL Server is restarted.)

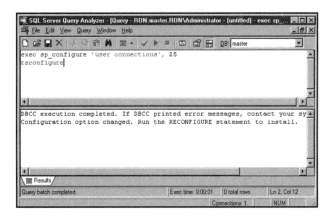

FIGURE 5-4

The Query Analyzer window allows you to enter stored procedure commands and view the results.

You can type in the command in the top window and see the result in the lower window. After you type in the command, you cause the relational engine to execute it by clicking on the first green arrow icon. You may also type Ctrl+E (^E) or Alt+X to cause the command to be executed. In Figure 5-4, the number of user connections has been reconfigured to 30.

In the following pages, rather than showing the Query Analyzer window, I'll just point out the command to you. So, for example, to use `sp_configure` to change the number of user connections to 30, you'll just see

```
exec sp_configure 'user connections', 30
```

which you can then type into the Query Analyzer and execute.

Dynamic and Static Options

Some of the sp_configure options are dynamic, in the sense that they can take place immediately and do not require the SQL Server to be stopped and restarted. The remainder, though, are static and do require stopping and restarting SQL Server to make them take effect.

Advanced Options

To see a list of configuration options you can set with sp_configure, just issue

```
exec sp_configure
```

by itself in the Query Analyzer. The result, by default, only shows a standard subset of the configuration options. To see all of them, you must issue

```
exec sp_configure 'show advanced options', 1
```

and then

```
exec sp_configure
```

will show you the complete list of options. In the following pages, you'll learn which of the options are advanced.

User Options Bit Mask

There is another method of using the sp_configure stored procedure, and that is to send it a bit mask for a set of options. In this alternative, the "user options" string is sent as a parameter, followed by a number holding the sum of a set of options that are either on or off. Those options have values of 1, 2, 4, 8, 16, 32, 64, 128, 256, 512, and 1024 when they are On. You send sp_configure the number that sums up all the ones you want turned On. For example if you want the options with 2 and 8 On, and all the rest Off, you just enter 2 + 8 = 10 as the parameter:

```
exec sp_configure 'user options', 10
```

Obviously, the "user options" parameter is a bit more tricky than the others, because you have to make sure you have all the numbers together, or else you may accidentally turn off some option without realizing it. All the "user options" choices appear in the Server Properties dialog box.

Using the Extended Stored Procedures

In addition to the system stored procedure sp_configure, the Server Properties dialog box makes use of a few extended stored procedures as well. It uses xp_regread and `regwrite` to read from and write to the Registry, and it uses `xp_msver` to get version information.

For example, to get the folder that holds the SQL Server 7 installation on the current machine, the Properties dialog box executes

```
exec xp_regread 'HKEY_LOCAL_MACHINE', 'SOFTWARE\Microsoft\MSSQLServer\Setup',
'SQLPath'
```

In the preceding command,

```
HKEY_LOCAL_MACHINE\SOFTWARE\Microsoft\MSSQLServer\Setup
```

is the Registry key being read, and `'SQLPath'` the value. Figure 5-5 shows you one example of the Registry keys.

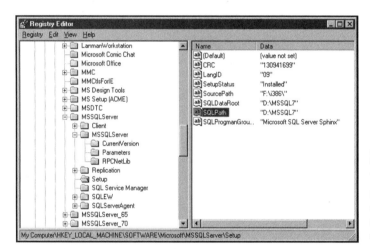

FIGURE 5-5

The Server Properties dialog box will use the extended stored procedure `xp_regread` *to read and write to the Registry.*

These stored procedures are called extended stored procedures because they call routines in binary .DLLs that are external to the database system. Ordinary stored procedures like `sp_configure`, which begin with the `sp_` prefix, act against the SQL Server database using SQL commands.

General Tab

With this in mind, you're ready to tackle the configuration options. The General tab is a mostly informational display, as you can see in Figure 5-6.

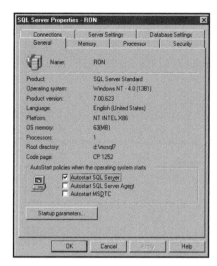

FIGURE 5-6

The General tab displays some information along with choices concerning whether to automatically start SQL Server and SQL Agent.

Enterprise Manager gets the information about the current machine from the extended stored procedure xp_msver, by executing:

```
exec xp_msver N'productversion', N'Language', N'platform', N'WindowsVersion',
N'ProcessorCount', N'PhysicalMemory'
```

The uppercase N makes the strings into Unicode strings (for more about Unicode, see Chapter 12, "Data Definition").

The real configuration options on this page concern whether to start SQL Server and SQL Agent automatically. You initially set these values when you installed SQL Server. If you change either of them, the Properties dialog box will use xp_regwrite to write to the:

```
HKEY_LOCAL_MACHINE\SYSTEM\CurrentControlSet\Services\MSSQLServer
```

key, and it will change the Start value.

WARNING

Do not write to the Registry to change these values. Use the Properties dialog box. That way you'll ensure that you won't accidentally change something you shouldn't.

Startup Parameters

You can also set startup parameters for SQL Server from this dialog box. If you click on the Startup Parameters button, you can add parameters in the dialog box shown in Figure 5-7.

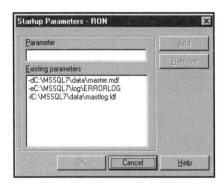

FIGURE 5-7

You can modify the startup parameters for SQL Server.

SQL Server will start up looking for the master database in the path specified by –d. It will write the error log to the file and path specified in the –e parameter and look for the master database transaction log in the –l parameter.

NOTE

SQL Server 7's startup parameters are called "startup options" in the Books Online documentation.

If any of these parameters are incorrect, SQL Server will not start correctly, and it will leave an error message in the NT Application log, which you can view with the Windows NT Event Viewer.

For example, changing the –d parameter to something like C:\MSSQL7\FOOBAR\MASTER.MDF will result in an error message like that shown in Figure 5-8.

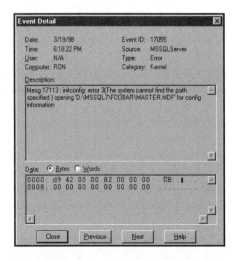

FIGURE 5-8

The Windows NT Event Viewer's Application log will contain error messages if SQL Server's startup parameters are not correct.

The Server Properties dialog box gets this parameter information from the

`HKEY_LOCAL_MACHINE\SOFTWARE\Microsoft\MSSQLServer\MSSQLServer\Parameters`

key in the Registry, using the `xp_regenumvalues` extended stored procedure.

Other startup parameters are available, including trace flags with the –T parameter, and –f for starting SQL Server from the command line in minimal mode. You'll return to startup parameters at the end of this chapter.

NOTE

In prior versions of SQL Serve, it was possible to configure more memory for certain configuration options that was available on the server, and SQL Server would not start. In that case, you would have to use the –f startup parameter to start SQL Server with a minimal configuration. Then you would have to use ISQL to make a single connection to the database and issue the `sp_configure` command to reconfigure the offending parameters. (Later service packs for SQL Server 6.5 made this over-configuration impossible.) With SQL Server 7, however, this is no longer necessary. It is not possible to configure SQL Server 7 in such a way that the SQL Server will not start.

Memory Tab

Normally, SQL Server will dynamically configure its own use of memory, as shown in the Memory tab in Figure 5-9.

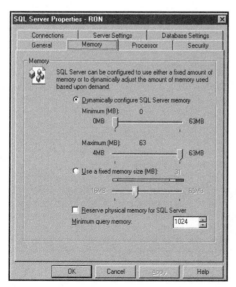

FIGURE 5-9

SQL Server can dynamically configure its own memory usage.

You can cause SQL Server to use a fixed amount of RAM if you want, by using the slide bar shown in the dialog box. Note how the slide bar turns yellow and then red as you start starving NT of memory on the high end, and yellow on the low end if you underallocate RAM for SQL Server.

WARNING

The memory setting is considered an advanced option. You should normally let SQL Server dynamically allocate its own memory usage. Only in cases where you are certain that you want SQL Server to use a specified amount of RAM should you change this option.

If you change the memory allocation, the Server Properties dialog box will send:

```
exec sp_configure 'memory', <number of megabytes>
```

to SQL Server.

For Windows NT only, you also have the option of reserving memory for SQL Server, meaning that it will keep memory it has used and not give it back to other processes. The command to make this happen is:

```
exec sp_configure 'set working set size', 1
```

The Maximum Query Memory option allows you to choose the maximum amount of additional memory queries can use, in addition to their normal 1MB. If you have some queries that are extremely complex, involving hashing or sorting operations, you may benefit from increasing this value.

Processor Tab

The processor tab, as shown in Figure 5-10, allows you to specify the number of processors for SQL Server to use on a multiprocessing computer.

NOTE

The Processor options apply to Windows NT only, not to Windows 98 and Windows 95.

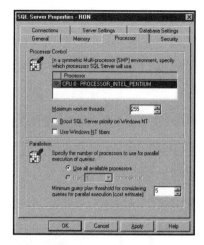

FIGURE 5-10

You can configure the use of multiple processors using the Processor tab.

Processor Control

You can specify which processors SQL Server will use in the first window of the dialog box. This option is also called the "affinity mask." If you change it, the Server Properties dialog box will send

```
exec sp_configure 'affinity mask', <integer value>
```

where the integer value indicates which set of processors to use. (For more information about this option, see "affinity mask" in the Books Online.)

The Maximum Worker Threads option sets the maximum number of NT threads SQL Server will use. Normally each connection gets a thread, but when the number of connections to the server exceeds the number of threads, SQL Server will pool the threads. The command for setting this option is:

```
exec sp_configure 'max worker threads', <integer value>
```

The Boost SQL Server Priority on Windows NT option, if on, causes NT to give SQL Server a higher priority than other processes on the computer. This is almost never desirable, and you should leave it off. Its command is:

```
exec sp_configure 'priority boost', <1 or 0>
```

The Use Windows NT Fibers option allows SQL Server to use fibers, a subcomponent of NT threads.

WARNING

The Processor Control choices are all advanced options. SQL Server 7 has been optimized to make best use of multiprocessing servers. Do not change the settings unless your research indicates that you should.

Parallelism

The Number of Processors to Use for Parallel Execution of Queries option explains itself. SQL Server 7 can process some queries in parallel, and this option allows you to restrict the number of processors such queries can use. Its command is:

```
exec sp_configure 'max degree of parallelism', <integer value>
```

The Maximum Query Plan Threshold option sets the cost mark for parallel queries. If a query can make use of parallelism, and its cost exceeds this setting, then the relational engine will parallelize it. The command for this setting is:

```
exec sp_configure 'cost threshold for parallelism', <integer value>
```

WARNING

The Parallelism settings are also advanced options. Under normal circumstances you should not change them.

Security Tab

The Security tab lets you choose the type of SQL Server login security you would like to impose. The dialog box is shown in Figure 5-11.

NOTE

The Security options apply only to Windows NT. You must use SQL Server login security in Windows 98 and Windows 95.

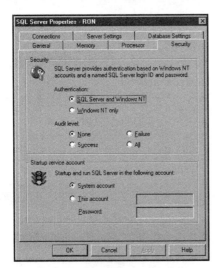

FIGURE 5-11

You can set a number of registry security options with the Security tab.

Security

The choices in the Security box relate to the type of security you want for SQL Server logins. Under Windows NT, your choice consists of whether to add SQL Server's own authentication to Windows NT. If you do, thereby using a "mixed" mode of both security options, SQL Server will first check to see if a new login is a SQL Server login, and if so, check the password. If it is not a SQL Server login, then SQL Server will request Windows NT to validate the login. If that also fails, the login is denied.

NOTE

SQL Server running under Windows 98 and Windows 95 does not support Windows NT authentication, or "integrated" security. Under those operating systems, you must use SQL Server's authentication.

If instead you choose SQL Server security, you need to assign those logins passwords within SQL Server, and in order to log in, the users or their applications will have to supply the passwords.

The Server Properties dialog box sets this type of security by reading and writing from the

HKEY_LOCAL_MACHINE/SOFTWARE\Microsoft\MSSQLServer\MSSQLServer

key, 'LoginMode' value.

You can also indicate the degree of login auditing you want. The results of the logins will be written to either the SQL Server log, or the Windows NT application event log, or both, depending on how you configure logging.

Startup Service Account

The account that you have SQL Server start up with is important. SQL Server, as a service on Windows NT Server, must log in just as any domain user must. However, services can log in under a special account known as the Local System account. It has administrator privileges on the local machine, but no network privileges. If you leave this as SQL Server's login, it will be restricted to operations that do not involve other servers. To let SQL Server participate in remote procedure calls, replication, distributed queries, or any other operations that involve other servers, you must give it a domain login.

This portion of the dialog box reads and writes to the

HKEY_LOCAL_MACHINE/SYSTEM\CurrentControlSet\Services\MSSQLServer

key, and the 'Start' value.

> **TIP**
>
> When you give SQL Server a Windows NT domain login, you must make sure that you give it an account that belongs to the local administrators group and has rights to log on as service. For directions on how to give SQL Server and SQL Executive such an account, see Chapter 9, "Security."

Connections Tab

When SQL Server handles requests for data, it does so by making connections with clients. Each client requesting data opens a connection with SQL Server and then later closes it, normally when the client is finished with its request. In a network client/server environment, the number of users, and therefore the number of connections to SQL Server, will vary throughout the day. In a Web application, an Internet server application such as Microsoft's IIS will make connections with SQL Server, and it may manage the connections itself or let Microsoft Transaction Server (MTS) manage them.

For all these and other cases, you have a fairly large number of configuration settings that govern these connections, as shown in Figure 5-12.

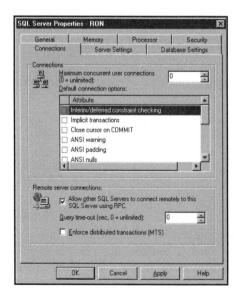

FIGURE 5-12

You make a number of configuration choices in the Connections tab.

Connections

Your first choice in the Connections tab, Maximum Concurrent User Connections, refers to the maximum number of connections that SQL Server will allow for the entire server at any given time. Leaving the value at 0 allows SQL Server to manage that number itself, allocating a small amount of RAM per connection. Normally you can leave this value at 0, unless you are more comfortable setting a maximum. Remember, the number of connections does not translate into the number of simultaneous users, because some applications may use more than one connection. The Transact-SQL command that sets this option is:

```
exec sp_configure, 'user connections', <integer value>
```

Default Connection Options

The defaults for all connections are shown in the list. These apply to each connection, although the client can change them after making the connection. In addition, some of them are set by the Data Source Name (DSN) for the ODBC connection as well. (For more information about DSNs, see Chapter 6, "Connectivity.")

All of these connection options can be set with the 'user options' parameter to sp_configure:

```
exec sp_configure 'user options', <integer bit mask value>
```

where the integer bit mask value is a number that sums up the numeric values for all the various options you want turned on. Also, each of them has a corresponding SET command that can be used for temporarily overriding the configuration. In the following list, after each option is described, you'll see the sp_configure number along with the corresponding Transact-SQL command to set the option for a particular session.

- ◆ Interim/deferred constraint checking: By turning this on, you cause SQL Server to disable its deferred checking of foreign key constraints and therefore apply a stricter type of referential integrity checking. (For more on referential integrity, see Chapter 12, "Data Definition.")

    ```
    exec sp_configure 'user options', <n + 1>
    SET DISABLE_DEF_CNST_CHK  ON
    ```

- ◆ Implicit transactions: If you want SQL Server to automatically start transactions for a number of commands that normally do not use them, set this option on. The SQL Server ODBC driver and OLE DB Provider automatically set this option off. (For more on transactions, see Chapter 16, "Transactions.")

    ```
    exec sp_configure 'user options', <n + 2>
    SET IMPLICIT TRANSACTIONS  ON
    ```

- ◆ Close cursor on commit: This option, when set, will automatically close a cursor at the end of a transaction. The SQL Server ODBC driver and OLE DB Provider automatically set this option off. (For more on cursors, see Chapter 16, "Transactions.")

```
exec sp_configure 'user options', <n + 4>
SET CURSOR_CLOSE_ON_COMMIT ON
```

◆ ANSI warning: This option, when on, causes SQL Server to give warnings under certain conditions when SQL Server would normally not issue a warning. The SQL Server ODBC driver and OLE DB Provider automatically set this option on, so it is probably a good idea to have this on for all connections.

```
exec sp_configure 'user options', <n + 8>
SET ANSI_WARNINGS ON
```

◆ ANSI padding: Data in fixed-length character columns that were created with this option ON will be padded with trailing blanks to fill out the width of the column. When the option is off, fixed length character columns will not be padded with trailing blanks. The SQL Server ODBC driver and OLE DB Provider automatically set this option on, so it is probably a good idea to have this on for all connections.

```
exec sp_configure 'user options', <n + 16>
SET ANSI_PADDING ON
```

◆ ANSI nulls: This option governs how the equals (=) and not equals (<>, !=) operators evaluate nulls. When it is on, comparing anything with a null gives an unknown result. (For more on null values, see Chapter 12, "Data Definition.") The SQL Server ODBC driver and OLE DB Provider automatically set this option on, so it is probably a good idea to have this on for all connections.

```
exec sp_configure 'user options', <n + 32>
SET ANSI_NULLS ON
```

◆ Arithmetic abort: When on, this causes a query to terminate if numeric results overflow a data type's ability to store, or if the query causes a division by zero.

```
exec sp_configure 'user options', <n + 64>
SET ARITHABORT ON
```

◆ Arithmetic ignore: When on, this causes SQL Server to return error messages for the same conditions as arithmetic abort.

```
exec sp_configure 'user options', <n + 128>
SET ARITHIGNORE ON
```

◆ Quoted identifier: When on, this causes SQL Server to interpret double quotes as indicating an identifier (table or column name) in a SQL statement, rather than as delimiting a string. The SQL Server ODBC driver and OLE DB Provider automatically set this option on, because this is ANSI SQL-92 standard behavior. (For more information about the use of quoted identifiers, see Chapter 12, "Data Definition.")

```
exec sp_configure 'user options', <n + 256>
SET QUOTED_IDENTIFIERS ON
```

◆ No count: When on, this turns off the display of the number of rows returned when you execute a query in the Query Analyzer or ISQL.

```
exec sp_configure 'user options', <n + 512>
SET NOCOUNT ON
```

◆ ANSI null defined: When on, this causes a session to ignore a database's default and make columns in new tables default to allowing nulls if their nullability is left undefined.

```
exec sp_configure 'user options', <n + 1024>
SET ANSI_NULL_DFLT_ON ON
```

◆ ANSI null defined OFF: When on, this causes a session to ignore a database's default and make columns in new tables default to prohibiting nulls if their nullability is left undefined. It is the opposite of the preceding value.

```
exec sp_configure 'user options', <n + 2048>
SET ANSI_NULL_DFLT_OFF ON
```

Remote Server Connections

The Remote Server Connections region contains three settings to govern how the current server will interact with other servers.

When Allow Other Servers to Connect Via RPC is on, remote servers can log into the current server to execute stored procedures remotely. The command to set this is:

```
exec sp_configure 'remote access', <1 or 0>
```

If the value is off, remote servers cannot log into the server.

The Query Timeout option governs how much time the current server should allow for processing a query sent by a remote server, before timing out.

```
exec sp_configure 'remote query timeout', <number of seconds>
```

The last option, Enforce Distributed Transactions, allows the current server to participate in transactions governed by the Microsoft Distributed Transaction Coordinator.

```
exec sp_configure 'remote proc trans', <1 or 0>
```

Server Settings Tab

The Server Settings tab contains just a few miscellaneous server settings, as shown in Figure 5-13.

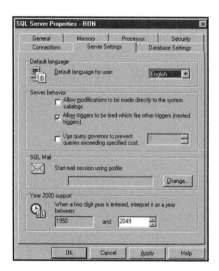

FIGURE 5-13

The Server Settings tab gives you a few miscellaneous server settings.

Default Language

The Default Language option allows you to pick the default language to be used for error messages.

```
exec sp_configure 'remote proc trans', <language id number>
```

Server Behavior

By default, no one is allowed to modify system tables, also called the system catalog. If it becomes necessary for the system administrator to change a system table, then you can turn on the Allow Modifications option. The command for setting this is:

```
exec sp_configure 'allow updates', <1 or 0>
```

> **WARNING**
>
> Modifying system tables is very risky. If you make a mistake, you can prevent SQL Server from running, corrupt a database, or just lose some data. This is a good one to leave unchecked.

It is possible to allow or disallow triggers to fire other triggers, and this is the "nested triggers" option. (For more about triggers, see Chapter 18, "Triggers.") The command that sets this option is:

```
exec sp_configure 'nested triggers', <1 or 0>
```

The Query Governor Option

The Query Governor is a new option with SQL Server 7.0 that allows you to determine the maximum cost that any query should be allowed to take. The cost is the Query Analyzer's numerical estimate of the overall relative expense of a query, based on the query engine's analysis of the joins and other operations required to execute the query. (For more information about the Query Analyzer's costing, see Chapter 19, "Tuning Queries.")

> **NOTE**
>
> The Query Governor does not limit the amount of time that a query will take. It only limits queries based on the cost estimate made by the Query Analyzer.

You can also set the server-level Query Governor amount using sp_configure, as follows:

```
exec sp_configure 'query governor cost limit', <limit>
```

You can also set it per connection in Transact-SQL, using

```
SET QUERY_GOVERNOR_COST_LIMIT <value>
```

SQL Mail

SQL Mail is a facility within SQL Server that allows you to send e-mail and pager notifications to e-mail accounts. To communicate with the mail system, however, SQL Server must have a valid e-mail profile name, and that is what you provide here. The Server Properties dialog box will write the result into the

HKEY_LOCAL_MACHINE\SOFTWARE\Microsoft\MSSQLServer\MSSQLServer'

key, 'MailAccountName' value.

> **NOTE**
>
> The SQL Mail option is available under Windows NT only.

Year 2000 Support

In queries, you can insert or modify dates into SQL Server data without specifying the century part of the year. For example, you can execute the following:

```
UPDATE Titles

        SET pubdate = '6/12/19'

        WHERE title_id = 'BU1032'
```

By default, SQL Server will update the year value as 2019, not 1919. In fact, the default is to interpret any one or two-digit year number that is less than or equal to 49, as meaning the year 2049. You can change that setting using this tab, or by issuing:

```
exec sp_configure 'two digit year cutoff', <cutoff>
```

Note that this becomes a server-wide setting.

Database Settings Tab

The last tab contains settings directly related to database management, as shown in Figure 5-14.

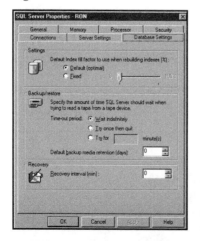

FIGURE 5-14

The Database Settings tab contains some defaults for database management.

Settings

The initial database size sets the default initial size in megabytes for all new database files. (For more on database files, see Chapter 7, "Managing Databases.")

```
exec sp_configure 'database size', <integer number of megabytes, 1 to 10,000>
```

The default index fill factor concerns the amount of free space SQL Server should keep when creating new indexes. This setting only governs the initial amount of fill, and after some database activity, the index fill factor will change.

```
exec sp_configure 'fill factor', <integer percentage>
```

Backup/Restore

The wait time options for reading a tape are DB-Library-only settings. The Server Properties dialog box will read and write this setting from the:

```
HKEY_LOCAL_MACHINE\SOFTWARE\Microsoft\MSSQLServer\MSSQLServer
```

key, `Tapeloadwaittime` value.

The default media backup retention concerns the number of days you would like SQL Server to maintain backups before deleting backup files.

```
exec sp_configure 'media retention', <number of days>
```

Recovery

Finally, the recovery interval is the amount of time that SQL Server should use for determining when to flush all cached data pages to disk, called a checkpoint. As soon as SQL Server estimates that it would take the amount of time you've set to recover if the server were suddenly shut down and restarted (as in a power loss), it will issue a checkpoint. This setting helps you keep the amount of recovery time down in the event of a disaster.

```
exec sp_configure 'recovery interval', <number of minutes>
```

If the truncate log on checkpoint option is set, however, checkpoints are issued every minute, no matter what, and the recovery interval setting no longer applies. (For more information on the transaction log and recovery, see Chapter 7, "Managing Databases.")

More sp_configure Options

The Server Properties dialog box does not contain all the server configuration options that you can set with sp_configure. If you issue:

```
exec sp_configure 'show advanced options', 1
go
exec sp_configure
```

in the Query Analyzer, you'll see a list of all the configuration options available to the sp_configure stored procedure. The Server Properties dialog box does not make use of all of them.

The Server Properties Query

You can use the SQL Profiler to find out that the Server Properties dialog box actually uses the following SQL command to find all the configuration options:

```
select v.number, v.name, minimum = v.low, maximum = v.high,
          dynamic = c.status & 1, config_value = c.value,
          run_value = r.value
from master..sysconfigures c, master..spt_values v,  master..syscurconfigs r
where v.type = 'C' and v.number = c.config and v.number >= 0 and
          v.number = r.config and
          (c.status & 2 = 0 or exists
          (select * from syscurconfigs where config = 518 and value = 1))
          order by v.name
```

Figure 5-15 shows the results of the query. The results show each option, its various values and ranges, as well as whether it is dynamic.

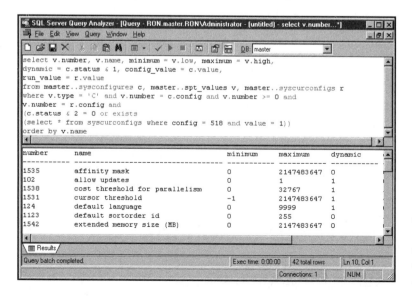

FIGURE 5-15

The results of the actual SQL query used by the Server Properties dialog box

Note that the fifth column indicates whether a configuration value is dynamic. You can cause the results of the Query Analyzer to show in a grid by clicking on the second green arrow icon.

The Remaining `sp_configure` Options

The following list contains the remaining `sp_configure` options.

NOTE

Some of the following configuration items may not be available on Windows 9x.

WARNING

Many of the following settings are advanced options. You should not change them unless you have good reason and are confident that the new values you are assigning will be correct or within a reasonable range. Advanced options cannot be read or changed unless you enable them with `sp_configure` and the "show advanced options" parameter.

- **cursor threshold:** This advanced setting determines how the query optimizer returns rows to a client. If the number of returned rows is greater than the threshold, then the query optimizer will process the query asynchronously. This means it will start returning rows to the client before the query is finished.
- **default sortorder id:** A read-only option, this shows the current sort order of the server. You must use the Setup program to change the server's sort order.
- **extended memory size:** An advanced option available only on SQL Server Enterprise Edition for a future version of Windows NT. It determines how much memory to use as an extended memory cache.
- **index create memory:** This advanced option specifies the amount of memory to use for sorting during the creation of indexes.
- **language in cache:** This specifies the number of languages that can be held in cache.
- **Language-neutral full text:** This advanced option tells SQL Server whether to use the language neutral word breaker on Unicode data.
- **Lightweight pooling:** An advanced option to allow SQL Server to user Windows NT fibers on SMP systems.

- **Locks:** This advanced option specifies the maximum number of locks that the server will hold across all databases. The default of 0 lets SQL Server dynamically allocate memory for locks as it needs it.

- **Max async IO:** This sets the maximum number of disk I/O requests that SQL Server can have outstanding against a file. The default is 32; increasing this number can sometimes help improve SQL Server performance for disk-intensive operations.

- **Max text repl size:** This option sets the maximum size of a replicated text column for insert and update operations. The default is 65,536 bytes.

- **Min memory per query:** An advanced option to specify the minumum memory for SQL Server to use in processing any query.

- **Min server memory:** An advanced option to specify the minimum memory allocated to SQL Server.

- **Network packet size:** This is a dynamic option that specifies the default size of network packets. The default is 4,096 bytes. Microsoft has found this to be generally the optimum.

- **Open objects:** This sets the maximum number of open objects for the server. The default is 500. If you receive error messages about too many open objects, you'll want to increase this number.

- **Remote login timeout:** This advanced option determines how long the server should wait as it tries to log into another server remotely, before timing out. The default is five seconds.

- **Resource timeout:** This advanced option specifies the number of seconds the server should wait for a resource to be released. When the time is exceeded, a warning message results. If transactions are taking more than the default 10 seconds to finish, you'll see error messages concerning logwrite or bufwait timeouts, and you'll need to increase this value.

- **scan for startup procs:** An advanced option that determines whether SQL Server should scan for startup stored procedures when starting. (For more about startup stored procedures, see Chapter 17, "Stored Procedures".)

- **Show advanced options:** As you saw earlier, setting this on shows you and allows you to change the advanced configuration options.

- **Spin counter:** This advanced option specifies the number of times SQL Server will retry to obtain a resource. The default is 10 for a one-processor machine, and 10,000 for more than one processor.

◆ **Time slice:** An advanced option, this sets the CPU time in milliseconds that a particular process can take before scheduling itself out. If it takes longer than this time, the SQL Server kernel will kill the process. The default value is 100 milliseconds.

◆ **Unicode comparison style:** This read-only option shows you the sorting option for Unicode data.

◆ **Unicode locale id:** Another read-only option, this shows the locale for sorting Unicode character data.

Recovering from a Bad Configuration

You can configure SQL Server in such a way that it may lock up and/or refuse to start. Generally this will result from configuring the "locks" parameter too high, because it actually causes SQL Server to allocate memory. If it does, you can overcome this by starting SQL Server with a minimal configuration and resetting the configuration parameters.

To start SQL Server with a minimal configuration, make sure that the SQL Server service is stopped. Enter the NT command window and type:

```
D:\>sqlservr -f
```

This will start SQL Server with a minimal configuration, in single-user mode, and independent of the Windows NT Service Control Manager. The minimal configuration ignores any mistaken values you may have assigned to the configuration options. Leave SQL Server running. You can shut it down later using Ctrl+C (^C).

After you've started the service, you can connect to the server in another NT command window using isql.exe (the command-line isql utility). You can then run the sp_configure stored procedure to move the settings back to normal.

For example, if you've set the number of locks so high that SQL Server can no longer start up, just start SQL Server in minimal mode. In another NT command window, start isql and issue:

```
1> sp_configure 'locks', 5000
2> go
1> reconfigure
2> go
```

For more information about startup parameters, see the following section.

The Windows NT Services Dialog Box

If you have installed SQL Server on Windows NT, you can use the Services utility from the Control Panel to set a couple of the same configuration options that you already saw in the Server Properties dialog box. Go to the Windows NT Start menu and choose Settings, Control Panel, and then the Services icon to see the Services dialog box shown in Figure 5-16.

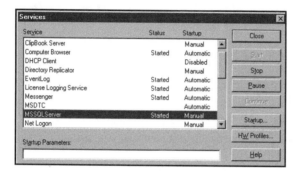

FIGURE 5-16

The Services dialog box gives you access to some SQL Server configurations.

NOTE

There is no equivalent to the Services dialog box in Windows 98 and Windows 95, because they do not have services, and SQL Server runs on those operating systems as just another executable.

Scroll down so that MSSQLServer is highlighted. This is the actual SQL Server service name as known to Windows NT. You can start and stop SQL Server from here, but for now, click on the Startup button, and you'll see a dialog box similar to that in Figure 5-17.

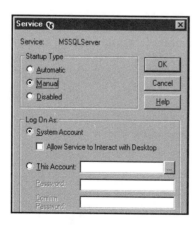

FIGURE 5-17

You can choose some configuration options from the Service dialog box for SQL Server.

Here you can choose whether to have SQL Server start automatically when Windows NT starts, whether to default it to a manual startup, and even whether to disable the service. The disabling option is only available from this dialog box.

In addition, you can determine whether to have SQL Server log in under a local system account, or as a domain account. This is the same as the Startup Service Account option on the Enterprise Manager Server Properties dialog box.

However, there is one very interesting addition: the check box to Allow Service to Interact with Desktop. When this is checked (and it's only valid for the local system account option), if SQL Server executes some external program such as Notepad, you'll be able to see the Notepad GUI interface on the desktop. When it's unchecked, such external programs are not visible on the desktop.

Other Startup Parameters

The −f option on starting SQL Server is called a startup parameter. Startup parameters also configure SQL Server in various ways.

You've already seen the startup parameters -d, −e, and −1 in the General tab of the Enterprise Manager Server Properties dialog box early in this chapter. Here are some additional startup parameters:

c	Prevents SQL Server from running as a service. This speeds up the startup process if you're running SQL Server from the command console.
f	As you saw earlier, this starts SQL Server with a minimal configuration.
m	Starts SQL Server in a single-user mode, allowing only one connection to the server.
n	Tells SQL Server not to log errors into the NT application vent log.
p<precision level>	Configures the maximum number of digits in SQL Server for the numeric and decimal data types. The default is 28 digits, but you can increase it up to 38.
s<alternate Registry key>	Tells SQL Server to use an alternate location for Registry information for the server.

T<trace number>	Tells SQL Server to start up with a particular trace flag. For more information about trace flags, see "Trace Flags" in the Books Online.
x	Instructs the SQL Server relational engine to disable keeping CPU and cache-hit ratio statistics. This is for maximum throughput on CPU-intensive queries.

Summary

SQL Server 7.0 is far easier to configure than earlier releases because SQL Server can dynamically configure its own memory. Nevertheless, you can still control a number of options, and it's important to know what configuration options are available, even if you don't use them right away. After your server is configured, you'll need to connect to it. A number of issues are associated with SQL Server connectivity, which you can find out about in the next chapter.

Chapter 6

Connectivity

In This Chapter

♦ Modeling SQL Server connectivity

♦ The database driver layer

♦ The networking components layer

♦ Testing connectivity

In this chapter you'll learn the basics about connecting and communicating with SQL Server. To start off, you'll build a conceptual model of SQL Server's client/server communications, a framework that you can use to understand SQL Server connectivity.

Modeling SQL Server Connectivity

Microsoft has done a good job of hiding much of the complexity of client/server communication, but as a result some choices—such as the choice of "Network Protocols" when installing—can be very perplexing. We need a conceptual model within which to understand how SQL Server client/server communication works.

Client software communicates with SQL Server by sending requests and receiving data from the server. The client makes requests, and the server responds. It turns out that this communication has to pass through a series of connectivity layers on the client, from your application down to the network level, and then back up again through a parallel series of layers on the server side. In the process, your request must be wrapped with instructions to the server on how to decode it, and similarly the results coming back from the server must be decoded and unpacked on your client machines.

Let's build your conceptual model by understanding these layers as solutions to two problems.

The first problem is one of database communications. Every DBMS, SQL Server included, must be general purpose. But client software is often special purpose, developed for vertical markets and in-house use. So how can these widely varied clients communicate with the database server? The answer will be a layer for database communications.

The second problem is one of network communications. After you have a common language or protocol between a database server and its clients, how do you physically get that communication across the network? Just having the client emit the requests, or having the server generate results, is not enough to translate it into the proper network communications. The solution here will be another layer, the network library.

Database Communications

The purpose of client/server architecture is to distribute application processing between client and database server. The server takes on the tasks of data access and data management, and the client takes on the task of presenting data to and receiving input data from the user. The client and the server both run interactively, simultaneously, as processes on their respective machines. So your first problem is that there must be a method of communication between the client and the server processes—an interprocess communication, as shown in Figure 6-1—that will pass data back and forth from client to server.

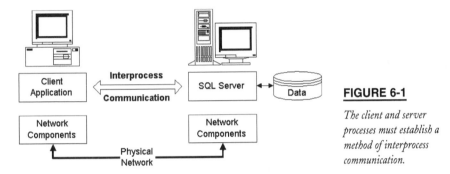

FIGURE 6-1

The client and server processes must establish a method of interprocess communication.

There are two broad classes of interprocess communication over networks: connection-based, and broadcast. The connection-based sort establishes a two-way line of communication between the client and the server that starts, persists for a time, and then ends. SQL Server client/server communication is connection-based.

NOTE

The term interprocess communication (abbreviated as IPC) in a client/server context applies generally to any method of communication between two processes. It is not necessary for the two processes to be on the same machine, and in the case of client/server communication, most often they are not. Further, communication does not need to happen in real time; so network delays are allowed.

The client software must open a connection, a communication line, to the database server. Once the connection is opened and the server sends an acknowledgement back to the client, the client can send requests for data and receive responses from the server. A client may make its requests one at a time to just one server, or to many servers. The server must handle multiple connections, process all their requests separately, and return the results back to the original client.

If all you have is the client on one machine, and the server on another, connected by a network, with no other components as shown in Figure 6-1, you still cannot establish interprocess communication. You must establish a common data language between the client and its server, as well as get that protocol back and forth between the machines. You need more components.

The Tabular Data Stream

The client cannot communicate directly with the server DBMS. If it could, then the DBMS would have to be rewritten for every new client application, to understand its requests for data. Instead, the DBMS has to establish rules for all clients who want to communicate with it.

In fact, every DBMS has a proprietary, low-level communications protocol, called a logical data stream protocol. With SQL Server, the logical data stream is called the tabular data stream, or TDS.

With TDS, the client can quickly detect what the data stream contains: It can tell whether the incoming stream of data is actually query results, a description of data, an error message, or a status code, for example. The TDS protocol embeds tokens in the data stream delimiting the commands that the client is sending to the server. In the return communication from server back to client, TDS tokens describe the structure (columns and data types) of result sets, error messages, statuses of requests, and so forth. Although the SQL commands and results that travel back and forth between client and server may be text, the TDS protocol wraps and intermingles that text with tokens that describe the text.

You can see some of the TDS stream passed between SQL Server and a client by using the Windows NT Network Monitor service. (You can install it by adding it as a service using the Network Neighborhood dialog box, Services tab.) Figure 6-2 shows a sample of the data stream wrapped in a network packet that is returned when a simple SELECT * FROM AUTHORS is sent to the pubs database.

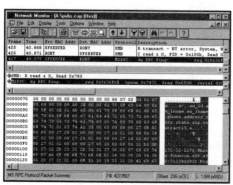

FIGURE 6-2

The TDS data stream returns a list of columns, their data types and length, and the data.

In the figure, the text in the right-hand column gives a character translation of the hexadecimal data shown on the left. The highlighted segment shows the results set being returned to the client after the SQL query, "select* from authors."

Now look at the addresses in the left-hand column and find the address 0x000000C0. Travel across the row until you see the hex value 0x0B near the end of the bytes starting at address 0x000000C0. That's the length of the au_id column: 0x0B = 12 bytes. In the next line, the values 0x28 and 0x14 indicate the length of the au_lname and au_fname columns, respectively, and so on. These are some of the tokens that the TDS stream uses to describe the data that it is returning.

Database API Components

Now the client application cannot be expected to send and receive TDS. If it did, then every client application would have to contain code to translate all its data requests into the TDS stream, and it would also have to contain code to interpret the TDS data stream coming from the server. Rather, it's better to abstract that task away from the client and insert a special database driver to do those tasks. You can now expand your model to include that driver. A logical view of that relationship for SQL Server is shown in Figure 6-3.

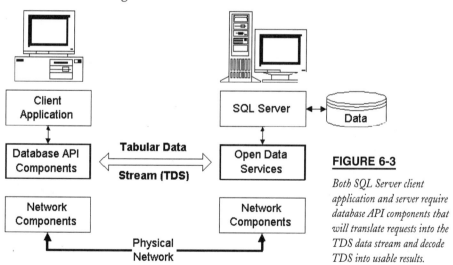

FIGURE 6-3

Both SQL Server client application and server require database API components that will translate requests into the TDS data stream and decode TDS into usable results.

The database API components add an abstraction layer that relieves the application from having to interpret the low-level TDS protocol and present standardized interfaces to the client. I will cover these interfaces later; they include DB-Library, ODBC, and OLE DB. The client software makes calls to the database API components, whose drivers generate TDS to send to SQL Server.

Figure 6-3 also shows something on the server side to translate TDS, and for SQL Server that is Open Data Services. Let's look at ODS next.

Open Data Services

Microsoft Windows NT has built-in support for client/server computing, in the form of Open Data Services (ODS). ODS acts as a network connection handler for SQL Server.

As an ODS application, SQL Server loads the ODS driver (Opends70.dll) and relies on it to establish an NT thread for each new connection. SQL Server also relies on ODS to decode the TDS tokens and make calls to SQL Server's event handlers for each request.

ODS manages the network by listening for new connections, cancellations, and failed connections and disconnects. It listens for data requests and returns result sets, messages, and status codes back to the client as TDS. ODS has an event-driven programming interface. Based on the types of events it receives, it calls SQL Server event handling routines. The types of events involved are connection and disconnection requests, language events, and server-to-server remote procedure calls.

When SQL Server is ready to send results back to the client, it hands them over to ODS, which encodes them in TDS. SQL Server calls an ODS function to translate result sets, error messages, and such into the TDS data stream. Then it calls functions in the appropriate server network library to send the TDS to the client.

You have solved one initial problem, namely that of what language or protocol each client must use with SQL Server, but you haven't solved the other problem, that of network communications. There's nothing included in the database driver that is network-specific, something that will package the necessary TDS stream, send it from client to server, or return it from server back to the correct client.

IPC Components

In other words, the tabular data stream (TDS) is just a logical protocol, in the sense that it defines the format of data. It has no mechanism to maintain communication between client and server, or to interface with the network components on client or server.

In fact, because SQL Server was originally designed to be able to interact with a number of different networks, developers specifically chose not to embed network-specific code into the database API components. Therefore a new component to complete the interprocess communication—namely, the network library—is necessary, as shown in Figure 6-4.

The client IPC component layer communicates with the server's IPC component layer, for purposes of initiating, maintaining, and ending a connection, as well as sending commands from the client and sending results from the server.

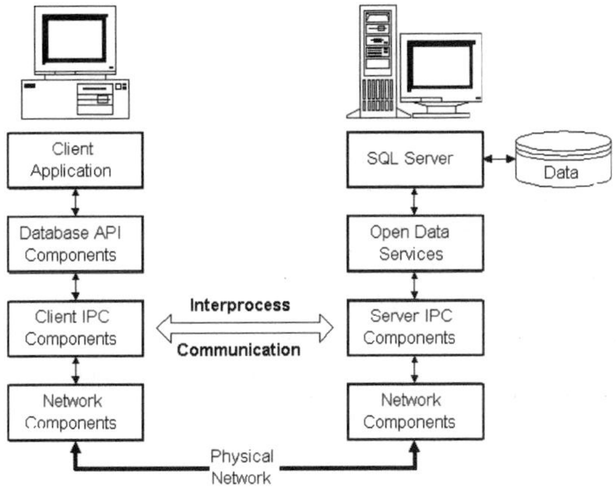

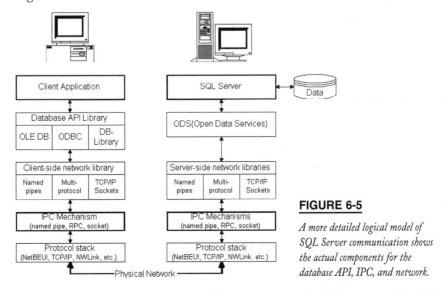

FIGURE 6-4

The client and server IPC components complete the communications path by establishing interprocess communication between client and server.

The client and server IPC components take TDS data from the database API components and package it into a network format that can be sent between the server and client using the network components, namely each machine's protocol stack and transport protocol. When receiving network data, the IPC components remove the network information and return pure TDS to the client and server database APIs components.

Your model is complete but still a bit general. What are the exact components that fill the roles outlined in Figure 6-4? Let's take the model and drill down for a more specific look.

The SQL Server Connectivity Model

A more detailed logical model of Microsoft SQL Server connectivity is shown in Figure 6-5.

FIGURE 6-5

A more detailed logical model of SQL Server communication shows the actual components for the database API, IPC, and network.

The diagram in Figure 6-5 shows more detail about the actual implementation of SQL Server's client/server communication. From the client side, the client writes connection requests, database commands, to the database driver, namely the ODBC, OLE DB, or DB-Library driver. These drivers translate those requests and commands into TDS to send to SQL Server. The client software does not need to know any TDS or network details to do this, although it might set some parameters by way of configuration.

The database driver interfaces to the IPC layer, which contains the network library. When the database driver requests a connection, the network library establishes a method of communication with the server by choosing an IPC mechanism. For example, the named pipes network library communicates with SQL Server by reading from and writing to SQL Server's named pipe. After a connection is established, the database driver calls network library functions that convert the TDS stream into network packets and hand them over to the network stack to send to the server via the physical network.

The different network libraries all present the same interface to the database driver, so the driver does not need to know which network library is active. You can change network libraries without affecting any database driver code.

You end up with a series of lower-level layers that act somewhat like interchangeable parts. Both network libraries and the underlying network transport protocols can change without your having to change your application code or database driver.

The end result is a rather elegant solution to database communication problems. By abstracting out the database API layer, the server establishes a standard data stream protocol with which to communicate with its clients, and the clients are relieved of the burden of having to interpret the low-level TDS data stream. Then by abstracting out the IPC layer and using network libraries that choose specific IPC mechanisms, the database driver can write to a common network interface, using one of several IPC mechanisms over one of potentially many network transport protocols. The end result is to make the client/server software application portable across many different networks.

Server-to-Server Communication: Linked Servers

The modularity and interchangeability of these communication layers makes it easy to connect one SQL server to another. In SQL Server 7.0, the query engine communicates with the storage engine by means of OLE DB. Therefore the query engine can act as an OLE DB client to another server, thereby communicating directly with the other server's storage engine, as shown in Figure 6-6.

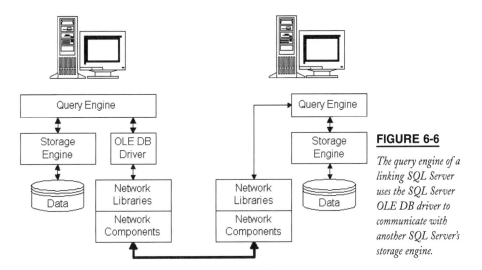

FIGURE 6-6

The query engine of a linking SQL Server uses the SQL Server OLE DB driver to communicate with another SQL Server's storage engine.

Linked servers replace remote servers and remote stored procedures from earlier versions and makes distributed queries possible. The query engine of the main SQL Server either registers the other server as a linked server or uses the OPENQUERY() function. In either case, the connection process identifies the proper OLE DB driver to use to link to the other server. Then the linking server's query engine uses the OLE DB driver to communicate with the other server; in the case of another SQL Server, as shown in the figure, it will be to the storage engine of the other server. (For more information about linked servers, see Chapter 23, "Distributed Data.")

The Database Driver Layer

SQL Server listens to three different database API drivers: ODBC, OLE DB, and DB-Library. ODBC is currently the most popular for applications. OLE DB as a native interface to SQL Server is new with SQL Server 7.0 and will assuredly grow in popularity. DB-Library is the original SQL Server database driver. Once very popular, it has taken on a less significant role for SQL Server 7.

ODBC Connectivity

ODBC is currently the main database API driver used by most SQL Server client software. Standing for Open Database Connectivity, it has evolved through several iterations. Its purpose is to present a database-independent method for accessing relational database and text file data. Because you can pass queries through ODBC that contain the SQL dialect of the back-end database, though, ODBC does not completely succeed in achieving database independence.

ODBC replaced DB-Library as the preferred database driver and will soon be replaced by OLE DB, which is still in its infancy. For now, though, ODBC is the most common database interface to SQL Server.

Client applications use ODBC to connect to SQL Server data sources either by referencing a stored collection of connection information called a data source name (DSN) or by supplying connection information in a connection string at run time. The former type is often called a DSN connection, and the latter a DSN-less connection.

A DSN-less connection must rely on either the application's or the user's providing a server name, a user login id, a password (if not using a trusted connection), and optionally a default database. A DSN connection, however, can store all this information so that the application just references the DSN name, and the ODBC driver will extract the connection information from the DSN.

In this chapter, you'll focus on making a DSN connection. (You can make DSN-less connections by calling ODBC directly from a C++ or VB program, using RDO or ADO from VB, or ADO and DAO from VB or Access. Because this is more an application programming issue, and not directly related to SQL Server, I won't cover it in this book.)

Installing ODBC on a Client

ODBC is strictly a client-side system: You'll only use the SQL Server ODBC database driver with client software. You'll find it on your server after installing SQL Server, but that is for using client software on the server. Similarly, to have clients in a LAN environment access SQL Server, you must have the SQL Server ODBC driver on each client machine, and that is achieved by running the SQL Server Setup program from the CD or a network. You don't need to install all the management tools on the client machine, but to get the ODBC driver and supporting ODBC DLLs, as well as the network libraries, you must use the Setup program.

For Windows 9x and NT, you need the 32-bit ODBC drivers. To get the latest ODBC drivers from Microsoft, you can download the Microsoft Data Access Components (MDAC) from the Microsoft Web site. Microsoft Office and Visual Studio will automatically install a base set of ODBC drivers and the core ODBC components (see the text that follows).

The Structure of ODBC

On the client computer, ODBC loads in a series of layers. The actual SQL Server ODBC driver is just one among several components, as shown in Figure 6-7.

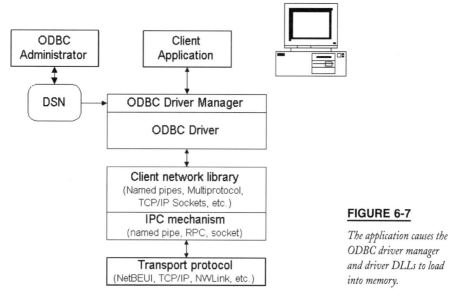

FIGURE 6-7

The application causes the ODBC driver manager and driver DLLs to load into memory.

When the client software starts up, it makes initial connection calls to ODBC. That will cause the ODBC driver manager DLL to load into memory. If it is a DSN-type connection, the ODBC driver manager will look in the Registry (or in INI files for 16-bit Windows) for the DSN and extract the connection information, which includes the name of the database driver. The driver manager then causes the SQL Server ODBC driver to load into memory and makes calls to it to establish a connection to the server.

The ODBC driver then emits the required TDS data stream and calls the network library to package the request and send it to the server. As results come back, the ODBC driver receives the TDS returned from the server and returns a translated version back to the client software. The core ODBC components are shown in the ODBC Data Source Administrator About tab. Figure 6-8 shows version 3.51.

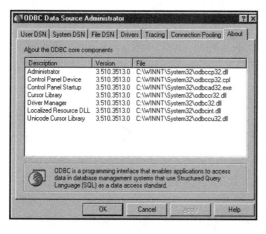

FIGURE 6-8

The Data Source Administrator shows the core ODBC components.

You can find this dialog box by choosing Settings from the Start menu, then Control Panel, and then double-clicking on the ODBC32 icon. You can use the ODBC Data Source Administrator to create and test data source names (DSNs) and save them.

The first three components support the Data Source Administrator. The other DLLs are the following:

♦ The cursor library, odbccr32.dll, which supports building client-side cursors within ODBC for the client software to manipulate

♦ The driver manager, odbc32.dll, which is the thin wrapper that manages ODBC drivers for the client software

♦ A localized resource DLL, odbcint.dll, for internationalization

♦ The Unicode cursor library, odbccu32.dll, which performs the same function as odbccr32.dll, but for Unicode

An important component that is not shown in Figure 6-8 as a core component is the ODBC trace DLL, odbctrac.dll, which you'll learn more about as you dissect the process of creating a DSN. In addition, on 16-bit clients, two generic "thunking" DLLs must be loaded to translate between 16-bit and 32-bit addresses.

NOTE

Because the ODBC drivers usually reside on the client machine, not the server, they must follow the operating system of the client. For a Windows 3.x machine or MS-DOS, you must use 16-bit ODBC drivers. You can install the 16-bit SQL Server ODBC driver, as well as the 16-bit ODBC driver manager, from the SQL Server Setup program.

Running the ODBC Data Source Administrator

SQL Server 7 supplies version 3.5 of the ODBC Administrator, a newer version of the utility. You can start the Administrator program by choosing Settings from the Start menu, then Control Panel, and then double-clicking on the ODBC32 icon.

When you double-click on the ODBC32 icon, you'll bring up the Administrator dialog box, as shown in Figure 6-9.

In the figure, the dialog box is not listing ODBC drivers. Instead, it shows User DSNs created by Microsoft Office. It may be confusing, but the first column of the list shows the DSN names, and the second column lists the associated ODBC driver. It just happens that Microsoft Office, in this case, makes default DSN names that are similar to the names of their drivers.

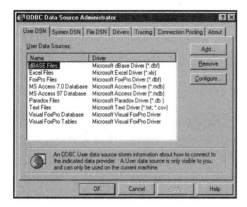

FIGURE 6-9

The opening dialog box of the ODBC Data Source Administrator is the User DSN tab.

A User DSN is a named link to a data source that is restricted to the current network user's use. Therefore, if someone logs into the current client machine under a different login, a user DSN set up for the other NT or Windows 9x account will not be visible. A System DSN is a similar named link, but it is available to all logins on the current machine. A File DSN is a link that is stored in a separate file. The aim of a file DSN is to be available on a network to a number of users. Unfortunately, not many applications yet recognize a file DSN.

However, you're not looking at the ODBC drivers themselves. To see the drivers, click on the Drivers tab, as shown in Figure 6-10.

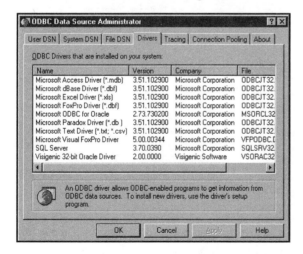

FIGURE 6-10

You can find the installed ODBC drivers listed in the Drivers tab.

SQL Server 7 Setup supplies the SQL Server and Oracle drivers. What's useful in this dialog box is that the version numbers and DLL names are provided for each driver.

Notice that although many drivers have numbers that match the current ODBC version (3.5 or thereabouts), the SQL Server driver has a version of 3.70.0390. The way to read the SQL Server driver version is to take the 3 as referring to ODBC 3.0+, the 70 as meaning SQL Server 7.0, and the remaining number as the same number as the latest SQL Server installed service pack, and the build number when you inspect `@@version`.

NOTE

The SQL Server ODBC drivers have been updated for each service pack of SQL Server. You need to make sure you are running with the proper SQL Server driver from the service pack.

Normally the System DSN is the best choice of DSN type, because User DSNs can cause considerable confusion if a client machine must be shared. Also, many applications that need ODBC data sources will only recognize System DSNs, ignoring User and File DSNs.

Creating a DSN

To create a DSN for SQL Server, click on the Add button and in the Create New Data Source dialog box, and select the SQL Server driver, as shown in Figure 6-11.

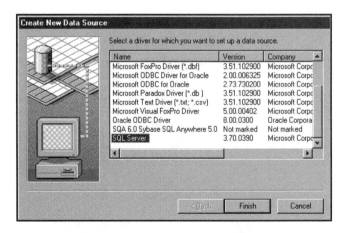

FIGURE 6-11

Your first choice when creating a new DSN is to pick the ODBC driver.

It's always worth a chuckle to see this one–dialog box "Wizard." The Back button never works, and there's no Next button, just a Finish button. Choose the SQL Server driver, and then click on the Finish button, and you're launched into a more familiar wizard, one embedded in the SQL Server ODBC driver, as shown in the next dialog box, Figure 6-12.

When you choose a data source name, it's probably most useful to somehow embed DSN information into the DSN name. For example, a DSN for the Pubs database on the SQLAdmin server might have the name PubsSQLAdmin.

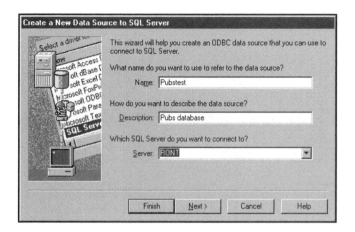

FIGURE 6-12

The first dialog box of the SQL Server ODBC Data Source Wizard asks for a data source name (DSN) and a SQL server.

The next option asks for connectivity information, as shown in Figure 6-13.

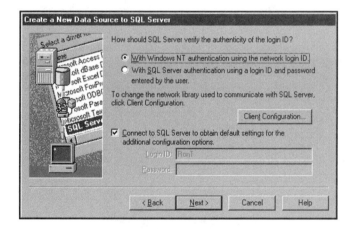

FIGURE 6-13

The next dialog box asks for connectivity information.

If you choose to use Windows NT authentication, the login id and password at the bottom will be disabled. The check box on the lower part of the dialog box asks whether you would like to get the server's default settings for many of the options on ensuing dialog boxes. If you choose SQL Server level authentication but leave this check box unchecked, you will not be able to enter a login id and password here. If you check this and use SQL Server authentication, the wizard will log into SQL Server to obtain server-side defaults and apply them to subsequent dialog boxes.

A button for Client Configuration allows you to specify what client-side network library you would like to use with this DSN, as shown in Figure 6-14.

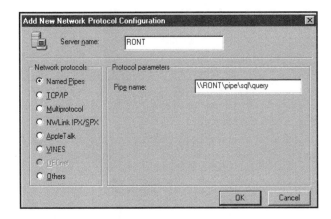

FIGURE 6-14

You can specify which network library to associate with a DSN.

Remember, even though the dialog box says "network protocols," they are really network libraries. (See "The Networking Components Layer" later in this chapter.)

The dialog box that follows lets you set a default database and make some choices about default settings, as you can see in Figure 6-15.

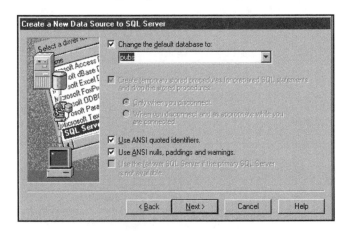

FIGURE 6-15

Next, you choose some defaults.

It's always a good idea to specify a default database for a DSN. The settings here are interesting.

The first one, to create temporary stored procedures for prepared SQL statements, will allow ODBC to use the server's tempdb database for storing prepared stored procedures. This is not normally a problem, but with frequent aborts, that code can fill up tempdb, so many users prefer to leave this option unchecked.

Using ANSI quoted identifiers and nulls, padding, and warnings lets you choose to have a closer ANSI SQL compliance than is the default for SQL Server. The ODBC driver defaults to having these checked. These options correspond to the following Transact-SQL commands:

```
SET QUOTED_IDENTIFIER ON
SET ANSI_PADDING ON
SET ANSI_WARNINGS ON
```

Your application can reset these choices. (For more information about these ANSI settings, see Chapter 13, "Data Manipulation.")

The final option refers to the failover server in a Wolf Pack cluster. If you're using SQL Server Enterprise Edition on a cluster, with NT 4 Enterprise, you can use this option. The next dialog box contains an additional group of settings, as you can see in Figure 6-16.

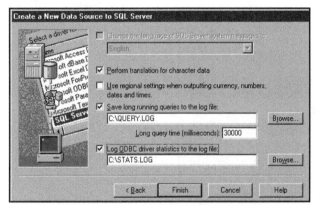

FIGURE 6-16

Additional settings and logging options

You can change the language for SQL Server error messages that this client will receive, based on the number of languages installed on the server. You can cause a translation of upper-order characters from the server character set to the local character set of the client. Also, you can have monetary amounts, dates, and times formatted for display based on the local client settings, rather than the server's. This should only be checked for applications that display but do not update data.

The final options on the dialog box let you establish some logging. These options let you log long-running queries and statistics from the current DSN.

The query statistics are loaded into a tab-delimited file that you can import into SQL Server or read from a spreadsheet, as you can see in Figure 6-17.

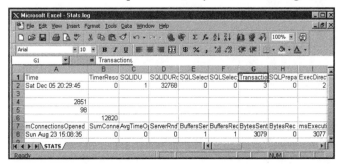

FIGURE 6-17

You can also collect client-side statistics about ODBC calls.

The columns accumulate counts of the various kinds of calls recorded by the SQL Server ODBC driver.

> **NOTE**
>
> The new SQL Server ODBC driver also allows you to test the DSN, a useful feature not often found in ODBC drivers.

When you click on the Finish button, the last dialog box shows you the options you've chosen in a summary fashion (see Figure 6-18).

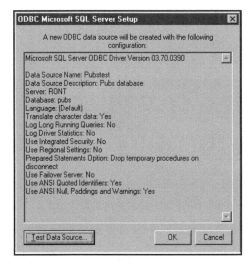

FIGURE 6-18

You get a summary list of features and the ability to test the DSN in the last dialog box.

A confirmation dialog box shows you the tests that the driver runs, and whether the test succeeded, as you can see in Figure 6-19.

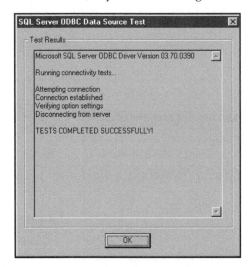

FIGURE 6-19

The confirmation of a successful DSN test

ODBC Registry Keys

Both User DSN and System DSN names are stored in Registry keys, for the 32-bit SQL Server ODBC driver. The ODBC Driver Manager reads these keys to determine what the stored connection values should be.

User DSNs are stored in:

HKEY_CURRENT_USER\Software\ODBC\ODBC.INI

whereas System DSNs are stored in:

HKEY_LOCAL_MACHINE\SOFTWARE\ODBC\ODBC.INI

The values associated with the pubscopy DSN you saw in the previous section are shown in Figure 6-20.

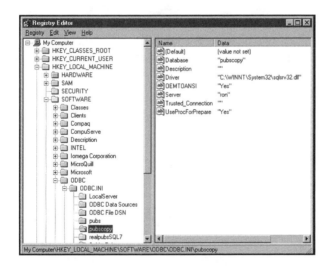

FIGURE 6-20

The Regedit values for the sample pubscopy DSN

File DSNs, of course, are stored on disk and not in the Registry.

DB-Library Connectivity

DB-Library is the oldest database driver for SQL Server but is being retired by Microsoft. In SQL Server 6.5, it had complete functionality, but the SQL Server 7 version has not been enhanced to take advantage of SQL Server 7. Consequently, none of the new Transact-SQL language features of SQL Server 7 are permitted through DB-Library.

You can configure DB-Library using the Client Configuration utility, as shown in Figure 6-21.

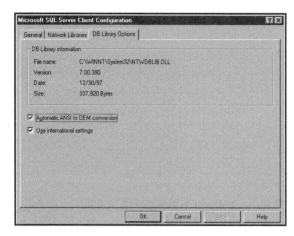

FIGURE 6-21

The configuration options for DB-Library

DB-Library also resides on the client computer, and you're given two options for configuring the client. The first affects ANSI to OEM, the translation of upper-order characters in character columns between the ANSI ISO character set on SQL Server, and the OEM (MS-DOS) character sets on client computers. This option is only helpful if you have some MS-DOS clients that store ASCII characters above the value 127 in their character columns.

The other option is to use international settings. This option, when checked, allows DB-Library to set monetary, date, and time formats based on the SQL Server, rather than the localization file sqlcommn.loc.

The Networking Components Layer

Many network libraries are available for SQL Server communication. As you saw in Chapter 3, "Installing," you choose the server network libraries from the Network Protocols dialog box, as shown in Figure 6-22.

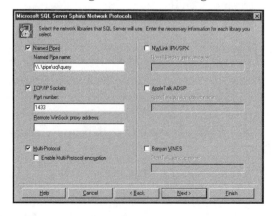

FIGURE 6-22

When installing SQL Server, you can choose one or more network libraries for SQL Server.

Both the client and the server use network libraries. The client software uses one network library for any given connection, but SQL Server can use more than one at a time. That's why you can choose more than one of the network libraries to be active at the same time.

Each network library implements a distinct method of interprocess communication, called an IPC mechanism. For example, the named pipes network library defaults to creating a named pipe called \\.\sql\pipe\query, the multiprotocol library uses the Windows RPC (remote procedure call) mechanism, and the TCP/IP Sockets network library (also called Windows Sockets) defaults to listening on port 1433.

WARNING

In order for interprocess communication to take place between client and server, their network libraries must match. You must make sure that the client's network library matches one of the network libraries loaded on the

The network libraries between client and server must match because a named pipes network library cannot decode information packaged by a TCP/IP Sockets network library, and neither of them can decode information packaged by multiprotocol. They can't decode each other's information because they don't use the same IPC mechanism.

The network libraries work like interchangeable parts. You can change a client's default network library, and the database driver will work with it. That's because every network library has the same set of function calls. You can see a list of those functions in Figure 6-23.

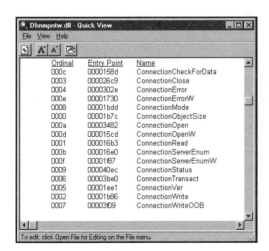

FIGURE 6-23

You can use Windows Explorer's Quick View on a network library DLL to see its function calls.

You can view this yourself by using Windows Explorer to find the named pipes client network library Dbnmpntw.dll in the MSSQL\BINN folder. Select the DLL, right-click, and choose Quick View. Then scroll to the Export Table, which will contain a list of the library's function calls.

Note that all the function names relate to connections. Among other things, to maintain interprocess communication, the client network library can enumerate servers on the network, open a connection to a server, write and read data, check status and errors, and close the connection.

If you compare this list with other client network library DLLs, you'll see that the function names are the same. Only the ordinals and entry points change. With the same function names among all the libraries, they can be used interchangeably. The SQL Server network libraries differ from the client's. If you take a look at Figure 6-24, you'll see the Export table for the server-side network library DLL.

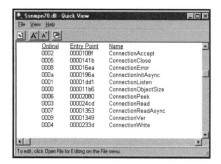

FIGURE 6-24

The function names for SQL Server's network libraries differ from the client's.

In this figure, you can see that there are functions to accept, listen for, read, write, and close a connection, among other things. Again, all the server-side network libraries have the same set of function calls, differing only in ordinal and entry point.

Network Protocols

When you choose the network libraries, you are not choosing the network transport protocols to run on your server. Protocols were chosen during the installation, and the list can be edited from the desktop Network Neighborhood dialog box, Protocols tab, as shown in Figure 6-25.

If you want to see the order in which they will be accessed, see the Bindings tab.

Network Libraries

It is possible for a network library to support more than one network transport protocol. The diagram in Figure 6-26 shows the relationship of the available networking libraries and the underlying transport protocols.

FIGURE 6-25

You can find a list of your network protocols in the Network Neighborhood dialog box.

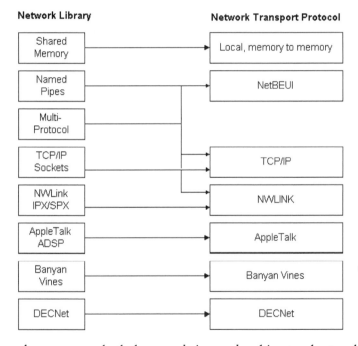

FIGURE 6-26

The named pipes and multiprotocol networking libraries support multiple transport protocols.

As you can see, both the named pipes and multiprotocol network libraries implement IPC mechanisms that support three transport protocols: NetBEUI, TCP/IP, and NWLink. Having a network library support more than one network protocol makes it possible to only one network library supporting a context where the server is connected to a variety of PC networks.

Which network library is best? Named pipes is the default net-library for fresh installations. However, the Books Online entry, "Named Pipes vs. TCP/IP Sockets" indicates that TCP/IP Sockets has lower overhead than named pipes. Certainly for larger or heavy-usage networks, there seems to be a trend to using the TCP/IP Sockets library. Then again, multi-protocol is the only one to offer data encryption on the network. Your choice will depend on the application.

Shared Memory

The shared memory network library is new with SQL Server 7 and is used by SQL Server 7 on Windows 9x for local connections. (SQL Server on Windows NT uses named pipes for local connections, and the named pipes network library is not available for Windows 9x.)

Named Pipes

Named pipes was SQL Server's first network library, starting with SQL Server on OS/2. It can be used even when network communication is not required. For example, when you run SQL Server client software, such as Enterprise Manager or the Query Analyzer on the same NT machine as SQL Server, the IPC connection will be made through a local named pipe, because no network communication is needed.

On the other hand, Windows 98 and 95 do not support the server-side functions of named pipes, so SQL Server does not use the named pipes network library on Windows 9x at all. When you run both client and SQL Server software on a Windows 9x machine, the IPC connection is made through shared memory.

Client and Server on the Same Machine

When you run the SQL Server management tools, such as Enterprise Manager or the Query Analyzer, on the same machine as SQL Server, no physical network connection is made between the client and server processes. However, SQL Server still uses the network libraries to establish interprocess communication, even on one machine, as you can see illustrated in Figure 6-27.

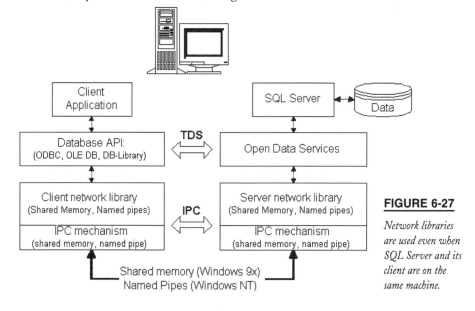

FIGURE 6-27

Network libraries are used even when SQL Server and its client are on the same machine.

All the standard SQL Server tools, such as Enterprise Manager, operate as client software to SQL Server. To run them on the same machine as the server, the database API drivers must be present, as well as the client network library DLLs. Enterprise Manager and the Query Analyzer use the OLE DB database driver, OSQL uses ODBC, and ISQL uses DB-Library.

Notice in the figure that only the shared memory and named pipes network libraries are shown. On Windows 9x, clients make local connections to SQL Server through the shared memory IPC mechanism, whereas on Windows NT, a local named pipe mechanism is used. No physical network is used, because the IPC mechanism is local. If you use the NT Network Monitor to observer a local connection, you will find that no network packets are sent from the client to the server.

Multiprotocol

The multiprotocol network library uses Windows RPC mechanisms, and it supports encryption over the network. The encryption is 40-bit Windows NT encryption. This encryption may be necessary because all other network libraries send commands to SQL Server as text, and receive character data in text format. You can use the Windows utility NetMon to detect those packets and read their contents.

NOTE

Only named pipes and multiprotocol support Windows NT authentication and dynamic enumeration of servers on the network.

The remaining network libraries (NWLink IPX/SPX, AppleTalk, Banyan Vines, and DECNet) use only one underlying networking protocol.

Client and Server Network Libraries

Client and server network libraries have different implementations. When you install SQL Server and include the management tools, the SQL Server setup program installs the server-side networking libraries as well as the client-side networking libraries. It defaults the client network library to named pipes, so if you remembered to choose named pipes as one of the server-side networking libraries, you can connect to SQL Server.

WARNING

You should not remove named pipes as one of the server-side network libraries on an NT installation. If you do, you will not be able to make a local connection to the server. You can easily add it just by running Setup, adding the named pipes network library, and then stopping and restarting SQL Server.

You can test the network library pairing yourself. Just remove named pipes as a SQL Server network library, and make sure that your client software has named pipes as the default client network library. You will then not be able to connect. The following table shows each network library and the corresponding .DLL files that it requires.

Network Library	Client DLL	Server DLL
Shared Memory	DBMSSRHN.DLL	SMSSSH70.DLL
Named pipes	DBNMPNTW.DLL	SSNMPN70.DLL
Multiprotocol	DBMSRPCN.DLL	SSMSRP70.DLL
TCP/IP Sockets	DBMSSOCN.DLL	SSMSSO70.DLL
NWLink IPX/SPX	DBMSSPXN.DLL	SSMSSP70.DLL
AppleTalk ADSP	DBMSSDSN.DLL	SSMSAD70.DLL
Banyan Vines	DBMSVINN.DLL	SSMSVI70.DLL
DECNet	DBMSDECN.DLL	SSMSDE70.DLL

Network Libraries and the Registry

To determine which network libraries are active on a given SQL server, you use REGEDIT.EXE to inspect the

HKEY_LOCAL_MACHINE\SOFTWARE\Microsoft\MSSQLServer\MSSQLServer

key and then the ListenOn value, as shown in Figure 6-28.

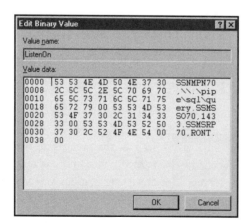

FIGURE 6-28

You can inspect the Registry entries for network libraries using the Regedit utility.

The values show the DLL names for the shared memory network library, followed by the DLL names and network addresses for named pipes, TCP/IP sockets, and NWLink IPX/SPX.

Configuring the Client Network Library

From the client side, you can detect and configure the client's default network library by running the SQL Server Client Configuration tool, as shown in Figure 6-29.

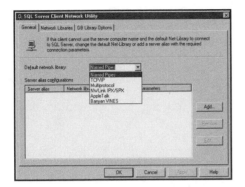

FIGURE 6-29

You can set the client network library on the General tab of SQL Server's Client Configuration tool.

Your client machine can use only one networking library for any given server, but it does not have to use the same one for all of them. By clicking on the Add button on the General tab, you can add a server name and then choose the network library you want your client to use as the default, as shown in Figure 6-30.

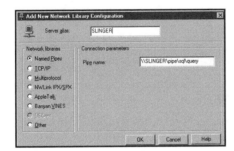

FIGURE 6-30

You can associate a network library for each server.

Finally, you can get a list of all the available network libraries on your machine by clicking on the second tab, as shown in Figure 6-31.

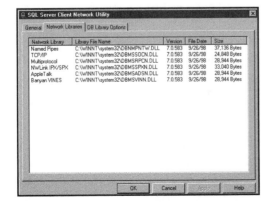

FIGURE 6-31

The Network Libraries tab shows all the installed network libraries.

You can use this dialog box to determine the version of each of the network libraries. This may help in troubleshooting, because these libraries may be updated as time goes on, just as the ODBC and OLE DB drivers are, and some problems may be resolved just by updating the drivers.

Testing Connectivity

Tools that come with SQL Server provide a number of ways to test connectivity. Most of the tools are quite small programs, making them convenient and portable.

Testing ODBC

You have a number of ways to test an ODBC connection to SQL Server, and they vary in complexity. As with readpipe, you test from the client, and the client machine could be the same as the server machine.

- ◆ When you create an ODBC data source name (DSN) using version 3.6 of the ODBC Administrator and the SQL Server 7 ODBC driver, you can test the connection during the definition, as you saw earlier in this chapter.

- ◆ SQL Server comes with one tool specifically built to test ODBC connections, called ODBCPING.EXE. ODBCping will simply log into a server long enough to make a connection, and then disconnect. Like makepipe and readpipe, it is a very small utility (32KB), so it's very portable. It also is installed with the management tools.

- ◆ To use ODBCping to test an ODBC connection, just issue it from a command window. The syntax of ODBCping is quite simple:

```
ODBCping[-S Server    -D DSN] [-U Login Id] [-P Password]
```

All three parameters are required. The first parameter is either a server name or a data source name (DSN), the second is a SQL Server login id, and the last is a password. Consequently, you can test both DSN and DSN-less connections. For example, to test a DSN named "SQL70," the sa login, and a password of 123, you could call ODBCping as:

```
ODBCping-DSQL70 -Usa -P123
```

Similarly, to make a DSN-less connection to a server named "DBServer," sa login, and password of 123:

```
ODBCping-SDBServer -Usa -P123
```

◆ You can also use OSQL.EXE, the ODBC version of ISQL.EXE. It uses ODBC to connect to SQL Server. Because it is a full-fledged utility, and you can use it to submit queries and receive results, it's a somewhat larger utility (133KB) than ODBCping. To use OSQL.EXE to log into a server and get the current version, you could just type the commands shown in Figure 6-32.

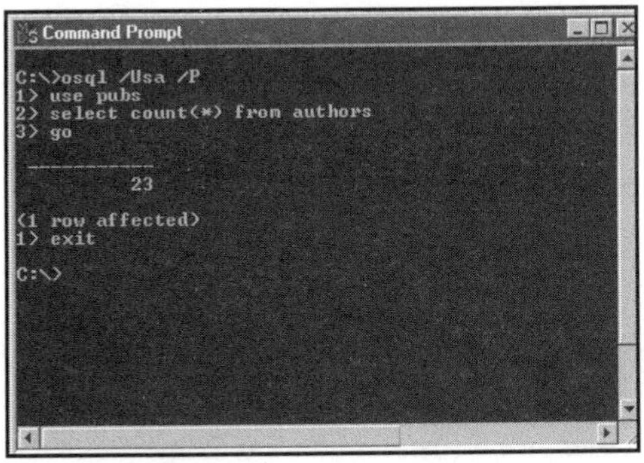

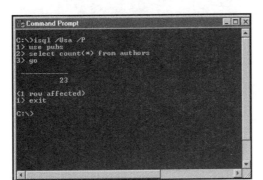

FIGURE 6-32

You can test a DB-Library connection with ISQL.EXE.

You can learn more about OSQL and ISQL in Chapter 13, "Data Manipulation."

Testing DB-Library

The only SQL Server 7 utility remaining that uses DB-Library is ISQL.EXE, the command line utility. If you can log into SQL Server using it, then you have verified that the connection is valid. For example, to log into a server and get the current version, you could just type the commands shown in Figure 6-33.

FIGURE 6-33

You can test a DB-Library connection with ISQL.EXE.

By logging in and performing any operation, you've shown that the database driver is working. As mentioned previously, you can learn more about OSQL and ISQL in Chapter 13, "Data Manipulation."

Testing Named Pipes

To test network named pipes between two computers, or local named pipes on a single machine, you can use the makepipe.exe and readpipe.exe programs that come with SQL Server. They are installed by default when you install either SQL Server or its management tools. Makepipe sets up a pipe on the server computer and returns any data sent to it. Readpipe sends and receives data from the pipe, echoing results to the screen.

1. On your server computer, start up an NT Command Prompt window, and issue the makepipe command. The syntax of the command is:

   ```
   makepipe[/h] [/w] [/p<pipe name>]
   ```

   When you issue the command, you can use /h or /? to get the command syntax, or /p with a pipe name to create a pipe with a name of your choosing. The /w option will cause the server to wait a specified number of seconds before responding to the client. If you issue the command with none of the options specified, then the command will use the default wait time of zero seconds and pipe name of "abc." Figure 6-34 shows makepipe with a pipe name of "testpipe" waiting for readpipe.

FIGURE 6-34

The makepipe.exe program will wait for a client to read the pipe.

2. From the client computer (which may also be the server) on which you've installed at least the Diagnostics tools from among the SQL Server management tools, start up a command prompt again and issue the readpipe command. The syntax of the command is:

   ```
   readpipe[/h][/n<iter>][/{q t}][/w][/s<Server>][/p]<pipe>][/d<Data>]
   ```

   Again, you can use /h or /? to get the syntax and /n for the number of times you want to send and receive data from the pipe. The /q option will poll rather than write, whereas /t will override polling. The /w option is the wait time, /s, the server name, /p, the pipe name, and /d, the data to send and receive. Figure 6-35 illustrates reading the pipe made in the previous figure, with three iterations, and the data "hi there."

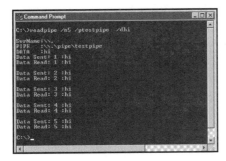

FIGURE 6-35

You can repeat the number of messages with readpipe.

3. From a separate client machine, just enter the server name following the /s, as in:

```
readpipe/n5 /sSQLAdmin /dhi
```

4. If you send a message string that includes spaces, just enclose the string with double quotes:

```
readpipe/n5 /sSQLAdmin /d"hi there"
```

An ODBC Checklist

Use the following checklist to test the ODBC configurations on client machines.

❑ All 16-bit clients have 16-bit ODBC drivers installed.

❑ All 32-bit clients have 32-bit ODBC drivers installed.

❑ The SQL Server ODBC driver on each client machine matches the correct SQL Server build.

❑ The client DSNs are set up as the correct type (user, system, or file).

❑ The client DSNs specify a default database.

❑ The ODBC Connection was tested during setup or has been tested using a tool such as ODBCping.

Summary

Many components make up SQL Server 7 connectivity. SQL Server 7 makes extensive use of ODBD and OLE DB. It uses OLE DB most notably to enable distributed queries and linked servers. Despite the number of components, SQL Server 7 comes with an adequate collection of tools to help set up and diagnose connectivity. These chapters finish your coverage of setting up your SQL Server. Now it's time to take a look the methods and tools for administering SQL Server 7.

PART III

Administration

Chapter 7

Managing Databases

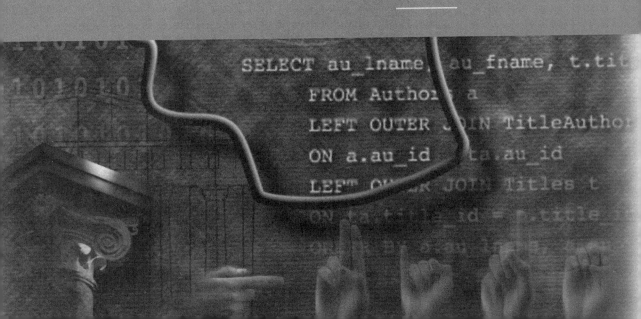

In This Chapter

◆ Managing servers

◆ Databases

◆ Creating a database

◆ Copying, renaming, and dropping a database

◆ Detaching and reattaching a database

◆ The DBCC command

SQL Server 7 makes servers and databases easier than ever to manage. This allows you to manage far more databases than ever before. In this chapter, you will learn about the tools available for building and managing databases. In the following chapters, you'll learn how to manage database backups, security, and data transfer, as well as how to schedule maintenance tasks.

Managing Servers

The central management tool for SQL Server is Enterprise Manager, a graphical utility that has the capability of managing many SQL Servers across an enterprise. You can use Enterprise Manager to configure a particular SQL Server, as well as manage its databases. (For more information about configuring SQL Server, see Chapter 5, "Configuring.")

Enterprise Manager runs as an MMC snap-in, as does the OLAP Services tool (see Chapter 25). Enterprise Manager becomes useful when you can register SQL Servers and connect to them using it. Then its tools give you administrative control of the servers, both local and remote.

SQL Server Groups

When you first bring up SQL Server Enterprise Manager after a fresh install, the local server will be registered and one or two groups will appear. Figure 7-1 shows the results of a new installation where SQL Server 7 was installed on a server that already had SQL Server 6.5 installed.

FIGURE 7-1

Enterprise Manager will show a group for the local SQL Server 6.5 server, if there is one, as well as the local 7.0 server.

Note the two default SQL Server groups: SQL Server and SQL 6.5. The 6.5 group contains a reference to the local (but not running) SQL Server 6.5.

NOTE

The local 6.5 server cannot run at the same time on the same machine as SQL Server 7.0, and the 7.0 Enterprise Manager cannot directly administer a 6.5 server. However, if you do register a 6.5 server in the 7.0 Enterprise Manager, when you attempt to connect to it, EM will bring up a copy of the 6.5 Enterprise Manager that you can use to directly administer the 6.5 servers.

You can create new groups at this point, or later. Server groups help you organize the servers to which you might connect; a sample set of groups is shown in Figure 7-2.

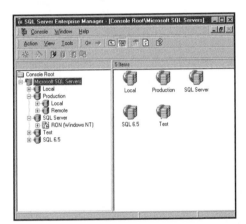

FIGURE 7-2

You can use groups to help organize the servers to which you connect.

To move a server from one group to another, edit its Registration Properties, which you can do by right-clicking over the server name and choosing Edit Registration Properties. The resulting dialog box is shown in Figure 7-3.

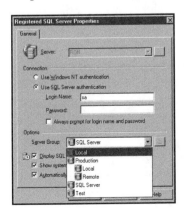

FIGURE 7-3

You can edit a server's registration properties, and change its group, in the Server Registration Properties dialog box.

So, for example, to move the current server from the SQL Server group to the Local group, just change the selection in the Server Group list box.

Registering a Server

When you register a SQL server, you can use either the Register Server Wizard or the Registration Properties dialog box. If you deselect the Wizard, you'll see the properties dialog box. To register a new server, right-click on the group name and choose New SQL Server Registration, pick the same choice from the Action menu, or click on the Register Server icon on the toolbar. You'll see the Properties dialog box, as shown in Figure 7-4.

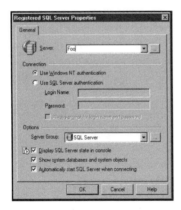

FIGURE 7-4

When you register a SQL server without the Register Server Wizard, you fill out the Registration Properties dialog box.

From this dialog box, you enter a name for the server, based on the name the server is known to broadcast on the network (usually the computer name.)

If you are working with a local server, you can use the string "(local)" or the period (.) to stand for the local server name. If your NT login has privileges on the server, then you can use NT authentication to register the server. If you want to register a remote server, you can enter the server name directly, choose from the list, or browse the server using the browse icon next to the server name.

TIP

It often takes some time for servers to broadcast their name on the network. If you know a server is running but don't see it in the list, then just enter the name directly.

Note that below the Server Group entry, you have three check boxes. The first shows the server state in the console, which you would normally want to see.

NOTE

The server state may not show up under Windows 95 and 98 on remote servers, because they lack NT network facilities.

The second choice lets you decide whether to show system databases and tables. Every SQL Server installation has a number of system databases, and every database has a number of system tables (see the next section in this chapter). You can hide them from your Enterprise Manager view by unchecking this check box.

T IP

If you do not see the system tables (master, model, msdb, and tempdb) in Enterprise Manager, but you want to, check the second option in the Registered Server properties dialog box.

The third option lets you automatically start the given server when connecting, if it is not already started.

Enterprise Manager and the Registry

The reason all this activity is called registering a server is because when you finish registering a server, all of the relevant information, including login information, is stored in your machine's Registry. If you choose the local registration, the information will be stored in

`HKEY_CURRENT_USER\Software\Microsoft\MSSQLServer\SQLEW\Registered Servers X`

The Enterprise Manager registration will be available only to those using your login on the current machine.

If you choose the shared registration, then your Enterprise Manager server registration will be available to all logins on the current machine, and the information will be stored in the Registry key,

`HKEY_LOCAL_MACHINE\Software\Microsoft\MSSQLServer\SQLEW\Registered Servers X`

WARNING

If you explore the Registry keys, do not change any values unless you must. If you make a mistake, the results may be unpredictable.

Enterprise Manager Utilities

When you open a server, you'll see the set of nodes shown in Figure 7-5.

FIGURE 7-5

Enterprise Manager organizes its facilities into five nodes.

As you explore Enterprise Manager's five nodes shown for each registered server, you find all the system, sample, and user databases in the Databases node (see the next section, "Managing Databases," in this chapter.)

All of the other nodes contain activities or storage covered in other chapters of this book. For example, the Data Transformation Services node contains entries for local DTS packages, repository packages, and metadata. (For more information about DTS, see Chapter 10, "Importing and Exporting Data.") The Management node contains entries for SQL Server Agent (see Chapter 11), backup (see Chapter 8), current activity (see Chapter 20), database maintenance plans (covered in this chapter), SQL Server logs (see Chapter 3), and the Web Publishing Wizard.

The Security node contains entries for logins and server roles (see Chapter 9), and linked and remote servers (see Chapter 23). Finally, the Support Services node contains the Distributed Transaction Service (see Chapter 23), and SQL Mail (see Chapter 11).

You've taken a broad-brush look at the major nodes within a server. Now, let's drill down into the Databases node.

Managing Databases

All SQL Server 7 data is stored in databases. A database is simply a collection of tables and other objects that have some bearing on them. The tables contain data organized in rows and columns, and the other objects either constrain or manipulate the data.

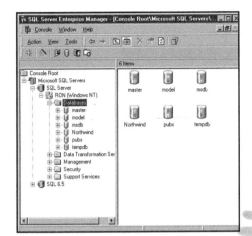

FIGURE 7-6

SQL Server's setup program installs six default databases.

WARNING

If you do not see all six databases when you open the Databases node in the Enterprise Manager tree control, you may have the Show System Databases and System Objects option unchecked in your registration of the server. To see all databases, as well as system objects, right-click over the server's name in the tree control and choose Edit SQL Server Registration. In the server registration Properties dialog box, make sure you have the option checked.

When you drill down to the database level using Enterprise Manager, you'll meet six databases already installed by the Setup program, as shown by Figure 7-6.

Let's take a closer look at those six databases.

The Installed Databases

Of the six databases SQL Server creates upon installation, four of them are system tables, and the remaining two, pubs and Northwind, are sample databases that contain sample data. The master database is absolutely essential for the operation of SQL Server, so let's start with it.

NOTE

You cannot add or alter tables in master, though you can update its data. Changing data in the master database is very risky; one false move may corrupt your entire installation.

The Master Database

The master database holds a set of global system tables. These system tables contain references to all the databases, logins, server configuration (character set and sort order) related to this installation of SQL Server. They contain references to the databases in the system, but not to any specific database contents.

The Model Database

The Model database is a small, mostly empty database whose configuration provides defaults for all subsequent databases created by this server. Its function is similar to that of a template. It contains all the database-specific system tables, which will be copied whenever you create a new database.

You can customize the model database so that certain objects (tables, indexes, and so on) will show up in every subsequent new database.

The Msdb Database

The SQL Agent uses the msdb database to schedule jobs and alerts. SQL Server also keeps a history of online backups and restores in this database.

The Northwind Database

The Northwind database is an upsized and converted version of the Jet sample database. You can use it as a model for how to work with an upsized Jet database, or for comparing queries between Access and SQL Server 7.

The Pubs Database

The pubs database is a sample database, consisting of a small set of data about authors, publishers, and books.

The Tempdb Database

The tempdb database is a database for storing temporary tables. Because the tables in tempdb are not persistent, tempdb does not use the same system tables that user-created databases require.

NOTE

All users share tempdb, and when any user disconnects, that user's temporary tables are deleted. When you shut down and restart SQL Server, tempdb is re-created.

> **TIP**
>
> Unlike in previous releases of SQL Server, the tempdb database in SQL Server 7.0 cannot be placed in RAM. Tempdb consists of disk files like any other SQL Server 7 database. If you must place tempdb in RAM, you can create a RAM disk and place it there.

Database Objects

Because all data in a database is stored in tables, tables are the most fundamental component from the preceding list. Any given table belongs to only one database, just as any given database belongs to only one SQL Server. You can see the complete drill-down from server to database to tables in Figure 7-7.

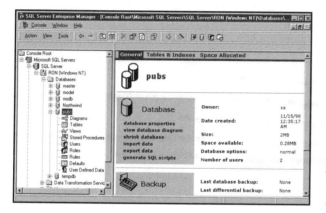

FIGURE 7-7

The database objects and tables for the Pubs database

Note how the right pane of Enterprise Manager displays (in HTML pages) some useful information about the database selected. Within the database, as you can see in the dialog box, every database contains a number of objects:

- ◆ Database diagrams: Visual diagrams of the database that you create
- ◆ Tables: Both system and data tables for the database
- ◆ Views: Saved selections of data derived from tables, that can be accessed like tables
- ◆ Stored procedures: Compiled Transact-SQL code to manage data
- ◆ Users: The database user names that have permission to access database objects
- ◆ Roles: The database roles that database users can have in the database
- ◆ Rules: Named constraints on data that can be applied to tables
- ◆ Defaults: Default rules bound to table columns (now obsolete)
- ◆ User-defined data types: Data types derived from the SQL Server base data types

You'll learn more about database diagrams, tables, views, rules, defaults, and user-defined data types in Chapter 12, "Data Definition." You'll learn more about database users and roles in Chapter 9, "Security," and more about stored procedures in Chapter 17, "Stored Procedures."

> **NOTE**
>
> Two prominent components are missing from each database's list: indexes and triggers. They belong to tables and can be found by using the menus and

How SQL Server Uses Its Databases

To understand how SQL Server databases work, you need to understand three fundamental points:

1. Every SQL Server database contains two types of tables: system tables and application data tables.
2. Every SQL Server installation contains two types of databases: system databases and user-created databases.
3. Every SQL Server database contains two types of files: data files (for all the tables) and log files (for the transaction log).

> **NOTE**
>
> Dramatic external and internal changes have been made to the SQL Server 7 storage engine that DBAs experienced with SQL Server 6.5 need to be aware of. Externally, all SQL Server databases are now stored in files, not devices. Every database stores its data on database files, and its transaction log on transaction log files. Unlike on SQL 6.5 devices, a database file can have only one database stored on it, and a transaction log file can have only one transaction log stored on it. Further, database and transaction logs cannot be stored together on the same file. Finally, database and log files can automatically grow and shrink, or optionally you can specify initial and maximum sizes for them.
>
> Internally, as you will learn more about in Chapter 12, "Data Definition," SQL Server stores all its data on 8K pages, rather than the 2K-page size of all earlier releases. Also, pages use a bitmapped addressing technique and no longer use linked lists. Last, SQL Server 7 adds fixed and variable Unicode character data types.

1. System and Data Tables

First of all, every SQL Server database, without exception, contains two types of tables: system tables and user tables. The system tables, called the system catalog, consist of metadata that describes all the data tables in the database, along with all the other objects, such as constraints, triggers, and stored procedures. The data tables consist of the tables you create to contain your data. In a way, you can view the system tables as containing the data tables, in the sense that they contain all the metadata about the data tables. You can see a diagram of this relationship in Figure 7-8.

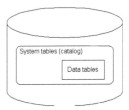

FIGURE 7-8

Every database consists of system tables and data tables.

You add your own data into data tables that you create using SQL Server's Transact-SQL language, and the SQL Server database engine ensures that the system tables are kept up to date. For instance, one system table contains a list of all the objects in the database, including tables (the sysobjects table), as well as all the columns of your tables (the syscolumns table), and so on. When you add a new table, SQL Server will add that table's characteristics into the appropriate system tables. As you would expect, the sysobjects table also contains rows for itself as well as the syscolumns table.

All information about a database is contained in the database's catalog. A database's catalog only contains information about that database, and not any other databases.

2. System and User Databases

The second point to understand is that every SQL Server installation contains two types of databases: system databases and user databases. The master, model, msdb, and tempdb databases are system databases, and the pubs database is a sample user database. You can see a diagram of this relationship in Figure 7-9.

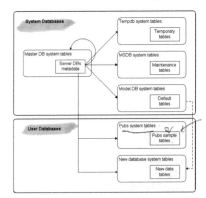

FIGURE 7-9

The master database contains metadata about all databases.

As you can see from the diagram, the system databases include master, model, msdb, and tempdb. The user databases consist of the pubs sample database (and the Northwind sample database, not shown) plus any new databases that you create.

The master database, like every SQL Server database, has a set of system (catalog) tables and a set of data tables. However, the master database's data tables contain metadata about all the databases in the system, including the master database itself. That accounts for the curved arrow from master's own data tables back to itself. (It also can contain information about other servers in the system, such as linked servers.)

A dashed arrow from the model database to the user databases shows that a number of default settings for a new database is taken from the model database.

3. Database and Transaction Files

Every SQL Server database contains tables and a transaction log. The transaction log contains a hidden history of all transactions on the database. All changes to data, with a few exceptions, take place as transactions, and SQL Server will write those changes out to the database's transaction log before applying the changes to the data. When SQL Server writes the transaction log, it forces the writes to go directly to disk, bypassing any memory cache. SQL Server also changes the data, but often many of those data changes will simply be made to the memory cache and not written immediately to disk.

If your system should crash during a transaction, when SQL Server restarts it can recover the database to the state before the crash and take care of the transaction. If the transaction was not yet committed, SQL Server can use the transaction log to back out any changes. If the transaction was committed, SQL Server can use the transaction log to make sure that all the data is written correctly, and it will apply any changes to data that were in memory and lost in the crash.

Each time SQL Server starts, it makes sure it recovers all databases. You will not be able to access a database until the recovery process is complete.

In every database, SQL Server stores the transaction log on a separate set of files from database data. Data and system tables are stored on data files, and the database's transaction log is stored on files of a different kind, namely log files. You can see a conceptual diagram of a SQL Server 7 database and its files in Figure 7-10.

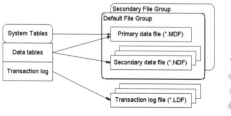

FIGURE 7-10

SQL Server 7 stores database data and transaction logs on two distinct types of files.

As you can see in Figure 7-10, the transaction log is stored on one or more transaction log files, which will default to the extension .LDF.

The storage of database data and system tables is a bit more complex. SQL Server 7 introduces the notion of file groups, which are named collections of files belonging to a single database. A database always has a default file group, and the first file in it must be the primary data file, for which the default extension is .MDF (probably short for "main data file"). The primary data file will be created on the database's default file group when the database is created, and SQL Server will place and keep the system tables on the primary data file.

Any given file group, including the default file group, can have more than one file on it. The additional files are called secondary data files, and there can be more than one on any file group. In addition to the default file group, you can add other file groups with secondary data files.

NOTE

You can control what data SQL Server stores on these data files by using the file name when you create a table or an index. By placing these files judiciously across SCSI drives, you can distribute your data for maximum throughput.

By default, SQL Server will create data and log files that automatically grow and shrink depending upon the need for space. This is very handy for small databases, because you do not need to anticipate disk space needs. It is also especially useful for transaction logs, because every time a backup is performed, the transaction log will be emptied of inactive transactions, and then it can automatically shrink.

However, the activity of growing and shrinking data and log files may be noticeable for large databases, so it is wise to specify the size of your large data files and not rely on SQL Server growing them. That way, the activity of changing the file size will not affect performance.

Creating a Database

When you create a new database, you must make some decisions related to storage: what file groups and files to store the data on, and what file to store the transaction log on.

You can create a new database using the Enterprise Manager Database Properties dialog box, or by using the Create Database Wizard. The Wizard simply does in five steps what the Properties dialog box does in two, so it's actually simpler to use the Properties dialog box.

right click Databases under
MS SQL Servers / SQL Server Group / My computer

To create a new database, right-click over the Database node in Enterprise Manager, and choose New Database. You'll be presented with an empty Database Properties dialog box, as you can see in Figure 7-11.

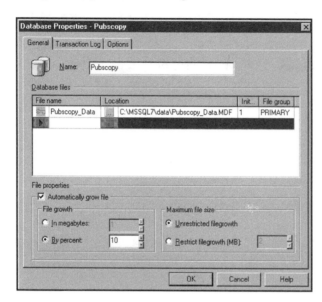

FIGURE 7-11

You specify the data file names and locations for a new database in the General tab.

In this case, you'll create a new database called Pubscopy, which you will use to make a copy of the pubs database. The initial file size defaults to 1MB, with one file in the default PRIMARY file group.

NOTE

You can find out the properties of any given database by right-clicking over the database name in Enterprise Manager and choosing the Properties option from the menu. (You can also select the database name and choose Action/Properties from the Enterprise Manager menu.)

Note also that the main data file is on the primary file group. You can add new data files for the Pubscopy database, putting them on the primary or a new file group, as you see fit.

The options at the bottom of the tab let you specify whether to let each file grow automatically in size, and by how much, either a percentage or an amount. You can also specify a maximum size for each data file or let it grow without restriction.

TIP

For smaller database files, and with a large amount of free disk space, you may want to let your database files automatically grow and shrink. However, if you expect to have large data files and limited disk space, you may want to specify the maximum size of your data files in order to monitor their growth. It can be better to get an error message that the file has reached its limit, than an error message indicating the file has filled up the disk.

Transaction Log Tab

The Transaction Log tab shows the same information for the transaction log files, as you can see in Figure 7-12, except that transaction log files cannot be collected into file groups.

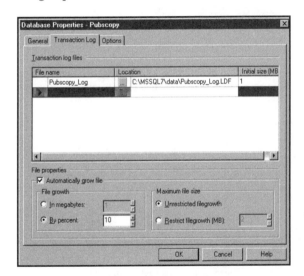

FIGURE 7-12

You can specify the file names and locations for one or more transaction log files in the Transaction Log tab.

In this case, there is no file group selection, because transaction logs do not reside on file groups.

WARNING

The SQL Server 7 Books Online recommends against using Windows NT file compression on data or transaction log files (see the "Physical Database Files and Filegroups" topic.) SQL Server 7 relies on writing the transaction log directly to disk, without the intervention of caching, which compression will cause. If you use NT compression on transaction logs, it is possible that a system crash will not have completely written log data, and the system may lose transactions.

Like data files, transaction files can automatically grow and shrink, and you can apply the same growth factor and size limits to your transaction files.

TIP

As with data files, if you expect the transaction file to stay small, and you back it up often (thereby removing inactive transactions), you may want to let it automatically grow and shrink. However, you may want to prevent it from filling up the disk by placing a maximum size on it.

WARNING

When you shrink a transaction file or files, they may not immediately reduce their size. Transaction log files can take a longer time to shorten.

The Options Tab

The Options tab gives a number of options you can set per database. Each of these options governs the database in question only, and not any other databases. Figure 7-13 shows the Options tab.

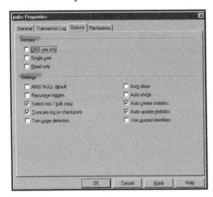

FIGURE 7-13

The Options tab offers settings choices for each database.

Each of the choices in the Options dialog box also correspond to commands of the stored procedure `sp_dboption`. As I discuss each option, you'll also see the `sp_dboption` call that corresponds to the dialog box choice. You should also know the `sp_dboption` command because you may need to include it in a script so that you can automate these choices.

NOTE

You can determine what options have been set for a database by using the `DATABASEPROPERTY()` System function. However, you cannot set those options using it.

Access

DBO Use Only. You can make the database so that only people whose SQL Server logins are mapped to the database owner role can use it. This effectively blocks out all other users from any access to the database. You'll learn more about this in Chapter 9, "Security." The sp_dboption equivalent of this choice is:

```
exec sp_dboption "pubs", "dbo use only", 1
```

Read Only. You can make the database read-only with this option, so that no one, including the system administrator, can modify it. The equivalent is:

```
exec sp_dboption "pubs", "read only", 1
```

Single User. With this option, SQL Server will allow only one connection to access the database at a time. However, it does not distinguish just who that connection has to be; it could be anyone, so it's first come, first served. The equivalent command is:

```
exec sp_dboption "pubs", "single user", 1
```

Settings

ANSI Null Default. When this option is on, SQL Server will default to making all columns of new tables nullable, unless you specify otherwise in the CREATE TABLE statement, or the New Table dialog box. The default setting is off, so SQL Server by default will make all columns of new tables to not allow nulls, unless you specify otherwise. See Chapter 12, "Data Definition," for more on this setting. The equivalent command is:

```
exec sp_dboption "pubs", "ANSI null default", 1
```

Recursive Triggers. A new feature of SQL Server 7 is that it will allow triggers to call themselves, indirectly, when they make changes to the trigger's table. For more information on this option, see Chapter 18, "Triggers." The equivalent command is:

```
exec sp_dboption "pubs", "recursive triggers", 1
```

Select Into/Bulk Copy. This option enables nonlogged operations. The SELECT .. INTO is a Transact-SQL extension to the SQL language that lets you create and populate a new table from a SELECT statement. The insert activity into the new table will not be logged in the transaction log, so it cannot be recovered or rolled back. You'll learn more about the SELECT statement in Chapter 13, "Data Manipulation." The Bulk Copy option is what is called "fast bulk copy," where inserts due to BCP are also not logged. You'll learn more about BCP in Chapter 10, "Importing and Exporting Data." The sp_dboption version of this is:

```
exec sp_dboption "pubs", "select into/bulk copy", 1
```

Truncate Log on Checkpoint. Sometimes you will have databases that do not contain volatile data and do not need to be backed up. In that case, you will not need to save the transaction log. This option will cause SQL Server to truncate the transaction log, that is, delete completed and inactive transactions from the log, whenever a checkpoint occurs. A checkpoint is the name for the operation when SQL Server writes all cached data changes from memory to disk. The equivalent command is:

```
exec sp_dboption "pubs", "trunc. log on chkpt.", 1
```

Torn Page Detection. SQL Server 7 has a minimum I/O size of 8KB, because that's the page size. However, it is possible that only part of a SQL Server page might be written to disk. If the Torn Page Detection option is on, SQL Server will check every 512-byte portion of a page, matching the 512-byte sectors written to disk, to make sure the entire page was written correctly. If a torn page is detected, SQL Server will raise an error and kill the connection. Although there is little overhead in setting this option on, there is no need to use it if your server has a battery-backed hard disk caching controller. The command for setting this is:

```
exec sp_dboption "pubs", "torn page detection", 1
```

Auto close. If you check this option, the database will be closed and taken off line when the last user exits and all resources are freed. This way, you can cause a Desktop SQL Server to optimize resources on a less powerful machine than a server.

```
exec sp_dboption "pubs", "autoclose", 1
```

Auto shrink. This option will automatically shrink database files to remove unused space. The default is off. The Transact-SQL equivalent is:

```
exec sp_dboption "pubs", "autoshrink", 1
```

Auto create statistics. When on, SQL Server will automatically create statistics on unindexed columns. The default is on; the equivalent command is :

```
exec sp_dboption "pubs", "auto create statistics", 1
```

Auto update statistics. When on, SQL Server will automatically update index statistics. The default is on; the equivalent Transact-SQL command is:

```
exec sp_dboption "pubs", "auto update statistics", 1
```

Use quoted identifiers. When on, SQL Server will interpret the use of double quotes as identifiers for table and column names. When off, it will interpret double quotes as string terminators. The default is off; the equivalent command is:

```
exec sp_dboption "pubs", "quoted identifier", 1
```

Other `sp_dboption` Settings

A number of choices do not show up in the dialog box. In the following list, the name you see is the parameter for the `sp_dboption` system stored procedure for setting the option.

♦ ANSI nulls: Treat NULLs in ANSI-SQL standard (= NULL returns NULL).

♦ ANSI warnings: Send warnings according the ANSI standards.

♦ Concat null yields null: Make concatenating a NULL with a string yield NULL.

♦ Cursor close on commit: Close cursors when a transaction is committed.

♦ Default to local cursor: cause cursor declarations to default to being local cursors.

♦ Merge publish: Enable merge replication for this database.

♦ Offline: Take a database offline so that it can be placed on a removable medium such as a CD-ROM.

♦ Published: Enable replication publishing.

♦ Subscribed: Enable replication subscribing.

The Permissions Tab

The Permissions tab lets you set database-wide permissions for users. For more information about this tab and other security issues, see Chapter 9, "Security."

Other Database-Related Stored Procedures

You can find out more about a database from a number of stored procedures. For example,

```
exec sp_heldb [<table name>]
```

shows you general information about a database. If you leave the parameter empty, you get information about all databases, as you can see in Figure 7-14.

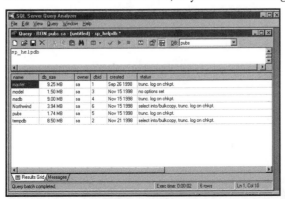

FIGURE 7-14

The `sp_helpdb` *stored procedure displays general information about a database.*

Note that `sp_helpdb` shows the options set by `sp_dboption` in the status clause. To inquire about free space in a database, you can issue

```
exec sp_spaceused
```

which will show you how space is used, as you can see in Figure 7-15.

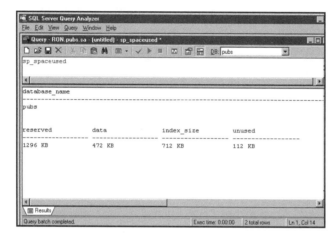

FIGURE 7-15

You can detect allocated and unused space by using `sp_spaceused`.

The command nicely points out how much of the data is free. `sp_spaceused` is very handy because it tells you the space used by the database's or table's indexes. You can also use `sp_helpfile` to show the files for the database, as shown in Figure 7-16.

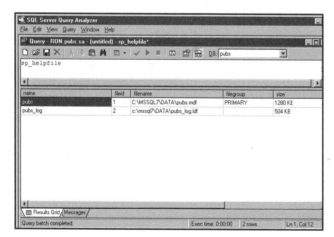

FIGURE 7-16

You can find out the files for the current database using `sp_helpfile`.

Plus, you can use `sp_helpfilegroup` to get information about your file groups.

Finally, to get information directly from the system tables, just query `sysfiles` directly, as you can see in Figure 7-17.

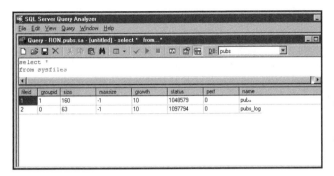

FIGURE 7-17

You can get information about your database and transaction log files from the database's own sysfiles *system table.*

The sysfiles system table contains file information about the current database.

WARNING

Microsoft recommends you use the ANSI information schema views instead of querying system files directly. However, no information schema view corresponds to the information in sysfiles.

Database Diagramming

To get a diagram of a database, you can use the Database Diagramming tool built into SQL Server 7's Enterprise Manager. To use it, all you need to do is drill down to a particular database in Enterprise Manager's tree view, right-click, and choose New Database Diagram. At that point, the Database Diagram Wizard will start up. As you walk through the wizard's steps, you can choose the tables you want to see in the diagram. For example, in the Pubs database, you can choose all the tables, as shown in Figure 7-18.

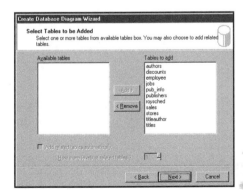

FIGURE 7-18

In the Database Diagramming Wizard, you can choose the tables you would like to see in the diagram.

When you finish the wizard, it will create a diagram and automatically arrange the tables, as you can see in Figure 7-19.

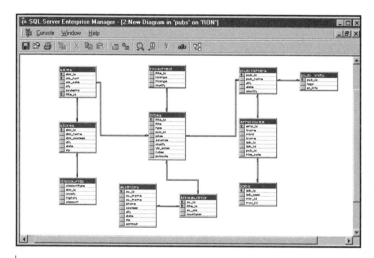

FIGURE 7-19

The wizard will arrange the diagram's tables automatically.

NOTE

The Database Diagramming Tool is considered a physical modeling tool because it maintains a one-to-one relationship between entities in the diagram and the tables in the database, and because it is specific to SQL Server databases.

After you have a set of tables, you can add, edit, and delete relationships between the tables by dragging and dropping from a primary key to a foreign key.

In addition, if the tables already have a foreign key relationship, the diagramming tool will automatically draw the appropriate one-to-many relationship, as you can see in the figure. The "one" side of the relationship is represented by the key symbol, and the "many" side is represented by the infinity symbol.

Copying, Renaming, and Dropping a Database

In addition to creating a database, you can also copy a database using backup and restore (see Chapter 8, "Backup and Restore"), or DTS (see Chapter 10, "Importing and Exporting Data").

You can rename a database using the sp_renamedb stored procedure. To do that, however, you must first put the database into single-user mode. First change the database to single user in the Database Properties dialog box, and then execute

```
exec sp_renamedb pubscopy, pubscopy2
```

You will see the changed name in the Enterprise Manager tree control, and then you can take the renamed database out of single-user mode.

You can delete a database using Enterprise Manager by right-clicking over the database name in the tree view and choosing Yes in the dialog box. You can also issue the T-SQL Drop Database command:

```
DROP DATABASE newcopy
```

WARNING

In prior releases of SQL Server, dropping or deleting a database did not delete the corresponding data files. In SQL Server 7.0, however, dropping a database does delete the data files.

This command comes in handy if you must drop the database but you cannot access it from the Enterprise Manager tree view.

Installing a Database from a Script

The Transfer Manager shown previously is an efficient way to copy a database from one server to another.

Often, however, you'll be given a set of scripts to install the database. SQL Server contains a script for installing the pubs database as MSSQL\INSTALL\INSTPUBS.SQL.)

Detaching and Reattaching a Database

You can also detach a database and its files from SQL Server using the sp_detach_db stored procedure, as in:

```
exec sp_detach_db 'pubs', 'true'
```

or with named parameters,

```
exec sp_detach_db @dbname= 'pubs', @skipchecks = 'true'
```

The second parameter tells SQL Server to run UPDATE STATISTICS against the database before detaching, so that all statistics are up to date, in case you are moving the database to a read-only medium such a as CD-ROM.

To reattach a detached database, use the sp_attach_db system stored procedure, as in:

```
EXEC sp_attach_db 'pubs', 'c:\mssql7\data\pubs.mdf',

                  'c:\mssql7\data\pubs_log.ldf'
```

or with named parameters,

```
EXEC sp_attach_db @dbname = N'pubs',

                @filename1 = N'c:\mssql7\data\pubs.mdf',

                @filename2 = N'c:\mssql7\data\pubs_log.ldf'
```

T IP

Detaching and attaching is the preferred way to move databases from one server to another, and one disk to another. However, the tempdb database cannot be detached, so if you want to move it to another disk drive, you must use the ALTER DATABASE command to move the database one file at a time. For example, if you want to move the tempdb database from drive C: to D:, issue something like the following for the data file:

```
ALTER DATABASE tempdb
MODIFY FILE ( name = 'tempdev', filename = 'd:\sqldata\tempdb.mdf')
```

Then for the log file, issue the following:

```
ALTER DATABASE tempdb
MODIFY FILE ( name = 'templog', filename = 'd:\sqldata\templog.ldf')
```

NOTE

As of the initial release of SQL Server 7.0, there is no way to detach and attach databases in Enterprise Manager.

The DBCC Command

Should the need arise, SQL Server provides you with a tool to diagnose and fix a database—the DBCC command. DBCC is short for "database consistency check." It's an internal SQL Server command that you can issue in stored procedures and scripts, and that you can also schedule. What follows now is a list of the most commonly used DBCC options.

SQL Server stores all its data on 8,192-byte pages. The DBCC CHECKDB, CHECKTABLE, NEWALLOC, and CHECKCATALOG commands will check the consistency of a database's data pages with their system tables and allocation maps. Many DBCC commands can only be executed by the sa login. See the Transact SQL Reference, "DBCC Command" for details.

DBCC CHECKDB Option (sa or dbo)

The CHECKDB option of DBCC checks an entire database to ensure that all pages are correctly allocated and used. It is the primary method of determining whether there is any corruption in the database. It checks the index and data pages for each table and makes sure that the pages are all correctly linked. It makes sure that the indexes are up to date and in proper order, that all pointers are consistent, and that the data information and page offsets are up to date. The syntax of the command is:

```
DBCC CHECKDB [(database_name [, NOINDEX])]
```

If you do not specify the database name, then DBCC will default to the current database.

To check the pubs database, you would issue the command as:

```
DBCC CHECKDB (Pubscopy)
```

If you only want to see error messages, then issue:

```
DBCC CHECKDB (Pubscopy) WITH NO_INFOMSGS
```

If you add the NOINDEX option, then only the data pages will be checked:

```
DBCC CHECKDB (Pubscopy, NOINDEX)
```

which can save some time.

DBCC CHECKTABLE Option (sa, dbo, or the Table Owner)

You can execute DBCC against a single table, with roughly the same syntax:

```
DBCC CHECKTABLE (table_name [, NOINDEX ¦ index_id])
```

This just restricts the DBCC operation to a single table, as in:

```
DBCC CHECKTABLE (authors)
```

DBCC CHECKCATALOG Option (sa or dbo)

You can check the system tables for a database with the CHECKCATALOG option. For example, the following command checks the system tables of the pubs database:

```
DBCC CHECKCATALOG (pubs)
```

For other DBCC commands related to indexes and other types of maintenance, see Chapter 12, "Data Definition."

DBCC Repairs

There are three kinds of repairs that DBCC can perform on a database or table: fast, rebuild, and allow data loss.

> **NOTE**
>
> To execute DBCC with repair options, the database must be in single-user mode.

Fast repairs. With this option, you instruct SQL Server to make minor, non-time-consuming repairs that will not result in any data loss. The format is

```
DBCC CHECKDB (Pubs, REPAIR_FAST)
```

Rebuild. This option causes SQL Server to make all the repairs of REPAIR_FAST, along with some time-consuming actions such as rebuilding indexes. The format is

```
DBCC CHECKDB (Pubs, REPAIR_REBUILD)
```

Allow data loss. This option does all the actions of REPAIR_REBUILD, plus correcting for allocation errors, fixing structural and page errors, and deleting corrupt text data type objects. It can result in some data loss. The format of this option is

```
DBCC CHECKDB (Pubs, REPAIR_ALLOW_DATA_LOSS)
```

> **T IP**
>
> You can wrap the DBCC repair options in a transaction. So you can begin a transaction, run DBCC with REPAIR_ALLOW_DATA_LOSS, inspect the results, and roll back the transaction if you cannot allow the objects to be dropped.

Summary

SQL Server 7.0 makes it easier and more intuitive to deal with servers and databases. Enterprise Manager is the graphical tool of choice for managing servers and databases, although most of its operations can also be duplicated using system-stored procedures. In addition, the DBCC command adds some maintenance options that are not contained directly in Enterprise Manager. The following chapters will take you through techniques for managing your data: through backup and restore, security, importing and exporting data, and scheduling tasks with SQL Server Agent. You'll start with backing up and restoring database data in the next chapter.

Chapter 8

Backup and Restore

In This Chapter

♦ Backup concepts

♦ Backup and restore techniques

♦ Database maintenance plans

You can't prevent disasters, but you can recover from them. The more carefully you lay and practice a disaster recovery strategy, the more effectively you'll be able to recover.

Your main tool for recovering from server or database disasters is to restore from one or more recent data backups. With a good backup and restore system, you can overcome a disaster by re-creating an acceptably recent state of the database and bringing it back online as quickly as possible.

Backup Concepts

To grasp the basic concepts of SQL Server backups, it's handy to review some basic terminology and disaster scenarios.

Some Terminology

A *backup* is just a specially formatted copy of your data that resides on disk or tape. (A database backup includes your data tables plus all the system tables, or metadata, necessary to re-create the database.) You can use it to restore your data in the case of a disaster. In SQL Server, you back up a single database or a database's transaction log at one time.

The process of backing up consists of copying to a disk file or tape drive. In either case, you must back up to a *device*; if you're backing up to a disk file, SQL Server will require you to supply a file name as a *disk device*. If you back up to a tape drive, you'll have to supply the name of the tape drive as the *tape device*. You can back up to several tapes in parallel, making what is called a *striped backup*.

> **NOTE**
>
> SQL Server 7 backups now use the Microsoft Tape Format, so SQL Server backups can share the same tape media with other backups

You can restore a backup to the same server or another server. If you run two servers in tandem, backing up from one and restoring to the other, the second server, the one that is not in production, is called a *warm standby*. If the first server fails, the second server can be brought into production.

For more hardware redundancy, you can use the Microsoft Cluster System (MCS), formerly known as "Wolfpack." MCS allows you to cluster two SQL Server computers together, running as one DBMS. If one of the systems fails, the other can take over immediately. Although clustering gives additional protection against hardware failures, it does not eliminate the need for backups. A cluster system cannot protect you against user errors and many types of database corruption.

The SQL Server Transaction Log

All SQL Server backup techniques involve a database's transaction log. The transaction log is SQL Server's mechanism for implementing transactions. In order to understand your backup options and needs, it is important to understand the role of transactions and the transaction log in SQL Server.

Every modification to data in SQL Server 7 takes place in the context of a transaction, one or more commands treated by the SQL Server as a whole. Either the whole set of actions succeed, or they all fail. SQL Server accomplishes this by writing each data change to the transaction log just before it changes the database. The transaction log operation is illustrated in Figure 8-1.

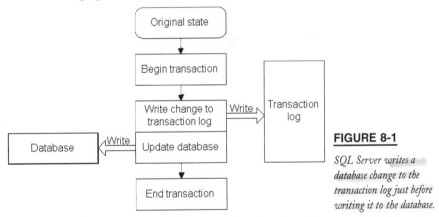

FIGURE 8-1

SQL Server writes a database change to the transaction log just before writing it to the database.

When SQL Server writes to the transaction log, it writes enough information to determine both the old and new states of the data. If a transaction fails in midstream, due to an error, or to an explicit ROLLBACK command, SQL Server can read the transaction log and undo all its changes by writing the old values back to the database in reverse order.

NOTE

For a fuller treatment of transactions, see Chapter 16, "Transactions." For concurrency issues, see Chapter 20, "Concurrency Tools."

Because SQL Server does not write its database changes out to disk immediately, the true current state of the database includes both the data pages on disk and the data pages in the data cache. Some disasters may involve a sudden crash when SQL Server cannot write its database changes from cache to disk. In that case, the data changes in cache memory will be lost. However, you can combine the data files on disk with the transaction log and get very close to the actual state of the database before the crash. The exact technique varies depending on the type of backup, but for all types of SQL Server 7 backup, the transaction log is essential.

Types of SQL Server Backups

SQL Server provides four kinds of backups:

1. In a *full database* backup, you back up the entire database along with its transaction log.

2. A *file* backup just backs up a file or file group. Backing up all files and file groups is equivalent to a full database backup.

3. In a *differential database* backup, you back up the changes in the database since the last full backup, plus all the changes to the transaction log that occur during the backup.

4. In a *transaction log* backup, you just back up a database's transaction log, which records transactions from the last full or differential database backup, or from the last transaction log backup.

To understand why there are so many backup strategies, it helps to look at what happens when a disaster occurs.

Consider first a typical time period for an OLTP database. It will have a number of transactions occurring during a certain time period, as you can see in Figure 8-2.

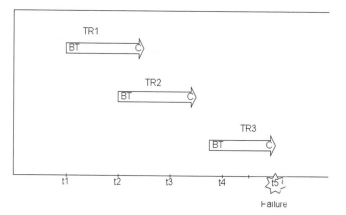

FIGURE 8-2

An OLTP system will have a set of transactions spread over a period of time, and you must prepare for a failure point.

Each of the arrows in the diagram represents a transaction. The diagram shows three transactions: TR1, TR2, and TR3. In each transaction, "BT" indicates the beginning of the transaction, and "C" stands for the commit, in other words the completion and acceptance of the transaction. The horizontal axis shows five time points, t1 through t5. At time t5, a failure of some kind occurs that is severe enough to prevent transaction t3 from completing. The failure is also severe enough to prevent any further activity on the server, either because it crashed, or because the DBA had to take it offline to repair it.

The span of time you are interested in is time t1 through t5, and a failure occurs at time t5. With no backup in the scenario, and when failure at t5 occurs, you are essentially sunk. The only way to recover is to rebuild the database from scratch.

Full Database Backup

So suppose you make a full database backup at time t1, as shown in Figure 8-3.

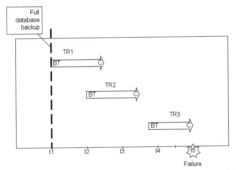

FIGURE 8-3

You make a full database backup at time t1, so now you can recover from a failure.

Now you have a full database backup. When the failure occurs at time t5, you can recover the data from your backup and make the refreshed system current as of time t1.

SQL Server 7 implements a fuzzy backup algorithm for full database backups. Unlike the database backups of earlier SQL Server releases (4.2x and 6.x), a SQL Server 7 fuzzy backup backs up all the data in a database plus all the transaction log changes to the data that took place after the backup process started. SQL Server 7 simply copies database pages sequentially through the database and adds those transactions to the backup that are necessary to restore the database to the same state as when the backup completed. Because a SQL Server 7 full database backup has all the data and the transaction log changes, the backup effectively gets a snapshot of the database at the time of backup completion. When the backup ends and gets the last completed transaction, it records that fact in the transaction log.

Earlier releases of SQL Server (4.2x and 6.x) took their snapshot of the database at the beginning of the backup and backed up the database one object at a time. As a result, other activity in the database could be blocked while the backup was occurring, and the backup would often not read the data pages sequentially. SQL Server 7's fuzzy backup gets around those problems.

> ### WARNING
>
> Because a SQL Server 7 fuzzy backup relies on the transaction log to pick up those changes to the database that occur after the backup begins, certain operations cannot occur during the backup. These operations include creating or deleting database files, creating indexes, using nonlogged operations such as SELECT INTO or fast bulk copy, or shrinking a database file.

Unfortunately, for the scenario in Figure 8-3, a full database backup is not enough for a full recovery. You will have lost all data from transactions that completed before the failure point at time t5. Notice that transactions TR1 and TR2 had their data committed, which means that the clients assumed the data made it into the database. However, if the most recent backup is only good for time t1, then these two transactions have been lost.

Because a full database backup can take more time than the other backups, and impact the performance of a production system, it is usually not suitable as the only backup strategy. It is better to supplement a full database backup with differential database backups and/or transaction log backups, because the latter are normally smaller, take less time, and have less impact on the production system.

File and File Group Backups

For large databases, in the tens and hundreds of gigabytes, it may be more convenient to back up individual files or file groups instead of the entire database. If you back up all the files or file groups of a database, and also backup the transaction log, it becomes the equivalent of a full database backup. When you restore the filegroups, you must also apply the transaction log to bring the database into a consistent state.

Differential Database Backup

A differential database backup is just like a full database backup, except that it only backs up the data pages that have changed since the last full database backup. A differential backup is smaller and faster than a full database backup, because it does not include the entire database, and therefore both the backup and the restore will normally be much faster than the full backup.

Because the differential backup is faster, you can use it more often. Consequently, you can use a differential backup to get you closer to the failure point, as you can see visualized in Figure 8-4.

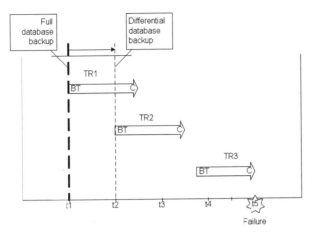

FIGURE 8-4

A differential backup at time t2 records all changes to the database since the full backup at time t1.

The differential database backup at time t2 records all the changed data in the database plus the changes to the transaction log since the start of the backup. So in this case, the differential backup at t2 records the transaction TR1 as unfinished. If you use the t2 differential backup to restore the database after the disaster at t5, and use only the first differential backup to recover the database, then transaction TR1 will have its changes rolled back. Based on the differential backup, SQL Server cannot detect whether the transaction finished, what other changes it made, and whether the transaction committed.

Now suppose you add the second differential backup at time t3, as shown in Figure 8-5.

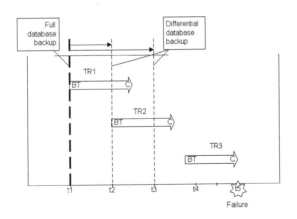

FIGURE 8-5

A second differential backup also records all database changes since the last full backup.

Differential database backups are cumulative. In other words, the differential backup at time t3 includes all the database changes since time t1, so it includes all the information of the differential backup made at time t2. Therefore each subsequent differential backup will normally be larger than the previous one.

The new differential backup made at time t3 now includes the fact that transaction TR1 completed, so the changes made to the data by TR1 are now part of the backup. You are a step closer to recovering to the point of failure.

However, transaction TR2 is incomplete at time t3. If you restore the database using the full database backup and the t3 differential backup, and recover the database, then you will have lost transaction TR2. One solution is just to do differential backups more often. However, there is still one more type of backup that can be used to bring you much closer to the state of things at the time of failure, namely the transaction log backup.

Transaction Log Backup

A transaction log backup backs up just the transaction log, and no data pages. It will back up the log from the time of the last completed full or differential database backup or transaction log backup. So if you add a transaction log at time t4, for example, you can bring a restored database closer to the state at the time of failure, as you can see in Figure 8-6.

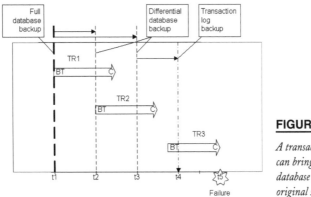

FIGURE 8-6

A transaction log backup can bring a restored database closer to its original state.

The transaction log backup now lets you recover transaction TR2, but transaction TR3 is still not recovered. Notice you could have done the same with another differential backup at time t4. In the current scenario, they both would achieve the same result.

NOTE

You can combine differential and transaction log backups. But remember that a transaction log backup only backs up the log starting from the most recent full database backup, differential database backup, or transaction log backup.

Transaction log backups have both an advantage and a disadvantage relative to differential backups. The advantage is that a transaction log backup sometimes can be used to recover the database almost to the exact state it was in at the time of failure.

One advantage of a transaction log backup is that if a failure does not bring down the server, one last transaction log backup of a database can be made before shutting down and restoring, as shown in Figure 8-7.

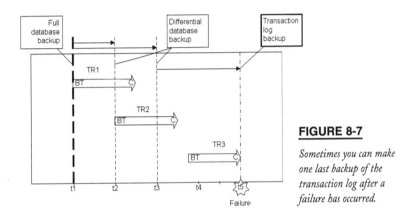

FIGURE 8-7

Sometimes you can make one last backup of the transaction log after a failure has occurred.

You make this type of transaction log backup right after everyone is off the system and just before you shut down the system and start your rebuild process. If transaction TR3 was completed, even though the data changes may only exist in cache, the transaction log will contain enough information to re-create the database with a completed TR3 if you can back the log up. If transaction TR3 is unfinished, in other words uncommitted, then all the user's changes will be lost.

One disadvantage of a transaction log backup system is that unlike differential backups, they are not cumulative. You must apply transaction log backups in the exact sequence with which they were first built, as you can see in Figure 8-8.

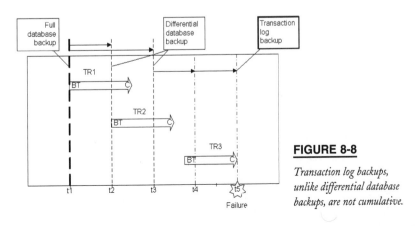

FIGURE 8-8

Transaction log backups, unlike differential database backups, are not cumulative.

As Figure 8-8 indicates, the transaction log backup at time t4 records the changes in the log from t3 to t4, whereas the transaction log backup at time t5 only records the changes from time t4 to t5.

To prevent the transaction log at t4 from rolling back transaction TR3, you restore it without recovery. "Without recovery" instructs SQL Server to leave the database in a read-only or recovery mode without resolving unfinished transactions from the transaction log. This allows you to restore the next transaction log, which contains data about the rest of the unfinished transactions. You can then restore the last transaction log with recovery, and SQL server will allow the database to come back online.

> **WARNING**
>
> You must restore every transaction log backup, except the last one, without recovery. You should only restore the very last transaction log in the sequence with recovery.

When you restore the database, you need to apply only the last of the differential backups after the full database backup. After the differential backups are done, you must then restore the transaction log backups in the exact sequence you created them, or else the restores will not succeed.

Of course, being cumulative, each subsequent differential backup is larger than the last one, whereas the size of a transaction log backup depends solely upon the amount of activity since the last backup.

Protecting from Disaster

Among the bad things that can happen to production databases are, more or less in order of severity:

1. Users may deliberately or inadvertently damage data.
2. A database may become corrupted.
3. A hard drive system may fail and make your data unrecoverable.
4. An environmental disaster may destroy your server.

Let's take a look at each of these scenarios.

User Error

In this scenario, when only the data is damaged, you will have to recover the database from a state prior to when the damage occurred. In that case, the more backups you have, the better off you are. Suppose you keep a full backup of the database in question every day, and a differential backup every hour. Then you can recover the database to within an hour of its final state. If you also keep transaction log backups every 15 minutes, then you can recover the database that much closer by applying the log backups after the differential backup.

If you have to discover the time the error occurred, you can progressively apply the backups to determine it. While it is not possible to apply only part of a backup, it is possible to restore to a given point in time, called point in time recovery. So once you know exactly when the mistake occurred, you can restore the given backup to just prior to that point.

Database Corruption

It is unlikely that SQL Server 7 databases will suffer much corruption, but it is possible. Prior releases of SQL Server (4.x, 6.x) used a linked-list mechanism for managing data pages that could often go bad. However, SQL Server 7 has a new set of bitmapped storage structures that are much more stable.

Nevertheless, if database corruption occurs, it will persist in the database and may be propagated to the backups. If it is just index corruption, you can drop and re-create the indexes. If it's data corruption, you may be able to export the data to another table, and rebuild the original table, without having to rebuild the entire database. If the corruption is more severe than that, you may have to rebuild the entire database up to the point the corruption occurred.

System Failure

It may happen that the entire database becomes inoperable, or a hard drive subsystem completely fails, and the database is lost. In this case, if the transaction log is on a separate drive, you may be able to back it up and use it when rebuilding the original database on a new drive. However, if the transaction log is also lost, then you'll only be able to recover to the state of your last good backup.

Environmental Failure

If you lose the entire server, you'll only be able to recover the database on a new server up to the point of your last good backup, that was stored externally. In other words, that was stored on tape or some other backup medium.

Backup and Restore Techniques

Now that you've gotten the basic concepts of SQL Server backups, let's take a look at some specific techniques for backing up SQL Server databases.

The Database Backup Wizard

The easiest way to make a full database backup is to use the Database Backup Wizard. Like all wizards, it guides you through the backup process in a step-by-step fashion. On the other hand, it can hide details that you might otherwise want to know.

When you choose the Backup Wizard, you must identify the database you want to back up, and the backup file name. You then select the type of backup you want, as shown in Figure 8-9.

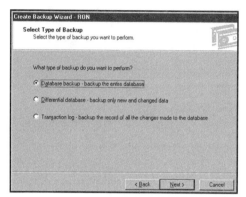

FIGURE 8-9

The Backup Wizard gives you three options for type of backup.

These three options match the types of backups I have previously discussed. Note, however, that file or file group backups are not listed.

In the next step, you must choose a backup device. Remember, a backup device is just a file. If none are listed in the dialog box as available, just click on the Add button and you'll be able to add one. You then choose the type of medium, disk or tape, and whether to initialize or overwrite the backup file. The last set of choices you must make in the Wizard also concern the medium you're using, as you can see in Figure 8-10.

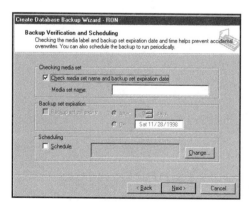

FIGURE 8-10

The last set of choices you make using the Backup Wizard concerns the backup medium.

If you are using a backup device with a lot of other backups on it, you'll want to verify that you are backing up to the correct one by entering a media set name and having SQL Server check it. You can also choose to have the backup expire at a certain date, if you want to prevent yourself from restoring backups older than a given amount of time.

Finally, you can have SQL Server verify the backup upon completion. This does not verify the data, just that the volumes are all present and readable.

WARNING

If you want to verify the integrity of the entire backup, you must restore the backup and then verify the database with DBCC.

The Backup Dialog Box

You can do all the same work as the Backup Wizard in a random order using the Backup Database dialog box. To get to this dialog box, select a database, and from Tools, choose Backup Database. You'll see the dialog box shown in Figure 8-11.

Tools / Backup DB

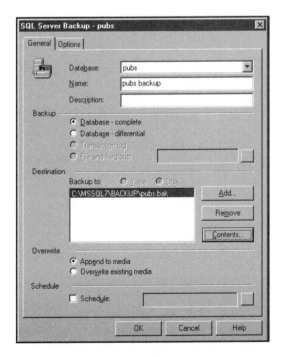

FIGURE 8-11

The Backup Database dialog box is another way to perform a backup.

Again, you can choose the kind of backup you want to do: full database, differential, or transaction log. Notice that this dialog box does include the file or file group types of backup.

Notice you have your choice of backup media and devices to use. If nothing is listed in the dialog box, just click on the Add button and you can either find a file or create a new backup file name. If you want to see what is on the listed backup file, click on the Contents button, and you'll get a list of all the different backups in the file, as shown in Figure 8-12.

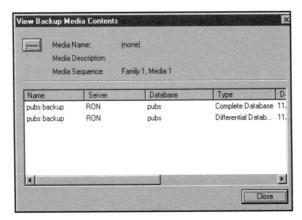

FIGURE 8-12

The Contents button shows you the backups in a given backup file.

The Options tab gives you the same set of media choices that the Wizard gave you, as you can see in Figure 8-13.

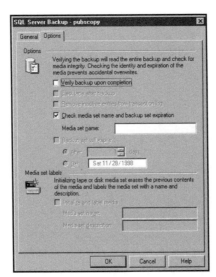

FIGURE 8-13

You make the remaining media set decisions in the Options tab.

After you've made these choices, click on the OK button; the backup will proceed.

The Transact-SQL BACKUP Command

The set of choices you just made in both the Backup Wizard and the Backup dialog box will actually execute this Transact-SQL command:

```
BACKUP DATABASE [pubs]
TO  DISK = N'd:\mssql7\BACKUP\pubsbak'
WITH  NOINIT ,  NOUNLOAD ,  NAME = N'pubs  backup',  NOSKIP ,
STATS = 10,  NOFORMAT
```

In this case, you backed up the database pubs to the disk medium, with a file name of pubsbak and no extension. In addition, you did not specify that the backup should initialize the file (and thereby destroy other backups). The NOUNLOAD option means that if a tape backup is being made, the tape will not be automatically unloaded from the tape drive. It is irrelevant for a disk file backup. The NAME is the backup set name; NOSKIP says not to verify the backup set name; the STATS = 10 option indicates the system should show progress every 10 percent of the way; and NOFORMAT specifies that the media header should not be written on all the volumes.

Numerous options are available on the BACKUP command, too many to cover here. The BACKUP command actually has three versions. For a full database backup, you just issue:

```
BACKUP DATABASE database-name
          TO backup-device
          WITH options
```

For a file or file group backup, you issue:

```
BACKUP DATABASE database-name
          database-file-name or file-group-name
          TO backup-device
          WITH options
```

For a differential backup, you add the keyword DIFFERENTIAL:

```
BACKUP DATABASE database-name
          TO backup-device
          WITH options, DIFFERENTIAL
```

For a transaction log backup:

```
BACKUP LOG database-name
          [WITH  NO_LOG or TRUNCATE_ONLY]
          TO backup-device
          WITH options
```

The Restore Dialog Box

There is no Restore Wizard, but there is a Restore dialog box, the other half of the
Backup dialog box. When you choose it from Tools, Restore Database, you'll see the
dialog box listed in Figure 8-14.

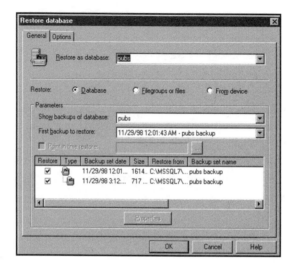

FIGURE 8-14

*You can restore from a full
database backup, a
differential backup, or a
transaction log backup using
the Restore dialog box.*

In this case, after you choose what type of restore to make, you must select a device
by clicking on the Select Devices... button and adding the device file name. If you are
working with a lot of backup sets, you can specify further choices, in addition to the
type of backup set.

The Choose Restore Devices dialog box is shown in Figure 8-15.

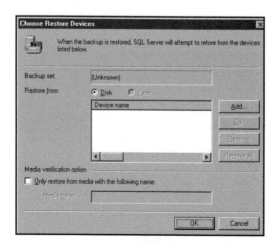

FIGURE 8-15

*The Select Devices button
leads to the Assign Restore
Devices dialog box.*

In this dialog box you specify the actual file or files, or tape devices, to be used for the restore. You can also verify the media set name, just as you could with the backup dialog boxes.

After you've selected a restore device, you can return to the original tabbed dialog box and look at the Options tab. The Options tab lets you choose what files to restore, as you can see in Figure 8-16.

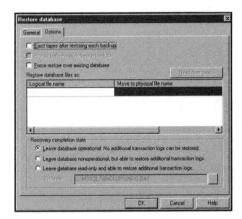

FIGURE 8-16

The Options tab specifies what database files you want to restore to on disk.

This dialog box holds a number of key choices. Because you're restoring a simple database backup into a database with the same name, you can work with the defaults. You don't need to eject tapes, because you're using a disk backup; you don't need to force a restore over the current database, because it's got the same name, and you do want to restore to the pubs database for now. In the next section, you'll see how to use this option to restore into a copy of the database.

The bottom items relate to restoring from transaction logs. If you choose to leave the database operational, that means SQL Server should do a recovery when the backup finishes. You want to keep this option for any full or differential database backups. However, if you are restoring a single transaction log, you'll want to make sure that only the last transaction log leaves the database in an operational, recovered state. For all the prior transaction log restores, you'll need to make sure you use one of the other operations.

NOTE

For more information about warm standby servers, see the 1999 release of the Back Office Resource Kit. It contains a utility to automate the warm standby process.

The Transact-SQL RESTORE Command

When you use the Restore dialog boxes to restore a backup, Enterprise Manager actually sends the Transact-SQL RESTORE command to SQL Server. In the preceding case, you actually sent the command:

```
RESTORE DATABASE [pubs]
FROM  DISK = N'd:\mssql7\BACKUP\pubsbak'
WITH  FILE = 1,
NOUNLOAD ,  STATS = 10,  RECOVERY
```

You restored the database pubs from the disk file pubsbak, first backup set, with the options not to unload the tape drive (which is ignored, in our case), to show progress every 10 percent, and to restore with recovery.

The last option, WITH RECOVERY or WITH NORECOVERY, is all-important with transaction log backups. Only the last transaction log backup in a sequence should be restored WITH RECOVERY.

Just as with BACKUP, there are numerous other options. The basic format of the RESTORE command, for restoring full database backups, is:

```
RESTORE DATABASE database-name
FROM backup-device-name
WITH options
```

For a file or file group restore:

```
RESTORE DATABASE   database-name
            database-file-name or file-group-name
FROM backup-device-name
            WITH options
```

For a differential backup:

```
RESTORE DATABASE database-name
FROM backup-device-name
            WITH options
```

For a transaction log restore:

```
RESTORE LOG database-name
FROM backup-device-name
            WITH options
```

Using BACKUP **to Copy a Database**

You can use the backup and restore dialog boxes to make a copy of a database, by restoring to a database with a different name. For example, using the preceding dialog boxes, you've backed up the pubs database to the backup file called pubsbak. In this section, learn how to use that backup to make a copy of the pubs database.

Just create a new database, called pubscopy. Initially the new database will be empty, save for the system tables that every new database has. Now choose the pubscopy database in Enterprise Manager, and bring up the Restore dialog box. Choose to make a restore from backups belonging to the pubs database, as shown in Figure 8-17.

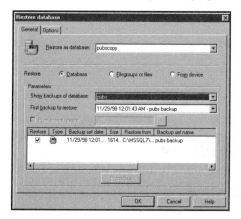

FIGURE 8-17

You can restore from a database of a different name. Start by specifying the other database in the Restore dialog box.

Notice that it finds the backup files. If you try the backup now, it will not work, because you cannot restore to a database of a different name without making extra choices on the Options tab.

Choose the Options tab, and notice the fields in Figure 8-18.

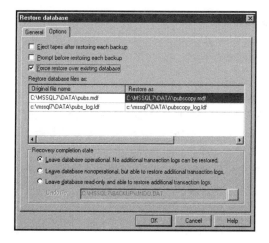

FIGURE 8-18

You need to force the restore to overwrite the current database.

Notice the check boxes: You want to force a restore over the existing database and to restore the database as pubscopy. Make sure you check the Restore As column and verify that the file names match the ones you want to use for this database. The actual command sent to the server was:

```
RESTORE DATABASE [pubscopy]
FROM  DISK = N'd:\mssql7\BACKUP\pubsbak'
WITH  FILE = 2,  NOUNLOAD ,  STATS = 10,  RECOVERY ,  REPLACE ,
MOVE N'pubs' TO N'd:\mssql7\DATA\pubscopy.mdf',
MOVE N'pubs_log' TO N'd:\mssql7\DATA\pubscopy_log.ldf'
```

Notice that the dialog box added the MOVE options to copy the pubs and pubs_log logical file names to the physical names that you overwrote in the dialog box.

Backing Up OLTP versus DSS Data

As you saw in Chapter 1, the current database industry deals with essentially two kinds of data: online transaction processing (OLTP) and decision-support data (DSS), though often they are mixed together. Recovering from server or database disasters requires different strategies for each type.

If a database contains any kind of OLTP data, it is transaction-based, and there's a good probability that a sudden halt to the server will cause some data to be lost. Often that's simply unacceptable, so you must provide a backup system that will restore the database or databases to a state very close to when the halt occurred.

If the database contains only DSS data, you may only need a single backup with a fresh set of DSS data. If and when a disaster occurs, you can restore from the current backup and bring the system back online.

If you have a mixed situation, then you may be able to partition the data into files or file groups and just provide recent backups of the OLTP portion. If you cannot do that, however, you'll need to find out what amount of lost data is acceptable and budget for that.

To restore a DSS system, you will probably only need database backups. To restore an OLTP system, though, you will have to use some combination of database backups and transaction log backups. In a pure DSS system, where there are no user transactions, a full database backup at time t1 would be sufficient to recover the database. If transactions TR1 and TR2 represent new builds of the system, however, then you will not be able to restore to a recent build with just a backup at time t1.

Emptying the Transaction Log

If you are not making transaction log backups, on occasion you may need to truncate the log so that it doesn't take up too much space on the disk. One way to do this is to set the Truncate Log on Checkpoint option in the Database Properties dialog box (see Chapter 7.)

If you do not truncate on checkpoint, however, you can still empty the log with the command:

```
BACKUP LOG Pubscopy WITH TRUNCATE_ONLY
```

This empties the inactive portion of the log and logs the operation.

If you've completely run out of disk space, and you need to truncate the log in order to free up disk space, and the preceding command does not appear to clear it out, you can issue:

```
BACKUP LOG Pubscopy WITH NO_LOG
```

which does the same thing but does not log the operation.

Database Maintenance Plans

SQL Server 7 makes it very easy to schedule backups using the construct of a database maintenance plan. There's a special node in the left pane of Enterprise Manager for them and a sophisticated Wizard you can use for their creation. Do not dismiss the Database Maintenance Plan Wizard just because it is a Wizard—it may indeed provide you with all you need for maintaining small to medium-sized databases.

You start the Maintenance Wizard in the usual way, by opening up the Wizards dialog box from the toolbar; you'll find it under Management. After an opening dialog box, you can choose your database, and then you'll see a number of data reorganization options, as shown in Figure 8-19.

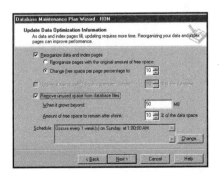

FIGURE 8-19

Your first set of choices concerns data reorganization.

These choices let you determine, for a given database, how often and in what way to reorganize index and data pages. You can also check data integrity, as shown in Figure 8-20.

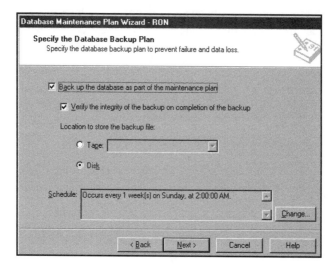

FIGURE 8-20

Your second set of choices concerns data integrity.

This is really the frequency and method for applying DBCC CHECKDB to your database. It's not until the next dialog box that you see backup options, as shown in Figure 8-21.

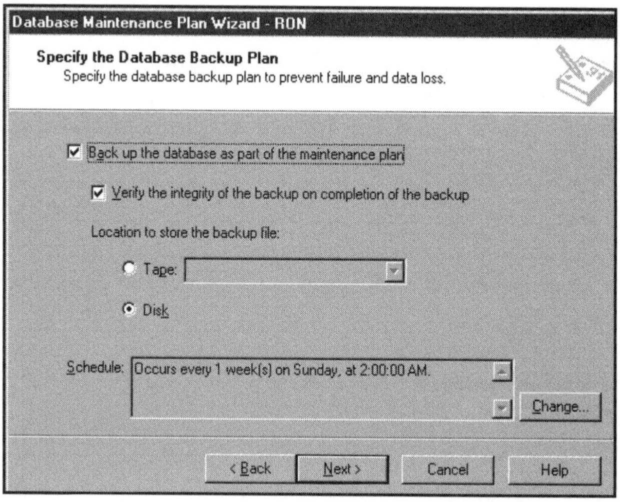

FIGURE 8-21

The next option concerns backup.

If you choose to back up the database as a part of the maintenance plan, then you'll get additional choices reflecting backup options. For example, you can verify the integrity (i.e., read the backup header) of the backup upon completion, and schedule the backup independently of the other maintenance steps. You can accept the default schedule or change it by clicking on the Change button.

The next dialog box lets you choose the destination directory of the backup, as shown in Figure 8-22.

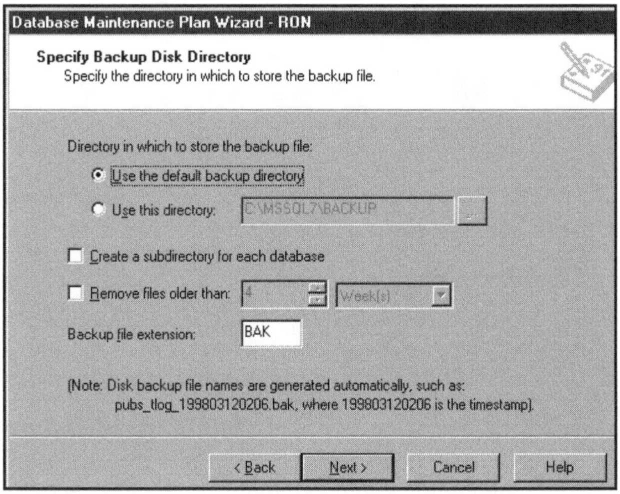

FIGURE 8-22

You can specify the backup directory and the age of the backups.

What's additional here is something you don't get in the regular backup dialog boxes: You can age the backups, so that backups older than a certain number of weeks will be deleted. The Maintenance Plan Wizard can do this because it will make all backups to individual disk files, where the time and date of the backup are in the file name. Because the backups are on separate files, it can delete the old ones.

The next dialog box also lets you specify a backup of the transaction log, as shown in Figure 8-23.

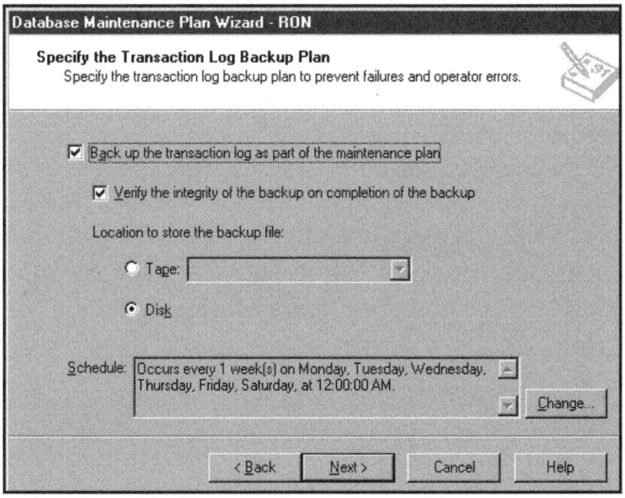

FIGURE 8-23

You can also specify transaction log backups as part of a maintenance plan.

You can accept the default schedule or change it by clicking on the Change button. The remaining dialog boxes are rather straightforward, so I won't go through them here.

After you're finished, the final maintenance plan will show up in Enterprise Manager under the Management node. When you select a plan, and inspect its properties, you'll see all of the Wizard's choices reflected in a tab dialog, shown in Figure 8-24.

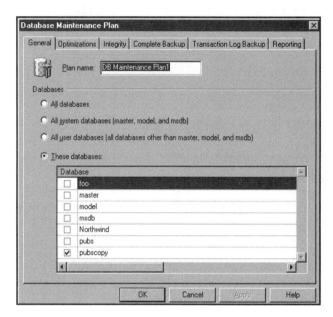

FIGURE 8-24

All of the steps of the Maintenance Plan Wizard are collected into the Properties dialog of the plan.

Maintenance plans can be very worthwhile for managing large sets of databases, or guiding end users through setting up their own maintenance.

Summary

You have several options available to you when backing up your SQL Server 7 database data. Full database backups, differential backups, and transaction log backups can each be used in appropriate situations. Your restore strategies must be coordinated to match the backup strategy of the database in question. In addition, you can include backup operations in database maintenance plans, using a Wizard to build them and then Enterprise Manager to manage them.

Chapter 9

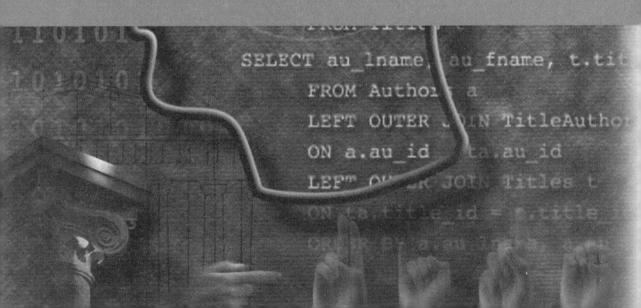

Security

In This Chapter

◆ Basic concepts of SQL Server security

◆ Authentication modes

◆ Logins

◆ Database components

Every user that connects to SQL Server must have a valid login id, and that login id must be registered with SQL Server. In this chapter, you start with the basic concepts and essential principles and then later go into the mechanics and commands.

Basic Concepts of SQL Server Security

SQL Server Security has many components and can become quite complex. In this section, you'll learn the basics of its security system.

Logins, the Server, and Databases

SQL Server security begins with logins, which have access to the server and its databases, as shown in Figure 9-1.

Server

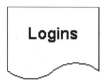

Logins

Databases

FIGURE 9-1

SQL Server security starts with logins, the server, and its databases.

Client applications connect to SQL Server by having a login that SQL Server can authenticate. That login may be a SQL Server login or a Windows NT login. SQL Server logins consist of a login name and password that are stored in SQL Server. Windows NT logins are Windows NT user names or groups that are registered by the system administrator or security administrator within SQL Server. With Windows 95 and 98, all you can use are SQL Server logins.

Authentication and Permissions

Once a login has access to a particular SQL Server, the user may perform server-level tasks or database-level tasks, as shown in Figure 9.2.

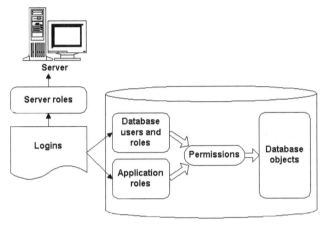

FIGURE 9-2

Logins can have two levels of access, the server level and the database level.

For server-level tasks, SQL Server 7 introduces the concept of *server roles*, which allow a given login to perform certain server-level activities. Server roles subdivide the system administrator tasks into specialized components. That way, a given login does not need all system administrator privileges just to do a few administrative tasks.

At the database level, access is a bit more complex. All data in a database is stored in and accessed by *database objects*. Every object in a database is owned by some entity, called the *database object owner*. These object owners are identified in the database as *database users*, though not all database users must own objects. Database users, in turn, can be associated with *database roles*. In addition to database users and roles, SQL Server 7 also introduces *application roles*, which contain sets of privileges that an application can switch to after logging in. To gain access to database objects, every login must be mapped either to a database user or to an application role.

NOTE

The upshot is that to gain access to a database, every login must have some explicit or implicit mapping to a database user or application role in that database.

Implementing Security

When you log into a fresh SQL Server installation, SQL Server security can seem invisible. When you use the sa login, or you use a trusted connection and your NT login belongs to that machine's NT Administrators group, you can immediately access all the databases and their objects (tables, views, stored procedures, and so forth). That's because every database object in all the standard databases is owned by a database user, present in each database, called *dbo* (abbreviation for *database owner*), and those privileged logins automatically map to the dbo of every database.

In other words, any login with system administrator rights can immediately see all the database objects of every database in the server. Therefore, implementing SQL Server security consists of using logins other than sa or an NT login with local Administrator rights.

WARNING

If you only use the sa login or an NT login that belongs to the local machine's Administrators group, you are bypassing SQL Server security.

Now let's take a more detailed look at how SQL Server security works.

Authentication Modes

If SQL Server is running under Windows NT, you can configure it to accept both Windows NT logins and SQL Server logins, or just Windows NT logins. As you saw in Chapter 5, "Configuring," you can choose this configuration setting in the Security tab of each server's Properties dialog box, as shown in Figure 9-3.

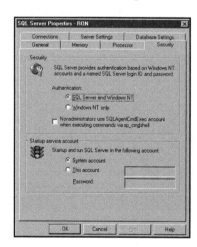

FIGURE 9-3

You can choose the type of security for Windows NT SQL Servers using the Security tab of each Server's Properties dialog box.

If SQL Server is running under Windows 9x, the only authentication mode it can use is the mixed SQL Server and Windows NT login authentication, but no Windows NT logins are allowed. So in effect, Windows 9x security is restricted to SQL Server login authentication only.

Consequently, SQL Server really has three total security authentication modes:

- ◆ SQL Server authentication only (Windows 9x) (equivalent to "standard" security on SQL Server 6.x)
- ◆ SQL Server and Windows NT authentication (equivalent to "mixed" security on SQL Server 6.x)
- ◆ Windows NT authentication only (equivalent to "integrated" security on SQL Server 6.x)

Logins

SQL Server has two kinds of logins, as shown in Figure 9-4.

Server

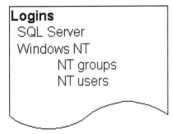

Logins
SQL Server
Windows NT
     NT groups
     NT users

Databases

FIGURE 9-4

There are two kinds of logins: SQL Server and Windows NT.

SQL Server comes preinstalled with one SQL Server login, sa, short for system administrator. The sa login automatically has administrative rights over the entire SQL Server and its databases. No other SQL Server login has those rights, however.

Every SQL Server login requires a password. In the case of sa, it is initially set to blank (no password at all). Of course, it's a good idea to give sa a password immediately after installing a server.

SQL Server will also allow you to add Windows NT users and groups (both local and global groups) into SQL Server as logins. By themselves, Windows NT users and groups do not normally have any authentication rights to SQL Server. The server's system administrator has to explicitly identify those NT users and groups within SQL Server to give them authentication and thus the ability to log in. However, NT users and groups do not require passwords. Instead, SQL Server relies on Windows NT's password validation.

Creating a New Login

To add a new login, you can use the Create Login Wizard or use the Login Properties dialog box, both from Enterprise Manager. Because the wizard just takes a subset of all the choices of the dialog box and segments them into a sequence of steps, if you understand the Login Properties dialog box, it's easy to see what the wizard is requesting.

You reach the Login Properties dialog box for a new login by selecting the Login node of a server in the Enterprise Manager left pane, and then right-clicking and selecting New Login from the pop-up menu. (You can also select New Login from the Enterprise Manager Action menu.) The result is the dialog box in Figure 9-5.

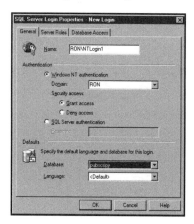

FIGURE 9-5

The Login Properties dialog box for a new login

In this figure, the dialog box shows both the Windows NT and SQL Server authentication modes available for this new login, because the server has been configured for both modes. The first choice you should make here is to decide which authentication mode the new login should have, if you're allowing both.

If you work with Windows NT authentication, you can choose the NT user or group domain from the Domain: pull-down list. You can then grant or deny access to the server for that login. After you choose a domain, the dialog box will prepend the domain name to the login name that you type.

You can also specify the default database and default language for the new login. The default database will be the database to which the login will have its context set when it first logs into this server. The default language is the language for error messages.

Changing the sa Password

One of the first things you should do when you install a new instance of SQL Server is change the sa password. Don't leave it blank! However, if you use Enterprise

Manager to change it and you register the server in Enterprise Manager using the sa password, your connection will no longer work. You will need to edit the server registration by going to the Edit SQL Server Registration dialog box, which you can find by selecting the server name in Enterprise Manager, and right-clicking or choosing the Action menu. Put the new sa password in, and your connection will be registered with the new sa password.

If you've forgotten an sa password, there's no way to retrieve it. If you've registered the server in Enterprise Manager, the sa password is stored in the registry, under

```
HKEY_CURRENT_USER\Software\Microsoft\MSSQLServer\SQLEW\Registered Servers X\SQL
Server
```

where the password is encrypted.

To get around this problem, you can reset the sa password in the Login Properties dialog box, and then enter the new password in the Edit SQL Server Registration dialog box.

NOTE

If you rebuild a SQL Server, or apply a SQL Server service pack, the sa password will remain unchanged. But if you uninstall and reinstall SQL Server, the sa password will revert to the default blank value.

Server Roles

If you want to grant this login the ability to manage the server, you can use the Server Roles tab of the Login Properties dialog box, shown in Figure 9-6.

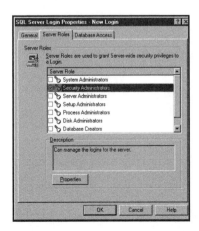

FIGURE 9-6

You can grant the login server administration capability using the Server Roles tab.

In prior releases of SQL Server, you would have to log into SQL Server as sa in order to do any kind of maintenance activity. With SQL Server 7, the sa functionality has been subdivided into a set of server roles. These server roles stand between the logins and the server, as shown in Figure 9-7.

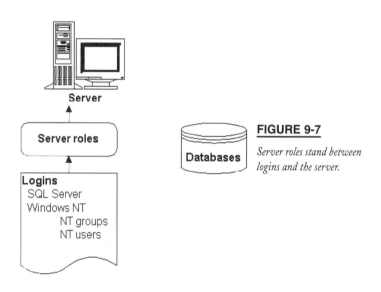

FIGURE 9-7

Server roles stand between logins and the server.

The server roles provided for SQL Server logins are:

sysadmin	All system administrative functions
serveradmin	Administer server configurations
setupadmin	Administer replication and extended stored procedures
securityadmin	Administer security
processadmin	Administer processes
dbcreator	Create, alter, and rename databases
diskadmin	Administer disk files

The sysadmin server role is equivalent to the sa login; in fact, the sa login is automatically given the sysadmin server role and cannot be removed from it.

NOTE

In prior versions of SQL Server, it was always possible to drop the sa login. In SQL Server 7, it is not possible to drop the sa login.

The number and nature of the server roles is fixed. You cannot add or modify their properties. However, you can get a good idea of what each role can do in the server by right-clicking over the role's name in Enterprise Manager and looking at the Permissions tab of the server role's Properties dialog box. Figure 9-8, for example, shows the permissions for the dbcreator server role.

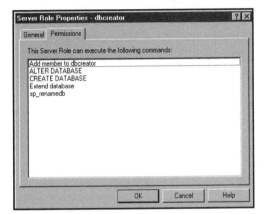

FIGURE 9-8

Each server role's Properties dialog box contains a list of the permissions for that role.

The addition of server roles makes it possible to delegate server administrative tasks to other logins and keep the number of people who must use the sa login or the sysadmin role to a minimum.

WARNING

The Administrators group of the server computer automatically has a login into the server and belongs to the sysadmin server role. So if an NT user belongs to the Administrators group of the local machine, that user can immediately log into the SQL Server and has sysadmin (and therefore sa) privileges. You can deny access to the BUILTIN\Administrators group to deny such users access to the server.

Security across Linked Servers

Login security is required for linked servers. When two or more SQL Servers are linked, the SQL Server login at one server can have permissions assigned on the linked server. In addition, the NT login of one server can delegate its security account to the linked server. For information about security across linked servers, see Chapter 23, "Distributed Data."

Database Access

Before you look at the Database Access tab, let's look in more detail at how SQL Server security works inside each database.

SQL Server data is contained in databases. Just connecting to SQL Server will not by itself allow access to the server's data. Consequently, there must be some means of mapping authenticated logins to data in databases. The way SQL Server accomplishes this is by three components inside a database: database objects, database users, and database roles, as shown in Figure 9-9.

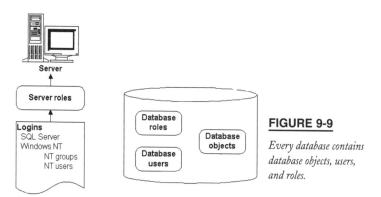

FIGURE 9-9

Every database contains database objects, users, and roles.

The database objects are the tables, indexes, triggers, defaults, constraints, rules, views, and stored procedures in the database. Database users are the names of the owners and users of the database objects. Database roles are groupings of users. Both database users and roles can be granted and denied permissions to the database objects.

Every database object is owned by exactly one database user. The only way you can access a database object is by either being the object's owner or having access to the object granted to you by the object's owner.

Every database has at least one database user, the dbo. The dbo owns all the system tables in a database, as well as all objects created by the sa login or sysadmin role.

NOTE

When you log in as sa or have a login that gives you the sysadmin role, you can automatically see all the objects in a database that are owned by dbo. These include all the system databases such as master, msdb, model, and tempdb, as well as the entire pubs database. Then all objects you create under such logins become owned by dbo.

Mapping a Login to a Database User

A SQL Server login gains access to a database object by having a login that maps to a database user, as shown in Figure 9-10.

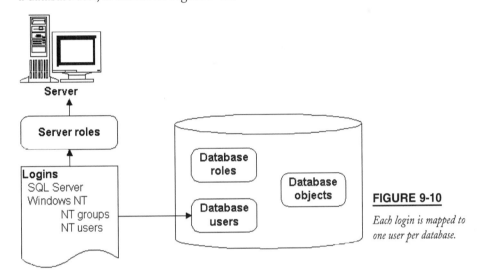

FIGURE 9-10

Each login is mapped to one user per database.

The sa login, NT user logins that are part of the local Administrators group, and any logins with sysadmin server roles are all automatically mapped to the dbo users in every database. Every other login must either be explicitly mapped to a database user to gain access to a database or implicitly mapped to the guest user or public role. You'll learn more about guest and public in the next sections.

NOTE

The key concept here is that without the mapping of a login to a database user, no login can access a database's data. You can map a login to only one database user per database, but you can map that login to more than one database at a time.

Database Users

Every database has at least one database user, namely the database owner, or dbo. The dbo owns all the system tables in the database, and every sa login or any NT login with the sysadmin server role automatically becomes the dbo in the database.

An optional database user is assigned the keyword guest. If you add a database user with that name to the database, then all logins that are not already mapped to some other user in the database become implicitly mapped to the guest database user. You can use the guest database user to establish a minimal public sort of access to a database. (There's another way to establish public access, and that is with the public database role.)

You can create a new database user by selecting the Database Users node of a database in Enterprise Manager, right-clicking, and choosing New Database User from the pop-up menu or the Action menu, as shown in Figure 9-11.

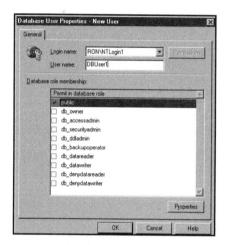

FIGURE 9-11

You can create a new database user in the Database User Properties dialog box.

In this dialog box, you must supply both the login id for this database user and the database user name. The Transact-SQL way of doing this is:

```
EXEC sp_grantdbaccess 'RON\NTLogin1', 'DBUser1'
```

Every database user can be given a set of permissions to the database objects. The dbo starts out automatically with all permissions, but you must explicitly set all permissions for other database users. However, you can take a shortcut by making your users members of one or more database roles.

Database Roles

Database roles are ways of grouping users together so that they inherit the permissions of the roles, so that you do not have to explicitly grant permissions for each database user.

There are three kinds of database roles:

Fixed standard Server	Subdivisions of dbo rights supplied by SQL Server
Custom standard	Roles created by the database administrator
Application	Roles for applications that bypass database users

The first set is the fixed standard database roles provided by SQL Server. Fixed by SQL Server, it cannot be changed. Similar to server roles, it subdivides the roles of the dbo. So, for example, the top fixed database role, db_owner, corresponds to the dbo database user rights. The following list shows this and the other fixed database roles:

db_owner	All dbo rights
db_accessadmin	Administer users, NT groups, and NT users
db_datareader	Read access to all data in the database
db_datawriter	Write access to all data in the database
db_ddladmin	Create, alter, and drop rights to all database objects
db_securityadmin	Manage roles, role membership, and permissions
db_backupoperator	Manage backups and restore
db_denydatareader	Cannot read data, but can make schema changes
db_denydatawriter	Cannot change any data in the database

The database user, dbo, is automatically a member of the db_owner role. You cannot add new fixed database roles.

With custom standard database roles, you define your own database roles and then grant permissions to each role. All permissions granted to these roles are inherited by their members, unless explicitly denied.

You can add your own custom database role by selecting Database Roles in the Enterprise Manager's left pane and choosing New Database Role from the pop-up menu that results from right-clicking, or from the Action menu. You can see the resulting dialog box in Figure 9-12.

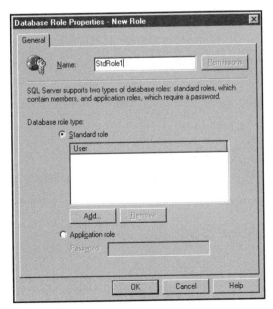

FIGURE 9-12

You can make a new custom database role or a new application role in the Database Role Properties dialog box.

At this point, simply choose a standard (custom) role, or an application role. The Transact-SQL for creating a new standard role is:

```
EXEC sp_addrole 'StdRole1'
```

For a standard role, you can add users to the role by clicking on the Add button, which results in the dialog box you see in Figure 9-13.

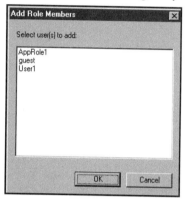

FIGURE 9-13

You can add users to a role with the Add Role Members dialog box.

To do the same thing with Transact-SQL, just issue:

```
EXEC sp_addrolemember 'StdRole1', 'User1'
```

Application roles are a special kind of role that can be used to switch the permissions that a login would normally have, based on a password sent to the sp_setapprole stored procedure. In this way, someone running an application could get permissions to database objects that they would never get using their own login.

You can add application roles using the same dialog box shown in Figure 9-11, but you must add a password that the stored procedure sp_setapprole will use.

In Transact-SQL, add an application role called AppRole1 with a password of '123' by issuing:

```
EXEC sp_addapprole 'AppRole1', '123'
```

Then for an application to use the database application role, it can issue:

```
EXEC sp_setapprole 'AppRole1', '123'
```

To drop an application role, you can use:

```
EXEC sp_dropapprole 'AppRole1'
```

To see why application roles can be useful, you might have a situation where users run an application against a database using Windows NT authentication. If the users log in without the application, you might deny them access to the database objects. However, when they run the application, the application can assume the application role that does give access to the database objects. The switch from the NT user's set of permissions to the application role permissions is done when the application executes the `sp_setapprole` stored procedure. What's significant is that the application can use the application role to gain new security without logging off and logging into SQL Server.

The Database Access Tab

You can use the final Database Access tab in the Login Properties dialog box to decide what databases this login can access, and what database user this login will be mapped to, as shown in Figure 9-14.

FIGURE 9-14

You grant a login the ability to access a database in the Database Access tab of the Login Properties dialog box.

Notice in the dialog box just shown that by granting access to the pubscopy database for the NT login `'DBUser1,'` SQL Server lists the database user as `'DBUser1,'` a database user that does not yet exist. The dialog box defaults to creating a user to match the NT login, or a SQL Server login, if there is no user with that name yet in the database. You can change the value to another user, including the dbo user. In addition, the dialog box defaults to permitting the new login the public database role. This dialog box permits you to assign as many database roles to a user that you like.

You can use the `sp_grantdbaccess` stored procedure to grant access and assign a default database user for the new login:

```
EXEC sp_grantdbaccess 'RON\NTLogin1', 'DBUser1'
```

To permit the new login to have a particular database role, use the `sp_addrolemember` stored procedure to add the database user to the role:

```
EXEC sp_addrolemember 'public', 'DBUser1'
```

Transact-SQL Summary

Here is a summary of the Transact-SQL commands that will reproduce the steps just described.

NT Login

To add the login 'DBUser1,' which is an NT user, on the domain 'RON,' you can use the sp_grantlogin stored procedure:

```
EXEC sp_grantlogin 'RON\NTLogin1'
```

To set its default database to pubscopy, use the sp_defaultdb stored procedure:

```
EXEC sp_defaultdb 'RON\NTLogin1', 'pubscopy'
```

To add it to a server role, for example the securityadmin role, use sp_addsrvrolemember:

```
EXEC sp_addsrvrolemember 'RON\NTLogin1', 'securityadmin'
```

To grant it database access to the current database, use sp_grantdbaccess:

```
USE pubscopy
EXEC sp_grantdbaccess 'RON\NTLogin1', 'DBUser1'
```

To add it to a particular database role, use sp_addrolemember:

```
EXEC sp_addrolemember 'public', 'DBUser1'
```

SQL Server Login

To add a new login using Transact-SQL, you must use a series of stored procedures. To add the login 'DBUser1,' which is an NT user, on the domain 'RON,' you can use the sp_addlogin stored procedure:

```
EXEC sp_addlogin 'SQLLogin1'
```

To set its default database to pubscopy, use the sp_defaultdb stored procedure:

```
EXEC sp_defaultdb 'SQLLogin1', 'pubscopy'
```

To add it to a server role, for example the securityadmin role, use sp_addsrvrolemember:

```
EXEC sp_addsrvrolemember 'SQLLogin1', securityadmin
```

To grant it database access to a particular database, use sp_grantdbaccess:

```
USE pubscopy
```

```
EXEC sp_grantdbaccess 'SQLLogin1', 'SQLUser1'
```

To add it to a particular database role, use `sp_addrolemember`:

```
EXEC sp_addrolemember 'public', 'SQLUser1'
```

Permissions

After a database has database users and roles, you can grant permissions to database objects through them. The upshot is that a login gains its access to database objects through database users and roles, as you can in Figure 9-15.

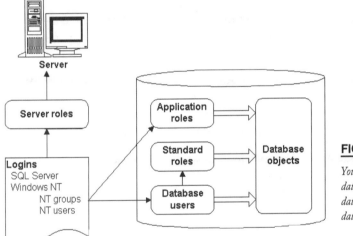

FIGURE 9-15

You can set permissions to database objects for both database users and database roles.

Every object in a database has an owner, and an object owner is always a database user. Database objects include tables, views, and stored procedures, most notably. Normally the creator of the object is its owner, and the owner of an object can grant and deny permissions to the object.

NOTE

The full name of every database object includes the database name, the owner name (a database user), and the object name. For example, in the pubscopy database, the full name of the authors table is pubscopy.dbo.authors, indicating the database name, the owner name, and then the table name. Consequently, two different users can each create a table or object with the same name in a single database, provided the user names are different. So, for example, you could have both pubscopy.user1.authors and pubscopy.user2.authors. However, no database user can create two objects with the same full name, because in that case the object owner names would be the same.

Assigning Permissions

Any login with the sysadmin or securityadmin server roles (therefore including the sa login) can assign permissions to database users and roles. Permissions are assigned with the GRANT, REVOKE, and DENY commands, and the content of the permission is chosen in the body of the command.

GRANT, REVOKE, **and** DENY

The three major permissions commands are GRANT, REVOKE, and DENY, and they can be applied to a database user or a database role on two levels—the database level or the object level.

When you GRANT a permission, it applies to the database user or role in question. If the role has the GRANT permission, and the permission is not otherwise denied, every database user will inherit the GRANT permission from the role.

When you REVOKE a permission, it removes the prior GRANT permission, if there was one, but does not explicitly prevent a database user from inheriting a GRANT from a database role. So you can REVOKE a permission from a database user, but if the user belongs to a database role that has a GRANT, the user will still have the permission.

The DENY action takes precedence over the GRANT action. When you DENY a permission to a database user or role, the permission is explicitly removed. Further, the DENY status overrides all other GRANT permissions in the various roles to which a database user may belong.

> **NOTE**
>
> The DENY command is new with SQL Server 7.0. Despite the fact that it is a Transact-SQL command only, and not part of the ANSI SQL-92 standard, it is a valuable addition.

Database Permissions

At the higher level, permission to a data definition statement such as CREATE or ALTER TABLE can be granted, revoked, or denied. This level corresponds to the action of assigning fixed database roles to a user. You can grant all of the following CREATE or BACKUP statements, or a subset of them, to a user or role:

CREATE

DATABASE

DEFAULT

```
            PROCEDURE

            RULE

            TABLE

            VIEW

    BACKUP

            DATABASE

            LOG
```

To grant user DBUser1 the rights to create a table, just issue:

```
GRANT CREATE TABLE TO DBUser1
```

in the current database. Alternatively, you can just make DBUser1 a member of the db_owner or db_ddladmin database role, and the database user could do the same thing. Finally, you could grant CREATE TABLE to a standard database role, and make DBUser1 a member of it, and also have the same effect.

You can set permissions for database users at the database level in Enterprise Manager in the Database User Properties dialog box, in its opening tab, as you can see in Figure 9-16.

FIGURE 9-16

You can set permissions at the database level using the Database User Properties dialog box.

You can assign database-wide permissions to a database role by using the Transact-SQL GRANT statement.

Object-Level Permissions

You can also grant permissions at the database object level. The kinds of permissions you can grant are:

```
Table or view    SELECT, INSERT, UPDATE, and DELETE

Stored procedure  EXECUTE
```

You can use the Properties dialog box of either the database user or database role in question to set the permissions, as you can see in Figure 9-17.

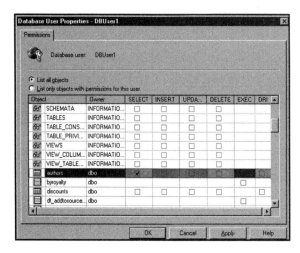

FIGURE 9-17

You can set object-level permissions in the database user or database role Permissions dialogs.

Note that the dialog box distinguishes between tables and views on the one hand, and stored procedures on the other. Stored procedures, such as byroyalty in Figure 9-17, only have EXECUTE permission; tables and views have SELECT, INSERT, UPDATE, and DELETE permissions; and tables have the DRI option (see the discussion of REFERENCES that follows.)

Using Transact-SQL, to grant DBUser1 the ability to SELECT against the Authors table, just issue:

```
GRANT SELECT ON Authors TO DBUser1
```

To allow DBUser1 to grant others the ability to also SELECT from the table, issue:

```
GRANT SELECT ON Authors TO DBUser1 WITH GRANT OPTION
```

instead.

These two commands grant SELECT capability for the entire table. It is possible to grant SELECT or UPDATE capability for just a set of columns, using

```
GRANT SELECT (au_id, au_lname, au_fname) ON Authors TO DBUser1
```

INSERT and DELETE statements apply to the entire table, so only SELECT and UPDATE permissions can be restricted to a subset of the table's columns.

There is a further twist to granting INSERT and UPDATE permissions to a table, if the table has one or more foreign keys. If those keys point to referenced tables from which the database user or role lacks SELECT permission, then you also have to grant REFERENCES permission to the user. For example, if you grant UPDATE permission to the DBUser1 database user on the pubscopy Titles table,

```
GRANT UPDATE ON Titles TO DBUser1
```

and if DBUser1 lacks SELECT permission on the Publishers table, then the INSERT and UPDATE statements will fail, because the foreign key reference cannot be validated. However, if you go one step further,

```
GRANT REFERENCES ON Titles TO DBUser1
```

now DBUser1 can INSERT and UPDATE the table, even though the database user lacks SELECT permission on the Publishers table. (This corresponds to the DRI column in the Database User Properties Permissions dialog box.)

Finally, when a database user belongs to many roles, and those roles conflict, you can specify what role a database user should be inheriting a permission from with the AS expression. For example, DBUser1 may want to extend SELECT on the Titles table to DBUser2, and use the StdRole1 to do it:

```
GRANT SELECT ON Titles TO DBUser1 AS StdRole1
```

NOTE

Remember that in the case of conflicts among role permissions, the DENY action takes precedence over GRANT.

Security Functions

A full set of security functions exist to find out the login name, user name, and role memberships for each login. As you'll see in the following examples, these security functions enable you to restrict what portions of database data a given login can have access to.

The more useful security functions are:

is_member()	Returns whether a login is a member of a certain database role.
is_srvrolemember	Returns whether a login is a member of a certain server role.
suser_sid	Returns the security id of a login or current connection.

`suser_sname`	Returns the login name of a login or current connection.
`user`	Returns the database user name.

You can use these functions to add a further level of security. Although you can restrict SELECT and UPDATE privileges to certain columns using the GRANT option, it does not allow you to restrict the rows selected. But with these functions, you can.

Suppose you want to allow all authors to only select the rows from the Authors table that belong to them. In other words, the author Marjorie Green should only be able to see her books, and no others, from the Authors table. To do this, if you set her login id to match some values in the data, you can use these security functions to limit the rows she sees to just hers.

For example, suppose all authors have as their NT logins the first initial of their first name, plus the last name, so that Marjorie Green's NT login is MGreen. Then the following view will restrict what she sees:

```
CREATE VIEW dbo.v_authors

AS

SELECT *

FROM authors

WHERE 'RON\'+SUBSTRING(au_fname,1,1) + LTRIM(au_lname) = LTRIM(suser_sname())
```

Here the security function `suser_sname()` returns the login "RON\MGreen," thereby restricting the rows that are returned. A login with no matching first and last name in the table will not see any rows at all. If the authors are on various domains, it may be necessary to create a view for each domain.

So to restrict the Authors table so that authors can see only their own data, you would DENY access to the Authors table, but GRANT access to the view, for those authors. You can also use the user name and the USER function to get the same effect.

Summary

The SQL Server 7 security system can seem complex at first, but becomes intuitive when you understand that every login for SQL Server must map to some database user. Then permissions are assigned to the database users, or to the database roles that they play. SQL Server 7 also lets you subdivide the sa login into several server roles, the dbo database user into several database roles, and adds DENY to the list of commands that you can use to set permissions.

Chapter 10

Importing and
Exporting Data

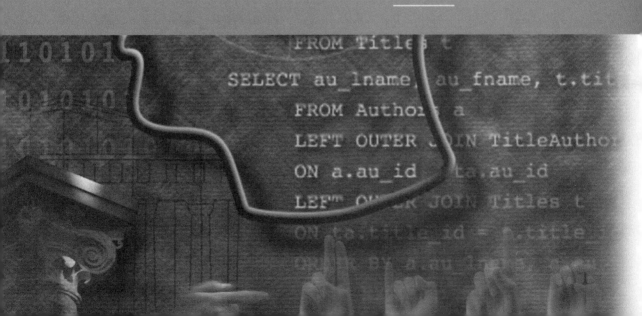

In This Chapter

- ◆ Data Transformation Services (DTS)
- ◆ The DTS Import and Export Wizards
- ◆ The DTS Package Designer
- ◆ The Bulk Copy Utility
- ◆ The BULK INSERT command

SQL Server 7.0 gives you several new tools for importing and exporting data. Most noteworthy is the Data Transformation Services utility, DTS, which allows you to add highly customized transformations to data that you pump from one data source to another. SQL Server 7.0 enhances the traditional SQL Server import/export BCP utility (short for Bulk Copy Program) and improves its performance. SQL Server 7.0 also adds a new way to import BCP-formatted data from Transact-SQL in the BULK INSERT command. In this chapter, you'll take a look at each of these methods, starting with DTS.

Data Transformation Services (DTS)

The Data Transformation Services utility copies data from one data source to another. It is primarily aimed at the process of transforming the data during the copying process. This is a common task in data warehousing applications, where data must often be staged, cleansed, and transformed before it can be added to the central data store.

DTS supports a very flexible configuration. It can copy and transform data from any OLE DB or ODBC data source to another. It is not restricted to having SQL Server at either end of the process. In addition, it comes with its own drivers for text data.

> **NOTE**
>
> Because the focus of DTS is on transforming data from a wide variety of data sources, it only copies tables and their (possibly transformed) data. It does not copy database objects such as triggers, stored procedures, rules, defaults, constraints, and user-defined data types. For copying an entire database, either a restore from a backup or the Database Transfer Utility are more appropriate tools.

DTS has a native interface in Enterprise Manager, taking up one of the nodes of the Enterprise Manager for each server. It also can be invoked externally, either as an executable, or through its object model, as you'll see later in this chapter.

DTS Concepts

To use DTS, you build a DTS package. Each DTS package contains information about your source and destination data sources and the data to transfer. In addition, the package defines the transformations of the data as a set of tasks, called steps. You can store DTS packages in three different formats:

1. In the msdb database in the native DTS format
2. In the msdb database's Microsoft Repository as a repository object
3 As a COM-structured external disk file

When you use the third method, you can run the transformation independently of SQL Server, using the dtrun.exe utility, as you'll see later in this chapter. When you execute a package, the underlying DTS data pump is used to copy and transform the data, as shown in Figure 10-1.

FIGURE 10-1

The DTS process consists of the DTS package, which defines the steps for the data transformation to take.

The steps of a DTS process can execute queries and transform data using VBScript and/or JavaScript. In addition, any one of the steps can call an external executable. With all these tools and a relatively unlimited number of steps available, you can encapsulate some very sophisticated data transfer operations in a DTS package.

The DTS Import and Export Wizards

The best place to start DTS is through the DTS Import Wizard and Export Wizard. These two wizards are not mere wrappers around a properties dialog box. Rather, they provide a very useful way to build a sophisticated DTS package. They can be used to quickly create a relatively simple package, or to jump-start a more sophisticated set of transformations.

Data Source

The only difference between the DTS Import and Export Wizards lies in their opening dialog boxes. Once you're past that, you specify a source for your data and a destination. The source dialog box is shown in Figure 10-2.

→ import "Table 1" from Access → SQL

For importing. open the destination db then choose
① Tools/ Data Transformation Services / Import Data
② Source: Microsoft Access, find the file name. next
③ Destination: Microsoft OLEDB Provider for SQL Serv
click the right db name, next next.
④ choose the table. run, next. finish

FIGURE 10-2

*You first specify a data
source in the DTS Wizards.*

No matter whether you choose the Import or Export Wizard, each one asks you to specify the data source location first. Under the Source: list control, you can see quite a large number of possible data source types, ranging from the SQL Server 7.0 OLE DB provider, through Oracle, various desktop databases, and text. Be sure to specify the particular database in the Database: control down below.

Advanced OLE DB Data Source Configuration

The Advanced button brings up a dialog box that allows you to configure the OLE DB data source, as shown in Figure 10-3.

FIGURE 10-3

*You can configure OLE DB
data sources in the Advanced
Properties dialog box.*

This dialog box lets you customize your OLE DB connection. The options change depending upon the OLE DB provider in question.

Destination

After you've chosen the data source OLE DB provider and database, you next make the same choices for the destination of the DTS transfer. The destination dialog box exactly corresponds to the data source dialog box, as you can see in Figure 10-4.

*To export Demographics table from Location db, SQL
to Access. Similar process as import. Just be sure
a file name as the destination. (eg. Table1. mdb) — Not*

FIGURE 10-4   *create a new file name! Then the*

The Destination dialog box   *new table will be within the same*
exactly corresponds to the   *db as Table 1*
Data Source dialog box.

Again, you can customize the OLE DB parameters through the Advanced tab.

Copy, Query, or Transfer

The next dialog box asks you to decide whether to copy data directly from the data source, create a query that will build the data from the data source, or transfer the data, as shown in Figure 10-5.

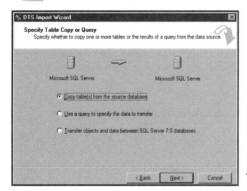

FIGURE 10-5

You next decide whether to build the initial source data from a simple copy, a query, or a transfer.

Tables

If you choose a copy, you then can decide which tables in the database to copy, as shown in Figure 10-6.

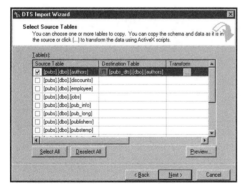

FIGURE 10-6

You can choose from all the tables in the database, but not the views.

The dialog box lists all the user tables in the database, but it excludes views and system tables from the list.

WARNING

If you choose a SQL Server data source to copy, only tables can be chosen, not views. If you want to copy from a view, choose to import from a query instead.

Notice that after you choose a table in the list, the dialog box places an assumed table (of the same name) in the Destination Table column and enables a button in the Transform column. You can change the table to any other table in the destination database.

NOTE

Each table you choose in the Select Source Tables dialog box becomes a distinct transformation step if you save the Wizard's work as a package.

Customizing the Transformation of Table Data

The Transform button leads to a dialog box that lets you customize the table copy process, as shown in Figure 10-7.

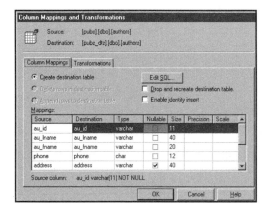

FIGURE 10-7

You can customize a transformation using the Transformations tab of the Column Mappings and Transformations dialog box.

In the Column Mappings and Transformations dialog box, you can specify whether to create the destination table, delete all the current rows in the destination table before copying the source data into it, or appending rows onto the destination table. In addition, you can change the particular mappings of source column to destination column.

The data type, nullability, size, precision, and scale columns refer to the destination table. If you're creating a new table, you can redefine the data here.

WARNING

If your destination table does not allow NULL in a given column but your source table contains some NULLs in the data for that column, you'll have to use the Transformations tab to catch them in a script.

The Transformations Scripting Tab

You can expand on the kinds of transformations you can apply to the data using the Transformations tab, as shown in Figure 10-8.

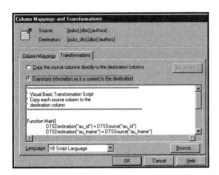

FIGURE 10-8

The Transformations tab has further customization options.

The default option is to simply copy the data from source to destination. You can script the transformation by choosing the "Transform information" option button, resulting in a VBScript or JavaScript editing window. Figure 10-9 shows the VBScript window with a script customized to remove the NULLs from the state column in the publishers table and replace them with a space.

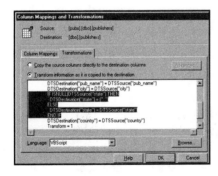

FIGURE 10-9

The VBScript window shows an example of a customized transformation.

The script replaces:

```
DTSDestination("state") = DTSSource("state")
```

with:

```
IF ISNULL(DTSSource("state") THEN

        DTSDestination("state") = ("   ")
ELSE

        DTSDestination("state") = DTSSource("state")
END IF
```

In the Wizard window, you must remember that the ISNULL function is a valid VBScript function. As you'll see later, the DTS Designer has a VBScript window that lists all the valid functions while you're building the script.

Advanced Transformation

If you do not choose to write a script, you can click on the Advanced button to bring up a last set of transformation options that you can choose, as shown in Figure 10-10.

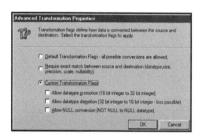

FIGURE 10-10

The Advanced Transformation Properties dialog box contains a final set of transformation options.

The default choice is the first option button. The second button will require exact matches of column properties between source and destination tables. The third option allows you to set custom transformation flags relating to changing actual data values. You can allow promotion and demotion of 16-bit integers to 32-bit integers. However, the demotion can possibly lose data, as it loses precision.

The last option is quite interesting. With it, you can allow a conversion of a value in a source column that does not allow NULL to a NULL in the destination column, when it does allow NULL.

WARNING

The last Advanced option would suggest that it might change a NULL in the source data to some other value (perhaps a default value, or spaces) in the destination column. However, the option does not allow that. Instead, it does the reverse: it will allow a value in the source data to become NULL in the destination column.

Using a Query

If you chose to use a query rather than copy a table in the second step of the wizard, you can specify a configuration that does not match the table set. In that case, a blank query dialog box will come up, as you can see in Figure 10-11.

FIGURE 10-11

You can insert a valid SQL query into the Query dialog box.

In the figure, you can see a Transact-SQL statement that does not match any single table or set of tables in the source database. Here is where you can put in the SQL statement that would define a view, for example, if you wanted to export from a view.

You can use the Browse button to find a SQL query stored as a text file, and you can also use the query builder to make a very simple query. Figure 10-12, for example, shows how you could get the same set of columns for a query using the query builder.

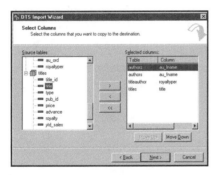

FIGURE 10-12

The DTS query builder can build a limited SQL SELECT *statement.*

You can then specify the sort order in the next dialog box, and then you can add qualifications to the WHERE clause, as you can see in Figure 10-13.

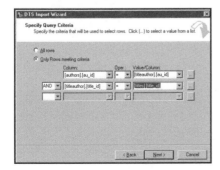

FIGURE 10-13

You can add join conditions in the last part of the DTS query builder.

In order to make the query use inner or outer joins, you'll have to use the equality operator rather than the SQL JOIN syntax.

The buttons to the right of each line allow you to choose a distinct value for the initial column listed. Note that there is a maximum number of conditions that the query builder can allow. The resulting choices are shown in Figure 10-14.

FIGURE 10-14

The result of the query builder is a standard SQL SELECT statement.

You could then customize the result and change the simple equi-joins to match the SQL JOIN syntax. Even though there is no means of saving the query, you can save it with the package at the end of the Wizard.

After the query is built, the next statement takes you to the same Select Source Tables dialog box that you saw previously when just copying tables. Now you can customize the transformation, map the query to a different table, and so on, just as you saw previously with the tables.

Transfer

You can also transfer an entire database's data, with objects and security, from one database to another. This option is the equivalent of the Transfer utility in SQL Server 6.5. There are quite a number of options to decide when doing it, as you see when you reach the very next dialog box after choosing the transfer option in the Wizard, as shown in Figure 10-15.

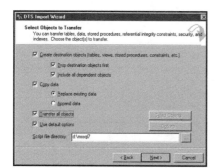

FIGURE 10-15

When transferring a database, you have the option of selecting fewer than all the objects.

The first set of options concerns whether to create the destination objects, and if so, whether to drop them on the destination first, or fail otherwise. A second set of options concerns the data: You can just copy the schema and leave the data behind, or append data to the destination objects.

The last two options concern object selection and various defaults. If you uncheck the "Transfer all objects" check box and click on the Select Objects button, you'll get a dialog box to change your object selection, as shown in Figure 10-16.

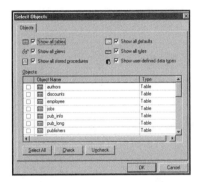

FIGURE 10-16

You can select just a subset of the objects.

The list will show all the objects in the database. The default is to copy them all, but you can select a subset when you enter this dialog box. You can also change various default settings by unchecking the "Use default options" check box and clicking on the Options button. You'll see the dialog box shown in Figure 10-17.

FIGURE 10-17

You can select just a subset of the objects.

With this dialog box, you can change security and table options. You might not want to transfer security options, if your sole concern is with data. Also, if you're adding to existing tables, there may be no need to bring over indexes and other table features. Finally, you can change the default that have DTS use quoted identifiers when making the transfer. There's no harm here, and it's required to use quoted identifiers if any of the tables or columns contain spaces or special characters.

Save, Schedule, or Replicate

For both the table and query options, your next choice is how to run the DTS package, as shown in Figure 10-18.

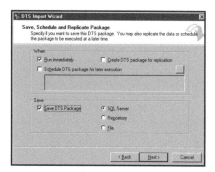

FIGURE 10-18

You have a number of ways to run and save a DTS package.

Run Immediately will run the current package right after the Wizard ends but will not save your work.

Create Replication Publication will create a publication on the source server to replicate the same data, rather than run it as a DTS package. This allows you to use the DTS Wizard as a method of building replication articles.

If you Save the Package on SQL Server, the package will be stored in the msdb database as a package or in the respository, or you can save the package externally as a file.

You can also schedule the package. If you check this option, you can go ahead and click on the button to the right and bring up a scheduling dialog box, as shown in Figure 10-19.

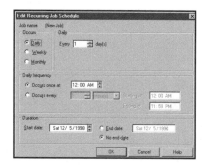

FIGURE 10-19

You can schedule a DTS package using the DTS Edit Recurring Job Schedule dialog box.

Saving a DTS Package from the Wizards

If you choose to save a DTS package, you'll be presented with the dialog box shown in Figure 10-20.

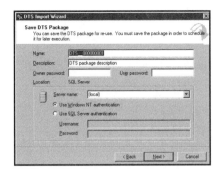

FIGURE 10-20

The initial save dialog box lets you put a password on your DTS package.

In this dialog box, you choose a name, description, and password for the DTS package. You then specify a SQL Server in which to save the package. Note that you can specify an owner password, required to edit the package, as well as a user password, to run the package.

Running the DTS Package

When you run the DTS package later, or choose to Run Immediately from the wizards, you'll see a dialog box that tracks the progress of the steps in the DTS package, as shown in Figure 10-21.

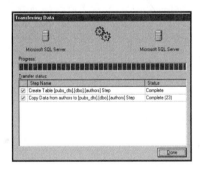

FIGURE 10-21

Running a DTS package produces a dialog box that tracks the progress of each step.

Running the Wizards Externally

You can also run the DTS Import and Export utilities externally, from a Windows NT command prompt, or from the Windows NT Run menu. What you use is called the dtswiz utility, and it is separately documented in the Books Online. To run the import wizard locally, you could just issue:

```
dtswiz
```

followed by the set of options:

/i or /x	For import or export (optional)
/s<servername>	The server name (optional)

/u<SQL Login>	SQL Server login (if using SQL Server authentication)
/p<password>	Password (if using SQL Server authentication)
/d<database>	Database on the server (optional)
/r<provider name>	Name of the OLEDB provider (optional)
/y	Flag to hide the SQL Server system databases
/n	Trusted connection (optional)

So, for example, to match the choices you made in your example Wizard import, you could issue:

```
dtswiz /i
```

using a trusted connection, or:

```
dtswiz /i /SRON /Usa /P123
```

using a SQL Server login.

NOTE

You can run the DTS Wizard without specifying Import or Export, as in

```
dtswiz
```

You'll get a Wizard dialog box that does not specify either Import or Export.

The DTS Package Designer

You can also use the DTS Package Designer to further refine the packages you've built using the DTS Import and Export Wizards, or you can use the Designer to build a new package from scratch.

Refining a Wizard Package

If you start with one of the DTS Wizards and save the package on SQL Server, you can go to the Data Transformation Packages node in Enterprise Manager and find either Local or Repository Packages. Both are stored in the server's msdb database. You can open up a particular package by selecting the package in question, right-clicking on the package, and choosing Edit Package. For the query package you built earlier in this chapter, you can see the resulting dialog box in Figure 10-22.

* If you didn't save any package befor, there are 0 items in either Local or Repository Packages; rightclick either one, choose "New Package" you'll open the DTS Package Designer.

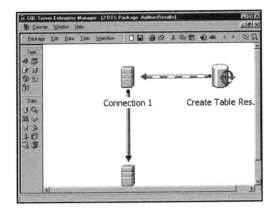

FIGURE 10-22

You can edit a saved DTS package using the Package Designer.

In this case, the Designer shows the query contributing to Connection 1, and the query results going to the Connection 2. At this point, you can revise each of the objects on the DTS Designer surface by right-clicking and choosing Properties.

To revise the query, for example, just edit the query properties. Another dialog box, one that contains the query, comes up, as shown in Figure 10-23.

FIGURE 10-23

You can reedit a query's properties in the DTS Designer.

This query builder is considerably more advanced than the Wizard version, allowing all valid SQL queries (including INSERT, UPDATE, and DELETE in addition to SELECT). In addition, you can test the query online and verify its results.

Creating a New Package

You can create a new DTS Designer package directly from Enterprise Manager by right-clicking over the Local Packages node and choosing New Package from the resulting menu. Or you can just clear the designer surface if you're already in it. You'll then be presented with a blank design surface with sets of icons above and on the left side of the surface, as you can see in Figure 10-24.

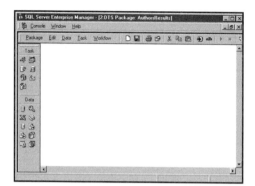

FIGURE 10-24

You have two significant toolsets of icons in the DTS Designer.

The toolset icons at the side indicate objects, while the menu and icons on the top let you select particular actions.

Creating Connections

To make a simple transformation, you can start by dragging out two SQL Server icons onto the surface. For each one, you'll get a familiar dialog box in which you define the connection, as shown in Figure 10-25.

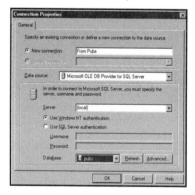

FIGURE 10-25

You can give your own name to the connection in the Connection Properties dialog box.

T IP

When the Connection Properties dialog box first comes up, type your own name into the New Connection text box, or else you'll have a very cryptic default name for the connection. If you want to change the name of the connection later, bring up the Properties dialog box and click on New Connection. You can then enter a more descriptive name.

Adding a Transformation Step

Once you've got the connection objects defined, you can select both and then click on the Transform icon (the gear with arrow icon) on the top toolbar, resulting in a transformation, as shown in Figure 10-26.

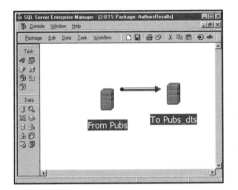

FIGURE 10-26

You can create a transformation by selecting the two connections and clicking on the arrow icon on the top toolbar.

WARNING

There is an important feature of Wizard-based packages that only shows up in the DTS Designer. If you make a transfer of several tables using a Wizard, each will be a distinct transformation in the Designer, each with its own set of connection objects. Because their names will be rather cryptic, you'll want to rename them.

Editing a Transformation

You can now edit the Transformation by right-clicking over it and choosing Properties. This dialog box repeats many of the things you saw previously in the DTS Wizards.

The resulting Properties dialog box has four tabs: the first tab defines the source table or query; the second defines the destination table columns; the third defines the mapping of the columns, and the last lets you set various advanced options. The third tab, transformations, allows you to map columns, as you can see in Figure 10-27.

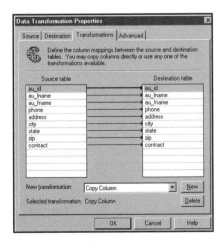

FIGURE 10-27

You can see the mapping of a transformation's columns in the Transformations tab of the Data Transformation Properties dialog box.

Unfortunately, a column-to-column mapping like the one in Figure 10-27 cannot be used with automation (scripting). To get automation, group all the mappings together by deleting the lines between the columns, and selecting all the table columns from both sides. Next, change the type of transformation from Copy Column to ActiveX script, as shown in Figure 10-28.

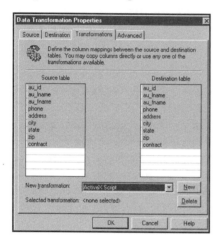

FIGURE 10-28

To get scripting, delete all the mappings, select all or a subset of the columns, and choose the ActiveX script transformation.

Now click on the New button, and you'll be presented with the VBScript editing dialog box shown in Figure 10-29.

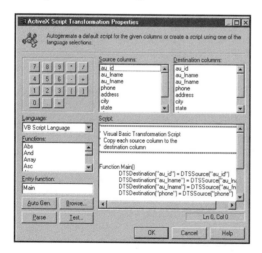

FIGURE 10-29

You can build a script using the DTS Designer VBScript editing utility.

Notice that this dialog box not only shows the source and destination columns but also provides a list of VBScript (and JavaScript and PerlScript) functions.

In addition to editing the VBScript for a transformation, you can also edit the flags for the transformation by right-clicking over the line connecting the two sides and choosing Flags. The resulting dialog box is shown in Figure 10-30.

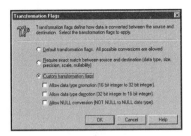

FIGURE 10-30

The Flags dialog box gives you some more control over the transformation.

These flags give you a number of advanced options that normally should not be required. For example, you can force the data types to match exactly between source and destination. This might be useful if you are concerned that mistakes might be made between numeric values—for instance, perhaps you would not want a decimal value from a text source truncated to an integer, because then the data loses its accuracy.

Data Lineage

When you save a DTS package to the Repository, you can keep track of changes you make to packages, as well as version your data rows, with the data lineage feature.

You can enable data lineage for a DTS package by checking the "Show lineage" option in the Advanced tab of the package's Properties dialog box. To Utilize this option, you must save the package to the repository, not to SQL Server or an external file.

After you've enabled data lineage, when you later change the package, versions will be stored in the repository. You can view past versions for any package by right-clicking over the package name and choosing Versions. You can also browse versions by selecting the Metadata node of DTS in the left pane of Enterprise Manager, selecting the Package option from the right pane, and drilling down into the package name below.

The BCP Utility

In addition to the Data Transformation Services, SQL Server 7.0 provides an enhanced version of the legacy SQL Server import/export utility, *BCP*, the *bulk copy program*. BCP imports and exports data between a SQL Server table or view and a text file. It runs as a command line utility and has no GUI interface. In past versions, it used DB-Library, but the version that comes with SQL Server 7 uses ODBC.

BCP as a Command Line Utility

The BCP utility copies data one table at a time from or to a database. You have the option of storing the external data in character format (as text, in delimited ASCII files) or in the native data type format. The character format is a true text format, easily read and edited by other applications; the native format can only be read by SQL Server. The native format has the advantage of slightly faster copying time.

To use BCP, the user must have SELECT permissions against the tables in question as well as the database's system tables. You use BCP by starting the NT command window (the MS-DOS box) and then changing to the appropriate subdirectory.

Because BCP is a command-line utility, it operates in a character, not a GUI, mode, and you add parameters to the command in order to make choices. The full syntax of the command is:

```
bcp <database.owner.table> <in | out | format> <text file> <flags>
```

The flags include:

Flag	Description
-S<server name>	The server name (optional if local)
-U<SQL login>	SQL Server login id
-P <password>	SQL Server password
-f<format file>	Format file (optional)
-b batch_size	
-n	Native format (optional)
-E	Keep identity values
-c	Character format (optional)
-t<field terminator>	Text file field terminator

Many more flags are available, but these should suffice for the most part.

WARNING

BCP is annoyingly case-sensitive. All the option letters in the preceding list must be in exactly the case you see them.

The remaining options allow you to override the defaults, giving you the ability to define your own row and column terminators, a range of rows, a particular format file and error file, and a maximum number of errors.

TIP

You can use either a dash (–) or a forward slash (/) to indicate a parameter for BCP. Sometimes a slash may look better because it matches the NT Command prompt utility standard:

*Start/ Programs/ Accessories/ Command Prompt.
② C:\> bcp pubs..authors out au_out.txt /c /P ✓   (output: Fig.10-32).
③ notepad. open, C:\
the file "au_out.txt is there.

IMPORTING AND EXPORTING DATA   *Chapter 10*   **275**

Bulk Copying Data Out from SQL Server

The example shown in Figure 10-31, uses the default behavior to copy out the authors table. It uses the command   *

```
bcp pubs..authors out au_out.txt /c /P
```

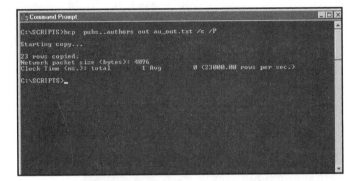

FIGURE 10-31

You can export data to a text file with defaults by leaving off the flags.

Note that the /c flag was required. You must specify either character or native format. Character format is a pure text file; native format stores noncharacter data such as numbers and dates in a binary format. Only character data is fully editable in a program like Notepad or usable by non-SQL Server installations.

If you then examine the results in Notepad, you'll see something like that shown in Figure 10-32.

FIGURE 10-32

You can examine the results of the query in Notepad.

BCP's default is to give the data a tab column delimiter and end each line with a newline. Our command specified that the data should be in character format.

To copy in native format, you simply substitute the /n for the /c in the preceding command:

```
bcp pubs..authors out au_out.txt /c /P
```
⟨/n⟩   output: massy. hard to read.

Using a Format File

The copies you've seen so far assume that the external file and internal SQL table have the same structure. When that is not the case, you can use the BCP format file and change it to fit the data.

To create a format file in older versions of BCP, you had to avoid specifying either /c or /n in a command and walk the BCP prompts until the program asked for the name of a format file. With SQL Server 7.0, all you have to do is specify that you want a format file:

译 p 275

⊕ bcp pubs..authors format au_out.txt /fau_out.fmt /c /P   output: Fig 10-33.

In this command, format is used in place of in or out, and /f specifies that the file au_out.fmt will be the format file.

The resulting format file looks like that shown in Figure 10-33.

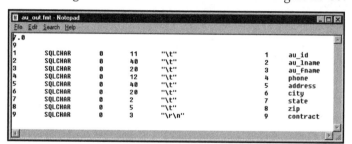

FIGURE 10-33

You can view the format file produced by the prior command.

You can learn these things from the format file shown in the figure:

1. The version of BCP used is 7.0.
2. There are nine columns of data in the host file, au_out.txt.
3. The first column in au_out.txt is of the character data type.
4. The first column has a prefix length of zero, meaning there is no special prefix.
5. The length of the first data column is 11 characters.
6. The data columns are terminated by the tab (\t) character.
7. The first column of au_out.txt corresponds to the first column in the server table.
8. The server column name for the first column of au_out.txt is au_id.
9. The remaining columns can be read in the same way as the first.

Let's say, for example, that you wanted to import a text file like au_out.txt into a table that is very much like the authors table, except it does not have the zip code, and it has the last name and first name reversed. You could revise the format file as shown in Figure 10-34.

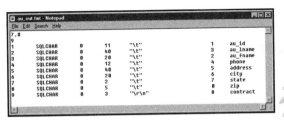

FIGURE 10-34

By changing values in the format file, you can change the mapping of text columns to table columns.

Notice that the column order for au_lname and au_fname are reversed; the second column of the text file imports into the third column of the table, and vice versa. Also notice that the zip column is 0, and the ninth column of the text file imports into the eighth column of the table. The zero in the zip column tells BCP not to import that column.

WARNING

Although BCP can be useful, it is notoriously difficult with which to work. The syntax is extremely unforgiving, and the error messages are often not helpful.

The BULK INSERT Command

SQL Server 7.0 adds one more interesting advance with the BULK INSERT command. This is a new Transact-SQL command that imports data from a bcp-formatted text file into SQL Server, but you do not need to invoke BCP externally to use it.

The basic syntax of the BULK INSERT command is simply

```
BULK INSERT <table name>
    FROM <data file>
    WITH <options>
```

The options available match the options you can use with BCP.

For example, to import the au_out.txt file you just created into the pubscopy database, set the database options to allow Select Into/Bulk Copy, using the Database Properties dialog box, Options tab. Then make an empty copy of the authors table using

Just use Query Analyzer, (choose pubs database)

```
SELECT *
    INTO au_copy
    FROM authors
```

Next, use the BULK INSERT command to populate the new table:

```
BULK INSERT au_copy
    FROM 'c:\scripts\au_out.txt'
```

depends on the subdirectory you saved the file.

Summary

The Data Transformation Services utility provides a full capability for data transfer between a wide variety of data sources. Because it is quite easy to use, scriptable, and portable, it can handle most data import and export needs. SQL Server 7 also includes the command line utility, BCP, which can also be used for importing and exporting data, though it is more difficult to use than DTS. From within Transact-SQL, you can use the BULK INSERT command to import data from external data files.

In the coverage of SQL Server 7 administration issues, you have one important topic left: scheduling jobs with SQL Server Agent, the subject of the next chapter.

Chapter 11

SQL Server Agent

In This Chapter

♦ SQL Server Agent overview

♦ Alerts

♦ Operators

♦ Jobs

♦ Configuring SQL Server Agent

♦ Multiserver administration

SQL Server Agent is SQL Server 7.0's scheduling and alerting utility. It represents a significant enhancement over SQL Executive, the SQL Server 6.0/6.5 scheduling and alerting tool. SQL Server Agent provides you with the ability to schedule administrative and other jobs, which you can execute once or on a recurring basis. In addition, SQL Server Agent lets you send messages as alerts when these jobs succeed or fail, or when SQL Server encounters errors.

Perhaps most significant of all SQL Server Agent's enhancements is the ability to do multiserver administration. If you administer a significant number of SQL Server 7.0 servers, you can define jobs for them on a single administrative server and have the jobs execute on the other servers automatically, without having to enter those jobs on each of the other servers.

In this chapter, you'll learn about the features of SQL Server Agent and techniques you can use for multiserver administration.

SQL Server Agent Overview

Two fundamental kinds of recurring tasks occupy database administrators' time: responding to errors within SQL Server and performing database maintenance. SQL Server Agent is a utility that gives you a method of automating these periodic tasks. You can have SQL Server Agent respond to SQL Server errors by defining alerts and perform maintenance by scheduling jobs. You can have both types of tasks notify operators, as shown in Figure 11-1.

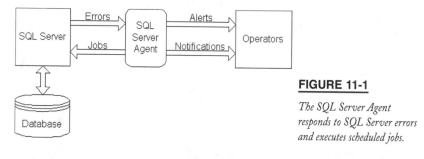

FIGURE 11-1

The SQL Server Agent responds to SQL Server errors and executes scheduled jobs.

A SQL Server Agent alert is a named error condition that triggers some kind of messaging action when a SQL Server error occurs. Alerts are based on SQL Server events or performance conditions. The events are errors (error numbers, severity levels, or the message text), whereas the performance conditions are thresholds based on performance counters. When an event or condition fires an alert, you can have SQL Server send a message to an operator, which is an e-mail address, pager e-mail, or network account to which you want the message sent, or you can place a message in the Windows NT event log.

In SQL Server Agent, you can also schedule jobs. Each job consists of a set of one or more named steps that contain a set of one or more commands. You can control the sequence and flow of the steps, so that the entire job may be aborted if one of the steps fails. The steps' commands can be Transact-SQL commands, batches, or scripts, as well as ActiveScript scripts and external Windows NT commands. You can assign many schedules to a job. In any given schedule, you may assign a one-time or recurring execution. In addition to scheduling a job, you can execute it on demand. You can have SQL Agent notify an operator upon completion or failure of the job.

SQL Server Agent runs as a service on the same server as SQL Server, and you can use Enterprise Manager to manage it. Because it is a separate service, it has its own login into Windows NT and Windows 95/98.

Alerts

The best way to approach alerts initially is through Enterprise Manager. Just open a registered SQL Server and drill down to the nodes under SQL Server Agent, and select the Alerts node. *management / SQL Server Agent / Alerts*

Demo Alerts

A fresh installation of SQL Server 7 comes with a demo set of alerts, as you can see in Figure 11-2.

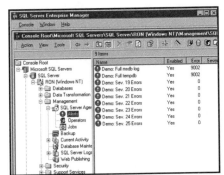

FIGURE 11-2

A number of demo alerts come with a new installation of SQL Server 7.

Two of the errors that trigger an alert are given the error number 9002, which states that the file is full:

```
The log file for database '%.*ls' is full. Back up the transaction log for the
database to free up some log space.
```

However, one is for the msbd database, and the other for the tempdb database. The remaining alerts are based on any errors with severity levels between 19 and 25, which is the range of fatal errors. In other words, you can use these alerts to be notified of any fatal error.

You can view the properties of any alert in the list by right-clicking over the alert and choosing the Properties option from the pop-up menu. For the first alert, the demo on a full msdb database, you'll see the tabbed dialog box shown in Figure 11-3.

FIGURE 11-3

The demo alert on a full msdb database has these properties.

In this case, you can see that this alert is defined as a SQL Server event alert, based on the error number 1105. The properties dialog box keeps a few statistics for this alert as history. You'll take a look at the Response tab momentarily. To see more about this dialog box, let's create a new alert from scratch.

Creating a New Alert

You can create a new alert by right-clicking over an alert or over the Alerts node in the Enterprise Manager tree view and selecting New Alert. The resulting dialog box, as shown in Figure 11-4, contains a new alert properties dialog box.

FIGURE 11-4

You use the alert properties dialog box to create a new alert.

After you've entered an alert name, notice that the type of alert can be one based on a SQL Server event or a performance condition.

NOTE

A second way to create a new alert is to use the Create Alert Wizard. Because the wizard is just a light duty, step-by-step guide to filling out the New Alert Properties dialog box, I won't include it here.

Event Alerts

If you choose a SQL Server event, you must associate the event with some error number, severity level, or message text. If you want to search for error numbers, just click on the small button to the right of the Error Number text box, and you'll get the Manager Server Messages dialog box, as shown in Figure 11-5.

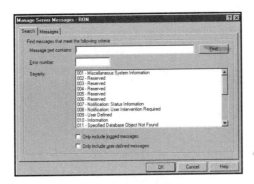

FIGURE 11-5

The Manager Server Messages dialog box has a Search tab to help you find a particular error message.

If you click on the Find button, you'll get a list of all SQL Server 7 system error messages, as you can see in Figure 11-6.

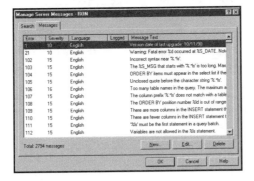

FIGURE 11-6

You can choose an error from the list of all SQL Server 7 system error messages.

Many of the error messages are truncated by this window. You can see an entire message by double-clicking on it.

On the other hand, if you choose the Messages tab instead of the Search tab, you
can choose from the set of user-defined error messages on the system, as shown in
Figure 11-7.

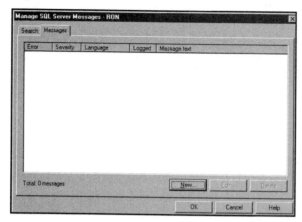

FIGURE 11-7

*The Messages tab shows you all
the user-defined error messages
created on this SQL Server.*

You can create your own error message by clicking on the New button and using an
error number greater than 50000, as you can see in Figure 11-8.

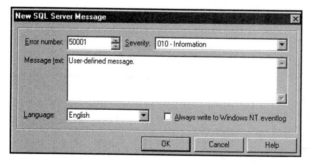

FIGURE 11-8

*You can create a new error message
from the Messages tab.*

The New Message dialog box lets you add a new message by picking a new message
number, choosing a severity level, giving it a message text, choosing a language, and
deciding whether to write the occurrence to the Windows NT event log. If you want
to add a message in a different language, you must first add the message in English;
then you can add the message in another language for the same error number.

The stored procedure that this dialog box runs behind the scenes is sp_addmessage.
The actual command sent to SQL server is:

```
EXEC msdb.dbo.sp_sem_add_message 50002, 10, 'Message from 50002', '', true
```

which reflects the error number, severity level, message text, language, and whether to
log the message to the NT event log. The language defaults to the installed language,
US English.

Once you've defined the new message, you can then assign it to the alert.

Performance Conditions

You may define a performance condition instead of a SQL Server event. If you do, the Alert Properties dialog box changes its appearance, as shown in Figure 11-9.

FIGURE 11-9

The New Alert Properties dialog box changes its appearance if you choose an alert based on a performance condition instead of a SQL Server message.

The counters available are the same as those available to the NT Performance Monitor. First you choose an object, which has a particular set of counters available. For instance, to monitor how much memory SQL Server is using, choose the SQL Server: Memory Manager object, and the associated Total Server Memory counter. You could then send an alert if it exceeds a certain number, say 500KB, as shown in Figure 11-10.

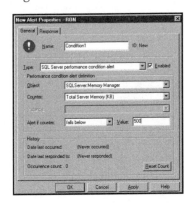

FIGURE 11-10

You associate a counter with an object, and define a threshold, when setting up a performance condition alert.

You can use the Instance text box to choose a particular database, for those counters that are database-specific.

Deleting an Alert

You can delete an alert by right-clicking over the alert name in Enterprise Manager and choosing Delete. If you have the associated error message being logged to the Windows NT event log, the dialog box will check to see whether you wish to continue to have the error message logged, even though the alert is no longer present.

Scripting an Alert

When you've created an alert, you can script out the Transact-SQL code necessary to create one of the alerts by right-clicking over the alert and choosing Script. The dialog box that results is shown in Figure 11-11.

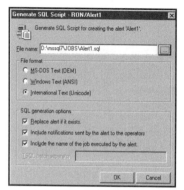

FIGURE 11-11

When you script out an individual alert, you must supply a file name for the script.

The action of creating an alert uses the sp_add_alert stored procedure, and the scripting action reverse-engineers the script necessary to re-create the same alert using that stored procedure. So for example, the actual script for the Alert1 you created earlier, with the Unicode option, is:

```
-- Script generated on 8/8/98 10:29 PM
-- By: sa
-- Server: RON
IF (EXISTS (SELECT name
                FROM msdb.dbo.sysalerts
                WHERE name = N'Alert1'))
            ---- Delete the alert with the same name.
            EXECUTE msdb.dbo.sp_delete_alert @name = N'Alert1'
BEGIN
EXECUTE msdb.dbo.sp_add_alert @name = N'Alert1',
            @message_id =        50002,
            @severity = 0,
            @enabled = 1,
            @delay_between_responses = 0,   @include_event_description_in = 0,
            @database_name =       N'pubs',
            @event_description_keyword = N'Message from Alert1',
      @raise_snmp_trap = 0,
            @category_name =       N'[Uncategorized]'
END
```

> **NOTE**
>
> You can script out all the alerts by right-clicking over the Alerts node in the left pane of Enterprise Manager and choosing Script All.

Verifying an Alert Message

If you have chosen to send an alert's message to the Windows NT event log, you can verify that the message alert is in effect by using the RAISERROR command. For the Alert1 you just created, execute the following command in the Query Analyzer, in the pubs database:

```
RAISERROR (50002, -1, -1)
```

Then, in the Windows NT event viewer, application log, you will find the alert results, as shown in Figure 11-12.

FIGURE 11-12

The Windows NT event viewer can be used to verify that an error message was logged.

This does not really put the alert to work, though, if you don't send an alert to some operator. So let's take a look at defining an operator.

Operators

After you've defined an alert, to make the alert do something, you must define an operator to which the alert can send a message. An operator is an e-mail address, pager address, or network address registered with SQL Server Agent.

Creating a New Operator

SQL Server 7 does not come with any demo operators. You can define a new operator by selecting the Operators node (under SQL Server Agent) in Enterprise Manager, right-clicking, and choosing New Operator from the pop-up menu. The General tab of the New Operator Properties dialog box appears, as shown in Figure 11-13.

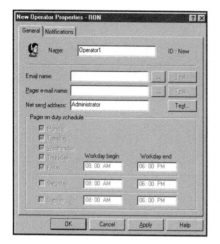

FIGURE 11-13

You define a new operator in the New Operators Properties dialog box.

You fill in the new name, which will be the name by which you'll identify the operator later in either alerts or jobs. Then you can choose an e-mail address, pager e-mail address, or network name. If you choose the e-mail or pager address, the dialog box will find your installed e-mail system and let you choose from your local and global address books, as you can see in Figure 11-14.

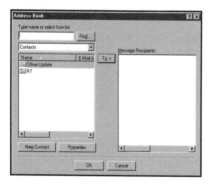

FIGURE 11-14

You can select an e-mail address from your local or global address books.

NOTE

After you choose an e-mail, pager, or network address, you can test each one. Each will send a message that basically notifies the receiver that it's just a test and they can ignore the message.

Scripting an Operator

You can script an operator using the same technique that you can use for alerts: Simply right-click over the operator name and choose Script. The resulting script, however, will also include the assignment of alerts to that operator. For example, the following script will re-create your sample Operator1 with an assignment to Alert1:

```
-- Script generated on 8/9/98 12:05 PM
-- By: sa
-- Server: RON
IF (EXISTS (SELECT name FROM msdb.dbo.sysoperators
            WHERE name = N'Operator1'))
            ---- Delete operator with the same name.
            EXECUTE msdb.dbo.sp_delete_operator
                @name = N'Operator1'
BEGIN
EXECUTE msdb.dbo.sp_add_operator @name = N'Operator1',
            @enabled = 1,
            @netsend_address = N'Administrator',
            @category_name = N'[Uncategorized]',@weekday_pager_start_time = 80000,
            @weekday_pager_end_time = 180000, @saturday_pager_start_time = 80000,
            @saturday_pager_end_time = 180000, @sunday_pager_start_time = 80000,
            @sunday_pager_end_time        = 180000,
            @pager_days = 62
EXECUTE msdb.dbo.sp_add_notification
            @alert_name = N'Alert1',
            @operator_name = N'Operator1',
            @notification_method = 1
END
```

Notice that the `sp_add_operator` stored procedure defines the operator, with default operator pager times. The `sp_add_notification` stored procedure associates that operator with Alert1.

Associating Operators to Alerts

You can associate an operator with a set of alerts by choosing the Notifications tab of the Operator Properties dialog box, as you can see illustrated in Figure 11-15.

FIGURE 11-15

You associate an operator with your defined alerts in the Notifications tab.

In Figure 11-15, the operator called Operator1 has been assigned the alert Alert1. You can disable this particular operator from receiving a notification without removing his or her assignments by clearing the check box entitled "Operator is available to receive notifications." As with alerts, a statistical history is kept of the notifications that this operator has received.

Verifying an Alert to an Operator

You can verify an alert to an operator by executing the RAISERROR you saw used to verify that the alert wrote to the Windows NT Application Event Log. Assuming the alert you built in the last section, and the operator called Operator1, with a network address (the login of Administrator on the local machine), issuing the RAISERROR command results in the network message shown in Figure 11-16.

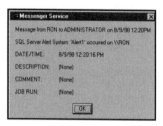

FIGURE 11-16

When you fire an alert using net send, SQL Server Agent sends a network message to the login.

Deleting an Operator

To delete an operator, simply right-click on the operator in Enterprise Manager. The resulting dialog box will detect if that operator has been associated with any alerts or jobs, as shown in Figure 11-17.

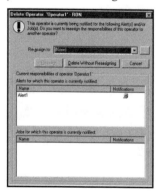

FIGURE 11-17

If you delete an operator with alerts or jobs assigned to it, you will be asked whether you want to reassign the alerts.

This dialog box lets you reassign an operator's alerts and notifications to another operator, just prior to deleting. If you do not want to reassign and wish to simply continue with the delete, just click on the Delete Without Reassigning button.

You may have noticed that operators are involved with jobs as well as alerts, so now it's time to consider SQL Server Agent jobs.

Jobs

You can automate your database maintenance and other tasks using SQL Server Agent jobs. A job is a set of one or more steps, which contain the actions in the sequence you want them executed. Each step can contain one action of several types: The step could be a Transact-SQL script, an ActiveScript script (that is, a VBScript or a JScript), or a call to an external Windows executable.

Creating a New Job

You can create a new job by selecting the Jobs node in Enterprise Manager, right-clicking over it, and then choosing New Job from the pop-up menu.

> ### NOTE
>
> You can also use the Create Job Wizard to create a simple, one-step job. Because it simply helps fill out the New Job Properties dialog box, I won't cover the wizard here.

The resulting New Job Properties dialog box has four tabs to help guide you through the process, as you can see in Figure 11-18.

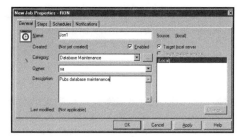

FIGURE 11-18

You create a new job by filling in the New Job Properties dialog box.

You give the job a name and choose a category for the job. The categories provided by a fresh installation are: Database Maintenance, Full Text (if installed), various replication categories, the Web Assistant category, and a catch-all Uncategorized.

The full-text category will show up if you've installed the Full Text search engine. The replication categories are used by SQL Server replication, and the Web Assistant category is used by the SQL Server Web Assistant. (For more information about replication, see Chapter 24 "Replication.") An additional category called Uncategorized can be used for miscellaneous jobs. You can also create your own new categories. (See "Managing Job Categories" later in this section.)

After specifying a category, you can provide a description and also enlist a target server if you've defined any. (For more information about target servers, see the "Multiserver Administration" section later in this chapter.)

Defining Job Steps

After you've filled in the General tab, click on the Steps tab to define job steps. The initial dialog box will be blank; you add a step by clicking on the New button, which brings up the dialog box to define a step, shown in Figure 11-19.

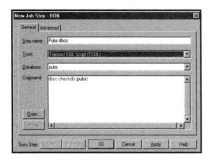

FIGURE 11-19

You define a step using the New Job Step dialog box.

The figure shows a step that will do a DBCC of the pubs database, using the Transact-SQL type of step. The types of steps available are ActiveScript, Operating System command, various replication commands, and Transact-SQL script, the default. These are the only types available; you cannot define your own types of commands.

Transact-SQL Scripts

The Transact-SQL Script type allows you to enter a set of Transact-SQL batches, or to load a script from disk. The script, when loaded, can consist of more than one batch, which is a significant improvement over SQL Server 6.5's SQL Executive, which could execute only one Transact-SQL batch.

> ### WARNING
>
> If you load a Transact-SQL script from disk into a job step, a copy of the script is loaded into the step and stored in the msdb database for execution. If you change the script on disk, the changes will not be reflected in the job step. To make the step execute what's on disk, see the next section.

Note that every Transact-SQL script must be associated with a particular database, at least to start with. Of course, you can change the database context within the script.

Operating System Command (CmdExec)

You can execute external Windows executables and operating system commands using the Operating System Command (CmdExec) type. This is handy for calling external programs and can allow you to execute scripts and save the results on disk. To call an external script, you can make a call to OSQL, as shown in Figure 11-20.

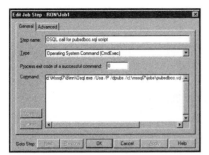

FIGURE 11-20

You can call an external script using the Operating System Command type.

The dialog box will not show the entire command, which is as follows:

```
d:\Mssql7\Binn\Osql.exe /Usa /P /dpubs /id:\mssql7\jobs\pubsdbcc.sql
/od:\mssql7\jobs\pubsdbcc.rpt
```

> ## WARNING
>
> Be careful to make sure there are not any hidden carriage returns. If your command looks like it has word wrap, that could indicate an embedded carriage return, which will make the Operating System command type fail. You must scroll the window to see an entire command.

ActiveScript

You can also choose ActiveScript, which gives you an editing window within which to choose the type of script, to load a script, or just to type one in. You can see an example of the window in Figure 11-21.

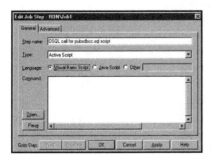

FIGURE 11-21

You can enter a script such as VBScript using the ActiveScript type of command.

The dialog box shows the script necessary to execute a dbcc on the pubs database.

Advanced Tab

When you choose the Advanced tab, you can determine how the job should behave if there is an error or if the step succeeds, as shown in Figure 11-22.

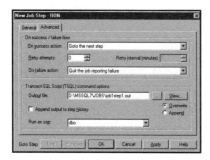

FIGURE 11-22

You can determine what action to take based on whether the step succeeds or fails in the Advanced tab.

Most important from the standpoint of the job, this dialog box lets you choose what actions to take based on success or failure. In the job shown in the figure, you're going to do a backup right after the DBCC, so you'll quit the job if the DBCC fails but go to the next step if it succeeds.

You can also determine what output file to save the output in, and whether to append or overwrite what's already in the file. You can create a file for each step or use one file for all the steps, as shown in the figure. In addition, you can run as a particular user within the database.

WARNING

You can also go to a particular step rather than quit. This adds a lot of power but also allows you to create potential problems. It's possible to create a sequence of steps in which some steps could never be reached, because they are always skipped. Similarly, you could create an infinite loop. If you do, SQL Server Agent will warn you when you try to save the job.

In your current example, Job1 has two steps, one for a DBCC of pubs, and the second for a backup. You only want the backup to be done if the DBCC succeeds, as shown in Figure 11-23.

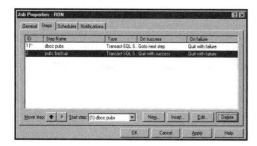

FIGURE 11-23

You can quit a sequence early upon failure.

Because step 1 will go to the next step on success but quit with failure, the backup will only be done if the first step succeeds.

Note that you can move the steps around and even choose a different starting step in this dialog box.

Schedules

You can create one or more schedules for a job. Therefore you can schedule a job under one particular pattern and add another pattern as well. For example, you could schedule an incremental backup of a database every day at noon, as well as Monday through Friday at 5:00.

> **NOTE**
>
> SQL Server 6.5's SQL Executive could apply only one schedule per job. The ability to have many schedules for a single job is another example of a significant enhancement in SQL Server 7.

To add schedules, just choose the Schedules tab and click on the New Schedule button. You'll see the dialog box shown in Figure 11-24.

FIGURE 11-24

You can schedule a job for any number of patterns.

After you give the schedule a name, you have a number of options. For example, you can enable or disable a particular schedule, have the job execute whenever SQL Agent starts up, or have it execute whenever the CPU becomes idle. Or you can have the job execute one time or on a recurring basis. If you choose recurring, you'll see a familiar scheduling dialog box that allows you to create just about any repeating pattern throughout a daily, weekly, or monthly period of time. You get to the recurring dialog box by clicking on the Recurring option button and then clicking on Change. The resulting dialog box is shown in Figure 11-25.

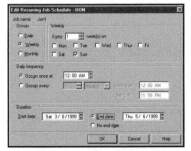

FIGURE 11-25

You can create a recurring schedule by clicking on the Change button.

Notifications

The final tab of the Jobs dialog box is the Notifications portion. Here you can determine what operators to notify based on success or failure of a job. Again there are quite a number of options, as you can see in Figure 11-26.

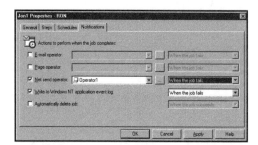

FIGURE 11-26

You can determine who to notify upon completion of each job.

In this case, the dialog box shows that you'll notify Operator1 with a network message whenever the job does not complete successfully. Alternative choices are upon successful completion and both types of completion.

> **NOTE**
>
> You can also have a job automatically delete itself upon completion!

Scripting a Job

Just as with alerts and operators, you can also script out a job. You can do this by right-clicking on a job and choosing Script. You can also script out all jobs by right-clicking over the Jobs node and choosing Script All.

The resulting script will re-create the original job. Scripts for jobs are much more complex than those for alerts and operators, especially when the jobs contain more than one step. For your sample two-step job, the resulting script is as follows:

First the script begins a transaction, deletes any job with the current name, and proceeds to re-create the job if it does not exist:

```
BEGIN TRANSACTION
    DECLARE @JobID BINARY(16)
    DECLARE @ReturnCode INT
    SELECT @ReturnCode = 0
IF (SELECT COUNT(*) FROM msdb.dbo.syscategories
            WHERE name = N'NewCategory') < 1
            EXECUTE msdb.dbo.sp_add_category N'NewCategory'
    -- Delete the job with the same name (if it exists)
```

```
SELECT @JobID = job_id
        FROM    msdb.dbo.sysjobs
        WHERE (name = N'Job1')
IF (@JobID IS NOT NULL)
BEGIN
```

Then the script checks to see whether this is a multiserver job, and aborts the script if it is:

```
-- Check if the job is a multi-server job
IF (EXISTS (SELECT   *
            FROM    msdb.dbo.sysjobservers
            WHERE   (job_id = @JobID) AND (server_id <> 0)))
BEGIN
  -- There is, so abort the script
  RAISERROR (N'Unable to import job ''Job1'' since there is already a multi-
server job with this name.', 16, 1)
    GOTO QuitWithRollback
END
ELSE
  -- Delete the [local] job
  EXECUTE msdb.dbo.sp_delete_job @job_name = N'Job1'
  SELECT @JobID = NULL
END
```

Now the script adds the job and its steps:

```
BEGIN
  -- Add the job
  EXECUTE @ReturnCode = msdb.dbo.sp_add_job
            @job_id = @JobID OUTPUT ,
            @job_name = N'Job1',
            @owner_login_name = N'sa',
            @description = N'Pubs database maintenance',
            @category_name = N'NewCategory',
            @enabled = 1,
            @notify_level_email = 0,
            @notify_level_page = 0,
            @notify_level_netsend = 2,
```

```
                @notify_level_eventlog = 2,
                @delete_level= 0,
                @notify_netsend_operator_name = N'Operator1'
    IF (@@ERROR <> 0 OR @ReturnCode <> 0) GOTO QuitWithRollback
    -- Add the job steps
    EXECUTE @ReturnCode = msdb.dbo.sp_add_jobstep
                @job_id = @JobID,
                @step_id = 1,
                @step_name = N'dbcc pubs',
                @command = N'dbcc checkdb (pubs)',
                @database_name = N'pubs',
                @server = N'',
                @database_user_name = N'',
                @subsystem = N'TSQL',
                @cmdexec_success_code = 0,
                @flags = 0,
                @retry_attempts = 0,
                @retry_interval = 1,
                @output_file_name = N'',
                @on_success_step_id = 0,
                @on_success_action = 3,
                @on_fail_step_id = 0,
                @on_fail_action = 2
     IF (@@ERROR <> 0 OR @ReturnCode <> 0)
                GOTO QuitWithRollback
    EXECUTE @ReturnCode = msdb.dbo.sp_add_jobstep
                @job_id = @JobID,
                @step_id = 2,
                @step_name = N'pubs backup',
                @command = N'backup database pubs to pubsbak',   @database_name = N'pubs',
                @server = N'',
                @database_user_name = N'',
                @subsystem = N'TSQL',
                @cmdexec_success_code = 0,
                @flags = 0,
```

```
                @retry_attempts = 0,
                @retry_interval = 1,
                @output_file_name = N'',
                @on_success_step_id = 0,
                @on_success_action = 1,
                @on_fail_step_id = 0, @on_fail_action = 2
 IF (@@ERROR <> 0 OR @ReturnCode <> 0)
                GOTO QuitWithRollback
 EXECUTE @ReturnCode = msdb.dbo.sp_update_job
                @job_id = @JobID,
                @start_step_id = 1
 IF (@@ERROR <> 0 OR @ReturnCode <> 0)
                GOTO QuitWithRollback
```

Then the schedules:

```
 -- Add the job schedules
 EXECUTE @ReturnCode = msdb.dbo.sp_add_jobschedule
                @job_id = @JobID,
                @name = N'Schedule1',
                @enabled = 1,
                @freq_type = 8,
                @active_start_date = 19980809,
                @active_start_time = 0,
                @freq_interval = 1,
                @freq_subday_type = 1,
                @freq_subday_interval = 0,
                @freq_relative_interval = 0,
                @freq_recurrence_factor = 1,
                @active_end_date = 99991231,
                @active_end_time = 235959
 IF (@@ERROR <> 0 OR @ReturnCode <> 0)
                GOTO QuitWithRollback
 -- Add the Target Servers
 EXECUTE @ReturnCode = msdb.dbo.sp_add_jobserver
                @job_id = @JobID,
                @server_name = N'(local)'
 IF (@@ERROR <> 0 OR @ReturnCode <> 0)
```

```
            GOTO QuitWithRollback
END
COMMIT TRANSACTION
GOTO    EndSave
QuitWithRollback:
  IF (@@TRANCOUNT > 0) ROLLBACK TRANSACTION
EndSave:
```

It is instructive to read through the script and see how the quit conditions are set. Each sp_add_jobstep stored procedure has four parameters that govern the actions that occur after a step executes. The following list contains the parameters from step 1:

```
@on_success_step_id = 0,
@on_success_action = 3,
@on_fail_step_id = 0,
@on_fail_action = 2
```

The first pair of parameters states that on success, the execution should go to the step with id 0 (the default), and the action is 3, which is "go to the next step." The second pair deals with failure, and the action is 2, meaning "quit the job with failure," and the id is 0, which is just the default.

Job History

After you've saved a job, it will execute when you specified, provided that the SQL Server Agent is running. In addition to the scheduled time, you can execute a job at any time by right-clicking over the job and choosing Start from the menu.

You can see a job's history by right-clicking over the job name and choosing Job History. The resulting dialog box is shown in Figure 11-27.

Note that for a job containing many steps, you'll often need to collapse the list by

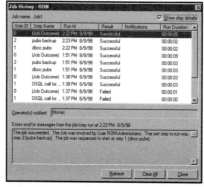

FIGURE 11-27

You can see a job's history with all steps or without the steps.

unchecking the Show Step Details check box in the upper-right corner.

Managing Job Categories

Recall that the New Job Properties dialog box requires that you classify every job into some category. It is possible to manage job categories, in particular to create your own categories, by right-clicking over the Jobs node in the Enterprise Manager tree view and choosing Job Categories from the menu. The resulting tree-view dialog box, shown in Figure 11-28, lets you add and delete categories.

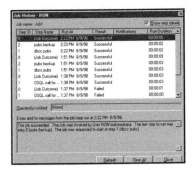

FIGURE 11-28

You can add your own job categories.

When you add a category, you just pick a new name and potentially add some jobs to it, as shown in Figure 11-29.

FIGURE 11-29

You can add a category and optionally add some existing jobs to it.

You must check the Show All Jobs check box to see the jobs, and then you can move jobs from their current category to this one by checking the Member box and clicking on the Apply and then OK buttons. In the figure, you've moved Job1 from the Database Maintenance category to NewCategory.

Configuring SQL Server Agent

In addition to creating jobs, alerts, and operators, you can set a number of configuration values for SQL Server Agent.

> **TIP**
>
> No jobs or alerts will be active unless SQL Server Agent is running. Therefore, it's often a good idea to make SQL Server Agent start automatically whenever the server starts.

The General Tab

To configure SQL Server Agent, just right-click over it in the Enterprise Manager tree view, and choose Properties. The resulting tabbed dialog box is shown in Figure 11-30.

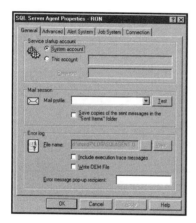

FIGURE 11-30

You can configure settings for SQL Server Agent by bringing up its Properties dialog box.

First and foremost, you can determine the login that SQL Server Agent uses, either a local system account or an NT domain account. This choice is very similar to the configuration for the SQL Server service. (See Chapter 5, "Configuring" for more details.)

In addition, if you want to use e-mail or pager notification, you must specify a SQL Mail profile. (See the next section on Configuring SQL Mail for more details.)

Finally, this tab ends with some choices concerning where to store the SQL Server Agent error log, and how much information to include. By default, the error log only includes errors and not trace information. If you enable the trace information, all output from all jobs will be included in the trace file. This may help in diagnosing problems with a particular job.

> **WARNING**
>
> If you choose to include trace information in the error log, you should only do it for short periods of time and for selected jobs, because the file may grow large quickly.

The Advanced Tab

The Advanced tab adds a number of interesting choices, as shown in Figure 11-31.

FIGURE 11-31

The Advanced tab lets SQL Server Agent govern the SQL Server Service, among other things.

Note that you can have the SQL Server Agent restart if stopped unexpectedly, and you can also restart SQL Server if it is stopped unexpectedly! You can forward events to a different server, which is useful for multiserver management.

Finally, you can specify what conditions constitute an idle CPU. Since you can make some jobs execute when the CPU is idle, here is how you define what idles means.

The Alert System

In the Alert System tab, you can specify special prefixes for the paging system, among other things, as shown in Figure 11-32.

FIGURE 11-32

You can specify a number of alerting options in the Alert System tab.

In addition, you can specify a fail-safe operator, which is an operator that will be reached if the designated operators cannot be reached (because they've turned off their pagers or are out of the region, for instance).

The Job System Tab

You can set a number of defaults for the jobs using the Job System tab, as shown in Figure 11-33.

FIGURE 11-33

You can also configure defaults for the job system.

You can limit the size of the job history log, which prevents job history from consuming the disk, in addition to clearing out a job history log.

The Shutdown timeout interval specifies how long SQL Server Agent should wait before shutting down after a job has finished.

The final option, "Non-SystAdmin job step proxy account," lets you specify how other users can use the Operating System command type (CmdExec) and ActiveScript type in their SQL Server Agent steps. Because SQL Server Agent runs with administrator privileges, you will not want other users to create jobs that have steps executing an external Windows NT command with the SQL Server Agent's network rights. By checking this box, you prevent that from happening.

The Connection Tab

Finally, you can specify how SQL Server Agent should log into SQL Server in order to execute jobs, as shown in Figure 11-34.

FIGURE 11-34

You can specify how SQL Server Agent logs into SQL Server in the Connection tab.

Because SQL Server Agent has to log into Windows, it can also log into SQL Server using its Windows NT login, or a particular SQL Server login.

NOTE

Since Windows 95/98 does not have Windows NT authentication, SQL Agent must log in with a SQL Server login that has the sysadmin role.

You can also enter the local server by name.

Multiserver Management

One of the most useful features of SQL Agent is the ability to make a server a remote manager of many other servers. This proves most useful in a production environment. You can administer the SQL Agent jobs for many different servers across a network from one central machine observing the results of the jobs and detecting when they fail.

Let's start with some terminology. In SQL Agent, the server you use to administer the other servers is called the *master* server or *MSX* server. The servers you administer are all called *target* servers, or *TSX* servers.

You *enlist* a server as a target server for a master server, and when you remove it, you *defect* the server. (Yes, "defect" is the term, sort of like someone "defecting" to an enemy country!) A master MSX server can administer multiple target servers, but a TSX target server can have only one master at a time. In order to change a target server's master, you have to defect it from one, and then enlist it with another.

TIP

If the number of servers you administer is at all large, or they are at remote locations, it's best to dedicate a SQL Server machine to being the master server, rather than using a production server. You don't want to be doing maintenance for a customer on the same machine that's supposed to be monitoring other servers!

Requirements

When engaging in multiserver administration, you must meet a number of requirements:

- ◆ All servers, master and targets, must be running SQL Server 7.0
- ◆ SQL Server and SQL Agent should use domain accounts, not the local system account, to log into Windows NT

◆ Make sure SQL Agent is running on all servers

◆ Ensure that SQL Agent start up automatically with SQL Server on each server

It's also a good idea to configure SQL Agent to auto-restart SQL Agent if it stops unexpectedly, in the Advanced tab of the SQL Agent Properties dialog box. (For more information on the SQL Agent Properties dialog box, see the sections earlier in this chapter. For more information about giving SQL Server and SQL Agent domain rather than system accounts, see Chapter 5, "Configuring".)

Setting Up a Master/Target Server

You can set up a Master/Target server relationship by using the Make MSX Wizard. (There are two wizards to assist in this activity, one for the MSX server and one for the TSX servers. When you run each wizard, it's assuming you're acting on the current server.)

You can access the Make MSX wizard by clicking on the "wand" icon on the toolbar and choosing the wizard from the management node of the Wizards list, or by right-clicking over SQL Agent and choosing Muliserver Administration, as shown in Figure 11-35.

FIGURE 11-35

You can find multiserver administration by right-clicking over SQL Agent.

When you bring up the wizard, a welcoming screen will remind you of the requirements necessary for setting up the master/target relationship. The first step by the wizard is to create an operator that will be defined as the operator for the multiserver jobs, as you can see in Figure 11-36.

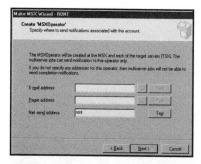

FIGURE 11-36

Your first step is to define an MSX operator for the target jobs.

So far in this chapter, you considered local jobs. With multiserver management, you're defining SQL Agent jobs for target servers. The operator can be notified about the status of the jobs.

Note that as with local operators, you can have an e-mail, pager, or network notification sent. But in this case, it's the target server that will be sending the notification to an operator defined on the master server. In this way, you can be notified about remote jobs.

Next, choose one or more SQL Servers to enlist in as target servers, as shown in Figure 11-37.

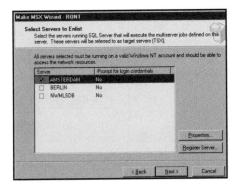

FIGURE 11-37

Your first step is to define an MSX operator for the target jobs.

SQL Server detects the other SQL Server 7 servers that you've registered in your Enterprise Manager and lists them. If you want to add a server, just click the Register button and you'll get the same dialog box that you see for registering a server in Enterprise Manager. You can edit the current registration by clicking the Properties button.

After you click on the Next button, you'll see a brief dialog box in which you can add descriptions for the target server names. After you add a description, you're at the end, and when you click on Finish, the process of enlisting takes place, as shown in Figure 11-38.

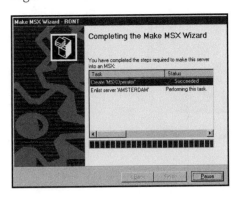

FIGURE 11-38

When you click on the Finish button, the process of enlisting other servers starts.

If the process succeeds, you'll see a new set of nodes in Enterprise Manager under SQL Agent jobs, as shown in Figure 11-39.

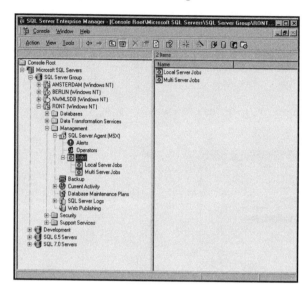

FIGURE 11-39

You now see local jobs and multiserver jobs.

You're now ready to create multi-server jobs, which you can do using much of the same logic as local jobs.

Creating Multiserver jobs

To create a multiserver job, just right-click over the multiserver jobs node, and choose New Job. You'll get the familiar tab dialog box with the target server option enabled on the first tab, as shown in Figure 11-40.

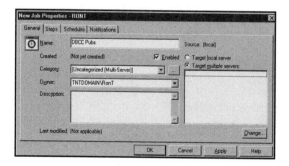

FIGURE 11-40

Notice that the target server option is now enabled.

To add a target server for this job, just click on the Change button, and you'll see the dialog box shown in Figure 11-41.

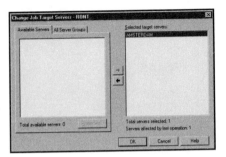

FIGURE 11-41

You can add a target server from the available enlistees.

At this point, you can add jobs in the usual fashion, as I covered earlier in this chapter.

After you've got one or more target servers set up, and want to execute some jobs, you can actually download instructions to them. Just right-click over the jobs and select Download from the menu. You'll see the dialog box shown in Figure 11-42.

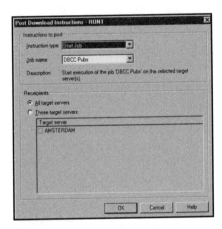

FIGURE 11-42

You can download instructions to the target server jobs.

After you've set up the target server jobs, you can treat them the same as local SQL Agent jobs. You can script them out, for example, using the same commands to script local jobs. Further, the remote jobs make their history available to the job listing in the master server.

"Defecting" (Removing) a Target Server

You can remove —defect —a target server either from the master server or from the target server itself. You must defect a target server if you want to make it the target of another master server. To defect a target server, just right-click on the target server, select Defect from the menu, and you'll see the dialog box shown in Figure 11-43.

FIGURE 11-43

You can remove or "defect" a target server from target server itself.

Using master and target server is easy and intuitive (except for the "defecting" terminology), and will no doubt prove one of the most popular features of SQL Agent.

Summary

You can schedule maintenance jobs using SQL Server Agent, SQL Server 7.0's scheduling and alerting utility. You can define several steps for each job and control the flow among the steps. If any step fails, you can alert operators using SQL Agent's alerting capability. In addition, you can define other alerts based on errors that occur within SQL Server, and notify operators when those errors occur, as well as write them to the NT event log.

One of the most useful enhancements to SQL Agent is its capability for multiserver administration. You can define jobs on a central server that act on remote servers, and have the results returned back to the central server for inspection.

You've seen the essential tools SQL Server 7 provides for database administration in this part. Now it's time to move on to a new set of topics centered around database data: data definition and manipulation, starting with the next chapter.

PART IV

Managing Data

Chapter 12

Data Definition

In This Chapter

◆ The SQL Server 7.0 relational and storage engines

◆ Enterprise Manager's data definition tools

◆ Defining tables

◆ Defining views

◆ System tables and ANSI views

◆ Column constraints

◆ Referential integrity constraints

◆ Metadata functions

After you're confident of the installation, configuration, and management of your SQL Server, you're ready to build an actual database. In this chapter, you'll learn the essentials of data definition, the SQL Server 7 utilities and Transact-SQL language tools for defining the data to be stored in a database. Because data definition implements the design constraints, you'll start with an overview of database design, followed by the specific commands to implement design features and constraints. In the following chapters, you'll examine data manipulation and the many aspects of the Transact-SQL language, wrapping up with stored procedures and triggers.

The SQL Server 7.0 Relational and Storage Engines

There are a lot of factors to keep in mind when building databases in SQL Server. The context for understanding those factors begins with a fundamental fact about SQL Server's architecture, namely that at its core, SQL Server consists of two independent subsystems, the relational engine (sometimes called the query engine), and the storage engine, as shown by Figure 12-1.

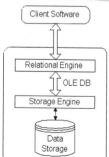

FIGURE 12-1

The SQL Server RDBMS consists of two independent subsystems: the relational engine and the storage engine.

The relational engine processes queries, whereas the storage engine stores and retrieves data. (In prior releases of SQL Server, query processing and data storage were intermingled in one monolithic engine.) The relational engine communicates with the storage engine via the low-level OLE DB. (For more information about the SQL Server 7 architecture, see Chapter 2, "Architecture.")

The Relational Engine

The relational engine processes two fundamental types of queries: data definition (called DDL, short for data definition language), and data manipulation (called DML, short for data manipulation language).

You use DDL commands to define the databases, tables, indexes, and constraints that make up your application's data source. For example, `CREATE TABLE, CREATE INDEX`, and so on are DDL commands. You use DML commands to manipulate data and populate tables with data. `SELECT, INSERT, UPDATE,` and `DELETE` are DML commands.

Whenever you communicate with SQL Server's relational engine, you use the Transact-SQL language, the dialect of SQL that belongs to SQL Server. Let's take a closer look at the relationship of the relational engine, Transact-SQL, and the SQL language.

The Relational Model

In 1969, the IBM mathematician E.F. Codd first formulated the theory of relational database systems. He based his ideas on the application of set theory to data structures. During the 1970s, researchers worked out most of the fundamental operations that could be applied to data organized in sets. A few prototype relational database systems were built, and many more were proposed, but the first commercial relational database systems, including IBM's mainframe DB2, were introduced in the early 1980s. Since that time, the relational DBMS has become the dominant method for storing database data.

The relational model of database storage is a well-developed theory of how data should be stored and manipulated. If you store data in the relational format, and if you follow the relational model's rules, then the results of performing relational operations on the data can be predicted with mathematical certainty.

It's important to learn about the relational model because it plays a role in how SQL Server 7 is designed and implemented. (For more information about the relational model, see Chapter 1, "Background.")

The SQL Language

Researchers knew that relational databases would need a query language, a well-defined set of commands to populate and query the database for data. Several were proposed during the 1970s, including SQL by IBM, and by the early 1980s the winner was SQL (short for "structured query language.") SQL won out because of support by IBM.

As the 1980s proceeded and other relational database products came on the scene, they all adopted the SQL language. Eventually, by the end of the decade, vendors cooperated on an ANSI committee to formulate the SQL language, resulting in ANSI Standard SQL. The first SQL standards, SQL-86 and SQL-89, began as least common denominators of the major SQL dialects. By 1992, however, the ANSI committee forged ahead of the vendors and made a blueprint for vendors to develop their SQL dialects in the future, called SQL-92.

Transact-SQL

When it comes time to start defining database tables and loading them with data, your main relationship with SQL Server will be through its query interface language, called Transact-SQL. The commands in Transact-SQL allow you to define tables, populate them with data, and retrieve data back from them.

Most of your contact with SQL Server's data will be through Transact-SQL, the SQL Server dialect of the SQL language. Because a standards body defines and maintains standard SQL, each new release of SQL Server gradually gets closer to the standard, and SQL Server 7 is no exception. Since the SQL standard does provide some guidance to the future of Transact-SQL, it's important to note where Transact-SQL conforms to the standard, and where it deviates.

NOTE

In this and the following chapters, as you learn Transact-SQL commands, you'll also learn when SQL Server implements and deviates from the SQL standard.

Influences on the Relational Engine

The SQL Server 7 relational engine is influenced by both the relational model and the ANSI SQL standard, as you can see in Figure 12-2.

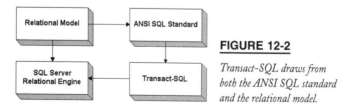

FIGURE 12-2

Transact-SQL draws from both the ANSI SQL standard and the relational model.

As Microsoft develops new releases of SQL Server, it revises some Transact-SQL commands and adds new commands to bring it closer to the ANSI SQL standard. Since the standard SQL commands are more generally known and often better defined, it is usually better to develop your queries using the versions of Transact-SQL commands that conform to the ANSI SQL standard.

> **TIP**
>
> It's important to know which commands in Transact-SQL conform to the SQL standard. If there's a choice between formulating a Transact-SQL command using the ANSI SQL syntax on the one hand and in a nonconforming way on the other, usually it's better to choose the ANSI SQL way. The code will be more maintainable, and often more readable.

Both the relational engine and the ANSI SQL committee take many ideas from the relational model. The ANSI SQL committee bases its standard on the operations and rules of the relational model, more or less. Behind the scenes, there is pressure on the ANSI SQL committee to bring its standard in line with the relational model, so the relational model in turn has influence on the direction of the SQL standard.

In addition, database vendors such as Microsoft implement relational algorithms in their database query engines. Industrial and academic researchers have built and refined these algorithms for over 25 years, so vendors often adapt them into their products. In this way, the relational model has a direct influence on SQL Server's relational query engine, and an indirect influence on Transact-SQL through the ANSI SQL standard.

> **TIP**
>
> A good understanding of the relational model is very helpful when designing databases. Neither Transact-SQL nor the ANSI SQL standards treat database design; they simply work with tables you've already decided upon. The relational model, however, is defined at a level where design decisions can be analyzed and examined.

The Storage Engine

The storage engine stores and retrieves data for the query engine. In order to improve performance of the storage engine, and solve a number of SQL Server 6.x and prior problems, SQL Server 7 has changed the on-disk storage structures.

Storage Structure Limits

First of all, SQL Server 7 has a larger page size (8K bytes instead of the older 2K bytes), and this change has a ripple effect throughout SQL Server 7's storage structures. Extents are now 64KB (8 pages of 8K bytes each). A single row in a page can now occupy up to 8,060 bytes, which is increased from the older maximum of 1,962. Character and binary columns can extend to 8,000 bytes, up from 255.

With more rows on a page, it seems natural that SQL Server 7 should lock rows. In fact, row locking is the default, and SQL Server will automatically escalate to page or table locking depending on its analysis of the query.

Database and Log Files

As you learned in Chapter 7, data storage changes dramatically. Database devices are thankfully gone in SQL Server 7, replaced by operating system files. Every SQL Server 7 database has at least one data file and one transaction log file, and unlike the old database devices, every SQL Server 7 database file can only contain data from one database. By default, SQL Server 7 will automatically grow and shrink data and log files, although you can override that.

One surprise is that you cannot put tempdb in RAM; it resides on disk like all other databases. You can move it and other databases from one local disk drive to another with the enhanced ALTER DATABASE command. In addition, you can detach a database from one server, copy its files, and attach it to another server with the new sp_attach_db and sp_detach_db system stored procedures.

Indexes

There is an important, though less visible, change to indexing. Clustered indexes always keep a unique clustering key for each row in a table and will create a unique key (a uniqifier, in Microsoft parlance), if the indexed columns lack one. If there is a clustered index on a table, all nonclustered indexes on the table will use the clustering key to locate rows in the table. The benefit is that page splits will not require any updates to the nonclustered indexes. But because each nonclustered index contains copies of the clustering key, it's very important to keep clustered indexes as narrow as possible. For more information about indexing, see Chapter 19, "Tuning Queries."

With these changes in mind, let's take a closer look at the process of defining tables in a database, starting with the tools in Enterprise Manager.

Enterprise Manager's Data Definition Tools

For working with data tables, two convenient sets of tools come with Enterprise Manager. The first set (known as the data tools in Visual Studio), are graphical methods of creating and querying tables. The second set are the dialogs of the Query Analyzer. It's good to know how to create tables and constraints using both sets of tools.

Let's take a look at the data tools first, and then at the Query Analyzer.

Using the Data Tools

The data tools show up in connection with several activities: designing a table, opening a table, and working with a database diagram. (For more information about database diagramming, see Chapter 7, "Managing Databases.")

Designing a Table

When you right-click on a table name in Enterprise Manager, you have two ways to inspect the table's properties. One, the Table Properties dialog box, shows you the essentials of a table, but you cannot change any of the values. For example, Figure 12-3 shows the authors table properties.

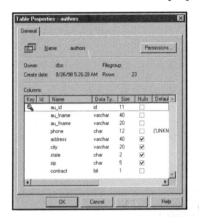

right click a table name then "properties".

FIGURE 12-3

You can inspect but not change a table's properties using the Table Properties dialog box.

However, if you choose Design Table, rather than Properties, you will get the Design Table window shown in Figure 12-4.

Table and Index Properties.

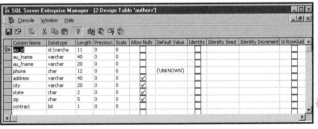

FIGURE 12-4

You can inspect and change a table's column properties in the Design Table window.

The Design option does allow you to change a number of table properties that I'll cover in detail later in this chapter: column name and order, data type, length, precision, scale, nullability, default value, identity (with seed and increment), and whether the column is a rowguid.

NOTE

When you make changes to a table using the Design Table dialog box, the changes are applied as a script to the underlying table. You can save just the script by clicking on the save change script icon in the dialog box's toolbar.

In addition to seeing a table's column properties through this dialog box, and potentially changing them, you can also inspect further properties of a table by clicking on the Table and Index Properties icon, also on the toolbar. The resulting dialog box is shown in Figure 12-5.

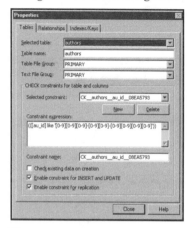

FIGURE 12-5

You can also inspect further table and index properties from the design table dialog box.

You can see the table's constraints, relationships, and indexes and keys from this dialog box. I will make reference to this dialog box often in this chapter.

NOTE

The properties dialog box based on the Design Table dialog box contains much more information than the standard Table Properties dialog box.

Opening a Table

In addition to the Design Table dialog box, you can also right-click on a table name and choose Open Table. You can either enter a top set of rows or see all the rows. If you inspect all the rows of the Authors table, you'll see a grid like that shown in Figure 12-6.

FIGURE 12-6

You can inspect and change a table's data by choosing Open Table.

The resulting window is a data grid: You can change the data inline. Each row's data will be changed when you move to a different row.

The Data window is really a full-blown query designer. Just click on the second, third, and fourth icons on the toolbar: the Show/Hide Diagram Pane, the Show/Hide Grid Pane, and the Show/Hide SQL Pane icons, and you'll see something like that in Figure 12-7.

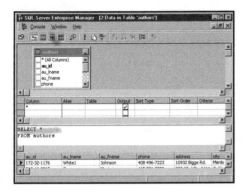

FIGURE 12-7

The Open Table window is actually a full SQL query designer.

You can enter SQL text, or build a query from the Grid pane, similar to the way you can build queries in Access and MS Query.

As you'll see in the next section, a number of important disadvantages to the query builder result from the Open Table choice. You cannot load and save Transact-SQL scripts, nor can you determine the cost of a query as you can in the Query Analyzer.

Let's now take a look at the somewhat more useful Query Analyzer.

Using the Query Analyzer

The SQL Server Query Analyzer is a graphical query tool and is the successor to the ISQL_w tool in SQL Server 6.x. You can bring up the Query Analyzer by choosing Tools from the Enterprise Manager and then finding the Query Analyzer.

NOTE

In SQL Server 6.5, there is an icon specifically for executing ISQL_w within Enterprise Manager. In SQL Server 7.0, the Query Analyzer uses an independent window and can be launched from Enterprise Manager or the Start, Programs menu.

The resulting Query Analyzer window, as shown in Figure 12-8, essentially is waiting for you to enter Transact-SQL text.

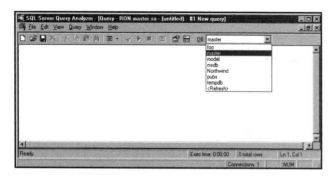

FIGURE 12-8

You can enter Transact-SQL text into the Query Analyzer.

Note that when you bring up the Query Analyzer initially from Enterprise Manager, it will use your current EM login to start the query. If you start Query Analyzer from the Start menu, then you'll have to explicitly name the server and choose either SQL Server or Windows NT authentication.

When you first start the Query Analyzer, it will place you in some database. It's always a good idea to make sure right away that you have the database context set, as you can see in the list box shown in Figure 12-8. If you inspect the icons across the toolbar, you'll get a sense of the many uses of the Query Analyzer.

The first icon lets you spawn another query window that will be the child of the current window, and it will use the same characteristics of your current connection, although with active queries, each window will have its own distinct connection.

You can load and save Transact-SQL scripts with the open and save icons. These scripts are normally saved as text files with a .SQL extension. Unlike the query builder in the data tools (see the preceding section), the Query Analyzer can handle all legal Transact-SQL commands.

You can clear the query window of all commands using the red X icon. You can also cut, copy, paste, and search text with the next set of icons. If you enter a command and click on the right green arrow, you'll see the results, as shown in Figure 12-9.

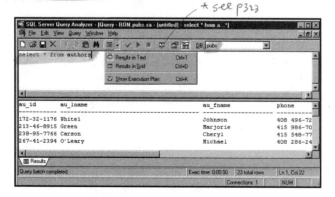

FIGURE 12-9

The results can be output either to text or to a grid.

You can choose the grid option by selecting from the Execute mode icon, as you can see in the figure. You can parse the query only, with no execution, by clicking on the blue check mark.

The right green arrow causes a query or selected part of a query to execute. You can also use Ctrl+E (^E) or Alt+X to execute a query from the keyboard.

If you choose the Display Estimated Execution Plan icon, you'll see the graphical showplan for the query (for more information about graphical showplan, see Chapter 19, "Tuning Queries").

You can also inspect the current properties of the Query Analyzer by clicking on the Current Connection Options icon on the toolbar, and you'll see the tabbed dialog box shown in Figure 12-10.

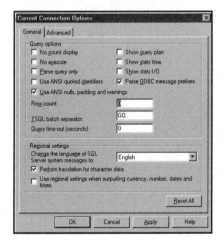

FIGURE 12-10

You can adjust the connection options in the Query Analyzer.

Many options are available here in the General tab:

- ◆ No count display: Drop the rowcount display from the query results text output.
- ◆ No execute: Parse and build the query plan without executing the query.
- ◆ Parse query only: Check just the syntax of the query.
- ◆ Use ANSI quoted identifiers: Restrict the use of double quotes for identifiers.
- ◆ Use ANSI nulls, padding, and warnings: Make = NULL return a null, pad strings with trailing blanks, and issue ANSI warnings about NULL values being eliminated from query results.
- ◆ Show query plan: Show the textual query plan along with query text results.

◆ Show stats time: Show execution times for the query.

◆ Show stats I/O: Show the logical and Physical I/Os for the query.

◆ Parse ODBC message prefixes: remove the standard ODBC driver prefixes and just present the error messages in the results pane.

In addition, you can limit the rows returned by the query, though this is not as efficient as SELECT TOP (see the next chapter). You can also change the Transact-SQL batch separator (though that is of dubious value), and you can set a query timeout. (The default of 0 indicates no timeout.) Finally, you can change the language for error messages on this query connection, translate character data if needed between character sets (the default), and select regional settings for the display of date, time, money, and numbers.

In the Advanced tab, you can choose a number of format options for the textual output, as shown in Figure 12-11.

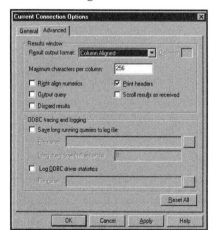

FIGURE 12-11

You can also set formatting options for the textual results pane.

In the Advanced tab you can tweak how the textual results look in the lower pane of the Query Analyzer: column-aligned or delimited by comma, tab, or your own character.

You can pick the maximum number of characters to display in a column, align number display, and otherwise control the appearance of the results. Finally, you can log the long-running queries or driver statistics for this Query Analyzer session.

Now let's use both the Query Analyzer and the Design Table dialog box to define database tables.

Defining Tables

All data in relational databases is stored in tables. In this section, you'll learn how tables are structured and created, and the boundary conditions for data types stored in SQL Server. To do this, you'll rely both on SQL Server's database diagramming utility, and on the Transact-SQL commands. It's important to learn both ways of doing things, because the Enterprise Manager GUI tools may not always be available to you, whereas the Transact-SQL interface to SQL Server is always available.

Creating a Table

One way you can create a table is by right-clicking on the Tables node in Enterprise Manager, in your chosen database, and choose New Table from the diagram. After you enter a table name, you'll be presented with the Design Table dialog box, in which you can fill out the characteristics of the table, as you can see in Figure 12-12.

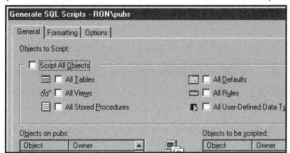

FIGURE 12-12

You can create a new table using the New Table dialog box.

The fields you fill in here match the options you can use in the CREATE TABLE command.

Although it can be very convenient to use the GUI tools to define a table, often database developers and administrators choose to use the CREATE TABLE command. For example, instead of the dialog box that preceded, you could submit the following command in the Query Analyzer (or from isql.exe or osql.exe):

```
CREATE TABLE Customer
    (cust_id        INT NOT NULL,
    cust_name CHAR(30) NULL)
```

The reason many developers prefer the command-line approach is that it can be stored in a script and rerun on demand.

Naming a Table

SQL Server table names must conform to the rules for all identifiers. That is, they can be up to 128 characters in length and include the usual letter and number characters, as well as the legal symbols of underscore (_), at-sign (@), and pound sign (#). A table name must always begin with an alphanumeric character.

Database and Table Owner

The full reference to a table consists of the database name, followed by the owner name and then the table name, as in the following example:

```
SELECT *
FROM pubs.dbo.authors
```

If you are already in the context of the database, you do not need the database reference. If you own the table, you do not need to include the owner. The combination of owner name and table name must be unique in any given database.

Temporary Tables

If you start the name of a table with a poundsign, SQL Server will create a temporary table, for your session only, in the tempdb database. It will delete the table automatically when your session ends. No one else can see or access your temporary table.

If you prefix the table with two pound signs, the temporary table becomes a global temporary table, also created in the tempdb database, and others can see and access the table. SQL Server will delete it when the session that created it ends.

Quoted Identifiers

If you want to include spaces in your table name, you can use two techniques: one that is ANSI standard, and one that is T-SQL specific.

You can surround a complex table name with double quotes if you use what is called quoted identifiers. That is, with the QUOTED IDENTIFIER setting ON, you can reference a table with double quotes, as in the following example:

```
SET QUOTED_IDENTIFIER ON
CREATE TABLE "Customer Table"(
        cust_id     INT     not null,
        cust_name CHAR(30) )
```

However, once you are using quoted identifiers, you can no longer use double quotes as string delimiters in queries. For more information about the use of quoted identifiers, see Chapter 13, "Data Manipulation."

SQL Server 7 also introduces a technique first used in Microsoft Access, whereby you can refer to a complex table name using left and right brackets, as in the following example:

```
CREATE TABLE [Customer Table](
        cust_id     INT     not null,
        cust_name CHAR(30) )
```

NOTE
The advantage of the bracket technique is that it does not depend on the setting of QUOTED IDENTIFIER. The disadvantage is that it is not ANSI SQL standard.

Naming Columns

Column names must also obey the same limitations as table names. If you want to include spaces in a column name, then use the square brackets or quoted identifiers, as shown in the following code:

```
CREATE TABLE [Customer Table](
          [cust id]    INT     not null,
          [cust name] CHAR(30) )
```

Choosing Column Data Types

Every database's columns have data types that limit the kind of data that can be stored in them. You've already seen this in the CREATE TABLE command; now let's explore data types more thoroughly.

Table 12-1 shows the data types available for SQL Server.

Table 12-1 SQL Server Data Types

Name	SQL Name	Range	Sample
Binary			
binary	binary(n)	1 to 8000	0xa1
binary varying	varbinary(n)	1 to 8000	0xa1
Character			
character	char(n)	1 to 8000	'string'
character varying	varchar(n)	1 to 8000	'string'
unicode character	nchar(n)	1 to 4000	N'string'
unicode varchar	nvarchar(n)	1 to 4000	N'string'
Date			
datetime	datetime	01/01/1753 to 12/31/9999	'Jan 15, 1996 09:01:22.1'
small datetime	smalldatetime	01/01/1900 to 6/6/2079	'Jan 15, 1996 09:01'
Logical			
bit	bit	0 or 1	1

Money

money	money	+–$922,337,203, 685,477.5807	$314453789.22
small money	smallmoney	+–$214,748.3647	$453789.22

Exact Numeric

decimal	decimal(p, s)	+1E38 to –1E38–1	1234.56
numeric	numeric(p, s)	+1E38 to –1E38–1	1234.56

Approximate Numeric

float	float(n)	+–2.23E-308 to 1.79E+308	123.456
real	real	+–1.18E-38 to 3.40E+38	123.456

Integer

integer	int	+2,147,483,647 to –2,147,483,648	12334556
small integer	smallint	+32,767 to –32,768	-2345
tiny integer	tinyint	0 to 255	12

Special

cursor	cursor	N/A	N/A
image	image	length up to 2,147, 483,647 bytes	
sysname	sysname	N/A	N/A
timestamp	timestamp	N/A	N/A
text	text	length up to 2,147, 483,647 bytes	'string'
ntext	ntext	length up to 1,073, 741,823 bytes	N'string'

User-Defined Types

You can create new data type names of your own, based on one of SQL Server's data types. In the pubs database, you'll find three examples. User-defined types allow developers to impose some constraints on a column's data. However, they limit the kinds of queries that can be done with the data, so the general trend is to avoid them.

Row Limits

Because SQL Server stores all data in 8K pages, the maximum single row length is 8,060 bytes. The remainder of the 8,192 bytes is used for overhead.

Default Values

You can also specify whether you want a column to default to a value when you don't specify the value in an Insert command. For example, in the Customers table, you can specify a default value of blank for the name using the following code:

```
CREATE TABLE Customer (
          cust_id       INT,
          cust_name     CHAR(30) DEFAULT 'New Customer')
```

Default values are important when considering NULLs.

NULLs

When you create a table, you can specify whether the columns can accept a NULL, which means there is no value at all in the column for that row. The NULL is not technically a value at all, just a marker indicating that no value is present. You can use NULL to indicate that a value is missing or is unknown.

You can make a column allow a NULL by using the NULL qualifier after the name of the column:

```
CREATE TABLE Customer (
          cust_id               INT       NOT NULL,
          cust_name     CHAR(30) NULL )
```

You can use a NOT NULL along with a default value, as in the following code:

```
CREATE TABLE Customer (
          cust_id               INT       NOT NULL,
          cust_name     CHAR(30) NOT NULL DEFAULT 'New Customer')
```

In this case, the cust_name column will default to an empty string but will never be NULL. You can detect whether a particular value has the NULL marker with the IS NULL construct, as you'll see later when I cover the SQL SELECT command.

WARNING

Allowing NULL in a table is controversial. The meaning of NULL can be ambiguous (not entered, unknown, just missing, not relevant, and so on). Many developers prefer to disallow NULL entirely in all columns and add default values instead.

Identity Property

You can have an automatically incrementing column in a table using the Identity keyword, as in the following code:

```
CREATE TABLE Customer (
        cust_id        INT IDENTITY(1,1) NOT NULL,
        cust_name    CHAR(30)        NOT NULL Default '')
```

> ### NOTE
>
> You cannot insert values directly into a column when it has the identity property, unless you first override the property by using the SET IDENTITY_INSERT <tablename> ON command. In order to use SET IDENTITY_INSERT, you must be the table owner or aliased to the table owner.

You can only have one identity column per table, and it must not allow NULL. The identity property works with all numeric (integer, smallint, tinyint, decimal, numeric, and float) data types. The parentheses after the IDENTITY keyword are optional and indicate the seed value (the initial value of the incrementing number), and then the increment amount. Both must be integer values.

The Uniqueidentifier Data Type

SQL Server 7 offers an alternative to the IDENTITY property in the uniqueidentifier data type. It produces a column that stores a unique GUID (globally unique identifier) in the column, sometimes called the ROWGUIDCOL property. As with identity, you can have only one per table. The data in the column stores 32 hexadecimal digits, which makes it a 16-byte-wide column (four times the width of an integer). When you display it, SQL Server inserts four dashes. For example, you could create the table Customer with a cust_id that is a Uniqueidentifier:

```
CREATE TABLE Customer (
    cust_id uniqueidentifier,
    cust_name CHAR(30)        )
```

You can use the NEWID() function to get SQL Server to populate the row with a GUID value:

```
INSERT INTO Customer
VALUES (NEWID(), 'New Customer')
```

When you display the result, you'll see the new ID:

```
cust_id                                 cust_name
...................................... ...............................

1E3602A4-F87F-11D1-84C6-204C4F4F5020 New Customer
```

SQL Server will automatically change the result of the GUID to a string for display purposes.

> **NOTE**
>
> Unlike the IDENTITY property, the Uniqueidentifier data type does allow NULLs. However, if you want to use it as a primary key, you must disallow NULL when you create the table.

Unicode Character Data

New to SQL Server 7 are the Unicode data types: NCHAR, NVARCHAR, and NTEXT. Unicode data is stored in two bytes per character, instead of the usual one byte per character. With two bytes available per character, every language character that Unicode supports can be assigned a unique value, thereby solving the problem of having multiple character sets that do not translate all characters. As you'll see in the next chapter, you can specify that a string be interpreted as Unicode by prefixing it with the uppercase N. The following brief script stores a unicode value and checks its length.

```
CREATE TABLE Customer (
        cust_id      INT,
        cust_name NCHAR(30)    )
INSERT INTO Customer
        VALUES (1, 'New Customer')
SELECT DATALENGTH(cust_name)
        FROM Customer
```

In the last statement, the DATALENGTH() function returns the length of the cust_name value, and it shows 60 bytes, two bytes per character.

Computed Columns

You can define columns to a table that actually just compute the values from other columns in the same table. These are called computed columns. SQL Server does not actually store the computation but calculates it at run time, much as a SELECT statement would. In the following table, for example, the penalty column computes 0.1 times the amt_due column:

```
CREATE TABLE Customer (

            cust_id        INT,

            cust_name CHAR(30),

            amt_due money,

            penalty AS amt_due * .1          )

INSERT INTO Customer

            VALUES (1, 'New Customer', 10.00)
```

So now when you look at the table, you'll see:

```
cust_id     cust_name          amt_due          penalty

..........  ...............    .............    .........

1           New Customer       10.0000          1.00000
```

Scripting a Table

You can reverse-engineer a table's CREATE TABLE script at any time by right-clicking on a table name, choosing All Tasks, and then choosing Generate SQL Scripts. The resulting dialog box is shown in Figure 12-13.

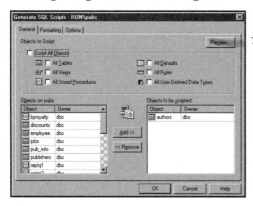

FIGURE 12-13

The Generate SQL Scripts dialog box lets you reverse-engineer scripts for an entire database.

After you've chosen a table, just click on the Preview button to see the script, and you'll see something like the script shown in Figure 12-14.

FIGURE 12-14

The script for the Customers table shows the entire Transact-SQL commands for dropping and creating the table.

These scripts can be stored on disk, and they prove much more flexible (and permanent) than a set of GUI steps.

In addition to the table creation scripts, an additional Format tab on the Generate SQL Scripts dialog box lets you format the scripts. A third tab called Options lets you decide whether to include security, indexes, triggers, and primary and foreign keys. In addition, the Options tab lets you choose various disk file options, such as saving in Unicode format, as well as saving all scripts in one file, or creating one script file per table.

Determining Table Size

You can determine the size that a table takes up with the `sp_spaceused` stored procedure. If you add a table name to the procedure, as in

```
exec sp_spaceused Authors
```

then you'll see something like the results shown in Figure 12-15.

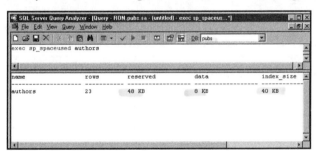

FIGURE 12-15

You can use the `sp_spaceused` *system stored procedure to determine the amount of database space used by a table.*

You learn that SQL Server has reserved 48KB for the authors table, which includes 8KB of data and 40KB for indexes.

You can also find out about table space usage from the right-hand pane in Enterprise Manager, the Tables and Indexes link, as shown in Figure 12-16.

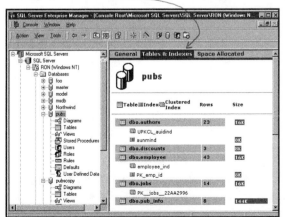

FIGURE 12-16

You can also inspect space usage of tables in the Enterprise Manager.

Copying, Renaming, and Deleting a Table

When you copy, rename, or delete a table, SQL Server takes care of references to the table in the database's system tables.

Copying a Table

w̄ Query Analyzer.

There is no GUI way to copy a table. However, you can use Transact-SQL to copy a table with the Insert command:

? or into

```
SELECT  *
            INTO Authors_copy
            FROM Authors
```

This will extract all the rows from the authors table and put the results into a new table called authors_copy.

> ### WARNING
>
> In order for the Select Into command to work, the new table must not yet exist, and you must have the Select Into/Bulk Copy database option set. You can set this option in the Options tab of the Database Properties dialog box, or with the stored procedure `sp_dboption`.

Renaming a Table

There are two ways to rename a table. In the Enterprise Manager, if you right-click on the top of a table's name in the Scope pane and pick Design Table from the menu, you'll get a dialog box to modify the table. Then choose the Properties button on the button bar, and you'll see the dialog box shown in Figure 12-17.

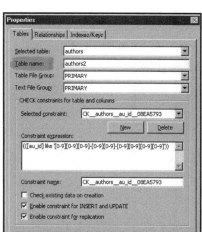

right click a table name & then choose "rename".

FIGURE 12-17

You can rename a table using the table's Properties dialog box.

Here you simply enter the new name in the Table Name field.

You can also call the SQL Server system stored procedure sp_rename in ISQL/W:

```
exec sp_rename Customer, Customer_copy
```

Obviously, you can't rename a table if there's already a table with the new name!

Dropping a Table   2 ways.   ①

To drop a table using Enterprise Manager, just right-click on the top of the table name in the database tree view, and choose Delete. A dialog box will ask you to confirm the delete.

NOTE

You'll find that SQL Server and the ANSI SQL standard distinguish dropping a table from deleting from a table. To remove a table entirely from a database, the customary term is to DROP the table, to distinguish it from the DELETE command, which removes rows from the table.

Alternatively, you can use the SQL DROP TABLE command:

②

```
DROP TABLE Customer_copy
```

WARNING

When dropping tables, be careful about dependencies. If you are trying to drop a parent table that has other tables referencing it with foreign key constraints, SQL Server will not allow the drop to occur. You must drop the child tables first. (Foreign key constraints are explained later in this section.)

Changing a Table's Structure—the ALTER TABLE Command

You can use the SQL ALTER TABLE command to add and drop columns to a table, and also add and drop constraints.

To add a new column called Address to our Customer table, you could submit:

```
ALTER TABLE Customer
        ADD Address VARCHAR(50) NULL
```

With the Alter Table command, you can add and drop columns, and also modify their characteristics, such as changing a data type:

```
ALTER TABLE Customer
                ALTER COLUMN Address CHAR(20) NULL
```

Also, you can drop the column:

```
ALTER TABLE Customer
                DROP COLUMN Address
```

> **WARNING**
>
> Any columns you add using ALTER TABLE will be placed at the end of a table, so you cannot insert them in any position you want. However, using the Design Table dialog box, you can place the columns in the order you desire.

Now let's take a closer look at database views.

Defining Views

Views are virtual tables. They are really queries, but you can refer to them as though they were tables. For example, the following code creates a view:

```
CREATE VIEW CA_Authors AS
                SELECT * FROM Authors
                WHERE state = 'CA'
```

You can then select directly from CA_Authors:

```
SELECT * FROM CA_Authors
```

→ same output as: select * from authors where state = 'CA'

and see only the California authors. Views can be used to limit the number of rows or columns that users can see. A DBA can grant rights to a view and not to the original table, thereby hiding sensitive information from the user.

You can inspect views in Enterprise Manager by drilling down to the Views node within a database and selecting Properties. The resulting dialog box will be something like that shown in Figure 12-18.

right click a view name then choose Properties.

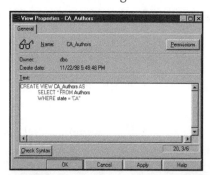

FIGURE 12-18

You can edit a view when you inspect its properties.

From here you can edit the view, check its syntax, and also set permissions for the view.

You can also change a view in Transact-SQL using the ALTER VIEW command, as in the following code:

```
ALTER VIEW CA_Authors AS
         SELECT au_lname, au_fname FROM Authors
         WHERE state = 'CA'
```

This has the advantage that permissions do not need to be reset for the view.

> **TIP**
>
> If you drop and re-create a view, it gets a new ID in the sysobjects table and requires you to reset its permissions. If you use ALTER VIEW, the ID stays the same and you don't need to reset permissions.

Updatable Views

SQL Server 7 supports updates against views, provided the view is against one table and does not contain any computed columns. Once those assumptions are in place, you can execute the Transact-SQL INSERT, UPDATE, and DELETE commands against the view.

> **WARNING**
>
> If you try to update a view that does not allow updates, the error messages may be cryptic, especially on the client. Be extra careful when trying to update views.

Using WITH CHECK OPTION in Updatable Views

If you have a view that shows only a subset of a table's data, and you update the column on which the view depends, you may get surprising results. For example, if you update a view that contains only authors with state = 'CA', and you change a state value to 'NY', the resulting row will disappear! That's because it no longer fits the view.

To prevent updating view definition columns, compile the view using the WITH CHECK OPTION switch:

```
CREATE VIEW CA_Authors AS
         SELECT au_lname, au_fname FROM Authors
         WHERE state = 'CA'
WITH CHECK OPTION
```

Partitioned Views

You can make a union of a set of views, provided the views are union-compatible, and then select from or update the view.

```
CREATE VIEW All_Authors AS
        SELECT * FROM CA_Authors
UNION
        SELECT * FROM NY_Authors
```

When you update a partitioned view, SQL Server is smart enough to know from your values to what table the new or changed row belongs.

Functions in Views

You can add a function to a view and have it return the result of the function by including the input in the view declaration. For example:

```
CREATE VIEW TypeYTDSales (TitleType, AvgYTDSales)
AS
SELECT type, AVG(YTD_Sales)
FROM titles
GROUP BY type
```

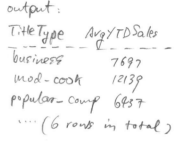

output:

TitleType	AvgYTDSales
business	7697
mod-cook	12139
popular-comp	6437

.... (6 rows in total)

Creating Views with Encryption

You can also create a view with encryption, just as you can with triggers and stored procedures. Just add the WITH ENCRYPTION option to the view declaration:

```
CREATE VIEW CA_Authors
WITH ENCRYPTION
AS
        SELECT au_lname, au_fname FROM Authors
        WHERE state = 'CA'
```

The purpose of encryption is to store the view definition in an encoded format that cannot be read using Enterprise Manager tools. This can be useful if you're delivering the database as a product and the view definition contains proprietary information.

System Tables and ANSI Views

According to the relational model, all data about a database's tables should be kept in system tables. SQL Server 7 has two broad categories of system tables. Every database has a set of catalog tables, which describe and govern all the data tables; and some databases, such as master and msdb, have data tables that act as system tables for the entire server. You can see each database's system tables and the system databases by making sure that you have the option to see them checked. Just right-click on the server name in Enterprise Manager, choose Edit SQL Server Registration, and you'll find the check box for system tables at the bottom of the dialog box, as you can see in Figure 12-19.

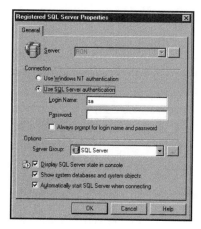

FIGURE 12-19

To make sure you can see the system tables and databases, have the option checked in the Edit SQL Server Registration dialog box.

Once you've got that option checked, you can drill down into any database, including the system databases as well as the user databases, and see the system tables, as shown in Figure 12-20.

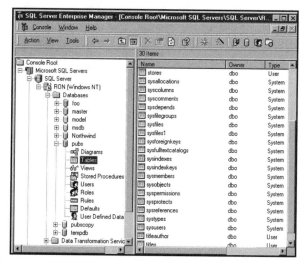

FIGURE 12-20

The system tables in the pubs database all begin with the sys prefix.

The System Catalog

The system catalog is the set of tables in the master and msdb databases. The tables in master keep track of the server-wide data. For example, the master database has a sysdatabases table to track the databases on the server, and a syslogins table to keep track of the server's logins. You can query these tables directly or rely on the system stored procedures.

The Database Catalog

Each database has a catalog that consists of a set of system tables as well, and these are the ones you see in Figure 12-20. All the database's objects are listed in sysobjects, for example, while all the users are in sysusers. As with the system catalog, you can query these tables directly or rely on the system stored procedures.

> **WARNING**
>
> Do not attempt to update the system tables directly unless it is absolutely necessary. A slight error might make the database suspect and unusable. In any case, some of the system tables are actually not persistent, and cannot be updated.

ANSI Information Schema Views

Based on the system tables, a set of ANSI views are defined in each database and inherited from the model database; they extract a limited set of information from the database system tables. These views can be seen in the tree view of Enterprise Manager, under the SQL Server Views node.

Each view has the owner INFORMATION_SCHEMA, and the owner must be referenced to identify the view. For example, to see a list of all the tables in a database, you query the TABLES view with:

```
SELECT *
FROM INFORMATION_SCHEMA.TABLES
```

The advantage of the ANSI view is that it returns a table that you can manipulate; the disadvantage is that the owner name must be referenced, making the typing rather tedious. Also, the ANSI information schema views do not return as extensive a set of information as the built-in system stored procedures, such as sp_help or sp_helpconstraint.

You can see the ANSI information schema views by looking under the Views node in Enterprise Manager.

Column Constraints

Constraints are the most important ways of limiting values in a table's column. You can enforce uniqueness, specify a range of values that the column must conform to, or specify that a foreign key column's value in one table must match one of the values of a candidate key column in another table. With constraints, you can further limit the values of a column beyond the stated limits of the column's data type.

Indexes

SQL Server will also use indexes as an indirect, shortcut method of finding data from tables without having to scan the table directly. Indexes are the primary tool for enhancing the performance of queries. For more information about using indexes to enhance query speed, see Chapter 19, "Tuning Queries."

There are two kinds of indexes you can add to a table: clustered and nonclustered.

Clustered Indexes

A clustered index actually rearranges the data into a sort order matching the columns making up the index. SQL Server will keep a table's data stored in the order you specify in a clustered index.

You can create an index using the T-SQL command, CREATE INDEX. For example, the following command creates a clustered index on the cust_id column of the Customer table:

```
CREATE CLUSTERED INDEX cust_id
        ON Customer(cust_id)
```

Obviously, a table can have only one clustered index!

Nonclustered Indexes

You can create additional nonclustered indexes. They do not affect the physical order of the data, but they can greatly improve query performance. For example, you can also create a nonclustered index using the T-SQL CREATE INDEX command:

```
CREATE NONCLUSTERED INDEX cust_name
        ON Customer(cust_name)
```

A table can have many nonclustered indexes. Adding nonclustered and clustered indexes is one of the most often used tools in query optimization.

All nonclustered indexes will go through a table's clustered index if the table has one.

Deleting Indexes

You can delete an index with the DROP INDEX command:

```
DROP INDEX cust_name
```

You can also drop an index in Enterprise Manager.

Getting Index Information

You can use Enterprise Manager to work with indexes. Just right-click on a table, choose Design Table, and then click on the Properties button on the toolbar. Figure 12-21 shows the resulting dialog box.

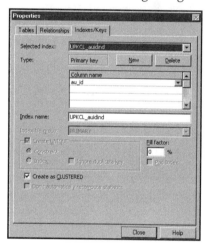

FIGURE 12-21

The Indexes/Keys tab of the Design Table Properties dialog box lets you add and modify indexes.

You can also use the sp_helpindex system stored procedure. For example,

```
exec sp_helpindex Authors
```

gives a list of all the indexes on the authors table, along with a description and a list of the keys columns making up each index.

Uniqueness Constraints

SQL Server enforces the uniqueness of values within a column by using indexes. When you create a unique index on a column or combination of columns, SQL Server will force-reject all inserts or updates to the table that would result in duplicate values.

Unique Indexes

You can use an index to enforce uniqueness. In that case, you can add an index with the UNIQUE keyword:

```
CREATE UNIQUE INDEX cust_name
           ON Customers(cust_name)
```

> **TIP**
>
> You can use a unique index to specify that a particular column or set of columns is an alternate key.

Primary Keys

You can tell SQL Server to designate a column or combination of columns as a primary key. When you choose the PRIMARY KEY keyword, SQL Server will automatically assign and name a primary key constraint. The primary key will consist of a unique index. Then SQL Server will enforce unique values in the column. Once you specify a primary key, SQL Server will also let you declare referential integrity constraints.

If the table has no other clustered index, SQL Server will default to making the primary key a clustered index. You can override this when you declare the primary key.

> **NOTE**
>
> In line with the relational rule of entity integrity, to use any column or set of columns as a primary key, you must define them as NOT NULL. No primary key value can ever be unknown.

You can declare a primary key at table creation time:

```
CREATE TABLE Customer (
           cust_id      INT      PRIMARY KEY,
           cust_name CHAR(30) )
```

Also, you can append the constraint to the CREATE TABLE statement:

```
CREATE TABLE Customer (
           cust_id       INT NOT NULL ,
           cust_name     CHAR(30) NULL ,
           CONSTRAINT PK_customer PRIMARY KEY  CLUSTERED (cust_id)
```

If you do not specify a name for the primary key constraint, SQL Server will create one—usually the letters "PK" followed by two underscores, then the table name and two more underscores, and then a set of digits. The primary key constraint name must be unique among all database objects.

You can also use the ALTER TABLE command to create a PK constraint, and add the constraint to the table after it has been created.

```
ALTER TABLE Customers
        ADD CONSTRAINT PK_Customers
            PRIMARY KEY (cust_id)
```

SQL Server will default to making the primary key constraint a clustered index. However, it's always better to spell it out:

```
ALTER TABLE Customers
        ADD CONSTRAINT PK_Customers
            PRIMARY KEY CLUSTERED (cust_id)
```

You can also put the "Clustered" keyword in the CREATE TABLE statement.

Once you've declared a primary key, then the unique character of that key becomes part of the data integrity of the table. If a duplicate key is ever added, the integrity of the table will be violated. It is SQL Server's job to make sure that never happens.

Check Constraints

Beyond column uniqueness, you may need to restrict the ranges or formats of data values in certain columns. For example, you might want to specify that the royalty percentage in the titleauthors table can never be zero or less. You can add such a constraint in Enterprise Manager by entering the Design Table mode and going to the Properties dialog box, as in Figure 12-22.

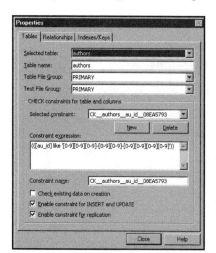

FIGURE 12-22

You can add and modify check constraints in the same Design Table Properties dialog box, on the Table tab.

In this case, you'll see the constraint name "CK_titleauthor_royaltyper," and the condition placed in the window.

Alternatively, you can issue the following ALTER TABLE command in order to add the constraint:

```
ALTER TABLE Titleauthor
        ADD CONSTRAINT CK_titleauthor_croyaltyper
        CHECK (royaltyper > 0)
```

To drop the constraint, you can either use the same dialog box or issue the following code:

```
ALTER TABLE titleauthor
        DROP CONSTRAINT CK_titleauthor_croyaltyper
```

You can also see constraints by using sp_help. For example, executing:

```
exec sp_help Authors
```

shows you a constraint called "CK__authors__au_id__02DC7882," which has the following restriction:

```
((au_id like '[0-9][0-9][0-9]-[0-9][0-9]-[0-9][0-9][0-9][0-9]'))
```

Effectively, this says every author ID must be like 999-99-9999, that is, a Social Security number.

Rules

Rules are a way you can add constraints without redefining them each time. Once a rule is established, it can be bound to particular columns. Rules, however, are not ANSI SQL standard, and so the trend is to just use the CHECK constraints.

Referential Integrity Constraints

Referential integrity refers to the validation of foreign key values when one table has columns referring to another. The referring table has the values that need to be validated; the referenced table has the values that the validation is done against. The purpose of the foreign key constraint is to prevent any unmatched references on the stated column.

Declarative Referential Integrity

Referential Integrity can be enforced in two ways: either through Declarative Referential Integrity (DRI), which is the same as a foreign key constraint, or by triggers. (SQL Server releases prior to 6.0 had to use triggers only. You can apply foreign key constraints to SQL Server 6.0 or later.)

Since three kinds of actions can occur to a table (insert, update, and delete), and a primary-foreign key relationship always involves two tables, a foreign key constraint can affect a total of six actions. Those actions are insert, update, and delete, on the primary key table and on the foreign key table.

With Declarative Referential Integrity, foreign key constraints apply to the Update and Delete of a Primary key in the referenced table, and the Insert and Update of the foreign key in the referencing table. Let's look at a specific example. In the Pubs database, the Titles table has the pub_id foreign key, which refers to the publishers table, as shown in Figure 12-23.

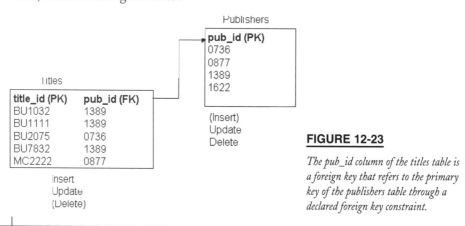

FIGURE 12-23

The pub_id column of the titles table is a foreign key that refers to the primary key of the publishers table through a declared foreign key constraint.

NOTE

The name of a foreign key column does not have to match the name of the primary key it is referencing. A table can have only one primary key, but it can have many foreign keys.

When you add a foreign key constraint to a table, SQL Server imposes restrictions on the values that can be added to the table. It requires that any row inserted or updated in the table have a matching value in the referenced table.

Data Change	Action SQL Server Takes
Insert into referencing table	Reject if the FK value is not present in the parent table as a PK.
Update of referencing table	Reject if change of FK to an unmatched PK value in the parent table.
Delete from referenced table	Reject if any child table row with that value as FKs.
Update of referenced table PK	Reject change to PK if there are any child rows with that value.

Why aren't there actions for delete of a row from the referencing table, or insert of a row into the referenced table? Consider the titles and publishers example: Adding a new publisher has no effect on titles, so there's nothing to restrict; and deleting a row from titles can never produce an unmatched foreign key, so there's nothing to restrict there either.

> **NOTE**
>
> SQL Server's Declarative RI only tests for invalid foreign key values and restricts the actions mentioned. If you want additional things tested, or if you need to perform such actions as changing statuses, then you will need to write triggers for them.

Finding Keys and Constraints in a Table

You can get a list of all the constraints on a table by using the `sp_helpconstraint` system stored procedure. For example:

```
exec sp_helpconstraint Authors
```

gives a list of all the constraints, including primary key, unique key, check constraints, and defaults.

In addition, you can select from the ANSI information schema views. For example, to get a list of constraints in a database, you can issue:

```
SELECT constraint_name, table_name, constraint_type
FROM INFORMATION_SCHEMA.TABLE_CONSTRAINTS
```

For check constraints, you can access the `CHECK_CONSTRAINTS` view:

```
SELECT constraint_name, check_clause
FROM INFORMATION_SCHEMA.CHECK_CONSTRAINTS
```

> **NOTE**
>
> The information from ANSI views is not as extensive as from `sp_helpconstraint`. The advantage of the ANSI view is that a table is produced, not a textual report, so the results can be saved and manipulated, even joined with other data.

Metadata Functions

You can use a number of functions in your Transact-SQL to determine the properties of tables, columns, and other objects in the database.

Database Objects Metadata Functions

Every object in a database is given both a name and an object ID. Both are stored in the sysobjects system table, but the object name is only stored once. All the other references to the object in other system tables, and by SQL Server's relational engine, are made to the object ID. That's why it's so easy to rename an object: Only the name need be changed in sysobjects.

If you know the name of an object, you can get its ID using the OBJECT_ID() function:

```
SELECT OBJECT_ID('Authors')
```

Conversely, if you know the object ID, you can get the name with the OBJECT_NAME function:

```
SELECT OBJECT_NAME(453576654)
```

An interesting use of these functions is to find out whether an object exists before trying to drop it:

```
IF NULLIF(OBJECT_ID('dbo.junk'),0) > 0
            DROP TABLE dbo.junk
CREATE TABLE dbo.junk(id int)
```

A more sophisticated object function is the OBJECTPROPERTY() function. It is extremely extensive, and with it you can find out any property of any object. For more information, see the Books Online, "OBJECTPROPERTY."

Column Metadata Functions

There are also some column functions. The COL_LENGTH() function returns the length of a column, as in:

```
SELECT COL_LENGTH('Authors', 'au_id')
```

The COL_NAME() function returns the name of a column, based on its order:

```
SELECT COL_NAME(OBJECT_ID('Authors'), 2)
```

With the COLUMNPROPERTY() function, you can determine the property of any column, provided you supply the ID of the table, the column name, and the property in question:

```
SELECT COLUMNPROPERTY(OBJECT_ID('Authors'), 'au_id','AllowsNull')
```

A return value of 0 means false and 1 means true.

Finally, the TYPEPROPERTY() function returns properties of any datatype. For example,

```
SELECT TYPEPROPERTY('int', 'precision')
```

returns a 10, indicating that the integer data type can handle 10 decimal digits.

Index Metadata Functions

There are two index metadata functions. The first, INDEX_COL(), determines whether there is an index on a column:

```
SELECT INDEX_COL('Authors', OBJECT_ID('UPKCL_auidind'), 1)
```

Finally, the INDEXPROPERTY() function lets you determine the properties of an index:

```
SELECT INDEXPROPERTY(OBJECT_ID('Authors'),'UPKCL_auidind' , 'IsUnique')
```

The INDEXPROPERTY() function also returns a 1 if true, 0 if false.

Summary

SQL Server 7.0's Enterprise Manager gives you several tools you can use to define tables. You can use them to inspect and change table properties, create and modify views, and add and modify constraints. Next, let's take a look at data definition. *manipulation*

Chapter 13

Data Manipulation

In This Chapter

◆ The INSERT command

◆ The UPDATE command

◆ The DELETE command

◆ The SELECT command (single-table)

◆ The SELECT command (multitable)

◆ Full-Text Search

◆ A query checklist

In addition to defining the tables that will hold data, SQL Server provides a set of Transact-SQL commands to populate those tables with data. These commands are often collectively referred to as data manipulation language, or DML. In this chapter, you'll learn about the various DML commands to insert, update, delete, and select data from database tables. Let's start with the SQL INSERT command.

The INSERT Command

You can use the SQL INSERT command to add data to a table. The INSERT command essentially takes place in two steps. First, you state what table or view you want to insert the data into. In the second step, you specify the data you want to insert.The basic Transact-SQL syntax of the INSERT command is

```
INSERT [INTO] table-or-view
            (column-list) VALUES ({DEFAULT | constant-expression } list)
            | select-statement
            | execute-statement
            | DEFAULT VALUES
[OPTION query-hints]
```

(For the complete syntax, see the Books Online.)

For the first step, specifying what you want to insert data into, you begin the command with INSERT, followed optionally by INTO, and then a table source. The INTO is ANSI standard but optional in T-SQL. Since it aids in reading the statement, you'll use the ANSI format. A table source is either a table or a view. (You'll see more about inserting into views in a few pages.)

> **NOTE**
>
> You can insert into only one table at a time. Even in the case of a view, only one of the tables in the view can be updated. See "Updating a View" in the next section for more information.

For the second step, specifying the data you want to insert, you must supply one of these items:

1. A column list followed by VALUES and a list of values
2. A SELECT statement
3. An EXECUTE statement (T-SQL only)
4. The keyword DEFAULT VALUES

Among these four options, only the third, the SELECT INTO with an EXECUTE, is not ANSI-92 standard SQL. Let's consider each of these options one at a time.

1. A Column List Followed by VALUES and a List of Values

Recall the Customer table from the last chapter:

```
CREATE TABLE Customer
          (cust_id      INT NOT NULL PRIMARY KEY,
          cust_name CHAR(30) NULL)
```

You can insert data into this table using the column list as follows:

```
INSERT INTO Customer (cust_id, cust_name)
          VALUES (123, 'Sweet Potato Consortium')
```

This inserts one row with a cust_id of "123" and a customer name of "Sweet Potato Consortium."

The keyword INTO is optional in both T-SQL and the ANSI standard. Sometimes you can make your statements more readable by including it.

If the table has default values declared for any of the columns, you can spell that out in the column list. For example, let's redefine the Customer table as follows:

```
DROP TABLE Customer
CREATE TABLE Customer
```

```
          (cust_id      INT NOT NULL PRIMARY KEY,
          cust_name     CHAR(30) NOT NULL DEFAULT 'New Customer')
```

Then you can use the keyword DEFAULT in place of the column value:

```
INSERT INTO Customer (cust_id, cust_name)
          VALUES (123, DEFAULT)
```

1a. Inserting into a Table with an IDENTITY Column

You cannot specify the column name of the IDENTITY column. To see this more clearly, let's re-create the Customer table with an IDENTITY column:

```
CREATE TABLE Customer
          (cust_id      INT IDENTITY NOT NULL PRIMARY KEY,
          cust_name     CHAR(30) NULL)
```

Now you must not mention the cust_id column:

```
INSERT INTO Customer (cust_name)
          VALUES ('Sweet Potato Consortium')
```

Of course, SQL Server will just insert the next sequence number as the cust_id. You can override this with the SET IDENTITY_INSERT setting:

```
SET IDENTITY_INSERT Customer ON
INSERT INTO Customer (cust_id, cust_name)
          VALUES (123, 'Sweet Potato Consortium')
```

The setting will remain on for the current connection, until you turn it off.

2. Inserting from a SELECT Statement   2 tables

You can insert the results set of a SELECT statement into a table by using SELECT in place of a column list and values. For example, let's redefine the Customer table slightly:

```
CREATE TABLE Customer
          (cust_id      CHAR (8) NOT NULL PRIMARY KEY,
          cust_name     CHAR(30) NULL)
```

Here you've changed cust_id to be a character rather than an integer. Then you can use the Pubs Publishers table to insert a set of data:

```
INSERT INTO Customer
```

```
SELECT pub_id, pub_name
FROM pubs.dbo.publishers
```

The columns in the SELECT statement must match up with the columns in the Customer table.

If you insert into a table with an IDENTITY column, just make sure that the SELECT statement's columns match all the remaining non-IDENTITY columns in the table:

```
INSERT INTO Customer
        SELECT pub_name
        FROM pubs.dbo.publishers
```

3. An EXECUTE Statement (T-SQL Only)   2 tables.

If you have a stored procedure that returns a result set, you can insert its results into a table also, just as you can with the INSERT/SELECT statement. Let's drop and re-create the Customer table with a character id:

```
DROP TABLE Customer
CREATE TABLE Customer
        (cust_id     CHAR (8) NOT NULL PRIMARY KEY,
        cust_name    CHAR(30) NULL)
```

Now create a stored procedure that returns the id and name from the Publishers table:

```
CREATE PROC usp_PubidPubname
AS
        SELECT pub_id, pub_name
        FROM pubs.dbo.publishers
```

Now you can do the insert using the EXEC statement:

```
INSERT INTO Customer
        EXEC usp_PubidPubname
```

NOTE

The INSERT with EXECUTE form is an invaluable Transact-SQL enhancement to the SQL language. It allows you to insert the results of a stored procedure into a table or view. It is not ANSI-92 standard, because the Transact-SQL EXECUTE statement behaves differently from the ANSI SQL EXECUTE statement.

4. The Keyword DEFAULT VALUES

If you define a table with default values, you do not have to specify the data values in a list. For example, let's re-create the Customer table with defaults:

```
DROP TABLE Customer
CREATE TABLE Customer
          (cust_id      INT IDENTITY NOT NULL PRIMARY KEY,
          cust_name     CHAR(30) NOT NULL DEFAULT 'New Customer')
```

Then you can use a simpler form of INSERT just to get a row that has all default values:

```
INSERT INTO Customer
          DEFAULT VALUES
```

Of course in this example, the cust_id column has the IDENTITY property, so all the rows will have unique values.

Inserting into a View

You can insert into a view, provided the view contains only one table. If the view contains any aggregate functions, or more than one table, you cannot use it in an INSERT statement. For rules about inserting into views having more than one table, see the INSERT statement in Books Online.

An interesting problem can occur with an INSERT if the defined view restricts the set of rows. For example, consider the following view:

```
DROP TABLE Customer
CREATE TABLE Customer
          (cust_id      INT NOT NULL PRIMARY KEY,
          cust_name     CHAR(30) NOT NULL DEFAULT 'New Customer',
             state      CHAR(2) NOT NULL DEFAULT 'NY')
CREATE VIEW Customer_CA_View        AS
          SELECT * FROM Customer
             WHERE state = 'CA'
```

The Customer_CA_View gives us a view of California customers. If you insert a New York customer:

```
INSERT INTO Customer_CA_View (cust_id, cust_name, state)
          VALUES (123, 'Sweet Potato Consortium', 'NY')
```

the INSERT is successful, but when you select from the view:

```
SELECT * FROM Customer_CA_View
```

you'll find the row you just inserted is now missing, because the view won't show it! To prevent disappearing rows, you can define the view with the WITH CHECK OPTION:

```
DROP VIEW Customer_CA_View
CREATE VIEW Customer_CA_View AS
            SELECT * FROM Customer
                WHERE state = 'CA'
            WITH CHECK OPTION
```

Now the insert will fail with error 550:

```
Server: Msg 550, Level 16, State 44000
The attempted insert or update failed because the target view either specifies
WITH CHECK OPTION or spans a view which specifies WITH CHECK OPTION and one or
more rows resulting from the operation did not qualify under the CHECK OPTION
constraint.
 Command has been aborted.
```

> **TIP**
>
> If you have views that will allow updating, it's a good idea to create them using the WITH CHECK OPTION.

INSERT and Transaction Atomicity

SQL Server treats each INSERT statement as a transaction or a logical unit of work. Either the statement entirely succeeds, or it entirely fails. If the INSERT statement appends data to a table that violates any constraint or trigger, then the entire statement fails, and no rows at all will be appended. For more information about transactions, see Chapter 16, "Transactions."

If an INSERT statement fails due to an arithmetic error, SQL Server will return an error message, terminate the command, and abort the current batch. An arithmetic overflow or a divide by zero will trigger the arithmetic error, just as is the case when SET ARITHABORT is ON.

The UPDATE Command

To change data in a table, you can use the UPDATE command. The basic syntax for the command is:

```
UPDATE table or view
            SET assignment-commalist
            [WHERE conditional-expression]
            [FROM table-expression]
            [OPTION query-hints]
```

(For the full syntax of the command, see Books Online.)

The purpose of the UPDATE command is to change data in a single table or view. You must first enter UPDATE and then the table or view name. A single UPDATE statement can update only one table or view. Then you must specify what changes you want, using assignment statements to assign new values to the current values. Optionally, you can restrict the range of your update to a subset of the table's rows with the WHERE clause. Finally, Transact-SQL has an additional FROM clause to handle cases where you update one table from another. The FROM clause is not ANSI standard and can always be replaced with ANSI equivalents, as you will see in the examples that follow.

Let's rebuild the Customer table again, this time with two rows:

```
DROP TABLE Customer
CREATE TABLE Customer
        (cust_id         INT NOT NULL,
        cust_name        CHAR(30) NOT NULL DEFAULT 'New Customer',
        state    CHAR(2) NOT NULL DEFAULT 'NY')
INSERT INTO Customer (cust_id, cust_name, state)
        VALUES (123, 'First row', 'NY')
INSERT INTO Customer (cust_id, cust_name, state)
        VALUES (456, 'Second row', 'CA')
```

You can change the state of all the rows in the Customer table with:

```
UPDATE Customer
        SET state = 'CA'
```

However, this will change all the rows in the table. To restrict the range of the update, you specify the range of the change in the WHERE clause:

```
UPDATE Customer
        SET state = 'CA'
        WHERE cust_id = '123'
```

Practice :
alter table customer
add state char(2)

To change multiple columns, you can make a comma-delimited list of the columns in the SET clause:

```
UPDATE Customer
          SET state = 'CA', name = 'New customer'
          WHERE cust_id = '123'
```

(handwritten annotation: cust_name)

Each UPDATE statement, like each INSERT, takes place as a transaction, a logical unit of work. If the statement succeeds, all updates are done, but if it fails, no rows will be updated. An UPDATE may fail if the statement violates a constraint or trigger for one or more rows. It will also fail if it attempts to change a value to an incompatible data type or insert NULL into a column that does not allow NULL.

If the UPDATE statement fails due to some error that the compiler can catch (such as an arithmetic overflow), it will fail and abort the current batch.

Searched versus Positioned UPDATE

The UPDATE statement you've looked at so far is called a searched update, because it is restricted in its scope by a WHERE clause. If you are using the UPDATE in a cursor, and you use the WHERE CURRENT OF option, you can use what's called a positioned update. In a cursor, the UPDATE...WHERE CURRENT OF will change only the current row. For more information about cursors, see Chapter 15, "Basics of Transact-SQL Programming."

Conditional UPDATE: the CASE Expression

If you want to make a conditional update, say change the state to 'CA' if the cust_id is 123, but change it to 'FL' if the cust_id is 456, then you can use either a simple CASE expression:

```
UPDATE Customer
          SET state = CASE cust_id
              WHEN 123 THEN 'CA'
              WHEN 456 THEN 'NY'
          END
```

Alternatively, you could use the searched CASE expression:

```
UPDATE Customer
          SET state = CASE
              WHEN cust_id = 123 THEN 'CA'
              WHEN cust_id = 456 THEN 'NY'
          END
```

(handwritten annotation: Note, If there are 3 records in the table, and only mention two records here, the another "state" will be "null".)

For more information about the CASE statement, see Chapter 15, "Basics of Transact-SQL Programming."

UPDATE a Table from One or More Tables: ANSI SQL

You can update one table from one or more other tables in one of two ways in SQL Server. You can use the ANSI standard method with a correlated subquery, or the Transact-SQL-only FROM clause.

To see this more clearly, suppose you create an additional table called Customer_update and change its states:

```
SELECT *
        INTO Customer_update
        FROM Customer
UPDATE Customer_update    SET state = 'AL'
        WHERE cust_id = 123
UPDATE Customer_update    SET state = 'WA'
        WHERE cust_id = 456
```

Suppose the task is to update the Customer table's state column from the Customer_update's state column.

The ANSI SQL-92 standard method, supported by SQL Server, could be implemented as follows:

```
-- Incomplete version
UPDATE Customer
        SET state = (SELECT state
                        FROM Customer_update cu
                        WHERE cu.cust_id = Customer.cust_id)
```

This query will set the state column of each Customer row equal to the state column of Customer_update, for that particular cust_id. It's called a correlated subquery because the Customer table is referenced in the subquery but named only in the outer query.

However, a source table like Customer_update often would have fewer rows than the target table Customer, and the preceding query will attempt to insert NULL for those rows that do not have a cust_id in Customer_update. Therefore, it's best to add a qualifier on the end, restricting the update to just those cust_ids that are in Customer_update:

```
UPDATE Customer
          SET state = (SELECT state
                            FROM Customer_update cu
                            WHERE cu.cust_id = Customer.cust_id)
          WHERE EXISTS (SELECT *
                            FROM Customer_update cu
                            WHERE cu.cust_id = Customer.cust_id)
```

This is the ANSI standard method of updating one table from another.

The UPDATE FROM Clause (T-SQL Extension)

There is a simpler and sometimes more efficient Transact-SQL method of updating one table from another using the FROM clause in the UPDATE statement. However, as you'll see later, using it can be risky.

The idea of the FROM clause is to add a reference to another table in the UPDATE statement, and join it with the original table:

```
UPDATE Customer
          SET state = cu.state
          FROM Customer_update cu
          WHERE Customer.cust_id = cu.cust_id
```

You can also replace the WHERE clause with the INNER JOIN:

```
UPDATE Customer
          SET state = cu.state
          FROM Customer
          INNER JOIN Customer_update cu
          ON Customer.cust_id = cu.cust_id
```

If you don't include the join in the WHERE clause, the results will be unpredictable.

As an alternate formulation, you can mention the original table a second time in the FROM clause and use its alias in any further WHERE clause:

```
UPDATE Customer
          SET state = cu.state
          FROM Customer c, Customer_update cu
          WHERE c.cust_id = cu.cust_id
```

However, there is a major problem with the FROM clause. For it to work properly, you must never have any duplicates on the join columns in it. In other words, suppose there were duplicate ids in the Customer_update table:

```
UPDATE Customer_update
            SET cust_id = 123
            WHERE cust_id = 456
```

Now in the Customer_update table you've got:

cust_id	cust_name	state
123	first test row	AL
123	second test row	WA

Which row should be used? According to your original UPDATE...FROM statements, you want to update the rows in Customer where the cust_id matches, but now you have two that match. Rather than report the ambiguity, the T-SQL UPDATE...FROM construct will simply choose one of them and give the result in Customer. For example:

```
BEGIN TRAN
            UPDATE Customer
                SET state = cu.state
                FROM Customer c, Customer_update cu
                WHERE c.cust_id = cu.cust_id
SELECT Cust_id, state from Customer
ROLLBACK
```

results in:

Cust_id	state
123	WA
456	CA

This time it chose the second row of Customer_update as the source of the value, changing the state to 'WA'. However, you can't count on any rule here.

By way of contrast, the ANSI SQL-92 form, in SQL Server, detects the ambiguity. For example:

```
UPDATE Customer
            SET state = (SELECT state
                FROM Customer_update cu
```

```
            WHERE cu.cust_id = Customer.cust_id)
    WHERE EXISTS (SELECT *
            FROM Customer_update cu
            WHERE cu.cust_id = Customer.cust_id)
```

gives the error message:

Server: Msg 512, Level 16, State 21000

Subquery returned more than 1 value. This is illegal when the subquery follows =,

!=, <, <= , >, >=, or when the subquery is used as an expression.

The subquery following the SET keyword returns two rows, and you can't set one row equal to a value in two rows. So the ANSI version detected that the directions were ambiguous—your statement did not specify which one of the two rows to use.

Of course, if you choose one of them, say with a MAX() function, then the update will succeed, as you can see in these statements:

```
UPDATE Customer
        SET state = (SELECT MAX(state)
            FROM Customer_update cu
            WHERE cu.cust_id = Customer.cust_id)
    WHERE EXISTS (SELECT *
            FROM Customer_update cu
            WHERE cu.cust_id = Customer.cust_id)
```

WARNING

Updating one table from another using the Transact-SQL UPDATE/FROM extension can be simpler and even more efficient than using the ANSI SQL-92 version. However, if there are any duplicate rows in the source tables, the Transact-SQL extension will not detect the fact, and you can receive unpredictable results. When you make your command follow the ANSI SQL standard using UPDATE/WHERE EXISTS, it will detect the ambiguity and refuse the update until you provide a method for choosing among the duplicates.

Cascading UPDATE

A cascading UPDATE is the action of changing the primary keys of a secondary table to the new values set in a primary table. Cascading updates are not supported by SQL Server's DRI, and only a limited version, restricted to updates of one row, can be implemented in triggers. For an example, see Chapter 18, "Triggers."

The OPTION Clause

You can add query hints in the OPTION clause to force the query analyzer to use certain indexes. For more information, see Chapter 20, "Concurrency Tools."

Updating a View

You can update a view, with essentially the same rules for inserting into a view. The view can only contain one table. If the view contains any aggregate functions, or more than one table, then you cannot update it. For more information about updating a view, see the CREATE VIEW statement in Books Online.

The same problem of disappearing rows can occur with an UPDATE of a view if the view restricts the set of rows, as discussed above about inserting into views. The rows can seemingly disappear. For example, consider the following view:

```
DROP TABLE Customer
GO
CREATE TABLE Customer
            (cust_id      INT NOT NULL PRIMARY KEY,
            cust_name     CHAR(30) NOT NULL DEFAULT 'New Customer',
            state CHAR(2)  NOT NULL DEFAULT 'NY')
CREATE VIEW Customer_CA_View      AS
            SELECT * FROM Customer
                WHERE state = 'CA'
```

The Customer_CA_View gives you a view of California customers. If you insert a California customer:

```
INSERT INTO Customer_CA_View (cust_id, cust_name, state)
            VALUES (123, 'Sweet Potato Consortium', 'CA')
```

the INSERT is successful. Now change the state:

```
UPDATE Customer_CA_View
            SET state = 'NY'
            WHERE cust_id = 123
```

Now when you select from the view:

```
SELECT * FROM Customer_CA_View
```

you'll find the row you just updated is missing. To prevent disappearing rows, you can define the view with the WITH CHECK OPTION.

> **TIP**
>
> If you have any views that will allow updating, it's a good idea to create them using the WITH CHECK OPTION.

The DELETE Command

The purpose of the DELETE statement is to remove rows from a table. The DELETE statement operates like the UDPATE statement minus the SET statement. You specify the table name and then add a restriction to the rows you want deleted.

> **NOTE**
>
> The DELETE statement does not remove or delete a table. The command to remove a table from a database is DROP TABLE.

The basic syntax of the Transact-SQL DELETE command is:

```
DELETE [FROM] table-or-view
            [FROM table-expression]
            [WHERE conditional-expression]
            [OPTION query-hints]
```

(For the full syntax of the command, see Books Online.)

Notice the two optional FROMs: The first is actually required by ANSI SQL-92 but is optional in Transact-SQL. The second, a FROM clause similar to one in the UPDATE statement, is a Transact-SQL extension. The two can sometimes cause confusion when they occur together. In the following examples, you'll continue your attempt to stay close to ANSI SQL.

The DELETE command removes rows based on the qualification you put in the WHERE clause. If you don't use a WHERE clause, all rows will be removed. For example, to remove all rows from the Customer table, you can write:

```
DELETE FROM Customer
```

Although it will remove all rows from a table, you can also use the more efficient TRUNCATE TABLE command, which does not write the deleted data to the transaction log:

```
TRUNCATE TABLE Customer
```

The TRUNCATE command will be more efficient with large tables in particular.

You can delete a restricted subset of the table's rows using the WHERE clause:

```
DELETE FROM Customers
            WHERE cust_id = 123
```

DELETE from One or More Tables: ANSI SQL

Just as SQL Server lets you update one table from another in two ways, it also lets you delete rows in two ways. The first, ANSI standard, method also uses a correlated subquery, whereas the Transact-SQL extension relies on DELETE's second FROM clause.

Using the additional table called Customer_update that you created in the UPDATE section, you can remove rows from Customer based on Customer_update as follows:

```
DELETE FROM Customer
        WHERE cust_id IN (SELECT DISTINCT cust_id
            FROM Customer_update)
```

You can interpret this as saying, "Delete every Customer row that has a customer id in the list of customer ids from Customer_update."

In addition to the IN function, you can use the WHERE EXISTS clause:

```
DELETE FROM Customer
WHERE EXISTS (SELECT *
        FROM Customer_update cu
        WHERE cu.cust_id = Customer.cust_id)
```

You can read this as saying, "Delete every row in Customer where there exists a customer id in the Customer_update table equal to its customer id."

The DELETE FROM...FROM (T-SQL Extension)

The Transact-SQL method of placing an additional FROM clause in the DELETE can be more efficient and easier to user than the ANSI version. Unlike the UPDATE statement, though, no ambiguities result.

Again, the idea of the second FROM is to add a reference to another table in the DELETE statement and join it with the original table:

```
DELETE FROM Customer
        FROM Customer_update cu
        WHERE Customer.cust_id = cu.cust_id
```

You can repeat the original table and reference it with an alias:

```
DELETE FROM Customer
        FROM Customer c, Customer_update cu
        WHERE c.cust_id = cu.cust_id
```

The use of the two FROMs can be confusing, as you can see. Some like to drop the first optional FROM, making the command somewhat simpler. However, it's almost always a good practice to stick with ANSI-compatible SQL if you can, and leave in the first FROM.

You can rewrite every DELETE statement that uses the Transact-SQL FROM into an ANSI standard format. For example, the Books Online contains the following example, which deletes the top 10 authors by referencing a derived table:

```
DELETE authors
FROM (SELECT TOP 10 * FROM authors) AS t1
WHERE authors.au_id = t1.au_id
```

In other words, the inner query gets the top 10 authors, and then the outer query references them. This is very powerful, but it is not ANSI standard. However, the following version does use the ANSI syntax:

```
DELETE FROM authors
        WHERE EXISTS (
            SELECT * FROM (SELECT TOP 10 * FROM authors) AS t1
            WHERE authors.au_id = t1.au_id)
```

You can read this as, "Delete every author's row where there exists a top 10 author id equal to that row's author id."

Cascading DELETE

A cascading DELETE is the action of deleting rows from a secondary table when rows in a primary table are removed. Cascading deletes are not supported by SQL Server's DRI and have to be implemented in triggers. For an example, see Chapter 18, "Triggers."

The `OPTION` **Clause**

You can add query hints in the `OPTION` clause, to force the query analyzer to use certain indexes. For more information, see Chapter 19, "Tuning Queries."

The `SELECT` **Command (Single-Table)**

You can issue the SQL `SELECT` command to retrieve data and inspect the results of inserts and updates. The `SELECT` command returns you a new table of data containing the results of the criteria that you specify. The table that the `SELECT` command returns to you is called the results set.

The basic syntax of the Transact-SQL `SELECT` command is:

```
SELECT select-list
          [INTO table-reference]
          [FROM table-reference
          [WHERE conditional-expression]
          [GROUP BY column-commalist]
          [HAVING conditional-expression]
          [WITH CUBE | ROLLUP]
          [ORDER BY column-commalist]
          [COMPUTE [BY] column]
          [FOR BROWSE]
          [OPTION query-hints]
```

In the preceding syntax, the WITH CUBE|ROLLUP, COMPUTE, and FOR BROWSE constructs are Transact-SQL extensions, not present in ANSI SQL-92.

The order of the components in the SELECT command is important. If you use the INTO syntax, for example, it must occur before the FROM clause. The GROUP BY must occur after the WHERE, and so on.

The SELECT command can become complex very quickly, mostly because you can include other SELECT commands inside it. Also, because the syntax is very flexible, there are often many ways to write the same query. In this section, you'll learn about the basics of the SELECT command, focusing on SELECTs from single tables. Following this section, another section will treat the more complex SELECTs from multiple tables.

A SELECT **Returns Results in a Table**

A SELECT statement always returns results to you as a table, often called a results set. This is in accordance with the relational model, which states that every operation on a set of tables should result in a table. In the Query Analyzer and ISQL, when you submit a SELECT command the results are returned and then displayed by the software on screen.

> ### NOTE
>
> The table holding a SELECT command's results set is a SQL Server table, and so it cannot have any rows exceeding 8,060 bytes in length. It can, however, have 4,096 columns, four times the 1,024 column limit for base tables.

Notice that all the parts of the command are optional, except the word SELECT itself! You can send a truly minimal SELECT command to the Query Analyzer or ISQL as follows:

```
SELECT 'Hi there'
```

You'll get a one-row, one-column table as the result set:

```
- - - - - - - -

Hi there

(1 row(s) affected)
```

The Query Analyzer returns with the message that one row was affected, which in this case means that the result set is a table consisting of only one row.

The dotted line above the string "Hi there" is a separator supplied by the query software, not part of the results. It's meant both to separate and indicate column titles. You can add a column name in the query window as follows:

```
SELECT 'Hi there' AS Message
```

and the result will now be:

```
Message
- - - - - - - -
Hi there
```

Transact-SQL also allows you to put the string beforehand, as follows:

```
SELECT 'Message' = 'Hi there'
```

Also, Transact-SQL allows you to drop the keyword AS:

```
SELECT 'Hi there' Message
```

As is often the case, the best practice is to stay close to the SQL standard, and use the AS construct to name columns. Most of the time, you'll be selecting data from a table, and Transact-SQL will provide you with the column names by default.

Column Specification

You specify the columns of the results set in the SELECT clause, followed normally by the table or tables from which you want the data to come. For example, a table called Publishers in the Pubs database has columns pub_id and pub_name:

```
SELECT pub_id, pub_name
        FROM Publishers
```

In this case, you'll see the returned data in the results pane:

```
pub_id pub_name

------ ----------------------------------------
0736   New Moon Books
0877   Binnet & Hardley
1389   Algodata Infosystems
1622   Five Lakes Publishing
1756   Ramona Publishers
9901   GGG&G
9952   Scootney Books
9999   Lucerne Publishing
(8 row(s) affected)
```

Instead of naming all the columns, you can use the asterisk as a wild card to indicate all columns:

```
SELECT *
        FROM Publishers
```

The default behavior for ANSI SQL and Transact-SQL is to return a results set table that allows duplicate rows. In other words, the results set is a table that does not have a primary key. For example, if you select the author id and state from the Authors table, you'll get unique rows, because the author id is a primary key:

```
SELECT au_id, state
        FROM Authors
```

But if you just select the state, as in the code that follows, duplicate values will show in the results:

```
SELECT state
          FROM Authors
```

```
state

-----

CA

CA

CA

CA

CA

KS

etc.
```

```
(23 row(s) affected)
```

NOTE

The SQL SELECT behavior of returning duplicate rows in results set tables is not in accordance with the relational model and is a common object of criticism of the SQL language by relational theorists.

The SELECT command does have a mechanism for preventing duplicate rows in the results set. You can remove duplicates using the DISTINCT keyword:

```
SELECT DISTINCT state
          FROM Authors
```

```
state

-----

CA

IN

KS

MD

MI

OR

TN

UT
```

```
(8 row(s) affected)
```

Now the results set has unique rows. The DISTINCT keyword applies to the entire row, and not to any single column.

NOTE

If you install SQL Server with a case-sensitive sort order, column and table names will be case-sensitive. Therefore you must name your columns in the SELECT statement exactly the way they were first created in the database.

SELECT TOP N

A new and much-needed feature in SQL Server 7 is the TOP keyword, which you can use to get the first or "top" number or percentage of rows. For example, to get just one row from the Authors table, you can issue the command:

```
SELECT TOP 1 *
        FROM Authors
```

SQL Server will return just the first row in the table that it finds.

NOTE

The word "TOP" suggests an order, but really it just limits the number of rows returned to the result set, so its meaning is really closer to "first" than "top."

Sometimes, though, you really do want the top number, in the sense of greatest. In that case, you need to use the ORDER BY clause:

```
SELECT TOP 10 title_id, ytd_sales
        FROM Titles
        ORDER BY ytd_sales DESC
```

You can also change the requirement to percent, as in:

```
SELECT TOP 10 PERCENT title_id, ytd_sales
        FROM Titles
        ORDER BY ytd_sales DESC
```

The percent here refers to the number of rows. The preceding query returns two rows because there are 18 rows in the table, 10 percent of which is 1.8, which rounds up to 2 rows. SQL Server will round up when deciding the number of rows in a percentage to return.

If you want to include ties, when there is more than one row that would satisfy the requirement, just add the WITH TIES clause:

```
SELECT TOP 5 WITH TIES title_id, ytd_sales
          FROM Titles
          ORDER BY ytd_sales DESC
```

This query actually returns eight rows, not five, because the fifth through the eighth all have the value 4095. The WITH TIES clause causes them to be added to the results set:

```
title_id ytd_sales
........ ...........

MC3021   22246

BU2075   18722

TC4203   15096

PC1035   8780

BU1032   4095

BU7832   4095

PC8888   4095

TC7777   4095
(8 row(s) affected)
```

SELECT INTO (T-SQL Extension)

After you've specified the table, you can also specify a named target location for the results set table using the Transact-SQL extension, INTO. If you use the INTO clause, it must come before the FROM clause, and it must name a table that does not yet exist:

```
SELECT DISTINCT state
          INTO Authors_states
          FROM Authors
```

If the target table already exists and you just want to add additional rows to it, use the INSERT...SELECT formulation instead.

NOTE

The SELECT...INTO construct is not a fully logged operation, and so by default SQL Server databases will not allow it. You can use the sp_dboption stored procedure or Enterprise Manager to set it. For more information, see Chapter 7, "Managing Databases."

In order for you to SELECT...INTO a table, your database must have the Select Into/Bulk Copy option turned on. However, you can SELECT INTO a temporary table without the option being on:

```
SELECT *
        INTO #Authors_temp
        FROM Authors
```

Select * from #authors_temp ↓

The temporary table actually resides in the Tempdb database, and it does have the Select Into/Bulk Copy option on by default.

> **WARNING**
>
> Do not confuse SELECT...INTO with the singleton SELECT of embedded SQL. The singleton SELECT retrieves exactly one row and populates a set of variables.

The FROM Clause

In the FROM clause, you can name a table or a view. If the table or view name has blanks in it, you'll have to use square brackets or quoted identifiers to identify it. (For information about nonstandard table names, see Chapter 12. For more information about quoted identifiers, see "Delimiting Strings," which follows.)

Let's take an example. Suppose you have a table called "Too Much," and you want to select from it. You can use the Transact-SQL extension introduced in SQL Server 7 of square brackets to identify the table, as in:

```
SELECT *
        FROM [Too Much]
```

use [ ] or " "
if there is "space" (blanks) in a table/view name

(The table name will be case-sensitive on a case-sensitive server.)

In addition, if QUOTED_IDENTIFIERS is ON, you can also use double quotes:

```
SELECT *
        FROM "Too Much"
```

> **NOTE**
>
> Usually it is more trouble than it is worth to allow embedded spaces or other nonstandard characters in table or column names. Unless your application uses legacy or upsized tables with embedded spaces, you're better off using standard Transact-SQL identifiers. For more on identifiers, see Chapter 12.

Derived Tables

The SELECT statement returns a table called the results set. This is actually a table derived from the base tables you mention in your FROM clause. Is there any way to make use of the results set table? The answer is yes, using what are called "derived tables" in the FROM clause. Here's a simple example:

```
SELECT *
        FROM (SELECT * FROM Authors) AS T1
```

You have to use an alias for the inner SELECT, giving it in effect a table name. Then you can use that name in other parts of the SELECT statement. Because most uses of derived tables involve multitable SELECTs, I'll cover derived tables later in this chapter.

Aggregate Functions

If you want to see just the number of rows for a column, you can use the COUNT() function:

```
SELECT COUNT(*)
        FROM Authors
```

output. ---- *(23 records in total)*
       23

> **TIP**
>
> Using COUNT(*) is generally better than using COUNT() with a specific column name, because it gives the query engine the flexibility to find out the row count any way it can. It might, for example, just read an index instead of scanning the table.

Count (*)
or
Count (State)

Based on all of the preceding considerations, if you want to see the count of a set of unique values, you can combine DISTINCT and COUNT():

```
SELECT COUNT(DISTINCT state) AS state_count
        FROM authors
```

turns out: *State_count*

               8

In addition to counting the number of values in the rows of a table, you can also get other data using T-SQL functions known as aggregate functions. For example, in the pubs Discounts table, you can find the maximum, minimum, sum, and average of the discounts:

```
SELECT
        MAX(discount)          AS maxdiscount,
        MIN(discount)          AS mindiscount,
        SUM(discount)          AS sumdiscount,
```

→ Important

Turns out:

maxdiscount	mindiscount
10.50	5.00
sumdiscount	avgdiscount
22.20	7.40

```
AVG(discount)            AS avgdiscount
FROM Discounts
```

There are some important things to think about when using aggregate functions with NULLs.

The COUNT() function, for example, considers all NULLs as just one distinct value. Consider the Discounts table, which has a number of NULLs:

```
SELECT *
        FROM Discounts
```

Turns out:

discounttype	stor_id	lowqty	highqty	discount
Initial Customer	NULL	NULL	NULL	10.50
Volume Discount	NULL	100	1000	6.70
Customer Discount	8042	NULL	NULL	5.00

The COUNT() function will only count a NULL once, so:

```
SELECT COUNT(stor_id)
        FROM Discounts
```

returns a count of only two rows, not three. The MAX(), MIN(), SUM(), and AVG() functions will ignore NULLs entirely in their calculations, unless all the values are NULL. If all the values are NULL, then the result will also be NULL.

Column Arithmetic

You can perform arithmetic operations among numeric columns when you use the plus (+) or minus (−) signs:

```
SELECT title_id, ytd_sales, ytd_sales * 2      as ytd_sales x2'
        FROM Titles
```

title_id	ytd_sales	ytd_sales x 2	
BU1032	4095	8190	= 4095 × 2
BU1111	3876	7752	
BU2075	18722	37444	
BU7832	4095	8190	
MC2222	2032	4064	
MC3021	22246	44492	
MC3026	NULL	NULL	

Note that the ytd_sales value for MC3026, the last in the list, is NULL and the result of multiplying by two is also NULL.

In fact, you can use the SELECT statement as a very expensive calculator:

```
SELECT 5*55
...........
275
(1 row(s) affected)
```

You can also use the standard multiply (*), divide (/), and modulo (%) arithmetic symbols with numeric data types.

However, division will default to integer division (dropping remainders) when you divide two integers:

```
SELECT 15/11
...........
1
(1 row(s) affected)
```

The result returned is an integer, so the fractional remainder has been dropped. To get a noninteger result that keeps the remainder, you can change one of the operands to a noninteger data type, as in this code:

```
SELECT 15/11.0
...........
1.363636
(1 row(s) affected)
```

✗ Note: ① If no space between ' ', then no space between resulted first- and last name ② If use
select au-fname + ' ' + au-lname as aut-name
then aut-name will appear as the title for the result

For more information about conversions from one data type to another, see Chapter 15, "Basics of Transact-SQL Programming."

Concatenating Strings

You can combine character columns by concatenating them with the plus (+) sign. The following query concatenates the last names and first names of all the Authors rows and inserts a comma followed by a blank right after the last name:

```
SELECT au_lname + ', ' + au_fname
        FROM Authors
        WHERE state = 'CA'
```

Select au_fname + ' ' + au_lname
from authors
where state = 'ca'

Result: white, Johnson
Green, Marjorie

Result: Johnson White
Marjorie Green   *接上 ✗ Note*

An interesting problem arises when you try to concatenate a NULL with a string:

```
SELECT 'Hi there' + NULL    output:    ----
                                        null
```

The default behavior of SQL Server before Release 7 was to return just the original string, with nothing attached. However, the ANSI SQL-92 standard states that all operations involving a NULL should return NULL, including concatenation. So SQL Server 7 has added the CONCAT_NULL_YIELDS_NULL setting and defaults to setting it ON. When ON, the result of concatenating a NULL will be NULL. If you do not want that behavior, you can either change the setting:

```
SET CONCAT_NULL_YIELDS_NULL OFF
SELECT 'Hi there' + NULL
```

or you can set the database default with sp_dboption.

The WHERE Clause

You can use the WHERE clause to filter the rows that a query returns. This clause just adds a condition to the query, based on data values of the columns:

```
SELECT *
    FROM Authors
        WHERE state = 'CA'
```

Simple

As you would expect, you can use the standard comparison symbols =, <>, >, >=, <, <= for both strings and numbers.

You can use the AND and OR connectives to combine conditions in the WHERE clause, and the NOT operator to negate them. Note that you have to repeat the name of the object you're comparing:

```
SELECT au_id, au_lname
    FROM Authors
        WHERE state = 'CA' OR state = 'UT'
SELECT au_id, au_lname
    FROM Authors
        WHERE state = 'CA' AND NOT city = 'Berkeley'
```

or

and not

When the conditions become numerous or complex, it's a good practice to clarify how the conditions apply by using parentheses:

```
SELECT au_id, au_lname
    FROM Authors
```

```
WHERE (state = 'CA' OR state = 'UT')
      AND city = 'Berkeley'
```

Where (... or ....) ,
and ....

In the preceding query, the parentheses make it clear that you want rows with states of either CA or UT, that also have a city of Berkeley. Without the parentheses to clarify the conditions, you would get all rows that have a state of CA, along with all rows that have a state of UT and a city of Berkeley. This is caused by the normal order of precedence: an AND is evaluated first, then the OR.

Delimiting Strings

The ANSI SQL standard is to use single quotes to delimit string literals, and double quotes only for identifiers (such as table and column names that include blanks). If you want to find all authors whose last name is "Ringer," the ANSI standard would have you use just single quotes to delimit a string:

```
SELECT * FROM Authors
        WHERE au_lname = 'Ringer'
```

single quotes (' ') is needed here;
case not sensitive; double quotes (" ") work too.

Transact-SQL will normally also accept double quotes, but that is not standard ANSI SQL. You can test this behavior using the QUOTED_IDENTIFIER setting. For example, this code produces an error:

```
SET QUOTED_IDENTIFIER ON
GO
SELECT * FROM Authors
        WHERE au_lname = "Ringer"
Server: Msg 207, Level 16, State 42S22
Invalid column name 'Ringer'.
```

The command returns the error message because it was expecting the double quotes to be used to identify a column or table.

The QUOTED_IDENTIFIER setting is affected by the setting of ANSI_DEFAULTS. Setting ANSI_DEFAULTS to ON will also cause QUOTED_IDENTIFIER to be set ON, and you'll get the same error message.

NOTE

Because the ANSI defaults do not allow the double quote to be used, it's a good idea to stick to single quote marks. Since both the OLEDB and ODBC drivers default to setting ANSI_DEFAULTS ON, it's a good practice to use single quotes whenever possible to delimit strings.

But then there's a problem: what about looking for a title in the pubs Titles table named "The Busy Executive's Database Guide"? If you try:

```
SELECT * FROM Titles
        WHERE title =
            'The Busy Executive's Database Guide'
```

you'll get the error message,

```
Server: Msg 170, Level 15, State 42000
Line 3: Incorrect syntax near 's'.
Unclosed quote before the character string ''.
```

In this case, the query engine is unable to interpret what comes after the second quite mark, interpreting the first string as ending with the word "Executive."

The ANSI solution is to simply double up the apostrophe as two single quote marks:

```
SELECT * FROM Titles
        WHERE title =
            'The Busy Executive''s Database Guide'
```

Result:
1 row affected

However, embedding a sequence of two quote marks in a string whenever an apostrophe occurs is an unrealistic requirement for most applications.

NOTE

Because embedding a sequence of two quote marks in a string to cover apostrophes may place too great a burden on your applications, consider making sure that the QUOTED_IDENTIFIER setting is OFF. You can change this setting for the entire database by using sp_dboption. (For more information about sp_dboption, see Chapter 7, "Managing Databases.")

For more information about the effect of the ANSI settings, see Chapter 12.

The GROUP BY Clause

Sometimes you will want to retrieve summary data in the results set. The GROUP BY statement causes the results set to contain a list of groups from the original tables, rather than the raw data. That way, it can be used to collect summaries.

The GROUP BY helps solve a problem with the simple SELECTs you've seen so far. For example, suppose we want to know how many authors are in each state. We could start out with:

```
SELECT state, COUNT(state)
         FROM Authors
```

The idea here is that you want each state, then the count for the state next to it.

However, Transact-SQL returns the following error message:

Server: Msg 8118, Level 16, State 42000

Column 'Authors.state' is invalid in the select list because it is not contained

in an aggregate function and there is no GROUP BY clause.

What the error message is stating is that using the state column is incompatible with the COUNT() function. The COUNT() function treats the whole table as a single group and will return a single row into the results set; however, the state column will return one row for each state. You can't have a results set with one row and several rows at the same time!

However, if you use the GROUP BY statement and force a grouping for each state, then the query engine will give you a count for each group, which is what you want:

```
SELECT state, COUNT(state) As statecount
         FROM Authors
         GROUP BY state
```

```
state statecount
----- -----------
CA    15
IN    1
KS    1
MD    1
MI    1
OR    1
TN    1
UT    2
```

(8 row(s) affected)

Since the COUNT() (and any aggregate) function without any GROUP BY just treats the whole table as one group, when you add the GROUP BY, the COUNT() function applies to each group, and so you get a count for each grouped row in the results set. The same logic applies to all the other aggregate functions, such as MAX(), MIN(), AVG(), and SUM().

> **NOTE**
>
> What's important to remember is that GROUP BY does not sort similar rows together; rather, it makes a single row in the results set for each group in the original table.

There are some restrictions to GROUP BY. Any column named in the GROUP BY clause must be mentioned in the SELECT column list (excluding aggregate functions like COUNT(), of course). You can't group by an alias, though, and you can't GROUP BY columns that have the bit, image, ntext, or text data types.

All NULLs in the columns named in the GROUP BY will be collected together into one group.

It turns out that barring some minor exceptions, all GROUP BY statements could be replaced by subqueries. For example, you can also get a list of all states along with their counts by using this query:

```
SELECT DISTINCT state,
          (SELECT COUNT(state)
               FROM Authors a2
               WHERE a2.state = Authors.state) AS statecount
     FROM Authors
```

In this case, the subquery gets a total for each state, and the DISTINCT gets a results set with one row for each state. This is called a correlated subquery, and although it can replace the GROUP BY, it is not easier to read or maintain, and it is also usually slower. You'll learn more about correlated subqueries later in this chapter.

The HAVING **Clause**

The HAVING clause just filters the GROUP BY clause:

```
SELECT state, COUNT(state) As calcount
          FROM Authors
          GROUP BY state
          HAVING state = 'CA'
```

Result:
State   calcount
CA   15

This query returns just one row, because there's only one group in the results set that has the state 'CA'. Like the GROUP BY, the HAVING clause can often be replaced by a WHERE clause, as it could have been in the preceding example:

```
SELECT state, COUNT(state) As calcount
        FROM Authors
        WHERE state = 'CA'
        GROUP BY state
```

order matters.

This query limits the rows to just the state of California first, and then does the grouping and count.

Sometimes, however, the HAVING is essential. Consider the problem of finding duplicates. The following SELECT command finds all the duplicate states in the Authors table:

```
SELECT state, COUNT(state) As statecount
        FROM Authors
        GROUP BY state
        HAVING COUNT(state) > 1
```

```
state statecount
----- -----------
CA     15
UT     2
(2 row(s) affected)
```

In this case, the HAVING clause places a condition on the aggregate, to list just those groups that have a total greater than one—in other words, the groups with duplicates. You could not use a WHERE clause instead, because the aggregate is not a column of the table.

The query you just saw is very useful for finding duplicates in any number of cases. For example, in earlier releases of SQL Server, database diagrams indicated that the combination of first and last name in the pubs Authors table should be unique. However, the pubs database was never implemented with a uniqueness constraint to do that. You can check to see whether the combination of first and last name in the Authors table is unique, by checking to see if there are any duplicates, and using the concatenation of the names to select and group by:

```
SELECT au_fname+au_lname,
        COUNT(au_fname+au_lname) As au_count
        FROM Authors
        GROUP BY au_fname+au_lname
        HAVING COUNT(au_fname+au_lname) > 1
```

Result:

0 row affected

In this query, you cannot use au_lname and au_fname by themselves, because they are column names and cannot be listed in the SELECT clause. However, you can concatenate them, group by the concatenation, and restrict the results to when the count of the concatenated group is greater than one.

CUBE **and** ROLLUP

There is an interesting addition to the GROUP BY option—the WITH CUBE and WITH ROLLUP operators. These cause additional rows to be added to the results set that contain aggregates across the columns named in the GROUP BY.

Let's take an example. The Titles table in the pubs database contains a publisher id, a type of book, and year-to-date sales columns. You can look at each publisher, with the type of book that it publishes and the total year to date sales for that type, using this query:

```
SELECT pub_id, type, sum(ytd_sales)
         FROM titles
         GROUP BY pub_id, type
         ORDER BY pub_id, type
```

pub_id type

....

pub_id	type	
0736	business	18722
0736	psychology	9564
0877	mod_cook	24278
0877	psychology	375
0877	trad_cook	19566
0877	UNDECIDED	0
1389	business	12066
1389	popular_comp	12875

(8 row(s) affected)

The results tell you the publisher id, the types of books its publisher has sold, and the total year-to-date sales for each type. Notice that there is an "UNDECIDED" type with no ytd_sales.

Now, let's get some aggregates. You'll start with ROLLUP, which is the simplest:

```
SELECT pub_id, type, sum(ytd_sales)
         FROM titles
         GROUP BY pub_id, type
         WITH ROLLUP
```

pub_id type

```
......  ...........  ..........
```

0736	business	18722
0736	psychology	9564
0736	NULL	28286 |-- Total for 0736 → *author's comments.*
0877	mod_cook	24278
0877	psychology	375
0877	trad_cook	19566
0877	UNDECIDED	0
0877	NULL	44219 |-- Total for 0877
1389	business	12066
1389	popular_comp	12875
1389	NULL	24941 |-- Total for 1389
NULL	NULL	97446 |-- Grand total

```
(12 row(s) affected)
```

Notice the extra rows for each publisher id. It has NULL for the type, indicating that it is the total; in other words, the total ytd_sales for the publisher 0736 is 28,286. What the ROLLUP operator does is generate subtotals and a grand total for the first column named in the GROUP BY, which in this query is the publisher id.

The CUBE operator just takes that one step further, generating aggregates for all the columns in the GROUP BY. Take a look at this query:

```
SELECT pub_id, type, sum(ytd_sales)
         FROM titles
         GROUP BY pub_id, type
       WITH CUBE
```

```
pub_id type

......  ...........  ..........
```

0736	business	18722
0736	psychology	9564
0736	NULL	28286 |-- Total for 0736 *comments*
0877	mod_cook	24278
0877	psychology	375
0877	trad_cook	19566
0877	UNDECIDED	0
0877	NULL	44219 |-- Total for 0877
1389	business	12066
1389	popular_comp	12875

```
1389   NULL         24941 -- Total for 1389
NULL   NULL         97446 -- Grand Total
NULL   business     30788 -- Totals for types:
NULL   mod_cook     24278 --   mod_cook
NULL   popular_comp 12875 --   popular_comp
NULL   psychology   9939  --   psychology
NULL   trad_cook    19566 --   trad_cook
NULL   UNDECIDED    0           --   UNDECIDED

(18 row(s) affected)
```

What the CUBE operator does is add totals for the second column, the types, in addition to what the ROLLUP operator had.

The CUBE and ROLLUP operators add a way to put aggregate totals in a results set without additional queries. For another discussion of the CUBE operator, see Chapter 25, "OLAP Services."

The ORDER BY Clause

Like all SQL commands, the SQL SELECT command is set-oriented. That means that the results set rows are returned with no particular physical order implied. There are no parts of the SQL SELECT command that let you access the physical order or position yourself within it. This is a rather strict rule of relational tables: You cannot count on, and do not need to reference, the physical order of the rows in a table. It may happen that the results are returned in a physical order, based on how they are stored. In fact, in past releases of SQL Server you could count on rows returning in their physical order. However, in SQL Server 7, parallel operations make it possible for the relational engine to return rows that are not in their physical order.

Consequently, in order to see your results set in a particular order, you must use the ORDER BY clause of the SELECT command:

```
SELECT au_fname, au_lname
       FROM Authors
           ORDER BY au_lname
```

The default order is ascending. To change the results so that they appear in descending order, just add the DESCENDING (or DESC) qualifier:

```
SELECT au_fname, au_lname
       FROM authors
           ORDER BY au_lname DESC
```

You can add ASCENDING or ASC to an ORDER BY, but it's not necessary, because it's the default.

You can also use integer numbers to indicate which column from the SELECT list to sort by:

```
SELECT au_fname, au_lname
        FROM authors
            ORDER BY 2
```

2nd column (au_lname)

> ### WARNING
>
> Using an integer to represent a column in the ORDER BY is called a "deprecated feature" in the ANSI standard, meaning it may be dropped in the future. It is never necessary to use numbers instead of column names anyway.

Transact-SQL provides an extension to the ORDER BY, allowing you to sort by columns that are not named in the SELECT list:

```
SELECT au_fname, au_lname
        FROM authors
            ORDER BY city
```

but it'll be much clear (the output) if include "city" in the select list

If you do sort by a column that isn't in the SELECT list, you can't use a number in place of the column name.

> ### NOTE
>
> When the sorting occurs for an ORDER BY, NULLs are listed first. You cannot ORDER BY columns that have text, ntext, or image data types.

You can order by more than one column, and when you do, each column takes its own ascending or descending attribute. Take a look at this query:

```
SELECT au_fname, au_lname
        FROM authors
            ORDER BY state ASC, au_lname DESC
```

It will sort the entire results set ascending by state, but within each state, descending by last name.

COMPUTE BY and FOR BROWSE

The COMPUTE statement adds subtotal and totals to the output of the SELECT command. In its simplest form, you could just get a total for a set of items with something like this:

```
SELECT title_id, ytd_sales
        FROM Titles
        COMPUTE SUM(ytd_sales)
```

After your results set, you'll see a grand total of ytd_sales as an additional results set:

```
title_id ytd_sales
-------- -----------
BU1032    4095
BU1111    3876
BU2075    18722
...
TC7777    4095
(18 row(s) affected)

sum
-----------
97446
(1 row(s) affected)
```

→ this part of the output is because of "compute sum(ytd - sales)

You can get subtotals out of the COMPUTE clause with its BY option. The following query will return a subtotal for each title's type:

```
SELECT type, title_id, ytd_sales
        FROM Titles
        ORDER BY type
        COMPUTE SUM(ytd_sales) BY type
```

To get both subtotals and a grand total, you can combine the two:

```
SELECT type, title_id, ytd_sales
        FROM titles
        ORDER BY type
        COMPUTE SUM(ytd_sales) BY type
        COMPUTE SUM(ytd_sales)
```

The COMPUTE clause is a Transact-SQL extension, and not ANSI standard. It is perhaps a little long in the tooth these days. When users want subtotals, they tend to use client software to do their summarizing, rather than SQL SELECT.

The FOR BROWSE option allows direct updating from a client application when using DB-Library. Like the COMPUTE statement, it is a Transact-SQL extension that is gradually fading from use.

The SELECT Command (Multitable)

When you reference two or more tables in a SELECT statement, you must meet a couple of new requirements:

- ◆ It must be clear to which table each column name belongs.
- ◆ The results set should be restricted by joining on some common column.

What should happen when you name two tables in a SELECT statement? The general idea is that you want data from both tables. But what should the query engine do with the two tables?

Recall that the SELECT statement always returns you a results set as a table. When you apply the SELECT command to two or more tables, it joins the two tables together to make your results set, based on how you direct it.

In fact, the default behavior of the SQL SELECT command is to join those two tables by producing a cross product or Cartesian product of the tables. A cross product is essentially a multiplication of the two tables, where each row of the first table is combined with every row of the second table, making the results set very large. It will then narrow down those results based on the conditions in the WHERE clause.

As you can imagine, normally you'll want to avoid cross products. So when referencing more than one table in a SELECT statement, you'll have to limit the results set to something meaningful by a condition in the WHERE clause, namely a join condition.

Table Aliases

Before you get started with joins and join conditions, you need to introduce the concept of table aliases. When you name two tables in a SELECT statement, the query processor must be able to determine to which tables each column belongs. So you'll often see SQL SELECT commands written as, for example,

```
SELECT Publishers.pub_id, Publishers.pub_name
        FROM Publishers, Titles
        WHERE Publishers.pub_id = Titles.Pub_id
```

Because each column name is preceded by the table name, no confusion is possible regarding to which table the column belongs. However, repeating the full table name is cumbersome. To make things more efficient, you can assign brief alias names to the tables and use them in place of the full table names:

```
SELECT p.pub_id, p.pub_name
        FROM Publishers p, Titles t
        WHERE p.pub_id = t.Pub_id
```

publishers p

↑

alias

Notice how much more readable even a short query becomes by using table aliases.

TIP

Using table aliases can considerably improve the readability and maintainability of your queries.

Cross Products

Now when you combine a SELECT of all columns from Publishers and Titles, as in this code:

```
SELECT *
        FROM Publishers, Titles
```

you will get 144 rows with all the columns from all the tables.

You can see where this number comes from by looking at the counts:

```
SELECT COUNT(*) AS pubcount
        FROM publishers
SELECT COUNT(*) AS titlescount
        FROM titles
SELECT COUNT(*) AS pubs_titles_count
        FROM titles, publishers
```

pubcount

8

titlescount

18

pubs_titles_count

144

The results are 8, 18, and 144, respectively. The last number is so large because it's the unfiltered cross product. Why such a large number?

You can see how the cross product works by observing the results of the following query:

```
SELECT TOP 10 p.pub_id AS Ppub,
              t.title_id,
              t.pub_id AS Tpub
        FROM  Titles t, Publishers p

Ppub title_id Tpub
---- --------- ----
0736 BU1032    1389
0877 BU1032    1389
1389 BU1032    1389
1622 BU1032    1389
1756 BU1032    1389
9901 BU1032    1389
9952 BU1032    1389
9999 BU1032    1389
0736 BU1111    1389
0877 BU1111    1389
(10 row(s) affected)
```

You can see how this cross product results set was built: all 8 pub_ids of the Publishers table were matched with the first title_id (BU1032) and pub_id of the Titles table, making the first 8 rows of the results set. Then all 8 Publishers pub_ids were matched with the next title, BU1111, making the next 8 rows of the results set, for a total of 16 rows. This continues for the remaining 16 titles, making a total of 144 rows in the results set.

Join Conditions

Now just looking at the preceding results, you should be thinking, why combine the Publishers pub_id 0736 with a row of the Titles table that has a pub_id of 1389? The answer is, you shouldn't! You should filter out the mismatches by adding a WHERE clause to the SELECT that requires the pub_ids of each table to match. This conditions is called the join condition. A join condition is just a filter on the cross product:

```
SELECT       p.pub_id AS Ppub,
     top 5         t.title_id,
```

```
                  t.pub_id AS Tpub
             FROM Publishers p, Titles t
             WHERE p.pub_id = t.pub_id
  Ppub title_id Tpub
  .... ......... ....
  1389 BU1032   1389
  1389 BU1111   1389
  0736 BU2075   0736
  1389 BU7832   1389
  0877 MC2222   0877
```

Here you can see the first 5 of the total 18 rows, and you can see that every Publisher pub_id matches every Titles pub_id.

Inner Joins

As an aid in clarifying join conditions, SQL Server adds the ANSI SQL-92 INNER JOIN keyword, which you can use instead of the WHERE clause:

```
SELECT      p.pub_id AS Ppub,
                t.title_id,
                t.pub_id AS Tpub
            FROM Publishers p
            INNER JOIN Titles t
            ON p.pub_id = t.pub_id
```

The word INNER is optional, but using it can add clarity to the query.

The JOIN condition just requires that you separate how you specify the tables, and take the join condition out of the WHERE clause and into the ON clause. If you want to add additional conditions, you can add a WHERE clause to the INNER JOIN query:

> **TIP**
>
> It's a good idea to use the ANSI SQL-92 JOIN syntax whenever you have multiple conditions, in order to clarify your code.

```
SELECT      p.pub_id AS Ppub,
                t.title_id,
                t.pub_id AS Tpub
            FROM Publishers p
            INNER JOIN Titles t
```

```
ON p.pub_id = t.pub_id
WHERE t.type = 'business'
```

These queries do not get you much, though, because you already know the pub_id in Titles. The gain comes when you try to get additional information from the Publishers table.

For example, suppose you want a list of every publisher and its titles. One way to do that is replace the Publishers pub_id with the name, pub_name, and replace the Titles columns with the title name, title, as you can see in Figure 13-1.

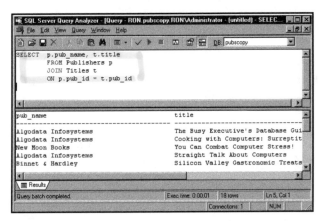

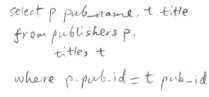

```
select p. pub_name, t. title
from publishers p,
     titles t
where p. pub-id = t. pub-id
```

FIGURE 13-1

An inner join allows you to combine information from either of the joined tables in your results set.

Cross Join

SQL Server 7 also adds a new ANSI SQL construct called CROSS JOIN, in case you really do want to have a cross product:

```
SELECT      p.pub_id AS Ppub,
            t.title_id,
            t.pub_id AS Tpub
       FROM Publishers p
       CROSS JOIN Titles t
```

Because this is also just the default behavior of the SELECT command, all the CROSS JOIN really adds is clarity, that you really do want a cross product!

Subqueries

One of the great features of the SELECT command is that you can combine SELECT commands together, embedding SELECTs within other SELECT commands.

A subquery is a SQL SELECT command embedded in another. Subqueries can solve some important problems. For example, if you want to know the names of all the publishers that have titles, you can just issue this statement to SQL Server:

```
SELECT DISTINCT p.pub_name
        FROM Publishers p, Titles t
        WHERE p.pub_id = t.pub_id
```

The DISTINCT clause gets rid of the duplicate names. This query actually has a second use: It can give all the titles with their publisher names, if you leave out the DISTINCT and add the title into the SELECT clause.

OK, so far so good. Now get the names of all the publishers that do not have titles. You might start by just negating the equals sign:

```
SELECT DISTINCT p.pub_name
        FROM Publishers p, Titles t
        WHERE p.pub_id <> t.pub_id
```

So now you want the names of all publishers in which the Publishers pub_id is not equal to the Titles pub_id. Unfortunately, this also results in a cross product: Each of the rows in Publishers gets paired with all the rows in Titles in which the ids are not the same!

To get the answer to all the publishers that do not have titles, you need to use a subquery. Let's start with the IN condition.

The IN Condition

You can think of finding all the publishers that do not have titles as finding all the publisher names that are not in a certain list. To do this, you can use the IN condition. In its bare-bones form, the IN condition just creates a list:

```
SELECT pub_name
        FROM Publishers
        WHERE pub_id IN('0736','0877')
```

Result: Pub_name
New Moon Books
Binnet & Hardly.

Same result where pub_id = '0736' or pub_id = '0877'

To find all the publisher names of the publishers that are in the Titles table, think about selecting the publisher names from Publishers, in which those publishers are in a list of the publisher ids in Titles. Since SQL allows you to put another SELECT statement inside the IN clause, you can write:

```
SELECT pub_name
        FROM Publishers
        WHERE pub_id IN(SELECT pub_id FROM Titles)
```

Same result as using exist condition (P396)

To find the publishers that do not have titles, just add the NOT operator in front of the IN clause:

```
SELECT pub_name
        FROM Publishers
        WHERE pub_id NOT IN(SELECT pub_id FROM Titles)
```

There are problems with the NOT IN condition, however, if the subquery ever returns any NULLs, as you'll see later.

Nesting SQL Queries

SQL Server's T-SQL allows you a lot of flexibility with embedding and nesting queries. For example, you can find the name of the publisher that has the highest-selling title using the following query:

```
SELECT pub_name
        FROM Publishers
        WHERE pub_id =
        (SELECT pub_id
            FROM Titles
            WHERE ytd_sales =
            (SELECT max(ytd_sales) FROM Titles) )
```

You can read this query as being evaluated from the inside out. The steps are:

1. Get the maximum ytd_sales from Titles.
2. Get the publisher id from Titles that has that maximum ytd_sales.
3. Get the publisher name from Publishers that has the publisher id found in step 2.

Unfortunately, this query will return an error if more than one pub_id in Titles has a title equal to the maximum ytd_sales. In addition, it is a little more complex than it needs to be. You can simplify it a bit by making a join condition between Titles and Publishers on pub_id:

```
SELECT pub_name
        FROM Publishers p, Titles t
        WHERE p.pub_id = t.pub_id
        AND t.ytd_sales =
            (SELECT max(ytd_sales) FROM Titles)
```

Now the query will not fail if there's more than one winner, and it's easier to follow.

> **NOTE**
>
> Oftentimes, complex SQL SELECT commands can be simplified, and it's an art to get both the simplest and most efficient command available.

The EXISTS Condition

Another condition you can use with subqueries to test for the existence of rows is the EXISTS function. For example, to find all the names of publishers that have titles, you could have used EXISTS:

```
SELECT pub_name
        FROM Publishers p
        WHERE EXISTS (SELECT pub_id
                        FROM Titles t
                        WHERE p.pub_id = t.pub_id)
```

Result:- 3 rows affected.
Same result is using in condition
P 394.

You can read this query as finding each publisher name for which a pub_id in Titles equals its pub_id. The reference inside the subquery to the outer Publishers table functions somewhat like the "in" pronoun in the previous sentence.

When a subquery makes a reference to a table in the outer query, it's commonly called a correlated subquery. The EXISTS condition almost always results in correlated subqueries.

You may recall from earlier in this chapter that the ANSI standard way to use the UPDATE and DELETE statements with more than one table is to use the EXISTS condition. It turns out that EXISTS is a very useful construct.

Using EXISTS versus NOT IN

You can use the EXISTS condition to fix an important problem in the ANSI SQL implementation of the IN condition.

A simple way to find out all the publisher ids that are not in Titles is to use the IN condition:

```
-- Find all pub_ids for publishers not in Titles
SELECT pub_id FROM Publishers
        WHERE pub_id NOT IN
                (SELECT pub_id FROM Titles)
```

The query returns five pub_ids, the ones not in Titles.

However, there is a serious problem here the NOT IN condition. To see it, change one of the pub_ids in Titles to NULL:

```
-- NULL a pub_id
UPDATE Titles SET pub_id = NULL
            WHERE pub_id = '0736'
```

When you re-execute the preceding SELECT, you'll get no rows returned! That's because the list of pub_ids returned by the subquery,

```
(SELECT pub_id FROM Titles)
```

now contains NULLs. It is a rule of ANSI SQL (and one that Transact-SQL follows) that if NULLs are present in a list, you can't know whether anything is NOT IN it. It makes sense: If you have a list of ids, but some of them are unknown, how can you tell which ids are not in the list?

But a correlated subquery using the EXISTS condition instead of IN will find the ones you want:

```
SELECT pub_id FROM Publishers p
      WHERE NOT EXISTS
        (SELECT pub_id FROM Titles t
            WHERE t.pub_id = p.pub_id)
pub_id
- - - - - -
0736
1622
1756
9901
9952
9999
(6 row(s) affected)
```

Compare to the "exists condition" example, p396

Notice that "0736" now shows up in your list: It is no longer in Titles!

There is a way around the problem of NOT IN returning no rows, and that is to add the qualifier that no NULLs should be returned by the subquery:

```
SELECT pub_id FROM Publishers
        WHERE pub_id NOT IN
            (SELECT pub_id FROM Titles
                WHERE pub_id IS NOT NULL)
```

Make sure you use the IS NOT NULL construct rather than the <> NULL, because the latter changes value depending on ANSI_DEFAULTS and ANSI_NULLS setting. For more information about ANSI settings, see Chapter 12.

Now restore the original values to the Titles pub_id column:

```
-- Restore the nullified pub_id columns
UPDATE Titles SET pub_id = '0736'
            WHERE pub_id IS NULL
```

> **WARNING**
>
> Use IS NULL rather than = NULL, and IS NOT NULL instead of <> NULL. While the = NULL will work in Transact-SQL, it is not ANSI standard and so will not work via ODBC when SET ANSI_DEFAULTS is ON. The IS [NOT] NULL construct always works and is ANSI standard.

Cross Tabulations

You can use correlated subqueries to produce cross tabulations. A cross tabulation, or crosstab, is a table that contains summaries of another table. For example, you can produce a table that contains summaries of the ytd_sales of Titles, based on the type of title, using queries for each column:

```
SELECT DISTINCT t.pub_id,
            'business' = (SELECT SUM(ytd_sales) FROM Titles t1
                WHERE t1.pub_id = t.pub_id AND t1.type =
                            'business'),
            'psychology' = (SELECT SUM(ytd_sales) FROM Titles t1
                WHERE t1.pub_id = t.pub_id AND t1.type =
                            'psychology')
            FROM Titles t
```

It will produce the following cross-tabulated results:

```
pub_id business     psychology
------ -----------  ----------
0736   18722        9564
0877   NULL         375
1389   12066        NULL
```

Because there are no business titles for publisher "0877" and no psychology titles for publisher "1389," their totals are NULL. You can evaluate a correlated subquery from the outside in, though with a few twists. The preceding query works by:

1. Getting the first distinct `pub_id` from Titles
2. Getting the sum of that `pub_id`'s `ytd_sales` for the two types
3. Repeating for each distinct `pub_id`

Self-Joins

Sometimes it's useful to join a table with itself. Suppose you want to find all the stores that have sold both BU1032, "The Busy Executive's Database Guide," and PS2091, "Is Anger the Enemy?" You might start with the query:

```
SELECT stor_id
    FROM Sales
    WHERE title_id = 'BU1032'
        AND title_id = 'PS2091'
```

Q. which store(s) sold both books?
→ won't work

However, that won't work. One thing you can do to get the correct answer is join the table with itself. That way you can name it twice and check for the id:

```
SELECT s1.stor_id
    FROM sales s1
    INNER JOIN sales s2
    ON s1.stor_id = s2.stor_id
    WHERE s1.title_id = 'BU1032'
    AND s2.title_id = 'PS2091'
```

output: stor_id

6380

solution 1

Alternatively, you can embed the JOIN condition in the WHERE clause:

```
SELECT s1.stor_id
    FROM Sales s1, Sales s2
    WHERE s1.stor_id = s2.stor_id
    AND s1.title_id = 'BU1032'
    AND s2.title_id = 'PS2091'
```

same output.

solution 2

In each case, the query works by finding each `stor_id` from sales with a title of BU1032, and then each `stor_id` with a title of PS2091. It then reports all the matching `stor_ids`.

This is called a self join, because a table is joined with itself. To see how this self join works, look at the data from the sales table joined with itself. You can see the top five rows of the each sales table side by side:

```
      Sales s1                  Sales s2

   stor_id title_id          stor_id title_id

   ....... .........         ....... .........

   6380    BU1032    6380    BU1032

   6380    PS2091    6380    PS2091

   7066    PC8888            7066    PC8888

   7066    PS2091            7066    PS2091

   7067    PS2091            7067    PS2091
```

When the self-join query is evaluated, it compares the Sales table with itself. The join condition is that the stor_id should be equal, so look at the first two rows, which have stor_id equal to "6380." The additional conditions are that the s1.title_id = "BU1032" and that s2.title_id = "PS2091."

What makes the self-join work is that SQL Server can look at the groups of rows side by side and try all the combinations to find a hit. You can see by inspection that s1's row 1 has a title_id of "BU1032" and s2's row 2 has a title_id of "PS2091," so you can add stor_id "6380" to the list of stores that has both of those titles. Now look at stor_id "7066." Since s1.title_id must be "BU1032," neither of the rows succeeds, so stor_id "7066" is eliminated.

Because the SQL language is set-oriented, it cannot simply process the rows of the Sales table one by one, from top to bottom, checking off whether each stor_id has the title_id in question. In fact, it would be easier to read the table from top to bottom, just as we do ourselves. However, because the SQL SELECT is set-oriented, it must deal with tables as unordered and cannot process them row-by-row.

The self-join is a case where the set-style operation is more awkward than the sequential row-by-row processing that nonrelational systems can do. In Transact-SQL, you can use a server-side cursor to do row-by-row processing, which you'll learn more about in Chapter 15, "Basics of Transact-SQL Programming."

You may not need to use a self join, though. The original example can be rewritten using a GROUP BY and HAVING join as follows:

```
SELECT stor_id
        FROM Sales
        WHERE title_id = 'BU1032' OR title_id = 'PS2091'
        GROUP BY stor_id
        HAVING COUNT(stor_id) > 1 ]
```

Solution 3

In this case, the initial three lines of the SELECT obtain all the stores with title ids of either "BU1032" or "PS2091", but the GROUP BY combined with the HAVING COUNT() eliminates those stores that only have one of them.

The UNION **Command**

Another way of joining two or more tables together is to use the UNION command. UNION works by taking the results of one SELECT and combining them with another SELECT, provided that the column orders and data types are compatible.

The syntax of the UNION command is pretty simple:

```
<select-statement>
UNION [ALL]
<select-statement>, etc.
```

In other words, you take one SELECT statement, UNION with another, and another, and so on. By default, the UNION will remove duplicate rows. If you want the duplicate rows to show up, you can use the ALL qualifier.

For example, you could create a union of two SELECTs on city and state from the Authors and Publishers tables, using their names:

```
SELECT au_lname+', '+au_fname, city, state
FROM Authors
UNION
SELECT pub_name, city, state
FROM Publishers
```

output : 31 rows.

city   state

names
(publishers or authors)

Note that the string formed by combining the first name and last name from Authors is compatible with and in the same order as the name from Publishers. Also, the city and state columns from each table also are in the same position in the SELECT list and have compatible data types. Because all the columns match up and have compatible data types, the UNION succeeds.

One handy feature of Transact-SQL is that you can create a view based on a UNION:

```
CREATE VIEW v_pubs_locations
AS
        SELECT au_lname+', '+au_fname AS author_name,
            city, state
        FROM Authors
        UNION
        SELECT pub_name, city, state
        FROM Publishers
```

The view definition will work provided you have a declared column name for each of the columns. That's why the preceding query has AS author_name added to the SELECT clause.

Creating views of UNION statements can come in handy if you have partitioned tables. For example, if you had all your first quarter's data in a table called Qtr1, and second quarter in table Qtr2, then you could create a view across all the quarters that users could access for the whole year's data. The view would simply create a union among all the relevant Qtr tables. Users would only need to name the view, and you could re-create the view when the underlying tables change.

Outer Joins

Sometimes you may want more information than a simple inner join gives you. Recall that you can get all the publishers' names and their titles using the query:

```
SELECT     p.pub_name, t.title
           FROM Publishers p, Titles t
           WHERE p.pub_id = t.pub_id
           ORDER BY p.pub_name
```

However, there may be publishers without titles, and titles without publishers. You may want a list of all the publishers with titles, combined, either with all the publishers that don't have titles and/or all the titles that don't have publishers. These combinations are provided by the outer join facilities.

Outer joins just add additional data to the inner join, data that is normally excluded by the join condition. Consider all the publishers and all the titles. Some publishers have titles, some publishers may not have titles, and some titles may not have publishers. So we really have three combinations. You've already found the inner join, namely the publishers that have titles. Let's assume that you form the inner join by accessing the Publishers table first and the Titles table second. If you add the publishers without titles to the inner join, then you get a right outer join. If you add the titles without publishers to the inner join, you get a left outer join. And if you add both publishers without titles and titles without publishers, you get a full outer join. To summarize:

Inner join:	All publishers with titles
Left outer join:	All publishers with titles, and
	all publishers without titles
Right outer join:	All publishers with titles, and
	all titles without publishers

Full outer join: All publishers with titles, and

all publishers without titles, and

all titles without publishers

You can get a general picture of how outer joins work using the Venn diagrams shown in Figure 13-2.

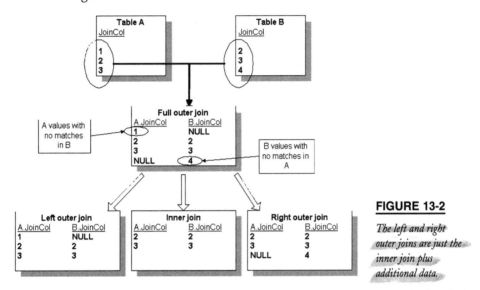

FIGURE 13-2

The left and right outer joins are just the inner join plus additional data.

In the diagram, note that Table A and Table B have a column in common, the JoinCol column, which is the basis of the join condition. Now combine the columns from each table into a new table, row by row. Create one row in the new table for each matching JoinCol value from each table. In addition, create one row in the new table for each unmatched value from either table, and use NULL as its pair to indicate the mismatch. The result is the full outer join table in the diagram. The inner join, left outer join, and right outer join are all just subsets of the full outer join.

The inner join results in a table that contains only the rows with matching join values between the two tables. The left outer join creates a table with the matching rows like the inner join, but adds the mismatches from the left or first table. The right outer join does the opposite of the left outer join: it creates a table containing all the matching rows like the inner join, but adds the mismatches from the right or second table.

Now let's take a look at how you can create these outer joins in Transact-SQL. You'll start by using the UNION operator to construct a left outer join.

Using UNION *to Construct an Outer Join*

In the past neither SQL Server nor the SQL standard had constructs for outer joins, and everyone had to use the UNION command.

As you saw earlier, you can find all the publishers with titles using the query:

```
SELECT p.pub_name, t.title
        FROM publishers p, titles t
        WHERE p.pub_id = t.pub_id
```

Now, the results do not include all the publishers without titles. To get just the publishers without any titles, you could issue:

```
SELECT p.pub_name
        FROM publishers p
        WHERE NOT EXISTS (SELECT * FROM titles t
            WHERE t.pub_id = p.pub_id)
```

as you saw previously.

There's a problem here. This query's columns will not match up with the one above it, because there's only one column in the second query. However, you can add just a blank string, and then the columns will match up:

```
SELECT p.pub_name, '     '
        FROM publishers p
        WHERE NOT EXISTS (SELECT * FROM titles t
            WHERE t.pub_id = p.pub_id)
```

So now, to get a list of all the publishers with titles and without titles, you could use the following query:

```
SELECT p.pub_name, t.title
        FROM Publishers p, Titles t
        WHERE p.pub_id = t.pub_id
UNION
SELECT p.pub_name, '     '
        FROM publishers p
        WHERE NOT EXISTS (SELECT * FROM titles t
            WHERE t.pub_id = p.pub_id)
```

The preceding query will put a blank title in the results set for publishers that have no titles.

You've seen how a UNION can produce a left outer join. You can make a right outer join by varying the second query, and a full outer join by combining all three queries.

Using the OUTER JOIN *Operators*

Transact-SQL follows the ANSI SQL-92 standard by providing a built-in syntax for outer joins. You replace the INNER on the JOIN command with OUTER, and precede it with LEFT, RIGHT, or FULL.

For example, you can get the same left outer join on Publishers and Titles using the following style of query:

```
SELECT p.pub_name, t.title
        FROM Publishers p
        LEFT OUTER JOIN Titles t
        ON p.pub_id = t.pub_id
```

The results are the same as the UNION version, except that the empty titles in the results set will contain NULL, not blanks.

The preceding query is a "left" outer join because the query includes empty rows from the leftmost table in the join condition, Publishers. In other words, the LEFT qualifier includes publishers with no titles. If you put the word RIGHT in place of LEFT, then it looks for titles that have no publisher:

```
SELECT p.pub_name, t.title
        FROM Publishers p
        RIGHT OUTER JOIN Titles t
        ON p.pub_id = t.pub_id
```

Finally, you can get a full outer join using the FULL keyword.

```
SELECT p.pub_name, t.title
        FROM publishers p
        FULL OUTER JOIN titles t
        ON p.pub_id = t.pub_id
```

NOTE

The LEFT and RIGHT keywords give results based on the order that the tables are referenced in the JOIN clause. The LEFT outer join adds unmatched values to the inner join results from the first table mentioned in the JOIN clause. Therefore, you must take care to use LEFT and RIGHT based on how you place the table names in the JOIN clause. The actual term OUTER is optional, but it is much clearer to include it.

Chaining Outer Joins

You can chain OUTER JOIN clauses in a SELECT statement. For example, the Authors table and the Titles table are connected by a linkage table called TitleAuthor. The author name is in the Authors table, and the quantity sold for each title is ytd_sales in the Titles table. If you want a list of all author names who have written titles, along with the title names, and you also want to include the authors that have not written any books, you'll need an outer join across three tables:

```
SELECT au_lname, au_fname, t.title
        FROM Authors a
        LEFT OUTER JOIN TitleAuthor ta
        ON a.au_id = ta.au_id
        LEFT OUTER JOIN Titles t
        ON ta.title_id = t.title_id
        ORDER BY a.au_lname, a.au_fname, t.title
```

The LOJ from Authors to TitleAuthor gets you all the authors, and the LOJ from TitleAuthor to Titles keeps the mismatched authors in the results set.

The Older Transact-SQL *= Outer Join Syntax

SQL Server also provides an older, alternate Transact-SQL notation to get a left and right outer join. It consists of the asterisk followed by an = sign (*=) to indicate a left outer join:

WARNING

The *= and =* constructs were built into Transact-SQL before SQL Server had the ANSI SQL-92 syntax available, so they are now considered outmoded. Also, they can give erroneous results if you chain a series of them together, and you cannot use them in combination with the ANSI JOIN. Therefore, it's best to avoid using them altogether.

```
SELECT p.pub_name, t.title
        FROM Publishers p, Titles t
        WHERE p.pub_id *= t.pub_id
```

This gives the same result as the LEFT OUTER JOIN ANSI syntax. A right outer join just uses =*. There is no equivalent construct for a full outer join.

Query Hints

You can add query hints after each table name in the SELECT command to force the query analyzer to use certain indexes. For more information, see Chapter 19, "Tuning Queries."

Full-Text Search

In addition to standard table/column SQL queries, SQL Server 7 comes with a Full-text Search service. You choose to install it during setup if you select the custom installation. The text search engine adds the ability to make searches of character and text columns in your tables that are more sophisticated than the standard SQL LIKE operator.

The search engine operates independently of SQL Server, and interacts with the storage engine in order to create its indexes. It gives a provider to SQL Server, but from the documentation it appears not to be an OLE DB provider. In other words, this is a very specific service written to interact with just SQL Server 7.

To use the search engine, you must create additional full-text indexes on columns you wish to search. Once you do that, you can use special full-text search functions in your SQL SELECT commands to perform the searches.

NOTE

The Full-Text Search service and engine is not installed by default. To install the Full-Text Search engine, you must make a Custom installation of SQL Server 7. If you choose a typical installation, the Full-Text Search service will not be installed. If you want to add the engine after an installation, you must uninstall and reinstall SQL Server 7. (Be sure to detach and reattach your databases using the sp_detachdb and sp_attachdb system stored procedures.)

If you choose to install the engine, you'll notice an additional service in the Support Services node of Enterprise Manager's console tree, called Full-Text Search. From there you can stop and start the Full-Text service, as well as inspect the service properties, as shown in Figure 13-3.

The Performance tab of the properties dialog box allows you to choose a relative system resource usage for the service when building its indexes. Full-text indexes and support data reside outside your database in the files shown in the General tab.

In addition to the service, you'll also notice that each database has been enabled for full-text search, shown by the new Full-Text Catalogs node shown in the Enterprise

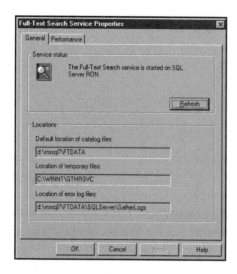

FIGURE 13-3

The Full-Text service properties dialog box shows the engine's support file locations.

Manager console tree for each database. When you create a full-text index on a table's columns, you create a catalog to store that data, and the name of the catalog will be shown in the right pane of the console when you select Full-Text Catalogs.

Creating a Full-Text Catalog in Enterprise Manager

A full-text catalog consists of choosing a table, a unique key, a set of one or more character columns in the table, and an optional schedule for populating the catalog with data.

WARNING

You can create a new full-text catalog in the usual two ways: there's a Full-Text Indexing Wizard, which you can invoke by going to the Wizards dialog box and choosing the Full-Text Indexing Wizard from the wizards list under Database. There's also a New Full-Text Catalog option, if you right-click over the Full-Text Catalogs node in Enterprise Manager. However, the GUI utilities are incomplete and at some point you will need to use the full-text stored procedures.

After you've installed the Full-text service, every database on the server will have the ability to store full-text catalogs. A new node in Enterprise Manager, called Full-Text Catalogs, contains the new catalogs.

To create a new catalog, you can either use the GUI tools or the full-text system stored procedures. If you choose the Full-Text Wizard, it will guide you through by asking first for a table, then a unique key column for the table, a set of columns, a catalog name, and an optional index population schedule. (The steps are fairly self-evident, so I won't cover them here.) After you've finished, you can use the catalog's Properties dialog box to inspect it. For example, the dialog box shown in Figure 13-4 shows a catalog called TitlesCat, for the Titles table of the pubscopy database.

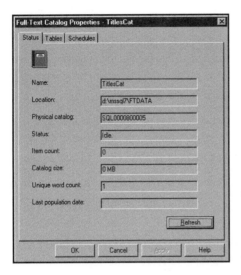

FIGURE 13-4

The General tab of a Full-Text Catalog Properties dialog box shows the file location and some catalog statistics.

The location is the default location set in the service properties (as mentioned earlier in this chapter.) The remaining tabs show that the catalog contains an index on the titles table, and any schedule for population.

NOTE

The Properties dialog boxes do not let you create or modify fully-functional catalogs. You must use the Wizard or, better yet, the stored procedures to have full control over your catalogs.

Now you can populate the catalog with data by right-clicking over the catalog and choosing Start Population from the pop-up menu. You have the choice of either a full or incremental population. Initially, the population must be full, but subsequent scheduled populations can be incremental.

Creating a Full-text Catalog with Stored Procedures

With the initial release of SQL Server 7, you can only gain full control over the creation and manipulation of full-text search using stored procedures. (Look for subsequent service packs to improve the GUI interface.) To create the same catalog as in the prior example using stored procedures, you need the following steps:

1. Make sure the current database has full-text search enabled:

```
USE Pubscopy
EXEC sp_fulltext_database 'enable'
GO
```

2. Add the catalog with `sp_fulltext_catalog`:

```
EXEC sp_fulltext_catalog
        @ftcat = 'TitlesCat',
        @action = 'create'
GO
```

3. To add the Titles table to the catalog, use `sp_fulltext_table`:

```
EXEC sp_fulltext_table
        @tabname = 'titles',
        @action = 'create',
        @ftcat = 'TitlesCat',
        @keyname = 'UPKCL_titleidind'
GO
```

Note that you must also specify a unique key that the search engine can use to identify rows.

4. Add one or more Titles columns to the catalog using `sp_fulltext_column`:

```
EXEC sp_fulltext_column
        @tabname = 'titles',
        @colname = 'notes',
        @action  = 'add'
GO
```

5. Activate the table for full-text indexing using `sp_fulltext_table`:

```
EXEC sp_fulltext_table
        @tabname = 'Titles',
        @action = 'activate'
GO
```

6. Populate the catalog with index data using `sp_fulltext_catalog`:

```
EXEC sp_fulltext_catalog
        @ftcat = 'TitlesCat',
        @action = 'start_full'
```

```
GO
```

You can add subsequent columns of that table using the `sp_fulltext_column` stored procedure. For example:

```
EXEC sp_fulltext_table
        @tabname = 'Titles',
        @action = 'deactivate'
GO
EXEC sp_fulltext_column
        @tabname = 'titles',
        @colname = 'title',
        @action  = 'add'
GO
EXEC sp_fulltext_table
        @tabname = 'Titles',
        @action = 'activate'
GO
EXEC sp_fulltext_catalog
        @ftcat = 'TitlesCat',
        @action = 'start_full'
GO
```

WARNING

Because the Full-Text service runs independently from SQL Server, the GO statements of a Transact-SQL script do not wait until all full-text processes are finished. Therefore, when running a script to create a full-text catalog, you may need to insert pauses using WAITFOR in order to let the full-text service finish its job.

Getting Information about Full-Text Indexing

After you've created some catalogs with tables and columns, you can get information about them using the full-text help stored procedures.

For example, to find out information about a full-text catalog, you can use `sp_help_fulltext_catalogs`:

```
EXEC sp_help_fulltext_catalogs 'TitlesCat'
```

To find out what tables are in a particular catalog, you can use `sp_help_fulltext_tables`:

```
EXEC sp_help_fulltext_tables 'TitlesCat'
```

To find out what columns are indexed for a given table, use `sp_help_fulltext_columns`:

```
EXEC sp_help_fulltext_columns 'Titles'
```

In addition, if you inspect the properties for a given table, you'll notice a new Full-Text tab, as shown in Figure 13-5

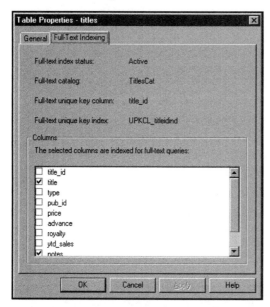

FIGURE 13-5

A table's Properties dialog box has a Full-Text Indexing tab that shows the indexed columns.

Dropping a Full-Text Catalog

You can drop a full-text catalog from Enterprise Manager by right-clicking over the catalog, and choosing Delete.

With stored procedures, you must first stop the catalog, drop the table from the catalog, and then drop the catalog. The following code segment for those actions was taken from the Profiler, using a trace of the Enterprise Manager drop action:

```
exec sp_fulltext_catalog N'TitlesCat', N'stop'
exec sp_fulltext_table N'[dbo].[titles]', N'drop'
exec sp_fulltext_catalog N'TitlesCat', N'drop'
```

Full-Text Queries

There are two fundamental constructs for querying data using full-text indexes; one for exact matches (`CONTAINS`), and one for free text (`FREETEXT`). Also, you can situate your query either in a WHERE clause using the CONTAINS or FREETEXT functions, or as derived tables using the CONTAINSTABLE or FREETEXTTABLE functions.

Queries using CONTAINS *and* CONTAINSTABLE

The CONTAINS function allows you to do exact and partial match searches, on a variety of bases.

For example, to find a match for the word "computer" in the TitlesCat catalog, you can issue:

```
SELECT *
        FROM Titles
        WHERE CONTAINS( *, 'computer')
```

The * inside the CONTAINS function will match all columns.

For the prefix "compute", just use:

```
SELECT *
        FROM Titles
        WHERE CONTAINS( *, '"compute*"')
```

The double-quotes allow you to subdivide the search value.

For a proximity condition, use something like:

```
SELECT *
        FROM Titles
        WHERE CONTAINS( *, '"compute*" NEAR "stress"')
```

For any word that is based on the verb compute, use:

```
SELECT *
        FROM Titles
        WHERE CONTAINS( *, ' FORMSOF(INFLECTIONAL, muckrake))
```

This will pick up entries with forms of the verb, such as "muckraking."

To get only hits with high ratings use the ISABOUT function:

```
SELECT *
        FROM Titles
        WHERE CONTAINS( *, ' ISABOUT(computers NEAR hype WEIGHT(.9))')
```

The CONTAINSTABLE function uses the same search conditions as the CONTAINS function, but returns its results as a table rather than as a logical value. So, for example, to find all columns with "computer" using CONTAINSTABLE, just issue something like:

```
SELECT *
        FROM CONTAINSTABLE(Titles, *, 'computer')
```

The return values are in a table with the key and a ranking:

KEY	RANK
PS1372	48
PC9999	48
PS7777	48
PC8888	48
MC3026	48
BU2075	48

```
(6 row(s) affected)
```

Notice that now the key can be used to join with the original titles table. For example, to find all titles with any form of the word "muckrake" in their notes, and that have been sold after January 1, 1994:

```
SELECT t.title
        FROM Titles t
        JOIN CONTAINSTABLE(Titles, notes, ' FORMSOF(INFLECTIONAL, muckrake)')
c
        ON t.title_id = c.[key]
```

Notice that you must use the brackets, or quoted identifiers, around the key column of the CONTAINSTABLE result set.

Queries using FREETEXT *and* FREETEXTTABLE

Using FREETEXT is much simpler than that of CONTAINS. FREETEXT will send a string to the full-text service where it will be parsed and weighted, with noise-words removed. Then an approximate match is found based on those weightings.

For example, to find a match for "computer hype", issue

```
SELECT notes
        FROM Titles
        WHERE FREETEXT( notes, ' "computer stress" ')
```

The command returns all rows with instances of either word.

Similarly then for FREETEXTTABLE:

```
SELECT t.title
        FROM Titles t
        JOIN FREETEXTTABLE(Titles, notes, ' "computer stress"') c
        ON t.title_id = c.[key]
```

> **NOTE**
>
> Full-Text search is a powerful but somewhat unfinished utility in SQL Server 7.
> It is likely that Microsoft will quickly add new features and better documentation
> with extended usage and user requests.

A Query Checklist

You can use the following checklist when inspecting your queries:

- ❏ Is ANSI standard SQL-92 followed whenever possible?
- ❏ Does each major clause of the query begin on its own line?
- ❏ Whenever two or more tables are in a query, is there a join condition present, either in the WHERE or JOIN clause? (In other words, cross products are avoided.)
- ❏ Are table aliases used to clarify queries?
- ❏ Are single quotes used in place of double quotes for literal strings?
- ❏ Are excessive parentheses avoided?
- ❏ Is an indentation standard followed?
- ❏ Is an uppercase/lowercase standard followed?
- ❏ Are columns named instead of SELECT * when only one or a few columns are needed in the results set?
- ❏ Is COUNT(*) used instead of COUNT(<some specific column>)?
- ❏ When an order to the rows is needed, does the SELECT include an ORDER BY and not rely on the natural ordering of the table?
- ❏ Is the ANSI SQL-92 standard OUTER JOIN syntax used instead of the *= or =* operator?

Summary

In this chapter you've learned the SQL language's DML commands, INSERT, UPDATE, DELETE, and SELECT, as implemented in SQL Server 7. The SELECT command can become quite complex, often due to the fact that there can be several ways to write a query that will solve a question. In addition to the standard options of the SELECT command, SQL Server 7 also has a Full-Text Search service that gives you the ability to do sophisticated text searches on character or text data. Next, let's take a look at the English Query utility, which you can use to automatically generate Transact-SQL SELECT statements.

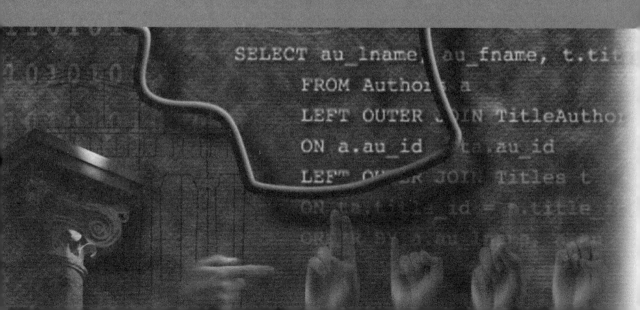

Chapter 14

English Query

In This Chapter

◆ Building an English Query

◆ Global properties

◆ Regression testing and English Query applications

English Query is a stand-alone utility whose primary purpose is to translate natural language query requests into SQL SELECT statements. You can then pass the SQL SELECT output statements to SQL Server and return data to the user. English Query can be used as a query generation tool, as well as a component of an application. In this chapter, you'll focus on the query generation capabilities of English Query.

Overview

The basic idea of English Query (which I'll occasionally abbreviate as EQ), is to load it with enough background information that it can interpret natural English requests as SQL queries. After you do this, you can compile the resulting information into an English Query application that can be run remotely.

To get started, you have to supply the English Query domain editor utility with information about the database in question and the relationships among the data elements. The EQ domain editor consists of three tabs, as shown in Figure 14-1.

The Files tab holds information about a project, which is stored as an .eqp file, and

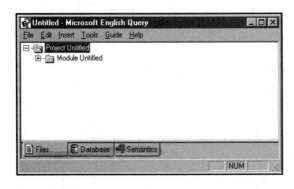

FIGURE 14-1

You specify three major components of an English Query application: files, database, and semantics.

the project's modules, which are stored as .eqm files. In the EQ domain editor, you must always work with one and only one project, which can be stored in one or more modules.

Having modules under projects gives a limited degree of multiuser capability to the domain editor. More than one user can work in a given EQ project, provided that each is editing a different module. Modules themselves are single-user.

The Database tab specifies the tables and columns of an ODBC data source that you can specify for query purposes. (You can also insert tables and fields of your own with no data source behind them.) Normally, you'll want to tie your EQ application to a particular database, so you'll want to have an actual data source at its base.

In the Semantics tab, you specify the semantic objects that EQ needs to interpret natural language requests. These include entities, relationships, dictionary synonyms, and special commands.

Once you've specified the database and semantics for your EQ application, you can test the application using the Test Application dialog box in the domain editor. You can either specify an actual data source or ask EQ to generate SQL statements without executing them. The testing tool lets you see what kinds of SQL SELECT statements will be created based on the English text submitted. For example, the dialog box in Figure 14-2 shows the results of submitting "list all the publishers" to the test tool.

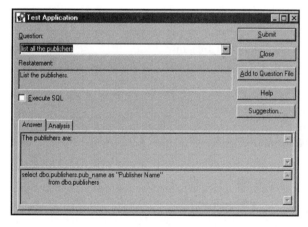

FIGURE 14-2

You can submit a natural language statement and see the resulting SQL SELECT statement using the Test Application dialog box.

EQ has taken the string "list all the publishers" and interpreted it as:

```
select dbo.publishers.pub_name as "Publisher Name"
        from dbo.publishers
```

This dialog box allows you to see how EQ will translate a free-form English statement into a more structured Transact-SQL statement.

This translation activity is the core part of English Query. Based on this, there are a couple of important uses you can make of EQ.

◆ First of all, you can use EQ to help you generate SQL SELECT statements for your own scripts and queries, especially when you would like an alternative way to state the query.

◆ Second, you can present a natural language query interface to end users and let EQ applications translate them into SQL statements that you send to SQL Server.

To get to either of these goals, you must first build an EQ application.

Building an English Query Application

In order to understand how to build an EQ application, let's start with some terminology and then look at the actual steps.

Terminology

To describe its activity, English Query uses a set of four key terms that come from the database design world but are used somewhat differently.

You start by specifying a *domain,* which is really just an actual or potential database. Do not confuse EQ domains with domains in the relational database sense of sources of attributes for entities. EQ domains are a universe of discourse for the set of queries and the EQ application. In English Query, each project deals with one domain.

Within a domain, you must then specify *entities,* which are any objects that can be involved in a relationship. Do not confuse EQ entities with the entities of an Entity-Relationship diagram: EQ entities correspond to both the entities and attributes of a relational database. Normally EQ entities include both the entities and attributes of your database design, but you can also include calculated, combined, or derived entities as well. You tie these entities to your database tables or columns.

Next, you need to specify the *relationships* between the entities. Again, do not confuse EQ relationships with relational database joins or foreign keys, which occur between tables (ER-style entities). EQ relationships occur between all entities, including attributes. Further, you classify EQ relationships in a way that allows EQ to perform natural language translations between them.

The last two key terms are optional. You can also add *domain commands,* which are specialized instructions or operating system commands that EQ will execute when one or more key verbs are stated in a natural language input. Finally, you can specify that EQ should read or write certain synonyms using *dictionary entries.*

Starting a New Project

When you start a new project, you can either specify a data source and have English Query import the table and fields for you, or you can simply start a blank project.

Suppose you start the project by specifying a data source, namely the Pubscopy database you created earlier. You'll be asked to specify an ODBC data source from either a file or machine DSN, or to make a new one.

When EQ loads information from your database, it will check the tables for primary keys. If a table is missing a primary key, EQ will report the fact, as you can see in Figure 14-3.

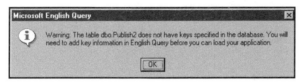

FIGURE 14-3

English Query will notify you if a table lacks a primary key.

The error message is somewhat benign: EQ will continue to load table and field data, but you need to add the keys in order to test or compile the EQ application. You give the project a name when you save it; the first module name will default to the same name as the project. So when you save a project as Pubscopy, EQ will create Pubscopy.eqp for the project, and Pubscopy.eqm for the first module.

Correcting Missing Keys

You must specify missing primary keys for tables that lack them. In the Pubs and therefore Pubscopy databases, the discounts and roysched tables do not have primary keys. You can add a key to an EQ table reference by clicking on the Database tab, finding the table in the tree view, editing the table information, and bringing up the Add Keys dialog box. For example, to edit the discounts table information, open up the tree view, select the discounts table, right-click, and choose Edit; you'll see the dialog box shown in Figure 14-4.

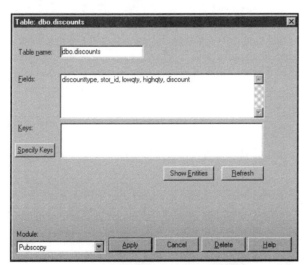

FIGURE 14-4

You must first bring up the Edit dialog box for a table to add key information.

Now just click on the Specify Keys button, and you can add the appropriate keys from the list of fields, as shown in Figure 14-5.

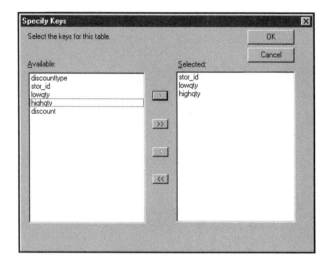

FIGURE 14-5

For the discounts table, you can add the title_id, lowqty, and highqty columns as the keys.

You can then do the same for the roysched table, choosing the title_id, lorange, and hirange fields as the keys.

Of course, you can also just delete the tables from the Database tab, after which EQ will let you compile and test the application. However, you would not be able to include references to those ranges if you deleted those tables.

TIP

If you are not going to use one or more sets of tables in the EQ application, just delete them from the Database tab.

Working with Joins

In addition to correcting keys, you'll also want to add or review the joins between tables. The joins will help EQ determine how to answer queries that involve more than one table.

Most joins are already detected by EQ when you load your tables. For example, you'll notice the two joins from the titleauthor table—one to authors and one to titles—in the titleauthor joins node, as shown in Figure 14-6.

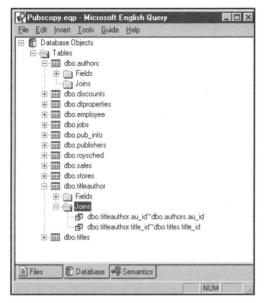

FIGURE 14-6

English Query determines two joins for the titleauthor table automatically when loading the tables.

Note that EQ uses a tilde (~), not an equal sign, to indicate the join. This is because the join might be an equijoin, or it might also be an outer join.

NOTE

A join in English Query is always listed from the referencing (foreign key) table to the referenced (primary key) table. Therefore, to find the join in the Database tab, drill down into the foreign key table.

You can add your own join to any table by right-clicking over the Joins node and choosing Insert Join. In the resulting dialog box, shown in Figure 14-7, you next choose the destination table.

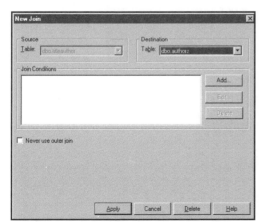

FIGURE 14-7

When you add a join, the first step is to select the destination table.

Now click on the Add button so that you can specify the actual join condition, as shown in Figure 14-8.

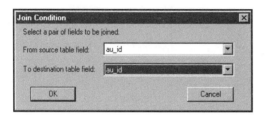

FIGURE 14-8

You specify the actual join condition in the Join Condition dialog box.

You need to remember which table is source and which is destination; the source table is the referencing foreign key table, and the destination table is the referenced primary key table.

The resulting dialog box now lets you inspect your join, as you can see in Figure 14-9.

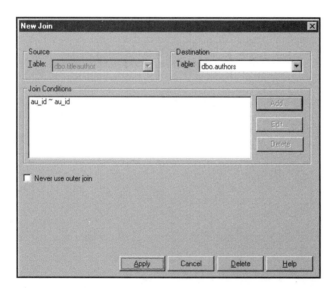

FIGURE 14-9

The resulting join condition is now listed in the dialog box.

After you apply the condition, you can return to edit the join as well as delete it.

Outer Joins

By default, EQ will allow outer joins. You can prevent outer joins one by one, using the check box in the New or Edit Join dialog box, as illustrated in Figure 14-9. You can also make a global decision about outer joins in the Advanced tab of the Global Options dialog box (shown later in this chapter).

> ## WARNING
>
> Making the correct decision regarding outer joins in English Query is very important, because it will affect the results of queries. Never allowing an outer join will make it impossible for users to phrase questions requesting outer join–like results.

Semantics

The last tab on the English Query designer is the Semantics tab, where you define a verbal correlation between database data and common English terms.

There are four types of EQ semantic objects: *entities*, relationships, domain commands, and dictionary entries. Semantic entities are synonyms or names for your database entities (tables and columns). Semantic *relationships* are verbal relationships between the semantic entities. *Domain commands* are external commands or actions that you can invoke, and *dictionary entries* are synonyms that you can force to be substituted by EQ when evaluating user language.

> ## NOTE
>
> There is no automated way to add semantic entities or relationships, so you have to add them manually.

Initially no semantic entities are defined, so it's not possible for EQ to answer certain questions. For example, if you choose Tools, Test Application from the menu and then issue the question, "how many titles are there," you'll see a result like that shown in Figure 14-10.

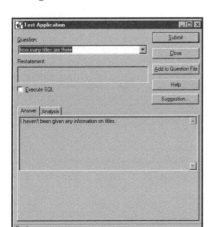

FIGURE 14-10

Without any semantic objects, English Query cannot answer simple questions like "how many titles are there?"

To get an answer to this question, you have to define the semantic object so that English Query can translate user English into queries about data. Add the title entity, as shown in Figure 14-11, by right-clicking over the Entities node in the Semantics tab and choosing Insert Entity.

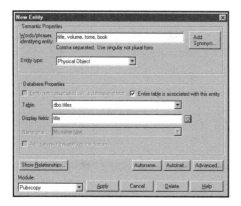

FIGURE 14-11

Adding a new semantic entity consists of listing the words users can use to identify the entity, linking it to data, and specifying the return values.

This dialog box has quite a few options. You can add a set of terms, in the singular form, that EQ will parse from the user's input. Then you give the entity a type, from a list of none, person, geographical location, animate object, physical object, and day or time. This helps EQ with its parsing of natural English.

You can associate the semantic entity with the data defined in the Database tab, either an entire table or a column. If you choose a table, you can then choose the columns to display when the table data is selected.

Testing an Application

Once you apply your new semantic entity, you can test a query against the entity's data, as shown in Figure 14-12.

FIGURE 14-12

Once a semantic entity is defined, you can query it.

The Analysis tab gives some additional detail about the entities and relationships used, whereas the Suggestion button will ask about any ambiguities detected in the user's question.

Semantic Relationships

To add a semantic relationship, you need more than one entity. Consequently, the next step is to define another semantic entity; let's choose authors. To follow the example here, add the authors semantic entity as shown in Figure 14-13.

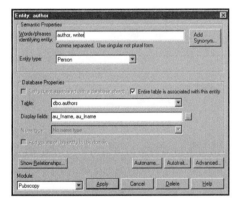

FIGURE 14-13

Adding the author semantic entity makes defining a semantic relationship possible.

Now you can define a semantic relationship between authors and titles. Specifically, you'll add the semantic relationship that authors write titles. First of all, bring up the new semantic relationship dialog box as shown in Figure 14-14, and add the semantic entities author and title.

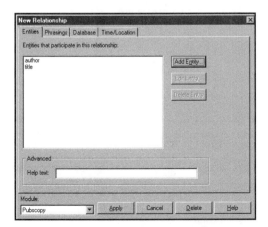

FIGURE 14-14

You start a relationship definition by adding the semantic entities to the list.

Next, choose the Phrasings tab and click on the Add button, so that you can specify a verb phrasing, as shown in Figure 14-15.

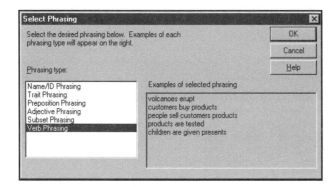

FIGURE 14-15

You next choose the type of phrasing.

In our case, the model "customers buy products" matches our goal of creating an "authors write titles" relationship.

The next dialog box, shown in Figure 14-16, asks for verb phrasing, in which you choose the subject and verb as well as an optional object or preposition reflecting the relationship.

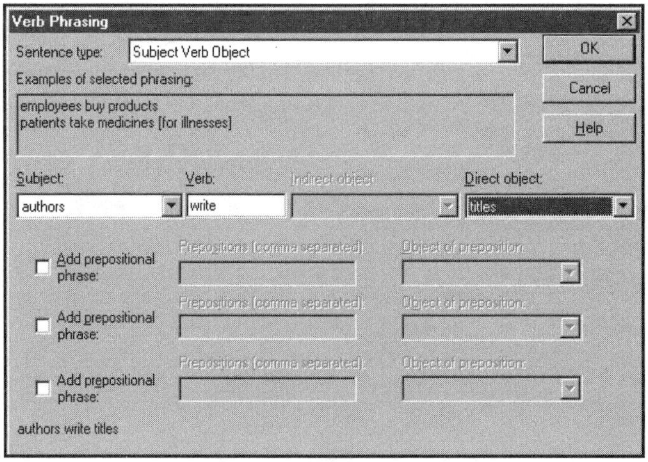

FIGURE 14-16

You then create the actual verb phrase pattern for the relationship.

Note that you could add up to three prepositional phrases to further qualify the relationship. Finally, you choose the table that holds the join for the relationship, titleauthor, in the Database tab of the dialog box.

Once all these steps are taken, you can ask a question like "how many authors do not have titles?" to see the result shown in Figure 14-17.

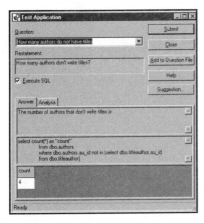

FIGURE 14-17

With a relationship defined, you can query across entities.

Note that EQ provides a more exact paraphrase, and then the actual SQL SELECT command. It's a good idea to review the resulting SELECT structure to make sure EQ has interpreted the initial question correctly. Note that you can also have EQ return the result set for further verification, as shown in the figure.

Column Entities and Relationships

Numerous kinds of questions arise that this simple semantic relationship cannot handle, such as "Who wrote 'The Busy Executive's Database Guide'?" The problem here is that the name of a title is not related to the title. So you need to add a new semantic entity, title name, and associate it with the title.

So in this case add the new entity, title_name, and associate it with the title, as shown in Figure 14-18.

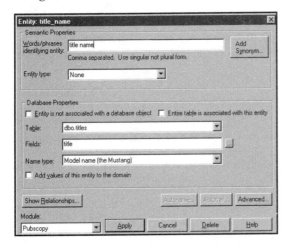

FIGURE 14-18

You can add a column of the table as a semantic entity.

Note the choices here: title name is not really any entity type, nor is it associated with an entire table. Nonetheless, you do associate it with the titles table and the title column. The name type, as a model name, is the closest in format to a title name.

Once the new entity is in place, you can ask the original question and get an answer, as shown in Figure 14-19.

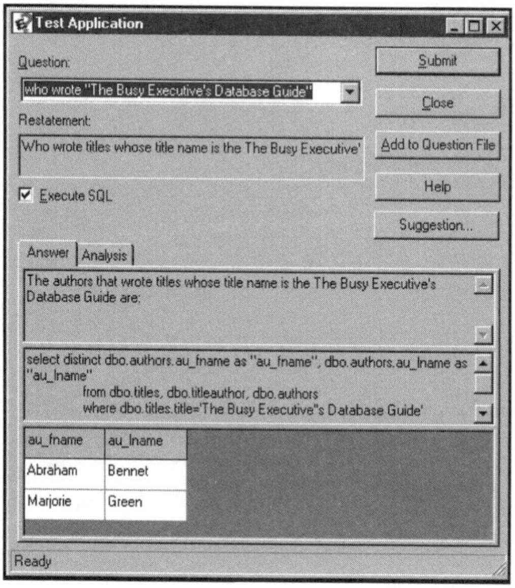

FIGURE 14-19

You can now ask more detailed questions about authors and titles.

Now EQ can correctly interpret the question "Who wrote 'The Busy Executive's Database Guide'?"

Here is where English Query is really displaying its technology. You specified that the title_name semantic entity was a name type of entity, and that it belonged to the titles semantic entity. EQ is then able to parse the question and realize that it is asking for a name of a title and thus produce the question. In other words, EQ takes:

```
Who wrote "The Busy Executive's Database Guide"?
```

and is able to interpret it as

```
Who wrote titles whose title name is the The Busy Executive's Database Guide?
```

Once the interpretation is in place and all semantic entities are associated with table entities, it's a short step to the corresponding SELECT statement:

```
select distinct dbo.authors.au_fname as "au_fname",
```

```
dbo.authors.au_lname as "au_lname"

        from dbo.titles, dbo.titleauthor, dbo.authors

        where dbo.titles.title='The Busy Executive''s Database Guide'

        and dbo.titles.title_id=dbo.titleauthor.title_id

        and dbo.titleauthor.au_id=dbo.authors.au_id
```

The crucial step is the initial translation of the user's question into a semantically parsed version. This depends upon your having correctly defined the semantic entities and relationships so that EQ can interpret the questions correctly. Unfortunately, this can be a daunting task.

Outer Joins Revisited

If you define your table joins to allow outer joins, then English Query can interpret some commands as an outer join. For example, EQ interprets the imperative,

```
Show me all the authors
```

as

```
Show the authors
```

and builds a SELECT statement to return all author first and last names, as you defined.

Now change the imperative slightly to add titles:

```
Show me all the authors and their titles
```

is interpreted by EQ as

```
Show the authors and the titles they write
```

which returns a left outer join of all authors, with titles left blank for those authors that have no titles, as seen in Figure 14-20.

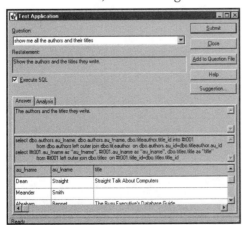

FIGURE 14-20

If you phrase a question carefully, EQ can return an outer join.

Formatted, the SELECT statement looks like:

```
select dbo.authors.au_lname, dbo.authors.au_fname,
dbo.titleauthor.title_id
            into #t001
            from dbo.authors
            left outer join dbo.titleauthor
            on dbo.authors.au_id=dbo.titleauthor.au_id
select #t001.au_fname as "au_fname",
            #t001.au_lname as "au_lname",
            dbo.titles.title as "title"
            from #t001 left outer join dbo.titles
            on #t001.title_id=dbo.titles.title_id
```

That is, there's an LOJ between authors and titleauthor, to get all the authors, whether they've written a title or not, and then another LOJ between titleauthor and titles, which actually just picks up the title names. The second LOJ is not actually required but is harmless.

Now let's rephrase the question to imply no outer join. If you submit,

```
Show me all the authors that have titles
```

EQ interprets it as

```
Which authors write titles?
```

Now we elaborate,

```
Show me all the authors that have titles, and their titles
```

EQ reinterprets this as

```
Show the authors that write titles and the titles they write.
```

The resulting SELECT is:

```
select dbo.authors.au_fname as "au_fname",
            dbo.authors.au_lname as "au_lname",
            dbo.titles.title as "title"
            from dbo.titles, dbo.titleauthor, dbo.authors
            where dbo.titles.title_id=dbo.titleauthor.title_id
            and dbo.titleauthor.au_id=dbo.authors.au_id
```

which does not use the outer join at all. In other words, a careful phrasing of the question you send to EQ can distinguish between a request for an outer join and a request for a regular join.

It seems reasonable that sometimes users should not be able to ask for outer joins, so at times you may want to turn the option off. However, English Query is pretty good at interpreting the commands correctly, at least at a simple level, so there may be no need to restrict outer joins from careful users.

Global Properties

You can set global properties for an English Query application by selecting the dialog box from Edit, Global Properties on the menu. The resulting dialog box's opening tab is shown in Figure 14-21.

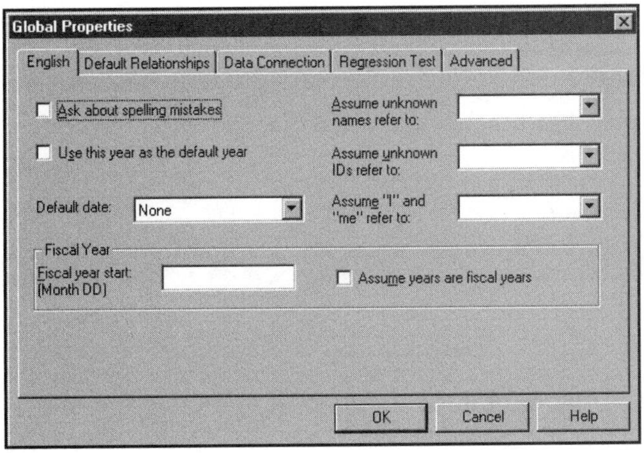

FIGURE 14-21

The English tab of the Global Properties dialog box lets you set some options for interpreting users' English and some defaults.

The assumptions allow EQ to determine otherwise ambiguous references such as "I" and "me" as well as set default dates and the fiscal year. Once the fiscal year is defined, values can be queried in terms of quarters.

If you have two or more relationships that each have the same semantic entities in them, EQ may have trouble determining what relationship to use. In the Default Relationships tab, you can choose one of the relationships as the default, for instance, primary relationship. The Data Connection tab contains the ODBC string and data source information EQ uses in building the data tables and executing SQL. The Regression Test tab contains file references for regression tests (see the next section for more).

The final, Advanced, tab, shown in Figure 14-22, collects some important default settings.

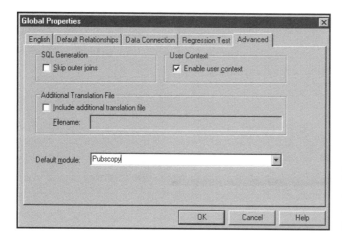

FIGURE 14-22

In the Advanced Global Properties tab, you can set a global outer join option.

You can cause all SQL generation in the entire application to avoid outer joins using this option. Although this may improve performance against large data sets, it also removes an important option from the user. You can also remove a user context and provide a translation file.

WARNING

The Skip outer joins option in the Advanced tab of the Global Properties dialog box, if checked, causes all resulting SQL SELECT commands to not use outer joins.

Regression-Testing an English Query Application

In addition to the ad hoc testing window that you've used so far to test your semantic entities and relationships, you can set up a regression test on an English Query application.

The regression test will compare the results of two files that contain queries from two different versions of an EQ application. This allows you to determine whether any changes you've made to the semantic entities or relationships have undone the results you are expecting.

If you choose Tools, Regression Test from the menu, you'll see the dialog box shown in Figure 14-23.

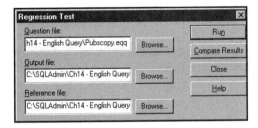

FIGURE 14-23

A regression test compares different output files.

The default locations for three types of files are listed. You need these things:

♦ A question file

♦ An output file

♦ A reference file

You create a question file by clicking on the Add to Question File button in the Test Application dialog box, as shown in Figure 14-24.

TIP

The English Query documentation is not very clear on how to create a reference file. All you need to do is copy an initial output file, .eqo, and give it the extension .eqs.

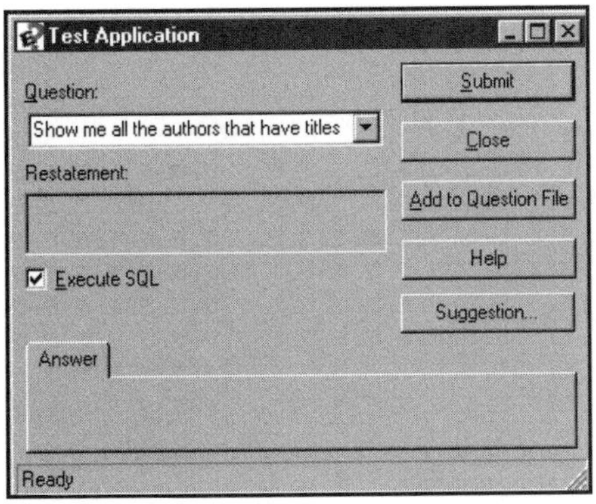

FIGURE 14-24

You can add to a question file in the Test Application dialog box.

The output file is created after you build the EQ application. Just choose Tools, Build Application from the menu. After you've created your reference file, you can then compare the answers later as you refine your model.

Summary

English query provides a way of taking natural language input from end users and sending SQL queries to SQL Server. You can optionally return a resulting translation into a more exact data retrieval statement to the user for approval. In any case, you can submit the resulting query to SQL Server and return the data to the user. Let's now turn to the other parts of Transact-SQL, the parts that make it a simple but effective programming language.

Chapter 15

Basics of Transact-SQL Programming

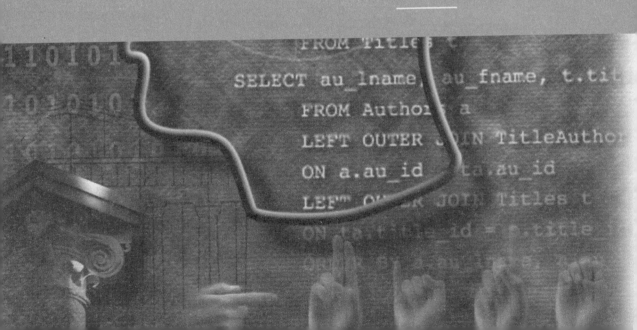

In This Chapter

♦ Batches, scripts, stored procedures, and triggers

♦ Transact-SQL basics

♦ Dynamic SQL (EXEC)

♦ Cursors

As the dialect of the SQL Language that comes with SQL Server, Transact-SQL also has traditionally provided database developers with constructs for writing programs. The same relational engine that executes SQL queries and updates executes these programs.

You can store and execute Transact-SQL programs in basically three formats: as scripts stored as text files, as stored procedures in the database, and as triggers attached to tables.

In this chapter, you'll learn the basic mechanics of the Transact-SQL programming language. This includes the concepts of batches, variables, flow control, cursors, and how to trace a script using the Transact-SQL debugger. Then in the following three chapters, you'll learn more about transactions, stored procedures, and triggers.

Batches, Scripts, Stored Procedures, and Triggers

All Transact-SQL commands are executed in groups called batches. A batch is a set of commands that the SQL Server query processor has compiled together and will execute as a group.

You've already been using batches. Whenever you send one or more unseparated SQL commands to SQL Server through the Query Analyzer, they form a batch. For example, the following two commands, executed together, form a *batch*:

```
SELECT * FROM authors
UPDATE authors
          SET contract = 1
          WHERE contract = 0
```

→ one batch

In addition, when you highlight a set of commands and execute them, the higlighted portion will also form a batch.

The idea is that the SQL Server relational engine will check the entire set of commands for syntax and build query plans for each before executing them. If there's a fatal error (a syntax error, for example), then the entire batch will fail. SQL Server will not selectively execute just the commands that pass muster.

A script can contain many batches, whereas a stored procedure and trigger can contain only one batch. You can separate one set of commands in a script from another, ensuring that they are in different batches, by using the GO keyword. For example, the GO keyword makes the following two commands occur each in its own batch:

```
SELECT * FROM authors
GO
UPDATE authors
          SET contract = 1
          WHERE contract = 0
GO
```

> ↘ *two batches.* ↙

NOTE

GO is not a command, because nothing is executed by SQL Server. The GO statement just tells the SQL Server query processor to treat a set of commands as a separate batch.

The SQL Server query processor will compile, build a query plan, and execute the SELECT statement. When finished, the query processor will move on to the next command and do the same.

You can see another use of batching Transact-SQL commands in OSQL and ISQL. Before the GUI SQL Server Query Analyzer existed, the only interactive tool for querying SQL Server was the command-line ISQL. SQL Server 7 still has ISQL.EXE, which uses DB-Library, and it also gives you OSQL, which uses

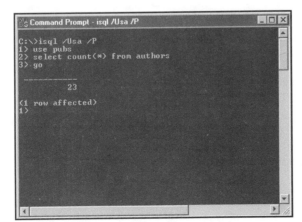

FIGURE 15-1

The GO keyword makes a series of commands into a batch to submit to SQL Server.

ODBC. You execute each from the NT MS-DOS command window. Figure 15-1 shows the use of ISQL with a couple of commands.

Here the GO keyword terminates a set of commands, and then ISQL executes them. In ISQL and OSQL, you submit commands one at a time and then the GO keyword sends them off as a batch to SQL Server. In the Query Analyzer, though, you can enter a series of commands and selectively decide which ones should become a batch.

There are a number of important limitations on what you can include in a batch:

◆ You must leave the CREATE DEFAULT, CREATE PROCEDURE, CREATE RULE, CREATE TRIGGER, and CREATE VIEW statements as one entire batch.

◆ If you use ALTER TABLE in a batch to add a new column to a table, you can't reference the new columns until a new batch is run.

There is a maximum batch size limit, in terms of explicit data values that can be inserted or updated in a single batch, of 128 times the network packet size. Since this size is usually about 4K, most often the maximum size of a batch will be 400K.

A script is a text file stored on disk outside of SQL Server that contains a set of one or more batches. Normally, script files have a .SQL extension. You can build scripts in the Query Analyzer. There's a Load SQL Script button on the toolbar, and the disk icon will save your queries as a script. Inside a script, as well as in the ISQL/W window, you can have one or more batches.

NOTE

A good way to permanently store your T-SQL code is as a script in an external text file. As external files, they can be stored in a source code control system such as Visual SourceSafe. In addition, scripts can be scheduled for execution by SQL Agent, as you learned in Chapter 11.

You can automate the use of a script by calling it from ISQL or OSQL. For example, suppose the following batch forms a script called Script1.SQL:

```
SELECT COUNT(*) FROM authors
GO
UPDATE authors
        SET contract  = 1
        WHERE contract = 0
GO
```

Then to execute the script, you can include a reference to the file in the command line, as shown in Figure 15-2.

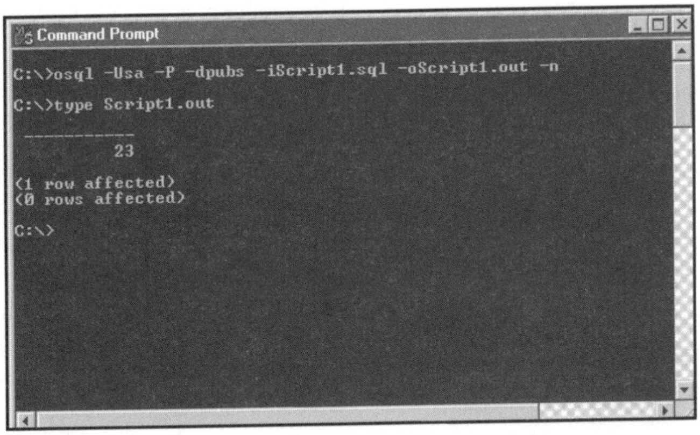

```
C:\>osql -Usa -P -dpubs -iScript1.sql -oScript1.out -n

C:\>type Script1.out

           23

(1 row affected)
(0 rows affected)

C:\>
```

FIGURE 15-2

You can execute a script using the command line SQL utilities ISQL.EXE and OSQL.EXE

TIP

The advantage of using OSQL.EXE over ISQL.EXE is that OSQL uses ODBC and therefore lets you use the new features of SQL Server 7. Since ISQL.EXE uses DB-Library, which has not been updated for SQL Server 7, you will not be able to use a number of newer SQL Server 7 features.

You can see that if you include this command in an NT command file, you can schedule it or make it a part of a series of commands.

NOTE

You'll learn about *stored procedures* and triggers—alternatives to scripts—in Chapters 17 and 18. A stored procedure is a single batch of commands that is compiled and stored in a SQL Server database that you can execute on demand. By way of contrast, a *trigger* is a form of stored procedure that is also compiled and stored in a SQL Server database, but that is attached to a table and only executes when the table is updated.

Transact-SQL Basics

The Transact-SQL language contains many of the same constructs that you will find in other programming languages, such as C++ or Visual Basic. There are ways to insert comments, declare variables, control the flow of a program, and so on. Let's start with comments.

Comments

You have two ways of commenting text in Transact-SQL. To command a group of lines, use /* followed by */:

```
/*
This is a comment line 1
This is a comment line 2
*/
SELECT COUNT(*)
        FROM Authors
```

The /* */ commenting system is rather difficult to type, so Transact-SQL also contains a single-line-only form of commenting with two dashes:

```
-- This is a single line comment
-- followed by a second line
SELECT COUNT(*)
        FROM Authors
```

You can use the two dashes to comment out a command:

```
-- Don't execute the following:
-- SELECT COUNT(*)
--        FROM Authors
```

or to append notes to the end of the command:

```
SELECT COUNT(*) -- Get the count
        FROM Authors
```

Variables

Transact-SQL has two kinds of variables: local variables and system functions. The local variables are variables local to a Transact-SQL batch. There are no variables that span batches. The system functions used to be called "global variables" in prior releases of SQL Server, but the SQL Server 7 documentation has renamed them.

Local Variables

Local variables are temporary locations in memory that you can name and use to store data in. What's local about a local variable is that its scope is limited to the current batch, and its visibility is limited to the current session. No other batch from any other user can see your batch's local variables.

Local variable names must begin with a single @ sign, and they must be explicitly declared and assigned a data type. The DECLARE statement registers the variable name and assigns it a SQL Server data type. With SQL Server 7, you can use the SET statement to assign it an initial value:

```
DECLARE      @sample char(10)
SET              @sample = 'hello'
```

TIP

If you do not initialize a variable with a value, SQL Server will initialize it to NULL.

You can also use the SELECT statement:

```
DECLARE      @sample char(10)
SELECT           @sample = 'hi there'
```

If this seems an odd use of the SELECT command, it is, but until SQL Server 7 it was the only way to assign values to local variables in Transact-SQL.

TIP

SQL Server 7 now extends the SET statement as an alternative and clearer way to assign values to variables.

You can also then use the SELECT command to display the result:

```
declare  sample  char(10)     > output:  sample
SELECT       @sample  'Sample' /           - - - -
                                            Null
```

System and Configuration Functions

In addition to local variables, which you can create, SQL Server contains a set of read-only system-wide "variables," which belong to a group of system functions and configuration functions. These functions are really reports about system characteristics. Many apply only to your current session. These system and configuration functions begin with two at-signs, @@. Unlike local variables, you cannot declare any system or configuration functions of your own.

Here are some of the more commonly used system functions that take the "@@" prefix:

@@error   The error number resulting from the last SQL command

@@identity   The last identity value used in an INSERT

@@rowcount   The number of rows processed by the preceding command

`@@trancount`	The transaction nesting level

Here are some of the commonly used configuration functions that take the `"@@"` prefix:

`@@nestlevel`	The nesting level of a stored procedure or trigger
`@@spid`	The current process id
`@@servername`	The name of current server *mycomputer*
`@@version`	The SQL Server version
`@@fetch_status`	The status of previous fetch statement

You use a system function by displaying its value. For example, to find the current version of your system, just use:

```
SELECT @@version
```

Similarly, to find the current server name, you can issue:

```
SELECT @@servername
```

The PRINT Statement

You can send output from your program to your client software using the PRINT statement. Often PRINT statements are used to display current values or simply to send messages. As a simple example, here's some sample text output:

```
PRINT 'Hi there'
```

The PRINT statement accepts only literal strings. The basic syntax of the PRINT statement is:

```
PRINT literal-text | local_variable | system function | string-expression
```

The addition of the string-expression at the end is new with SQL Server 7. It means that in addition to printing out just literal text or single variables, you can also print more complex expressions such as:

```
PRINT GETDATE()
```

and concatenations:

```
PRINT 'My version is ' + @@version
```

The PRINT statement will also convert numeric expressions to strings:

```
PRINT 3
PRINT 3 + 4    → Output : 7
```

However, you cannot mix a string and a number in the expression. For example, the following statement will not work:

```
PRINT 3 + 'hi there'
```

To accomplish such a mixed display, you need to use a conversion function.

Conversion Functions, CAST() and CONVERT()

Transact-SQL contains a number of conversion functions, as well as an all-purpose CONVERT() function, to translate data from one type to another. SQL Server 7 extends Transact-SQL to include the ANSI SQL CAST() function that duplicates most of the functionality of the nonstandard CONVERT().

To print a concatenation of a string with an integer, for example, you can use either CAST() or CONVERT():

```
PRINT CONVERT(CHAR(1),3) + ' hi there'
PRINT CAST(3 AS CHAR(1)) + ' hi there'
```
output: 3 hi there

The basic syntax of the CONVERT() function is:

Convert (char   (1),   3)

```
CONVERT (data-type[(length)], convert-expression)
```

In other words, you specify the data type you want the conversion to result in, followed by the expression you want converted. The resulting value will be returned by the function.

The CAST() function works similarly, reversing the order of the parameters and using an AS instead of a comma:

```
CAST (convert-expression AS data-type[(length)])
```

cast (3   as char   (1))

NOTE

Though it can be difficult to break the habit of using the CONVERT() function, using the CAST function will be better for you over the long run, because it is ANSI standard. In this text, I will mostly use the CAST function.

The CONVERT() and CAST() functions are fully documented in the *Transact-SQL Reference Manual*. You'll see more examples in the next few pages. In fact, one of the most common uses for conversion is with date and time functions.

Date and Time Functions

SQL Server stores both date and time together in a single data type. The date part stores the usual day, month, and year in a format that automatically tracks the century. The time part stores the time from midnight to the milliseconds.

To be more specific, the date is stored internally as an integer where the value 0 is equivalent to January 1, 1900. Positive integer values indicate the number of days forward from that date, ending at December 31, 9999. Negative numbers proceed backward to January 1, 1753. The time part of the DATETIME data type is an integer storing the number of milliseconds from midnight, but only to an accuracy of three milliseconds.

> **NOTE**
>
> The reason why January 1, 1753, is the earliest date that the DATETIME value can store is rather obscure. In late 1752, the English-speaking world changed from the Julian to the Gregorian calendar, bringing it into line with Continental Europe, and losing several days. Apparently someone at Sybase decided that was reason enough to terminate the DATETIME year range at that point, and Microsoft has inherited that decision.

Because the date part of the DATETIME data type is stored as an integer, all dates are stored with the century implicit in the data value.

To fill a variable with a DATETIME value, or to insert or update a DATETIME value, all you need to do is supply a string that obeys a readable format. For example, the following code stores a DATETIME value to a variable:

```
DECLARE @Mydate DATETIME
SET @Mydate = 'December 1, 1952 10:52:22.2'
```

To get the current date and time in a DATETIME variable or column, you can use the GETDATE() function:

```
DECLARE @Mydate DATETIME
SET @Mydate = GETDATE()
select @mydate
```

output:
2001 -10-04   16:17:11

Default Date and Time

Sometimes you will want to simply store a time, or simply store a date. If you just load the time, you'll get the default base date value of January 1, 1900:

```
DECLARE @MyTime DATETIME
SET @MyTime = '12:12:12'
```

```
SELECT @MyTime

..........................

1900-01-01 12:12:12.000

(1 row(s) affected)
```

And if you just store the date, you'll get the default time of 12:00 midnight.

Two-Digit Years

If you supply a string value with only a two-digit year, SQL Server defaults to storing any entry with two-digit years 50 or over as 19xx, and less than 50 as 20xx:

```
DECLARE @EarlyDate DATETIME,
          @LaterDate DATETIME
SET @EarlyDate = 'December 1, 62'
SET @LaterDate = 'December 1, 22'
SELECT @EarlyDate AS EarlyDate, @LaterDate AS LaterDate

EarlyDate                  LaterDate

..........................  ..........................

1962-12-01 00:00:00.000    2022-12-01 00:00:00.000
```

Date Arithmetic

With SQL Server 7, you can perform date arithmetic. In other words, you can add or subtract days:

```
SELECT GETDATE(), GETDATE() +1

..........................  ..........................

1998-06-24 22:02:35.497    1998-06-25 22:02:35.497

(1 row(s) affected)
```

Or you can add or subtract a portion of a day:

```
SELECT GETDATE(), GETDATE() - .5

..........................  ..........................

1998-06-24 22:02:35.497    1998-06-24 10:02:35.497

(1 row(s) affected)
```

NOTE

The default date arithmetic is to add or subtract days or parts of days. You can add or subtract months, hours, and so on by using the DATEADD() and DATEDIFF() functions.

CONVERT() *and* CAST() *with* DATETIME

Because date and time are stored together, you can use a date or time function to extract a portion of the entire data value when you want to get just the date or just the time. For example, to see just the date, you can use either the CAST() function or the CONVERT() function:

```
DECLARE @MyDate DATETIME
SET @MyDate = GETDATE()
SELECT CONVERT(VARCHAR(11), @MyDate)
SELECT CAST(@MyDate AS VARCHAR(11))
```

However, when extracting the time, the CONVERT() function includes an extra style option that allows you to specify the format in more detail:

```
DECLARE @MyDate DATETIME
SET @MyDate = GETDATE()
SELECT CONVERT(VARCHAR(24), @MyDate, 108)

-----------------------
22:27:37

(1 row(s) affected)
```

The CAST() function does not have a style option, and cannot display just the time part of the DATETIME datatype.

Other DATETIME *Functions*

Other functions include the DAY(), MONTH(), and YEAR() functions, which return integers indicating those values from a given date. More generally, the DATEPART() function returns integers indicating all those date options plus time values of hour, minute, second, millisecond, and so on. DATENAME() returns the name corresponding to the integers returned for the dates.

Errors

You can detect whether an error has occurred by using the @@error system function. When an error occurs in T-SQL, if the error has a number, SQL Server will put that number into the @@error system function. The variable holds that value until the next T-SQL statement executes. When a T-SQL command succeeds, SQL Server sets the value of @@error back to 0.

For example, in the following code, a divide by zero error is triggered and the error number captured:

```
DECLARE @myerrnum int, @char_err varchar(30)
SELECT 5/0
SELECT @myerrnum = @@error
IF @myerrnum !=0
BEGIN
        PRIN T '------------'
        PRINT 'Encountered error ' + CONVERT(char(10),@myerrnum)
END
GO
```

The result shows that you captured the error number:

```
Server: Msg 8134, Level 16, State 1, Line 0
Divide by zero error encountered.
------------
Encountered error 8134
```

Not all errors in T-SQL will set the @@error variable. What's important is that good T-SQL code should check the @@error variable often, especially after SQL statements that update data.

Error Levels

When an error occurs, and the error has a number, SQL Server will also return a severity level, which is just called "Level," and a state. Levels 1 through 14 are informational, 15 is a warning, and 16 and above are errors, though not necessarily fatal errors. The state is an arbitrary number from 1 to 127, and is ignored by SQL Server.

Raising Errors

Sometimes it's advantageous to raise errors directly. With the RAISERROR command, you can send an error message, and SQL Server will default the error number to 50000:

```
RAISERROR ('An error has occurred', 16,1)
```

It will return the default error number of 50000:

```
Server: Msg 50000, Level 16, State 42000
An error has occurred
```

You can define you own error messages (with a number of 50000 or above) using the sp_addmessage stored procedure. For example, you could add a new message called "Important business rule violated" using the following code:

```
EXEC sp_addmessage 50001, 16, 'Important business rule violated'
```

Then you can raise the error directly:

```
RAISERROR (50001,16,1)
Server: Msg 50001, Level 16, State 42000
Important business rule violated
```

The error level that the error will take is determined by the RAISERROR statement, not the sp_addmessage definition. Consequently, you can define a serious error but only raise it as an informational one:

```
RAISERROR (50001,10,1)
Important business rule violated
```

The RAISERROR command also has a mechanism for printing out variable values inside the command. For example, the statement:

```
RAISERROR ('The first value was %d and the next one was        %s.',0, 1,
10, 'hi there')
```

prints out this:

```
The first value was 10 and the next one was hi there.
```

This comes in handy when you are trying to communicate error data back to the user, and it is particularly valuable in triggers.

Conditional Execution

Conditional execution allows Transact-SQL to have branches of code that execute based on some condition.

Jumping to a Label with the GOTO *Statement*

There is a way to make code execution jump unconditionally to a location in the program, a location called a label. To do this, you use the GOTO statement, which is not at all the same as the GO statement! Instead, GOTO makes an absolute jump. For example, the following code jumps past the first PRINT statement and only executes the second print statement.

```
GOTO MyLabel
PRINT 'Hi there'
```

```
MyLabel:
        PRINT 'Done'
```

When SQL Server first parses and compiles this code, it checks that the name following the GOTO statement exists once somewhere in the same batch with a colon after it. When it executes, it simply jumps to the location of the label.

The IF *Statement*

You can use the IF/ELSE statement to conditionally execute statements:

```
IF @X > 0
        PRINT 'X > 0'
```

You can also combine IF with an ELSE branch:

declare @x char (1)

```
IF @X > 0
        PRINT 'X > 0'

ELSE
        PRINT 'X <= 0'
```

output: X <= 0

NOTE

There is no ENDIF construct in Transact-SQL. In addition, there is no ELSEIF construct, although you can easily embed IF statements within other IF statements.

One very nice feature of Transact-SQL is the ability to embed SQL SELECT statements in an IF clause:

```
IF (SELECT MAX(price) FROM Titles) > 20
        PRINT 'Maximum > 20'
ELSE
        PRINT 'Maximum <= 20'
```

This adds a great deal of power to conditional expressions.

Combining IF *and* GOTO

Combining the GOTO with the IF statement can be handy for emergency jumps when an error occurs, as the following code illustrates:

```
        -- Do some work
        IF @@error != 0        -- An error occurred
```

```
        GOTO Errorhandler -- Jump to the label
    -- Do some more work and finish
    RETURN
Errorhandler:
    RAISERROR ('Serious error has occurred, 16 ,1)
RETURN
```

This error handling has its greatest use in the context of tranactions within stored procedures and triggers. I'll cover transactions, stored procedures, and triggers in more detail in the next few chapters.

Statement Blocks

When you want to execute more than one statement within a branch of an IF statement, and certain other places, you must block them together with BEGIN/END pairs:

```
IF (SELECT MAX(price) FROM Titles) > 20
    BEGIN
        PRINT 'Maximum:'
        SELECT MAX(price) FROM Titles
    END
```

output: Maximum: _____
22.9500

Note that the following statement is quite different:

same output

```
IF (SELECT MAX(price) FROM Titles) > 20
        PRINT 'Maximum:'
        SELECT MAX(price) FROM Titles
```

The second SELECT statement will be executed no matter what the truth value of the IF statement is.

Looping

In addition to conditional execution, T-SQL has the WHILE construct for causing iterations or repetitions in code. To use the WHILE statement, you have to specify some condition and then place the repeating code in between a BEGIN/END block.

Here is a very simple WHILE loop that just counts from one to ten:

```
DECLARE     @Ctr integer
SET             @Ctr = 1
WHILE       @Ctr <= 10
```

```
BEGIN
        PRINT @Ctr
        SET @Ctr = @Ctr + 1
END
```

output: 1
2
3
4
5
...
10

This is about as bare-bones as a WHILE loop can be. Note that you must supply some condition, which in this case requires the counter variable @Ctr. Further, there has to be something going on inside the loop to change the condition so that it can eventually become false and the loop quit. In the preceding loop, the counter gets incremented by one every time it passes through, so that eventually the counter variable exceeds 10, the WHILE loop's condition fails, and the loop quits.

The WHILE statement must have some condition that evaluates to true or false. Then the interior of the loop must be blocked off by a BEGIN/END pair. What's very important to see is that the SELECT statement increments the counter so that the loop will come to an end. If you don't do that, your loop will execute indefinitely.

Quitting a Loop Early with BREAK

Inside a WHILE loop, it is sometimes necessary to quit the loop early with the BREAK statement. For example, the following code quits the preceding loop early:

```
DECLARE @Ctr integer
SET          @Ctr = 1
WHILE @Ctr <= 10
        BEGIN
                PRINT @Ctr
                SELECT @Ctr = @Ctr + 1
                If @Ctr = 5
                        BREAK
        END
```

output: 1
2
3
4

The BREAK statement executes when the @Ctr variable reaches 5, causing the loop to cease and move execution on to the next set of statements, if any, after the WHILE loop.

Repeating a Loop with CONTINUE

You can make the WHILE loop restart execution at the top of the loop with the CONTINUE statement. The following loop does not print out the number 5:

```
DECLARE @Ctr integer
SET          @Ctr = 0
```

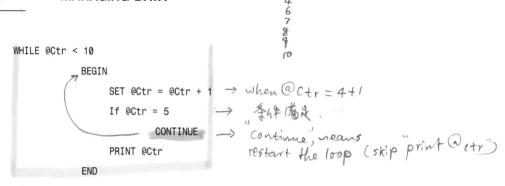

Make sure you see what the CONTINUE statement is doing. If @ctr equals 4, the loop still adds 1 to it and then executes the CONTINUE statement, skipping the PRINT and jumping back up to the WHILE. As a result, the number 5 never prints.

Simulating the *C* SWITCH *or VB* CASE *Statement*

Transact-SQL does not have an equivalent statement to the SWITCH statement of the C language, or the CASE statement of Visual Basic. However, you can simulate them with a series of IF statements, with GOTO, or a WHILE statement.

For example, if you have a series of conditions that you want to test, and you want them to execute in sequence, all you need is a series of IF statements:

```
-- Assume @x is an initialized integer
IF @X = 1
            -- Perform action 1
IF @X = 2
            -- Perform action 2
--etc.
```

However, even if @x is 1, the preceding code will test it against the remainder of the IF statements. You can get past this using labels:

```
IF @X = 1
        BEGIN
            -- Perform action 1
            GOTO BreakOut
        END
IF @X = 2
        BEGIN
            -- Perform action 2
```

```
            GOTO BreakOut
        END
--etc.
Breakout:
```

You could get the same effect without labels and GOTOs by using the BREAK statement in a WHILE loop:

```
WHILE 1=1
BEGIN
        IF @X = 1
        BEGIN
            -- Perform action 1
            BREAK
        END
        IF @X = 2
        BEGIN
            -- Perform action 2
            BREAK
        END
        --etc.
BREAK
END
```

In the preceding loop, the BREAK just before the last END statement ensures that the loop excutes only once.

> **NOTE**
>
> The CASE construct in Transact-SQL is an expression that you can embed in SQL expressions. It is not equivalent to the C SWITCH statement or VB CASE statement.

Dynamic SQL (the EXEC statement)

Sometimes you may need to assemble a SQL command out of strings and then execute it. You can do this using what's often called dynamic SQL, the ability to send a string to the SQL Server relational engine to execute. Look at the following code, for example:

```
EXEC ('SELECT * FROM Authors')
```

You can tell SQL Server to execute a string using the EXECUTE command and placing the string within parentheses following it. Normally, however, you'll have variables loaded with the appropriate values and have SQL Server execute the variable:

```
DECLARE @SQLString VARCHAR(255), @TableName VARCHAR(20)

SET @TableName = 'Authors'

SET @SQLString = 'SELECT * FROM ' + @TableName
EXEC (@SQLString)
```

As you'll see in Chapter 17, this capability comes in handy when accepting query conditions through stored procedure parameters.

A Limitation

There is an important limitation to dynamic SQL. SQL Server executes dynamic SQL in a different context from the current session. Consequently, the executing string does not have any ability to access your currently declared variables, nor can the executing string return any value back to your variable.

For example, suppose you want to load the variable @max_sales with the maximum year-to-date sales from the Titles table. A simple way is this:

```
DECLARE @max_sales INT
SELECT @max_sales = (SELECT MAX(ytd_sales) FROM Titles)
```

However, suppose you had to assemble the query using a table that's coming into the code in a variable:

```
DECLARE @TableName VARCHAR(50),
          @max_sales INT, @SQLString VARCHAR(200)
SET @TableName = 'Titles'
SET @SQLString =
          'SELECT @max_sales = (SELECT MAX(ytd_sales) FROM ' +
          @TableName + ')'
EXEC (@SQLString)
```

Unfortunately, even though the @SQLString variable contains the same string of the code just prior to the preceding lines, the EXEC query cannot read the @max_sales variable. Because it executes in a different context, it cannot recognize the @max_sales variable and returns an error message:

```
Server: Msg 137, Level 15, State 42000
```

```
Must declare variable '@max_sales'.
```

Nor can an EXEC change the value of a variable. For example, look at the following Transact-SQL code:

```
DECLARE @Ctr INT
SET @Ctr = 1
EXEC ('DECLARE @Ctr INT
          SET @Ctr = 2')
PRINT @Ctr
```

No matter what you try, there's no way to get the query in the EXEC to change the value of a variable in the calling batch.

The Workaround

The main way to get around this problem is to store data in a table rather than variables. For example, the following code uses a temporary table:

```
DECLARE @Ctr INT
CREATE TABLE #TmpTbl (Ctr INT)
INSERT #TmpTbl VALUES (1)
EXEC ('UPDATE #TmpTbl
          SET Ctr = 2' )
SELECT @Ctr = (SELECT Ctr FROM #TmpTbl)
DROP TABLE #TmpTbl
```

All this is due to the fact that the execution context of the EXEC command is different from the current batch. Note that the query:

```
SELECT @Ctr = (SELECT Ctr FROM #TmpTbl)
```

relies on there being only one row in the table. If there are more than one, you must do something to ensure that the second SELECT returns only one row. A common technique for this is to add the MAX() function:

```
SELECT @Ctr = (SELECT MAX(Ctr) FROM #TmpTbl)
```

Cursors

Normally, all you will need to access data is the standard set of SQL statements. Occasionally, however, you will need to use row-by-row processing, which you can do in a cursor. A *cursor* is a temporary table that can be processed in a sequential, row-by-row manner.

SQL Server's Transact-SQL is called set-oriented because it uses the set-oriented rules of the SQL language. In other words, every SQL command regarding data (INSERT, UPDATE, DELETE, and SELECT) affects an entire table at once. At no time do those statements give you a position within the table's rows whereby you could navigate the table. So for row-by-row processing, a special cursor construct is needed.

A SQL cursor must be declared and opened, and then the rows can be fetched and potentially updated one by one. Unfortunately, the ANSI SQL and Transact-SQL versions of the command diverge, making the command quite complex.

ANSI SQL Cursor Syntax

The basic syntax of the ANSI SQL-92 DECLARE CURSOR command is:

```
DECLARE cursor-name [cursor-type] CURSOR
        FOR select-statement
        [FOR {READ ONLY ¦ UPDATE [OF column-list]}]
```

The cursor-type options are INSENSITIVE for a read-only cursor and SCROLL for an updateable cursor. The final FOR READ ONLY would override the SCROLL option, and the UPDATE OF column-list allows you to restrict the updatable columns.

Transact-SQL Cursor Syntax

The basic syntax of the Transact-SQL version is:

```
DECLARE cursor-name CURSOR
        [scope-option] [fetch-option] [cursor-type]
        [locking-type]
        FOR select-statement
        [FOR UPDATE [OF column-list]]
```

The Transact-SQL version puts all the options after the CURSOR name.

WARNING

You cannot mix the two types of syntax for cursor declarations. A good practice is to use the ANSI version whenever possible, because it has the best chance of never changing in future releases of SQL Server.

The Scope Option

Transact-SQL allows you to make a cursor LOCAL to the current batch, trigger, or stored procedure, or GLOBAL. A GLOBAL cursor can be referenced from a later batch of commands and is the default. Therefore, you can have a cursor span multiple batches.

The Fetch Option

Transact-SQL also allows you to define the FETCH options with FORWARD-ONLY or SCROLL. SCROLL means the same in Transact-SQL as in the ANSI version, namely an updateable cursor. A FORWARD-ONLY cursor is limited to the FETCH NEXT statement and is the default.

The Cursor Type

Transact-SQL lets you define three types of cursors: STATIC, KEYSET, and DYNAMIC. A STATIC cursor makes an entire copy of the data to the tempdb database and does not reflect any subsequent updates to the underlying tables.

A KEYSET cursor copies a set of keys (called a keyset) from the table or tables, based on primary keys or unique indexes, into tempdb. Changes to the underlying tables are tricky. Any changes to the nonkey values are visible to the cursor. However, any new rows to the tables will not be seen, and attempting to fetch a deleted row will return an error (@@FETCH_STATUS - 2). In addition, changes to a row appear as a DELETE followed by an INSERT, so attempting to FETCH a row after updating it will return the same error.

A DYNAMIC cursor does not copy any data to tempdb, and your cursor has complete access to all rows, changed or new.

The Locking Type

The Transact-SQL locking type options are READ ONLY, SCROLL_LOCKS, and OPTIMISTIC. The READ ONLY option does not incur any locks. The SCROLL_LOCKS option causes exclusive row locks to be acquired for each row when updated.

The OPTIMISTIC option does not cause SQL Server to lock any rows. Rather, it obtains a timestamp from the table or tables involved, or else it computes a checksum on the row in question. If the row has been changed while the cursor has been operating, then an attempted update will fail.

NOTE

There is a degree of interaction between the fetch option (FORWARD_ONLY and SCROLL) and the cursor type (STATIC, KEYSET, and DYNAMIC). If neither of these options are specified, then the default fetch option is FORWARD_ONLY. If the fetch option is not specified and any of the cursor types are, then the default fetch option is SCROLL.

WARNING

You cannot mix the ANSI SQL cursor syntax and the Transact-SQL syntax. If you specify an ANSI cursor type following the DECLARE statement, you cannot use any of the Transact-SQL options following the CURSOR keyword, and vice versa.

Fetching a Row

After you've declared a cursor, you must open it before you can access any rows. When it is first opened, you are not positioned anywhere in the cursor result set. To navigate, you use the FETCH statement. When a cursor is read only, you can only use the FETCH NEXT construct:

```
FETCH NEXT FROM AuCursor
```

If the cursor is updateable, you can also use FETCH with the NEXT, PRIOR, FIRST, LAST, ABSOLUTE, and RELATIVE options. For example,

```
FETCH FIRST FROM AuCursor INTO @au_id
```

In addition to a simple FETCH , you can add the INTO clause to specify one or more variables to load with data:

```
FETCH FIRST FROM AuCursor INTO @au_id
```

Updates within Cursors

You can make two kinds of updates while updating a cursor: UPDATE and DELETE. Interestingly, you cannot make an INSERT from a cursor!

An UPDATE or a DELETE made with a cursor open applies to the table, not the cursor. In addition, you're restricted to acting on one row only, namely the row your cursor is positioned on. For that reason, they are called positioned updates and deletes.

To make an update or delete, you use the regular statement and specify the table name, but instead of FROM, you use WHERE CURRENT OF and add the cursor name. For example, to update a row in a cursor called AuCursor, you could write:

```
UPDATE Authors
        SET contract = 1
        WHERE CURRENT OF AuCursor
```

Further, to delete the current row, you would issue:

```
DELETE Authors
        WHERE CURRENT OF AuCursor
```

Cursors in Action

Let's look at an example. The following cursor prints out the first and last author ids from the Authors table:

```
DECLARE @au_id char(11)
DECLARE AuCursor SCROLL CURSOR
        FOR SELECT au_id FROM Authors
        FOR READ ONLY
OPEN AuCursor
        FETCH FIRST FROM AuCursor INTO @au_id
        PRINT @au_id
        FETCH LAST FROM AuCursor INTO @au_id
        PRINT @au_id
CLOSE AuCursor
DEALLOCATE AuCursor
```

The preceding cursor was opened for SCROLL, but then the FOR READ ONLY overrides that and keeps you from updating the cursor. You need the SCROLL option in order to do the FETCH LAST.

Unfortunately, the preceding sequence of code assumes that data will be returned into the cursor. It may happen, however, that no rows come back from the cursor's SELECT clause. To protect your code from that happening, you can do a "priming read" to make sure there's data before trying to do anything:

```
DECLARE @au_id char(11)
DECLARE AuCursor SCROLL CURSOR
        FOR SELECT au_id FROM Authors
OPEN AuCursor
```

```
-- Find out if there's any data
FETCH NEXT FROM AuCursor INTO @AuthorID
-- Loop as long as there is data
WHILE (@@FETCH_STATUS <> -1)
BEGIN
          -- Get the first row in the cursor
          FETCH FIRST FROM AuCursor INTO @AuthorID
          -- Get the last row in the cursor
          FETCH LAST FROM AuCursor INTO @AuthorID
          -- This fetch causes an end of data
          FETCH NEXT FROM AuCursor INTO @AuthorID
END
CLOSE AuCursor
DEALLOCATE AuCursor
```

The preceding script makes use of the system variable @@FETCH_STATUS, which contains −1 for no data, 0 for data, and −2 if the fetched row was deleted. It selects the author id and author last name into a temporary table, extracts the first row and then the last row, and prints them. Finally, it causes the @@FETCH_STATUS to become a −1 when it exceeds the last row, and the loop ends.

Cursors are sometimes handy, but they are notoriously slow. Often developers use a cursor merely because they do not know how to do the equivalent in SQL. More often than not, what's being done in a cursor could more easily be done in standard SQL. An exception is when a DBA writes a procedure to execute DBCC against all the tables of a database by walking through a cursor of table names.

Another bad reason to use cursors is denormalization. For example, suppose the Titles table had au_id1, au_id2, and au_id3, instead of the intermediate Titleauthors table. A business rule then might be that if the first author drops out or become inactive, then if the second is still active, move it into the au_id1, and move au_id3 into au_id2, and so on. A developer might be tempted to do this in a cursor, one row at a time, because there may be no SQL statements that could do this to all the rows at once.

Whatever the case, the use of cursors is a red flag. If the DBA or developer is savvy, he or she will operate only on small tables and be quick.

TIP

When you see cursors, you can pounce on them as likely places for slow performance, concealing denormalization or weak SQL.

An exception to the rule that cursors should generally be avoided is when you can use them to run through a list for maintenance purposes. For example, the following cursor runs DBCC CHECKTABLE against the tables in a database:

```
DECLARE @table_name varchar(50)
DECLARE tables_cursor CURSOR
    FOR SELECT table_name FROM information_schema.tables
            WHERE table_type = 'BASE TABLE'
OPEN tables_cursor
FETCH NEXT FROM tables_cursor INTO @table_name
WHILE @@FETCH_STATUS <> -1
BEGIN
            EXEC('DBCC CHECKTABLE(' + @table_name + ')')
            FETCH NEXT FROM tables_cursor INTO @table_name
END
CLOSE  tables_cursor
DEALLOCATE tables_cursor
```

Cursor Variables

SQL Server 7 now allows you to assign variables to point to cursors. These new variables are called cursor variables, variables that reference a cursor. The following code declares a cursor using the variable @Crsr:

```
DECLARE @Crsr CURSOR
SET @Crsr = CURSOR FOR
            SELECT au_lname
            FROM authors
            WHERE au_lname LIKE 'R%'
OPEN @Crsr
WHILE (@@fetch_status = 0)
            BEGIN
                FETCH NEXT FROM @Crsr
            END
CLOSE @Crsr
DEALL.OCATE @Crsr
```

Not much is gained by using a cursor variable if you're using it all in the same batch. However, you can also get a cursor variable populated from a stored procedure, thereby relieving your code from having to re-create the cursor each time. For more about cursor variables and stored procedures, see Chapter 17, "Stored Procedures."

Summary

Transact-SQL provides you with a small but powerful programming language that you can use to control the scripts, stored procedures, and triggers you write for SQL Server. You can declare variables, convert data, manage errors, and control execution paths using the many constructs provided by SQL Server 7.0. You've seen how they work for small batches of code. Let's now turn to another set of Transact-SQL constructs dealing with transactions. After that, you'll take a look at stored procedures and triggers.

Chapter 16

Transactions

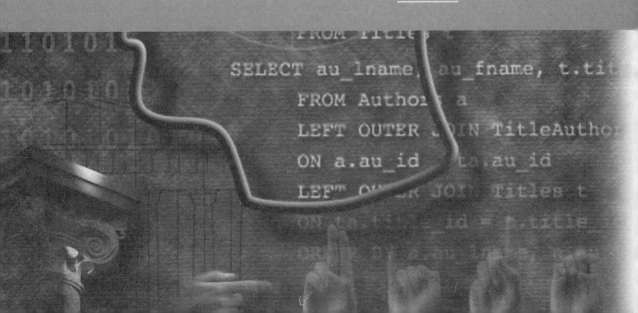

In This Chapter

- ◆ Transaction concepts
- ◆ Transaction mechanisms
- ◆ Working with transactions
- ◆ Programming transactions
- ◆ Transaction isolation levels
- ◆ Tutorial: Reproducing the concurrency problems

Transaction Concepts

A transaction is commonly defined as a logical unit of work. What that really means is that a transaction is a grouping of one or more DBMS commands that are treated as a whole.

By treating all data change commands in transactions, a DBMS can ensure that all changes to the database completely succeed or completely fail, it can keep a database consistent, it can handle multiple users, and it can recover from disasters.

> **NOTE**
>
> In this chapter, I'll refer to both data modification (DML) and data definition commands (DDL) as data change commands.

Completeness, Consistency, Recovery, and Concurrency: the ACID properties

In the ideal case, there are four goals of a DBMS that correspond to the properties of a transaction. We'd like all changes to the database to be complete, leave the database in a consistent state, recover those changes if a sudden halt occurs, and allow multiple users.

These four central goals of a DBMS correspond to the ACID properties of a transaction. The ACID acronym stands for

- ◆ Atomicity: Either all the transaction's changes happen, or none of them do.
- ◆ Consistency: The transaction does not violate any database constraints.

♦ Isolation: Concurrently executing transactions do not interfere with each other's changes.

♦ Durability: The changes of a committed transaction will survive disasters.

The atomicity property implies that all the transaction is committed, or none of it is. This corresponds to the "logical unit of work" requirement. The atomicity property satisfies the goal of keeping data modification commands complete. In other words, there are no partially successful data changes if all transactions are atomic.

A transaction should also leave the database in a consistent state. Consistency here is relative to the data integrity constraints enforced by the transaction. The database may enter an inconsistent state during a transaction, but it will always return to a consistent state at the end.

NOTE

You may make the database inconsistent yourself with a set of bad commands, so to a great degree consistency depends on your writing correct data modifications to the database. However, assuming your commands are correct, in no case should the DBMS ever let a transaction put the database into a state that violates either declared constraints or the constraints you enforce with your commands.

Further, all transactions should be isolated from each other: No transaction can detect data changes from other transactions until it is finished. Isolation supports concurrency: Because transactions can execute in isolation from each other, many different transactions can execute at the same time.

Last, all transactions must be durable: If the system crashes during a transaction, SQL Server will either finish the transaction during its recovery phase when it restarts or undo all the changes if the transaction must be rolled back. This corresponds to the goal of recovery: Because transactions are durable, SQL Server can recover from a crash that may have left the database in an inconsistent state.

NOTE

You can set varying levels of isolation for your transactions. You'll learn more about them in the section "Isolation Levels" toward the end of this chapter.

Two Examples of a Transaction

Consider the following two examples of a transaction. In each of these examples, the database will enter an inconsistent state during the change and return to a consistent state when the transaction finishes.

1.   Suppose you issue a command to delete some rows out of a table. (The actual number deleted will be three rows.)

```
DELETE FROM Sales
WHERE ord_date < 'Jan 1 1993'
```

When this statement executes, SQL Server will have to delete one row, then another, and then the last row. SQL Server must ensure that this command's transaction is:

   ◆ Atomic, so that the command either completely deletes all three rows or deletes none of them

   ◆ Consistent, so that even if the database enters an inconsistent state during the deletes, when the transaction finishes SQL Server will return the data base to a consistent state

   ◆ Isolated, so that all other transactions will see either all three rows or none of them, and no other transactions will see only a partial deletion

   ◆ Durable, so that if the server crashes after one or two of the three rows are deleted, SQL Server will finish the deletion upon recovery or roll back the transaction if it was uncommitted.

2.   Suppose you INSERT a row into the sales table, and you also want to update the running-total ytd_sales column in Titles to reflect the additional year-to-date sales for that title. In this case, the transaction consists of two statements:

```
INSERT INTO Sales
(stor_id, ord_num, ord_date, qty, payterms, title_id)
VALUES ('7067', '1234', GETDATE(), 3, 'Net 60', 'BU1032')
UPDATE Titles
SET ytd_sales = ytd_sales + 3
WHERE title_id = 'BU1032'
```

In this example, after the INSERT has finished but before the UPDATE is done, the Sales table will have the new row, but the title's ytd_sales will not have been updated. SQL Server must ensure that the transaction consisting of the preceding two commands is:

- ◆ Atomic, meaning that they both entirely succeed or both entirely fail
- ◆ Consistent, so that the database will not end up with a new row and an incorrect value in the Titles.ytd_sales column
- ◆ Isolated, so that no other transaction will see the new Sales row but not the new value of Titles.ytd_sales during the current transaction
- ◆ Durable, so that if the server crashes before the UPDATE finishes, SQL Server can recover the database to a consistent state

If SQL Server should halt suddenly (crash, lose power, reboot, or what have you), SQL Server must recover from the disaster. The process of recovery consists in part of dealing with all transactions that were executing at the time of the crash. Either SQL Server must completely finish each transaction's changes, or else it must undo its changes, thereby recovering the system to a consistent state.

NOTE

As you can see, transactions in SQL Server can consist of single statements or of a group of statements. Every INSERT, UPDATE, and DELETE command is a single-statement transaction. SQL Server will not let any of the commands partially succeed; they either completely succeed or completely fail.

Similarly, SQL Server provides you Transact-SQL commands to define your own multistatement transactions. In the midst of the transaction, you can determine in your code whether to commit the transaction or roll it back.

In both single-statement and multistatement transactions, SQL Server will preserve all the ACID properties of the transaction.

Transaction Mechanisms

SQL Server implements the ACID properties of transactions with two mechanisms: the transaction log and locking. The transaction log allows SQL Server to maintain atomicity, consistency, and durability. SQL Server uses locking to support isolation of transactions, as well as consistency, so that it can process many concurrent transactions at the same time.

The Transaction Log

SQL Server implements database transaction through the use of a special log file, called the transaction log. For every transaction, which includes every data change statement, SQL Server writes its changes to the transaction log. In addition, SQL Server makes calls to the Windows operating system to ensure that every write to the transaction log is a direct write to the disk drive, bypassing any NT disk cache.

NOTE

SQL Server does not do a checkpoint with each transaction. Rather, SQL Server performs a checkpoint whenever it calculates that the time it would take to recover from a system halt would exceed a value called the recovery interval. For information about setting the recovery interval, which is a server configuration option, see Chapter 5, "Configuring."

In the meantime, changes to the data are made initially to SQL Server's own cached data in RAM. Some time later the cached data is written to disk. The process of writing that changed data in SQL Server's cache to disk is called checkpointing.

The general flow of a SQL Server transaction is shown in Figure 16-1.

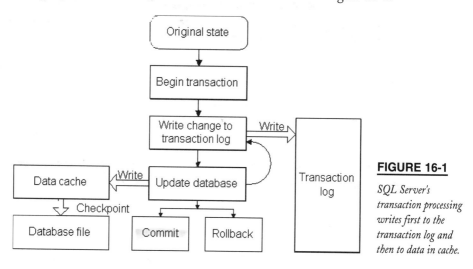

FIGURE 16-1

SQL Server's transaction processing writes first to the transaction log and then to data in cache.

When a transaction begins, SQL Server first writes data changes to the transaction log, then changes the data (in its RAM cache), and then either terminates the action in a commit state or performs a rollback.

For a single statement transaction consisting of just one Transact-SQL data change command (INSERT, UPDATE, or DELETE, for example), the commit state will automatically be reached if the command succeeds. This is called autocommit. If the command fails for some reason, then a rollback process starts.

As you'll see in the next few pages, for an implicit transaction, and for an explicit multistatement transaction, you must supply the command to either commit or rollback. You can see a diagram of the commit process in Figure 16-2.

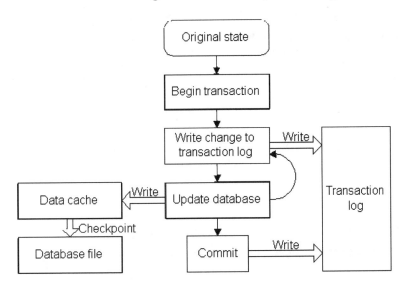

FIGURE 16-2

The commit process writes both to data and to the log.

Note that the commit process adds writing the commit state to the transaction log.

When a transaction is rolled back, SQL Server must read the transaction log and undo the changes to the data, as shown in Figure 16-3.

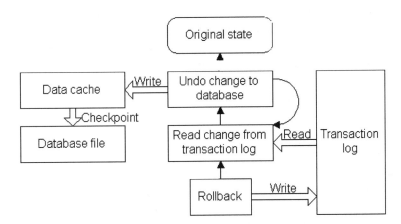

FIGURE 16-3

The rollback process must read the transaction log and undo the changes.

You can read the diagram from the bottom up. When the rollback process starts, it writes the rollback fact to the transaction log, reads the old data from the transaction log, and changes the data back to the original state.

When a transaction is finished (committed or rolled back), its record in the transaction becomes inactive. Inactive transactions stay in the transaction log until the log is backed up or truncated.

NOTE

For more information about backing up, restoring, and truncating a transaction log, see Chapter 8, "Backup and Restore."

Atomicity, Consistency, Durability

Three of the four ACID properties of transactions are implemented using the transaction log.

SQL Server enforces atomicity, and achieves the goal of completeness of commands, by writing all changes to the transaction log. If an error occurs, the transaction log can be used to roll the transaction back, thereby ensuring that no command ever just partially succeeds.

It enforces consistency in transactions again by not allowing any inconsistent state of the database during the transaction to ever surface after the transaction is finished.

Finally, transactions gain durability by having the transaction log as a disk file that is always available for recovery. If a transaction stops in midstream because the server has suddenly halted, SQL Server can find out what to do by reading the status of unfinished transactions from the transaction log. During the recovery process, SQL Server will finish an uncompleted commit, roll back an uncommitted transaction, and finish rolling back an uncompleted rollback.

Non-logged Operations

Not all changes to data are logged by SQL Server. Certain non-logged operations are also available. If you check the Select into/bulk copy in the Database Properties dialog box of Enterprise Manager, or use the system stored procedure sp_dboption to do the same, you allow two non-logged operations. The first, SELECT INTO, is the special use of the SELECT command to provide rows for the INSERT command, discussed in Chapter 13, "Data Manipulation."

The second, bulk copy, allows non-logged inserts to be made with BCP, the command-line bulk copy program. Only new data page allocations are recorded in the transaction log.

A third option is the BULK INSERT statement, which can be called from Transact-SQL. For more information about BCP and BULK INSERT, see Chapter 10, "Importing and Exporting Data."

Locking

SQL Server enforces the remaining ACID property, isolation, using locking. A lock is a hold placed on a data resource by a transaction, such that write and sometimes read activities by other transactions are prevented. SQL Server prevents other transactions from overwriting an unfinished transaction's changes by placing locks on the portions of data it is changing. As long as the locks are in place, no other transaction can change the data with which the current transaction is working.

Types of Locks

SQL Server has several types of locks, against several kinds of database resources. The basic types of locks are:

- ◆ Shared: Others can read, but no others can write to the resource.
- ◆ Update: Others can read, and these locks will escalate to exclusive.
- ◆ Exclusive: No others can read or write to the resource.

Read-only operations such as a SELECT command only need to make shared locks on data, because the command never changes any data.

To change data, the INSERT, UPDATE, and DELETE commands must gain an exclusive lock on the resource (row, page, or table). If there are already shared locks on the resource, the command's transaction cannot get an exclusive lock. But it can get an update lock, which is compatible with other shared locks. The update lock is a promissory note on getting an exclusive lock as soon as all the other shared locks are released.

In addition to these data-oriented types of locks, SQL Server will also issue intent locks, which indicate an intent to gain a shared or exclusive lock on a resource. Finally, SQL Server also has schema locks for making changes to the structure of a table.

SQL Server allows a transaction to lock data at the row, page, extent, and table levels. Normally, SQL Server 7 locks at the row level and escalates the locking level as it determines necessary.

Locking Hints

You can provide hints in your SQL queries indicating the type of lock you want. For example, with no hints, the following SQL SELECT command will accumulate a shared lock on each row that it reads during its execution and release all the locks once it finishes:

```
SELECT *
        FROM Authors
```

You can add a hint by adding WITH (<hint>) onto the end of the FROM clause:

```
SELECT *
        FROM Authors WITH (NOLOCK)
```

Now the SELECT will release each row's shared lock right after it reads the data.

Some other hints are:

HOLDLOCK	Hold all shared locks until the transaction completes
PAGLOCK	Use page locking
ROWLOCK	Use row locking
TABLOCK	Get a table lock
TABLOCKX	Get an exclusive lock on the table
UPDLOCK	Get an update lock and hold until transaction completes

NOTE

Other locking hints are available, but they interact with transaction isolation levels. For these other hints, see "Isolation Levels" later in this chapter.

Transaction Modes

All single-statement commands to modify data are placed in transactions by SQL Server. Normally, the transactional elements of a single-statement command are invisible to you, and SQL Server commits a successful command and rolls back a failed command.

When you have many commands that you would like to submit together as one transaction, you must add your own commands to start the transaction, and either commit or roll it back.

The command to explicitly commit a transaction is COMMIT, and the one to explicitly roll back a transaction is ROLLBACK.

Normally, in SQL Server, a single data modification command will form a transaction that commits automatically, and you don't have to add the COMMIT command. This is called the autocommit mode and is the SQL Server default. So unless you state otherwise, SQL Server will automatically commit your successful INSERT, UPDATE, DELETE, and other DML statements.

If you do not want SQL Server to autocommit, you can opt instead for implicit transactions. With the IMPLICIT_TRANSACTIONS setting ON, you assume that all your commands are implicitly in a transaction. You must explicitly add a COMMIT or ROLLBACK to the commands to end the transaction.

NOTE

When SET IMPLICIT_TRANSACTIONS is ON, you must explicitly add COMMIT and ROLLBACK to your individual commands to finish the implicit transaction. When the setting is OFF, and you're in autocommit mode, the COMMIT (and ROLLBACK if the command fails) are automatically performed by SQL Server.

Suppose, for example, you execute the following script in the Query Analyzer:

```
SET IMPLICIT_TRANSACTIONS ON
CREATE TABLE Test1
        (id INT, name CHAR(20))
go
INSERT INTO Test1
        VALUES (1,'hi')
go
```

If you do not add a COMMIT to the end of the sequence, when you disconnect, your table commands will all be rolled back and the table will not be present in the database. Indeed, until you issue the COMMIT, no other user can see the table. Alternatively, you can add the ROLLBACK command, and every data modification in your session since the last COMMIT or ROLLBACK will be rolled back.

NOTE

SQL Server defaults to the autocommit mode, where you do not need to explicitly add COMMIT or ROLLBACK to your statements. In other DBMS products, for example Oracle with SQL*Plus, you normally must explicitly commit or roll back. Most SQL Server users go with the default autocommit mode.

Programming Transactions

In SQL Server, every single-command INSERT, UPDATE, or DELETE that you submit is implicitly wrapped in a transaction. If you issue a sequence of data-changing commands, you will get a sequence of transactions, one for each command.

Sometimes, though, you'll want to have a transaction apply to an entire set of commands. To make a transaction wrap around a group of commands, you have to explicitly start and stop the transaction. You must use the BEGIN TRANSACTION command, available in several forms:

```
BEGIN TRANSACTION
BEGIN TRAN
BEGIN TRAN <transaction name or variable>
```

The BEGIN and at least TRAN are required. You can add a name if desired, either explicitly or through a character variable.

When you're ready to complete the transaction and save the work, you can issue any of the following:

```
COMMIT TRANSACTION
COMMIT TRAN
COMMIT TRAN <transaction name or variable>
COMMIT WORK
COMMIT
```

Only the word COMMIT is required. The TRAN or TRANSACTION are optional, except when you're committing a named transaction.

Parallel to the COMMIT, to end a transaction and remove all the work, you can use any of the following:

```
ROLLBACK TRANSACTION
ROLLBACK TRAN
ROLLBACK TRAN <transaction name or variable>
ROLLBACK WORK
ROLLBACK
```

> **NOTE**
>
> The SQL-92 standard does not provide for a BEGIN TRANSACTION statement and therefore relies on explicit COMMIT and ROLLBACK commands to end implicit transactions. The SQL-92 specification only supports the behavior of SET IMPLICIT_TRANSACTIONS ON. SQL Server's autocommit mode is a Transact-SQL extension.

Nested Transactions

You can include transactions within transactions, and name each one. However, the behavior of COMMIT differs from that of ROLLBACK within a nested transaction.

COMMIT Behavior

For example, the following script adds two rows to the Publishers table:

```
BEGIN TRAN foo
INSERT INTO Publishers
            VALUES ('9997', 'test', 'test', 'NY','USA')
            BEGIN TRAN  bar
                INSERT INTO Publishers
                        VALUES ('9998', 'test', 'test', 'NY','USA')
            COMMIT TRAN bar
COMMIT TRAN foo
```

Notice how the inner COMMIT names the inner transaction. However, the inner COMMIT has no effect, really, because it's just the last COMMIT that really commits the transaction.

But notice a curious thing: The COMMITs do not really need the transaction names. For example, putting some nonsense names on the COMMITs in the previous transaction has no effect:

```
BEGIN TRAN foo
INSERT INTO Publishers
VALUES ('9997', 'test', 'test', 'NY','USA')
PRINT @@TRANCOUNT
            BEGIN TRAN  bar
                INSERT INTO Publishers
```

```
                  VALUES ('9998', 'test', 'test', 'NY','USA')
                  PRINT @@TRANCOUNT
          COMMIT TRAN yoyodyne
COMMIT TRAN wuwu
```

> **WARNING**
>
> Only use transaction names on the outermost parts of a transaction. Transaction names are ignored when used on inner transactions.

The @@TRANCOUNT *Function*

You can determine the transaction nesting level with the @@TRANCOUNT function. The value of @@TRANCOUNT is zero when there's no transaction in progress, and it increases by one for every nested transaction. So taking the preceding script and inserting a PRINT @@TRANCOUNT:

```
BEGIN TRAN foo
INSERT INTO Publishers
          VALUES ('9997', 'test', 'test', 'NY','USA')
          PRINT @@TRANCOUNT
          BEGIN TRAN  bar
              INSERT INTO Publishers
                      VALUES ('9998', 'test', 'test', 'NY','USA')
              PRINT @@TRANCOUNT
          COMMIT TRAN bar
COMMIT TRAN foo
```

results in the values 1 and 2, respectively.

ROLLBACK *Behavior*

ROLLBACK does not behave the same way as COMMIT in a nested transaction.

First of all, a ROLLBACK by itself will roll back an entire transaction. Take, for example, the following script:

```
BEGIN TRAN foo
INSERT INTO Publishers
```

```
                VALUES ('9997', 'test', 'test', 'NY','USA')
            BEGIN TRAN  bar
                INSERT INTO Publishers
                        VALUES ('9998', 'test', 'test', 'NY','USA')
            ROLLBACK
COMMIT TRAN foo
```

The ROLLBACK actually rolls back the entire transaction and sets @@TRANCOUNT to 0. Consequently, the last COMMIT is acting with no parallel BEGIN TRANSACTION and produces an error.

Further, you cannot ROLLBACK a transaction name:

```
BEGIN TRAN foo
INSERT INTO Publishers
            VALUES ('9997', 'test', 'test', 'NY','USA')
            BEGIN TRAN  bar
                INSERT INTO Publishers
                        VALUES ('9998', 'test', 'test', 'NY','USA')
            ROLLBACK TRAN bar
COMMIT TRAN foo
```

Not only does the attempt to ROLLBACK TRAN bar fail, but nothing at all is rolled back, and the whole transaction is committed. However, because there's only one COMMIT at the end, @@TRANCOUNT is not set back to 0 but remains at 1.

WARNING

Only use transaction names on the outermost parts of a transaction. Transaction names are ignored when used on inner transactions.

When you have several nested transactions, all it takes to roll all of them back is a ROLLBACK by itself:

```
BEGIN TRAN foo
INSERT INTO Publishers
            VALUES ('9997', 'test', 'test', 'NY','USA')
            BEGIN TRAN  bar
                INSERT INTO Publishers
                        VALUES ('9998', 'test', 'test', 'NY','USA')
```

```
ROLLBACK TRAN

COMMIT TRAN foo
```

This time a single ROLLBACK ends both transactions. Since the COMMIT at the end has no matching BEGIN TRAN, it produces an error.

Savepoints

The only way to have a partial ROLLBACK in a transaction is by using a savepoint. A savepoint is a named point in the transaction to which you can roll back. You create a savepoint by using the following syntax:

```
SAVE TRANSACTION <savepoint-name or savepoint-variable>
```

For example, the following script rolls back the inner transaction but keeps the outer. Consequently, the transaction only inserts one row:

```
BEGIN TRAN foo
INSERT INTO Publishers
            VALUES ('9997', 'test', 'test', 'NY','USA')
            SAVE TRAN bar
                INSERT INTO Publishers
                        VALUES ('9998', 'test', 'test', 'NY','USA')
            ROLLBACK TRAN bar
COMMIT TRAN foo
```

NOTE

Only use ROLLBACK in nested transactions to roll back the entire transaction or to roll back to a savepoint.

In the preceding script, the ROLLBACK to the savepoint reduces @@TRANCOUNT by 1, so the COMMIT at the end matches up with the BEGIN TRAN, and the single row is committed to the table.

Errors and Transactions

What happens when errors occur in a transaction? It depends on whether the error is fatal or not, and whether the transaction is contained in one batch or spans batches.

Fatal Errors

When SQL Server encounters a fatal error, it aborts the remainder of the current batch. If your transaction occurs in that batch, and the error is in your transaction, then the count in @@TRANCOUNT will be higher than 0. If you end your session, the transaction will be rolled back. For example, the following script will abort after inserting one row in the table:

```
BEGIN TRAN foo
        INSERT INTO Publishers
            VALUES ('9997', 'test', 'test', 'NY','USA')
        INSERT INTO foobar -- Publishers
            VALUES ('9998', 'test', 'test', 'NY','USA')
COMMIT
```

The second INSERT is fatal and aborts the batch, so the COMMIT is not executed. However, the @@TRANCOUNT is left at 1, so any subsequent COMMIT or ROLLBACK will act on the transaction. If you suspect this may be happening, you will need to check that @@TRANCOUNT is 0 before beginning the next transaction:

```
WHILE @@TRANCOUNT > 0
BEGIN
        COMMIT
END
```

When your transaction spans batches, fatal errors will only abort a batch, not your transaction. For example, the following transaction succeeds in inserting one row:

```
BEGIN TRAN foo
        INSERT INTO Publishers
        VALUES ('9997', 'test', 'test', 'NY','USA')
go
        INSERT INTO foobar -- Publishers
        VALUES ('9998', 'test', 'test', 'NY','USA')
go
COMMIT
```

The second INSERT encounters an error and aborts the batch, but the COMMIT is in its own batch.

Non-Fatal Errors

If the error is nonfatal, only the command that encountered the error will fail, and the rest of the transaction will proceed. For example, in the following code, the second INSERT produces a nonfatal error (a primary key violation):

```
BEGIN TRAN foo
        INSERT INTO Publishers
        VALUES ('9997', 'test', 'test', 'NY','USA')
        INSERT INTO Publishers
        VALUES ('9997', 'test', 'test', 'NY','USA')
COMMIT
```

The first INSERT succeeds, because the primary key violation only affects the second INSERT and is not a fatal error.

You can force all errors, not just fatal errors, to abort the current batch by setting XACT_ABORT ON:

```
SET XACT_ABORT ON
BEGIN TRAN foo
        INSERT INTO Publishers
        VALUES ('9997', 'test', 'test', 'NY','USA')
        INSERT INTO Publishers
        VALUES ('9997', 'test', 'test', 'NY','USA')
COMMIT
```

Now no rows at all are inserted, because of the XACT_ABORT setting.

However, you may want the transaction to proceed in spite of nonfatal errors. For catching nonfatal errors, you can just use the @@ERROR function instead:

```
BEGIN TRAN foo
        INSERT INTO Publishers
        VALUES ('9997', 'test', 'test', 'NY','USA')
        IF @@ERROR <> 0
            RAISERROR ('First INSERT failed', 0, 1)
        INSERT INTO Publishers
        VALUES ('9997', 'test', 'test', 'NY','USA')
        IF @@ERROR <> 0
            RAISERROR ('Second INSERT failed', 0, 1)
COMMIT
```

You can test for the @@ERROR value to continue the transaction.

Transaction Isolation Levels

SQL Server executes a transaction by actually changing the data as you see it, but not as other users see it. That way, other users have a consistent picture of the data and only see the data as it was before your transaction changed it, or after your transaction changed it. In a word, your transaction is isolated from everyone else's, satisfying the third component of the ACID properties of transactions.

SQL Server could maintain a maximum amount of users in the database if it just let all transactions change everything, and did not care. But then there would be no transaction isolation, and concurrency problems would result.

Four Concurrency Problems

What problems would result if there were no transaction isolation? It's common to identify four problems that would occur without any isolation, and therefore without any locking.

1. The Lost Update Problem

This problem results from one transaction losing an update it made. You can see an example in the following representation of two transactions side by side, where Transaction TranA loses its update:

TranA		TranB
BEGIN TRAN	t1	BEGIN TRAN
UPDATE Table1	t2	
	t3	UPDATE Table1
	t4	COMMIT
COMMIT	t5	

In the lost update problem, TranA loses its update because TranB manages to update the same data after TranA. TranB succeeds in its update even though TranA's transaction had not finished! So even before TranA commits its transaction, it has lost its update.

2. The Dirty Read Problem

This is also called the uncommitted dependency problem. Suppose you have a transaction that bases its changes on certain values in the data. With no transaction isolation, all other transactions will expose their changes to data before they commit, and they might even roll those changes back. Therefore your transaction may make changes based on data values that were in fact rolled back, and in a sense never in the database at all. Here is a dirty read scenario:

TranA		TranB
BEGIN TRAN	t1	BEGIN TRAN
SELECT		
	t2	UPDATE Table1
SELECT	t3	
	t4	ROLLBACK
COMMIT	t5	

TranA experiences a dirty read at time t3, because it sees the results of TranB's UPDATE. However, TranB rolls back the transaction, so anything that TranA does on the basis of its earlier dirty read is wrong.

3. The NonRepeatable Read Problem

This is also called the inconsistent analysis problem. In this problem, TranA is summing up a set of values, and TranB changes them in such a way as to make TranA's results wrong. Here's an outline:

TranA		TranB
BEGIN TRAN	t1	BEGIN TRAN
SELECT @sum =		
	t2	UPDATE – 10
		UPDATE + 10
SELECT @sum =	t3	
	t4	COMMIT
COMMIT	t5	

TranA is summing up the values from two rows in a table. It gets the first row at time t1. TranB at time t2 takes 10 from the row that TranA just read and adds 10 to another row. Then TranA reads the other row at time t3 and gets the new, higher value. The end result is that TranA has a sum that is 10 too large, because it never caught the fact that TranB also subtracted 10 from a row it had read.

4. Phantom Rows

The last problem is one of a transaction seeing phantom rows. In other words, your transaction might see a certain number of rows in a table. A short time later, another transaction might insert a new row in the same table. The new row, called a phantom row, may cause conflicts with your transaction, which is assuming a given set of rows.

Here's an outline of the phantom rows problem:

TranA		TranB
BEGIN TRAN	t1	BEGIN TRAN
SELECT COUNT(*)		
	t2	INSERT
		COMMIT
SELECT COUNT(*)	t3	
COMMIT		

Since TranA sees the new INSERT at time t3, the transaction may incur an error or otherwise conflict with the row that was inserted.

> **NOTE**
>
> As you saw earlier in this chapter, transaction isolation is accomplished by locking. However, locking can have an adverse impact on performance and concurrency. So there's a need for transaction isolation, and therefore locking. With locks on data, fewer simultaneous users can engage in transactions, because they simply will have to wait until other transactions release their locks before being able to proceed.

Isolation Levels

Because transaction isolation can impact concurrency, Transact-SQL allows you to control a transaction's isolation level. You can control the isolation level of your transactions using the SET TRANSACTION ISOLATION LEVEL command, followed by the level name.

There are four distinct transaction isolation levels, READ UNCOMMITTED, READ COMMITTED, REPEATABLE READ, and SERIALIZABLE.

All these levels differ in what they allow.

♦ READ UNCOMMITTED: Allows lost updates, dirty reads, nonrepeatable reads, and phantom rows.

♦ READ COMMITTED: Does not allow dirty reads or lost updates; allows nonrepeatable reads and phantom rows.

♦ REPEATABLE READ: Does not allow lost updates, dirty reads, or non repeatable reads; allows phantom rows.

♦ SERIALIZABLE: Does not allow any of lost updates, dirty reads, nonrepeatable reads, or phantom rows.

SQL Server defaults the isolation level to READ COMMITTED, which is a compromise to allow the maximum degree of concurrency, while allowing only nonrepeatable reads and phantom rows.

You can see the preceding facts in the following table:

	READ UNCOMMITTED	READ COMMITTED	REPEATABLE READ	SERIALIZABLE
Lost update	Y	N	N	N
Dirty read	Y	N	N	N
Nonrepeatable read	Y	Y	N	N
Phantom rows	Y	Y	Y	N

NOTE

Notice that the SERIALIZABLE isolation level is not subject to any of the four problems, whereas the READ UNCOMMITTED level is. SQL Server, by defaulting to the READ UNCOMMITTED level, does allow nonrepeatable reads and phantom rows. You can adjust a transaction level, balancing the need for transaction isolation against the need for concurrency. For more information about concurrency issues, see Chapter 20, "Concurrency Tools."

Isolation Level Locking Hints

An alternative way to set the isolation level is by using locking hints. Earlier in this chapter you saw how locking hints can be added to a query to force a certain type of locking. You can also add locking hints to force a certain isolation level:

♦ READUNCOMMITTED: Forces the READ UNCOMMITTED level, and is equivalent to the NOLOCK hint.

♦ READCOMMITTED: Forces the READ COMMITTED isolation level, and is the SQL Server default.

♦ REPEATABLEREAD: Forces the REPEATABLE READ isolation level.

♦ SERIALIZABLE: Forces the SERIALIZABLE isolation level.

Tutorial: Reproducing the Concurrency Problems

You can reproduce the four concurrency problems, and test out the isolation levels, using the following scripts. Each problem has two scripts. You run each script in its own Query Analyzer window.

Each script needs to run simultaneously with its pair. Rather than use some sort of semaphore system, each script waits for a certain time to begin, a time that you specify in the script. If that time is the same in each script, they will run in a coordinated fashion and reproduce the concurrency problems. Before you start each script, set the time in the first WAITFOR command to 30 seconds or a minute ahead of the current time and then launch the scripts.

All the following scripts set the transaction isolation level to READ UNCOMMITTED, the lowest level. You can change those levels to verify that raising a transaction isolation level solves the concurrency problems.

> **NOTE**
>
> You can find these scripts, along with all the source code for each chapter, on this book's CD.

1. The Lost Update Problem

You can reproduce the lost update scenario with the following two scripts:

```
-- Script 1: Lost Update Script for TranA
SET TRANSACTION ISOLATION LEVEL READ UNCOMMITTED
BEGIN TRAN
        WAITFOR TIME '18:43:00' -- t1
        WAITFOR DELAY '00:00:05' -- t2
        UPDATE Publishers
            SET pub_name = 'Yoyo Publishing'
            WHERE pub_id = '0877'
```

```
            WAITFOR DELAY '00:00:15' -- t4
COMMIT
-- Script 2: Lost Update script for TranB
-- Tran B Wins the update
SET TRANSACTION ISOLATION LEVEL READ UNCOMMITTED
BEGIN TRAN
            WAITFOR TIME '18:43:00' -- t1
            WAITFOR DELAY '00:00:10' -- t3
            UPDATE Publishers
                SET Pub_name = 'Tran A'
            WHERE pub_id = '0877'
            WAITFOR DELAY '00:00:05' -- t3
COMMIT
```

2. The Dirty Read Problem

Here are two sample scripts to reproduce the dirty read problem:

```
-- Script 1: Dirty Read for TranA
SET TRANSACTION ISOLATION LEVEL READ UNCOMMITTED
BEGIN TRAN
            WAITFOR TIME '19:24:30' -- t1
            SELECT pub_name FROM Publishers
                WHERE pub_id = '0877'
            WAITFOR DELAY '00:00:10' -- t3
            SELECT pub_name FROM Publishers
                WHERE pub_id = '0877'
            WAITFOR DELAY '00:00:10' -- t5
COMMIT
-- Script 2: Dirty Read for TranB
SET TRANSACTION ISOLATION LEVEL READ UNCOMMITTED
BEGIN TRAN
            WAITFOR TIME '19:24:30' -- t1
            WAITFOR DELAY '00:00:05' -- t2
            UPDATE Publishers
                SET pub_name = 'Yoyodyne'
                WHERE pub_id = '0877'
```

```
            WAITFOR DELAY '00:00:10' -- t4

ROLLBACK
```

3. The Nonrepeatable Read Problem

Here are two scripts to re-create the nonrepeatable read problem:

```
-- Script 1: Nonrepeatable Read for Tran A
SET TRANSACTION ISOLATION LEVEL READ UNCOMMITTED
BEGIN TRAN
            WAITFOR TIME '19:49:00' -- t1
            DECLARE @sum int
            SET @sum = 0
            SELECT @sum = (SELECT ytd_sales
                FROM Titles
                WHERE title_id = 'BU1032') -- 4095
            WAITFOR DELAY '00:00:10' -- t3
            SELECT @sum = @sum + (SELECT ytd_sales
                FROM Titles
                WHERE title_id = 'PS2091') -- 2045
            WAITFOR DELAY '00:00:10' -- t5
            PRINT @sum
COMMIT

-- Script 2: Nonrepeatable Read for TRAN B
SET TRANSACTION ISOLATION LEVEL READ UNCOMMITTED
BEGIN TRAN
            WAITFOR TIME '19:49:00' -- t1
            WAITFOR DELAY '00:00:05' -- t2
            UPDATE Titles
                SET ytd_sales = ytd_sales - 10
                WHERE title_id = 'BU1032'
            UPDATE Titles
                SET ytd_sales = ytd_sales + 10
                WHERE title_id = 'PS2091'
WAITFOR DELAY '00:00:10' -- t4
COMMIT
```

The sum of the two values should be 6140, but with no transaction isolation, the result is 6150.

4. Phantom Rows

Here are two scripts to reproduce the phantom rows problem:

```
-- Script 1: Phantom row problem for TRAN A
SET TRANSACTION ISOLATION LEVEL READ UNCOMMITTED
BEGIN TRAN
          WAITFOR TIME '19:18:30' -- t1
          SELECT COUNT(*) FROM Publishers
          WAITFOR DELAY '00:00:10' -- t3
          SELECT COUNT(*) FROM Publishers
COMMIT

-- Script 2: Phantom for TranB
SET TRANSACTION ISOLATION LEVEL SERIALIZABLE
BEGIN TRAN
          WAITFOR TIME '19:18:30' -- t1
          WAITFOR DELAY '00:00:05' -- t2
          INSERT INTO Publishers
               VALUES ('9998', 'Hi There', ' ', ' ', ' ')
COMMIT
```

Summary

The concept of a transaction is vital to understanding how SQL Server works. Every change that SQL Server makes to database data will be done in the context of a transaction. The transaction log is used to maintain the integrity of transactions. You can set the degree of isolation for transactions in Transact-SQL, and program your own transactions in scripts. Now let's take a look at stored procedures.

Chapter 17

Stored Procedures

In This Chapter

♦ Basic concepts

♦ Working with stored procedures

♦ Examples

Stored procedures are batches of Transact-SQL code that you can store in a SQL Server database. You can execute them at will or schedule them for execution later.

Stored procedures have a number of important uses. They can be efficient: SQL Server can execute a stored procedure more efficiently than a script, if the stored procedure execution plan is already in RAM. In addition, stored procedures can help you embed intelligence into the database. They can provide a level of security: you might only grant permissions to stored procedures, and not to tables. Also, stored procedures can be more flexible, easier to invoke and schedule, than scripts.

Basic Concepts

A *stored procedure* is a batch of Transact-SQL code that you cause SQL Server to store in the database.

When you create a stored procedure, SQL Server parses the source code to check for valid syntax. If there are no syntax errors, SQL Server then stores the source code in the database's syscomments system table.

When you invoke the stored procedure for the first time, SQL Server compiles the source code into an execution plan. It resolves any references to database objects in the stored procedure, making sure, for example, that all references to tables and columns are correct.

NOTE

SQL Server 7 introduces a fundamental change in the way that stored procedures are compiled. It compiles a stored procedure into an execution plan at initial run time, not at the creation time. This is called deferred name resolution.

In prior releases of SQL Server, a partial execution plan was built at creation time, so any attempt to create a stored procedure that referenced nonexistent objects would fail. With SQL Server 7, the fact that this resolution phase comes after creation means that you can create a stored procedure that makes references to nonexistent objects. If the stored procedure references any nonexistent object at run time, the stored procedure will fail at that time.

After the names are resolved, SQL Server will build a query plan, and optimize it. SQL Server will choose the order to access tables, what indexes to use, and methods for building result sets. The resulting execution plan will be cached in memory for use by the current procedure and subsequent calls to the stored procedure. If there are changes to table or index statistics, or the stored procedure is somehow marked to be recompiled, the very next invoking of the stored procedure will cause it to recompile. Also, if the stored procedure goes unused, it could be aged out of the memory cache. The next time it is invoked, the execution plan will have to be rebuilt.

Accessing Stored Procedures in Enterprise Manager

You can enter a stored procedure directly into ISQL/W and create the new stored procedure. Or you can edit the stored procedure directly from Enterprise Manager.

To use the Enterprise Manager to write a stored procedure, just select Stored Procedures in the database tree view, right-click on any stored procedure and choose the Properties option, as shown in Figure 17-1.

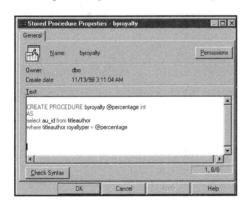

databases/pubs/stored procedure, right click on one name.

FIGURE 17-1

You can view or edit a stored procedure from its Properties dialog box.

In this case, you're looking at the `byroyalty` stored procedure in the Pubs database.

Types of Stored Procedures

There are several types of stored procedures: system stored procedures, application stored procedures, extended stored procedures, and triggers, which are also a form of stored procedure.

System Stored Procedures

You have already used a number of system stored procedures, namely the stored procedures that begin with `sp` (`sp_helpdb`, `for example.`) These are created by scripts that run at the end of the SQL Server installation process.

You can find a list of all the system stored procedures for your server by finding the stored procedures node of the master database, as shown in Figure 17-2.

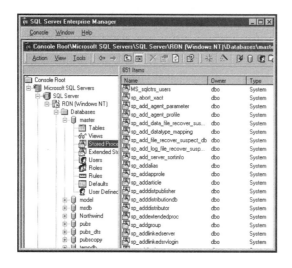

FIGURE 17-2

The system stored procedures are located in the Master database.

Normally you access a stored procedure in its own database. The system stored procedures that begin with sp, however, reside in the master database and are automatically available to all users on the system, at least to invoke. (Some users check to make sure that the sa is running them.)

NOTE

Generally you'll see a database's stored procedures attached to the application database, and not to the master database. Some more advanced DBAs will, however, rewrite the system stored procedures in master and save them under a new name. It is also possible for a DBA to rewrite a system stored procedure in master and make it behave in a customized manner.

Extended Stored Procedures *master db has 3 extended stored proced*

Extended stored procedures also reside in the master database but are really just wrappers around the calling interface to a DLL. They are prefixed by xp_ instead of sp_.

One noteworthy extended stored procedure is xp_cmdshell, which calls the CMD.EXE executable. It allows you to make calls to external programs, as you can see in the following:

```
EXEC master.dbo.xp_cmdshell 'dir d:\mssql\binn'
```

Working with Stored Procedures

The Transact-SQL command to write a stored procedure is the CREATE PROCEDURE statement, with some executable code:

```
CREATE PROCEDURE usp_TestProc AS
        BEGIN
        PRINT 'This is a stored procedure'
        END
```

create it w̄ location database.

In the preceding stored procedure, the code following the AS statement, between the BEGIN and END, becomes the executable code of the stored procedure. It gets compiled and stored in the current database.

You can remove a procedure with DROP:

```
DROP PROCEDURE usp_TestProc
```

NOTE

Since the sp_ prefix has a special meaning for stored procedures, it's good to adopt some naming convention that will make the difference between user-defined stored procedures and the system stored procedures that come with SQL Server. My convention will be to use usp_, standing for user stored procedure. This is better than a name like "rptq1," which could really be anything. However, SQL Server does not enforce any standard, other than the fact that stored procedures cannot use reserved SQL names.

The basic syntax of the CREATE PROCEDURE command is

```
CREATE PROC[EDURE] procedure-name [group-number]
[parameter-list [= parameter-default] ] [OUTPUT] ]
[WITH procedure-options]
[FOR REPLICATION]
AS
```

You use CREATE PROCEDURE or CREATE PROC, followed by a valid SQL Server identifier, to name the procedure.

You can also use a group number, consisting of a semicolon followed by a number, to group as set of procedures together. This is most useful if you want to be able to drop an entire group with one DROP command. You'll look at the remaining options later in this chapter.

Executing a Stored Procedure

To execute a stored procedure, you use the EXECUTE command (usually abbreviated as EXEC.) For the preceding stored procedure, just issue

```
EXEC usp_TestProc
```

and you'll see the result,

```
This is a stored procedure
```

Stored procedures can contain the full complement of Transact-SQL commands, including loops, transactions, and cursors.

The EXEC statement is not required if this is the only command you're executing, or if this is the first line in the batch. However, it's a good practice to add it because it clarifies that you're executing a stored procedure.

Creating or Altering

When you use the CREATE PROC statement, you may want to completely remove any existing stored procedure with the same name. If you do, you can detect it with the OBJECT_ID() system function:

```
IF NULLIF(OBJECT_ID('usp_TestProc'), 0 ) > 0
            DROP PROCEDURE usp_TestProc
go
CREATE PROCEDURE usp_TestProc AS
            BEGIN
            PRINT 'This is a stored procedure'
            END
```

However, when you drop and re-create a procedure, the new procedure will inherit none of the permissions and dependencies of the old procedure. To make sure that you're really just modifying the old procedure and not replacing it, you can use the ALTER PROCEDURE command:

```
ALTER PROCEDURE usp_TestProc AS
            BEGIN
            PRINT 'This is a stored procedure'
            END
```

Return Values

Stored procedures gain utility because they can return information to the caller. There is a set of default return values called *status codes,* but you can get more utility by returning your own.

Status Codes

Every stored procedure, when it does not return a value explicitly, returns a status code. You can examine that status code and test it for errors. For example, you could rewrite your call to the preceding stored procedure as:

```
DECLARE     @iStatus int
EXEC        @iStatus = usp_TestProc
PRINT       @iStatus
```

output: This is a stored procedure
0

These system-generated status codes are:

Value	Meaning
0	Procedure was executed successfully
−1	Object missing
−2	Datatype error occurred
−3	Process was chosen as deadlock victim
−4	Permission error occurred
−5	Syntax error occurred
−6	Miscellaneous user error occurred
−7	Resource error, such as out of space, occurred
−8	Nonfatal internal problem encountered
−9	System limit was reached
−10	Fatal internal inconsistency occurred
−11	Fatal internal inconsistency occurred
−12	Table or index is corrupt
−13	Database is corrupt
−14	Hardware error occurred

However, if you are detecting errors in your stored procedure, you will probably want to return your own status code.

Custom Return Values

A stored procedure can return values to the caller. For example, the following stored procedure returns a zero for success and other numbers for failure:

```
ALTER PROCEDURE usp_TestProc AS
        BEGIN
        PRINT 'This is a stored procedure'
        IF @@ERROR <> 0
                RETURN(1)
        ELSE
                RETURN(0)
        END
```

Now you can call the stored procedure with the following syntax:

```
DECLARE @ReturnVal int
EXEC @ReturnVal = usp_TestProc
PRINT @ReturnVal
```

Result Sets

In addition to returning status codes and return values, stored procedures also return result sets to the caller. This is obvious when, for example, you include a SELECT statement in a stored procedure:

```
ALTER PROCEDURE usp_TestProc AS
        BEGIN
        SELECT *
                FROM Authors
        END
```

*(handwritten annotations: (create); ① creat this stored procedure in pubs database. or "execute usp_"; ② then call it (use * Syntax).; ③ Output: contents of the table author; select * from publishers (or, of two tables).)*

and then call it using the Query Analyzer. It will return the results of a SELECT, PRINT, or FETCH statement to the output window. If you include two SELECT statements, then both result sets will be returned.

What's a bit surprising is that a stored procedure will also return a result set to any client software. If the stored procedure returns more than one result set, you need to make sure that the client software can handle it.

Many data access methods now support multiple result sets. However, often client applications cannot handle more than one result set, and will only return the first result set. You'll need to write your stored procedures accordingly.

Parameters

Stored procedures can also take parameters. You list the input parameters for a stored procedure after the CREATE statement, and before the AS statement. For example, the following stored procedure takes a parameter called cParm, which must be a string, and returns the string in reverse order.

```
IF NULLIF(OBJECT_ID('usp_ReverseString'), 0 ) > 0
        DROP PROCEDURE usp_ReverseString
go
CREATE PROC usp_ReverseString
        @cParm varchar(100)        No default value
AS
BEGIN
        -- Declare a result and counter variable
        DECLARE     @cResult varchar(100),
                    @iCtr int
        SET         @iCtr = DATALENGTH(@cParm)
        SET         @cResult = ''
        WHILE @iCtr >= 1
          BEGIN
            SET @cResult =
                    @cResult + SUBSTRING(@cParm,@iCtr,1)
            -- decrement the counter
            SET @iCtr = @iCtr - 1
          END
        -- Display the result
        PRINT @cResult
END
go
```

You can call this stored procedure in a number of ways.

First, you can call it by passing a literal value as a parameter:

```
EXEC usp_ReverseString 'hello'   ← literal value
```

Or you can pass a variable containing the value:

```
DECLARE @cMyParm varchar(100)
SELECT @cMyParm = 'hello'
EXEC usp_ReverseString @cMyParm
```

If you know the name of the parameter variable inside the stored procedure, you can pass it as a "named parameter," either:

```
EXEC usp_numconv @cParm = 'hello'
```

or

```
DECLARE @cMyParm varchar(100)
SELECT @cMyParm = 'hello'
EXEC usp_NumConv @cParm = @cMyParm
```

To add one or more parameters, you need only add them in the CREATE command, with a comma:

```
CREATE PROC usp_ReverseString
          @cParm varchar(100), @cParm2 Varchar(20), etc.
```

Default Parameter Values

If you do not specify a default value for the parameter, then all calling commands must supply a parameter value. However, you can specify a default value, making the call of the parameter optional. For example, the following code supplies a parameter:

```
ALTER PROC usp_ReverseString
          @cParm varchar(100) = 'hello'   Default value
AS
BEGIN
          -- Declare a result and counter variable
          DECLARE      @cResult varchar(100),
                       @iCtr int
          SET          @iCtr = DATALENGTH(@cParm)
          SET          @cResult = ''
          WHILE @iCtr >= 1
```

If no default value for the parameter, supply a value when call:

Exec usp_ReverseString 'hello'

specify a default value, all the procedure:

Exec usp_ReverseString

Supply a value for the parameter, the procedure will use it instead of default)

```
BEGIN
        SET @cResult =
                @cResult + SUBSTRING(@cParm,@iCtr,1)
        -- decrement the counter
        SET @iCtr = @iCtr - 1
    END
    -- Display the result
    PRINT @cResult
END
```

So now you can call the procedure without a value:

```
EXEC usp_ReverseString
```

and the procedure will use the default value. If you supply a parameter value, the stored procedure will use it instead of the default.

Output Parameters

In all the previous examples, the parameter sent to the procedure is sent by value; that is, a copy of the value is sent to the procedure. If you call the procedure with a variable as a calling parameter, and the procedure changes the receiving parameter internally, the calling program will not see any change in its variable.

For example, let's change the usp_ReverseString procedure to change the value of the incoming parameter:

```
ALTER PROC usp_ReverseString
        @cParm varchar(100) = 'hello'
AS
BEGIN
        -- Declare a result and counter variable
        DECLARE    @cResult varchar(100),
                   @iCtr int
        SET        @iCtr = DATALENGTH(@cParm)
        SET        @cResult = ''
        WHILE @iCtr >= 1
          BEGIN
            SET @cResult =
                @cResult + SUBSTRING(@cParm,@iCtr,1)
```

```
            -- decrement the counter
            SET @iCtr = @iCtr - 1
         END
      -- Change the parameter value
      SET @cParm = @cResult
END
```

If you call it with a variable:

```
DECLARE @cMyParm varchar(100)
SELECT @cMyParm = 'hello'
EXEC usp_ReverseString @cMyParm
```

you will see no change to your @cMyParm value due to what the stored procedure does.

In order to change that value, a special type of parameter, called an output parameter, can be used to communicate a changed value back to the caller's own parameter variable. To do this, you must use the keyword OUTPUT or OUT on each end of the calling:

```
ALTER PROC usp_ReverseString
            @cParm varchar(100) = 'hello' OUTPUT
AS
BEGIN
            -- Declare a result and counter variable
            DECLARE      @cResult varchar(100),
                         @iCtr int
            SET          @iCtr = DATALENGTH(@cParm)
            SET          @cResult = ''
            WHILE @iCtr >= 1
              BEGIN
                SET @cResult =
                         @cResult + SUBSTRING(@cParm,@iCtr,1)
                -- decrement the counter
                SET @iCtr = @iCtr - 1
              END
            -- Change the parameter value
            SET @cParm = @cResult
      END
```

Now you can capture the changed input parameter by passing the input parameter's value to the stored procedure as a variable, and using the OUTPUT keyword in the procedure call:

```
DECLARE @cMyParm varchar(100)

SELECT @cMyParm = 'foobar'

EXEC usp_ReverseString @cMyParm OUTPUT

PRINT @cMyParm
```

Additional Considerations

The following sections describe a number of additional considerations you should take into account about stored procedures.

Limits of Stored Procedures

Every stored procedure can contain only one Transact-SQL batch. Therefore, all the limitations on a batch apply to a stored procedure. For example, you cannot alter a table to add new columns to a table and then reference the new columns in the same stored procedure.

In addition, you cannot use any of the following commands in a stored procedure:

```
CREATE DEFAULT
CREATE PROCEDURE
CREATE RULE
CREATE TRIGGER
CREATE VIEW
```

Note that as a result, a stored procedure cannot be used to create another stored procedure.

Encryption

You can use the WITH ENCRYPTION option on the CREATE PROCEDURE and ALTER PROCEDURE statements to cause SQL Server to store an encrypted version of the source code in the database.

Recompilation

You can also add the WITH RECOMPILE option, which will cause the stored procedure to be recompiled every time it is invoked.

Cursor Variables and Stored Procedures

You can declare an OUTPUT parameter variable to be of the cursor data type. This way, you can return a cursor to a calling program that has also declared a variable to be of the cursor data type.

Temporary Stored Procedures

Just as with temporary tables, you can create temporary stored procedures. If you prefix the stored procedure name with a single pound sign (#), then it will be a private stored procedure, one that can only be executed by the user of the current session. If you prefix the name with two pound signs (##), then it becomes a global stored procedure that everyone can execute.

Temporary stored procedures do not follow the same security rules for permanent stored procedures. A private temporary stored procedure can only be run by the owner (the user that created it) and permission to run it cannot be granted to other users. A global temporary stored procedure is available to all users, and the owner cannot deny others access to it.

Permissions

When you initially create a stored procedure, EXECUTE permissions default only to the user of the stored procedure, the user that created it. You must then explicitly grant permission for others to execute it. Execute permissions are checked at run time.

Autostart

You can make stored procedures become a part of the SQL Server's startup process using the sp_procoption system stored procedure. You can also use sp_procoption to make a stored procedure nonupdateable, so that it must be dropped and re-created rather than changed.

Stored Procedure Source Code

To see the source code of a stored procedure, just issue the system stored procedure sp_helptext, followed by the name of the stored procedure. For example,

```
sp_helptext byroyalty
```

If you want to see the code for a system stored procedure, you have to change to the Master database and then call sp_helptext.

SET *Options*

Because client software can change the values of a number of SET options, you must take care to write your stored procedures so that they will not be affected by changes in the settings. For example, client software could change any of the following settings:

```
SET QUOTED_IDENTIFIER ON
SET TEXTSIZE 2147483647
SET ANSI_DEFAULTS ON
SET CURSOR_CLOSE_ON_COMMIT OFF
SET IMPLICIT_TRANSACTIONS OFF
```

So, for example, always use single quotes as string terminators, and use IS NULL or IS NOT NULL rather than = NULL or <> NULL.

Examples

The following sections contain some examples of stored procedures. The first simulates a cascading delete of an author, and the second is an example of a system stored procedure that gives additional information about the tables in a database.

Cascade Delete

When you use SQL Server's declarative referential integrity (DRI), you cannot create a trigger to do a cascading delete. Because the trigger executes only after constraints are satisfied, any attempt to delete the primary key in a referenced table will violate the constraint, and the trigger will never fire.

On the other hand, you can use a stored procedure to delete all the rows of the referenced table first, and then delete the primary key row. For example, the following stored procedure will cascade the delete of an author from the Authors table, by first deleting the author ids from the Titleauthor table:

```
ALTER PROC usp_DeleteAuthor
@au_id CHAR(11)
AS
BEGIN
BEGIN TRAN
IF EXISTS(SELECT * FROM TitleAuthor WHERE au_id = @au_id)
        DELETE FROM TitleAuthor
```

```
                   WHERE au_id = @au_id
               IF @@ERROR <> 0
                     BEGIN
                     RAISERROR('Could not delete row from Titleauthor - Abort', 16, 1)
                     GOTO Errorhandler
                     END
DELETE FROM Authors
                   WHERE au_id = @au_id
       IF @@ERROR <> 0
               BEGIN
               RAISERROR('Could not delete row from Authors - Abort', 16, 1)
               GOTO Errorhandler
               END
COMMIT
RETURN
Errorhandler:
               ROLLBACK TRAN
               RETURN
END
```

To test the stored procedure without actually deleting any rows, you can use the following script:

```
BEGIN tran
SELECT * FROM authors
          WHERE au_id = '172-32-1176'
EXEC usp_DeleteAuthor '172-32-1176'
SELECT * FROM authors
          WHERE au_id = '172-32-1176'
ROLLBACK
```

The following output fragment shows the row present and then missing, as you would expect.

```
au_id       au_lname                                          au_fname
----------- ------------------------------------------------- --------------------
172-32-1176 White                                             Johnson


au_id       au_lname                                          au_fname
----------- ------------------------------------------------- --------------------
```

The ROLLBACK in the script causes the delete to be rolled back.

Creating a System Stored Procedure

There is a current system stored procedure that comes with SQL Server 7 called sp_tables, which gives a small amount of information about the tables in a database: just the table name, owner, and type, as you can see in Figure 17-3.

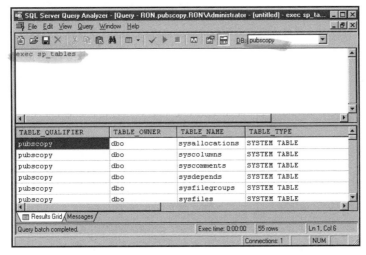

FIGURE 17-3

The sp_tables *system stored procedure gives a limited amount of information about a database's tables.*

The following stored procedure gives a little more information, by adding the primary key:

```
CREATE PROC sp_helptables
AS
SELECT s1.name AS 'Table name',
        CONVERT(sysname,USER_NAME(uid)) AS 'Owner',
        CASE xtype
        WHEN 'S' THEN 'System'
        WHEN 'U' THEN 'User'
        WHEN 'V' THEN 'View'
        ELSE '' END AS 'Type',
        (SELECT OBJECT_NAME(s2.id)
            FROM sysobjects s2
            WHERE s2.parent_obj = s1.id
```

```
                    AND xtype = 'PK') AS 'Primary Key'
FROM Sysobjects s1
WHERE s1.type IN ('U', 'S', 'V')
```

The result is shown in Figure 17-4.

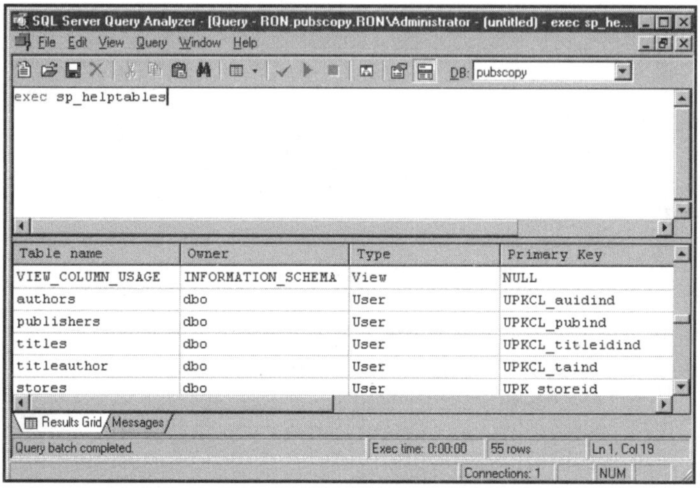

FIGURE 17-4

The new system stored procedure sp_helptables also shows the primary key.

You'll see another example of a new system stored procedure in the next chapter, "Triggers."

Summary

Stored procedures are the most effective way to embed repeatable code inside SQL Server. Once you've created a stored procedure, you can invoke it by name, schedule it, and call it from other stored procedures or triggers. In SQL Server 7.0, only the source code of a stored procedure is permanently stored in the database. When you first invoke it, it will be compiled into an execution plan that will be stored in memory cache. That execution plan can be reused by subsequent invokings of the stored procedure. Let's now take a look at triggers, which are a form of stored procedure.

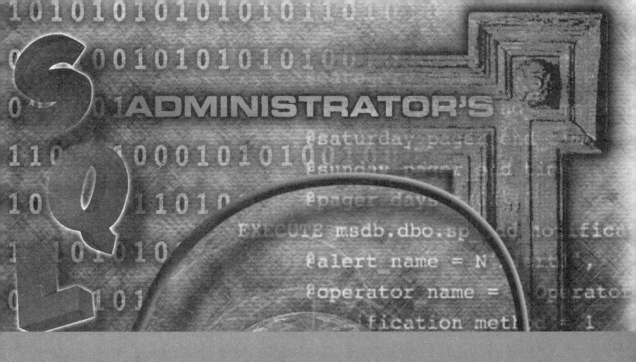

Chapter 18

Triggers

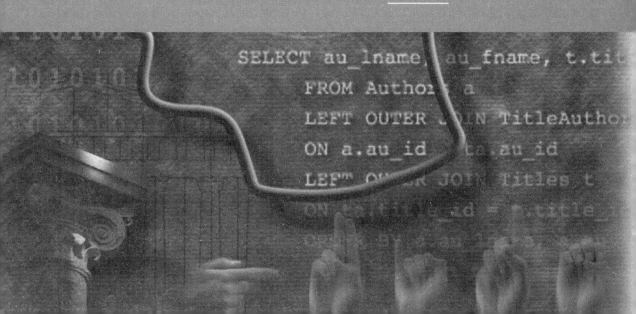

In This Chapter

♦ How triggers work

♦ Writing triggers

♦ Structural aspects of a trigger

♦ Functional aspects of a trigger

♦ Triggers checklist

♦ Tutorial: multiple-row updates

How Triggers Work

Triggers are limited forms of stored procedures associated with tables. They contain code that will execute whenever selected changes occur to a given table.

Every table can have multiple numbers of three types of triggers: insert, update, and delete. Each type binds to the appropriate SQL INSERT, UPDATE, or DELETE command. The number of triggers is limited by the setting for the maximum number of open objects in a database. SQL Server replication, for example, installs its own triggers on replicated tables. For more information about replication, see Chapter 24, "Replication."

Triggers can also fire themselves recursively. You have to enable this per database using the Database Properties dialog box or the sp_dboption system stored procedure.

Also, by default, trigger execution can be nested up to 32 levels. In other words, one trigger can make a change to another table that fires another trigger, and so on, for up to 32 levels. You can remove the option entirely using the Server Properties dialog box of Enterprise Manager, or the sp_configure system stored procedure.

> **NOTE**
>
> SQL Server 7 allows multiple insert, update, and delete triggers on a table. Prior versions of SQL Server allow only one insert, update, or delete trigger per table. If you would like to enforce the earlier behavior, you can use the sp_dbcmptlevel stored procedure to set the compatibility level to 65 or 60. For more information about compatibility levels, see Chapter 5, "Configuring."

Triggers execute (or "fire") after all other constraints in a table have succeeded. If any of the table's constraints fail, including foreign key constraints, the calling code is aborted and the trigger does not fire.

Before SQL Server had foreign key constraints, the only way to enforce referential integrity was through triggers. If a database uses declarative referential integrity (DRI), then triggers are not needed, provided that the choice is to restrict invalid changes to data. However, if a database developer needs other kinds of actions on data, including cascading referential constraints, the only way to implement that is by writing triggers.

> **NOTE**
>
> It is essentially a database developer's decision whether to use triggers for referential integrity, or DRI. It is possible to build a SQL Server 7 database and use triggers only for RI.

You can use triggers to:

◆ Compare before and after versions of the data

◆ Compare data with other tables and columns

◆ Modify other tables or columns

◆ Execute stored procedures

◆ Revert an invalid input

> **NOTE**
>
> Some third-party utilities and design tools will write triggers to enforce constraints and referential integrity. ERWin, S-Designor, and VisioModeler are all database design tools that can jump-start trigger writing.

Inserted and Deleted Tables

To help detect data changes within the trigger, SQL Server exposes two virtual tables to the trigger process: the Inserted and Deleted tables. Each of these tables has the same column structure as the original base table.

For an INSERT instruction, all the new data is in the Inserted table. For a DELETE statement, all the data to be deleted will be in the Deleted table. For an UPDATE statement, all the old rows are in the Deleted table, and the changed rows are in the Inserted table.

Using these two tables, your trigger can detect exactly what has been changed by an operation. Trigger code can select from these tables to see what's new or deleted. The Inserted and Deleted tables are not shared. They exist only for the duration of the transaction.

When Triggers Fire

Triggers fire after foreign key and all other constraints on a table. If any of the constraints fail, a trigger will not execute. For example, if you insert a row into titleauthors with an invalid title_id, SQL Server will reject the insert at that point and no triggers will fire. Only if an insert, update, or delete operation passes all the constraints will the triggers then fire.

After all constraints are passed, SQL Server actually executes the commands against the database within a transaction and then lets the trigger decide whether to roll back. If the trigger does nothing, the transaction gets committed.

From a logical standpoint, you can view the action on a table as follows:

1. A user issues an INSERT, UPDATE, or DELETE into the table.
2. The SQL Server relational engine checks to see that the command passes all constraints.
3. If the command passes all constraints, SQL Server executes any related triggers.
4. The relational engine places each trigger within the command's transaction.
5. For the trigger, SQL Server reads the transaction log and creates an Inserted table and places all the inserted or newly changed rows into it.
6. At the same time, SQL Server reads the transaction log and creates a Deleted table containing all the deleted or "old" rows.
7. Then SQL Server executes the trigger code.
8. If the trigger issues a ROLLBACK, then SQL Server rolls back the transaction.
9. If the trigger does not issue a ROLLBACK, SQL Server either commits the transaction or repeats the actions starting in step 5 until all triggers have executed or a ROLLBACK was issued.

Writing Triggers

To write a trigger using Transact-SQL, you just use the CREATE TRIGGER statement with some executable code:

```
CREATE TRIGGER dbo.tr_authors_diu
ON dbo.Authors
FOR INSERT, UPDATE, DELETE
AS
            PRINT  'Trigger trig_test fired'
```

To fire this trigger, you just need to execute an insert or an update:

```
UPDATE dbo.Authors
            SET contract = 1
            WHERE contract = 1
```

The trigger will execute even though the rows keep their same values. The UPDATE statement is still writing to the table!

The basic syntax of the CREATE TRIGGER statement is:

```
CREATE TRIGGER trigger-name
            ON base-table-name
            [WITH ENCRYPTION]
            FOR DELETE and/or INSERT and/or UPDATE
            [WITH APPEND]
            [NOT FOR REPLICATION]
            AS
                trigger-code
```

You must supply a trigger name, state whether the trigger is for delete, and/or insert, and/or update, and then follow the AS statement with one Transact-SQL batch.

Just as with regular stored procedures, you can compile the trigger with encryption. The NOT FOR REPLICATION clause prevents the trigger from firing when a replication login changes the table. The WITH APPEND option is only needed if you have the sp_dbcmptlevel setting below 70. Otherwise, SQL Server 7 will always append a trigger to the table.

If you try to create a trigger that already exists, SQL Server will return an error. You can drop the trigger first and re-create it, as in this example:

```
IF NULLIF(OBJECT_ID('dbo.tr_authors_diu'),0) > 1
            DROP TRIGGER dbo.tr_authors_diu
go
CREATE TRIGGER dbo.tr_authors_diu
ON dbo.Authors
```

```
FOR INSERT, UPDATE, DELETE
AS
        PRINT  'Trigger trig_test fired'
```

Or if you wish to replace a trigger without having to drop and re-create, just use ALTER TRIGGER:

```
ALTER TRIGGER dbo.tr_authors_diu
ON dbo.Authors
FOR INSERT, UPDATE, DELETE
AS
        PRINT  'Trigger trig_test fired'
```

For the ALTER TABLE to succeed, a trigger with that name must already exist in the database. You have to leave the trigger on the same table, so the ALTER TRIGGER must also use the same table name that the CREATE TRIGGER used.

Creating and Editing Triggers

SQL Server gives you two tools you can use to create or edit a trigger: Enterprise Manager and the Query Analyzer.

Enterprise Manager

You can create new triggers and edit existing triggers using Enterprise Manager. To do this, drill down into the tables in a database, right-click over a table that has the trigger you want to edit, choose Task, and then choose Manage Triggers. You'll get the Trigger Properties dialog box shown in Figure 18-1.

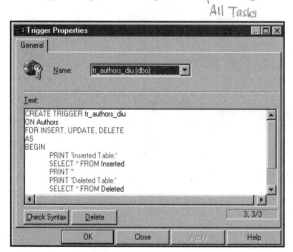

FIGURE 18-1

You can edit a trigger using the Trigger Properties dialog box.

To edit an existing trigger for that table, select the trigger from the drop-down list.

To make a new trigger, choose <new> from the list. You then fill in the new name of the trigger in the body of the trigger text, as shown in Figure 18-2.

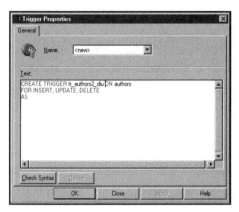

FIGURE 18-2

To create a new trigger, you must enter a trigger name in the body of the trigger.

The Trigger Properties dialog box provides color syntax highlighting and the ability to check the syntax. When you save the trigger, the dialog box will ask for the trigger name. When the Trigger Properties dialog box saves the trigger, it executes the create trigger code, thereby creating the trigger.

The Query Analyzer

Just as with a stored procedure, if you edit and save a trigger directly to the database like using the Trigger Properties dialog box, you lose your control of source code changes. An alternate way to create and edit a trigger is to use scripts and the Query Analyzer. You can save the trigger code in an external text file, load it into the Query Analyzer window, and execute the code to create the trigger. When you do this, it's best to drop and recreate the trigger, as shown in Figure 18-3.

drop & create trigger ←

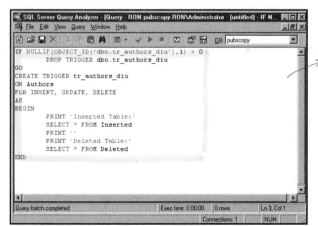

- output: The commands completed successfully.
- right click authors table.
  all tasks ... the trigger is there.

FIGURE 18-3

When executing a script in the Query Analyzer, it's best to drop and recreate the trigger.

Naming Triggers

A number of possible naming conventions are available for naming triggers. If you save triggers externally as scripts, each in its own text file, then you can store those scripts in source code control systems.

If you store each trigger in its own file, then it works out well if the name of the file is also the name of the trigger. What I've found out over time is that if you begin the name of a trigger with something like tr_, then add the name of the table, and then the type of trigger, the files will sort themselves out in your directories. All the trigger files will sort with tr_, then by table, and then by the type.

Creating Triggers from the Command Window

You can also then just run the scripts from a batch file to re-create the triggers. For example, if the trigger tr_authors_diu is saved on disk as tr_authors_diu.sql, you can apply it to SQL Server using OSQL, as shown in Figure 18-4.

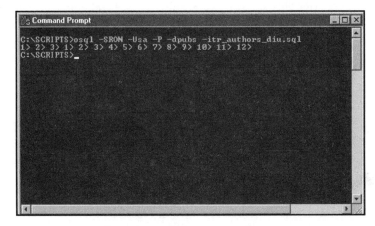

FIGURE 18-4

You can use OSQL to apply a trigger script to SQL Server.

By using OSQL.EXE or ISQL.EXE, you can run these scripts remotely, start them from a command file, or execute them from SQL Agent, as external commands. For more information about OSQL.EXE and ISQL.EXE, see Chapter 7, "Managing Databases."

Detecting Rows Changed

To determine how many rows were changed by a trigger, just add a check for the @@rowcount global variable:

```
ALTER TRIGGER tr_authors_diu
ON Authors
FOR INSERT, UPDATE, DELETE
```

```
AS
BEGIN
            DECLARE @rowschanged int
            SET @rowschanged = @@rowcount
            PRINT 'Number of rows changed: ' +
                    CONVERT(char, @rowschanged)
END
```

Now when you issue the preceding UPDATE, you will see something like this:

```
Number of rows changed: 19
```

Displaying the Inserted and Deleted Tables

The next example shows the same trigger enhanced to display the Inserted and Deleted tables, and to check for a changed column:

```
ALTER TRIGGER tr_authors_diu
ON Authors
FOR INSERT, UPDATE, DELETE
AS
BEGIN
            PRINT 'Inserted Table:'
            SELECT * FROM Inserted
            PRINT ''
            PRINT 'Deleted Table:'
            SELECT * FROM Deleted
END
```

First, let's do an INSERT:

```
INSERT INTO Authors
            VALUES ('111-11-1111', 'Test lname', 'Test
                fname','test phone', 'test address',
                'test city', 'CA', '00000', 1)
```

→ insert a new row (and the trigger will print out the output.) same w the update & delete

The trigger will show you the new row in the Inserted table, and no rows in the Deleted table, as you can see in Figure 18-5.

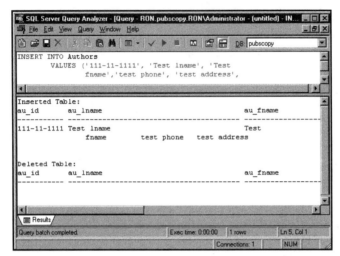

Now, try an UPDATE:

```
UPDATE Authors
        SET au_lname = 'Test2'
        WHERE au_lname = 'Test lname'
```

and you'll see the new and old values in the Inserted and Deleted tables, respectively, as in Figure 18-6.

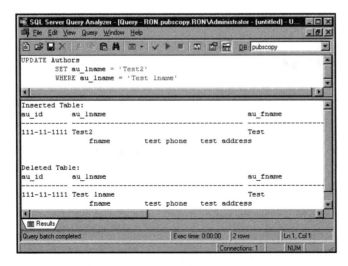

Finally, the DELETE:

```
DELETE FROM Authors
        WHERE au_lname = 'Test2'
```

Figure 18-7 now shows the deleted values in the Deleted table.

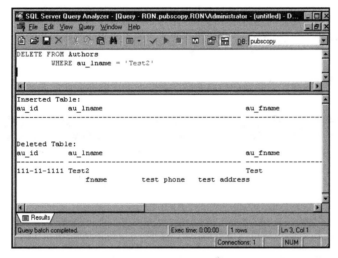

FIGURE 18-7

A DELETE statement populates just the Deleted table.

Now try this query:

```
DELETE FROM Authors
        WHERE au_lname = 'Not_a_name'
```

The trigger fires anyway! *but 0 rows affected*

When a WHERE condition on an UPDATE or DELETE returns no rows, relevant triggers will fire, no rows are changed, and the Deleted and Inserted tables will be empty. So a trigger will fire, even though no rows were really changed! The lesson here is that you can make your trigger code more efficient by detecting whether zero rows, one row, or more than one row has been changed, and then what the changes actually are.

For example, the following version of your trigger quits early if there are no rows changed:

```
ALTER TRIGGER tr_authors_diu
ON Authors
FOR INSERT, UPDATE, DELETE
AS
```

```
BEGIN
        IF @@ROWCOUNT = 0
                RETURN
        PRINT 'Inserted Table:'
        SELECT * FROM Inserted
        PRINT ''
        PRINT 'Deleted Table:'
        SELECT * FROM Deleted
END
```

WARNING

In a case-sensitive SQL Server, the Inserted and Deleted tables must be written all lowercase.

Detecting What Column Has Been Changed

SQL Server includes two functions to help find out what column has been changed. The first function, the UPDATE() function, works with insert and update triggers. It takes one of the table's column names as an argument and returns true if that column was included in the SQL statement. In other words, the UPDATE() function does not find out whether the column was actually changed, just that it was referenced in the statement. For example, you could test to see if the au_lname column was in an INSERT or UPDATE statement with this trigger:

```
ALTER TRIGGER tr_authors_diu
ON Authors
FOR INSERT, UPDATE, DELETE
AS
BEGIN
        IF @@ROWCOUNT = 0
                RETURN
        IF UPDATE(au_lname)
                PRINT 'au_lname in INSERT/UPDATE'
END
```

The problem with the UPDATE() function is that its usefulness is very limited for an update trigger, because an UPDATE statement might reference a particular column without changing it. With an insert trigger, though, the UPDATE() function does tell you that the column was in the INSERT statement, so the user is not relying on default values.

A mixed alternative can be found with the COLUMNS_UPDATED() function, new with SQL Server 7. To use this function, you must know the column order of the table, and the column order must not change while the trigger is in effect. If you use some tool like the Design Table dialog box in Enterprise Manager, or the Visual Data Tools in Visual Studio, you can change the order of columns in a table.

If the second column of the Authors table has been changed, the value of COLUMNS_UPDATED() will be the hex value of 0x0200, which is decimal 512. So you can rewrite the preceding trigger to use COLUMNS_UPDATED() as:

```
ALTER TRIGGER tr_authors_diu
ON Authors
FOR INSERT, UPDATE, DELETE
AS
BEGIN
        IF @@ROWCOUNT = 0
            RETURN
        IF (COLUMNS_UPDATED() & 512) = 1
            PRINT 'Updated au_lname'
END
```

To get other columns in the list, you must add the values together. The first and second column, for example, would be 256+512, which is 768, or hex 0x0300, and so on.

SET **Options**

Just as with stored procedures, you must take care to write your triggers so that they will not be affected by changes in SET settings. For example, client software could change any of the following settings:

```
SET QUOTED_IDENTIFIER ON
SET TEXTSIZE 2147483647
SET ANSI_DEFAULTS ON
SET CURSOR_CLOSE_ON_COMMIT OFF
SET IMPLICIT_TRANSACTIONS OFF
```

So, for example, always use single quotes as string terminators, and use IS NULL or IS NOT NULL rather than = NULL or <> NULL.

Disabling a Trigger

With SQL Server 7, you can disable a trigger with the ALTER TABLE statement:

```
ALTER TABLE Authors
DISABLE TRIGGER tr_authors-diu
```

Then you can re-enable it with

```
ALTER TABLE Authors
ENABLE TRIGGER tr_authors-diu
```

— should be an underscore.

Also, you can disable all triggers on a table with the ALL keyword:

```
ALTER TABLE Authors
DISABLE TRIGGER ALL
```

You can test whether a trigger is enabled with the OBJECT_PROPERTY() function, which you'll learn about next.

Finding Triggers in a Table

You can use the sp_helptrigger stored procedure to find triggers for a particular table, as shown in Figure 18-8.

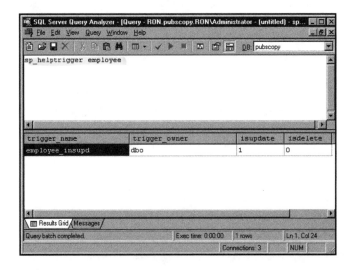

FIGURE 18-8

The sp_helptrigger *stored procedure gives some information about a particular table's trigger.*

Unfortunately, it does not show all the triggers in a database. You can use the following script, included on this book's CD, to get a list of all triggers in the database:

```
-- Single query to find all triggers in a database with tables
--   complements sp_helptrigger <table name>
SELECT      OBJECT_NAME(parent_obj) AS 'Table',
            name AS 'Trigger name',
            CASE
            WHEN ObjectProperty(id,'ExecIsDeleteTrigger') = 1 AND
                    ObjectProperty(id,'ExecIsInsertTrigger') = 1 AND
                    ObjectProperty(id,'ExecIsUpdateTrigger') = 1
                    THEN 'Delete, Insert, Update'
        WHEN    ObjectProperty(id,'ExecIsInsertTrigger') = 1 AND
                    ObjectProperty(id,'ExecIsUpdateTrigger') = 1
                    THEN 'Insert, Update'
        WHEN    ObjectProperty(id,'ExecIsDeleteTrigger') = 1 AND
                    ObjectProperty(id,'ExecIsInsertTrigger') = 1
                    THEN 'Delete, Insert'
        WHEN    ObjectProperty(id,'ExecIsDeleteTrigger') = 1 AND
                    ObjectProperty(id,'ExecIsUpdateTrigger') = 1
                    THEN 'Delete, Update'
        WHEN    ObjectProperty(id,'ExecIsInsertTrigger') = 1
                    THEN 'Insert'
        WHEN    ObjectProperty(id,'ExecIsUpdateTrigger') = 1
                    THEN 'Update'
        WHEN    ObjectProperty(id,'ExecIsDeleteTrigger') = 1
                    THEN 'Delete'
            ELSE '' END AS 'Type',
            CASE WHEN ObjectProperty(id,'ExecIsTriggerDisabled') = 0
                        THEN 'Y       ' ELSE 'N       ' END AS Enabled
    FROM Sysobjects
    WHERE ObjectProperty(id, 'IsTrigger') = 1
```

```
ORDER BY OBJECT_NAME(parent_obj), name
```

The output is a little more informative, as you can see in Figure 18-9.

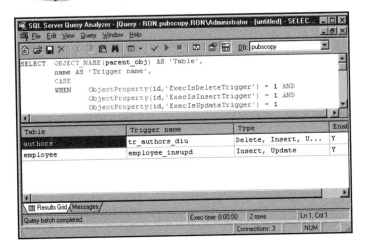

FIGURE 18-9

The new query shows more information about all the triggers in a database.

Structural Aspects of a Trigger

The purpose of a trigger is to change data according to the actions of the command to which it is responding. From a structural or "white box" standpoint, the trigger should follow good normal coding practices, plus some special considerations that apply just to triggers.

◆ First of all, if no rows are changed, the trigger should not do anything. Therefore the trigger's code should check the @@ROWCOUNT system function and exit immediately if no rows are affected.

◆ A trigger should check to see if the command it is serving actually changed the values it is concerned with. It is possible in an update trigger, for example, that the column or columns the trigger is supposed to manipulate weren't actually updated, so there's nothing for the trigger to do.

◆ A trigger needs to test every significant SQL command for success, and if any fail, it may require that the transaction be rolled back. Therefore the trigger code should check the value of the @@ERROR variable after each command that affects data and exit with a rollback if the command fails.

◆ The trigger should follow good indenting and consistent upper- and lowercase coding standards.

Let's look at an example. The following trigger comes with the Pubs database and applies to the Employee table:

```
CREATE TRIGGER employee_insupd
ON Employee
FOR insert, UPDATE
AS
--Get the range of level for this job type from the Jobs table.
declare @min_lvl tinyint,
    @max_lvl tinyint,
    @emp_lvl tinyint,
    @job_id smallint
select @min_lvl = min_lvl,
    @max_lvl = max_lvl,
    @emp_lvl = i.job_lvl,
    @job_id = i.job_id
from Employee e, Jobs j, inserted i
where e.emp_id = i.emp_id AND i.job_id = j.job_id
IF (@job_id = 1) and (@emp_lvl <> 10)
begin
    raiserror ('Job id 1 expects the default level of 10.',16,1)
    ROLLBACK TRANSACTION
end
ELSE
IF NOT (@emp_lvl BETWEEN @min_lvl AND @max_lvl)
begin
    raiserror ('The level for job_id:%d should be between %d and %d.',
        16, 1, @job_id, @min_lvl, @max_lvl)
    ROLLBACK TRANSACTION
end
```

- ◆ Notice that the Pubs `employee_insupd` trigger does not check to see whether any rows are actually updated, even though it is an update trigger.
- ◆ The trigger also is not checking to see whether the columns it is really concerned with, `job_id` and `empl_lvl`, are affected. Consequently, the trigger will execute its checking even if the update did not affect those rows.
- ◆ There is no error handling. Since all the trigger is doing is SELECT statements, that seems harmless, even though SELECTs can fail.

526 | *Part IV*   **MANAGING DATA**

◆ There is no consistent indenting, nor are any uppercase/lowercase conventions followed in the code.

Let's tidy up the trigger:

```
CREATE TRIGGER employee_insupd
ON Employee
FOR INSERT, UPDATE
AS
BEGIN
IF @@ROWCOUNT = 0
            RETURN
--Get the range of level for this job type from the Jobs table.
DECLARE @min_lvl TINYINT,
   @max_lvl TINYINT,
   @emp_lvl TINYINT,
   @job_id SMALLINT
SELECT      @min_lvl = min_lvl,
               @max_lvl = max_lvl,
               @emp_lvl = i.job_lvl,
               @job_id = i.job_id
            FROM Employee e, Jobs j, inserted i
            WHERE e.emp_id = i.emp_id AND i.job_id = j.job_id
IF (@job_id = 1) and (@emp_lvl <> 10)
            BEGIN
RAISERROR ('Job id 1 expects the default level of 10.',16,1)
                ROLLBACK TRANSACTION
            END
ELSE
            IF NOT (@emp_lvl BETWEEN @min_lvl AND @max_lvl)
                BEGIN
                        RAISERROR ('The level for job_id:%d should
be between %d and %d.', 16, 1, @job_id,                    @min_lvl,
@max_lvl)
                ROLLBACK TRANSACTION
                END
END
```

Notice how the consistent indentation, the use of upper- and lowercase, and the change to the test for no rows help the readability of the trigger. Also, a BEGIN/END pair was added to clarify the end point of the trigger.

There are still problems with this trigger, though, as will become apparent soon as you consider the functional aspects of a trigger.

Functional Aspects of a Trigger

The most subtle and perhaps important part of trigger functionality is checking to see that the trigger handles multiple row changes as well as single row changes. In other words, the trigger should work properly whether one or many rows are inserted, updated, or deleted.

It is actually quite difficult to write triggers to handle multiple rows, so testing multiple row updates is a very good way to find a trigger bug.

Single-Row Updates

If you make a single-row change to the Employees table that satisfies and then violates the trigger's constraints, you can see the trigger in action:

```
UPDATE Employee
        SET job_id = 1
        WHERE emp_id = 'PMA42628M'
```

This command will violate the first branch of the trigger and produce the following message:

```
Server: Msg 50000, Level 16, State 1, Procedure employee_insupd, Line 19
Job id 1 expects the default level of 10.
```

Another update statement will violate the second branch of the trigger:

```
UPDATE Employee
        SET job_lvl = 10
        WHERE emp_id = 'PMA42628M'
```

and produces the following message:

```
Server: Msg 50000, Level 16, State 1, Procedure employee_insupd, Line 25
The level for job_id:13 should be between 25 and 100.
```

So the trigger seems to be operating fine for single-row updates, though more testing might still turn up a bug. But now let's look at multiple-row updates.

Multiple-Row Updates

To perform a multiple-row test, you need to send an UPDATE that changes two rows. If you look at two Employee ids in particular, namely 'PMA42628M' and 'PTC11962M':

```
SELECT emp_id, job_id, job_lvl
        FROM Employee
        WHERE emp_id = 'PMA42628M' OR emp_id = 'PTC11962M'
```

you see that one has a job level of 35 and the other, 215:

```
emp_id     job_id job_lvl
.......... ....... ........
PMA42628M 13      35
PTC11962M 2       215
```

Now, looking at the Jobs table tells you that job_id 2 has a range of 200–250, and job_id 13 has a range of 25–100. So suppose you try to change them both to, say, 36? (You'll wrap the change into a transaction so that you don't have to reset your changes to the data.)

```
BEGIN TRAN
UPDATE Employee
        SET job_lvl = 36
        WHERE emp_id = 'PMA42628M' or emp_id = 'PTC11962M'
SELECT emp_id, job_id, job_lvl
        FROM Employee
        WHERE emp_id = 'PMA42628M' OR emp_id = 'PTC11962M'
ROLLBACK
```

The trigger works, because job_id 2 cannot have a value of 36:

```
Server: Msg 50000, Level 16, State 1, Procedure employee_insupd, Line 25
The level for job_id:2 should be between 200 and 250.
```

But let's change the query slightly, changing them both to, say, 216:

```
BEGIN TRAN
UPDATE Employee
```

```
                SET job_lvl = 216
                WHERE emp_id = 'PMA42628M' or emp_id = 'PTC11962M'
SELECT emp_id, job_id, job_lvl
                FROM Employee
                WHERE emp_id = 'PMA42628M' OR emp_id = 'PTC11962M'
ROLLBACK
```

Now the UDPATE succeeds and the embedded SELECT shows you the result:

```
emp_id      job_id  job_lvl
..........  ......  ........

PMA42628M 13     216
PTC11962M 2      216
```

What happened? Why did the trigger fail? If you look more closely at it, you can see that the trigger loads variables with values and then just tests them:

```
SELECT        @min_lvl = min_lvl,
              @max_lvl = max_lvl,
              @emp_lvl = i.job_lvl,
              @job_id = i.job_id
        FROM Employee e, Jobs j, inserted i
        WHERE e.emp_id = i.emp_id AND i.job_id = j.job_id
```

Well, if there are two rows in the Inserted table, a situation that a multiple-row UDPATE will cause, which ones get loaded into the variables? Recall that when you load a variable using a SELECT statement, the last row affected gets the value. So the trigger ends up testing both rows with the same limits. Both job_id 2 and job_id 13 follow the rules of the one that came later in the table, namely job_id 2. So both rows in your case just get tested for a job_level between 200 and 250. There's the bug!

You can solve the problem by doing all the testing in the query and not relying on loading variables. So here's a rewrite of the trigger:

```
ALTER TRIGGER employee_insupd
ON Employee
FOR INSERT, UPDATE
AS
BEGIN
IF @@ROWCOUNT = 0
RETURN
```

```
--Get the range of level for this job type from the Jobs table.
IF EXISTS (SELECT * FROM inserted
                WHERE job_id = 1 and job_lvl <> 10)
           BEGIN
                RAISERROR ('Job id 1 expects the default level of 10.',16,1)
                ROLLBACK TRANSACTION
           END
ELSE
           IF EXISTS
           (SELECT * FROM inserted i, Employee e, Jobs j
                WHERE e.emp_id = i.emp_id AND i.job_id = j.job_id
                AND NOT (i.job_lvl BETWEEN j.min_lvl AND j.max_lvl))
                BEGIN
                        RAISERROR ('Job level out of range',16,1)
                        ROLLBACK TRANSACTION
                END
END
```

If you now retry the tests, the trigger handles multiple row updates properly. All it took was rewriting the code so that all rows are tested. Here's a case where better SQL produces the best result.

Notice that the error message now does not report which job level is out of range, which may seem a disadvantage. In fact, without variables, you cannot load up the RAISERROR statement so that it will output the proper values. However, the original error message was just a single-row message. If more than one row violated the trigger, it could only report the one row.

In order to report many rows out of range, another SELECT statement could return them, but as a result set, not an error message. In this case, it's probably better to simply have a generic message.

NOTE

Once you understand how to handle multiple rows in triggers, you're on your way to mastering one of the most subtle aspects of Transact-SQL programming!

A Triggers Checklist

The following list covers a number of problems to look for in a trigger:

Structural:

- ❏ Does the trigger name follow the application's naming standards? Naming standards make code objects easier to find, learn about, and maintain.
- ❏ Does the trigger follow good SQL coding standards? Following coding standards can make it much easier to maintain it.
- ❏ Does the trigger completely avoid user intervention? Triggers should never wait for user input.
- ❏ Does the trigger remove complex or lengthy code to a stored procedure? Placing complex code in a stored procedure can make the trigger easier to understand and maintain.
- ❏ Does the trigger exit immediately if there are no rows updated? If there are no rows to update, there's no point in going through the remainder of the code.

Functional:

- ❏ Is trigger execution fast enough? All triggers should perform as fast as possible, otherwise performance of the system as a whole will be adversely affected.
- ❏ Does the trigger handle a sufficient sample of multiple-row updates correctly? Multiple-row updates are the Achilles heel of triggers, and an excellent test of their robustness.
- ❏ If any triggers are used for referential integrity, have you checked all possible combinations? It's easy to overlook all the combinations.
- ❏ Does the trigger always give descriptive and accurate error messages? The trigger can also be a means of explaining what went wrong with a command.
- ❏ Does the trigger avoid returning system error messages? System error messages tend to be cryptic and sometimes no help to the user or developer.
- ❏ Have all triggers been tested? Unless you've tested them all, you don't know what will happen when the system gets into production!

Tutorial: Multiple-Row Updates

Here's another exercise you can use for practice regarding multiple-row updates.

For example, take the following trigger. It is called `tr_sales_u`, which is short for "sales update trigger." It is meant to fill an important gap in the Pubs database. Currently there is no way to keep the `Titles.ytd_sales` value up to date on the basis of sales recorded in the Sales table. The purpose of this trigger is to handle just one aspect of that, namely when the values of the Sales.qty column are updated with the SQL UPDATE command. If there's an increase in the sales quantity, then the Titles.ytd_sales value should also increase. The cases for the SQL INSERT and DELETE are similar, but to keep the trigger example simple, let's just focus on the UPDATE. Here's an initial version of the trigger:

```
CREATE TRIGGER tr_sales_u ON sales FOR UPDATE
AS
        DECLARE @errmsg varchar(100), @qtyamt int,
            @insqtyamt int, @delqtyamt int
    IF @@ROWCOUNT = 0
        RETURN
    IF UPDATE(qty)
      BEGIN
        SELECT @insqtyamt = qty FROM inserted
        SELECT @delqtyamt = qty FROM deleted
        SELECT @qtyamt = @insqtyamt - @delqtyamt
        UPDATE Titles
                SET ytd_sales = ytd_sales + @qtyamt
                FROM Titles, Inserted, Deleted
                WHERE Titles.title_id =
                        Inserted.title_id
      END
    ELSE
        RETURN
    IF @@ERROR != 0
        BEGIN
                SELECT @errmsg = 'Update failed'
                GOTO Errorhandler
        END

        RETURN
Errorhandler:
        RAISERROR(@errmsg, 16,1)
        ROLLBACK TRANSACTION
    GO
```

From a structural standpoint, notice that the trigger does follow a coding standard, and it has proper indentation.

First, notice that the trigger exits immediately if no rows are affected. It does this by testing the @@ROWCOUNT function. The execution of triggers is a performance drain, so if no rows are affected, the trigger should exit as quickly as possible.

Second, tr_sales_u uses the UPDATE() function to check if the Sales.qty column was changed. If the qty column wasn't affected, there's no work to do, so the trigger just exits.

Notice the trigger does test its UPDATE command for errors, and if an error occurs due to the UPDATE command, the trigger immediately jumps to the Erorrhandler label and rolls back the transaction. Also notice that the trigger will only roll back if an error sends it to the Errorhandler label. Just before the label, a RETURN statement guarantees that the trigger will commit the transaction and exit normally.

The Multiple Row Update Bug

You can find a bug in the preceding trigger by executing a multiple-row update. Let's look at the data first. To start with, notice that stor_id '6380' in Sales has two orders, for title_id 'BU1032' and 'PS2091'. Let's create stored procedure to see the results:

```
CREATE PROC usp_showvalues
AS
PRINT 'Show the qty value in Sales:'
SELECT stor_id, ord_num, qty, title_id
  FROM Sales
  WHERE stor_id = '6380'
PRINT 'Show the ytd_sales value in Titles:'
SELECT title_id, ytd_sales
  FROM Titles
  WHERE title_id IN ('BU1032', 'PS2091')
GO
```

It returns the results:

```
Show the qty value in Sales:
stor_id ord_num                 qty     title_id
------- -------------------- ------- --------
6380    6871                       5     BU1032
6380    722a                       3     PS2091
```

Show the ytd_sales value in Titles:

```
title_id ytd_sales
........ ...........

BU1032   4095

PS2091   2045
```

Now, let's do an update across more than one row:

```
BEGIN TRANSACTION
EXEC usp_showvalues
PRINT ''
PRINT 'Multiple row update:'
PRINT 'Change qty to 5 for store 6380'
UPDATE Sales
         SET qty = 5
         WHERE stor_id = '6380'
PRINT ''
EXEC usp_showvalues2
ROLLBACK TRANSACTION
```

which will change the quantity of both to 5 (note that BU1032 already is 5). Now look again at the results in Titles. The correct results should be:

```
title_id ytd_sales
........ ...........

BU1032   4095

PS2091   2047
```

With the current trigger, your results should be different from these. So what happened? Well, the trigger did its calculation of the @qtyamt variable for only one row. The trigger statements:

```
SELECT @insqtyamt = qty FROM inserted
SELECT @delqtyamt = qty FROM deleted
```

filled the variables with single values that get applied to all the rows. So the amount to increment does not get recalculated for each of the updates.

A New, Improved Trigger

The better solution is to rewrite the trigger so that it can capture multiple rows. The following version uses a correlated subquery rather than a variable:

```
ALTER TRIGGER tr_sales_u
ON sales
FOR UPDATE
AS
DECLARE @errmsg varchar(100), @qtyamt int,
          @numrows int
SELECT @numrows = @@rowcount
IF @numrows = 0
          RETURN
IF UPDATE(qty)
   IF @numrows = 1
          UPDATE Titles
          SET t.ytd_sales = t.ytd_sales + i.qty - d.qty
              FROM Titles t, Inserted i, Deleted d
              WHERE t.title_id = i.title_id AND
                    t.title_id = d.title_id
   ELSE
          UPDATE Titles
          SET ytd_sales = ytd_sales
              + (SELECT SUM(i.qty)
                    FROM Inserted I
                    GROUP BY i.title_id
                    HAVING Titles.title_id =
                           i.title_id)
              - (SELECT SUM(d.qty)
                    FROM Deleted d
                    GROUP BY d.title_id
                    HAVING Titles.title_id =
                           d.title_id)
IF @@error != 0
          BEGIN
          SELECT @errmsg = 'Update of Sales failed'
             GOTO Errorhandler
          END
RETURN
Errorhandler:
```

```
                RAISERROR(@errmsg, 16,1)
                ROLLBACK TRANSACTION
GO
```

Now, re-execute the multiple-row update:

```
BEGIN TRANSACTION
EXEC usp_showvalues2
PRINT ''
PRINT 'Multiple row update:'
PRINT 'Change qty to 5 for store 6380'
UPDATE Sales
            SET qty = 5
            WHERE stor_id = '6380'
PRINT ''
EXEC usp_showvalues2
ROLLBACK TRANSACTION
```

Now you should see the results:

```
title_id ytd_sales
........ ...........

BU1032   4095
PS2091   2047
```

The correlated subquery handled the multiple rows just fine!

Summary

Triggers are a form of stored procedure that are attached to tables and execute based on data-change events against the tables. They always execute in the context of a command's transaction, but they only make use of the ROLLBACK command. Triggers can be used for referential integrity and other kinds of business rules validation.

You've come to the end of your treatment of managing data. Now it's time to see some of the issues related to SQL Server 7.0 performance.

ADMINISTRATOR'S

PART V

Performance

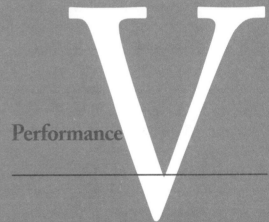

Chapter 19

Tuning Queries

In This Chapter

◆ Preparing some data for analysis

◆ Graphical showplan

◆ Textual Showplan

◆ Statistics I/O

◆ Index Analysis

◆ Index Distribution Statistics

Tuning the performance of your database can be one of the most challenging and complex of tasks, because there are so many variables. In the next several chapters, you'll look at several tools SQL Server 7 provides to help tune your performance.

Performance problems can arise from slow queries, blocked processes, and deadlocks. In this chapter, you'll take a look at tools for tuning queries. In the next chapter, you'll learn about the Current Activity tool for monitoring all SQL Server processes.

> **NOTE**
>
> Performance tuning and query optimization is a large and complex topic. See the References in Appendix A for further details and links.

Preparing Some Data for Analysis

Two Query Analyzer utilities can assist you in tuning your queries. The first is the Showplan utility, which allows you to infer relative performance among queries in either a graphical or textual way. The second is the Index Analysis option, which will suggest additional indexes to improve a query's performance. First, you need to create a large test data set and create some queries to tune.

Creating Test Data

The sample data set that comes with SQL Server in the pubs and Northwind databases is too small for a realistic test of query speed. It's easy to take a sample of that data, though, and create a much larger table. The following steps guide you through creating a large copy of the Publishers table in the pubscopy database.

1. First, make sure that you have Select Into/Bulk Copy turned on. You can find this option in pubscopy's Properties dialog box, Options tab.

2. Now you can create a large table. Let's take a simple table, such as the Publishers table, copy it to a new table, and increase its size all in one action. The Publishers table initially has only eight rows. If you join the table with itself in a query, it will greatly expand the number of rows. Execute the following query in the Query Analyzer. The query is located in the Ch19 folder of this book's CD as Publish2Create.SQL:

```
SELECT a.*
            INTO Publish2
            FROM Publishers a,
                Publishers b,
                Publishers c,
                Publishers d,
                Publishers e
```

The preceding query will create a new table called Publish2 with $8\wedge5 = 8 * 8 * 8 * 8 * 8 = 32,768$ rows.

NOTE

If your machine is not powerful enough to run the queries in this chapter, you can remove the last table reference in the query and end up with a table that only has 4,096 rows. You might find you need this if your CPU is not a P200 or greater, or if you are using the Desktop version of SQL Server.

---

3. To find the physical size of the table and verify the number of rows, execute this command:

```
sp_spaceused Publish2
```

SQL Server should report a space usage of about 1680KB.

4. Because you copied the original data many times into the Publish2 table, all the data is duplicate data, and there are no candidate keys available to choose as a primary key. However, you can create one by adding a new column with an identity property. The identity property will ensure that all the values are unique.

```
ALTER TABLE Publish2
            ADD newid INT IDENTITY(1,1)
```

The result is a table with unique values in the new_id column.

5. Now make the new column the primary key, with a nonclustered index:

```
ALTER TABLE Publish2
        ADD CONSTRAINT Publish2PK
        PRIMARY KEY NONCLUSTERED(newid)
```

Now you've got a table that's large enough for you to observe significant improvements in queries. The reason for making the index nonclustered will be explained later.

TIP

For generating test data, the Microsoft Back Office Resource Kit from Microsoft Press contains a utility called Filltabl.exe, which will generate test data. Another tool is TestBytes from LogicWorks (www.logicworks.com). You can download the shareware version from their Web site and use it to generate test data. Both of these tools work best when you have no primary or foreign key constraints on your tables.

Making a Test Script

What you need next are a few queries against the Publish2 table that will help illustrate the Showplan utility. The following script combines a variety of queries that you can analyze using Showplan and also use in the chapters following this one for performance testing. It's saved as Publish2Workload.SQL in the Ch19 folder of the book's CD. ?

```
-- Script to query the table Publish2
-- Count the number of USA entries
SELECT country, COUNT(country)
        FROM Publish2
        GROUP BY country
        HAVING country = 'USA'
GO
-- Insert a set of new rows
INSERT INTO Publish2
        SELECT p.pub_id, p.pub_name, 'Portland',
            'OR', 'USA'
        FROM publishers p
```

```
GO
-- Get a count of cities
SELECT city, COUNT(city)
          FROM Publish2
          GROUP BY city
          ORDER BY 2
GO
-- Change the city name of the new rows
UPDATE Publish2
          SET city = 'Salem'
          WHERE city = 'Portland'
          AND state = 'OR'
GO
-- Correlated Subquery to find count of publishers w/o titles
SELECT COUNT(DISTINCT pub_id)
FROM Publish2 p
WHERE NOT EXISTS
          (SELECT *
          FROM Titles t
          WHERE t.pub_id = p.pub_id)
-- Delete the new rows
DELETE Publish2
          WHERE city = 'Salem'
          AND state = 'OR'
GO
-- Outer Join method of finding all publishers w/o titles
SELECT DISTINCT p.pub_name, t.title
          FROM Publish2 p
          LEFT OUTER JOIN Titles t
          ON p.pub_id = t.pub_id
          WHERE t.title_id IS NULL
```

You'll use the preceding queries for studying query optimization in this chapter, and
for creating workload in the next several chapters.

Graphical Showplan

You can get a graphical picture of how SQL Server will execute a query using the Showplan option of the Query Analyzer. The Query Analyzer will display the query execution plan as a graph showing the number and type of steps that will be used to execute the query. In addition, you can zoom in on the details of each step and get an estimate of the relative cost of the query. The overall goal is to minimize the query cost.

The Execution Plan for a Single Table Query

To see an example of a query execution plan, let's start with the first query from the workload script (Publish2Workload.SQL):

```
-- Count the number of USA entries
SELECT country, COUNT(country)
            FROM Publish2
            GROUP BY country
            HAVING country = 'USA'
```

To see the execution plan (graphical showplan) for this query, click on the Display Execution Plan button, as shown in Figure 19-1, and then execute the query.

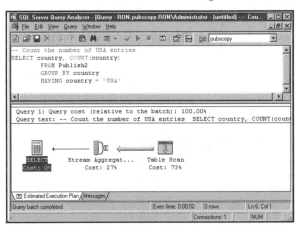

FIGURE 19-1

You can turn on the Graphical Showplan by choosing the Execution Plan toolbar button in the Query Analyzer.

Once you've chosen the option, you can execute the query either by clicking on the right green arrow or by pressing Control+E or Alt+X. The result will show the query execution plan in the lower results pane, as you can see in Figure 19-1.

NOTE

When you've checked the Execution Plan option, the query does not actually execute; instead, the execution plan is displayed.

The lower pane of the Query Analyzer window, which contains the output of the execution plan, is telling you that the query will be executed in the steps shown as nodes in the graph. You can read the steps from right to left. The first step will be a scan of the Publish2 table, followed by a stream aggregate (the COUNT operation in the query), producing the results of the SELECT statement.

The Execution Plan pane shows the query plan for the query, and you can read the plan in more detail by simply dragging your mouse over one of the nodes of the graph and seeing the result. Figure 19-2 shows the result for the Publish2 scan node.

FIGURE 19-2

The initial report from the execution plan estimates costs for the scan of the Publish2 table.

In this case, the plan estimates that the scan of the Publish2 table will cover 27,124 of the 32,768 rows, and total subtree cost is 0.223. The subtree cost is a relative estimate of the execution cost for this part of the query.

The next node of the execution plan is the stream/aggregate step, shown in Figure 19-3.

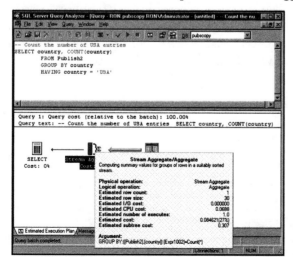

FIGURE 19-3

The execution plan report for the stream/aggregate node shows the estimated cost of the aggregation of the data.

The estimated cost for the aggregation, which is the COUNT() on the groups of rows in the table, is 0.084621, bringing the total subtree cost up to 0.307. As I mentioned earlier, that's a relative number, not an absolute number.

Finally, you can look at the last node of the query, the SELECT node, as shown in Figure 19-4.

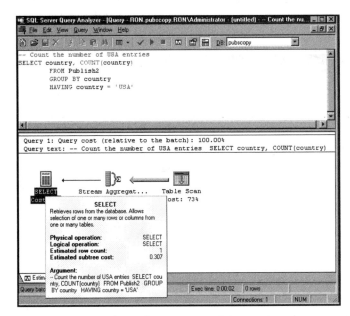

FIGURE 19-4

The SELECT node shows the total cost of the entire query.

As you can see, the final node estimates a return of one row, and a total subtree cost of 0.307, relatively speaking. You'll see this cost come down when you apply indexes using the Index Analysis tool.

The cost of the query is a relative number. Microsoft engineers have said that originally the number started out as the number of seconds on a reference machine. However, the number is not really translatable to other machines except in a relative sense. It's best to establish a benchmark query you wish to use as a reference, and take the numbers from there.

Also, the costing does not take into account the caching of data in memory, and execution plan reuse. You can clear cache memory with two DBCC commands, DROPCLEANBUFFERS and FREEPROCCACHE.

    DBCC DROPCLEANBUFFERS   remove all data from cache

    DBCC FREEPROCCACHE   remove procedure execution plans from cache

So far, you looked at a fairly simple query that SQL Server will execute in three steps: a table scan, a stream aggregate step, and a SELECT operation.

The Execution Plan for a Two-Table Query

Now let's take a look at a more complex query that involves a join operation, also from the workload script, Publish2Workload.SQL. The last query in the workload uses a LEFT OUTER JOIN to make a list of all the publishers that do not have titles:

```
-- Outer Join method of finding all publishers without titles
SELECT DISTINCT p.pub_name
          FROM Publish2 p
          LEFT OUTER JOIN Titles t
          ON p.pub_id = t.pub_id
          WHERE t.title_id IS NULL
```

When the execution plan of this query is formed, the results are shown in Figure 19-5.

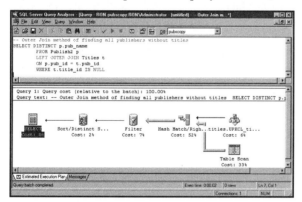

FIGURE 19-5

You can see the extra steps required to execute a LEFT OUTER JOIN *query.*

For the outer join, notice that the query only scans the clustered index for the Titles table, shown in the upper-right corner of the execution plan. It combines the results of that clustered index scan with the results of a scan of the Publish2 table, using a "Hash Match/Right Outer Join" operation, shown in Figure 19-6.

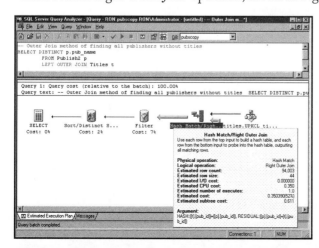

FIGURE 19-6

The Hash operation results in a total subtree cost of 0.661.

Notice at this point that the execution plan shows that a temporary table will be built, in order to create a matching set of rows with the outputs of the first two operations. The hash table contains a set of hash values, based on applying a hashing algorithm to the Publish2 (the top) table id. The hash table then ends up acting something like an index, but can be faster to build and more efficient for large tables.

NOTE

The use of hash operations in execution plans is new with SQL Server 7.

The query then filters and sorts the output, ending up with a total subtree cost of 0.667.

Remember from Chapter 13, "Data Manipulation," that there are two other ways to find the publishers that do not publish titles. One is using the NOT IN function, as in:

```
-- NOT IN method of finding all publishers without titles
SELECT DISTINCT p.pub_name
FROM Publish2 p
WHERE p.pub_id NOT IN
            (SELECT pub_id
            FROM Titles t
            WHERE t.pub_id IS NOT NULL)
```

This query has the execution plan shown in Figure 19-7.

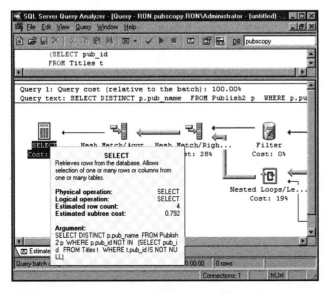

FIGURE 19-7

The NOT IN *execution plan has a total estimated cost of 0.792.*

Again, notice that the SQL Server relational engine is smart enough to use the index of titles, and not the table itself. The NOT IN subtree cost is 0.725 − 0.703 = 0.022, or about three percent less expensive than the LEFT OUTER JOIN.

Finally, you can compare a correlated subquery, NOT EXISTS, form of finding the same results:

```
-- NOT EXISTS method of finding all publishers without titles
SELECT DISTINCT p.pub_name
FROM Publish2 p
WHERE NOT EXISTS
            (SELECT *
            FROM Titles t
            WHERE t.pub_id = p.pub_id)
```

The execution plan results, with the total subtree cost, are shown in Figure 19-8.

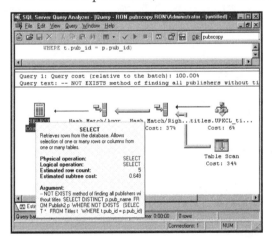

FIGURE 19-8

The NOT EXISTS *query has the fewest steps of all three queries.*

Notice now that the steps are fewer, although the total cost of the query is 0.648, slightly lower than NOT IN version.

You can summarize our findings in the following table:

	LOJ	NOT IN	NOT EXISTS
Number of steps	5	5	4
Total subtree cost	0.667	0.792	0.648

NOTE

In past releases of SQL Server, the NOT IN version of a query was noticeably slower than the equivalent NOT EXISTS. However, with SQL Server 7 you may find that there may no longer a penalty for using the NOT EXISTS form of a query.

Execution Step Operations

There are 68 operations that the SQL Server 7 relational engine can perform during a query. They're documented in Books Online/Optimizing Database Performance/Query Tuning/Using Showplan to Monitor a Database Query/Logical Operators.

You've already seen several of these operations in the prior examples. What each does in detail is an advanced topic in the field of query processing, but that the SQL Server engine exposes them is very valuable. It can help you determine exactly how a query is operating.

Textual Showplan

There is also a textual version of showplan that you can get as an output. It follows the same steps as the graphical version, but other information is presented in a tabular format.

The Query Options Dialog Box

You can get the textual showplan in two ways. First, you can set the option in the Options dialog box from the Query Analyzer. Just click on the toolbar button that says Query Options, and you'll see the dialog box shown in Figure 19-9.

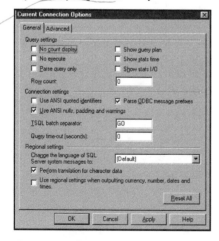

FIGURE 19-9

The Query Options dialog box lets you choose the textual showplan

For more information about the rest of these options, see the beginning of Chapter 12, "Data Definition." In order to show the textual showplan, just check the Show Query Plan check box. Make sure that in the Query Analyzer window, you no longer have the Execution Plan button selected, but instead have the Display Results in Window button selected. Now each query will not be executed, but a textual showplan will result instead. For example, your first query,

```
-- Count the number of USA entries
SELECT country, COUNT(country)
          FROM Publish2
          GROUP BY country
          HAVING country = 'USA'
```

produces the following textual showplan, which has been formatted to fit the
page:StmtText

```
------------------------------------------------------------  |--Stream
```
Aggregate(GROUP BY:([Publish2].[country])
                          DEFINE:([Expr1002]=Count(*)))
          |--Table Scan(OBJECT:([pubscopy].[dbo].[Publish2]),
                          WHERE:([Publish2].[country]='USA'))

(2 row(s) affected)

Only two steps are shown here, as opposed to the graphical plan, and the results are much more difficult to read. Also, all you see are the steps. More information is delivered by the SET SHOWPLAN_ALL command. First, let's look at the SET SHOWPLAN_TEXT command.

The SET SHOWPLAN_TEXT **Command**

You can get the same output as the one from the Query Options tab by using the SHOWPLAN_TEXT command, as follows:

```
SET SHOWPLAN_TEXT ON
GO
-- Count the number of USA entries
SELECT country, COUNT(country)
          FROM Publish2
          GROUP BY country
          HAVING country = 'USA'
GO
SET SHOWPLAN_TEXT OFF
GO
```

WARNING

The SET SHOWPLAN_ commands are independent of the Query Options dialog box. Make sure that you rerun the SET SHOWPLAN commands with the OFF operator to turn off the textual showplans.

The SET SHOWPLAN_ALL Command

You can get the additional textual showplan output by running the SET SHOWPLAN_ALL command. It operates the same way as SET SHOWPLAN_TEXT:

```
SET SHOWPLAN_ALL ON
GO
```

However, the results are far more extensive, and they can be returned in the form of a table, as shown in Figure 19-10.

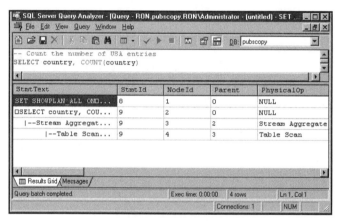

FIGURE 19-10

You can see the SHOWPLAN_ALL *results as a table in the Query Analyzer.*

Here you can ferret out most of the information of the graphical plan, but as with the other textual output, it is much more difficult to read initially.

Interleaving SHOWPLAN and Query Output: the SET STATISTICS PROFILE Command

Both the graphical and textual showplans do not actually execute a query. That's one reason the graphical version is called the estimated query plan. However, sometimes it's useful to have a query plan revealed for a query that actually executes.

You can have the textual output of showplan integrated with an executing query's output using SQL Server 7's new SET STATISTICS PROFILE ON command. It has the same result as textual showplan, but unlike the other showplan commands, the query is actually executed. For example, consider the following query:

```
SET STATISTICS PROFILE ON
GO
-- Count the number of USA entries
```

```
SELECT country, COUNT(country)
         FROM Publish2
         GROUP BY country
         HAVING country = 'USA'
GO
SET STATISTICS PROFILE OFF
GO
```

You'll see the same textual query plan after each query output.

> **TIP**
>
> You can use the SET STATISTICS PROFILE command to see the query plan for stored procedures that create and reference temporary tables. The other showplan commands, and the graphical execution plan, do not actually execute a query and therefore cannot show the plan of a stored procedure that does any data manipulation of a temporary table.

Show Execution Plan

You can also use the Query Analyzer's Show Execution Plan option for the same effect, except that the execution plan is graphical. Show Execution Plan will also execute the query, and return the graphical showplan on the Execution Plan tab of the Query Analyzer results pane.

To set Show Execution Plan on or off, use control-K (^K) to toggle the Show Execution Plan option off the Query menu, or the Show Execution Plan option in the Results icon. In each case, the graphical showplan will be put on the Execution Plan tab of the Query Analyzer results pane. Unlike SET STATISTICS PROFILE ON, the Show Execution Plan is graphical, not textual, and not interleaved with the query results.

Statistics I/O

In addition to the query plan, the Query Analyzer also has a way to show you how a query will use the disk. For these results, you actually have to run the query. Set the Query Options dialog box for Show stats I/O, as shown in Figure 19-11.

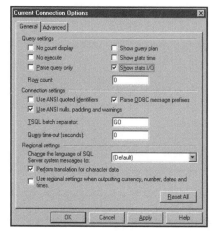

FIGURE 19-11

You can get textual output of execution statistics by selecting the Statistics I/O option in the Query Options dialog box.

The results, for your sample query, are shown in Figure 19-12.

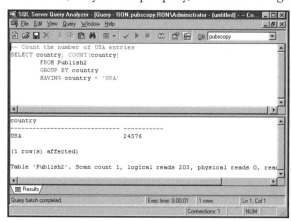

FIGURE 19-12

The Show Stats I/O option gives additional output indicating the number of physical and logical reads of the disk.

The stats I/O readout can tell you how much disk activity was actually used by a query. This can be extremely helpful in query tuning. You get an idea of how much activity there is against the data that is already cached, using the logical reads option. In the preceding query, that stands at 203 I/O's to cache. Also important, the physical reads option tells you how much of the I/O was due to reading pages from disk. Generally, if you cache most of your data, you want to reduce the number of logical reads as much as possible. If your query must go to disk, then you want to reduce the number of physical reads.

NOTE

The first time you run a query, it may have to read data from the disk into cache, and so it will give an artificially high number of physical reads. The second time the query runs, data will be in cache, and the number of physical reads may dramatically decline. However, the number of logical reads should stay constant.

Index Analysis

The Query Analyzer also has a utility that will recommend indexes for a query. It calls the same engine used by the Index Tuning Wizard and the SQL Profiler, which I'll cover in this chapter and in Chapter 21. First, let's talk about indexes in general, and then the Query Analyzer's Index Analysis utility.

SQL Server 7.0 Indexing

A table in SQL Server can have two kinds of indexes: at most one clustered index, and any number (up to 255) of nonclustered indexes.

> **NOTE**
>
> For information about creating and maintaining indexes, see Chapter 12, "Data Definition."

An index is a secondary data storage structure that contains information about accessing data in a table. In other words, one purpose of an index is to provide alternative, faster methods of searching a table. (Another purpose is to enforce a primary key or uniqueness constraint on a table, as you learned in Chapter 12.) An index can provide a faster means of finding data than scanning a table directly, because an index, containing just a small subset of the table's data, is almost always smaller than the table itself. Every index refers to just one table, but a given table can have many indexes. There are two kinds of indexes a table can have: clustered and nonclustered.

SQL Server 7 indexes have a B-tree structure, a tree-like set of levels that the index maintenance routines keep in a balanced structure. For example, let's look at a nonclustered index, shown in Figure 19-13.

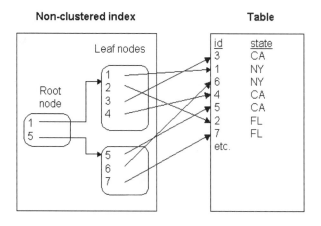

FIGURE 19-13

A nonclustered index does not reorder a table's data.

With a large number or rows, or a table with more than a few columns, an index is much smaller and easier to search than a table. In this case, because the index is nonclustered, the table keeps its original physical order.

A clustered index is an index that actually orders the rows and pages of the table so as to force a physical sorting order on the table. So if you rebuild that index and make it a clustered index, it will reorder the table, as shown in Figure 19-14.

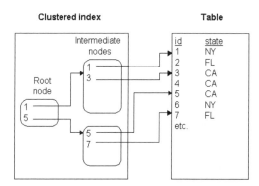

FIGURE 19-14

A clustered index reorders the table's rows.

Because a clustered index reorders the table, its leaf rows coincide with the actual rows of the table.

If there is no clustered index on a table, all the nonclustered indexes point directly to the rows of the table being indexed. Once there's a clustered index on a table, however, each nonclustered index uses the clustered index's key to find its way to the table. So if you continue your example, a clustered index on the id and a nonclustered index on the state column would end up looking like what you see in Figure 19-15.

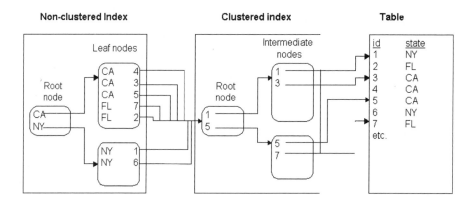

FIGURE 19-15

A nonclustered index seeks through a clustered index if one is available.

This process is carried out to minimize the changes to the nonclustered indexes due to page splits in the table. In earlier releases of SQL Server, prior to 7, every index would have to be updated when a change occurred and data had to be rearranged into new pages, because the leaf nodes of all indexes pointed to the pages. In SQL Server 7, the nonclustered indexes do not point to the pages and rows of the table directly, if there is a clustered index on the table.

T IP

When you have a table that will be queried for range scans, such as price or date, those columns are good candidates for a clustered index. However, remember to keep clustered index keys as narrow as possible.

You can find out the indexes on a table by using the `sp_helpindex` system stored procedure, or by looking at a table's properties in Enterprise Manager. For example, you can issue:

```
sp_helpindex authors
```

to get a list of all the indexes on the authors table.

WARNING

It's important to keep the keys of clustered indexes narrow, because they get copied into the nonclustered key. Always keep a clustered index as narrow as possible, on one column, and on something short, like an integer.

So what kinds of indexes should you build on a table? That takes you to the Index Analysis Utility.

The Index Analysis Utility

In addition to finding out about the query plan and I/O statistics, you can have the Query Analyzer recommend an index for a particular query. You just choose the Perform Index Analysis option from the menu, as shown in Figure 19-16.

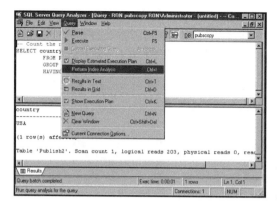

FIGURE 19-16

You can have the Query Analyzer recommend indexes for a query by choosing the Perform Index Analysis option from the Query menu.

When you execute a query using this option, the Query Analyzer has the Index Tuning Wizard analyze the query for possible indexes that might improve its performance. In the case of the preceding query, the results are shown in Figure 19-17.

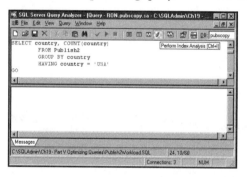

FIGURE 19-17

The Query Analyzer will allow you to build the recommended index for the selected query.

The suggested indexes will be numbered in the form `<tablename><sequence number>`. If you click on the Accept button, the Query Analyzer will create the index at that time.

If you now rerun the graphical query plan, the index causes a new result, as shown in Figure 19-18.

FIGURE 19-18

The new index dramatically decreases the cost of the query.

Notice that the query now just reads the index; it does not bother to read the table at all! The index changes the query into a "covered query," one in which the index covers the query and the table needn't even be read.

The Show stats I/O also shows a dramatic decrease, as shown in Figure 19-19.

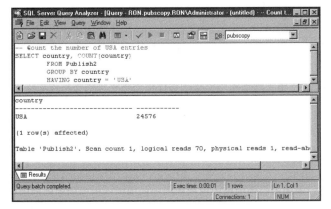

FIGURE 19-19

The new index also reduces the number of logical reads.

As you can see, the results have dramatically improved with the new index. The results of the new index for our sample query are summarized in the following table:

	Without Index	With Index
Query cost	0.307	0.151
Logical reads	203	70

In Chapter 21, where you will use the Profiler, you'll see how to get the actual time used by SQL Server for the query.

> ### NOTE
> Read-ahead reads are effectively physical reads and contribute to the cost of a query. If you see no physical reads, but you do see read-ahead reads, re-execute the query a couple of times to see if the number goes down.

The Index Tuning Wizard

You can use the Index Tuning Wizard to analyze and create indexes based on a workload. The Index Tuning Wizard calls the same engine used by the Index Analysis option in the Query Analyzer. To run the Wizard, you must first select a database within Enterprise Manager, and then bring up the Select Wizard dialog box (you can press the wand icon in the toolbar.) In the Management section, find the Index Tuning Wizard.

Once the Wizard is up, and you choose a server and database, you can also decide whether to keep all current indexes, and whether to perform a complete analysis (of the entire database). Generally you'll want to perform a complete analysis, unless your

---

NOTE

Do not confuse the Index Tuning Wizard with the Create Index Wizard. The latter just goes through the process of creating a single index.

---

database is so large that the analysis takes too much time.

Once you've made these decisions, the Wizard asks whether you want to use a workload file or create a workload file on your own. A workload file is just a script of queries that the Wizard can analyze, or a table of activity saved from the SQL Profiler.

If you choose a workload file, you can load it by browsing the disk. In your case, you'll use Publish2Workload.SQL, included in Ch19 on this book's CD. If you decide to create a workload file on your own, the Wizard will bring up the SQL Server Profiler, from which you can record activity into a .SQL script or a table.

Once you've decided to use your own workload file, the Wizard will present you with a selection dialog box to choose either a script or a table, as shown in Figure 19-20.

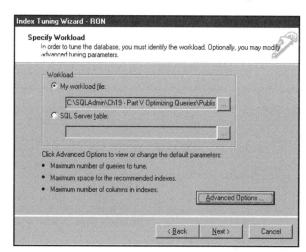

FIGURE 19-20

You can analyze a workload according to a table or a saved script.

Since you will use the script Publish2Workload.SQL, the next step will ask what tables to tune. The Wizard defaults to all tables, which in your case is not necessary. You'll just use the Publish2 table and the Titles table. When the Wizard finishes its job, it will present results in a dialog box like that shown in Figure 19-21.

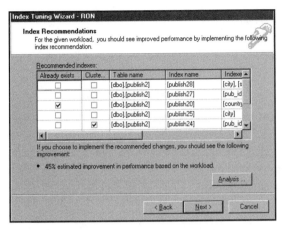

FIGURE 19-21

The Index Tuning Wizard recommends new indexes.

Notice in this case that the Wizard has recommended one new index, on the Publish2 pub_id. Those indexes listed with the check mark already exist in the database. The Analysis button gives more information about the projected usage of the indexes in a variety of reports, as shown in Figure 19-22.

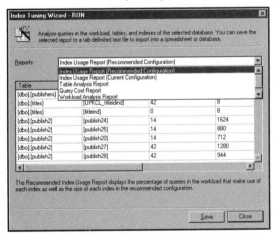

FIGURE 19-22

The Analysis dialog box shows you a number of reports that you can save on disk.

Once you close this dialog box and accept the recommendations, the Wizard will ask you whether you want to apply the changes now or schedule them for later. In addition, you can save the recommendations to a script file and apply and/or edit the script yourself.

Index Distribution Statistics

SQL Server 7 maintains a set of statistical data on each index, and also on selected unindexed columns, called distribution statistics. Using a sampling interval, the query engine reads the index keys and the table and determines the overall density of the key values.

A highly selective index is one whose key values return a small set of rows, and therefore it has a low density. A unique key, such as a primary key, has the highest selectivity, returning one row per key value. The more selective an index, the better it is for key-valued searches. Sometimes SQL Server will not use an index with low selectivity, because the query might require more I/O using the index than just scanning the table.

What's important is to have current distribution statistics on all your indexes and relevant columns, so that SQL Server 7's query optimizer can choose the best strategy for evaluating a query. Since it's possible for index statistics to go out of date, occasionally you'll need to rebuild them.

To rebuild the statistics for a given index, you can use the UPDATE STATISTICS command. In its most basic format, the command syntax is as follows:

```
UPDATE STATISTICS <table> [, <index>]
```

So to rebuild the statistics on the Publish2 table, just execute the following Transact-SQL command:

```
UPDATE STATISTICS Publish2
```

NOTE

SQL Server 7.0 always keeps indexes themselves in synch with their tables. It's just the distribution statistics that can become out of sync. For very dynamic tables, you should update the statistics on a periodic basis, such as every night.

To see the distribution statistics for a given table and index, just use the DBCC SHOW_STATISTICS command. For example,

```
DBCC SHOW_STATISTICS (publish2, publish20)
```

In the result, pay close attention to the All density column. That is an indicator of the selectivity. Selectivity and density are inverses; the lower the density figure, the higher the selectivity.

In addition to keeping statistics on indexes, SQL Server will also keep indexes on columns. You can let SQL Server automatically generate them, or you can create them yourself with the CREATE STATISTICS command. For example, the following command creates statistics on the country column of the Publish2 table:

```
CREATE STATISTICS country_stats
ON Publish2(country)
```

> **NOTE**
>
> General-purpose indexes should have high selectivity and therefore low density. Special-purpose indexes with low selectivity might still greatly help a particular query, however.

Summary

Query optimization is one of the most important performance considerations in a database application. SQL Server 7.0 provides you with an important set of tools to assist in that task: the new graphical showplan with estimated query cost, and the index tuning wizard. Next, let's take a look at another aspect of performance, monitoring current activity.

Chapter 20

Concurrency Tools

In This Chapter

◆ Locking in SQL Server 7

◆ Viewing locks

◆ The Current Activity Utility

◆ Blocking

◆ Deadlocks

Another performance problem arises when queries (extracts or updates) conflict with each other. To see how this can be so, consider two main requirements that SQL Server, as an RDBMS, must satisfy.

First of all, SQL Server must handle queries from many different sources at once, in other words, concurrently. But second, SQL Server must handle all queries in the context of a transaction, and each transaction must have a degree of isolation so that it maintains a consistent picture of the database.

SQL Server preserves the ACID properties of a transaction using a locking strategy. (You can learn more about the ACID properties in Chapter 16, "Transactions.") Queries can conflict with each other when the transaction of one query requires a resource that some other query's transaction has locked, resulting in the problems of blocking and deadlocks.

In this chapter, I'll cover the basics of SQL Server locking, tools to monitor concurrency, and how to monitor blocking and deadlocks.

Locking in SQL Server 7

SQL Server must ensure the consistency of the data as it appears to each transaction, and make it appear to the transaction that it is the only one on the database. While a transaction is running, if it changes data, no other transaction may change the same data at the same time. It may also be necessary that no other transaction can read the changes until the first transaction completes. After a commit or rollback occurs—finishing the transaction—other transactions can then read or change its results. To keep each transaction's data protected while it is operating, SQL Server places locks on its resources.

SQL Server Data Storage

To understand how SQL Server locks its resources, it's important to recall the fundamental units of storage in SQL Server 7. SQL Server stores all data, including tables, indexes, long text, and images, on 8K pages. Within those pages, you can have any number of data rows, or index keys. In addition, SQL Server will allocate those pages by groups of eight, each called an extent. A small table may reside on a single page or within a single extent, whereas a large table may span several extents. To sum up, the hierarchy of data storage is:

Table

Extent (eight contiguous pages)

Page (8K bytes)

Row or Key

For example, if you execute the sp_spaceused system stored procedure against the Publish2 table you saw created in Chapter 19, you'll get the following results:

```
name       rows    reserved  data      index_size   unused

.........  ......  .........  ........  ............ .......

Publish2   35806   3408 KB   1840 KB   1368 KB      200 KB
```

The Publish2 table occupies 3,408 / 8 = 426 8K pages, or 426 / 8 = 5.25 extents. These include 1,840 / 8 = 230 data pages, and 1,368 / 8 = 171 index pages. There are 200 / 8 = 25 pages of unused space in the table.

Resources

When SQL Server locks a portion of a data table or index, it can lock at any of these levels. There are two kinds of resources that SQL Server will lock: data and indexes. For each kind of resource, the levels match the data storage levels you just saw, as shown in the following matrix:

Resource	Lock Level	Description
Data	Row (RID, row id)	The lowest-level data lock
	Page (PAG)	The 8K storage unit for table data
	Extent(EXT)	A group of eight data pages
Index	Key (KEY)	The lowest-level index lock
	Page (PAG)	The 8K storage unit for indexes
	Extent(EXT)	A group of eight index pages
Both	Table (TAB)	The entire table, both data and indexes
	Database (DB)	The entire database, all tables and indexes

So when SQL Server 7.0 locks data in a table, it can do so at the row id (RID) level, the page level, or at the extent level. Similarly, when SQL Server locks an index, it can lock at the key range, index page, or extent level. However, if a transaction locks a table, it is also getting the same kind of lock on the table's indexes.

> **NOTE**
>
> Row locks for data and key range locks for indexes are new to SQL Server 7.0. Previous releases of SQL Server could only lock data at the page and table level, and indexes at the page level.

Lock Modes

There are two major kinds of lock modes that SQL Server can apply to a resource: the lock mode for actually reading or writing data, or more specialized lock modes that signal an intention to lock or prevent the schema of a table from being changed.

The read/write lock modes are:

- A shared lock, abbreviated with as S, allows others to read the data and also get a shared lock, but not write to it. This is the kind of lock required by the SQL SELECT statement.

- An exclusive lock, abbreviated as X, prevents others from gaining any kind of lock. An exclusive lock of a resource is what is needed to change any data, so it's required by an INSERT, UPDATE, or DELETE statement. When obtained, the exclusive lock can be the only lock on the resource.

- An update lock, abbreviated U, starts out as a special type of shared lock and becomes an exclusive lock. Only one update lock is allowed on a resource at a time. The update lock can escalate to an exclusive lock once there are no more shared (S) locks on the resource.

The more specialized lock modes are:

- An intent lock (I) mode indicates an intention to gain a read/write lock at a lower level. The intent lock modes can be combined with shared and exclusive, resulting in intent shared (IS) and intent exclusive (IX) lock modes.

- A schema lock mode, indicating that a table schema must be locked. There are two kinds of schema locks: schema stability (Sch-S), which prevents a table schema from being changed, and schema modification (Sch-M), which allows a transaction to change a table schema. There can be only one Sch-M lock on a table at a time, and only if there are no other locks on any portion of the table. An Sch-M lock is different from an exclusive lock on a table because it is not a lock of the table's data, but a lock on the schema.

SQL Server will select the type of lock automatically, and there's seldom any reason to override it.

Key Range Lock Modes

In addition to the lock modes for data just described, SQL Server has a special set of lock modes for locking a key range, that is, a range of key values in a table's index. Key range locking can be used to protect rows from being locked, without keeping a lock on the individual rows. Each key range lock designation is made up of the kind of range, combined with a row.

The row components are similar to the read/write data locks:

S	Protect the row for shared locks
U	Protect the row for update
X	Protect the row for exclusive
Null	No row is protected (abbreviated Nul)

The range components indicate the kind of locking made on the index:

IS	Intent shared lock on the index entry
IU	Intent-update lock on the index entry
IIN	Intent-insert with null resource
Null	No protection on index entries (abbreviated Nul)

When SQL Server reports that an index entry (key, page, extent) is locked, it will indicate the key range locked, followed by the type of protection given the data table rows. The combinations SQL Server will actually use are:

Nul-S	No index entries, shared lock on row
IS-S	Intent-shared for the index entries, shared lock on the row
IIN-Nul	Intent-insert with null resource, no lock on the row
IS-U	Intent-shared on the range of index keys, protect the row for update
IU-X	Intent-update on the index key range, lock the data resource exclusively

Viewing Locks

You can view the locks on a database using the `sp_lock` stored procedure:

```
sp_lock [process id]
```

When `sp_lock` runs, it will tell you the locks held by your process id.

To view the output of `sp_lock` in a meaningful way, let's set up an example. Assume you've defined a login called TestLogin that has been aliased to dbo in the Pubs or Pubscopy databases. Then bring up the SQL Server 7 Query Analyzer from the Start menu, and log in using TestLogin.

In the first query window, let's start with the following query, which you can find on this book's CD as Chap20\3windows.SQL:

```
-- Query window 1
BEGIN TRAN
SELECT *
            FROM authors WITH (SERIALIZABLE)
            WHERE au_id = '172-32-1176'
-- Execute the following to end the transaction
/*
IF @@TRANCOUNT > 0
   COMMIT
PRINT @@TRANCOUNT -- make sure this reads 0
*/
```

In the second query window,

```
-- Query window 2
BEGIN TRAN
UPDATE authors
            SET contract = 1
            WHERE au_id = '172-32-1176'
--ROLLBACK
```

Then in the third query window, execute:

```
--Query window 3
EXEC sp_lock
```

You should see the results of the third query looking like those in Figure 20-1.

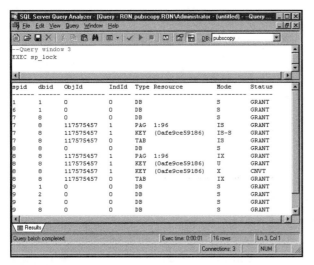

FIGURE 20-1

You can observe locks using the sp_lock *stored procedure.*

Notice that the first column is spid, short for server process id, the ids assigned by SQL Server to its connections. To find out more about spids and logins, just execute the sp_who2 system stored procedure from Enterprise Manager's Query Analyzer. You can see sample results in Figure 20-2.

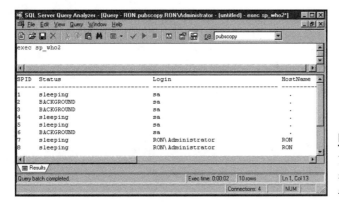

FIGURE 20-2

You can relate spids to login names using the sp_who2 *system stored procedure.*

The output of this sp_who tells you that spids 8, 9, and 10 are associated with TestLogin. Since spids are assigned in a first-come order, the first query window is spid 8, the second, 9, and the third, 10.

The First Transaction

Now you can see what kinds of locks the first query window produced. Normally locks are not held very long in SQL Server. But since the first query holds a transaction open and uses the SERIALIZABLE table hint on its SELECT command, it does not give up its locks and you can observe them. For spid 8, the locks from Figure 20-1 are:

spid	dbid	ObjId	IndId	Type	Resource	Mode	Status
7	8	0	0	DB		S	GRANT
7	8	117575457	1	PAG	1:96	IS	GRANT
7	8	117575457	1	KEY	(0afe9ce59186)	IS-S	GRANT
7	8	117575457	0	TAB		IS	GRANT

What this means is that the first query window, whose connection is spid 7, has a shared lock on the database with id 8, namely Pubscopy. Notice it has a shared lock on the entire database, which you can tell from the first row's data: the DB in the type column, and S in the Mode column. It's been granted the lock, which you can tell from the GRANT in the Status column.

Also, spid 7 has intent shared locks on the page of file id 1, page 96, which you can tell from the second row's PAG in the Type column, and the 1:96 in the Resource column. The IS lock simply indicates that this transaction may get a shared lock on data on that page.

The third row shows that spid 7 has a lock on the index for the Authors table, preventing any change to the table through a key range lock.

The final row shows that spid 7 has an (intent shared) lock on the entire Authors table. The id of the Authors table is 117575457, which you can determine by:

```
SELECT OBJECT_NAME(117575457)
```

NOTE

These locks are persistent because you did not commit the transaction. They will remain until the transaction is committed or rolled back. The sp_lock system stored procedure shows the locks that have been kept on the data by that transaction.

The Second Transaction

Now let's look at the results from the second query window, which does an update:

spid	dbid	ObjId	IndId	Type	Resource	Mode	Status
8	8	0	0	DB		S	GRANT
8	8	117575457	1	PAG	1:96	IX	GRANT
8	8	117575457	1	KEY	(0afe9ce59186)	U	GRANT
8	8	117575457	1	KEY	(0afe9ce59186)	X	CNVT
8	8	117575457	0	TAB		IX	GRANT

The second query, which contained an update statement, cannot finish until the first transaction commits or rolls back. Nevertheless, it does get some locks, including a shared lock on the database, an intent-exclusive lock on the page and table, and an update lock that will convert to an exclusive lock on the index. It is ready to act.

Commit the First Transaction

Go to the first query window, scroll down, find the COMMIT command and execute it. Now go to the third query window and re-execute sp_lock. When you commit the transaction in the first query window and then look to see what locks remain, you can see how the update lock of the second transaction became an exclusive lock. A subset of the sp_lock output now reads:

spid	dbid	ObjId	IndId	Type	Resource	Mode	Status
8	8	0	0	DB		S	GRANT
8	8	117575457	1	PAG	1:96	IX	GRANT
8	8	117575457	1	KEY	(0afe9ce59186)	X	GRANT
8	8	117575457	0	TAB		IX	GRANT

Because the update has already taken place, no exclusive lock is required on the page. However, since the transaction is still open, the IX locks on the page and table signal the possibility of reacquiring an exclusive lock on the page, and the key range exclusive lock protects the row and effectively keeps it locked.

To clean up, just execute the ROLLBACK command, and roll back the unfinished transaction.

The Current Activity Utility

You can also see locks and other activity in a graphical format using the Current Activity dialog box in Enterprise Manager. It shows locks along with blocking, which you'll explore in the next section.

Process Information Node

You can find the Current Activity dialog box by opening the Management node and then Current Activity within Enterprise Manager. If you restart the scenario created in the prior section, with the first transaction uncommitted, and the second transaction waiting, and drill down to Process Info, you'll see results like those in Figure 20-3.

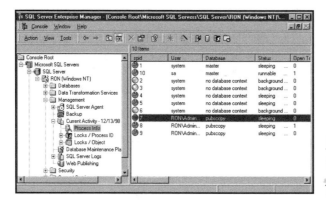

FIGURE 20-3

You can monitor current process information with the Current Activity utility.

The details pane of Enterprise Manager gives you information about each server process id (spid), by number. You can scroll to find out information for each spid. You can determine:

user name

database

status

number of open transactions

type of command

application name (if any)

wait time (time spent so far waiting)

wait type (i.e. status)

wait resources being used

CPU time (consumed so far)

physical IO (count)

memory usage

login time

last batch (sent)

host name

network library

network address

blocked by (spid number, if any)

blocking (spid number, if any)

TIP

To scroll the current activity information in the details pane, expand the Enterprise Manager window within the MMC console.

Too see details about any given spid's activity, you can either double-click over the spid in the details pane, or right-click and choose Properties. The dialog box in Figure 20-4 shows the details for spid number 7.

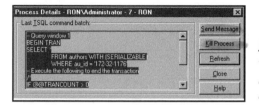

FIGURE 20-4

You can determine a spid's current transaction by examining its Properties.

The Locks/Process ID Node

The Locks/Process ID node shows you each spid that currently has locks. You can drill down to a particular spid to see what it has locked. Figure 20-5 shows the locks for spid 8.

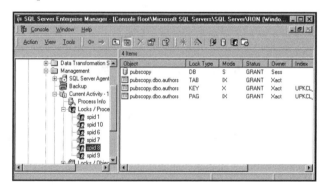

FIGURE 20-5

The Process ID/Locks node contains information about each spid's locks.

Notice how closely the detail matches that from the stored procedure, `sp_lock`.

The Locks/Object Node

The third node organizes the current activity information by object locked, as shown in Figure 20-6.

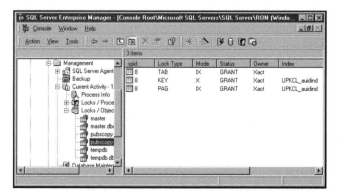

FIGURE 20-6

The Locks/Object node shows information about each locked object.

Again, if you double-click or inspect the properties of the lock, you'll see the transaction associated with this spid.

Current Activity Options

When you inspect the properties of a spid or locked object, and see the transaction, you'll notice the option to send a message and kill the spid.

Send Message allows you to send a message to a spid when you're on the Server Activity or Detail Activity tabs. This is a message sent over the network, perhaps to a blocking process. Kill Process brings up a dialog box in which a system administrator can terminate a blocking spid (process.)

The information in the Current Activity nodes is actually a snapshot of the moment in time when you first selected it. Consequently, it can get out of date. To extract current data, just right-click over the Current Activity node and choose Refresh.

> **NOTE**
>
> The Current Activity dialog box does not present lock activity in as compact a format as the sp_lock system stored procedure. Until it improves, you will probably find sp_lock and sp_blockinglocks more useful.

Let's now take a look at using the sp_who system stored procedure, to detect blocking.

Blocking

You've already seen an example of blocking, in the Update command in Query Window 2. It could not execute because it was waiting for the transaction in Query Window 1 to finish.

Blocking occurs when one transaction has a number of locks that another transaction wants, but the first transaction has not yet released them. As soon as the first transaction releases the locks, the second and other transactions will be able to finish.

> **NOTE**
>
> If a transaction cannot finish because it is being blocked by one of the transactions it is blocking, then a deadlock condition occurs and one of the transactions will be terminated. I'll cover deadlocks in the section after this one.

Simulating Blocking

To simulate a blocking condition, where one user's transaction blocks another user's activity, you can start a transaction from one query window but not commit it, and then try to access the same table from another query window. This is the same strategy you used before when looking at locks.

Close out the current windows you have in the Query Analyzer, and enter two more queries. First, execute the following query in one query window:

```
BEGIN TRAN
UPDATE authors
            SET contract = 0
            WHERE contract = 0
```

And in a second query window, execute the following:

```
SELECT *
            FROM authors
```

Now execute both queries. One will complete (but note, there's no commit!), and the other will hang. If you then consult the Server Activity tab, you'll see the first spid blocking the second.

Lock Timeout

The second transaction can wait indefinitely, or you can set a lock timeout that will cause the transaction's command to end after a stipulated period of time, using the `SET LOCK_TIMEOUT` command. The general syntax is:

```
SET LOCK_TIMEOUT <timeout_period>
```

where the timeout period is a number of milliseconds.

Now replace the second query window with:

```
SET LOCK_TIMEOUT 2000
GO
SELECT *
            FROM authors
```

You'll now see that the second query terminates after two seconds. Lock timeouts are set per connection, and you can get each connection's current lock timeout value from the `@@LOCK_TIMEOUT` system function.

The sp_who **System Stored Procedure**

You can also observe blocking from the sp_who stored procedure. For example, in the situation just described, where the unfinished UPDATE is blocking the SELECT statement, the result of executing sp_who is shown in Figure 20-7.

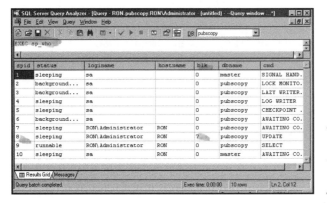

FIGURE 20-7

The output of the sp_who system stored procedure is clearer when sent to the grid format.

Here you can see from the blk column that spid 8 is being blocked by spid 7.

NOTE

You'll have to scroll the output or arrange the grid in order to see the blocking information for the sp_who system stored procedure. Blocking information is much more readily observable from the Current Activity utility.

You can also use the sp_who2 system stored procedure as an alternate to sp_who. It shows the same information as sp_who, but in a somewhat better format, as you can see in Figure 20-8

By having a Blocked by column, sp_who makes it much clearer which spid is the blocker, and which is the blockee.

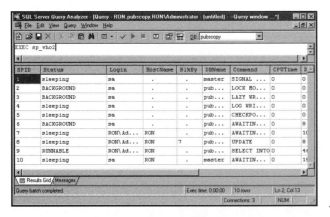

FIGURE 20-8

The output of the sp_who2 system stored procedure is somewhat clearer and more informative than that from sp_who.

What happens when a blocking process is also blocked, by the same process it is blocking? That's a deadlock, which takes you to your last topic.

Deadlocks

No discussion of concurrency issues is complete without a discussion of deadlocks. A deadlock is an impossible situation, a case where two transactions need each other's locked resources and neither can finish until they do. SQL Server periodically scans its locking information looking for deadlocks, and when it finds one, it will cancel one of the queries. In a transaction, you can test for message 1205 to determine whether your transaction has been rolled back due to a deadlock and needs to be restarted.

There are two kinds of deadlocks: a cycle deadlock and a conversion deadlock.

A Cycle Deadlock

A cycle deadlock occurs when one transaction has a resource exclusively locked that another transaction will need, and the second transaction has a resource exclusively locked that the first will need. It's impossible for either one of the transactions to finish, so a deadlock results.

To simulate a cycle deadlock, you can use two query windows again. Make sure that all transactions have been completed. In the first query window, enter the following:

```
-- Cycle Deadlock Step 1 - start transaction 1
BEGIN TRAN
UPDATE authors
          SET contract = 0
          WHERE contract = 0
-- Step 3 - now try to update the locked titles table
UPDATE titles
          SET ytd_sales = ytd_sales
          WHERE ytd_sales IS NOT NULL
```

In the second query window, enter the following:

```
-- Step 2- start a transaction 2
BEGIN TRAN
UPDATE titles
```

```
                SET ytd_sales = ytd_sales
                WHERE ytd_sales IS NOT NULL
-- Step 4 - now try to update the locked titles table
UPDATE authors
                SET contract = 0
                WHERE contract = 0
```

Execute the steps in sequence. In step 1, select the BEGIN TRAN through the first UPDATE statement, and execute it. Then do the same for the remaining steps, selecting the entire step and executing just that portion. The results in one of the windows will be something like that in Figure 20-9.

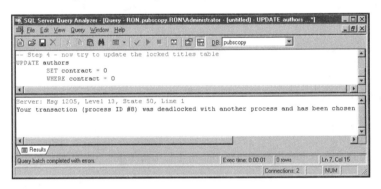

FIGURE 20-9

SQL Server detects deadlocks and will select one of the transactions as the victim.

You can't really predict which one will be chosen as the victim, so make sure to check both windows.

What happened is that each transaction is blocked by the other, and it becomes logically impossible for either transaction to finish. You can see this illustrated in Figure 20-10.

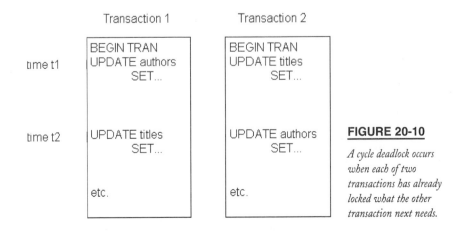

FIGURE 20-10

A cycle deadlock occurs when each of two transactions has already locked what the other transaction next needs.

Note that the transactions do not really need to be very similar at all or execute exactly simultaneously. However, the transactions must have some requirement to change data, and therefore use the UPDATE, INSERT, or DELETE commands. If each transaction only did SELECTs, no deadlocks would ever occur, because SELECT statements never require exclusive locks.

A good way to avoid cycle deadlocks is to always build similar transactions referencing the tables in the same order. Then two transactions will not have already locked what the other needs.

A Conversion Deadlock

A conversion deadlock occurs when each transaction has a shared lock on the same resource, and then each of them tries to escalate and change the data. Again, it becomes impossible for either of the transactions to finish, and a deadlock results.

To simulate a conversion deadlock, use two query windows again. In the first query window, enter the following:

```
-- Conversion Deadlock Step 1 - start transaction 1
BEGIN TRAN
SELECT *
          FROM authors WITH (SERIALIZABLE)
          WHERE au_id = '238-95-7766'
-- Step 3 - now try to change the data
UPDATE authors
          SET contract = contract
          WHERE au_id = '238-95-7766'
```

In the second query window, enter the following:

```
-- Conversion Deadlock Step 2 - start transaction 2
BEGIN TRAN
SELECT *
          FROM authors WITH (SERIALIZABLE)
          WHERE au_id = '238-95-7766'
-- Step 4 - now try to change the data
UPDATE authors
          SET contract = contract
          WHERE au_id = '238-95-7766'
```

In this case, one of the windows will return the same deadlock message.

What happened? After each transaction gets its shared locks, it holds them to the end of the transaction because of the HOLDLOCK optimizer hint. (For more about optimizer hints, see the section at the end of this chapter.) Then each tries to get an exclusive lock, while holding the shared lock. You can see this illustrated in Figure 20-11.

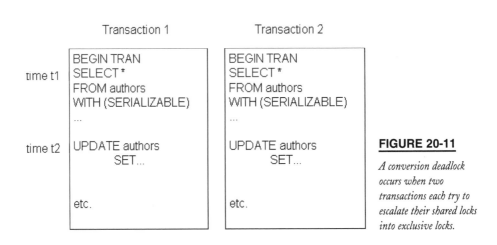

FIGURE 20-11

A conversion deadlock occurs when two transactions each try to escalate their shared locks into exclusive locks.

The reason you might want to hold a shared lock is to determine whether you want to do the update against some data, based on some condition that you look up first with the SELECT command.

> **NOTE**
>
> To avoid deadlocks, an application should keep transactions as short as possible and try to access resources in the same sequence across transactions.

Setting Deadlock Priority

When SQL Server detects this situation, it will choose one of the transactions as a deadlock victim, based on which one is the least costly to roll back. You can override this with the DEADLOCK_PRIORITY setting. The syntax is as follows:

```
SET DEADLOCK_PRIORITY <LOW | NORMAL | @var>
```

You can set a deadlock priority low, volunteering a transaction to be the victim, or else just set it back to normal. You can also put the strings 'low' or 'normal' into a variable and use that in place of the LOW or NORMAL keywords.

Locking Hints

As your final concurrency topic, you can add hints to queries to force a certain type of locking. Normally, SQL Server will do the correct job of locking, but occasionally you may have a query that needs a certain type of locking forced upon it, and you can do that with the locking hints.

There are essentially two types of locking hints: the first set deals with isolation levels, and the second set deals with physical locking.

Isolation Level Hints

You place a locking hint on a table in a query using the WITH syntax as in the following example:

```
SELECT *
        FROM authors WITH (SERIALIZABLE)
```

You place the hint right after the table name. The WITH is not required but is advisable for readability.

The isolation level hints match up with the isolation levels of transactions you learned about in Chapter 16, "Transactions." Since there are four isolation levels, there are four classes of hints, as you can see in the following table:

Isolation Level	Locking Hint
Read Uncommitted	READUNCOMMITTED (or NOLOCK)
Read Committed	READCOMMITTED
Repeatable Read	REPEATABLEREAD
Serializable	SERIALIZABLE (or HOLDLOCK)

NOTE

The NOLOCK hint is equivalent to the READUNCOMMITTED, and the HOLDLOCK hint is equivalent to the SERIALIZABLE. The NOLOCK and HOLDLOCK terms are not ANSI standard, so it's better to use their replacement terms.

The default isolation level for SQL Server is READCOMMITTED, so it's as though every query runs with that locking hint option. What this means is that in a transaction, a data read at the beginning of a transaction may not return the same results as when it is executed again later in the transaction. However, you will never read any uncommitted data. For more information, see the coverage of isolation levels in Chapter 16, "Transactions."

You can make the locking looser, by using READUNCOMMITTED, and your query will be able to read uncompleted (and therefore possibly phantom) data. This can be valuable if you want to scan a table but do not require exact data.

Or you can make your query require that it read the same each time in the transaction, with REPEATABLEREAD or SERIALIZABLE. Then the shared locks of the query will be held until the end of the transaction.

Physical Locking Hints

The locking hints that actually specify what locks to hold are:

```
READPAST
ROWLOCK
PAGLOCK
TABLOCK
TABLOCKX
UPDLOCK
```

The READPAST hint tells a query to skip past all exclusively locked resources in order to produce a fast result. For example, you could issue:

```
SELECT *
FROM Authors READPAST
```

and the SELECT will skip past any rows exclusively locked. However, the READPAST hint cannot read data from an exclusively locked table.

The ROWLOCK, PAGLOCK, and TABLOCK hints tell SQL Server to gain those levels of locks for the designated table. The TABLOCKX and UPDLOCK hints force exclusive locks, even if your query is just a simple SELECT-type table scan.

WARNING

SQL Server's query engine has been finely tuned to choose the best level of locking. Use locking hints with care, and only when you know for sure that your hints will improve a query or are the only way to get the data you need. As one of the people involved with the Microsoft relational engine said at a presentation, "hints are evil."

Summary

Database locking strategies are another way of managing and tuning performance. SQL Server 7 adds data page row locking and index key range locking to better manage concurrency. You can use the system stored procedures sp_who, sp_who2, and sp_lock to monitor current activity, along with the Current Activity utility in Enterprise Manager. Now let's turn to another tool for monitoring SQL Server performance, the Profiler.

Chapter 21

Profiler and Perfmon

In This Chapter

◆ The SQL Server trace architecture

◆ Creating a trace

◆ Some sample traces

◆ Profiling an application

◆ SQL Server and NT Performance Monitor

◆ Some useful Perfmon SQL counters

SQL Server 7 gives you two major tools to monitor your SQL server. SQL Server Profiler lets you trace SQL Server activity based on selected events emitted by the SQL Server query and storage engines. You can use the Profiler to analyze the behavior and performance of traced server activity, and you can replay the same traces on the server.

When you choose the Performance Monitor option from the SQL Server 7 menu, the NT Performance Monitor (a.k.a. "Perfmon") is loaded using a preselected set of SQL Server counters. In this chapter, you'll examine both utilities.

The SQL Server Trace Architecture

The purpose of making a trace in SQL Server 7 is to capture the events that are emitted from the SQL Server relational or storage engine. You capture those events into a queue that you've defined ahead of time, you can filter the queue, and then direct the queue to the Profiler screen, a table, or a file.

A good way to think about tracing SQL Server events is to picture them as captured in a two-dimensional table, as shown in Figure 21-1.

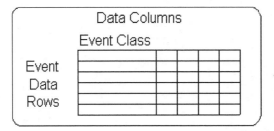

FIGURE 21-1

You can view the results of a trace as a two-dimensional table with queued data.

The table consists of columns that define the data elements that you'll collect. The rows contain the event data. Because the event rows are captured sequentially over time, they form a queue.

One of the columns in the table is the Event Class column, which contains the type of event. This column provides the outermost level of selection and definition for the results of the table.

Now, you could use all available columns for each event class, but that would be a waste of resources. Not every column is relevant for each event type. Consequently, when you define the queued results table of your trace, you define both the structure and content of the table. You define the structure by picking the data columns. You define the content of the resulting table by choosing the event classes you want to trace, and by optionally adding filtering to specifically include or exclude certain events.

After you've defined the results queue and added any filters, you can start collecting trace data. You can direct the results of the trace to the Profiler window, a trace file, or a data table in SQL Server. The overall architecture of the tracing system is shown in Figure 21-2.

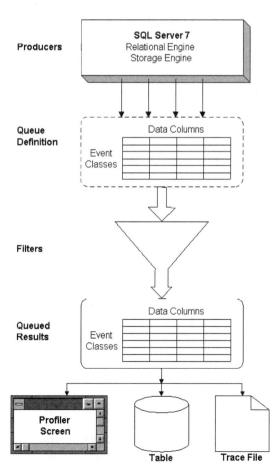

FIGURE 21-2

The overall architecture of the SQL Server tracing system stems from the Relational and Storage Engines emitting events that the tracing process can capture in a queue.

Client-Side and Server-Side Queues

In Figure 21-2, you can see all the various steps required to trace in SQL Server 7. The results of your trace can be queued up using the SQL Server Profiler utility, which is a client-side utility that stores the queued results temporarily. From the Profiler, you can also direct the results to a trace file or a table.

You can also use the 63 xp_trace extended stored procedures that come with SQL Server 7 to define a set of queued results on the server. No client software is involved, and the tracing is completely under server control.

To drill down into the process of defining a trace queue, let's take a look at the Profiler.

Creating a Trace

?where

You can create a new trace using the SQL Server Profiler by just choosing File, New, Trace from the menu. The Profiler will then present you with the Properties tabbed dialog box of your new Trace, as you can see in Figure 21-3.

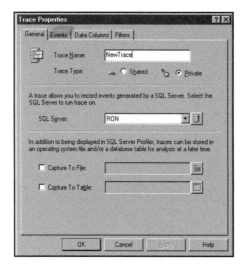

FIGURE 21-3

Starting a new trace in SQL Server Profiler takes you into the Properties dialog box.

Here you do the usual things, choosing a name for the trace and a particular SQL Server whose events you want to trace.

The option for a private versus shared trace is interesting. All trace definitions are stored in the Registry; a public trace will be stored in HKEY_LOCAL_MACHINE, and a private trace will be stored in HKEY_CURRENT_USER. If you use the Regedit utility to look for a private trace called NewTrace, as in the example, you'll find it in:

```
HKEY_CURRENT_USER\SOFTWARE\Microsoft\MSSQLServer\SQLServerProfiler\Client
\Queues\NewTrace
```

Your final choices are to store the trace results into a trace file or a SQL Server table. (Trace files have a default extension of .trc.) If you store to a SQL Server table, you'll be asked for both a SQL Server name and a database, as you can see in Figure 21-4.

FIGURE 21-4

You can save the trace results of one server in another server's table.

Although the first three choices are picklists, you can also define the name of the table in which you want to store the results.

When you first define a table, you normally pick the columns and then later limit the rows, but in the case of tracing, the columns you want often depend on the events you choose. Therefore, it's best to look at the events first, and then the data columns.

Event Categories and Classes

The Events tab lets you choose the event types you want to store in the queued results. Based on the types of events you choose, you can tailor the columns in the results queue to the various parts of the relational and storage engines in SQL Server. What are the types of events?

Each event type that you can trace is called an event class. Overall there are 43 event classes, and to make them more manageable Microsoft has grouped them into a set of event categories. The event categories are:

Cursors (5 event classes)

Error and Warning (4 event classes)

Locks (2 event classes)

Misc (6 event classes)

Objects (4 event classes)

Scans (1 event class)

Sessions (3 event classes)

SQL Operators (4 event classes)

Stored Procedures (4 event classes)

Transactions (2 event classes)

TSQL (6 event classes)

Within each category are usually several event classes, which are names of the types of SQL Server events that can be captured in a trace. For instance, within the SQL Operators category, there are four distinct event classes:

Delete

Insert

Select

Update

As you will most likely infer, the Delete event class captures all events of the SQL DELETE type, in other words, all the SQL DELETE commands submitted to the SQL Server.

Some of the event types are added by default. For example, in the NewTrace example that you've started, some Session and Transaction event types are filled in the Profiler by default, as shown in Figure 21-5.

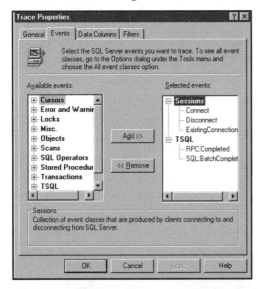

FIGURE 21-5

The Profiler will fill in some event classes (types) by default.

With these default types, the trace will contain information about each user's connection and disconnection event, as well as every completed RPC and SQL Batch. The SQL:BatchCompleted event class will show all the commands for each batch, along with their durations.

Data Columns

After you've chosen a set of events, what are the data columns available to you in the queued results table, and which of them should you choose?

For example, in the set of default event types in the NewTrace example, the columns chosen for the five event types are shown in Figure 21-6.

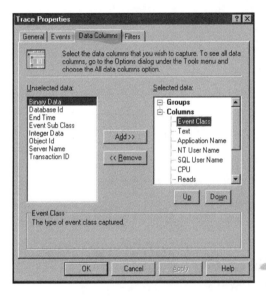

FIGURE 21-6

You tailor your choice of data columns to fit the event classes you've chosen.

Notice that the limited size of the dialog box makes it difficult to get a handle on all the available data columns. You can get a list of all the columns from the documentation or by removing all the columns and scrolling through them in the dialog box.

However, a more efficient way is to create a trace to a table that includes all columns, and then look at the results. If you saved such a trace to a table called AllColumns, you'd see a table like that shown in Figure 21-7, which shows all the data columns in a queued results table.

Two types of columns are available: a set of default columns that apply to every event type, and a set of customizable columns that may or may not be relevant for the event type in question. Every event has data for these columns:

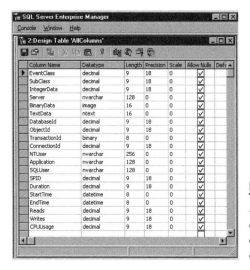

FIGURE 21-7

Saving a trace with all columns to a table is a convenient way to see all the available data columns.

EventClass	The event type
Server	The server name
DatabaseId	The ID of the database in use
TransactionId	The system ID of the transaction
ConnectionId	The connection ID assigned by SQL Server
Application	The client-supplied application name
SQLUser	The username
SPID	The server process ID
Duration	The duration in milliseconds of the event
StartTime	The event start, as a `datetime()`
EndTime	The event end, as a `datetime()`
Reads	The number of disk reads
Writes	The number of disk writes
CPUUsage	The CPU usage time in milliseconds

Each of these columns will collect data for all the event classes, but you still don't have to include them in your results queue.

NOTE

If you include the Server data column, then you'll see the database name in the Profiler. However, if you do not include the Server column, the Profiler will only show the numeric database ID.

The data columns that are customizable for each event type are:

SubClass	The event type subclass
IntegerData	Relevant integer data
BinaryData	Relevant binary data
TextData	Relevant text data (commands, batches, etc.)
Severity	Severity level
ObjectId	Database object id
NTUser	Windows NT username for the event

Again, each of these columns is optional, but in many cases they're critical. When you look at the Trace Wizard in a few pages, you'll see how they can be used.

Grouping

In addition to choosing the columns as such, you can place them in groups, causing the results of the trace to be grouped by identical values of the grouped items. This turns out to be very handy for organizing the results so that you can more easily understand the results.

Filters

After you've defined event classes and data columns, you can add filters on the last tab of the Trace Properties dialog box. One filter is put in by default, as you can see in Figure 21-8.

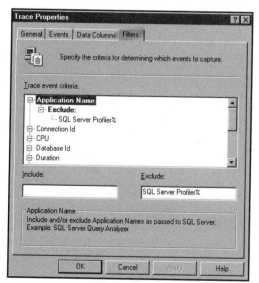

FIGURE 21-8

The Trace Properties dialog box excludes SQL Profiler event types by default.

For each event category, you can include or exclude certain items. When the value is a string, the Include and Exclude options are available, and you can just enter a string with the "%" wild card. When a numeric value is in question, as with the CPU usage, then the input boxes change to minimum and maximum values, respectively.

The reason for excluding SQL Server Profiler events is obvious: Unless you are specifically interested in how the Profiler behaves, Profiler events will simply clutter up your queued results.

Some Sample Traces

？where

A good way to experiment with some sample traces is to use the Trace Wizard, which you can invoke from either Enterprise Manager or the Profiler. When you start up the Wizard, you can choose from a total of six types of traces, as shown in Figure 21-9.

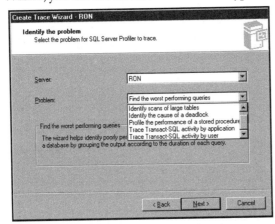

FIGURE 21-9

The Create Trace Wizard includes six types of traces.

The Trace Wizard then proceeds through a set of step-by-step choices that are a subset of the Trace Properties dialog box. For this choice, it will ask for a minimum duration for inclusion in the results set, in milliseconds, with the default set at 1000 (1 second.) If you are tracing briefer queries, be sure to set that lower. The Wizard makes automatic choices of event types and data columns, and it stores the resulting trace as a SQL Profiler trace in the registry.

Let's take a look at the events, data columns, and results for a couple of the Wizard's types.

Worst Performing Queries

The first trace chooses just the RPC:Completed and Batch:Completed event types, and it includes all the data columns. Let's run it using the query from the beginning of Chapter 19, "Tuning Queries":

```
-- Script to query the table Publish2
-- Count the number of USA entries
SELECT country, COUNT(country)
            FROM Publish2
            GROUP BY country
            HAVING country = 'USA'
GO
-- Insert a set of new rows
INSERT INTO Publish2
            SELECT p.pub_id, p.pub_name, 'Portland',
                   'OR', 'USA'
            FROM publishers p
GO
-- Get a count of cities
SELECT city, COUNT(city)
            FROM Publish2
            GROUP BY city
            ORDER BY 2
GO
-- Change the city name of the new rows
UPDATE Publish2
            SET city = 'Salem'
            WHERE city = 'Portland'
            AND state = 'OR'
GO
-- Correlated Subquery to find count of publishers w/o titles
SELECT COUNT(DISTINCT pub_id)
FROM Publish2 p
WHERE NOT EXISTS
            (SELECT *
            FROM Titles t
            WHERE t.pub_id = p.pub_id)
-- Delete the new rows
DELETE Publish2
            WHERE city = 'Salem'
            AND state = 'OR'
```

```
GO
-- Outer Join method of finding all publishers w/o titles
SELECT DISTINCT p.pub_name, t.title
          FROM Publish2 p
          LEFT OUTER JOIN Titles t
          ON p.pub_id = t.pub_id
          WHERE t.title_id IS NULL
```

The results of running the query with this trace are shown in Figure 21-10.

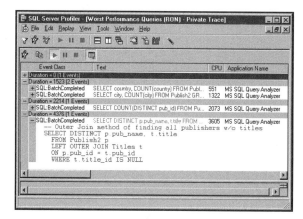

FIGURE 21-10

The results of a mixed query using the Worst Performing Queries trace

You can see that the duration of the longest query was 4.376 seconds, and it was the left outer join. Notice how the data appears in the results window, by duration. This is because the Wizard created the trace, with columns grouped by duration, as you can see from the Trace Properties in Figure 21-11.

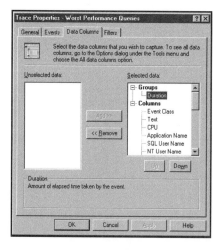

FIGURE 21-11

You can group data in the Data Columns tab of the Trace Properties dialog box.

Deadlocks

In the second example, the Create Trace Wizard option is "Identify the Cause of a Deadlock." Debugging deadlocks is a very trying task, and the Profiler will soon prove an essential tool in finding their causes. For this option, the Wizard chooses a couple of events from the Locks category (Lock:Deadlock and Lock:DeadlockChain), as well as RPC:Starting and SQL:BatchStarting. It also chooses all columns, grouped by the event class.

Let's run the trace created by the Wizard against the following two scripts for a cycle deadlock, taken from Chapter 20, "Concurrency Tools." In one query window, run this code:

```
-- Cycle Deadlock Step 1 - start transaction 1
BEGIN TRAN
UPDATE authors
          SET contract = 0
          WHERE contract = 0
-- Step 3 - now try to update the locked titles table
UPDATE titles
          SET ytd_sales = ytd_sales
          WHERE ytd_sales IS NOT NULL
```

In the second query window, enter this code:

```
-- Step 2- start a transaction 2
BEGIN TRAN
UPDATE titles
          SET ytd_sales = ytd_sales
          WHERE ytd_sales IS NOT NULL
-- Step 4 - now try to update the locked titles table
UPDATE authors
          SET contract = 0
          WHERE contract = 0
```

The result, in the Profiler window, is shown in Figure 21-12.

What's most interesting is that you can tell by reading the deadlock chain's three events that SPIDs 9 and 12 deadlocked, and on what commands.

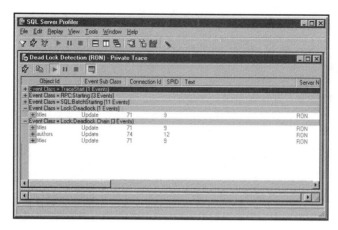

FIGURE 21-12

The results of the deadlock detection are grouped by event class.

Sample Profiler Traces

In addition to the six types of traces created by the Create Trace Wizard, six sample traces come with the Profiler. They are:

Sample 1TSQL

Sample 2TSQL (grouped)

Sample 3Stored procedures counts

Sample 4TSQL + Stored procedure steps

Sample 5TSQL by duration

Sample 6TSQL for replay

You can inspect these for events and columns as well. The sixth one, TSQL for replay, opens the vital replay option, so let's cover that next.

Profiling an Application

You can create traces with the end in mind of replaying them on a different computer, and you can walk through a script command by command in the trace window.

Replaying Traces

The ability to replay a trace is what gives the Profiler its name. By recording activity and then replaying it, you can create profiles of users and run them against a SQL Server in order to benchmark, test, or potentially even stress- or load-test the server.

To replay a trace, let's take a look at Sample 6 that comes with the Profiler. If you edit its trace properties, you'll see that it chooses just the events necessary to replay a trace into the Profiler, as shown in Figure 21-13.

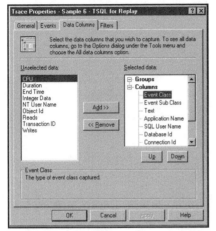

FIGURE 21-13

The TSQL for replay sample trace captures replay events.

Note that it captures cursor information, connect and disconnect data, as well as the RPC:Starting and SQL:BatchStarting events.

The data columns, shown in Figure 21-14, include the all-important text column, which will contain the text of RPCs and batches.

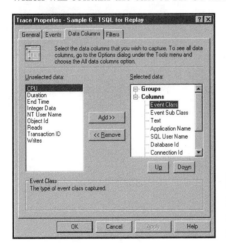

FIGURE 21-14

The data columns include the text column, to capture commands for replay.

No significant filters are on the trace. In order to run the trace and capture the results, you need to specify a trace file or table to hold the results for replay. Once you do that, you can reload it and replay it. When the query and tracing are done, just stop the trace and close the window. Then go to File, Open, Trace File and load the trace you just saved. Figure 21-15 shows the start of a replay using the results from the long script you used earlier in this chapter.

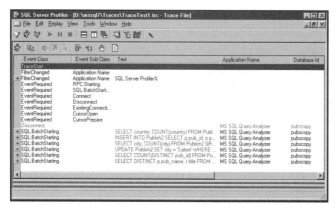

FIGURE 21-15

When you first load a saved trace file, it will show the commands that will be executed.

NOTE

The database ID column contains the name of the database Pubscopy, and not the numeric ID. (Recall, that's because the server name is also one of the columns.) Because that database ID is present, the replay knows that the commands take place in the Pubscopy database. If you don't save that column, the replay will probably not start in the proper database.

Look at the toolbar across the top of the execution window. When you start execution, you can execute a single step at a time, run to the cursor, and toggle break points. In fact, except for a watch window, you now have almost all the components of a debugger!

When you start the replay, you'll get an initial dialog box that asks you to identify the server and gives you an additional set of options, as you can see in Figure 21-16.

FIGURE 21-16

You must set a number of replay options right at the beginning.

The synchronization level option governs how accurately the Profiler will replay the trace. Full synchronization is the most accurate; in it, all events across all connections will be restarted in the order they originally restarted. You can scale this back for performance reasons to partial or no synchronization if you have a trace that does not require synchronizing.

The replay rate is a most fascinating choice, and Figure 21-17 shows the options.

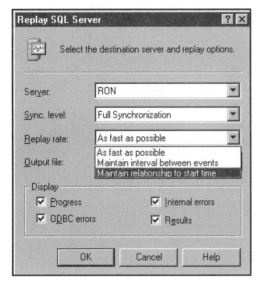

FIGURE 21-17

You can choose from a number of replay rate options.

If you replay the script As Fast as Possible, you are not repeating the "think time" that may have been present when the commands first ran. The second option, Maintain Interval between Events, allows you to replay with the same "think time" between the events, even if they do not take the same amount of time they originally did. The third option, Maintain Relationship to Start Time, will attempt to execute the commands such that the replay takes the same amount of time to complete as when it was recorded.

NOTE

The Replay Rate options are only of value if you plan to replay the script all at once. If instead you single-step or insert breakpoints, the replay rate is irrelevant.

Other options, as you can see in the figures, relate to displaying progress, errors, and the results of the commands. The Results option can make for voluminous output, so for queries returning large data sets, this one is best turned off.

When execution starts, you can control it from the toolbar at the top of the Execution dialog box. Figure 21-18, for example, shows the progress of your current replay after one step, with the results window expanded.

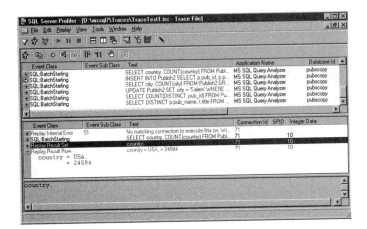

FIGURE 21-18

You can single-step one command at a time and inspect the results.

The fact that comments are also stored is a very nice touch! Note how the yellow arrow on the left shows the next statement to be executed. The pane below the replay script contains the results of each command. By expanding the result set, as shown in the figure, you can inspect the results of each command as it is replayed.

Playing Scripts

In addition to replaying a trace file, you can also simply play a script into the Profiler. Just go to File, New, SQL Script in the menu to create a script by hand, or to File, Open, SQL Script to load one from disk.

> **NOTE**
>
> To play a script, make sure you specify what database the script should be running against with a USE command.

For example, loading the script called Load.SQL, which you ran earlier in this chapter, results in the window shown in Figure 21-19.

You'll notice that now you're single-stepping through a script, debugging it as it runs, with information directly returned regarding the results of the script. You can now open another trace to record other events, such as deadlocks, while you run the current script!

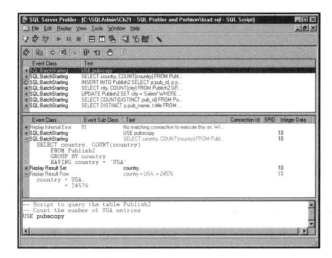

FIGURE 21-19

You can single-step through a script as well as a trace.

Using Traces with the Index Tuning Wizard

You can also load trace files from the Index Tuning Wizard, thereby using a trace as a means of tuning your database. For example, using the Load.SQL script's trace as a source for the Index Tuning Wizard, and performing an exhaustive analysis, results in the recommendations you see in Figure 21-20.

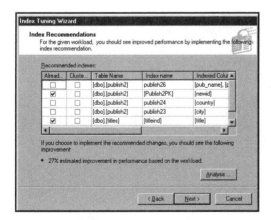

FIGURE 21-20

The Index Tuning Wizard recommends three new indexes on the Publish2 table.

Three new indexes are recommended, as you can see in the figure.

NOTE

You must run the Index Tuning Wizard from Enterprise Manager, not from the Profiler.

SQL Server and NT Performance Monitor

When you install SQL Server, it adds SQL Server counters to that server's NT Performance Monitor. These counters are added for various SQL Server objects, and you can use these counters to monitor server activity.

Exploring SQL Performance Monitor (Perfmon)

The Windows NT Performance Monitor is a graphical tool for monitoring certain kinds of counters on a regular basis. Perfmon, as it's commonly called, takes a sampling of the selected statistics on a configurable interval, the default being every three seconds. It presents results to you using a graph to show relative changes. In addition, it has an alerting facility for sending messages based on user-defined thresholds.

If you start Performance Monitor from the NT Administrative Tools menu, you will find SQL Server's counters but no default counters in place. However, when you first start up Performance Monitor from the SQL Server menu, you'll see a default set of counters established at installation time, as you can see in Figure 21-21.

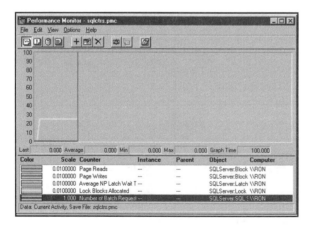

FIGURE 21-21

The SQL Server 7 menu starts NT Performance Monitor using the SQLCtrs.PMC configuration file.

If you start up the Windows NT Performance Monitor from the Administrative Tools section of the Start menu, you get the same utility but without the default choices of counters. Any changes you make to the configuration are saved and will not affect the configuration of Perfmon launched from the Administrative Tools menu. This way you can use the SQL Server version without interfering with a network administrator's Perfmon settings.

You can see the essential statistics for any given counter by selecting it on the bottom frame and then observing the Last, Average, Min, and Max values. You can use the buttons on the button bar at the top to add, edit, or delete one of the counters.

Each counter's name is displayed in the pane below the graph, with an associated color to identify its line in the graph.

> **TIP**
>
> You can press the Backspace key to highlight the graph line in white, for the selected counter in the lower pane. The Backspace key toggles the highlighting on and off.

SQL Perfmon Objects and Counters

The information displayed on the Perfmon screen is based on counters you select. The counters available in SQL Perfmon are organized by object, with each object containing a set of counters.

For example, if you double-click over the Lock Blocks Allocated counter in the lower pane of Perfmon, you'll see the dialog box shown in Figure 21-22.

FIGURE 21-22

You can view the properties of a counter by double-clicking over its name in the lower pane of the Perfmon dialog box.

You'll notice that the Lock Blocks Allocated counter belongs to the SQL Server:Lock Manager object, and it's using the Default scale. In the Edit Chart Line dialog box of Figure 21-22, you can only change the chart line properties and the scale. To get new counters on the chart, you have to add them in another dialog box.

To add a new counter of your own, just click on the plus sign on the toolbar, or choose Edit, Add to Chart from the menu. You'll bring up the Add to Chart dialog box, as shown in Figure 21-23.

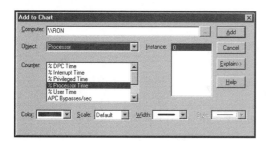

FIGURE 21-23

You add a new counter using the Add to Chart dialog box.

You can then pull down the Object: picklist to see the various objects available. Each object contains one or more counters available for monitoring, and sometimes the counters contain instances that further refine your choice.

> **WARNING**
>
> Be careful to inspect whether the Instance: box has entries in it whenever adding a new counter. If there are instances and you ignore them, you'll just be using a default value that may not be what you expected, and the graph will give you misleading information.

The SQL Server Objects

How many SQL Server counters are there? You can get an idea by looking at the number of SQL Server objects first, and then exploring their counters. You can see part of the list by scrolling down the Object: picklist, as shown in Figure 21-24.

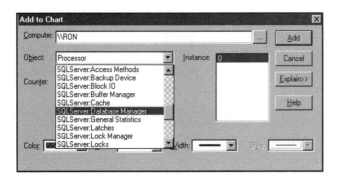

FIGURE 21-24

You can see most of the SQL objects in the Object: list.

Related Perfmon DBCC commands

The DBCC command has a SQLPERF option that can return a snapshot report of Perfmon counters. You can collect a group of them by executing this command:

```
DBCC PERFMON
```

This command returns a voluminous list of data that is much more difficult to interpret than the Perfmon graphs.

Another DBCC command with performance data is the:

```
DBCC SQLPerf (LOGSPACE)
```

command, which takes just the one argument. It returns the percent of transaction log space used in each of the server's database transaction logs.

Because all this information is available through the GUI Perfmon counters, I will skip over details about them. There are 16 SQL Server objects and at least 100 total counters, all of which are documented in the Books Online. Let's take a look at some useful counters.

Some Useful Perfmon SQL Counters

In the following sections, the Object list has been selected to show the SQL Server objects.

Cache Hit Ratio

The Cache Hit Ratio is a counter familiar to SQL Server 6.5 users. It reports the percentage of I/Os by SQL Server that find their target in SQL Server's RAM cache, as opposed to having to find them on disk. You can find this counter in the Buffer Cache object, as the Buffer Cache Hit Ratio. Generally you will want its value to be at least 90 percent, as shown in Figure 21-25.

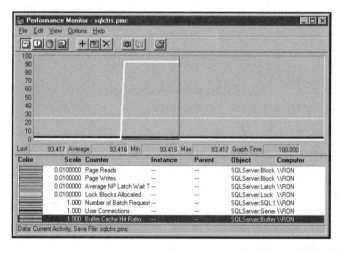

FIGURE 21-25

The Buffer Cache Hit Ratio should be at least 90 percent.

A consistently lower value here could indicate that you need more RAM on the machine, or you need to free up RAM for SQL Server, so that SQL Server can build a larger cache. A set of parallel cache hit counters are in the Cache object, as shown in Figure 21-26.

However, notice that these counters are much more specialized than the Buffer Cache Hit ratio, and that they all have instances. For example, the Cache:Cache Hit Ratio counter must apply to one of numerous types of SQL plans. It does not monitor the entire cache hit ratio.

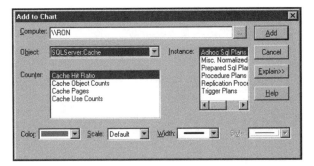

FIGURE 21-26

The Cache object's counters have instances.

NOTE

You can monitor the total amount of cache memory using the SQL Server:General Statistics:SQL Cache Memory(KB) counter.

General SQL Server Statistics

You can find a set of commonly used counters that apply to the entire server in the General Statistics object. One useful pair of counters from this object are User Connections and Connection Memory, which allow you to monitor the number of connections and the amount of RAM to support them.

Another pair is Total Server Memory and Target Server Memory, which monitor the amount of RAM currently used by SQL Server, as well as the amount of RAM SQL Server is willing to use. If the latter amount is much larger than what is available on the machine, that indicates that the machine may need more RAM.

Monitoring the Log Space Used

You can determine how much of your transaction log is being used with the Percent Log Used counter. Here is an example of where you must choose a database from the instance list, as you can see in Figure 21-27.

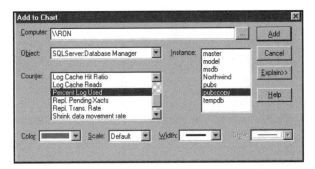

FIGURE 21-27

You must choose what database transaction log to monitor from the Instance list.

By choosing this object and the Pubscopy instance, you can monitor the percent log used of just that database's transaction log. To observe the percentage used, it can be useful to create some activity that will affect the counter.

The following script will add data to the transaction log, causing the file to grow and the percentages to change. The script simply fills a narrow table with INSERTs, each of which must first be logged. You can find the script on your CD as FilTrans.SQL.

```
CREATE TABLE FillTrans (
           id    int     IDENTITY PRIMARY KEY CLUSTERED,
           name varchar(100) )
GO
BEGIN
           DECLARE @count integer, @max integer
           SELECT @count = 1
           SELECT @max = 10000
           WHILE @count < @max
               BEGIN
                       INSERT INTO FillTrans (name)
                               VALUES ('This is filler text')
                       SELECT @count = @count + 1
               END
END
```

Now it's possible to monitor the log file. One sample reading is shown in Figure 21-28.

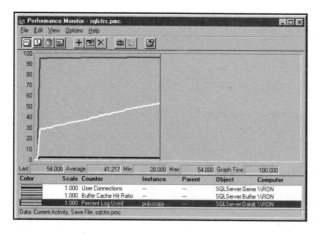

FIGURE 21-28

You can observe logged activity gradually filling the transaction log.

Perfmon Alerts

It's possible to have Perfmon send an alert when a certain threshold is reached—let's say when the transaction log is more than 50 percent full. To view the Alerts dialog box, go to View, Alert on the Perfmon menu or click on the Alerts icon on the toolbar. To add an alert, click on the Plus icon to bring up the Add to Alert dialog box, as shown in Figure 21-29.

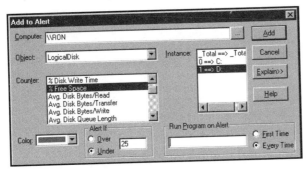

FIGURE 21-29

You can add alerts to your Perfmon settings.

You make the same kinds of choices in Alerts as you do in the original counters Chart dialog box, for Object, Counter, and Instance. In the preceding figure, the option shown is not a SQL Server counter but an NT counter to determine the percentage of free disk space. If your SQL Server database and log files grow and shrink automatically, you might want an alert if the free disk space goes below a certain percentage. You can see the condition in the Alert If dialog box at the bottom of the figure.

You can have these alerts written to a log, invoke a program, or notify you via a network. If you check the options button on the toolbar, the Alert Options dialog box comes up, as you can see in Figure 21-30.

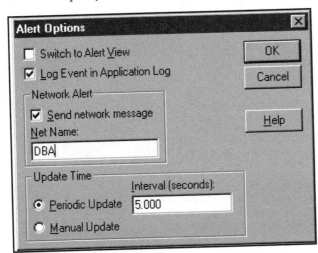

FIGURE 21-30

You can choose options for alerts in the Alert Options dialog box.

Summary

SQL Profiler and the NT Performance monitor give you two tools with which you can monitor SQL Server. SQL Profiler is a client utility that interacts with the underlying trace architecture built into SQL Server 7. You can use SQL Profiler to collect and filter events produced by server activity, save them to a file, table, or script, and even replay them step by step.

SQL Server 7 also gives you numerous SQL counters for the Windows NT Performance Monitor. Many of these counters collect SQL Server information that could not be known in any other way. To finish your survey of performance topics, let's next take a look at database load testing.

Chapter 22

Database Load Testing

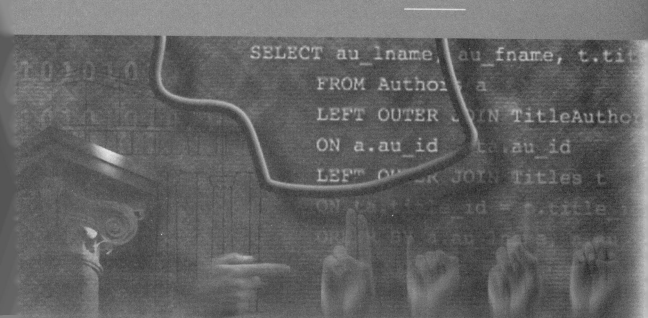

In This Chapter

- ◆ Overview
- ◆ Generating test data
- ◆ Simulating database load and stress
- ◆ Creating a load using heavy threads
- ◆ Using SQL Load Simulator 2
- ◆ Using Benchmark Factory

In this section, you'll explore some simple methods for creating load tests. You'll start by using T-SQL to create a large table from a small one, one that you can use in the exercises to follow. Then you'll see how to use the ISQL command line utility to run scripts and simulate load testing.

Overview

Load testing a software system is the activity of placing a load, determined by the users, on a system, and observing the response time. It is usually an attempt to answer the questions:

- ◆ How large a load (often, the number of users) can this system handle before response time becomes unacceptably slow?

    or

- ◆ Can this system handle a minimum load of N users at a time with adequate response time?

In the first case, you attempt to determine or predict the maximum load a system can bear, or its peak load, by fixing the required response time and varying the load. In the second case, you try to determine whether a system can hold up to a required level of use, by fixing the load and observing the performance. The basic variables involved are response time and the load, as shown in Figure 22-1.

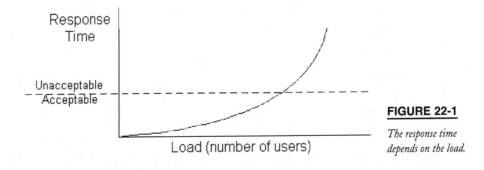

FIGURE 22-1

The response time depends on the load.

The average response time is a function of the number of users on the system. As you increase the number of users on the system, along the X axis of the figure, the response time also increases, along the Y axis, until at some point it becomes unacceptably large. That point is the load capacity of the system.

It's also assumed in this that users are performing some kind of typical activity. In other words, it's assumed that the load being placed on the system by the users reflects some kind of profile: a typical load, a benchmark query mix, or what have you.

Load versus Stress Testing

Often contrasted with load testing, the purpose of stress testing is to put a deliberately large load on a system to see whether it breaks, or at what point either it breaks or performance is no longer acceptable. You can create stress tests by just raising the load test volume.

NOTE

The Microsoft SQL Server group provides a free utility called SQL Hard Disk Test that will stress-test the hard drive of an NT machine, to see whether it can hold up to the intensive disk activity that a heavily loaded SQL Server can supply it. A new version of this utility will be out with the new Back Office Resource Kit. You can find this utility by searching for SQLHDTST.EXE on the Microsoft Web site.

Load Testing: Application versus Database Server

In client/server performance testing, it is important to distinguish application load testing from database server load testing. Application load testing acts on the entire client/server system, using typical client activity along with the backend server, whereas database load testing only tests the database server. The distinction turns on the subsystem you're talking about, as illustrated in Figure 22-2.

To load-test an entire client/server system, both application load testing and server load testing are needed. If you only load-test at the application level and find

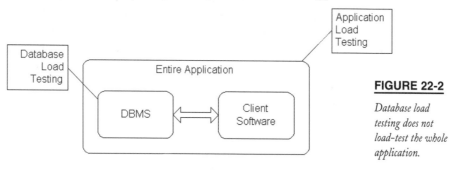

FIGURE 22-2

Database load testing does not load-test the whole application.

unacceptably slow response times, you will not know whether the problem is on the server side or the client side. But if you know that the database server is easily capable of 200 users at a time, for example, and the application response time becomes unacceptably slow at 10 users, say, then the problem obviously lies with the application. On the other hand, if typical queries on the database server have unacceptably slow response times with only 10 user connections, then a problem with the database is indicated.

In this chapter, you will consider load testing and load testing tools at the database server level, not the application level.

Load Test Strategies

The surest way to find out whether a client/server application or a database server subsystem can handle a particular load is to procure the required number of client machines and run the software on each of them. For example, to determine whether a system can handle 2,000 users, you could just get 2,000 computers and 2,000 users and run the software or query the database. There are two major strategies that are commonly used to automate load testing.

1. One strategy is to use a tool for client activity record-and-playback, which removes the need for humans at each station, though you still need a large number of workstations. This can be further broken down into a GUI playback and a script playback. The difference is that a GUI playback reruns the original software, whereas a script playback captures the messages sent to the server during recording into a script and then plays back that script without rerunning the original software. Because current GUI playback products usually limit playbacks to one instance per workstation, it is often impractical, and so testers turn to the second approach.

2. The other major strategy used for load testing is virtual users. Here you use a testing tool to send multiple requests to the server from a relatively small number of computers, making a single PC simulate a number of "virtual" users. This can remove the need to involve a large number of client PCs in the test.

Strategies and test types can be mixed and matched. Database server load testing can use record-and-playback, as long as the results of a recording are stored in a script. Then several instances of the scripts can be played back on a single computer, without invoking the original GUI software. Some database load testing tools make virtual user scripts by tracing database activity, using standard benchmarking scripts, or writing custom scripts meant to exercise certain aspects of the database. Normally application level testing would try to emulate the behavior of actual client software.

Load Testing Configuration

A good configuration for using database load test tools consists of at least three computers: a database server, a client computer, and a monitoring computer, as shown in Figure 22-3.

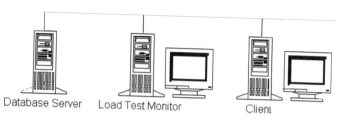

Database Server   Load Test Monitor   Client

FIGURE 22-3

A good load test configuration includes the database server, a monitor, and one or more client workstations.

With this configuration, you can easily detect and remove bottlenecks, perform data collection, and explore the capabilities of the load test tool.

Bottleneck Detection

The database server and client machine must each be monitored to make sure that they are not maximizing use of the machine's resources, specifically the CPU and RAM. So on each of these machines, you can track CPU and RAM usage with Task Manager, and you can track paging with NT's Perfmon.

You can use the monitor computer to gather statistics about the load test, and you can use the SMS Netmon utility to ensure that the network is not a bottleneck. (The Netmon utility comes with the Windows NT Resource Kit. An enhanced version, also called Netmon, comes with Microsoft SMS.)

Data Collection

The database server has the sample database with some tables of appreciable size. The client computers have the load testing tool installed, along with either client software or a query tool. The testing tool may also record a script, but it's used here to play a script back on the client software with a certain number of virtual users. The script may also be a set of SQL commands stored in a text file. Data is returned to the client machine.

The monitor machine collects data from the database server about the queries using SQL Profiler or a load test tool management utility. If you use the Profiler, you could capture the server data into a SQL database on the monitor computer, which you could in turn query for statistics. These results could be used to confirm the response time values reported by the testing tool. Using the Profiler might introduce a slight performance penalty when reading traces from the server.

You can make variations in a number of ways. If the client and monitor computers are identical in most respects but have different CPU speeds, you can make them swap roles in order to isolate the effect of CPU speed on load performance. You can also use Window NT's boot.ini to vary the amount of available RAM on the client machines.

Natural versus Synthetic Testing

When you use a database load test tool, you often have the option of running the load test against your own application's database or against a prepackaged database that the load test tool installs. Testing against your own application's database is called natural testing.

Testing against a packaged database that the load test tool installs is often called synthetic testing or benchmarking. The idea of a benchmark is to keep the back-end database constant so that you can vary the server machine, configurations, or database products.

Each type of testing has its advantages. A natural test gives you some evidence of how your actual application is likely to perform under a given load, which a synthetic test cannot. On the other hand, synthetic tests can reveal what a DBMS or server computer is capable of, and how it compares with alternative products or configurations.

Scripts

For natural load testing, where you are measuring load against an actual application, you'll want to create a realistic profile of user activity. You'll also want to realistically reproduce the production database server in your test environment.

Once a tool is loaded, a script must be prepared for submission to the server. Some tools base that script on a recording of client software activity, but in order to create a level playing field, the same script must be played for each testing tool. Therefore the scripts must contain a balance of queries. Script queries can include wait states called "think time," which gives the script a closer simulation of the user's activity.

Heavy and Light Threads

Each client computer runs a number of virtual users. How those virtual users are simulated depends on the load test software. They may use heavy or light threads, for example.

Heavy threads involves separate instances of an executable for each virtual user. This places a low practical upper limit on the number of virtual users a machine can simulate. The context switching between executables soon occupies a great deal of the client computer's CPU, keeping the number of realistic virtual users low.

Light threads occur in the context of a single multithreaded executable. Lightweight threads support much larger numbers of virtual users on a client computer than heavy threads, and while only a few of the database load test tools support lightweight threads, it is clearly the better technology.

It's important to control the number of queries and their think time. It does no good to raise the number of virtual users if the server is at its maximum. Conversely, it does no good to raise the number of virtual users if the client CPU is maximized as well.

Performing the Load Test

When queries are executed by client machines, you would normally increase the number of virtual users until:

1. A bottleneck is reached.

   or

2. The response time is no longer acceptable.

The bottlenecks are observed at each machine display. It is important to ensure that the queries are not maximizing CPU, RAM, or network usage. Many of the tools give reports of the response times for the scripts.

Load Testing Tools

The automated tools available for load testing are often specialized at either application or server testing levels. The following table for example, outlines the characteristics of a few database load test tools, based on information current as of press time.

Product	Company	Application Load Testing?	Server Load Testing?	Virtual Database User's	Lightweight Threads?	Operating System
Benchmark Factory	Client/Server Solutions	N	Y	Y	Y	Windows
SQL Load Simulator	Microsoft	N	Y	Y	Y	Windows

PreVue	Rational	N	Y	Y	Y	Unix
SQA Load Test	Rational	Y	N	N	N	Windows
Dynameasure	Bluecurve	N	Y	Y	N	Windows
LoadRunner	Mercury	Y	Y	Y	N	Windows

In the table, you can see the tools that support lightweight threads listed first, and then the others. The industry is moving fast: both Mercury's LoadRunner and Rational's Load Test are reportedly developing lightweight threaded versions, and Rational has announced that it is porting PreVue to Windows NT.

The database server level load test tools that support lightweight threads commonly simulate dozens and even hundreds of users on a single machine. They often run benchmarks or canned scripts that continuously bombard the server with activity.

Some of these tools can be very expensive. (The exceptions include SQL Load Simulator from Microsoft.) On the other hand, you may be able to lease some of the tools, rather than buy them.

In the final analysis, the only way to know for sure what tools achieve the goal of successfully performing a load test is to directly inspect them in a realistic configuration.

Generating Test Data

Sometimes you may not have a production database that you can use for testing. In that case, you will need to create the test data on your own. There are a number of ways to do this.

Using Transact-SQL to Create Large Data Sets

You can use Transact-SQL commands to create large data sets. Two commands stand out: SELECT INTO and the INSERT INTO. The major difference between them is that SELECT INTO is a nonlogged operation, so you don't unnecessarily fill the transaction log when creating the data.

Using SELECT INTO to Create Large Data Sets

If you have the Select Into/Bulk Copy option checked (see the Options tab in the Database Properties dialog box), you can use combinations of SELECT INTO. The basic idea is to select data from a table with a few rows to place into a new table that will have considerably more rows.

For example, the following query will create a new table called `Publish2` from the Pubs database's Publishers table:

```
SELECT *
        INTO Publish2
        FROM publishers
```

However, this table will only have eight rows, the same as the original table. You can exponentially increase that number by varying the command:

```
SELECT a.*
        INTO Publish2
        FROM publishers a, publishers b
```

The current query joins the Publishers table with itself, creating a cross-product. It selects just the first set of columns (a.*) and inserts the results into the new table, now resulting in 8 * 8 = 64 rows. By adding to the FROM clause, you can increase the number of rows. For example:

```
SELECT a.*
        INTO Publish2
        FROM publishers a,
             publishers b,
             publishers c,
             publishers e,
             publishers f,
             publishers g
```

creates $8 \wedge 6 = 262,144$ rows.

Using INSERT INTO *to Create Data Sets*

You can also insert the results of a table into itself, using INSERT INTO. For example, assuming that `Publish2` already has eight rows and no primary key, the following INSERT INTO will greatly expand the table:

```
INSERT INTO Publish2
            SELECT a.*
            FROM Publish2 a,
                 Publish2 b,
                 Publish2 c,
                 Publish2 d,
```

```
Publish2 e,

Publish2 f,

Publish2 g
```

This command will join `Publish2` with itself and insert the results back into the original table. Now the `Publish2` table will have 8 + (8 ^ 6) = 8 + 262,144 = 262,152 rows.

Creating a Primary Key

Both of these tables have a fair amount of duplicate data. With all the duplicates on `pub_id`, it can no longer be a primary key. However, you can add a new column and generate unique values with:

```
ALTER TABLE Publish2
        ADD new_id int IDENTITY
```

and the result is a table with unique values in the `new_id` column. You can make the new column the primary key, say with a nonclustered index:

```
ALTER TABLE Publish2
        ADD CONSTRAINT Publish2PK
        PRIMARY KEY NONCLUSTERED(new_id)
```

Now you've got a large enough table that you can query to test the load on the server. To see how big the table is, you can issue:

```
EXEC sp_spaceused Publish2
```

Automatically Generating Test Data

Although BCP can be used to load test data, there are tools for generating test data inside SQL Server itself. The Microsoft Back Office Resource Kit 2.0 from Microsoft Press contains a utility called Filltabl.exe that will generate test data.

Another tool is TestBytes from LogicWorks (**www.logicworks.com**). You can download the shareware version from their Web site and use it to generate test data.

Both of the tools just described tend to require that you have no primary or foreign key constraints on the tables.

Creating a Load Test Using NT Command Files

One interesting way to create load tests is using command files in Windows NT. Because NT provides the START command, one command file can launch another asynchronously, so the launching command file does not have to wait until the launched command file finishes before launching yet another command file.

To create this test, let's use the same script against the Publish2 table that you used in earlier chapters. In the next few pages, you'll learn how to call it from command files that will run somewhat simultaneously. Here is the script:

```
-- Script to query the table Publish2
-- Count the number of USA entries
SELECT country, COUNT(country)
          FROM Publish2
          GROUP BY country
          HAVING country = 'USA'
GO
-- Insert a set of new rows
INSERT INTO Publish2
          SELECT p.pub_id, p.pub_name, 'Portland',
               'OR', 'USA'
          FROM publishers p
GO
-- Get a count of cities
SELECT city, COUNT(city)
          FROM Publish2
          GROUP BY city
          ORDER BY 2
GO
-- Change the city name of the new rows
UPDATE Publish2
          SET city = 'Salem'
          WHERE city = 'Portland'
          AND state = 'OR'
GO
-- Correlated Subquery to find count of publishers w/o titles
SELECT COUNT(DISTINCT pub_id)
FROM Publish2 p
```

```
WHERE NOT EXISTS
            (SELECT *
            FROM Titles t
            WHERE t.pub_id = p.pub_id)
-- Delete the new rows
DELETE Publish2
            WHERE city = 'Salem'
            AND state = 'OR'
GO
-- Outer Join method of finding all publishers w/o titles
SELECT DISTINCT p.pub_name, t.title
            FROM Publish2 p
            LEFT OUTER JOIN Titles t
            ON p.pub_id = t.pub_id
            WHERE t.title_id IS NULL
```

The OSQL Command Line Utility

Next, you'll use the OSQL command line utility to execute the script. The syntax for OSQL is:

```
osql -U login_id [-e] [-E] [-p] [-n] [-d db_name] [-q "query"] [-Q "query"]
[-c cmd_end] [-h headers] [-w column_width] [-s col_separator]
[-t time_out] [-m error_level] [-L] [-?] [-r {0 | 1}]
[-H wksta_name] [-P password] [-R]
[-S server_name] [-i input_file] [-o output_file] [-u] [-a packet_size]
[-b] [-O] [-l time_out]
```

The number of parameters may seem overwhelming at first, but it does not take long to understand what they are used for. Also, the switches officially require a dash or hyphen, but you can also use a forward slash instead of the dash. For example:

```
SELECT COUNT(*)
            FROM authors
```

will execute in the Pubscopy database:

```
OSQL -Usa -P -dpubscopy -Q"SELECT COUNT(*) FROM authors"
```

and so will the following:

```
OSQL /Usa /P /dpubscopy /Q"SELECT COUNT(*) FROM authors"
```

You can see an illustration of OSQL command execution in Figure 22-4.

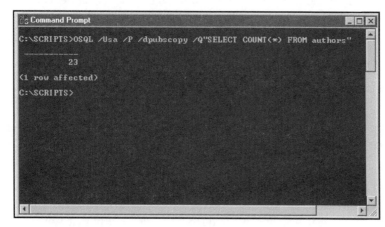

FIGURE 22-4

You can execute a single query using the OSQL command.

Note how OSQL quits as soon as it is finished. Note also that you must use double quotes around the string submitted with the /Q parameter.

You can extend the OSQL command to execute the load script by using the /i parameter:

```
OSQL /Usa /P /dpubscopy /iload.sql
```

or

```
OSQL -Usa -P -dpubscopy -iload.sql
```

Further, you can capture the output in a text file using the /o parameter:

```
OSQL /Usa /P /dpubscopy /iload.sql /oload.out
```

or

```
OSQL -Usa -P -dpubscopy -iload.sql -oload.out
```

Load Test Command Files

The next step is to create a command file that runs the OSQL command. If you make it accept a parameter, you can vary the name of the output file. So in the command file LoadTest.cmd:

```
REM LoadTest.cmd
OSQL /Usa /P /dpubscopy /id:\scripts\load.sql
              /od:\scripts\load%1.out
```

the %1 parameter allows you to vary the output file name. Whatever comes into this command as the value of the parameter will be appended to the output file name. If you call this command file with a 1, it will write the output to load1.out.

> **NOTE**
>
> Because this command must execute unattended, you must either use Windows NT authentication or supply a SQL Server login id and password in the command line.

The last step is to call the LoadTest.cmd file using the new command prompt command START, which will load batch files simultaneously. What you need is a driver batch file that will launch the queries, in such a way that you can vary the number of instances you want running. The following code in LoadDriver.cmd is one way of doing that:

```
REM LoadDriver.cmd
REM Drives the simple load test
FOR /L %%x IN (1,1,%1) DO  START /MIN LoadTest.cmd %%x
```

This code will loop using the FOR statement and start up an instance of the LoadTest command file the number of times you request. Each instance will start up minimized, so you'll only see the MS-DOS icons in the task bar, and not the entire command window.

> **NOTE**
>
> Unlike the ISQL and OSQL utilities, which accept either the dash or slash characters as option indicators, the FOR command requires the forward slash.

Running the Load Test

So now if you issue:

```
LoadDriver 10
```

in the command prompt, you'll get 10 instances and 10 output files for the query. In this way, you can simulate a series of 10 simultaneous users doing a short set of queries.

In addition, you can use a file compare utility to determine if any of them are different. For example you can issue:

```
fc /A load1.out load2.out
```

at the command prompt and inspect any differences of output. You could also use the Windiff utility.

Monitoring the Load

You can use the Windows NT Task Manager, Performance Monitor, and other tools to monitor the load test. Figure 22-5, for example, shows the results of running 10 command files, showing the User Connections, CPU time, and System:Processor Queue Length counters.

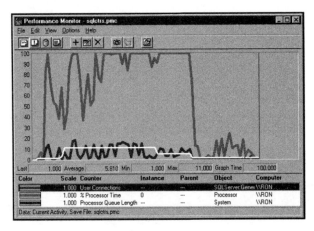

FIGURE 22-5

High CPU usage and Processor Queue length indicate an overloaded system.

This system is overloaded, and even though all the command files do seem to establish connections, the CPU usage and Processor Queue Length counters are both high.

You can find an excellent illustration of why this command-file based load test uses "heavy" threads using the NT Task Manager. Execute the Loaddriver command file with 10 threads, bring up Task Manager, choose the Processes tab, and click on the Image Name column title. Now when you run the load test, you'll see something like the screen shown in Figure 22-6.

If you scroll the Task Manager, you'll see an equal number of instances of CMD.EXE, each about 500K in size. Therefore, to simulate 10 virtual users, the command-file system must use 1724K + 500K ≈ 2200K * 10 ≈ 22MB of RAM!

For a counter-illustration, let's take a look at the SQL Load Simulator from Microsoft, a tool that uses lightweight threads.

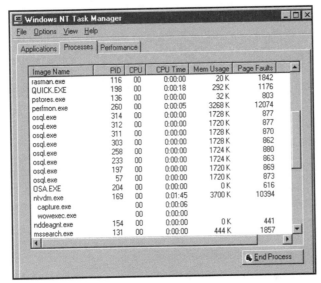

FIGURE 22-6

The command-file load test runs many instances of OSQL.EXE.

Using SQL Load Simulator 2

The SQL Load Simulator is a utility written by Microsoft's Mitch van Huuksloot. With it, you can execute a script with lightweight threads against an ODBC data source.

NOTE

The original version of the SQL Load Simulator was released with the Back Office Resource Kit, Part 2 in 1998. The newer version 2 has been located on the Microsoft Web site, but it moves around unpredictably. The most recent version is in the new Back Office Resource Kit (1999 version).

Preliminaries

When you first run the SQLLS.EXE utility, you must specify the script you would like to run. Each instance of the Load Simulator runs just one script (though you can run more than one instance of the Simulator itself on a single computer.) After that, you must identify an ODBC data source, the number of threads you want to run, and the amount of wait time between threads, as illustrated in Figure 22-7.

The Load Simulator will take your Transact-SQL script and create a number of connections to SQL Server, each executing that script. The number of connections matches the number of threads you specify. Then, the Simulator will simply repeat execution of each script within each connection, over and over again, as long as you run the session. You can insert a delay after each script execution, as shown in the dialog box.

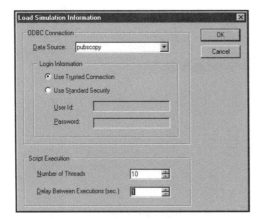

FIGURE 22-7

The SQL Load Simulator lets you specify the number of threads (virtual users) and the delay between sequential execution of each thread.

The Load Simulator Management Dialog Box

Once you've specified these parameters, the resulting dialog box sets up the threads and shows you what the simulator will be reporting, as you can see in Figure 22-8.

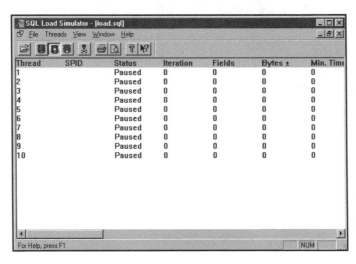

FIGURE 22-8

The Load Simulator shows you the threads and their statistics before execution starts.

NOTE

You can set an update interval, the frequency that the statistics will be updated, by choosing View, Update Interval from the menu. The default is 10 seconds, but when learning you may find it more revealing to set it lower, say to 3 seconds.

You start the simulation by pressing the green traffic light signal. You can tell whether the simulation is working by watching for errors in the results lines.

In Task Manager you can observe the Load Simulator's memory usage and see the evidence of lightweight threads, as shown in Figure 22-9.

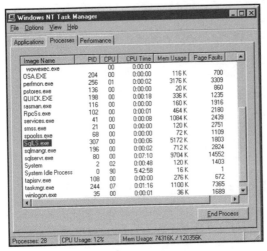

FIGURE 22-9

The Load Simulator is using only 5.1MB of RAM to simulate 10 virtual users.

Notice how much less RAM is used, and also the fact that only one instance of the Load Simulator is running. In other words, other executables are not needed to make the multiple connections to SQL Server. The Load Simulator will obviously use less CPU contention, less context switching, and less RAM than will command-file simulations or heavy-threaded load test tools.

After a certain period, you can inspect the results of the threads, the statistics accumulated by the Load Simulator, as shown in Figure 22-10.

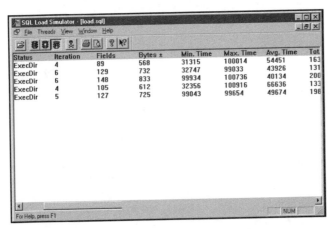

FIGURE 22-10

The Load Simulator displays the minimum, maximum, and average duration of the script iterations per thread.

The figure shows some of the statistics returned from the Load Simulator. In addition to the times, you can see the accumulated number of bytes passed back to the client, the total time, and a number of ODBC-related time data points: ODBC time, and execute and fetch times.

ODBC Statistics

You can also collect statistics from the ODBC driver to a log file through File, Open ODBC Statistics. It will require that you make another connection to the server. Once the dialog box comes up, wait until after your configured interval of refresh time, and you'll see the ODBC statistics collected on the client side, as shown in Figure 22-11.

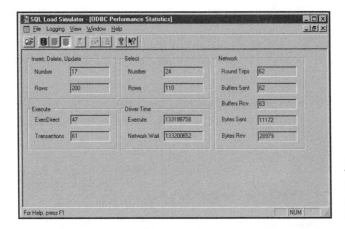

FIGURE 22-11

Sever ODBC statistics are available while running a load simulation.

These statistics are reported for all the connections made from the Load Simulator. It does not show them per thread, as the original dialog box does.

Load Simulator Output

To get output from the Load Simulator, you can print the statistics to a printer using the File, Print menu. You can save the Simulator results as a comma-separated file (.csv) using File, Save As from the menu.

Using VBScript with the Load Simulator

In addition, you can add VB Scripting to the Transact-SQL Scripts, by inserting the standard <% and &> delimiters. For example, you can insert a one-second wait time into the script with:

```
<%SCRIPT LANGUAGE="VBScript"%>

<%

Timer.Wait 1000

%>
```

Much of the Load Simulator object model is available inside the script. The Load Simulator has the following objects, with various methods and properties for each:

◆ DBCon object

◆ Simulation object

◆ Script object

◆ SQL object

◆ Timer object

 The properties and methods for each are documented in the Load Simulator's help file.

The Load Simulator is a limited but very effective lightweight thread tool for load-testing a database. A much more flexible and powerful tool can be found in Benchmark Factory.

Using Benchmark Factory

An important third party utility that you can use for database load and stress testing is Benchmark Factory (BF.) What places this tool above others is its ability to load test a database using lightweight threads and report the results in transactions per second (tps.)

Benchmark Factory gives you a choice of either a synthetic or natural load test. For synthetic load testing, BF supports various TPC and other standard benchmarks, such as AS3AP, TPC-B, TPC-D, TPC-D, and Wisconsin. Each has different purposes and structures. Benchmark Factory creates the target database to a size you specify, and then submits a query mix that you can adjust.

For natural load testing, you can identify your own application's database and then select certain standard queries that will be your own customized benchmark. In this section, you'll take the above query and create it as a benchmark against the pubs.Publish2 table, just as you did earlier in this chapter.

The Benchmark Factory application consists of a control center and one or more agents. The control center starts, monitors, and stops the agents, and it collects data from the database server. Each agent is capable of simulating one or more virtual users. For accurate results, you should place Benchmark Factory's control center on its own computer, and then place each agent instance on its own client machine. For learning purposes, you can run the control center and one agent on the database server.

Benchmark Factory is a complex product, but well documented. In this section, I'll cover just the essentials of getting a custom benchmark against the pubs database up and going.

Creating a New Project

When you first start a new project in Benchmark Factory, you have two options: a blank project or a benchmark project. You can create your own benchmarks with a blank project, or use the built-in benchmarks as the basis for a project, some of which are shown in Figure 22-12.

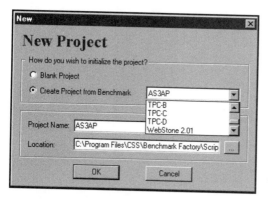

FIGURE 22-12

You can choose from a number of built-in benchmarks when you first start a Benchmark Factory project.

For a natural load test, you'll choose a blank project, and name it SQL7PubsLoadTest. When prompted for a project type, select Bfactory Database Script. The new project shows up in a tree control, as shown in Figure 22.13

FIGURE 22-13

Your new Benchmark Factory project is now listed in a tree control.

The next step is to add a new multi-user benchmark, so that you can run multiple virtual users for a load test. Now drill down to the available parts: multi-user scripts, right click over the multi-user scripts node, choose new, and in the popup dialog box, choose new multi-user test. The resulting multi-user benchmark wizard will start, as shown in Figure 22-14.

After filling in a name, the next dialog box you'll see is Transaction Selection. Click the Add button, so that you can add a transaction (i.e., a query to the database), thereby invoking the Transaction Wizard. Now add a name (in the example, I've added "Count the number of USA entries"). Click on the Next button, and select to create a dynamic part. (A static part here is a DLL written using BF's development system.) The dynamic transaction lets you enter a custom SQL command. On the next dialog box, add a query, such as the one shown in Figure 22-15.

FIGURE 22-14

You add a new multi-user benchmark using the Multi-user Benchmark Wizard.

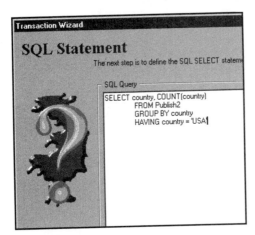

FIGURE 22-15

You can then add one or more transactions (queries) to the benchmark.

As you repeat the adding, each transaction (query) will be listed and then given a relative share to the mix. Figure 22-16 shows the result of adding just the one transaction.

Now click the Add button again, to repeat the add process. Choose a name, dynamic part, and add another query. At this point, the default is to give each transaction an equal share of the transactional activity. You can adjust this, so that you can create a customized profile of queries against the database as you can see in Figure 22-17.

After adding transactions, the next dialog box lets you choose the number of virtual users, as shown in Figure 22-18.

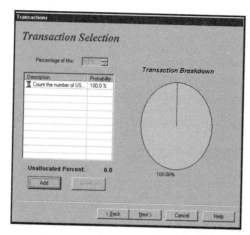

FIGURE 22-16

When you add your first transaction, it gets 100% of the mix.

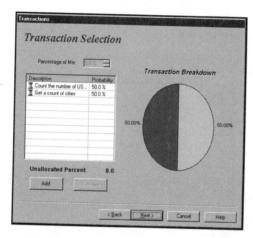

FIGURE 22-17

After you add a second transaction, you can adjust the mix.

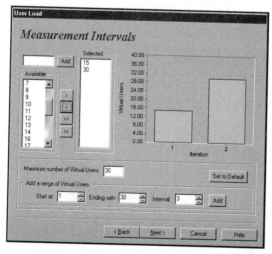

FIGURE 22-18

Next, you can customize the steps for the number of virtual users to be applied from each agent machine.

In this dialog box, you decide how the benchmark should operate. You can start with the defaults, where 1 user, then 4, and so on are run, or customize it, to say 15 and 30 users. Or you can start with the number you want to use. What's being decided is how each Benchmark Factory agent process will run on the other client machines. The selected box contains the list of how the benchmark will actually run the virtual users.

Next, you decide the timing, using the dialog box shown in Figure 22-19.

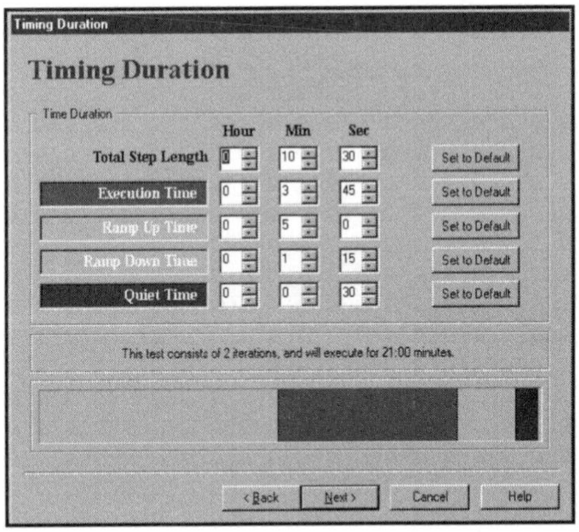

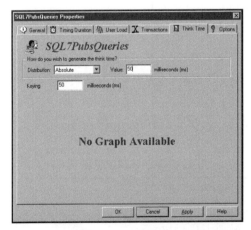

FIGURE 22-19

The next decision is the timing for the benchmark.

Each Benchmark Factory benchmark has a ramp up time, where connections are made to the database and queries are executed, but timings do not start. This gives the system some time to achieve a steady state before measurements are taken. The execution time is the time allotted for each step. The ramp-down time takes place after the execution phase has finished. This gives the system time to finish incomplete transactions or any backlogged activity. The quiet time is a beginning period in which each agent starts up but does not yet run the benchmark.

The last choice is think time, as shown in Figure 22-20.

FIGURE 22-20

Your last Wizard choice concerns the think time to be inserted between transactions.

"Think time" is a way time intervals between transactions to simulate the way users actually operate. With no think time, the transactions simply pummel the database with queries. By inserting think times, you can more easily simulate what happens in the real world. You can insert an absolute think time, or varied think times.

The Wizard is finished, and you can now place the benchmark in the queue by right-clicking over the multi-user benchmark and choosing to place it in the queue. It will show up in the queue in the upper-right pane of the Visual Control Center, as shown in Figure 22-21.

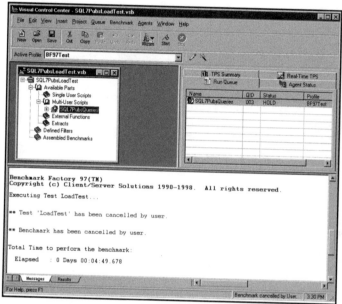

FIGURE 22-21

Before running, place the benchmark in the queue.

Make sure you have a connection defined to SQL Server. You can do this by clicking the Profile wand icon, and you'll see the dialog box shown in Figure 22-22.

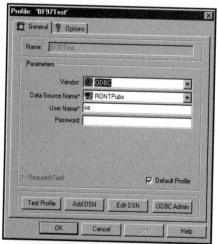

FIGURE 22-22

The Profile defines your connectivity through ODBC or DB-Library.

Now start up each agent on the client machines, or if you're just learning, you can start up one agent on your local machine. Next, choose Configure unassigned agents from the Agents menu on the Visual Control Center.

Once the agent or agents are up, click the start icon and the benchmark will commence. Be sure to check for error messages, which will show up in the lower pane of the control center.

Now observe the agents. As they start, each will go through the ramp up period, as shown in Figure 22-23.

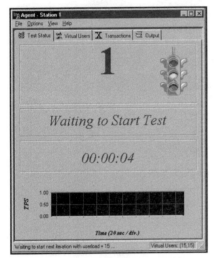

FIGURE 22-23

Each agent goes through the initial quiet period.

Figure 22-24 shows a ramping up period.

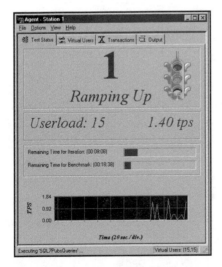

FIGURE 22-24

During ramping up, you can see some initial results.

During execution period, you can inspect the transaction per second measurement from each agent, or better yet, use the reporting tools in the Visual Control Center, as shown in Figure 22-25.

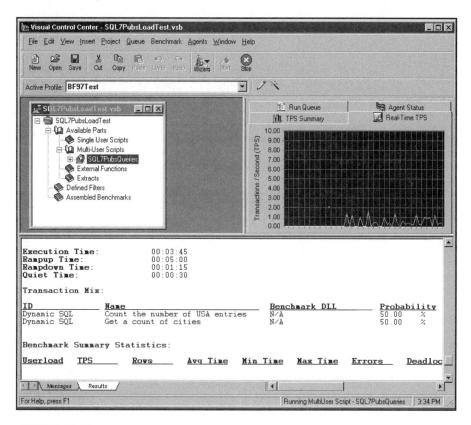

FIGURE 22-25

The Visual Control center lets you inspect the results.

You can get numerous other reports in the control center, but by far the most important is some sense of the transaction rate. In the examples of this chapter, all the work was done on a single computer, so it doesn't reflect the results from many different agents. You must run a number of agent machines in order to determine what SQL Server will actually be capable of.

Summary

Load testing is an important part of database application development. You can create synthetic load tests, based on standard benchmarks or canned databases, or you can make your own application-centric natural load tests using your own application benchmarks.

Also, load tests can use heavy threads, which amount to one executable per virtual user, or lightweight threads, which take advantage of Windows NT's multithreading. One inexpensive tool from Microsoft called the SQL Load Simulator is a useful lightweight thread tool that uses ODBC. One interesting load testing tool is Benchmark Factory, which uses lightweight threads and a sophisticated balancing system to return results for either canned benchmarks or customized tests against your own application.

Next, the final part of this book looks at integration. You'll start by examining distributed data.

PART VI

Integration

Chapter 23

Distributed Data

In This Chapter

◆ A model for distributed data

◆ Remote servers

◆ Distributed queries

◆ Distributed transactions

In this and the next two chapters, you'll examine some ways to integrate a SQL Server database with other SQL Server databases or data sources. You'll start with distributed queries and move on to replication and OLAP services.

SQL Server 7 greatly expands the capability to distribute data between several SQL servers as compared to prior releases of SQL Server. Distributing data among servers requires that the various SQL servers and other data sources be able to communicate with one other.

The key enabling technology for SQL Server 7 distributed data is OLE DB. Distributed data has been around in the DBMS world for several years, but prior releases of SQL Server could not really make use of it. SQL Server 7 now moves up to that technology.

A Model for Distributed Data

SQL Server uses OLE DB to distribute data across linked data sources. To understand the role of OLE DB in distributed SQL Server data, it helps to start with the goal of linked data sources, a feature pioneered by Microsoft Access, and then move on to the role of OLE DB in SQL Server 7.

The Microsoft Access Model of Distributed Queries

One of the more useful and innovative features of Access is its ability to link tables from ODBC data sources within its database framework. In other words, you can add a reference to a remote table to an Access database and then query that table just as you would an ordinary Access table in a database. Let's look at an example.

The Northwind database that comes with Access 97 has a table called Customers, which joins through the CustomerID primary key column with the Orders table, which has CustomerID as a foreign key. If you design a query across both these tables, you'll end up with something like the relationship shown in Figure 23-1.

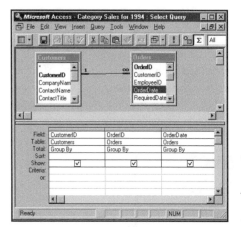

FIGURE 23-1

You can observe a simple join on Northwind CustomerID in Access's Design window.

The Access-specific SQL for this query is:

```
SELECT DISTINCTROW Customers.CustomerID, Orders.OrderID, Orders.OrderDate
        FROM Customers INNER JOIN Orders
        ON Customers.CustomerID = Orders.CustomerID
        GROUP BY Customers.CustomerID, Orders.OrderID,
        Orders.OrderDate;
```

Now suppose you want to join the Access Customers table with the Orders table on the remote SQL Server 7 Northwind database, not the local database. In other words, to join across data sources. In effect, the data is distributed across different data sources.

To accomplish this in Access 97, all you need to do is link the remote Northwind Orders table to the local Access database. Just choose File, Get External Data, Linked tables from the menu, and you'll be presented with the Link dialog box shown in Figure 23-2.

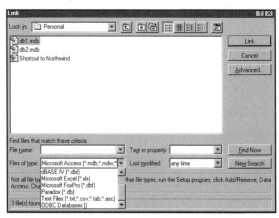

FIGURE 23-2

The Access Link dialog box lets you specify external ODBC data sources.

When you look at the list of file types, as in the figure, note that the last entry on the list is ODBC Databases. If you select this, the dialog box automatically opens the usual ODBC dialogs for choosing or creating a Data Source Name (DSN). (For more information about ODBC DSNs, see Chapter 6, "Connectivity.") If you specify a SQL Server DSN through which you can reach the SQL Server 7 Northwind database, you can add a reference to the Orders table to the Access database, as shown in Figure 23-3.

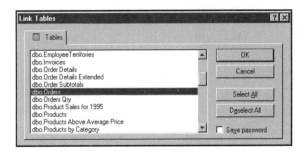

FIGURE 23-3

You can add a link to a SQL Server table in the Link Tables dialog box.

The figure shows the SQL Server tables. Once you choose to link the Orders table, it shows up in the Access database as a linked table that can be treated like a local table. Access names the linked table with the owner name, an underscore, and then the table name, so that you can reference the remote Orders table locally as dbo_Orders.

You can then design the same query as shown in Figure 23-1, but the new Access SQL syntax is:

```
SELECT DISTINCTROW Customers.CustomerID, dbo_Orders.OrderID, dbo_Orders.OrderDate
        FROM Customers INNER JOIN dbo_Orders
        ON Customers.CustomerID = dbo_Orders.CustomerID
        GROUP BY Customers.CustomerID, dbo_Orders.OrderID,
dbo_Orders.OrderDate;
```

This is remarkably easy and intuitive. You can reference the linked table just as you would any other table, and the table's data is queried remotely by the Access query engine behind the scenes. In fact, Access can do this with any number of ODBC data sources, so the linking is quite flexible.

This Access linking feature forms a model for distributed data in SQL Server 7. The differences are that SQL Server uses OLE DB rather than ODBC as the database API, and SQL Server links servers, not tables. In addition, SQL Server performs the linking at the server level, not at the client level, as does Access. Let's examine SQL Server 7's model for linked servers, starting with OLE DB.

OLE DB and SQL Server Communication

In order to understand how SQL Server 7 can communicate with other data sources, it helps to take a closer look at the database APIs used by clients accessing SQL Server data. The database APIs (OLE DB, ODBC, and DB-Library) are all interfaces that client software can write to and receive data from, without having to directly communicate with SQL Server in its own native tabular data stream (TDS).

Because ODBC, OLE DB, and DB-Library are all C/C++ interfaces that involve structures and pointers, it is common to use some kind of high-level middleware that client software can interface with, that will translate for development languages other than C and C++. For OLE DB, that is ADO, an automation server residing on the client that calls OLE DB providers but exposes a much simpler and easier-to-use interface to the client. For ODBC it is (currently) RDO, and for DB-Library, VB-SQL.

You can see a basic illustration of SQL Server 7 and its database APIs in Figure 23-4.

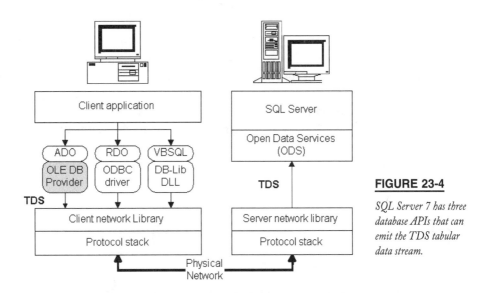

FIGURE 23-4

SQL Server 7 has three database APIs that can emit the TDS tabular data stream.

Each of the database APIs reside as driver DLLs on the client machine, emitting the TDS (tabular data stream) data protocol that can communicate with SQL Server. If the client is using OLE DB, then that driver will be the Microsoft OLE DB driver for SQL Server. In the figure, the OLE DB driver has been highlighted, because OLE DB is the key to how server-to-server communication is done.

Given that a client communicates to SQL Server using the database APIs, how can one SQL Server communicate with another? The answer is with OLE DB through the relational engine. Recall that in SQL Server 7, the relational engine communicates with the storage engine through the OLE DB interface, as shown in Figure 23-5.

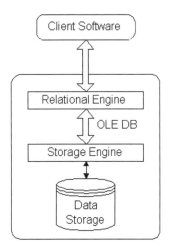

FIGURE 23-5

The SQL Server 7 relational engine uses the OLE DB interface to communicate with the storage engine.

It turns out that the relational engine uses the OLE DB interface to communicate with the storage engine. In other words, the relational engine uses the same low-level object interface to the storage engine that ADO uses to communicate with the OLE DB driver. In addition, the storage engine exposes data in OLE DB rowsets to the relational engine. Therefore, the relational engine can also use the same OLE DB driver that client software uses to communicate with other SQL Servers, as illustrated in Figure 23-6.

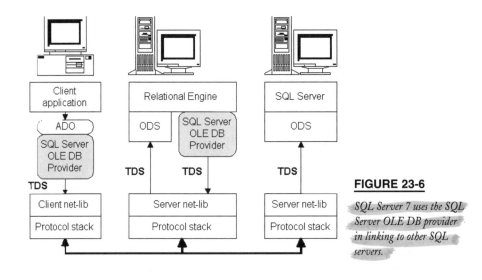

FIGURE 23-6

SQL Server 7 uses the SQL Server OLE DB provider in linking to other SQL servers.

Just as the SQL server OLE DB driver on the client emits TDS-formatted communications to the SQL server through the network, the same OLE DB driver on the SQL server can emit TDS to other SQL servers.

Since one SQL server's relational engine can use the OLE DB provider to connect and query another SQL server, or any OLE DB data source, you can use SQL Server 7 to distribute queries across many data sources. What's key is that SQL Server 7 does not have to use a third party product, or a distinct API, to distribute the query. It uses any OLE DB provider.

Because the communication is done at the server level, and by the relational engine, you can substitute other OLE DB data sources. In fact, SQL Server 7 comes with OLE DB drivers for numerous other data sources, such as Oracle, Jet, Site Server, and Index Server, as well as ODBC. All you need to do is specify the OLE DB provider driver you wish to use and the name of the data source. If your login security is satisfied, the relational engine can consume rowsets from the target data source.

So the final picture, including alternative data sources, is illustrated by Figure 23-7.

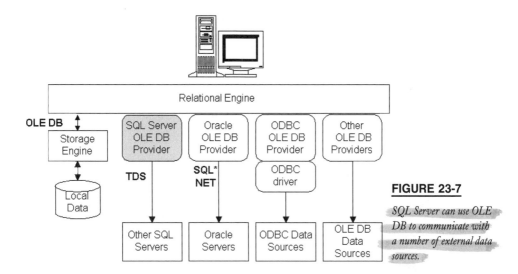

FIGURE 23-7

SQL Server can use OLE DB to communicate with a number of external data sources.

The ODBC OLE DB driver makes it possible to query any ODBC data source from a SQL server. The ability to add other OLE DB drivers as they are developed means that the number of data sources that SQL Server 7 can communicate with will increase over time.

> **NOTE**
>
> In a distributed query, SQL Server 7 will attempt to process (or delegate) as much of the query as possible on the remote provider or linked server. So if you have a query joining a 5-row local table with a 5 million row remote table, and the result will be 5 rows, the query processor will create a remote query to get 5 rows, not 5 million, from the remote table.

Remote Servers

Remote servers are a legacy mechanism by which you can make calls to another SQL server's stored procedures. It is restricted to communication between SQL servers. When you have another SQL server registered as a remote server, you can execute its stored procedures on the local server, provided you have permission. SQL Server 6.x replication uses remote server mechanisms, for example.

> **NOTE**
>
> Remote servers are a legacy feature of SQL Server 7, meant to support upgraded applications from prior releases of SQL Server. SQL Server 7 still supports remote servers, but for new applications, you are better off using the more flexible linked servers feature.

Remote servers are established in pairs. You must make each server recognize the other as a remote server before you can execute remote stored procedures.

Once you've established another SQL server as a remote server, any number of logins to the local server can use it. Since the local server is communicating as a client to the remote server, it must use some login. Therefore, after you establish the remote server, you need to also provide some security mapping of local logins to remote logins in order to use the remote server facility. Once the logins are mapped, users logging into the local server can execute stored procedures located on the remote server.

Configuring for Remote Access

Before you can establish another server as a remote server, you must make sure that each local server is configured to permit remote servers. You can check this by looking at the Connections tab of the local SQL Server's Properties dialog box in Enterprise Manager, as shown in Figure 23-8.

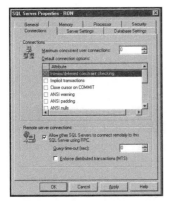

FIGURE 23-8

You can ensure that the local SQL Server can accept remote servers in the Properties dialog box.

In addition to the general configuration, you can also specify a default query timeout (with 0 indicating an indefinite wait), and whether by default the remote server should support distributed transactions. (For more information about distributed transactions and the MS Distributed Transaction Coordinator, see the final section of this chapter.)

You can do the same with the sp_configure stored procedure:

```
EXEC sp_configure 'remote access', 1
GO
RECONFIGURE
```

If you change any of these options, be sure to stop and restart SQL Server.

Adding a New Remote Server

You can establish a remote server from a SQL server using either Enterprise Manager or system stored procedures. In Enterprise Manager, just drill down to the Remote Servers node under the Security node, right-click, and choose to add a new remote server, as you can see in the dialog box shown in Figure 23-9.

FIGURE 23-9

When you add a new remote server, you can also specify login mappings.

In the figure, you can see how the login mappings are also applied in the dialog box. You can map all remote server logins to the local server to a single login, or you can make explicit mappings in the lower pane.

T IP

Always explicitly create login mappings to prevent any user on the remote server from having too powerful an access to the local server.

Using Stored Procedures to Add New Remote Servers

You can also use stored procedures to add new remote servers. Suppose you have two servers, Local1 and Remote1. On the Local1 server, execute something like this:

```
EXEC sp_addserver Local1, local
EXEC sp_addserver Remote1
RECONFIGURE
GO
```

Then stop and restart the Local1 server.

On the Remote1 server, do the converse:

```
EXEC sp_addserver Remote1, local
EXEC sp_addserver Local1
RECONFIGURE
GO
```

and stop and restart the server.

Now use the sp_addremotelogin stored procedure to make the login mappings. Matching the example in the previous section, and assuming that admin1 and admin have the same passwords, execute these statements on the Remote1 server:

```
EXEC sp_addremotelogin Local1, admin1, admin
GO
```

and stop and restart the Local1 server. Now you can execute Remote1 stored

> **NOTE**
>
> Profiler does not reveal the `sp_addremotelogin` logins and passwords when tracing, for security reasons.

procedures from the Local1 server.

To execute remote stored procedures, just prefix the fully qualified name with the server name. For example, to execute the `byroyalty` stored procedure on the remote server's Pubscopy database, just issue:

```
EXECUTE Remote1.Pubscopy.dbo.byroyalty 100
```

You can then drop the remote server with `sp_dropserver`.

Under the Hood

You can look "under the hood" at remote servers by inspecting at the `sp_addserver` stored procedure, located in the Master database. There you'll find the following code segment:

```
-- ADD THE SERVER (CHECKS PERMISSIONS, ETC)
    execute @retcode = sp_addlinkedserver @server
    if @retcode <> 0
        return @retcode
```

The `sp_addserver` stored procedure establishes a remote server by making it a linked server! That shows you that linked servers have replaced the remote stored procedure

> **NOTE**
>
> If you have legacy systems using remote stored procedure calls, you can replace them with regular query calls with the EXEC statement, using linked servers. See the next section.

technology. However, you may need it for legacy systems.

Remote servers go part of the way to handling distributed data. However, they are restricted to remote stored procedure calls only. There's no way for one server to directly reference another server's tables, even for read-only purposes, using remote servers. To accomplish true distributed data, you need distributed queries.

Distributed Queries

The Access model just described achieved distributed queries by linking tables. The legacy remote server technology achieves a kind of SQL Server to SQL Server linking but is restricted to executing remote stored procedures. In SQL Server 7, the relational engine can use the OLE DB driver to access any OLE DB data source using distributed queries. So what is a distributed query?

A query is distributed if it can reference the columns and tables of other data sources in the query. The OLE DB provider returns data from both relational and nonrelational data sources in the form of rowsets that can can be treated as tables by SQL Server. Consequently, SQL Server 7 queries can reference the columns and tables of any OLE DB data source. Some common OLE DB drivers are the SQL Server OLE DB provider, along with the Oracle, ODBC, and Jet OLE DB providers.

To achieve distributed queries, a SQL Server's relational engine uses an OLE DB provider driver. Distributed queries can be established in two ways. The first is an ad hoc fashion, establishing the connection in the query itself using the OPENROWSET function. The second way is by using the linked server technology provided by SQL Server 7. Let's take a look at each of these ways.

Ad Hoc Distributed Queries Using OPENROWSET

The OPENROWSET function can be used in place of a table in a query, provided that you pass parameters to it identifying the OLE DB data source and OLE DB provider. The syntax of the command is:

```
OPENROWSET ( <provider_name>,
            {<datasource, user_id, password> or 'provider_string'},
            {<catalog.schema.object> or <query>})
```

In other words, you provide the name of the OLE DB provider, then some means of identifying the data source, and then either a query or a particular table. You do not need to set up the other data sources as linked servers.

You use the OPENROWSET function in queries in the same way you would a virtual table:

```
SELECT a.*
        FROM (SELECT * FROM authors)
        AS a
```

Except that now the OPENROWSET function replaces the virtual table:

```
SELECT a.*
        FROM OPENROWSET(<parameters>)
        AS a
```

For more information about virtual tables, see Chapter 13, "Data Manipulation."

SQL Server OPENROWSET *Queries*

As a simple example for SQL Server, you can issue the following query to SQL server Local1 to some data from another SQL server, Remote1:

```
SELECT au.*
        FROM OPENROWSET('SQLOLEDB',
            'Remote1';'sa';'123',
            'pubs.dbo.authors')
        AS au
```

This style simply references the target table. You can refine it by specifying columns or even passing through a query:

```
SELECT au.au_lname, au.au_fname
        FROM OPENROWSET('SQLOLEDB',
            'Remote1';'sa';'123',
            'SELECT *
                FROM pubs.dbo.authors
                ORDER BY au_lname, au_fname')
        AS au
```

In the latter case, the ORDER BY is performed on the target server, not on the local server.

Jet OPENROWSET *Queries*

To use the OPENROWSET function with a Jet database, rather than specifying a server name, just enter the file location of the .MDB data source:

```
SELECT o.*
        FROM OPENROWSET('Microsoft.Jet.OLEDB.4.0',
            'c:\MSOffice\Access\Samples\northwind.mdb';
            'Admin';'',
```

```
        Orders)
    AS o
```

You can also reference Excel worksheets using the Jet OLE DB provider:

```
SELECT a.*
FROM OPENROWSET('Microsoft.Jet.OLEDB.4.0',
                'c:\MSOffice\Excel\OLEDBTest.xls';'';'',
                'Sheet1')
                AS a
```

Linked Servers

On a more permanent basis, you can store the OLE DB connection information in SQL Server as a linked server. The linked server technology in SQL Server 7 performs something of the same functionality for OLE DB that Data Source Names (DSNs) do with ODBC. With a linked server, you store the information necessary to make connections through OLE DB, with the local SQL Server behaving as a client to the linked server. (The term "linked server" is something of a misnomer. You are really establishing a linked data source, which may be database servers or other types of data sources.)

The process of establishing a linked server is similar to that for remote servers, with a slightly more elaborate security system. You can add a new linked server using either Enterprise Manager or stored procedures.

WARNING

Although the procedure for establishing linked servers is similar to that of remote servers, they are not compatible with each other. If you've already established some server as a remote server, you cannot also make it a linked server. To make it a linked server, first remove it as a remote server.

Adding a New Linked Server in Enterprise Manager

In Enterprise Manager, when you drill down to Security and select the Linked Servers node, you can right-click and choose Add New Linked Server. You'll then be presented with a dialog box similar to that shown in Figure 23-10.

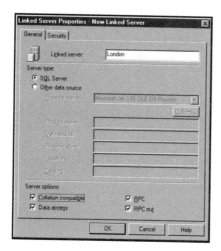

FIGURE 23-10

You can choose a SQL Server or another data source type in the New Linked Server dialog box.

The second tab of the dialog box contains important security information, as shown in Figure 23-11. You need to spell out how this server should log into the linked SQL Server or other data source.

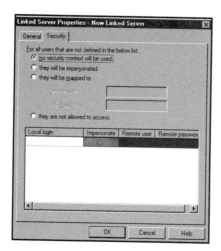

FIGURE 23-11

The Security tab allows you to map logins and set security defaults.

The upper part of the dialog box specifies how logins on the local server will behave if you do not explicitly map them to the linked servers logins. The selection defaults to "no security context," which means that all logins not explicitly mapped to the remote server will not be permitted to reference the linked server's data. Optionally, you can specify that they will be impersonated, meaning that the user's login id and password will be applied to the linked server, and if the linked server recognizes them, the user will have access. The third item allows you to specify a remote login id and password that all default users will have on the linked server.

The lower pane of the tab lets you explicitly map logins from the local to the remote server. You enter a local server login id and then decide whether to have it impersonate (reuse) its login on the remote linked server or map explicitly to a remote user and password.

Using the Linked Server Dialog Box with Non-SQL Server Data Sources

In setting up non-SQL Server data sources, the number of options increases. To set up an Access database as a linked server, enter the location of the database file in the General tab, but do not enter a product name or provider string, as shown in Figure 23-12.

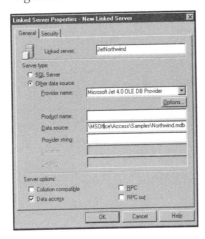

FIGURE 23-12

For a Jet database, do not enter a product name or provider string.

You can also set a number of options, shown in Figure 23-13, if you click on the Options button.

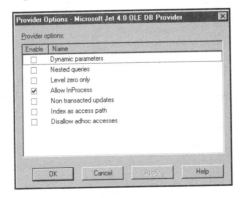

FIGURE 23-13

You can set a number of OLE DB provider options from the New Linked Server dialog box.

Then in the Security tab, enter the Admin login id and password, as shown in Figure 23-14.

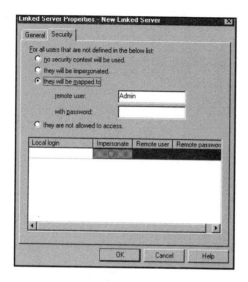

FIGURE 23-14

You specify the Admin login and a password in the Security tab.

In the preceding example, all users are given permission to the Jet database, by virture of being mapped to the Admin login and password.

Using Stored Procedures to Create Linked Servers

You can use a set of system stored procedures to add and remove linked servers. To add a linked server, just use sp_addlinkedserver. The syntax for sp_addlinkedserver is:

```
sp_addlinkedserver <servername>,
            [<serverproduct>,]
            [<OLE DB provider>,]
            [<data source>,]
            [<location>,]
            [<catalog>]
```

The server name is required, and some but not all of the remaining parameters are required. The actual calling is better done with named parameters, which revises the syntax a bit:

```
sp_addlinkedserver @server = <servername>,
            [@srvproduct = <serverproduct>,]
            [@provider = <OLE DB provider>,]
            [@datasrc = <data source>,]
```

```
[@location = <location>,]
[@provstr = <provider string>,]
[@catalog = <catalog name>]
```

When the linked server is another SQL server, the syntax is minimal. No location or catalog is required. Instead, just the server name and the OLE DB provider name are needed, as you can see in this code fragment:

```
USE master
GO
EXEC sp_addlinkedserver @server = 'London',
          @provider = N'SQL Server'
GO
```

Linked server information (like remote server information) is stored in the master database, so that's why the script sets the database context to master.

For an Access database, you need to add the location:

```
USE master
GO
EXEC sp_addlinkedserver @server = 'JetNorthwind',
          @provider = 'Microsoft.Jet.OLEDB.4.0',
          @location = 'C:\MSOffice\Access\Samples\Northwind.mdb'
GO
```

For an Oracle database, you can use the Oracle OLE DB provider:

```
USE master
GO
EXEC sp_addlinkedserver @server = 'OracleRemote',
          @provider = 'MSDAORA',
GO
```

Or you can use the ODBC OLE DB provider, spelling out the Oracle product name and the local ODBC DSN:

```
USE master
GO
EXEC sp_addlinkedserver @server = 'OracleRemote',
          @srvproduct = 'Oracle',
```

```
        @provider = 'MSDASQL',
        @datasrc = 'OracleDSN'

GO
```

Using Stored Procedures to Map Logins

Once you've established the linked server, you then have to establish a login using the sp_addlinkedserver stored procedure. The syntax for the stored procedure, showing named parameters, is:

```
sp_addlinkedsrvlogin [@rmtsrvname =] '<remote server name>'
    [,[@useself =] <use local login on remote>]
    [,[@locallogin =] '<local login>']
    [,[@rmtuser =] '<remote user>']
    [,[@rmtpassword =] '<remote password>']
```

The value of @useself is either 'true', indicating that the current local login id and password should be used on the linked server, or 'false', indicating that the remaining parameters will spell out the remote login id and password to be used.

For example, to establish that you want to connect to the SQL Server 'London' with everyone using their current SQL Server login ids and passwords, that is, impersonating themselves, just issue:

```
EXEC sp_addlinkedsrvlogin @rmtsrvname ='London', @useself = 'true'
```

However, to spell out a mapping of a specific user name to a remote login id and password, you could enter:

```
EXEC sp_addlinkedsrvlogin @rmtsrvname = 'London',
        @useself = 'false',
        @rmtuser = 'Login2',
        @rmtpassword = '123'
```

In the case of a Jet database, you supply remote user and password information sufficient to gain access to the database:

```
EXEC sp_addlinkedsrvlogin @rmtsrvname = 'JetNorthwind',
        @useself = 'false',
        @locallogin = 'Login1',
        @rmtuser = 'Admin',
        @rmtpassword = NULL
```

> **NOTE**
>
> The Profiler will record but not display the content of the `sp_addlinkedserver` and `sp_addlinkedsrvlogin` stored procedures, in order to protect password security.

Using Linked Servers

Once you've linked your servers, you can make distributed queries in two ways. One way is to simply reference the linked server tables that you have permission for, using a four-part name that specifies the server, catalog (database), schema (owner), and table.

For example, the following query joins the local Pubscopy Titles table from the remote Pubscopy Publishers table on the publisher id:

```
USE pubscopy
GO
SELECT p.pub_name, t.pub_id
            FROM [London].pubscopy.dbo.Publishers AS p
            INNER JOIN titles AS t
            ON p.pub_id = t.pub_id
```

If the linked server is not started, you'll get the error message,

```
Server: Msg 6, Level 16, State 1
Specified SQL server not found.
```

The other way is to send a query to the linked server and then use the results as a table, using the OPENQUERY function. The OPENQUERY function takes just two parameters, as you can see from its syntax:

```
OPENQUERY(<linked server name>, <fully qualified query>)
```

You can use the OPENQUERY function to send a query to the server and process the results locally:

```
SELECT *
            FROM OPENQUERY([London], 'SELECT *
                FROM pubscopy.dbo.titles')
```

All the previous examples have been shown using the SELECT statement, but other DML commands work as well. For example,

```
INSERT INTO [London].pubscopy.dbo.Publishers
            VALUES ('9998', 'Test', '','','')
```

Once linked servers are established, creating distributed queries is remarkably simple. But what about wrapping your distributed queries within transactions? That takes us to the topic of distributed transactions.

Distributed Transactions

When you cause a transaction to span more than one server, it's called a distributed transaction, just as a query that spans more than one linked server is called a distributed query. In SQL Server 7, a distributed transaction uses the Microsoft Distributed Transaction Coordinator (MS DTC) to do a two-phase commit (often abbreviated as 2PC).

NOTE

SQL Server 7 already allows transactions to span two databases. The transaction logs of each database are enlisted in the transaction, and the COMMIT or ROLLBACK is communicated to each database's transaction log.

First, let's take a look at how a two-phase commit works.

Two-Phase Commit

The only way to guarantee immediate, full transactional consistency across two servers is to have some kind of independent monitor that governs both servers and handles the decision as to whether the transaction is fully committed. That monitor might be an independent process, often called a transaction processing monitor or TPM. That is the role assumed by the Microsoft DTC, the Distributed Transaction Coordinator.

The way that the DTC can enforce an immediate commit across two or more servers is by inserting an additional prepare step in the transaction process. It's the presence of this additional step that leads to it being called a two-phase commit.

In phase one of the 2PC, the TPM (that is, the MS DTC) requests each server to prepare to commit. If any server reports that it cannot prepare to commit, the transaction is aborted. This preparation phase consists of each server making sure all locks are in place for a commit. You can see the flow of this first phase of a 2PC illustrated in Figure 23-15.

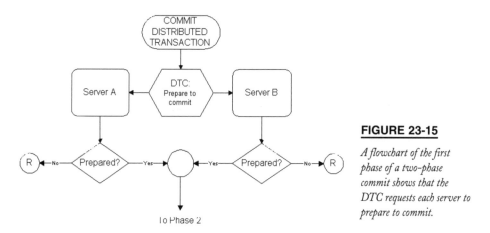

FIGURE 23-15

A flowchart of the first phase of a two-phase commit shows that the DTC requests each server to prepare to commit.

Then in phase two of the 2PC, the TPM tells each server to commit. Each server then reports back to the TPM indicating whether the commit succeeded. If they all did, the TPM registers the transaction as committed. If any server reports a failure to commit, the TPM will withhold the commit status for the transaction. You can see the second phase flowcharted in Figure 23-16.

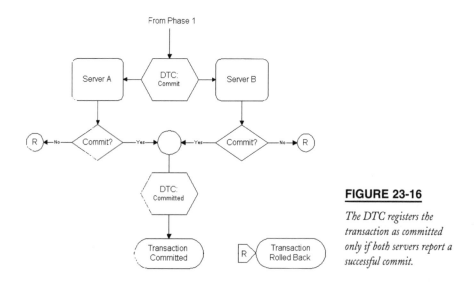

FIGURE 23-16

The DTC registers the transaction as committed only if both servers report a successful commit.

Once the DTC knows that each transaction has committed, it can record the entire distributed transaction as committed.

The MS Distributed Transaction Coordinator

The MS DTC comes as a service that you can start and stop on each server. In order to cause a distributed transaction to execute across more than one SQL server, you must have the DTC service running on each server. You can start and stop the DTC just as you would any other service.

Once the DTC is running, you can monitor it using the MS DTC Administrative Console, which you can invoke from the Microsoft SQL Server 7.0 menu. The resulting dialog box has one important tab that allows you to monitor existing transactions, as you can see in Figure 23-17.

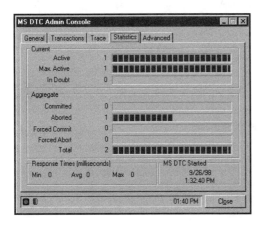

FIGURE 23-17

You can monitor the distributed transaction rate on a server using the MS DTC Administrative Console's Statistics tab.

The other tabs allow you to start and stop the DTC, as well as determine the frequency with which the Console refreshes.

Creating Distributed Transactions

In order to create a distributed transaction, you should first make sure that:

◆ Your servers are linked.

◆ The DTC service is running on each.

Then you create a distributed transaction in Transact-SQL by simply adding the word DISTRIBUTED to the BEGIN TRANSACTION statement.

For example, to create a transaction to span the Pubscopy databases on two linked servers, you could issue something like:

```
BEGIN TRANSACTION
INSERT INTO ServerA.Pubscopy.dbo.publishers
        VALUES ('9997', 'test', '','','')
```

```
INSERT INTO ServerB.Pubscopy.dbo.publishers
              VALUES ('9997', 'test', '','','')
COMMIT
```

The ability to distribute transactions across several servers makes it possible to extend your SQL Server OLTP data more widely than ever before.

Summary

One way to integrate SQL Server with other SQL Servers, as well as other data sources, is through OLE DB. SQL Server 7 uses OLE DB to bring distributed query processing to the SQL Server world, integrating query capability with nearly any OLE DB provider. You can establish an external OLE DB provider as a linked server and reference it as a table, or use the OPENROWSET function to identify the external provider. SQL Server 7's linked servers replace the legacy remote server technology. You can also create distributed transactions across linked servers.

Let's now turn to replication, another method of integrating SQL Servers.

Chapter 24

Replication

In This Chapter

♦ Replication overview

♦ Replication models

♦ Creating a publication

♦ Subscribing to a publication

♦ Removing replication

♦ Scripting replication

SQL Server 7 extensively expands and enhances the replication methods that originated with earlier releases of SQL Server. Most important is the introduction of merge replication, a type of replication that allows you to merge data from mobile users into a central database. SQL Server replication is a complex and broad topic, and in this chapter you'll learn the essentials of how to work with it.

TIP

SQL Server 7 replication is a vast and complex topic, and you can only scratch the surface in this chapter. The treatment of replication by the SQL Server 7 Books Online stands out as clear, well-written, and definitive. You can do no better than consulting those pages for more extensive coverage of replication.

Replication Overview

Replication is a method of transferring data from one server's database to another server's database. It can be from one server to a group of servers, or from a group of servers to one server. Further, the replication can take place on either a continuous or periodic basis.

The purpose of replication is to distribute data across several locations or servers. In the case of an application where data must be accessed from several different geographic locations, you can use replication to update servers at those several locations with current data from a central location.

In the case of an application where some data is subject to heavy demand, you can distribute the load by replicating data from one server to the others. For example, a number of applications may depend on a centralized customer table in a given customer database. You can replicate the needed customer data to the other applications on other servers, keeping them current.

SQL Server replication follows a publisher-subscriber model. A publishing node exposes its data to a distribution node, which can then publish the data to one or more subscribing nodes, as shown in Figure 24-1.

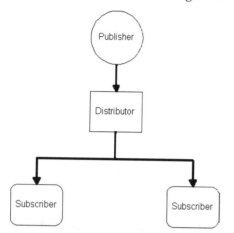

FIGURE 24-1

The data distribution model for SQL Server replication consists of a publisher and distributor sending data to one or more subscribers.

In addition, a publisher might also be a subscriber to many other publishers. Each of these nodes (publisher, distributor, and subscriber) is a distinct database. They may or may not exist on distinct servers. The diagram shows the logical components of a replication scenario without showing the physical implementation on individual SQL servers. It turns out that a publisher, a distributor, and several subscribers can all be on one SQL server, or optionally, each can be on its own database server. In addition, SQL Server 7 allows for publication from, and subscribing by, heterogeneous (that is, non-SQL Server) data sources.

The basic idea is that selected data is taken from the publisher and stored by the distributor on a continuous or periodic basis. Then the distributor sends the data to the subscribers.

Now add the following rule: A subscriber can also be a publisher to other subscribers. This becomes important when trying to implement replication solutions over slower links and two-way partitioned replication, as you'll see later in this chapter.

Types of Replication

There are fundamentally three types of SQL Server replication: snapshot, transactional, and merge.

In a snapshot replication, the publisher sends all its data at once to a subscriber, completely refreshing the subscriber's version of the data on a periodic basis. SQL Server does this by storing the data on the distribution server and then migrating it to each of the subscribers.

In a transactional replication, the distributor reads the publisher's transaction log and copies all transactions that need to be replicated to the distribution database. Then the distribution database applies those transactions to each of the subscribers. Since only copies of transactions are moved across the system, and it's done on a continuous basis, overall network traffic is much less than with the snapshot. However, the transactional replication usually requires an initial synchronization phase in which a snapshot of the publisher data is sent to each subscriber. Once that's done, everything after that is transaction-based.

In a merge replication, data is synchronized between an individual subscriber and the publisher. If conflicts arise, SQL Server resolves them by applying user-defined rules. As you'll see, however, merge replication cannot promise complete transactional consistency.

Replication Agents

SQL Server uses a set of agents to implement these three types of replication: a snapshot agent, a log reader agent, a distribution agent, and a merge agent.

The snapshot agent does the work of creating a snapshot of the publisher's data on subscribers. Running on the distributor database's server, it extracts the schema and data (in text format) from the publisher onto the distribution server. The distribution agent applies it to the subscribers, and updates subscriber status information in the distribution database.

The log reader agent is used in transactional replication. Running on the distribution database's server, it reads the publisher database's transaction log, copying those transactions that are marked for replication to the distribution database. When a publisher database has transactions that are marked for replication, they cannot be removed from the transaction log until the distributor has successfully copied them.

The distribution agent applies data from snapshot replication, or transactions from transactional replication, to the subscribers from the distribution database. The distribution agent can run on either the distribution server or the subscriber servers. It is not used in merge replication.

The merge agent is used in merge replication to synchronize data between publisher and subscriber. It synchronizes incremental changes to data that occur after an initial snapshot job has copied the publisher data to the subscriber. Conflicts are handled according to the rules established with the conflict resolver.

Push and Pull Subscriptions

In a push subscription, the publisher's data is taken by the distributor and sent to the subscribing servers by the distributor, without the subscribers requesting the data. In a push snapshot or transactional replication, the distribution agent runs on the distribution database's server. In a push merge replication, the merge agent runs on the distribution database's server.

In a pull subscription, each pulling subscriber requests data from the distributor whenever ready. In snapshot and transactional replication, pull subscriptions have the distribution agent on the subscriber. Similarly, in merge replication, pull subscriptions have their merge agent on the subscriber.

You can mix push and pull subscriptions in a single publication.

Snapshot Replication

Snapshot replication uses both the snapshot and distribution agents. The initial snapshot of the replicated data is gathered by the snapshot agent running on the distribution server and stores the intermediate data there as well. Then the distribution agent applies the data to the subscribers. When it's a push subscription, the distribution agent runs on the distributor, as shown in Figure 24-2.

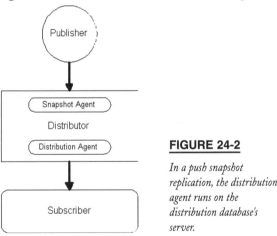

FIGURE 24-2

In a push snapshot replication, the distribution agent runs on the distribution database's server.

This is by way of contrast with a pull subscription, where the distribution agent runs on the subscriber.

The snapshot agent creates a new snapshot of all the replicated data each time it runs. This includes schemas to re-create necessary tables on the subscribers, as well as the actual data. If all the servers are SQL servers, then the data will be stored in native BCP format; otherwise, the data will be stored as clear text. The snapshot agent records its activity in replication tables in the distribution database.

In a push subscription, the distribution agent examines those tables, reads the location of the synchronization files, and then applies the schema and data to the subscribers. In a pull subscription, the distribution agent residing on the subscriber logs into the distribution server, reads the replication tables, but only applies the data to the one subscriber.

Transactional Replication

Transactional replication also uses the snapshot and distribution agents to set up an initial synchronization between publisher and subscriber. However, to apply transactions from a publisher to subscribers either continuously or periodically, it uses the log reader agent and distribution agent. As with snapshot replication, a push transactional replication places the distribution agent on the distribution server, as shown in Figure 24-3.

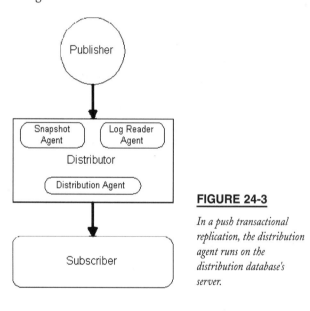

FIGURE 24-3

In a push transactional replication, the distribution agent runs on the distribution database's server.

Again, in a pull subscription, the distribution agent would run on each subscriber and apply snapshot and transactions to only the one subscriber.

Transactional replication also allows you to replicate stored procedure execution as well as table modifications. If your application makes changes to data through stored procedures and not through individual SQL statements, then you can replicate the stored procedure call with parameters rather than each individual INSERT, UPDATE, or DELETE statement from the transaction log. This can greatly improve the speed of the replication, because the amount of traffic involved is reduced to just the procedure call.

Immediate-Updating Subscribers

Normally, in both snapshot and transactional replication, subscribers do not change data. It is possible to let each subscriber sends updates back to the publisher using the two-phase commit (2PC) capabilities of the Microsoft Distributed Transaction Coordinator (MS DTC), as illustrated in Figure 24-4.

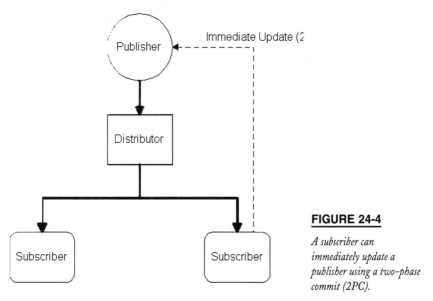

FIGURE 24-4

A subscriber can immediately update a publisher using a two-phase commit (2PC).

This happens only between one subscriber and the publisher at a time. The changes sent back to the publisher are then replicated out to the other subscribers in the usual fashion.

Merge Replication

Merge replication is a distinctive feature of SQL Server 7.0. Earlier releases of SQL Server included forms of both transactional and snapshot replication but did not have any form of merge replication. In merge replication, updates are accepted from both publisher and subscriber, and conflicts are arbitrated by a customizable conflict resolver.

Merge replication uses the snapshot agent to provide an initial snapshot of data to the subscriber, and then the merge agent thereafter to synchronize publisher and subscriber. It does not use the distribution or log reader agents. In a push subscription, the merge agent runs on the distributor's server, whereas in a pull subscription, the merge agent will run on the subscriber, as shown in Figure 24-5.

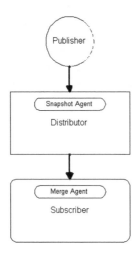

FIGURE 24-5

In a pull-style merge subscription, the merge agent runs on the subscriber.

Instead of reading the publisher's transaction log, the merge agent adds special system tables to the publisher database that will track data changes on the publisher. The merge process also adds a uniqueidentifier column with the ROWGUID property to each publishing table, and it joins that value with a ROWGUID column in the merge system tables. Further, the merge agent uses a generation column in the system tables to determine when subscribers were last updated.

To accomplish this, the merge replication installation process must make two changes to the publishing table. First, if each publishing table does not already have a uniqueidentifier column with the ROWGUID property, the merge process adds one. The uniqueidentifier column is needed to join with the merge system tables, allowing the merge agent to track changes in the data.

Second, the merge replication installation process adds insert, update, and delete triggers to each publishing table. These triggers track changes made to the table by writing to the merge system tables. The triggers are additive; they do not affect or impair any already existing triggers.

NOTE

Replication triggers could present a problem if your original triggers change the base table data and you do not have the recursive triggers option set at the database level.

You can customize the merge replication conflict resolution process by invoking stored procedures, using the merge agent's COM interface, or writing your own resolver.

Replication Models

The first step in physically implementing replication is to decide on the physical layout of your publisher, distributor, and subscriber databases. Since most of the time, subscribers will be on their own servers, the real decision is whether to put the distribution database on the publishing server or on a separate server.

One way to understand what this decision entails is to look at how the publisher, distributor, and subscriber databases are related to each other. The publisher and distributor are related in a one-to-one fashion, whereas the distributor and subscribers are related in a one-to-many fashion, as shown in Figure 24-6.

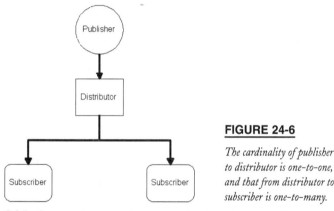

FIGURE 24-6

The cardinality of publisher to distributor is one-to-one, and that from distributor to subscriber is one-to-many.

SQL Server 7 replication normally involves no direct relationship between the publisher and subscriber; all replication goes through the distributor. The exception is for immediate-updating subscribers, which use the MS DTC, as described in the preceding section.

Local Distributor Model

You can make one server both publisher and distributor, as shown in Figure 24-7.

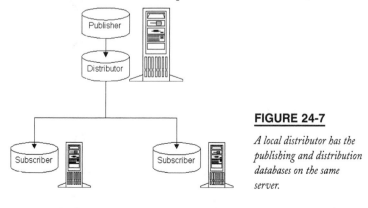

FIGURE 24-7

A local distributor has the publishing and distribution databases on the same server.

The advantage of putting both the publisher and distributor on the same server is ease of maintenance. The disadvantage is that all the distribution activity will bleed resources from the publication server. If the publication server has a significant load or is near load capacity, it's better to put the distributor on its own server.

Remote Distributor Model

A remote distributor separates the publishing and distribution servers, as shown in Figure 24-8.

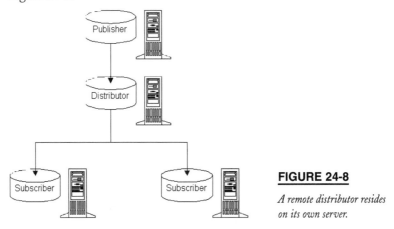

FIGURE 24-8

A remote distributor resides on its own server.

The advantage now is that the distribution activity is now done by a second server and no longer takes resources from the publishing server. However, you do have the added maintenance issues of having to deal with a second server. In addition, if you have more than one subscriber, a distributor on a second server can offload the transfer of data to subscribers from the publisher, and improve throughput.

In all types of SQL Server replication, a lot of activity goes on between the publisher and the distributor. The distributor will be extracting data from the publisher when making a snapshot, or reading the publisher transaction log for transactional replication, or synchronizing data in the case of merge replication. This activity is much more than will be occurring between the distributor and the subscribers. As a result, you will normally want the fastest connection possible between the publisher and distributor.

Central Subscriber Model

So far in your model, you've been looking at the publisher as the center of the hub, that is, at a central publisher model. The publisher serves as the hub of the data, which goes outward to all the subscribers. However, you can also set up a server to collect data from several publishers, as shown in Figure 24-9.

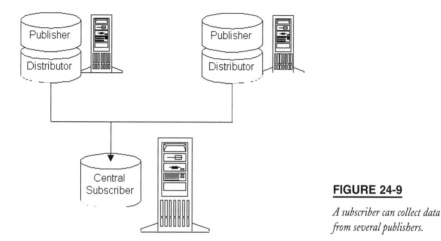

FIGURE 24-9

A subscriber can collect data from several publishers.

The central subscriber model only works if the data coming in is partitioned, in other words, if some guarantee exists that the primary keys in all the published tables differ for each publisher. That way, the subscriber will encounter no primary key conflicts.

Because every subscriber can also be a publisher, the central subscriber could then republish this data to other subscribers as well.

Subscribing Publisher Model

When you have a slow link between the publisher and the subscriber, you can implement a subscriber that further publishes the replicated data, as shown in Figure 24-10.

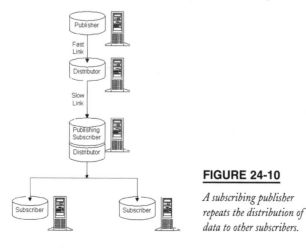

FIGURE 24-10

A subscribing publisher repeats the distribution of data to other subscribers.

The link from the distributor to the publishing subscriber can be slower than that between the publisher and distributor, because there will be less activity.

Configuring Distribution and Publication

SQL Server 7 makes it easy to install, configure, and remove replication with a set of replication wizards. Although it is much easier to use the wizards to work with replication, you can also use the replication system stored procedures.

Cases arise when having a script to reproduce a replication scenario is valuable—as a backup tool and as a method for automating client subscribers, for example. Once you've set up replication, you can extract scripts of the publication in question using Enterprise Manager, as you'll see.

To get started with replication, you must first identify the distribution database and enable the publishing server. To do that, you can click the wizards' wand icon on the toolbar, drill down to and open the Replication node of the tree view, select Configure Publishing and Distribution Wizard, and either double-click or click the OK button.

The Configure Publishing Wizard, in its second dialog box, asks for distributor information, as you can see in Figure 24-11.

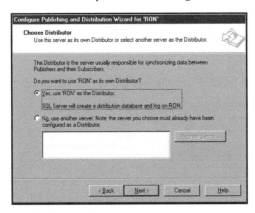

FIGURE 24-11

Your first configuration choice is the location of the distribution server.

The first option is to use the current server as the distributor. If you've already put the distributor on another server, then you can register the server at this point.

The next step is to identify which servers will be subscribers and publishers for this distributor. The default is all on the same server, but you can customize the settings, as you can see in the next dialog box, shown in Figure 24-12.

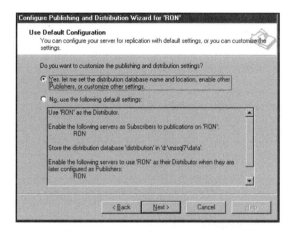

FIGURE 24-12

Setting up a more widely distributed system requires that you to choose Yes in this dialog box.

You can see many of the default settings in the edit box below the No option. Here the defaults will be to use the current server as subscriber, distributor, and publisher. If you choose the No option, then these default choices will be used and replication will be installed according to them.

Choosing Yes allows you to customize your file locations, database names, publishers, and subscribers. The very next dialog box is shown in Figure 24-13.

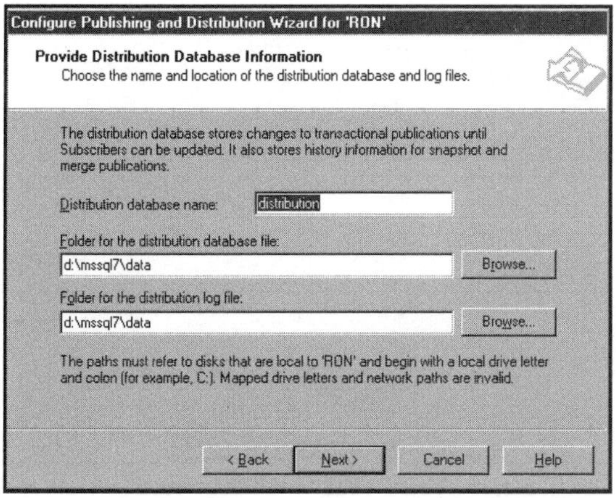

FIGURE 24-13

The first dialog box for the custom configuration path concerns the distribution database.

You can customize the distribution database name and locations. However, it's probably wise to always include some clue to the function of the database in its name, using something like "CustomerDistribution" as the name of the database.

The next dialog box after the distribution dialog box sets up a list of possible publishing servers for this distribution database, as shown in Figure 24-14.

FIGURE 24-14

The next dialog box lets you enable servers as publishers.

From here you can enable a given server as a publisher to this distribution server, or you can register a remote server and enable it. In addition you can set the login information for the publishing server by clicking on the Properties button in the Enable Publishers dialog box, the one with three dots (...), and you'll get the distributor Properties dialog box, as shown in Figure 24-15.

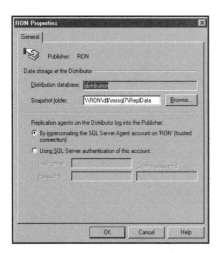

FIGURE 24-15

You can also set the logins and the location of the snapshot data in the distributor Properties dialog box.

NOTE

This dialog box is important because it is the only way in the wizard setup to specify the location of snapshot data.

The next step in the wizard is to enable databases on the publisher for publication, as shown in Figure 24-16.

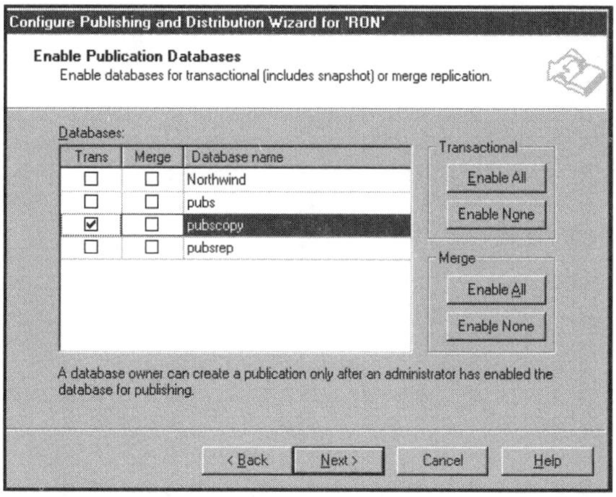

FIGURE 24-16

The next step is to enable databases for publication.

Note that you can enable both merge and transactional replication for each user database on the publishing server.

With distributor and publisher out of the way, all that remains is to enable subscribing servers, which is what the next dialog box does, as you can see in Figure 24-17.

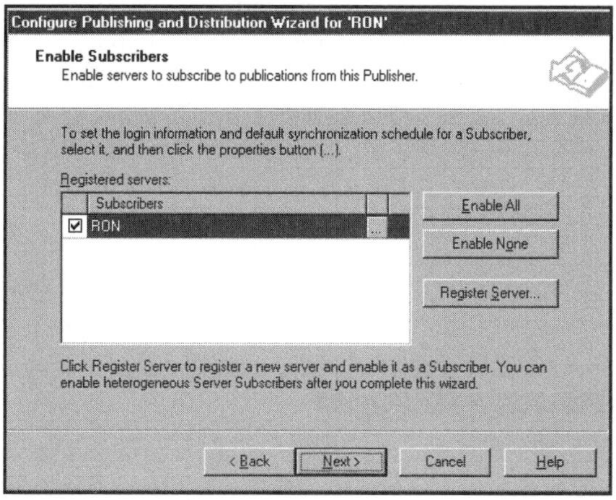

FIGURE 24-17

The last step is to enable the subscribing servers.

You can also set the account for the agent logins to the subscribing server by filling in the dialog box that results from clicking the Properties button.

Once you've gone through all these steps, the Finish dialog box will create the distribution database and install necessary files on publisher and subscriber to enable replication. Just click on the Finish button, and the wizard will complete its work.

When finished, you'll notice the new distribution database along with the Replication

Monitor node in the Enterprise Manager tree view, as shown in Figure 24-18.

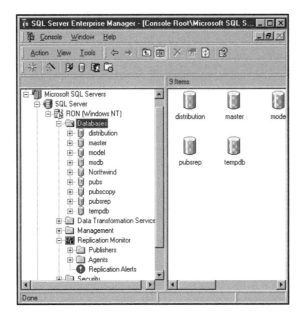

FIGURE 24-18

The distribution database and replication monitor now appear in Enterprise Manager.

The replication monitor utility gives you a way of monitoring the success or failure of replication jobs, as well as the communication status between publisher, distributor, and subscriber.

Creating a Publication

Once replication has been installed, and the major players identified and enabled, all that remains is to identify what data should be published. The way you do that in SQL Server 7 is to define a publication, which contains articles, and the easiest way to do that is with the Create Publication Wizard.

NOTE

SQL Server 6.x made a distinction between a publication and a set of articles, and a subscriber subscribed to an article. SQL Server 7 does still use the term "article," but subscribers only subscribe to an entire publication, not an article.

When you first bring up the wizard, it requests that you choose a database from the publishing server that contains the data for this publication, as shown in Figure 24-19.

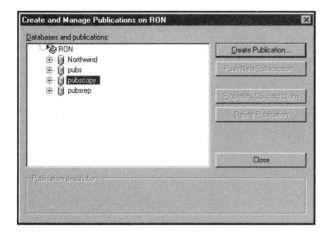

FIGURE 24-19

You must first choose the database containing the publication.

At this point, just click the Create Publication button to bring up the Create Publication Wizard opening screen. The next dialog box asks for the type of publication, as shown in Figure 24-20.

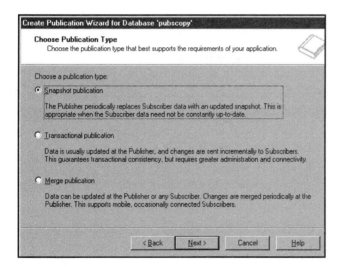

FIGURE 24-20

The first step in the Create Publication Wizard is to choose the type of publication.

Here the choice is among the major types of replication.

Snapshot and Transaction Replication

If you choose snapshot or transaction replication, your next choice will be whether to allow immediate-updating subscribers, as shown in Figure 24-21.

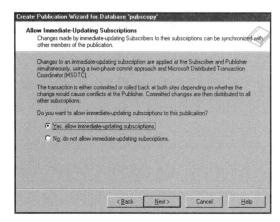

FIGURE 24-21

The next step in snapshot replication is to choose whether to allow immediate-updating subscribers.

Recall that immediate-updating subscribers can use the MS DTC service to update the publisher directly, without going through the distributor. The default is not to allow them.

No matter what your choice regarding immediate-updating subscribers, you next must stipulate whether you will have a homogeneous (all SQL Server 7) or heterogeneous (some non–SQL Server) data sources involved in the replication process. The dialog box is shown in Figure 24-22.

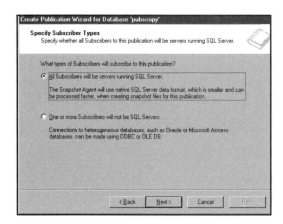

FIGURE 24-22

Next, you must stipulate whether some of the subscribers are not SQL servers.

Having all the subscribers as SQL servers makes it possible for replication to use the native BCP format. The native format of BCP stores numeric and binary data in a binary format, which takes up less space. If some of the subscribers are not SQL servers, then the character format must be used, which saves data as clear text that takes up more space than the native format.

The next choice is to specify the actual data for the publication's articles, as shown in Figure 24-23.

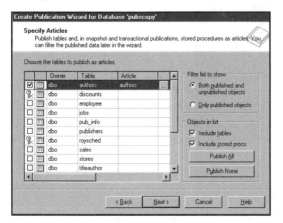

Notice that tables without primary keys cannot be published. Also notice that you can list stored procedures by checking the check box on the right. Replicating stored procedures can dramatically reduce the amount of data sent over the wire from publisher to distributor to subscribers.

Once you choose a particular table or stored procedure, note that the article name becomes filled in automatically. You can customize the article by double-clicking over its name (authors in the preceding dialog box). You'll get the article's Properties dialog box shown in Figure 24-24.

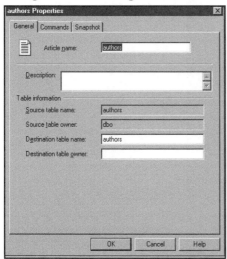

FIGURE 24-24

The article's Properties dialog box allows you to customize its name.

For a transactional replication, you'll see three tabs in the article Properties dialog box, whereas for snapshot replication, you'll only see two tabs, the General and the Snapshot tabs.

The Commands tab, for transactional replication, lets you specify options for the SQL DML commands that change the data, as show in Figure 24-25.

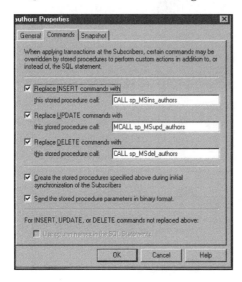

FIGURE 24-25

A transactional replication has article properties that let you choose command options.

The stored procedures will be created at the time of synchronization and used on the subscriber.

Further, on the third tab (or the second tab for snapshot replication), you can set some additional properties, as shown in Figure 24-26.

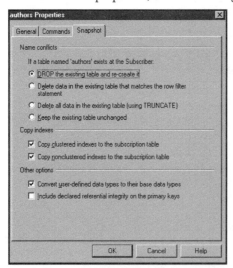

FIGURE 24-26

You can also explore other snapshot options in the article's Properties dialog box.

These options are very important for the snapshot publication and for the snapshot phase of a transaction replication.

First, you can stipulate how the snapshot should work if the table is found to exist in the subscriber database. You can re-create the table entirely or just replace the data that meets the filter condition you set on the publisher. You can use the second option to create a subscriber that receives data from several publishers, each filtered on some condition. You can also just truncate and not re-create the table, a choice that is slightly more efficient and could be useful if the publisher never changes the table structure. Finally, you can specify that the table not be changed at all if found to exist.

The other options allows you to copy indexes along with the data (which can enhance performance), convert user-defined data types to their standard SQL Server data types, and include declarative referential integrity (DRI) between tables on the subscriber as well.

If you chose to allow immediate-updating subscribers, then the dialog box shown in Figure 24-27 will appear.

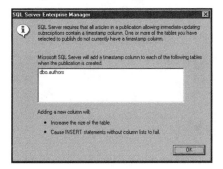

FIGURE 24-27

For immediate-updating subscribers, you must allow additional modifications to the table.

The wizard will add a timestamp column to the table in question in order to track changes and create a two-phase commit between subscriber and publisher when the subscriber updates published data.

Next, after choosing a publication name, you're asked whether you want to provide other options for the publication, as shown in Figure 24-28.

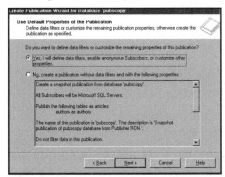

FIGURE 24-28

The next branch in the wizard concerns filters.

If you choose Yes, then you'll be asked to specify data filters, anonymous subscribers, or other custom properties. The first choice concerns data filters. If you say Yes to data filters, you'll be presented with the dialog box shown in Figure 24-29.

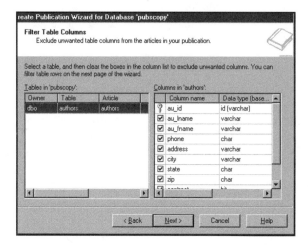

FIGURE 24-29

You can limit replication to a subset of an article's columns.

Much as in a view, you can let only some of the columns be exposed for replication. However, the primary key of the table must always be allowed to replicate.

Next, you can limit the rows being replicated. When you do, if you click on the article's Properties button, you'll see the dialog box shown in Figure 24-30.

FIGURE 24-30

You can also limit the rows with a condition.

Here you can enter any valid SQL SELECT condition.

One of your last choices, for snapshot replication, is whether to allow anonymous subscriptions. Anonymous subscriptions allow users to connect and receive replicated data without storing data about them in the distribution database. They are pull subscriptions only. The next option is to schedule the snapshot. If you decide to change the default schedule, you'll see the dialog box shown in Figure 24-31.

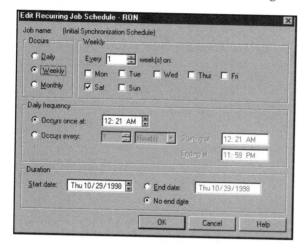

FIGURE 24-31

You can change the default schedule of the snapshot.

The next step is to decide on the access control list, shown in Figure 24-32.

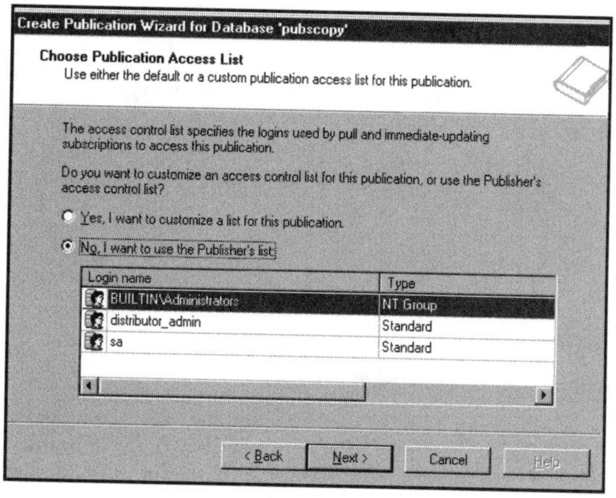

FIGURE 24-32

You can accept or change the default access control list.

The list contains logins that can be used in the replication process by pull subscriptions and immediate-updating subscribers. The final dialog box lets you finish and create the publication.

Merge Replication

When using the Create Publication Wizard for merge replication, you'll see most of the same dialog boxes as shown in the previous section, with some important exceptions:

In merge replication, for example, you cannot have any immediate-updating subscribers. Also, you cannot replicate stored procedure execution.

When you look at the article's Properties dialog box, you won't see a Commands tab, but you will see a new Resolver tab, as shown in Figure 24-33.

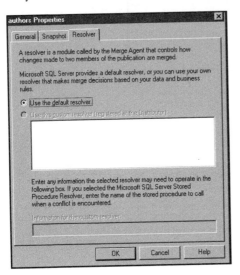

FIGURE 24-33

You can choose an alternate resolver in the article's Properties tab for a merge publication.

Another difference between merge replication and the other types is that you can define static or dynamic filters. A dynamic filter will be reevaluated for each subscriber, so you can add filters that contain a function such as susername(), which differs for each individual subscriber.

After you choose a dynamic or static filter and then specify a WHERE condition for the table, you'll then come to a dialog box that lets you define the filter in relation to other tables, as shown in Figure 24-34.

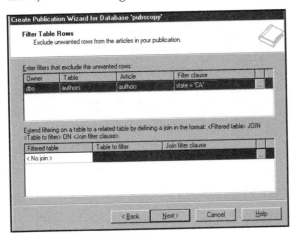

FIGURE 24-34

You can extend a filter in relation to other tables in merge replication.

This feature is unique to merge replication. The remaining dialog boxes are the same as for transactional and snapshot replication.

Publication Properties

When the publication is created, you'll see it entered in a new Publications node of the database in Enterprise Manager. You can then right-click and edit the publication's properties, as shown in Figure 24-35.

There are some important things to note about this dialog box, though. Unlike in

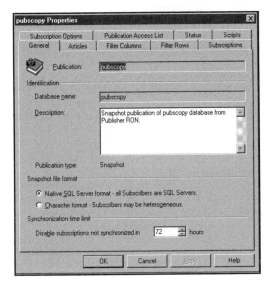

FIGURE 24-35

The Publication Properties dialog box summarizes the choices you made during the publication's creation.

most Properties dialog boxes, you cannot change the name of the publication. Further, if any subscriptions are already installed using this publication, then many of the properties cannot be changed.

Subscribing to a Publication

Once a publication has been created, all that remains is for subscriber servers to subscribe to it. This can be done in either a pull or push fashion.

In a pull subscription, once the snapshot of data is in place, the agent performing the ongoing replication resides on the subscriber server and does its updates whenever the subscriber determines. In the case of transactional replication, the distribution agent resides on the subscriber, and for merge replication, it's the merge agent on the subscriber.

In a push subscription, the agent performing the ongoing replication resides on the distribution server. The agent attempts to "push" the data on its own schedule, not on the subscriber's schedule. Compared to setting up replication and creating publications, creating a subscription is quite simple.

Creating a Pull Subscription

To subscribe in a pull fashion, start the Pull Subscription Wizard. After a welcoming dialog box, you'll be asked to identify a publication, as shown in Figure 24-36.

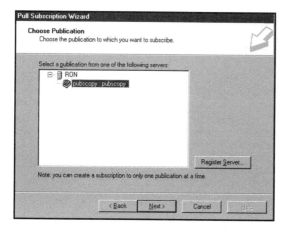

FIGURE 24-36

The first step in setting up a pull subscription is to identify the publication.

If you're working on the subscriber server, you can register the publisher, drill down to its publications, and choose one.

The next steps are to specify a synchronization login for the SQL Agent on the subscriber and choose when to start the snapshot. Finally, you need to choose how frequently the distribution agent should log in and get replicated data, as shown in Figure 24-37.

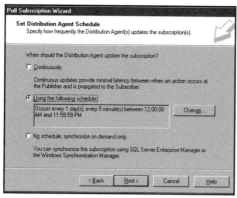

FIGURE 24-37

After specifying a SQL Agent login and when to perform the snapshot, you're asked to decide a frequency of update for the subscriber.

The options are fairly straightforward and don't need very much comment. The basic choice is between frequent access (and therefore low latency) and less frequent access (and higher latency). The final choice is to make sure the SQL Agent service is running on the subscriber. You then choose Finish and the subscription is in place.

Creating a Push Subscription

The push subscription steps are also simple, though they start with the assumption that you are on either the publication or distribution server. When the Create and Manage Publications dialog box comes up, just drill down to the publication, as shown in Figure 24-38.

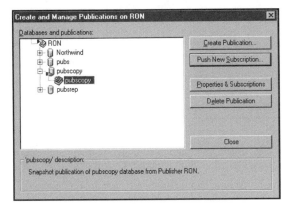

FIGURE 24-38

You must first find a publication before you can create a push subscription.

Click the Push New Subscription button, and the Push Subscription Wizard will start up. In this case, since you're pushing the data out to subscribers, you need to choose the subscribers from the dialog box after the welcoming dialog box, as shown in Figure 24-39.

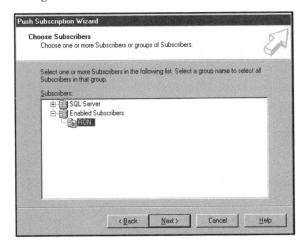

FIGURE 24-39

You need to choose the subscribers next.

If you have grouped the subscribers, you can just select the group. The next step is a simple one, but it brings up an important point: What is the name of the database on each subscriber server that will be receiving the data? This is illustrated in Figure 24-40.

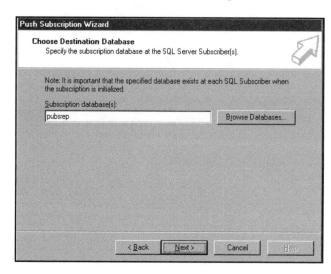

FIGURE 24-40

You must then choose a database name for all the subscribers.

What's important to realize is that a push subscription assumes that the receiving database is named the same on all subscriber servers. That will most likely be true; but when it's not, you'll have to either create distinct subscriptions or switch over to pull-style subscriptions.

The remaining steps are rather straightforward. You choose the frequency with which the distribution agent (in the case of transactional replication) will act to update the subscriber. Then you choose whether and when the subscription needs to be initialized. Finally, you make sure that the proper agent is running on the distribution server.

Removing Replication

You have a number of ways to remove replication, depending on how much you want removed.

Removing a Publication

You can remove a publication by drilling down into the database that houses it, finding the publication, right-clicking, and then choosing Delete. You'll be presented with a confirmation dialog box, notifying you that it will also delete all subscriptions.

Removing a Subscription

You can remove a pull subscription by drilling down into the subscriber database, finding the subscription, selecting it, right-clicking, and choosing Delete.

You can remove a push subscription by drilling down to the publication, right-clicking, choosing Properties, and then going to the Subscriptions tab, shown in Figure 24-41.

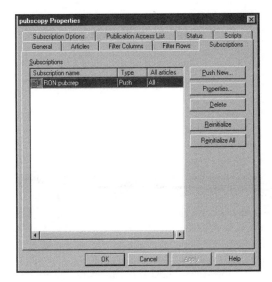

FIGURE 24-41

You can remove push subscriptions from the publication's Properties dialog box.

Removing Replication

You can remove replication entirely from a server by using the Disable Replication Wizard. Since the dialog boxes are very clear, there's no need to go through them here. However, it is worth thinking about scripting out your replication before removing it, just in case you forgot how you created it!

Scripting Replication

You can create a script that re-creates your publication by going to the Properties dialog box of any publication and choosing the Scripts tab, as shown in Figure 24-42.

You have the choice of three text formats, as well as whether to create or delete the publication. As with the other script generation tools in Enterprise Manager, you can preview the result of the re-created script or save to a file.

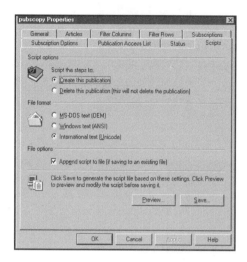

FIGURE 24-42

You can script out both the re-creation and the deletion of a publication.

Summary

Replication in SQL Server 7 uses a publisher/subscriber model, where a publishing database pushes data or has data pulled to one or more subscribers. The workhorse in this scenario is the distributor, consisting of a distribution database and distribution tasks. Quite commonly, the distribution system is put on a dedicated server, a distribution server.

SQL Server 7 provides three flavors of replication: transactional, snapshot, and merge. Both transactional and snapshot allow for immediate-updating subscribers, which allow a subscriber to change data and propagate the change to the publisher server, which will then replicate it to all the remaining subscribers. Merge replication uses a resolver that you can customize, which manages conflicts.

Now that you've looked at the interaction of many SQL Servers in replication, let's turn to your last topic in server integration, SQL Server 7's OLAP Services.

Chapter 25

OLAP Services

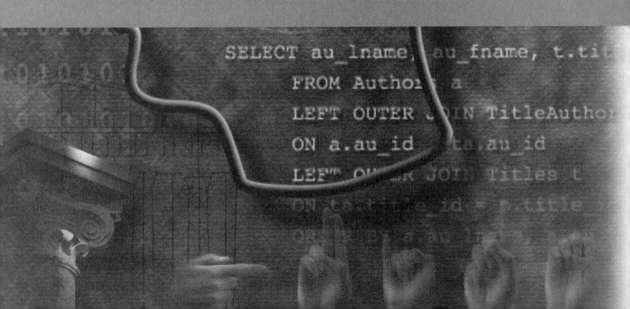

In This Chapter

♦ Microsoft SQL Server 7 OLAP Services overview

♦ From cross-tabs to cubes

♦ Building an OLAP data cube

♦ Inspecting the Foodmart sample cube

SQL Server 7 comes with a data analysis tool called OLAP Services (code-named "Plato" during development). OLAP stands for online analytical processing, and Microsoft OLAP Services allows you to perform sophisticated analyses on your data.

The entire tool is a complex product, consisting of both server and client components. A complete treatment would require another book! In this chapter, you'll take an introductory look at the overall architecture of OLAP Services, how you can build a data cube, and how you can use server-side OLAP facilities.

Microsoft SQL Server 7.0 OLAP Services Overview

The OLAP Services data analysis tools are meant to supplement a data warehouse or decision support system. The product consists of an OLAP Server service, a management tool similar to Enterprise Manager, and a client pivot table service. Let's take a brief look at these concepts.

Decision Support Systems

A decision support system, often known as a DSS system, is an application that allows users to query a comprehensive database for reporting and analysis purposes. You may hear the term DSS used in variety of ways: Someone may use it to refer to a database or collection of databases, or to an entire database application. The term goes back to the mid-1980s and originally referred to reporting systems that only executives or a few selected analysts would use. DSS systems are also thought of as read-only, because the data is being analyzed or summarized by its users, not changed.

A DSS system is based on, and generally contrasted with, an OLTP system, short for online transaction processing. It's transaction-based because the data is very dynamic and frequently changing. Most DBMS products were originally developed for OLTP systems and only later used for DSS purposes.

OLTP and DSS systems complement each other. Normally, OLTP systems do not contain very much history. In fact, it's common to archive old data out of OLTP systems when it's no longer being updated. This keeps the OLTP system from losing performance due to tables becoming too large.

On the other hand, querying history is something that DSS systems are often used very heavily for. Consequently, DSS systems tend to have much larger data sets that are queried often.

You can see a diagram of the complementary relationship between OLTP and DSS systems in Figure 25-1.

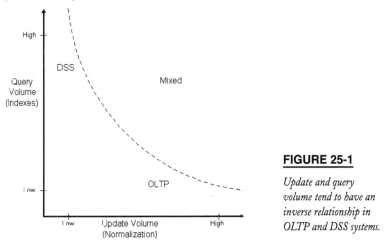

FIGURE 25-1

Update and query volume tend to have an inverse relationship in OLTP and DSS systems.

DSS systems have a high volume of queried data, and therefore more indexes, but a relatively small (and often nonexistent) update frequency. By contrast, OLTP systems have a relatively low query frequency and high update volume.

Data Warehouses

In the past several years, the capacity of DBMS systems to store data has grown, as well as the amount of stored data. Many organizations have benefited from storing all of an enterprise's data in one location for the purposes of building DSS systems. Thus a new form of DSS system, the data warehouse, came into being. A data warehouse is just that: a DBMS that stores all of an enterprise's data relevant for analysis in one central location.

The design and building of a data warehouse is a complex undertaking. Not only do you have to design a structure that will satisfy many reporting and analytical needs, but you often have to extract the data from a variety of database applications spread throughout an orgranization.

Consequently, data transfer and transformation become an important component of building a data warehouse. For this phase of the action, Microsoft SQL Server provides you the Data Transformation Services, or DTS. (For more about DTS, see Chapter 10, "Importing and Exporting Data.")

In very large organizations, it may be more efficient to let selected groups of users have copies of relevant parts of the data warehouse, called data marts. These data marts can be spread throughout the organization and queried without impeding the performance of each other or the main data warehouse.

Over the years, builders of data warehouses have settled on a couple of models for designing data warehouse tables. The core model is called the star configuration: A central fact table contains one or more quantitative data points called the measures. The fact table is surrounded by one level of lookup tables, called the dimensions. For example, a central fact table might be surrounded by product, time, location, demographic, and other dimensions, as illustrated in Figure 25-2.

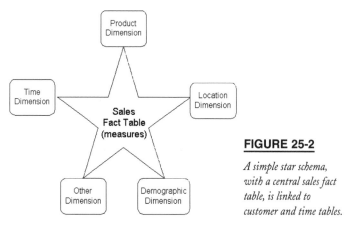

FIGURE 25-2

A simple star schema, with a central sales fact table, is linked to customer and time tables.

You could then realize the design of the start schema in a relational DBMS by making each of the dimensions a table. So if the purpose of the data warehouse is to track sales, then the central fact table should consist of individual sales facts with keys that link them to the dimensional lookup tables, as shown in Figure 25-3.

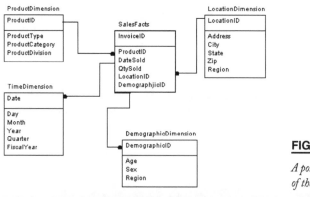

FIGURE 25-3

A possible ER diagram of the sample star schema

By keeping a narrow central fact table, you can store a much larger number of rows. Note for example the time dimension table: It contains the date and date parts, as well as the quarter and fiscal year. The time lookup table does not contain all possible dates, just the dates in the sales table. Then a simple single join, with no further calculations, can give you all the sales in a certain quarter of a fiscal year. The same reasoning applies to the location and product dimension tables.

Sometimes analysts need even more detail, causing the schema to need further satellite tables, causing what's called a snowflake structure. This might occur if the product dimension was also linked to a products table, for example. The disadvantage of a snowflake schema is the additional joins that are necessary to produce complex query results.

It can be a real challenge to define a good viable schema for a particular data warehouse. First, the designer must anticipate the requirements for analysis and make sure that sufficient data elements are included in the data warehouse to answer the kinds of queries the user will want to execute. Second, to implement the warehouse, data must often be collected from diverse data sources and cleansed so that it all meets a consistently high quality. Third, the data must be refreshed on a periodic basis so that the analyses can stay current.

NOTE

Often data warehouses are built using DBMS systems such as SQL Server that were originally architected as OLTP systems. However, some high-end DBMSs, such as Red Brick and NCR's Teradata, are designed exclusively for data warehouses. They contain no transaction capabilities, but excellent indexing and storage optimization features.

Once the warehouse is built, then users can query the data. However, since the underlying measures are quantities, much analysis of the data will involve aggregations of the data: sums, averages, means, and such.

A problem arises here: If all of these aggregations have to be recalculated for each query, the performance of the data warehouse system against a large data set will suffer.

OLAP Services to the Rescue

The OLAP technology in Microsoft OLAP Services provides a way to store those data warehouse aggregations so that analytical queries can perform much faster. It stores them in its own database in a cube structure, a flexible method of viewing data based on the dimensions and measures originally stored in the data warehouse.

Microsoft SQL Server OLAP Services is a middle-tier product that has both server-side and client-side components, as shown in Figure 25-4.

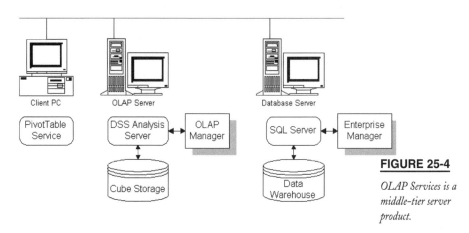

FIGURE 25-4

OLAP Services is a middle-tier server product.

It consists first and foremost of the DSS Analysis Server, a server-side Windows NT service that builds, stores, and maintains OLAP cubes. (In this chapter, you'll follow the Microsoft documentation and refer to it as the OLAP Server.) These data cubes are based on some external database, normally a data warehouse in SQL Server or some other relational DBMS. Since the DSS Analysis Server is an NT service, you can stop and start the service from the Control Panel, just as you would SQL Server.

You can build and maintain these data cubes on the OLAP Server using the OLAP Manager, a Microsoft Management Console snap-in that has a role analogous to Enterprise Manager in SQL Server. The aggregations can be stored in a relational database, in a relational OLAP (ROLAP) format, in a proprietary multidimensional OLAP format (MOLAP), or a hybrid relational/multidimensional (HOLAP) format.

In a production setting, you would probably keep the OLAP Server on its own server machine, as illustrated in the figure. However, you can run the DSS server on the same computer as SQL Server.

The PivotTable service is a client-side, in-process server that presents an interface that client software can use to gain access to stored cubes. It runs on the client and communicates directly with the OLAP Server.

Both the OLAP Manager and the PivotTable service make calls to the object model exposed by the OLAP Server.

So what are these data cubes that you can store in the OLAP Server? To get a clear understanding of this, you need to look at the difficulties in getting good analytical data using Transact-SQL, and how the data cubes overcome them.

From Cross-Tabs to Cubes

Why not just use the Transact-SQL language directly against data to analyze it? After all, you already analyze a lot of data using SQL. However, there is a certain rigidity in the SQL language when it comes to cross-tabulating data from a table. Many strategies can be used to overcome this, including the TRANSFORM() function in Access, and pivot tables in Excel. In fact, an OLAP cube can be seen as a cross-tab or pivot table on steroids, and more. Let's take look at the SQL language first.

Building a Cross-Tab in Transact-SQL

Some significant limitations to the SQL language show up when one is trying to make cross-tabulations of data. These limitations are inherent in the language and not limited to the Transact-SQL dialect.

What is a cross-tabulation? Consider the following query from the Pubs database's Titles table. It just gets a list of all the title IDs, publisher IDs, types, and year-to-date sales from the table, one row for each title:

```
SELECT title_id, pub_id, type, ytd_sales
        FROM Titles
```

Here are the first few rows of the results:

title_id	pub_id	type	ytd_sales
BU1032	1389	business	4095
BU1111	1389	business	3876
BU2075	0736	business	18722
BU7832	1389	business	4095
MC2222	0877	mod_cook	2032
MC3021	0877	mod_cook	22246

Now suppose you want to see some summary data. You want to see the total amount sold by each publisher, for each title. All you have to do is add a GROUP BY statement and drop out the title ID:

```
SELECT pub_id, type, SUM(ytd_sales) AS ytd_sales
        FROM Titles
        GROUP BY pub_id, type
```

The results are:

pub_id	type	ytd_sales

0736	business	18722
1389	business	12066
0877	mod_cook	24278
1389	popular_comp	12875
0736	psychology	9564
0877	psychology	375
0877	trad_cook	19566
0877	UNDECIDED	NULL

However, the results set, as it stands, does not present the data in a way that is easy to make comparisons. Since the publisher ID repeats, it is rather difficult to compare how a publisher ID did with one type versus another (though you could sort it on publisher id). Further, the only way to tell that a given publisher did not publish titles of a particular type, say business, is to read the entire table and see whether it is missing.

A better way to present the data is in a two-dimensional table with the numeric data in the cells. That is what a cross-tabulation can do, as you can see in the following data (to fit the data on the page smoothly, the "UNDECIDED" type has been omitted):

pub_id	business	mod_cook	popular_comp	psychology	trad_cook
......	....	....	....	....	....
0736	18722	0	0	9564	0
0877	0	24278	0	375	19566
1389	12066	0	12875	0	0

The publisher IDs are listed in the left-hand column, and each type has its own column across the first row. Then the numeric data occupies the body of the table.

You can see the rigidity of the SQL language in building this kind of cross-tabulation in the statement that produced the preceding data:

```
SELECT t.pub_id,
            ISNULL((SELECT sum(ytd_sales) FROM titles WHERE type = 'business' AND
    pub_id = t.pub_id), 0)
                AS 'business',
            ISNULL((SELECT sum(ytd_sales) FROM titles WHERE type = 'mod_cook' AND
    pub_id = t.pub_id), 0)
                AS 'mod_cook',
            ISNULL((SELECT sum(ytd_sales) FROM titles WHERE type = 'popular_comp'
    AND pub_id = t.pub_id), 0)
                AS 'popular_comp',
```

```
               ISNULL((SELECT sum(ytd_sales) FROM titles WHERE type = 'psychology' AND
➥ pub_id = t.pub_id), 0)
                    AS 'psychology',
               ISNULL((SELECT sum(ytd_sales) FROM titles WHERE type = 'trad_cook' AND
➥ pub_id = t.pub_id), 0)
                    AS 'trad_cook',
               ISNULL((SELECT sum(ytd_sales) FROM titles WHERE type = 'UNDECIDED' AND
➥ pub_id = t.pub_id), 0)
                    AS 'UNDECIDED'
FROM titles t
GROUP BY t.pub_id
```

Notice that each column must be explicitly mentioned, hard-coded, in the query. There's no way to make the number of cross-tabulated columns dynamic. If you add a new row to the original titles table and give it a new type, you must add a new clause to the SQL SELECT statement in order to show that new type in the cross-tabulation. Further, to decide how many types to include, you must first query the table.

A second problem arises from the use of correlated subqueries, which can be difficult to understand and less efficient to execute.

One is left thinking, there must be a better way!

The Transact-SQL CUBE Operator

You can make another attempt to get around the SQL language's rigidity by using the Transact-SQL CUBE operator. The CUBE creates additional rows in a SELECT statement with sums that include all the data of a cross-tab, though not in a cross-tab format.

For example, continuing with your desire to compare all the publisher IDs and their total year-to-date sales from the pubs Titles table, you could issue this code:

```
SELECT CASE WHEN (GROUPING(t.pub_id) = 1) THEN 'ALL'
            ELSE ISNULL(t.pub_id, '????') END AS 'Pub ID',
         CASE WHEN (GROUPING(t.type) = 1) THEN 'ALL'
            ELSE ISNULL(t.type, '????') END AS 'Title Type',
         ISNULL(SUM(t.ytd_sales), 0) AS 'Total Sales'
         FROM titles t
         GROUP BY t.pub_id,  t.type
         WITH CUBE
```

The actual use of the CUBE is rather simple. The query appears a bit more complicated because it's necessary to determine the grouping level to distinguish when NULL means a summary item as opposed to an actual value.

You'll see the following results:

```
Pub ID Title Type    Total Sales
...... ............  ...........

0736   business      18722
0736   psychology    9564
0736   ALL           28286
0877   mod_cook      24278
0877   psychology    375
0877   trad_cook     19566
0877   UNDECIDED     0
0877   ALL           44219
1389   business      12066
1389   popular_comp  12875
1389   ALL           24941
ALL    ALL           97446
ALL    business      30788
ALL    mod_cook      24278
ALL    popular_comp  12875
ALL    psychology    9939
ALL    trad_cook     19566
ALL    UNDECIDED     0
```

Unfortunately, you have to read the list quite carefully to interpret the data. Where the pub_ID is ALL, and the type is ALL, then the sum, 97446, is the sum of year-to-date sales for all publishers and all titles. Once you see that, the remaining rows are quite clear.

Nevertheless, despite the fact that the summaries are all present, the results set is still not as easy to read as a cross-tabulation.

Built-in Functions

Some products provide an alternative to writing hard-coded SQL SELECT cross-tabs by giving you built-in functions to transform a narrow, long table into a short, wide table, as you just did. Both Microsoft Access and SAS use the TRANSFORM() keyword, Access as a function and SAS as a procedure, to do the job.

For example, the same results set just shown using Transact-SQL can be done in Access using the following Access-specific keywords:

```
TRANSFORM Sum(dbo_titles.ytd_sales) AS [The Value]
SELECT dbo_titles.pub_id, Sum(dbo_titles.ytd_sales) AS [Total Of ytd_sales]
FROM dbo_titles
GROUP BY dbo_titles.pub_id
PIVOT dbo_titles.type;
```

Despite the fact that the TRANSFORM and PIVOT keywords are not standard SQL, the syntax is quite clear. Using these keywords, you do not have to hard-code the horizontal dimension's columns.

Pivot Tables

As an alternative to writing SQL statements to manipulate data into a cross-tab format, both Microsoft Excel and Access provide what are called pivot tables, a flexible and modifiable form of cross-tabulated data.

In Excel, for example, you can take the same titles data and create a pivot table, as shown in Figure 25-5.

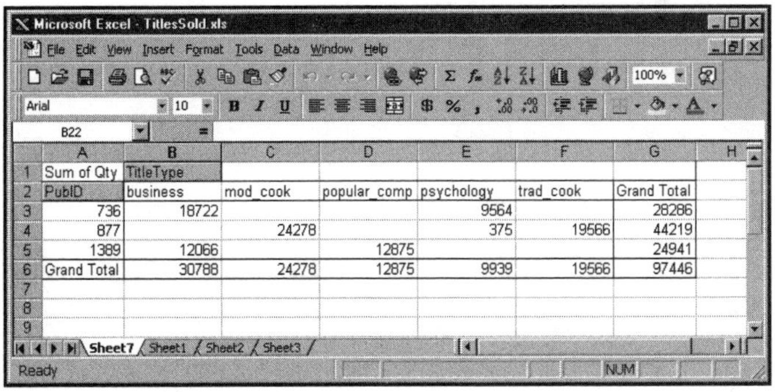

FIGURE 25-5

A pivot table in Excel matches the cross-tabs created earlier.

The flexibility of the pivot table stems from the ability to selectively change the appearance of the table by dragging and dropping the dimensions. For example, by simply dragging the TitleType to where the PubID column is, and dragging the PubID column title up to where TitleType was, you can invert the table, as shown in Figure 25-6.

With a pivot table, you can vary the appearance of your data quite easily. Now it's just a brief step to OLAP cubes.

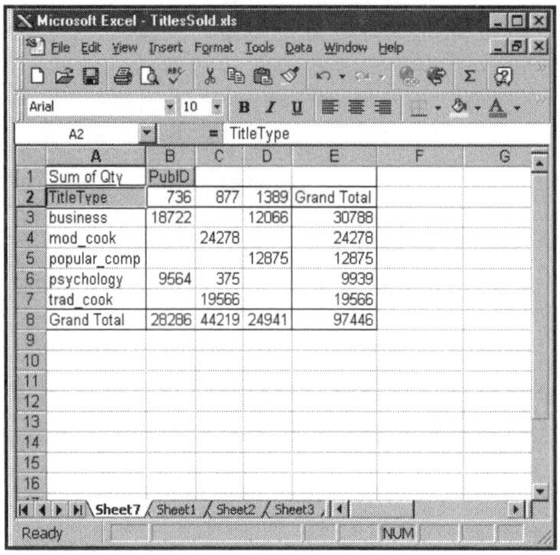

	A	B	C	D	E
1	Sum of Qty	PubID			
2	TitleType	736	877	1389	Grand Total
3	business	18722		12066	30788
4	mod_cook		24278		24278
5	popular_comp			12875	12875
6	psychology	9564	375		9939
7	trad_cook		19566		19566
8	Grand Total	28286	44219	24941	97446

FIGURE 25-6

The same table, now pivoted

Multidimensional Data

So far you've looked at data arranged in two dimensions, in order to keep the example simple. OLAP Services cubes can actually work with up to 64 dimensions. Let's take a look at how adding a third dimension to your example changes its appearance.

The actual data source you've used for your example includes the publisher ID and title type from the Titles table. It's easy to add another dimension, either from inside the titles table or from an external table such as Publishers. For an example, choose the publish date (pubdate).

You can reconstruct your original SQL cross-tab could as follows:

```
SELECT t.pub_id, CAST(t.pubdate AS VARCHAR(11)) AS pubdate,
            ISNULL((SELECT sum(ytd_sales) FROM titles WHERE type = 'business' AND
pub_id = t.pub_id), 0)
                 AS 'business',
            ISNULL((SELECT sum(ytd_sales) FROM titles WHERE type = 'mod_cook' AND
pub_id = t.pub_id), 0)
                 AS 'mod_cook',
            ISNULL((SELECT sum(ytd_sales) FROM titles WHERE type = 'popular_comp'
AND pub_id = t.pub_id), 0)
                 AS 'popular_comp',
            ISNULL((SELECT sum(ytd_sales) FROM titles WHERE type = 'psychology'
AND pub_id = t.pub_id), 0)
                 AS 'psychology',
```

```
                ISNULL((SELECT sum(ytd_sales) FROM titles WHERE type = 'trad_cook' AND
➡ pub_id = t.pub_id), 0)
                AS 'trad_cook',
                ISNULL((SELECT sum(ytd_sales) FROM titles WHERE type = 'UNDECIDED' AND
➡ pub_id = t.pub_id), 0)
                AS 'UNDECIDED'
FROM titles t
GROUP BY t.pub_id, t.pubdate
```

The CAST() function changes the appearance so that the results set includes just the date, not the time:

pub_id	pubdate	business	mod_cook	popular_comp	psychology	trad_cook	UNDECIDED
0736	Jun 12 1991	18722	0	0	9564	0	0
0736	Jun 15 1991	18722	0	0	9564	0	0
0736	Jun 30 1991	18722	0	0	9564	0	0
0736	Oct 5 1991	18722	0	0	9564	0	0
0877	Jun 9 1991	0	24278	0	375	19566	0
0877	Jun 12 1991	0	24278	0	375	19566	0
0877	Jun 18 1991	0	24278	0	375	19566	0
0877	Oct 21 1991	0	24278	0	375	19566	0
0877	Sep 26 1998	0	24278	0	375	19566	0
1389	Jun 9 1991	12066	0	12875	0	0	0
1389	Jun 12 1991	12066	0	12875	0	0	0
1389	Jun 22 1991	12066	0	12875	0	0	0
1389	Jun 30 1991	12066	0	12875	0	0	0
1389	Jun 12 1994	12066	0	12875	0	0	0
1389	Sep 26 1998	12066	0	12875	0	0	0

Now there are 15 rows because the date is included. However, the new time dimension makes the result more difficult to read.

The WITH CUBE query can be similarly expanded:

```
SELECT CASE WHEN (GROUPING(t.pub_id) = 1) THEN 'ALL'
                ELSE ISNULL(t.pub_id, '????') END AS 'Pub ID',
            CASE WHEN (GROUPING(t.type) = 1) THEN 'ALL'
```

```
        ELSE ISNULL(t.type, '????') END AS 'Title Type',
    CAST (pubdate AS VARCHAR(11)) AS pubdate,
    ISNULL(SUM(t.ytd_sales), 0) AS 'Total Sales'
    FROM titles t
    GROUP BY t.pub_id,  t.type, t.pubdate
    WITH CUBE
```

You end up with 75 rows instead of 18, because of the new dimension, also making the result much more difficult to read.

But in an Excel pivot table, you get a surprise: The result is actually fairly easy to handle, as shown in Figure 25-7.

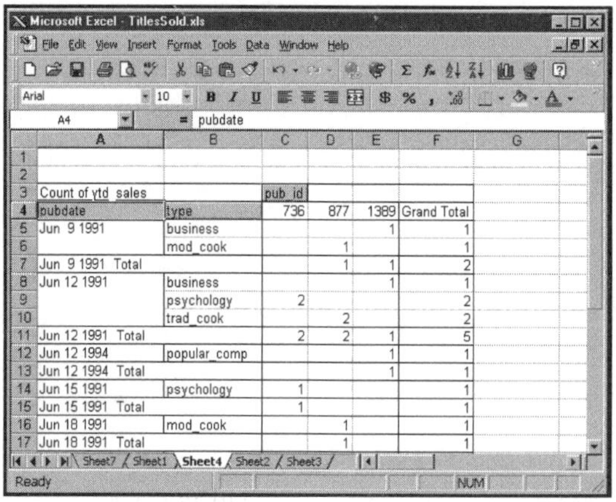

Count of ytd_sales		pub_id			
pubdate	type	736	877	1389	Grand Total
Jun 9 1991	business			1	1
	mod_cook		1		1
Jun 9 1991 Total			1	1	2
Jun 12 1991	business			1	1
	psychology	2			2
	trad_cook		2		2
Jun 12 1991 Total		2	2	1	5
Jun 12 1994	popular_comp			1	1
Jun 12 1994 Total				1	1
Jun 15 1991	psychology	1			1
Jun 15 1991 Total		1			1
Jun 18 1991	mod_cook		1		1
Jun 18 1991 Total			1		1

FIGURE 25-7

An Excel pivot table with three dimensions

The third dimension can be placed externally, or on either the column or the row (as shown in the figure.) Additional dimensions can be placed on either the column or the row, or in a special Page section in the upper left-hand corner.

Clearly, the pivot table is a superior way to present cross-tabulated data, especially when more than one dimension is present in the table.

OLAP Services Data Cubes

OLAP data cubes are simply the data forming the basis for pivot tables. They are based directly on database data and can include a large and extensive number of dimensions.

The major problem with an Excel pivot table is assembling, maintaining, and sharing large amounts of aggregated data. OLAP Services overcomes this by storing the data on a server, in an OLAP format. Multidimensional aggregated data can be stored on the original data server in a relational format (ROLAP), or on the OLAP server in a multidimensional format (MOLAP), or in a combination of the two, a hybrid format (HOLAP.)

Let's proceed to build a cube with OLAP Services using your original example.

Building an OLAP Data Cube

Building an OLAP Data Cube consists of identifying a data source, adding a cube name, and then building the cube by specifying dimensions and members. Microsoft DSS Services comes with a sample data warehouse, called Foodmart, in an Access .mdb database. While OLAP works best against a data warehouse, in this section you'll see how to build a simple cube from the Titles table of the SQL Server pubs database, as you used before. Keeping the data familiar will make the specific OLAP steps more clear. You'll explore the Foodmart cubes in the next section.

Creating an OLAP Database

The first step is to create a new database on the OLAP server. This is not a SQL Server database but rather a database that can hold multidimensional data, along with the definitions of dimensions and members for cubes, on the OLAP Server.

After you've started the OLAP Services Manager, you need to register the OLAP Server, just as you register a SQL Server in Enterprise Manager. You can right-click on the DSS analysis servers node, then choose Register server, and choose the name of the OLAP server you want to register. Like SQL Server, the OLAP Server takes its name from the name of the computer. Unlike SQL Server, the OLAP Server does not require you to log in to register it. Once the server is registered, you'll see it in the console, as shown in Figure 25-8.

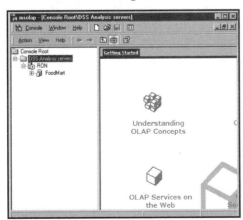

FIGURE 25-8

After you register the OLAP Server, you can drill down to the sample database.

You'll take a closer look at the Foodmart sample OLAP database in the next section.

For now, create a new OLAP database called Pubscopy, using the Pubscopy SQL Server database. Right-click on the server name, choose New Database, and enter the name Pubscopy. The result will be to add a new node under the server name, as shown in Figure 25-9.

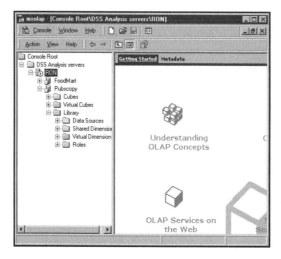

FIGURE 25-9

Adding a new database also adds nodes for Cubes, Virtual Cubes, and Library.

Notice that you can expand the Library node to show several nodes below it. The most important for you now is the Data Sources node, which provides you with a way to specify an external data source for the underlying OLAP data.

Right-click on Data Sources, choose New Data Source, and then fill in the resulting dialog box. The first tab of the dialog box is shown in Figure 25-10.

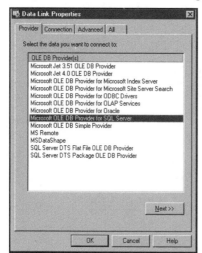

FIGURE 25-10

The first tab of the New Data Source dialog box lets you choose your driver.

To link the OLAP Services database to a relational database, if you specify an ODBC driver, you will need to create an ODBC DSN. (For more information on creating ODBC DSNs, see Chapter 6, "Connectivity.") In your example, since you use the SQL Server OLEDB driver, you do not need an ODBC DSN.

The next tab specifies the connection string, as you can see in Figure 25-11.

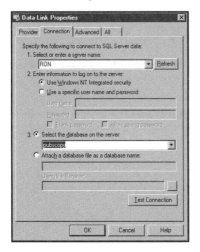

FIGURE 25-11

You specify the connection string in the Connection tab.

It's wise to also test the connection; use the Test Connection button at the lower right.

NOTE

You can also attach to a SQL Server database file without going through the server. You choose the Attach a Database File option and then identify the SQL Server .MDF file (main data file) on disk.

An Advanced tab for choosing a number of options is shown in Figure 25-12.

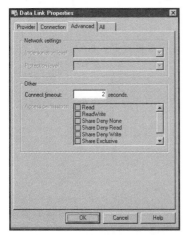

FIGURE 25-12

You can specify a number of connection options in the Advanced tab.

You can choose a number of network options, connection timeout, and access permissions for the connection. Once that's in place, the connection to a data source will show up under the Data Sources node.

Some Decisions

With a data source identified, it's now time to create some dimensions for the cube. You intend to create a TitlesSold cube. However, it's a good idea to decide first of all on what you want to measure and with what dimensions to summarize the data. Following your example in the previous section, you'll measure the year-to-date sold amount along three dimensions: publisher ID, publication date, and title type. The measure and the dimensions should really be created before the cube itself.

Creating Dimensions

You can create either private or shared dimensions. The advantage of a shared dimension is that it can be used in any number of cubes in the OLAP database. Let's create your three dimensions as shared.

Dimension One: Using the Dimension Wizard for Publisher ID

To create the publisher ID dimension, right-click on Shared Dimensions and choose New Dimension. You have the option of using the Dimension Wizard or the dimension editor. For your first dimension, choose the Wizard.

When the Dimension Wizard comes up, choose a single dimension table, and on the next dialog box, drill down and choose the titles table. This is a standard dimension, which you choose on the third dialog box, and then you can specify one level in the fourth dialog box, as shown in Figure 25-13.

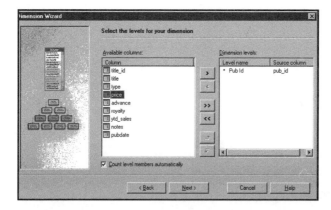

FIGURE 25-13

For a single value like pub_ID, there is only one level to the dimension.

The dimension could have more that one level if there were a combination of data values, such as city, state, and country, that would naturally group together. You'll see an example of that later when you create a related fourth dimension on the publisher location.

Give the dimension the name "PublisherID" in the last dialog box and click on Finish; the Wizard will create the dimension.

The Dimension Wizard leaves you in the dimension editor for further changes, or to create another dimension.

Dimension Two: Using the Dimension Editor to add Title Type

Stay in the dimension editor, or return to the editor by right-clicking on Shared Dimensions, choosing New Dimension, and then choosing Edit. In the dimension editor, you should see the PublisherID dimension.

Right-click on the PublisherID node, choose New Dimension, and in the resulting dialog box, drill down and identify the titles table. The result, after clicking on the OK button, is shown in Figure 25-14.

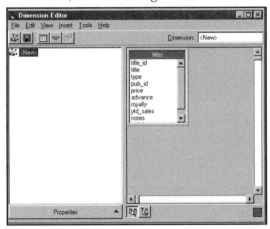

FIGURE 25-14

The next dimension uses the type column.

You can now click on the Insert Level icon on the toolbar, or right-click on the New node and pick New Level, and then choose the type column. Save the new dimension by clicking on the floppy disk icon on the toolbar, or File, Save As from the menu, and save the new dimension as TitleType.

Dimension Three: Publish Date

The third dimension in your example is a date, and time dimensions are treated specially by OLAP Services. There are natural groupings of a date into year, month, day, as well as quarter.

To see this, create the publish-date dimension using the Dimension Wizard. After you choose the titles table and then choose the time dimension, and pubdate as the column, you'll see the dialog box in Figure 25-15.

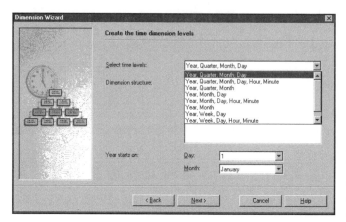

FIGURE 25-15

You can assign date columns a special structure in the Dimension Wizard.

The result of your choice will show up in the Dimension Structure box. Your choice here determines how aggregates for the date data will be formed when the dimensions are processed. For now, go with the default year, quarter, month, and day option. Finish the Wizard's dialog boxes by saving the new dimension as PublishDate.

You are now ready to create your first cube.

Creating a Cube

To create the cube, right-click on Cubes, choose New Cube, and start with the Cube Wizard. Step through the dialog boxes, selecting the titles table, and ytd_sales as the measure, as shown in Figure 25-16.

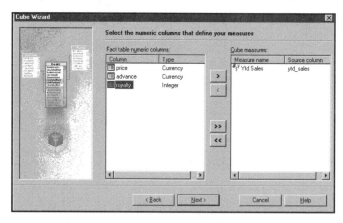

FIGURE 25-16

Measures consist of numeric data.

The OLAP process will calculate aggregates of the measure data along the dimensions you specify. So in the next dialog box, you choose the measures. For this example, choose all three, as shown in Figure 25-17.

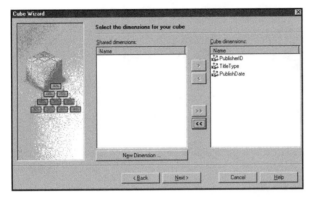

FIGURE 25-17

In this example, choose all three dimensions.

Finish the Cube Wizard by assigning the name TitleSales to the cube and saving it.

The resulting cube editor will show that you're using the Titles table as your fact table, and as the source of your dimensions, as you can see in Figure 25-18.

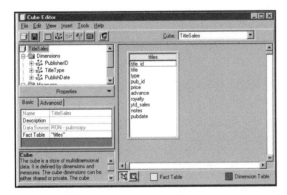

FIGURE 25-18

Your example has one fact table.

There are no dimension tables because you've defined all the dimensions so far from the one titles table. You'll add another dimension table shortly.

Designing Aggregations

Save the cube and do not accept any of the options. You need to process the cube after designing some aggregations. Right-click on the TitleSales cube name and choose Design Aggregations. The resulting Storage Design Wizard allows you to choose how to store the aggregations: in ROLAP, MOLAP, or HOLAP format, as you can see in Figure 25-19.

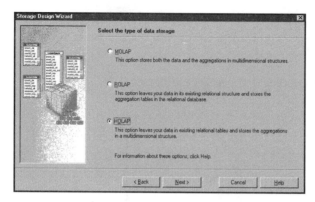

FIGURE 25-19

You must choose how to store aggregated data.

If you choose either relational OLAP or hybrid OLAP, the OLAP Services will create tables for aggregation back in your original SQL Server database. If you choose multidimensional OLAP, all aggregations will be stored in the OLAP Server's database.

Generally speaking, MOLAP will be better at storing aggregated data. However, the multidimensional format is proprietary and cannot be used outside of the OLAP Services server. You may want to use the aggregations, for example, in other queries on SQL Server. In the example, choose the HOLAP option.

The next dialog box in the Storage Design Wizard concerns the degree to which aggregations should be optimized, as shown in Figure 25-20.

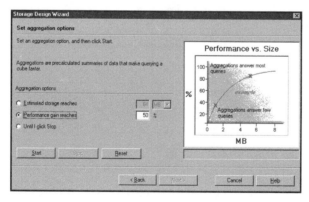

FIGURE 25-20

You specify the degree to which aggregations should be optimized.

Faster queries on large amounts of data will require a higher degree of aggregation. On the other hand, the greater aggregation will take up more space and more time to process them. The choice is a tradeoff, and the dialog box lets you decide.

For your example, choose 50% performance gain. Start the processing, which should take only a second or so, and then in the following dialog box, process the cube's dimensions.

Processing large cubes with extensive dimensions will require a powerful OLAP server with substantial RAM and virtual memory.

Browsing Cube Data

To browse cube data, right-click on the cube name, enter the cube editor, and choose View, Data from the menu. Now you can browse its data in a pivot table format as shown in Figure 25-21.

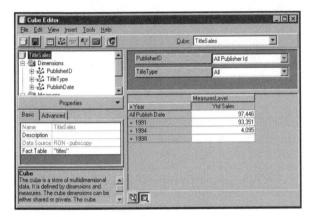

FIGURE 25-21

You can browse the cube data in a pivot table format after processing it.

T IP

If there is a message at the bottom of the screen saying that you can only browse sample data, then process the cube data from within the cube editor by choosing Tools, Process Cube.

The first instance shows the time dimension, publish date, in the left column and the measures in the right column. The other two dimensions, PublisherID and TitleType, are available but unused in the upper part of the right-hand pane.

You can now drill down for more granular detail on the dates. Because of the way you defined the dimension, the levels are year, quarter, month, and day.

In addition, you can drag any of the other two dimensions down and add them to the pivot view in order to gain a more detailed summary. In Figure 25-22, for example, the TitleType dimension was dragged down over the date dimension, and when dropped, it becomes a part of the left-hand column parameters.

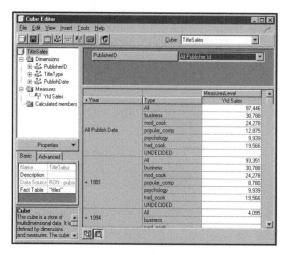

FIGURE 25-22

You can add the other dimensions to the table.

In addition, when other dimensions are in the upper pane, their values are available in a pull-down list and you can select a particular one. For example, the publisher ID in the figure is set at All Values, but you can choose a particular one to make the results more specific.

NOTE

You can also browse cube data in the OLAP Manager by selecting the cube name and then choosing the Data option.

Adding a Dimension Table to the Cube

So far, your cube has been unrealistically simple, getting all its dimension data from one table. Let's add a second table, the publishers table, which contains location data for publishers. So for your purposes, it is essentially a location table.

In the Library node, create a new shared dimension called PublisherLocation, based on the Publishers table. Over the Shared Dimension node start the New Dimension Wizard, select a single dimension table, select the publishers table, and then specify the levels from the outermost to innermost, as shown in Figure 25-23.

There's no point in choosing pub_name, because it's not a part of the hierarchy, though it is a member property, as you'll soon see. Save the dimension as PublisherLocation.

Now bring up the TitleSales cube in the cube editor, right-click on the Dimensions node, and choose the Dimension Manager, which will allow you to add the new shared dimension to the cube, as shown in Figure 25-24.

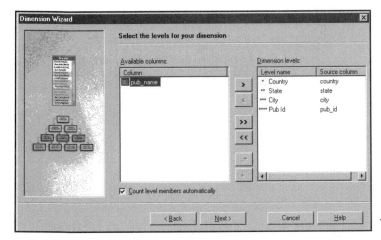

FIGURE 25-23

You must specify dimension levels from the outermost to innermost.

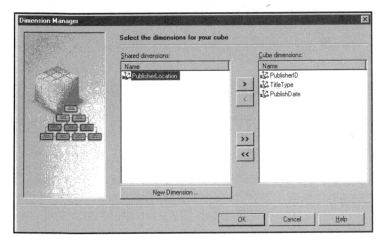

FIGURE 25-24

Now you can add the new dimension to the cube.

Once you move the PublisherLocation dimension to the other side, close the dialog box, and you'll see that the cube editor has picked up the join between the Titles and Publishers tables.

Because you've added an unprocessed dimension to the cube, you need to reprocess the cube. Save the cube, choose Tools, Process, and process the cube. You'll also have to redecide the storage structures.

Now when you browse the data, the new PublisherLocation dimension will show up in the upper-right pane. By dragging it down to the Publisher Date axis, you can now see a breakdown of year by location, as shown in Figure 25-25.

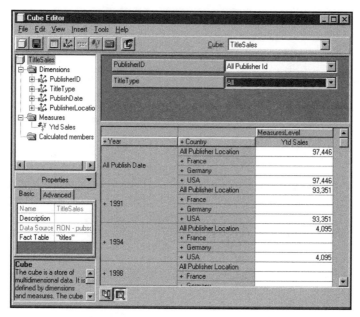

FIGURE 25-25

*Using the new
dimension to inspect
years by location*

You can double-click on areas that have plus signs (+); they will expand and contract so that you can drill down even further.

Virtual Dimensions and Cubes

You can also create virtual dimensions, based on other shared dimensions. You can create private dimensions, which are cube-specific. You can also create virtual cubes, which are cubes based on other cubes. Finally, you can add member properties to any level of a dimension; a member property is a coterminal value, like pub_name with pub_id.

Inspecting the Foodmart Sample Cube

The OLAP Services utility comes with a sample cube called Foodmart, which is based on a data warehouse stored in foodmart.mdb. Also, the online tutorial that you can start in the OLAP Manager takes you through the steps to build the Foodmart cube.

The Foodmart data warehouse is a Jet database, and you can see the related tables and their structure shown in Figure 25-26.

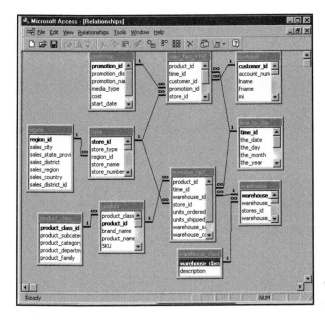

FIGURE 25-26

The Foodmart data warehouse has a snowflake structure.

The overall structure of the Foodmart data warehouse is a snowflake, because of the ancillary region, product_class, and warehouse_class tables. As you can infer from the relationships in the figure and by the table names, there are two fact tables, sales_fact and inventory_fact. The sales fact table has promotion, customer, time_by_day, store, and dimensions tables. The inventory fact table has store, region, time_by_day, warehouse, warehouse_class, product, and product_class dimension tables.

When you look at the OLAP database, you'll find that there are two cubes: one for sales and one for warehouse. Drilling down into the Sales cube, you'll notice a number of both shared and private dimensions, as you can see in Figure 25-27.

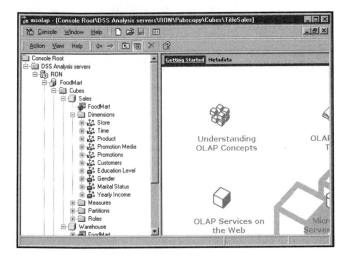

FIGURE 25-27

The sales cube has both shared and private dimensions.

One interesting feature is the number of demographic dimensions. The large number of dimensions makes for a somewhat complex cube, as you can see in Figure 25-28.

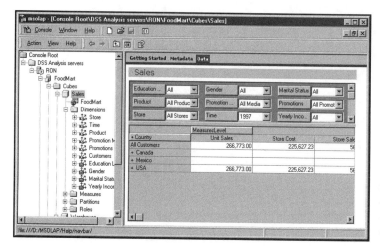

FIGURE 25-28

A large number of dimensions can make a cube complex.

The great advantage for analysis is the rapid speed with which you can retrieve summary data for different dimension choices. For more information specifically about the Foodmart database, work through the online tutorial in the OLAP Manager. The number of aggregations is fairly large, so you need to have at least 64MB of RAM on your computer, and a large amount of virtual memory.

Summary

The Microsoft OLAP Services is a complex and valuable data analysis tool that stands on its own and can analyze data from any number of data sources, not just SQL Server. Because it is meant for large data sets and runs as a Windows NT service, the OLAP Server should be placed on its own server machine.

Appendix A

References

References

The following pages contain notes and references for the preceding chapters. The references have a narrative format to tie them smoothly with the original chapters. The Bibliography appendix following this section has ISBN numbers for books and part numbers for Microsoft white papers.

Part I: SQL Server 7.0 Overview

Chapter 1, "Background", is based on industry-standard terminology and concepts. For an excellent survey of database systems in general, see *Fundamentals of Database Systems* (Elmasri and Navathe [1994]), Chapters 1-5. The best standard introduction to relational database management systems in general is C. J. Date's *Introduction to Database Systems* (Date [1995]), especially Chapters 1-3. For the distinction between presentation, business rules, and data access services, see Peter Hussey's "Designing Efficient Applications for MS SQL Server," Microsoft [1997a]. C. J. Date currently (1999) offers classes on the relational model and object/relational theory through the UCLA Extension.

For an excellent discussion about the distinction between client and server-based computing, see Peter Renaud's *Introduction to Client/Server Systems: A Practical Guide for Systems Professionals* (Renaud [1996]).

SQL Server's development over the years has been influenced by the relational database system model and the ANSI SQL standard, especially SQL-92. On the SQL-92 standard, see *A Guide to the SQL Standard* (Date and Darwen [1997]), as well as *Understanding the New SQL* (Melton and Simon [1993]).

One of the best ways to start learning about the relational model, database design, and normalization is with E. F. Codd's original papers, which are quite readable. Unfortunately, Codd's original paper, "Derivability, Redundancy, and Consistency of Relations stored in large data banks," (Codd [1969]) is out of print. (I got my copy by taking C. J. Date's class at the UCLA Extension.) Most people read his second relational DBMS paper, "A Relational Model of Data for Large Shared Data Banks," (Codd [1971]), which was published through the ACM and is now available as the very first paper in Stonebraker [1995]. C. J. Date has recently revisited Codd's early papers in a series of articles in *Intelligent Enterprise* magazine (Date [1998b]).

For Codd's latest thinking about the relational model, and what a DBMS ideally must have to be called relational, see Codd [1990]. For C. J. Date's latest developments for the relational model, extending it to include objects, see *Foundation for Object/Relational Databases* (Date and Darwen [1998a]).

I relied on Robert N. Stoll's *Set Theory and Logic*, (Stoll [1979]) for an understanding of set theory and relations.

On the distinction between conceptual, logical, and physical data modeling, see *Conceptual Database Design: An Entity-Relationship Approach*, (Batini et. al. [1992]). For additional discussion, as well as a thorough treatment of Object-Role Modeling (ORM), see Terry Halpin's *Conceptual Schema and Relational Database Design* (Halpin [1995]).

The literature on data warehousing is voluminous, and beyond the focus of this book. One of the most popular books is Ralph Kimball, *The Data Warehouse Toolkit*, (Kimball [1996]). For Microsoft's data warehousing perspective and goals, see the white paper "Microsoft SQL Server 7.0 Data Warehousing Framework" (Microsoft [1998h]).

Chapter 2, "Architecture," deals with some general concepts and then with SQL Server 7.0 specifically. For general concepts of database server architecture, see section 1.2 of *A First Course in Database Systems*, (Ullmann and Widom [1997]). Also see Elmasri and Navathe [1994], Chapter 2, for a more complex treatment of general database system architecture.

Ron Soukup unveils SQL Server 6.5 architecture in his *Inside Microsoft SQL Server 6.5* (Soukup [1997]), Chapter 3. Watch for its successor, by Kalen Delaney, due out some time after this book. SQL Server 7.0 architecture is outlined in the SQL Server Books Online, SQL *Server Architecture*. For more in-depth information about the storage engine, see "Microsoft SQL Server 7.0 Storage Engine" (Microsoft [1998m]). For more information about the query engine, see "Microsoft SQL Server 7.0 Query Processor" (Microsoft [1998l]).

Part II: Setting Up

Most of the chapters in this part deal with practical or functional aspects of SQL Server 7.0. For Chapter 3, "Installing", to find out more about the Microsoft Data Engine, see the white paper, "Microsoft Access 2000 Data Engine Options" (Microsoft [1998g]). For Chapter 4, "Upgrading", you can get further information and tips from the white paper: "Upgrading to Microsoft SQL Server 7.0" MS [1998r]. If you are migrating from Access, don't overlook "Migrating Your Microsoft Access Database to Microsoft SQL Server 7.0" (Microsoft [1998n]). For advanced issues related to Chapter 5, "Configuring", check out Henry Lau's papers: "Microsoft SQL Server 7.0 Performance Tuning Guide" (Microsoft [1998k]) and "SAP R/3 Performance Tuning Guide for Microsoft SQL Server 7.0" (Microsoft

[1998o]). The latter especially contains some interesting configuration recommendations.

Chapter 6, "Connectivity", covers a lot of difficult ground. For background concepts on client/server connectivity, see Renaud [1996]. For understanding all versions of SQL Server connectivity, the networking book in the Windows NT 3.51 Resource Kit (Microsoft [1997b]) is quite helpful.

At the database driver layer, for ODBC, see Kyle Geiger's *Inside ODBC* (Geiger [1995], especially section 6.2, "Microsoft SQL Server System Architecture". For more information about OLE DB connectivity, see the white paper "Microsoft SQL Server 7.0 Distributed Queries: OLE DB Connectivity" (Microsoft [1998i]).

For network libraries, I found the entire Chapter 8, "Client-Server Connectivity on Windows NT", of the Windows NT 3.51 Resource Kit Networking most helpful (Microsoft [1997b]). Network libraries were not well documented in previous releases of SQL Server, but SQL Server 7.0's Books Online *SQL Server Architecture* has a very good treatment.

Part III: Administration

For more information about SQL Server 7.0 administration issues, you can probably do best by consulting the online news groups and list servers. Two popular ones are: the Microsoft public news groups (microsoft.public.sqlserver.server, et. al.), and the Wynkoop list server at **http://www.swynk.com.** Look for more white papers from Microsoft as the year goes on, especially with the 1999 release of the Back Office Resource Kit. Of course, don't overlook the relevant chapters of *Administering SQL Server* in the Books Online.

Part IV: Managing Data

For further information related to Chapter 12, "Data Definition", see Date's overview of the SQL language in Chapter 8 of his *An Introduction to Database Systems* (Date [1995]). For authoritative treatments of the SQL language's DDL (data definition language), see *A Guide to the SQL Standard* (Date and Darwen [1997]), and *Understanding the New SQL* (Melton and Simon [1993]). For more information about the SQL Server storage engine, see "Microsoft SQL Server 7.0 Storage Engine" (Microsoft [1998m]).

For more in-depth treatment of data manipulation, the subject of Chapter 13 and following, you can start with Joe Celko's *Instant SQL Programming* (Celko [1995a]). You get a challenging introduction to the SQL language in Rozhenstein's

"The Essence of SQL: A Guide for Learning Most of SQL in the Lease Amount of Time" (Rozhenstein [1995]). For more advanced study, check out *Joe Celko's SQL Puzzles and Answers* (Celko [1997]), and Joe Celko's SQL For Smarties (Celko [1995b]). For more details about the SQL Server query engine, see "Microsoft SQL Server 7.0 Query Processor" (Microsoft [1998l]). For the Full-Text Search engine, see "Textual Searches on File Data Using Microsoft SQL Server 7.0" (Microsoft [1998p]).

You can get further information about English Query, the subject of Chapter 14, by consulting "Developing with Microsoft English Query in Microsoft SQL Server 7.0" (Microsoft [1998d]).

For more information about Transact-SQL programming, covered in Chapter 15, you can start with the excellent *Database Developer's Companion*, part of the product documentation for SQL Server 6.5 (Microsoft [1995]). For advanced techniques, see *Optimizing Transact-SQL: Advanced Programming Techniques* (Rozhenstein et. al. [1995]).

Database transactions, the subject of Chapter 16, is a complex topic. You can find excellent introductions to background issues in Chapter 13 of Date [1995] and Chapter 17 of Elmasri and Navathe [1994]. Ron Soukup (Soukup [1997]) has a good treatment of Transact-SQL issues including isolation levels. An approach covering the two-phase commit in detail can be found in *Principles of Transaction Processing* (Bernstein and Necomer [1997]). An exhaustive treatment of the entire subject can be found in Transaction Processing: Concepts and Techniques (Gray and Reuter [1993]).

For information about stored procedures (Chapter 17) and triggers (Chapter 18), it's difficult to find anything better than the *Database Developer's Companion* (Microsoft [1995]). There's also a wealth of information in Chapter 10 of Soukup [1997].

Part V: Performance

For general issues regarding database tuning and performance, see *Database Tuning: A Principled Approach* (Shasha [1992]). For general performance issues related to SQL Server, see "Microsoft SQL Server 7.0 Performance Tuning Guide" (Microsoft [1998k], and "SAP/R3 Performance Tuning Guide for Microsoft SQL Server 7.0" (Microsoft [1998o]).

For more information about query tuning, the subject of Chapter 19, see "Microsoft SQL Server 7.0 Query Processor" (Microsoft [1998l]), and "Index Tuning Wizard for Microsoft SQL Server 7.0" (Microsoft [1998f]). For basic concepts of query optimization, see Chapter 16 of Elmasri and Navathe [1994]. For a further in-depth treatment of the same, plus explanations of the various kinds of joins shown by SQL Server's graphical showplan, see *Principles of Database Query Processing for Advanced Applications* (Yu and Meng [1998]).

For additional reading related to Chapter 20, "Concurrency Tools", see Chapter 13 of Date [1995] for an excellent introduction to the issues. For more information on SQL Server's locking strategies, see "Microsft SQL Server 7.0 Storage Engine" (Microsoft [1998m]).

For further information about the issues covered in Chapter 21, "Profiler and Perfmon", at press time there are not yet any Microsoft white papers, but look for support for SQL Profiler in the 1999 release of the Back Office Resource Kit. Also consult Peter Lau's performance paper (Microsoft [1998k]) for suggestions on using NT performance counters.

For database load testing, the subject of Chapter 22, consult the Benchmark Factory white paper online at **www.benchmarkfactory.com.**

Part VI: Integration

Distributed queries, the subject of Chapter 23, is covered in "Accessing Heterogenous Data with Microsoft SQL Server 7.0" (Microsoft [1998b]) and "Microsoft SQL Server 7.0 Distributed Queries: OLE DB Connectivity" (Microsoft [1998i]).

For information about SQL Server 7.0 replication, the subject of Chapter 24, it's hard to beat the excellent treatment of Books Online. For more information, see "Replication for Microsoft SQL Server 7.0" (Microsoft [1998q]). For strategies and techniques related to merge replication, see "Developing Mobile Applications for Microsoft SQL Server" (Microsoft [1998c]).

Finally, for OLAP Services, dealt with in Chapter 25, there are numerous sources. For general OLAP concepts you can start with Codd's seminal paper, "OLAP Services: Providing OLAP to User-Analysts: An IT Mandate" (Codd et. al. [1993]). For more information about Microsoft's OLAP Services in particular, see "Microsoft SQL Server 7.0 OLAP Services" (Microsoft [1998j]). For supplemental information, see also "Microsoft SQL Server 7.0 Data Warehousing Framework" (Microsoft [1998h]), and "Implementing Large Decision Support Databases with Microsoft SQL Server 7.0" (Microsoft [1998e]).

Appendix B

Bibliography

Bibliography

In the following citations, titles are in italics and white papers and chapter titles in double quotes. Microsoft white papers are all listed under Microsoft, and the author's name mentioned if it was included in the paper. Both ISBN numbers for books and part numbers for Microsoft SQL Server 7.0 white papers are provided.

Batini C., Ceri S., and Navathe S. [1992] *Conceptual Database Design: An Entity-Relationship Approach*, Benjamin/Cummings, 1992. (ISBN 0-8053-0244-1)

Bernstein, Philip and Newcomer, Eric [1997] *Principles of Transaction Processing*, Morgan Kaufmann, 1997. (ISBN 1-55860-415-4)

Celko, Joe [1995a] *Instant SQL Programming*, Wrox Press, 1995. (ISBN 1-874416-50-8)

Celko, Joe [1995b] *Joe Celko's SQL For Smarties: Advanced SQL Programming*, Morgan Kaufmann, 1995. (ISBN 1-55860-323-9)

Celko, Joe [1997] *Joe Celko's SQL Puzzles and Answers*, Morgan Kaufmann, 1997. (ISBN 1-55860-453-7)

Codd, E. F. [1969] "Derivability, Redundancy, and Consistency of Relations stored in large data banks," August 19, 1969 (photocopy)

Codd, E. F. [1971] "A Relational Model of Data for Large Shared Data Banks," from Communications of the ACM, 13(6):377-387. Reprinted in Stonebraker [1995].

Codd, E. F. [1990] *The Relational Model for Database Management Version 2*, Addison-Wesley, 1990. (ISBN 0-201-14192-2)

Codd E. F., Codd S. B. and Smalley C. T. [1993] "Providing OLAP to User-Analysts: An IT Mandate," downloadable from **http://www.hyperion.com/whitepapers.cfm.**

Date, C. J. [1995] *An Introduction to Database Systems*, 6th Ed. Addison-Wesley, 1995. (ISBN 0-201-54239-X)

Date, C. J. and Darwen, Hugh [1997] *A Guide to the SQL Standard*, 4th Ed. Addison-Wesley, 1997. (ISBN 0-201-96426-0)

Date, C.J. and Darwen, Hugh [1998a] *Foundation for Object/Relational Databases*, Addison-Wesley, 1998. (ISBN 0-201-30978-5)

Date, C.J. [1998b] "Thirty Years of Relational," in *Intelligent Enterprise* at **http://www.intelligententerprise.com.**

Elmasri, R. and Navathe, S. [1994] *Fundamentals of Database Systems*, 2nd Ed. Benjamin/Cummings, 1994. (ISBN 0-8053-1748-1)

Geiger, Kyle [1995] *Inside ODBC*, Microsoft Press, 1995. (ISBN 1-55615-815-7)

Gray, Jim and Reuter, Andreas [1993] *Transaction Processing: Concepts and Techniques*, Morgan Kaufman, 1993. (ISBN 1-55860-190-2)

Halpin, Terry [1995] *Conceptual Schema and Relational Database Design*, 2nd ed., Prentice Hall, 1995. (ISBN 0-13-355702-2)

Kimball, Ralph [1996] *The Data Warehouse Toolkit*, John Wiley & Sons, 1996. (ISBN: 0471153370)

Melton, Jim and Simon, Alan R. [1993] *Understanding the New SQL: A Complete Guide*, Morgan Kaufmann, 1993. (ISBN: 1-55860-245-3)

Microsoft [1995] *Database Developer's Companion*, (Microsoft SQL Server 6.0/6.5 Documentation), Microsoft document No. 63901

Microsoft [1997a] "Designing Efficient Applications for MS SQL Server" by Peter Hussey, in SQL Server Developer's Kit, Microsoft TechNet, January 1999.

Microsoft [1997b] *Windows NT 3.51 Resource Kit: Networking*. Chapter 8, "Client-Server Connectivity on Windows NT" from Microsoft TechNet, January, 1999.

Microsoft [1998a] *SQL Server 7 Books Online* CD.

Microsoft [1998b] "Accessing Heterogeneous Data with Microsoft SQL Server 7.0", Microsoft part number: 098-80830.

Microsoft [1998c] "Developing Mobile Applications: Comparing Microsoft SQL Server 7.0 to Sybase Adaptive Server Anywhere 6.0" by Andrew Coupe, Microsoft part number: 098-81534.

Microsoft [1998d] "Developing with Microsoft English Query in Microsoft SQL Server 7.0," Microsoft part number: 098-80839.

Microsoft [1998e] "Implementing Large Decision Support Databases with Microsoft SQL Server 7.0," Microsoft part number: 098-81102.

Microsoft [1998f] "Index Tuning Wizard for Microsoft SQL Server 7.0," Microsoft part number: 098-82419.

Microsoft [1998g] "Microsoft Access 2000 Data Engine Options," Microsoft part number 098-81609.

Microsoft [1998h] "Microsoft SQL Server 7.0 Data Warehousing Framework," Microsoft part number: 098-80704.

Microsoft [1998i] "Microsoft SQL Server 7.0 Distributed Queries: OLE DB Connectivity," Microsoft part number: 098-82420.

Microsoft [1998j] "Microsoft SQL Server 7.0 OLAP Services," Microsoft part number: 098-80705

Microsoft [1998k] "Microsoft SQL Server 7.0 Performance Tuning Guide" by Henry Lau, Microsoft part number: 098-81529.

Microsoft [1998l] "Microsoft SQL Server 7.0 Query Processor" by Goetz Graefe, Jim Ewel, and Cesar Galindo-Legaria, Microsoft part number 098-80763.

Microsoft [1998m] "Microsoft SQL Server 7.0 Storage Engine," Microsoft part number 098-80769.

Microsoft [1998n] "Migrating Your Microsoft Access Database to Microsoft SQL Server 7.0," Microsoft part number: 098-82594.

Microsoft [1998o] "SAP R/3 Performance Tuning Guide for Microsoft SQL Server 7.0" by Henry Lau, Microsoft part number: 098-82427.

Microsoft [1998p] "Textual Searches on File Data Using Microsoft SQL Server 7.0," by Margaret Li and Frank Pellow, Microsoft part number: 098-81378.

Microsoft [1998q] "Replication for Microsoft SQL Server 7.0," Microsoft part number: 098-80829.

Microsoft [1998r] "Upgrading to Microsoft SQL Server 7.0," Microsoft part number: 098-82422.

Renaud, Paul E. [1996] *Introduction To Client/Server Systems: A Practical Guide For Systems Professionals*, John Wiley and Sons, 1996. (ISBN 0471133337)

Rozenshtein, David [1995] "The Essence of SQL: A Guide to Learning Most of SQL in the Least Amount of Time," SQL Forum Journal, vol. 4, no. 4.

Rozenshtein, D., Abramovitz A., and Birger E. [1995] Optimizing Transact-SQL: Advanced Programming Techniques, SQL Forum Press, 1995. (ISBN 0-9649812-0-3)

Shasha, Dennis [1992] *Database Tuning: A Principled Approach*, Prentice-Hall, 1992. (ISBN 0-13-205246-6)

Soukup, Ron [1997] *Inside Microsoft SQL Server 6.5*, Microsoft Press, 1997. (ISBN 1-57231-331-5)

Stoll, Robert N. [1979] *Set Theory and Logic*, Dover, 1997. (ISBN 0486638294)

Stonebraker, Michael [1995] *Readings in Database Systems*, 2nd ed., Morgan Kaufman, 1995. (ISBN 1-55860-252-6)

Ullman, Jeffrey and Widom, Jennifer [1997] *A First Course in Database Systems*, Prentice-Hall, 1997. (ISBN 0-13-861337-0)

Yu, Clement and Ming, Weiyi [1998] *Principles of Database Query Processing for Advanced Applications*, Morgan Kaufmann, 1998. (ISBN 1-55860-434-0)

Appendix C

What's On the CD?

What's On the CD?

The CD that accompanies this book contains the example projects from the book and an evaluation version of Microsoft SQL Server 7.

Running the CD

To make the CD more user-friendly and take up less of your disk space, no installation is required. This means that the only files transferred to your hard disk are the ones you choose to copy or install.

> **CAUTION**
>
> This CD has been designed to run under Windows 95/98 and Windows NT 4. Neither the CD itself nor the programs on the CD will run under earlier versions of Windows.

Windows 95/98/NT4

Because there is no install routine, running the CD in Windows 95/98/NT4 is a breeze, especially if you have autorun enabled. Simply insert the CD in the CD-ROM drive, close the tray, and wait for the CD to load.

If you have disabled autorun, place the CD in the CD-ROM drive and follow these steps:

1. From the Start menu, select Run.
2. Type **D:\CDInstaller.exe** (where D:\ is the CD-ROM drive).
3. Select OK.

The Prima License

The first window you will see is the Prima License Agreement. Take a moment to read the agreement, and click the "I Agree" button to accept the license and proceed to the user interface. If you do not agree with the license, click the "I Decline" button to close the user interface and end the session.

The Prima User Interface

Prima's user interface is designed to make viewing and using the CD contents quick and easy. The opening screen contains a two-panel window with three buttons across the bottom. The left panel contains the structure of the programs on the disc. The right panel displays a description page for the selected entry in the left panel. The three buttons across the bottom of the user interface make it possible to install programs, view the contents of the disc using Windows Explorer, and view the contents of a help file for the selected entry. If any of the buttons are "grayed out" it means that button is unavailable. For example, if the Help button is grayed out, it means that no Help file is available.

Resizing and Closing the User Interface

As with any window, you can resize the user interface. To do so, position the mouse over any edge or corner, hold down the left mouse button, and drag the edge or corner to a new position.

To close and exit the user interface, either double-click on the small button in the upper-left corner of the window, or click on the exit button (marked with a small "x") in the upper-right corner of the window.

Using the Left Panel

The left panel of the Prima user interface works very much like Windows Explorer. To view the description of an entry in the left panel, simply click on the entry. For example, to view the general information about Prima Publishing, Inc., click on the entry "Prima Publishing Presents".

Some items have subitems that are nested below them. Such parent items have a small plus (+) sign next to them. To view the nested subitems, simply click on the plus sign. When you do, the list expands and the subitems are listed below the parent item. In addition, the plus (+) sign becomes a minus (-) sign. To hide the subitems, click on the minus sign to collapse the listing.

NOTE

You can control the positon of the line between the left and right panels. To change the position of the dividing line, move the mouse over the line, hold down the left mouse button (the mouse becomes a two-headed arrow) and drag the line to a new position.

Using the Right Panel

The right panel displays a page that describes the entry you chose in the left panel. Use the information provided to provide details about your selection – such as what functionality an installable program provides. In addition to a general description, the page may provide the following information:

◆ World Wide Web Site: Many program providers have a web site. If one is available, the description page provides the web address. To navigate to the web site using your browser, simply click on the web address (you must be connected to the Internet).

◆ E-mail Address: Many program providers are available via e-mail. If available, the description page provides the e-mail address. To use the e-mail address, simply copy the address to the clipboard, and paste it into the address line of your e-mail program.

◆ Readme, License, and other text files: Many programs have additional information available in files with such names as Readme, License, Order, etc. If such files exist, you can view the contents of the file in the right panel by clicking on the indicated hyperlink (such as the word "here" displayed in blue). When you are done viewing the text file, you can return to the description page by reclicking on the entry in the left panel.

Command Buttons

Install. Use this button to install the program corresponding to your selection onto your hard drive.

Explore. Use this button to view the contents of the CD using the Windows Explorer.

Help. Click on this button to display the contents of the Help file provided with the program.

Read File. The Install button turns into the Read File button when you make a selection that has an Adobe Acrobat file attached. Clicking on the Read File button launches Adobe Acrobat Reader and opens the selected file. You must have previously installed Adobe Acrobat Reader, either on your own or from the disc included with the book.

Pop-Up Menu Options

Install. If the selected title contains an install routine, choosing this option begins the installation process.

Explore. Selecting this option allows you to view the folder containing the program files using Windows Explorer.

View Help. Use this menu item to display the contents of the Help file provided with the program.

The Software

This section gives you a brief description of the shareware and evaluation software you'll find on the CD.

NOTE

The software included with this publication is provided for your evaluation. If you try this software and find it useful, you must register the software as discussed in its documentation. Prima Publishing has not paid the registration fee for any shareware included on the disc.

Adobe Acrobat Reader. The free Adobe Acrobat reader enables you to read files in a common format: Adobe Acrobat (.pdx). Because of the wide availability of the Adobe Acrobat Reader, this file format is used frequently to ensure that the person receiving the file can open the file and view it. Adobe Acrobat preserves the format of text and graphics, and enables the Acrobat author to use live internet hyperlinks, email addresses, and cross-references to both other Acrobat files and to bookmarks within the current Acrobat file.

SQL Server 7 Evaluation Edition. The evaluation edition of Microsoft's SQL Server 7 is provided on the disc. You can install this software and use it to try out the various book projects. Pay particular attention to the system requirements necessary to run SQL Server 7, as discussed in the installation program screens. For example, if you are running NT, you must have Service Pack 4 (not included with this disc).

Benchmark Factory. Benchmark Factory is a framework used for developing and running multiple benchmarks. One analogy for the product is the carousel CD player, where each benchmark is a separate CD in the machine. In addition to providing a benchmark development environment, Client/Server Solutions provides pre-developed industry standard benchmarks, like the TPC-B&C, and AS3AP benchmark.

Index

A

B